The International Handbook on the Sociology of Education

The International Handbook on the Sociology of Education

An International Assessment of New Research and Theory

Edited by Carlos Alberto Torres
and Ari Antikainen

ROWMAN & LITTLEFIELD PUBLISHERS, INC.
Lanham • Boulder • New York • Oxford

ROWMAN & LITTLEFIELD PUBLISHERS, INC.

Published in the United States of America
by Rowman & Littlefield Publishers, Inc.
A Member of the Rowman & Littlefield Publishing Group
4720 Boston Way, Lanham, Maryland 20706
www.rowmanlittlefield.com

P.O. Box 317, OX2 9RU, United Kingdom

British Library Cataloguing in Publication Information Available

Library of Congress Cataloging-in-Publication Data

The international handbook on the sociology of education : an international
assessment of new research and theory / edited by Carlos
Alberto Torres and Ari Antikainen.
    p. cm.
Includes bibliographical references and index.
  ISBN 0-7425-1769-1 (cloth : alk. paper) — ISBN 0-7425-1770-5 (pbk.:
alk. paper)
  1. Educational sociology—Cross-cultural studies. I. Torres, Carlos
Alberto. II. Antikainen, Ari.
  LC189 .I53 2003
  306.43—dc21

                                                              2002004907

Printed in the United States of America

⊗™ The paper used in this publication meets the minimum requirements of
American National Standard for Information Sciences—Permanence of Paper
for Printed Library Materials, ANSI/NISO Z39.48-1992.

Contents

Introduction to a Sociology of Education:

Old Dilemmas in a New Century?

Carlos Alberto Torres and Ari Antikainen

THE SOCIOLOGY OF EDUCATIONAL SYSTEMS

All pedagogic action is, objectively, symbolic violence insofar as it is the imposition of a cultural arbitrary by an arbitrary power.

—Pierre Bourdieu and Jean-Claude Passeron, *Reproduction in Education, Society, and Culture* (London: Sage, 1990), 5

Misrecognition of the social determinants of the educational career—and therefore of the social trajectory it helps to determine—gives the educational certificate the value of natural right and makes the educational system one of the fundamental agencies of the maintenance of the social order.

—Pierre Bourdieu, *Distinction: A Social Critique of the Judgement of Taste* (Cambridge: Harvard University Press, 1984), 387

Many sociocultural phenomena require a special category of social space with its own system of co-ordinates.

—Pitirim A. Sorokin, *Social and Cultural Dynamics: Fluctuation of Forms of Art* (New York: Bedminster, 1962), 157

The twentieth century has been marked by the expansion of educational opportunities to children as well as to youth and adults in all social sectors in the world system. It has been the century of education, and the role of the state in the promotion of public education has been decisive. But the successes of public education in the new century run the risk of being undermined by the failures of neoliberal public policies that retreat from their liberal-democratic tradition, with serious implications for one of the central tasks of state: the education of the citizenry.

Particularly in the last decades, limited public resources have been spent in the provision of basic education for children, youth, and adults. The years of obligatory schooling have been extended significantly, particularly in developing countries. Initial and preschool education was provided to an increasingly broad gamut of families, especially families of few resources; access for children with learning deficiencies or disabilities was facilitated in many countries—with special education blooming in the last quarter century. Equal opportunity for the poor, immigrants, and indigenous peoples, as well as for girls and women, was substantially improved. Without a doubt, the last century has been marked also by the feminization of the educational enrollment, particularly in Latin America and Europe.

Along with the expansion of educational opportunities, improvement in efficiency took place, exemplified in the increased capacity to retain students in the initial and middle levels of the system, and in the capacity to promote them so that they continue advancing in the school system, arriving eventually at the level of postsecondary school and completing postsecondary study in ever increasing numbers.

Despite this progress, the themes of quality and relevance of education have been a secular preoccupation of thinkers, public intellectuals, teachers, leaders of teachers' unions, and members of the governmental bureaucracies. These concerns echo the demands expressed daily in schoolyards and classrooms, as well as in public forums by parents of different social sectors deeply interested in the education of their children.

One may argue that there are a number of reasons for this extraordinary school expansion, some of which are associated with the role of social sciences in facilitating social engineering through public policy.[1] Very importantly, with the constitution of public systems of education, the state adopted a critical role in the expansion of social welfare. Not surprisingly, the social sciences were called on to create a new social imaginary, new frontiers for society to evolve. Certainly these changes were not the gracious gift of enlightened elites to the majority of the population, but an attempt to coopt as much as to franchise large different social sectors around a notion of a social pact as social consensus. Education as Enlightenment played a major role in creating social consensus and legitimation for a smoother connection between democracy and capitalism. Thus the role of the state has been decisive for this process, and social sciences have been functional to state planning, particularly in periods of abundance of material, financial, and fiscal resources.[2]

We have argued elsewhere that the state, as a pact of domination and a self-regulated administrative system, plays a central role as mediator in the context of the crisis of capitalism, especially regarding the contradictions between accumulation and legitimation.[3] The discussion of the theories of the state is particularly important for education reform for several reasons. First, the definition, interpretation, and analysis of educational problems and their solutions depend to a large extent on theories of the state that justify and underlie the diagnostic and solution. In addition, the new kinds of state intervention, often defined as the neoliberal state, reflect a substantial change in the logic of public action and involvement of the state in the world system. At the same time, this change in the character of the state can also sponsor new visions about the nature and limits of the democratic pact, and of the character and role of education and educational policy in the global spread of capitalism.[4]

THE SOCIOLOGY OF THE WELFARE STATE AND EDUCATION AS PUBLIC POLICY

The material infrastructure of this youth world consists primarily of communication media, the prolonged system of education and the loosing grip of parents. The expansion of education was even more drastic than that of the welfare state and the pension system.

—Göran Therborn, *European Modernity and Beyond* (London: Sage, 1995), 251

The creation and operation of the welfare state was decisive for the consolidation of educational expansion. The welfare state represents a social pact between labor and capital. Its origins can be found in the institutional reorganization of capitalism at the beginning of the century in Europe, especially in the European social democracies, such as the Scandinavian countries.[5] The New Deal engineered during Roosevelt's administration in the United States represents a form of government in which the citizens can aspire to reach minimum levels of social welfare, including education, health, social security, employment, and housing. These services are considered a right of citizenship rather than a charity. Another central aspect is that this model operates under the assumption of full employment in an industrial economy following Keynesian models.[6] For many reasons, such as the populist experiences and the extreme inequality of income distribution in Latin America, state formations with a strong element of intervention in civil society have shared some similarities with the model of the welfare state. However, there is also an important divergence, especially the lack of state unemployment benefits. This state, which plays an important role as the modernizer of society and culture, is also a state that undertakes protectionist activities in the economy, supports the growth of internal markets, and promotes import substitution as a central aspect of the model of articulation between the state and society.

It is important to point out that, even in Latin America, Asia, and Africa, the expansion and diversification of education took place in states aspiring to resemble welfare states. These were interventionist states that considered educational expenditures an investment, expanded educational institutions, including a massive increase in enrollments, and enormously expanded educational budgets and the hiring of teachers—though not necessarily teachers' salaries and compensation. In many respects, given their declining salaries, teachers have been subsidizing educational expansion in many regions of the world.[7]

The role and function of public education was expanded, following the premises of the nineteenth-century liberal state that consolidated the nation and markets. In this liberal model of the state, public education postulated the creation of a disciplined pedagogical subject, and the role, mission, ideology, and teacher training models, as well as the founding notions of school curriculum and official knowledge, were all profoundly influenced by the predominant philosophy of the state—a liberal philosophy that was, despite its liberal origins, state oriented.[8]

Recent changes in the world system have shown that there is a new global economy, and globalization has emerged as the key factor intrinsically related to the process of social transformation in our era. The theme of globalization is pervasive in the theoretical contributions to this handbook seeking to understand the meaning of education in contemporary societies.[9] We turn now to a brief description of globalization.

GLOBALIZATION AND EDUCATION

Increasing globalization is a two-edged sword. On the one hand it is quite obvious that it removes competence from the national context and that it undermines the institutions which civil society and the democratic public hitherto have used for communication. On the other hand globalization opens up new possibilities for democratic influence on essential common issues which by their nature are about the notion of the nation state. Attempts to democratize are, therefore, forced to work for the establishment of democratic global structures, including international organs for civil society.

—O. Korsgaard, cited in Mayo, *Gramsci, Freire, and Adult Education*
(London: Zed, 1999), 175–76

Learning all age.

—Finnish proverb from the seventeenth century

Globalization has been defined as "the intensification of worldwide social relations which link distant localities in such a way that local happenings are shaped by events occurring many miles away and vice versa."[10] Held suggests, among other things, that globalization is the product of the emergence of a global economy, expansion of transnational linkages between economic units creating new forms of collective decision making, development of intergovernmental and quasi-supranational institutions, intensification of transnational communications, and the creation of new regional and military orders. The process of globalization is seen as blurring national boundaries, shifting solidarities within and between nation-states, and deeply affecting the constitutions of national and interest groups identities.

Some people see globalization as increasing the homogeneity of societies while others, on the contrary, see globalization increasing the hybridization of cultures and diversity. Still for others globalization is an evolving operation of power by multinational corporations and state power, while in contrast others see in globalization the linchpin for environmental action, democratization, and humanization. Some people see the concept of globalization as a contemporary ruse to describe the effects of imperialism or modernization, while others claim that modernization will open a new "global age" that differs from the "modern age." Although some theorists claim that globalization is the defining concept of a new epoch in the history of humankind, others disagree, claiming that the novelty and centrality of globalization has been greatly exaggerated.

For sociologists of education, the presence of globalization makes the study of education even more complex. Traditional preoccupations with the intersection of classes, race, gender, and the state in the social and cultural reproduction of societies become magnified with the dialectics of the global and the local.[11] Cultural studies, the political sociology of education, and the political economy of education, among the macro perspectives, or methodologies like life story, biographical accounts, or phenomenology of rituals in education among the microperspectives that prevail in sociology of education, have been trying to account for these changes in the dynamics between structure and agency in education, not always successfully.[12]

Changes in the world system, the phenomena of globalization, the growing ingovernability of Western democracies, and the new role of the state under deregulation in the neoliberal agenda are all crucial issues for critical educators. Critical intellectuals have discussed increasingly in the last quarter century the connections between democracy, capitalism, and education, as well as the possible contribution of education to citizenship and the construction of subjectivity and meanings. Educational rituals, codes, and meanings, or the process of people's making sense of their own life in terms of common sense à la Gramsci, cannot be dissociated from power and the permanent search for identity.

Thus there are serious concerns about the role of textbooks in the construction of official knowledge in the schools, the role of the explicit and hidden curriculum, particularly as articulated in the most recent developments in neoliberal educational reform, the role of teachers and technology in an increasingly global world not only undergoing drastic transformation but also subject to a polemic international movement for educational testing and standards, and the role of social movements in contesting social transformation and social policy, including education, have emerged as key themes for research and policy.

The importance of social movements has been indicated in the myriad of international mobilizations protesting against free trade deals, globalization based on the rule of international corporations, and the lack of international justice and equality. The mass mobilizations from the Seattle demonstrations, with its political premise of no globalization without representation, to the tragically emblematic violence in Genoa testify of the growing presence of this "globalization from below" based on resistance and contestation of public policy initiatives and international accords and alliances.

These are some of the issues that occupy the pages of this handbook, offering a state of the art of the concerns, challenges, and proposals in sociology of education in different parts of the world.

THE STRUCTURE AND CONTENT OF THIS HANDBOOK

The sentences of yesterday seem to deny all that has been on my mind: that it is through the senses that we will obtain what we need for higher reflection.

—Vivian Darroch-Lozowski, *Notebook of Stone* (Kapuskasing, Ont.: Penumbra, 1987), 37

The book is divided in three parts. The first part discusses new developments in social theory and methodology in the sociology of education. The second part offers a sequence of snapshots of the practice of sociology of education in different countries and regions of the world, as well as a focus on how the educational process is being analyzed by diverse audiences. The third part offers an appraisal of critical issues in sociology of education, including some of the thorniest debates in the field. These include questions of the origin and orientation of the ongoing movement for educational reforms worldwide, the question of parental choice in private and public education, key political issues regarding citizenship education, and the education of women in contemporary capitalist societies.

Part I: Social Theory and Methodology

In this part, a number of provocative chapters show some of the new developments and appraise old theories implemented in different social conditions in the past.

Honorio Martín Izquierdo and Almudena Moreno Mínguez offer a systematic appraisal of new developments in the sociology of education, classifying the paradigms according to their theoretical perspectives. After an overview of several approaches and research agendas that have been highly influential in the last quarter century, including Bourdieu and Passeron, Althusser's theory of ideological reproduction, Baudelot and Establet network theory, theories of economic correspondence, including the contributions of Bowles and Gintis, Collins's credentialist theory, Bernstein's class, codes, and control theory, the new interpretative sociology, Willis and the notion of conflict theories in the resistance to cultural reproduction, symbolic interactionism, and curriculum theories, they conclude with what they call a dual model of education, confronting the new developments of globalization to multicultural education.

Raf Vanderstraeten offers a systematic appraisal of system theory and its contribution to sociology of education, particularly what could be termed the "new social system theories." He moves from a systematic appraisal of system theories (with its references to communication, organizational dynamics, self-organization, autopoiesis, perception, and communication as pedagogical devices) to an exploration of its utility to the study of classroom interaction. As Martín Izquierdo and Moreno Mínguez attempted to do from a dialectical perspective, Vanderstraeten seeks from system theories to reach broad conclusions implying that the asymmetrical structure of the system of classroom interaction results in a heavy burden for the teacher, and that the "normalization" of educational interaction has a price in terms of enforcing a choice between adaptation and deviance. Finally, among other developments, the movement of testing and the setting of goals have unintended consequences that the author calls "secondary socialization," a byproduct of the organizational structure of schooling. Linking social system theory with a Niklas Luhmann perspective, Vanderstraeten turns his attention to the macro level of education and the different functions of the system, including functional differentiation, individualization, and educational growth. He concludes that from a perspective of functional differentiation the school system creates the foundations for hypostasizing its own function, and that each function system stimulates individuals to put forward expectations and claims in its own functional domain. This process in neofunctionalist fashion à la Talcott Parsons, submits Vanderstraeten, constitutes a basic foundation to explain educational expansion in contemporary societies.

AnneBert Dijkstra and Jules Peschar study the social capital theories and their empirical status in attainment and stratification research. After an overview of the concepts of human, cultural, and especially social capital in sociology of education, they give a more detailed exploration of the studies James Coleman introduced with Thomas Hoffer and developed. This concept was quickly adopted and became fashionable in sociology. Dijkstra and Peschar present their impression of the available empirical support for effects of the social capital on the distribution of educational attainment by reviewing research conducted in the United States and in the Netherlands, Canada, and South Korea. The fruitfulness and problems of the social capital concept, especially its ambiguity, is studied in Dijkstra's and Peschar's chapter in an elaborated way. The problems of diffuse concepts, collective and second-order resources, structural holes and structural closure, social capital being neutral, and outcomes of education are treated. Their conclusion about the potential value of the concept of social capital is far from negative, but they argue that more effort, both theoretical and empirical, is required before a balanced judgment about the value of the concept will be reached.

Steve Jordan offers a perceptive study of the uses of critical ethnography in the sociology of education, showing the growing importance of qualitative studies in the field, focusing on the last twenty-five years. Yet Jordan assesses contemporary ethnography inquiry as enmeshed in crises of representation, legitimation, and praxis. Facing this situation, Jordan undertakes a triple task: (1) to provide an overview of the origins of critical ethnography emerging as a critique of the positivism of conventional ethnography (and eventually linked to the postmodernist approach); (2) to provide an outline and evaluation of the major theoretical traditions from which critical ethnography has been drawn; (3) to provide insights of how critical ethnography might contribute to the development of sociology of education in the new century. Jordan argues for a broader and more expansive definition of the discipline to meet the challenges that global capitalism poses for both research and education in the contemporary world. An important hypothesis in Jordan's analysis is that the emergence of critical ethnography can be paralleled to the emergence of the "new sociology of education" as intertwined and complementary theoretical development. Despite its distinguished origins, many works in critical ethnography were "hijacked" by postmodernist thought. Looking at the connections between critical ethnography and the politics of research, Jordan focuses amply on the theme of the relationships between power and social inequality. Jordan concludes his analysis focusing on the connections between critical ethnography and sociology of education in a globalized epoch. Several contributions could emerge from critical ethnography, including mapping the contours of the new cultural economy that global capitalism has created; helping to revisit the central themes of the sociology of education, and providing a powerful methodology for the study "from below" of educational systems and classrooms.

David MacLennan studies the implications for sociology of education of sociocultural approaches to cognition. He examines the treatment of the subject both as a thinking and as a knowing subject. Particular emphasis is placed on Russian Jewish psychologist Lev Vygotsky and the sociocultural approach to cognition he is credited to have created. MacLennan argues that this approach has received surprisingly little attention in the sociology of education. His goal is to demonstrate that the activities of a thinking, knowing subject ought to be a central concern for the sociology of education, and that in developing a research program in this area, sociologists can and will benefit from the Vygotskian sociocultural approach to cognition. The analysis of the "zone of proximal development" and its influence in children's cognition, shows that cognition is cultural and develops over time. MacLennan links Vygotsky with Bourdieu and shows that the sociocultural theory of learning could be useful for a social theory of learning.

Gad Yair studies school organization and school effectiveness. Tackling paradigmatic assumptions of what he terms the "cumulative paradigm" in the study of school effects, Yair pinpoints several paradigmatic assumptions. First, it is assumed that the amount of exposure to learning opportunities determines student outcomes. Second, it is assumed that learning is progressive or gradual, building knowledge step by step, almost in hierarchical order, like building blocks. Third, it is assumed that instruction is a linear process in which the units (e.g., hours of instruction, teachers, etc.) are equivalent and therefore exchangeable (a teacher-proof system of instruction). Thus learning outcomes can be planned and predicted. Next, Yair shows the shortcomings of this paradigm. These paradigmatic principles are challenged because it is difficult to reconcile its assumptions with the belief that specific teachers have profound influences on teachers' lives. Similarly, this paradigm cannot explain the efficacy of short-term intervention programs affecting students' cognitive and noncognitive outcomes. In addition, the cumulative paradigm shows a simplistic and reductionist conception of learning. Finally, it cannot explain overachievement (both at the level of master teachers and exceptional students). To counteract this model, so pervasive in the bibliography on school effectiveness, Yair offers a "big bang" approach to the study of school effects. He proposes an approach to the study of decisive educational episodes, using a model of reconstructing life experience experimented by adult learners. He focuses on pragmatic decisions, self-empowerment, values, attitudes and beliefs, behavioral changes, and motivational mechanisms that affect outcomes. Yair concludes the study with a discussion of instructional production, the social distribution of instruction and its usage.

Ari Antikainen and Katja Komonen study the "biographical" approach, as an ideographical method, and the "life course" approach, as a nomothetical method, both coexisting in the sociology of education and reinterpreted as the emic and the etic in the contemporary enthnography. Tracing the origins of classical biographical studies in the field of sociology in the work of Thomas and Znaniecki in their classic *The Polish Peasant in Europe and America*, and showing also the contributions of the Chicago School, Ari Antikainen and Katja Komonen place their study in the context of their Nordic and European identities. Life course focuses on transitions in life, as a temporal and historical phenomenon. This methodology is based on several principles: historical time, timing in lives, linked lives, and human agency. The quantitative approach to life history has been named "event history analysis" that is intimately related to the life course perspective. This method has proven extremely helpful for the study of schooling and the changed life course. The authors show that since the 1970s, the interest in the biographical method has increased significantly, exemplified with a number of important studies.[13] Defining the biographical approach, the authors show that it is flexible and holistic, and can be approached from a number of different analytical perspectives. There are two separate analytical ways to study life stories, narrative analysis, and the analysis of narratives. This distinction can also be characterized as "life as told" and "life as lived." Key methodological and epistemological questions emerge in the use of these techniques, for instance, is there such a thing as a "true" story? The question of reliability of life stories, so well studied in the field, has not been theoretically and methodologically solved. Reality as a social construction and the narrative about different social constructions even in the theoretical perspective of social biographies, are not easily reconciled. Yet the authors wonder if there is a possibility of a new synthesis between life course methods and biographical studies, since both are characterized by theoretical and methodological pluralism.

Lawrence J. Saha and J. P. Keeves, tracing the contribution of the sociology of education to the discipline of sociology more generally, offer a systematic assessment of the time-honored contributions of quantitative techniques to the sociology of education. They focus primarily on methods of data analysis and conclude that many of the developments in mainstream sociology of new techniques for data analysis are closely correlated with the development of powerful computers that made possible the complex analysis of larger data sets, which the new analytical techniques demanded. Yet they argue that research in education has been the engine that has driven many of these new developments in sociological research techniques.

Part II: Sociology of Education in International Contexts: Regional Focus

Several case studies illustrate the development of sociology of education in specific regions of the world. While not an exhaustive and comprehensive survey, these studies offer useful insights on the development of the discipline and its concerns worldwide.

António Teodoro studies educational policies and new forms of government in a transnational period, with a particular concern for Western Europe and Portugal, a semiperipheral country in the world system. Teodoro argues that the school system has been crucial in the expansion of literacy; very early on, schooling became a global phenomena through isomorphism developed in the global world. Focusing on the notion of comparative education, Teodoro looks at four essential issues: the ideology of progress, the concept of science, the concept of the nation-state, and the definition of comparative methodology. The theoretical discourse is illustrated with historical analysis, and a brief but pointed analysis of the emergence and presence of the OECD in educational research and policy in the European Union.

Then Teodoro focuses on the Portuguese revolution of 1974, and the uses of the educational system to legitimate the new social order after the collapse of the Salazarista regime. In so doing, Teodoro considers the implications of those changes for the inception of Portugal in UNESCO and its connections with the World Bank proposals. Teodoro discusses the "new vocationalism" justified by the European mandate as part of Portugal's intention to join the OECD countries as participation in the examination program of national educational policies. Drawing on contributions from Boaventura de Sousa Santos, Alan Touraine, and Jürgen Habermas, the chapter offers a systematic and sharp analysis of the new forms of transnational regulation in the field of educational policies, what Teodoro has termed "low-intensity globalization." The author concludes his study by analyzing the challenges posed by hegemonic and counterhegemonic globalizations for a pedagogy of possibility and emancipation.

Jason Chang and Zhang Renjie show that the sociology of education has gradually gained recognition as an academic discipline in both Mainland China and Taiwan. Insisting that Chinese sociologists of education are not happy with simply practicing a discipline borrowed from the West, the authors show that there is a trend to craft a distinctive sociology of education that suits their own social contexts, in the context of a debate, prevalent in the region, between internationalization and indigenization, or (though not identical distinction) between the dynamics of the global and the local.

David Konstantinovski shows how education in the social transitions in Russia, instead of living up to the expectation of democratization, has resulted in growing inequality. Documenting empirically his claims, Konstantinovski holds up the notion of equal opportunity as nothing but a powerful myth. Yet the question of educational opportunity and equality are intimately related, and the myth of equal opportunity (alongside other myths) was an important part of Soviet Russia. Kontanstinovski explores two sets of questions: (1) to what extent the differentiation of the educational system in the post-Soviet period has been increased or decreased and (2) how this process of differentiation can be interpreted and evaluated in terms of social equity. Detailed empirical data supports the analysis through comparison of different age cohorts in schools. The author hints that educational opportunities are being taken advantage of differentially by diverse social groups; Russian youth understand these changes, particularly members of the old elite, which continues to rake in privileges. With the growing stratification of higher education, and the process of differentiation in secondary school, the author identifies serious challenges to equality in Russia.

Carlos Alberto Torres offers empirical evidence as well as normative and analytical arguments showing the progress, alongside the setbacks, of the Latin American educational systems. Key educational ideas that have been implemented in the region and have contributed to the educational tradition of Latin America are discussed. Several theories that have predominated in the educational environment throughout the century are revisited, including pedagogical positivism, spiritualism, humanism, normalism, the economics of education, particularly human capital approaches, the "New School," Paulo Freire and popular education, and the neoliberal agenda embodying the privatization movement. The chapter ends with several theoretical suggestions of how to rethink/unthink the pedagogical utopia and reinvigorate public education as a central component of the democratic pact in Latin American societies.

Martin Munk studies educational opportunity as institutionalized legitimate information capital in the welfare state, with special reference to the Danish state. He proposes the use of a cohort-historical approach to supplement the conventional sociocultural analysis of life changes and odds ratios for achieving differential social position. In short, to what degree social inequality between different birth cohort in Danish society exists over time, especially in education, work experience and employment is the leitmotiv of this chapter. The cohort study of inequality is based on a large register from *Statistics Denmark* regarding covariate and outcome variables, using descriptive cross-tabulations and multivariate logistic regression analysis. The theoretical model rests on Bourdieu's social and cultural capital theories associated with education. The conclusion is that despite the uniformity of the Danish educational system, its purported social equality, and open notions of social mobility, social inequality persists. The achievement of educational levels and better jobs still depends on social class origin, gender, and work experience and to some degree adult education. Yet the strength of association/odds rations vary over time by birth cohorts.

Part III: Critical Issues in Sociology of Education

Geoff Whitty and Sally Power analyze global and national influences in educational reform. They study the growing emphasis on parental choice and school autonomy in England, Sweden, Australia, New Zealand, and the United States. The focus of the study is recent reforms (what they aptly term "policy convergence") that have brought marketization into the educational systems of the developed world. Considering possible explanations of this new wave of reform, including the influence of identifiable New Right networks, the condition of postmodernity, the effects of globalization and changes in the mode of regulation of modern state, the chapter discusses the effects of the hidden curriculum on a range of issues, from forms of social solidarity to the formation of social identities. The authors conclude critically that the growing atomization and commercialization of schooling may result, in the end, in that the nation state will be increasingly confronted with the problem of maintaining social cohesion in civil society. The changing role of the state in education has been the subject of much research in the field, and Whitty and Power call our attention to this surging body of literature.

Their warning reveals the urgent need to develop new conceptions of citizenship and new approaches to education for citizenship in the global world. Their critical view shows that the reformist call of reasserting a sense of common citizenship by insisting on core programs of civic education in the schools, despite the increasingly heterogeneous nature of modern societies, pays insufficient attention to not only the effects of quasi-markets in exacerbating existing inequalities between schools (and society at large) but also underestimates the power of the hidden curriculum of the market to undermine any real sense of commonality in schools. They conclude with a ray of hope, discarding a "straightforward return to the old order of things" while suggesting that to avoid the atomization of educational decision making and the tendencies toward fragmentation and polarization, "we need to create new collective and experimental contexts within civil society, new institutional arrangements that are genuinely inclusive. Educators alone cannot do this. It needs global responses from social movements, though recognizing the specific policies, social context, culture, and the nature of contemporary societies."

AnneBert Dijkstra and Jaap Dronkers study the connections of governance and choice in education in the context of a theory of civil society as equilibrium. The Dutch arrangement for the articulation of private delivery and central regulation offers an example of exceptionality in the current debate worldwide. Exploring the origins of the Dutch educational arrangement, the authors show its uniqueness in the following terms: religious schools are not of one denomination; the principle of freedom of education or parental choice under conditions of equal funding was already established in the Constitution of 1917, and the equal subsidy to all religious and public schools has promoted the strong presence of elite private schools outside the state-subsidized sector. Thus an institutionalized hierarchy (e.g., the Ivy League type) in the Dutch schools does not exist. They test several explanations for the survival of religious education, including issues of segregation, central regulation, differences in educational administration, the resiliency of educational values in parent preferences, the "mild" conservatism of religious schools that is valued by many parents in light of Dutch secularism, and the question of effectiveness on academic achievement that is attributed to confessional schools. They conclude, after a brief criticism of public schools, that the Dutch case shows that promoting more parental choice in education and more competition between schools may improve the quality of teaching, decrease the level of bureaucratic control, and reduce school costs and hence savings.

Ingrid Jönsson discusses women's education in Europe, particularly focusing on women's educational attainment and differential expansion rates in Germany, Portugal, and Sweden. The author argues that in understanding the expansion of the number of women in educational systems, one must consider, in addition to the structure of the educational system, recent economic, demographic, social, and cultural changes in the European Union. Revisiting the notion of education as part of the welfare state, Jönsson analyzes the trends in female participation in upper secondary education and higher education. Then the author considers the participation in labor markets vis-à-vis educational attainment, trying to explain the differences in female participation in education. She focuses on the expansion of the educational systems, the structure of the systems, public social services, and ideologies of motherhood, and proposes a set of generalizations regarding women as full citizens in the European polity.

The Affective Education Research Group consists of European and Israeli researchers—Yaacov J. Katz, Alkistis Kontoyianni, Peter Lang, Isabel Menezes, Sean Neill, Arja Puurula, Claudia Saccone, Lisa Vasileiou, and Lennart Vriens—interested in the role of attitudes, feelings, beliefs, and emotions in educational processes. In their study of cultural similarities and differences in school culture, they widen their point of view from psychological to sociological and cross-cultural perspective. For the teacher survey and the student survey, conducted in 1998, 1,818 students and 1,100 teachers in five southern European countries (Greece, Israel, Italy, Portugal, and Spain) and in five northern European countries (England, Finland, Ireland, the Netherlands, and Northern Ireland) were interviewed. Based on the survey results and applying especially the ideas Ronald Inglehart and Andy Hargreaves have presented, the research group argues that the basic difference between the South and the North can be interpreted by the dichotomy of collectivism versus individualism and modern versus postmodern.

Sinikka Aapola, Tuula Gordon, and Elina Lahelma study the international representation of citizenship in school textbooks. Textbooks are institutionalized forms of authoritative texts in education, informing, organizing, and formulating different kinds of perception of the world by offering categorizations and thought structures for readers. For the authors, textbooks construct citizenship in mainly two ways: explicitly by presenting certain views of people and their behavior within particular subjects and implicitly, in the way the texts are constructed. Based on a comparative sample of school textbooks published in the 1990s in Finland, England, Sweden, and United States, they explore discursive representations of citizenship and embodiment in school textbooks, and their intertwined association with a hierarchical social organization of age and gender in school. In addition, they analyze, through a sample of biology books, the representations of sexuality and adolescence, as they are closely connected with representation of citizenship and embodiment (of heterosexuality, for the most part). An interesting finding is that biology textbooks do not usually separate sexuality from reproduction, and therefore sexuality is closely related to heterosexual intercourse. Sexual pleasure, on the other hand, as a central part of the sexual desire is omitted as irrelevant. They conclude that representations of citizenship are connected to construction of embodiment and to discourses of puberty, adolescence and gender. To achieve full citizenship, there is a need to understand diversity in the sexuality domain as well.

Reviewing these chapters may suggest that the new century brings with it old, unresolved preoccupations for sociologists of education but also new challenges. The point is not to fall into the trap of thinking that the only contribution of sociology of education is to offer alternatives to continuing social engineering in society. This would be similar to pouring old wine into new containers. The sociology of education should recognize that if it, as a discipline of study, is to survive the inevitable social and cultural transformation of the new century marked by globalization and neoliberalism, it should find ways to improve the understanding and critique of educational reform. Similarly, the sociology of education should make itself available and useful for the work of different agencies, including social movements, to transform and reverse the social, political, and economic exclusionary trends of nowadays. Sociology of education, if it is going to survive as a meaningful field of inquiry, thinking, and praxis, should help create a society, paraphrasing Paulo Freire, where it will be easier to love. Educational policies that reject neoliberal and neoconservative models, the creation of new structures of social solidarity, and the presence of a robust, participative democratic state are all ideals that will contribute to Freire's dreams. Surely the sociology of education has a role to play in empowerment and liberation.

NOTES

1. J. Boli and F. Ramirez, "Compulsory Schooling in the Western Cultural Context," in *Emergent Issues in Education: Comparative Perspectives,* ed. G. P. Kelly, R. Arnove, and P. Altbach (New York: State University of New York Press, 1992), 38; John Meyer, "The Effects of Education as an Institution," *American Journal of Sociology* 83, no. 4 (1977): 55–57.

2. There are always questions in times of fiscal retrenchment of the ability of social sciences to survive fiscal cut measures, including reduction of public expenditures and defunding of higher education. However, they are still central players in the institutional development of universities, which will guarantee their presence, at least in advanced capitalist societies, for a long time.

3. Carlos Alberto Torres, *Education Democracy and Multiculturalism: Dilemmas of Citizenship in a Global World* (Lanham, Md.: Rowman & Littlefield, 1998).

4. Carlos Alberto Torres, "La universidad latinoamericana: De la reforma de 1918 al ajuste estructural de los 1990," in *Curriculum universitario siglo XXI*, ed. C Torres, R. Follari, M. Albornoz, S. Duluc, and L. Petrucci (Paraná, Entre Rios: Facultad de Ciencias de la Educación, Universidad Nacional de Entre Rios, 1994), 13–54.

5. This argument has been explored in some detail in Carlos Alberto Torres, "Structural Adjustment, Teachers, and State Practices in Education: A Focus on Latin America," in *Educational Change and Educational Knowledge: Changing Relationships between the State, Civil Society, and the Educational Community,* ed. T. J. Popkewitz and A. Kazamias (Albany: State University of New York Press, 1999); Lois Weiner, "Schooling to Work," in *Post-Work: The Wages of Cybernation*, ed. S. Aronowitz and J. Cutler (New York: Routledge, 1998), 185–201; Harold L. Wilensky, *The New Corporatism: Centralization and the*

Welfare State (Beverly Hills: Sage, 1976); Wilensky, *The Welfare State and Equality: Structural and Ideological Roots of Public Expenditures* (Berkeley: University of California Press, 1975).

6. Wilensky, *Welfare State and Equality*; Wilensky, *New Corporatism*; Thomas Popkewitz, *A Political Sociology of Educational Reform: Power/Knowledge in Teaching, Teachers' Education, and Research* (New York: Teachers College, Columbia University, 1991); Robert Erikson, Erik J. Hansen, Stein Ringen, and Hannu Uusitalo, eds., *The Scandinavian Model: Welfare States and Welfare Research* (Armonk, N.Y.: Sharpe, 1987). This is well documented in the sociological literature. The twelfth World Congress of Sociology, which took place in Bielefeld, Germany (July 18–23, 1994), had "contested boundaries and shifting solidarities" as its central theme. See Neil Smelser, *International Sociological Association (ISA) Bulletin*, Spring 1993, 5.

7. C. A. Torres et al., "The State, Teachers Unions, and Educational Reforms in Six Pacific Rim Countries: Empirical Findings and Policy Recommendations" (presented at the international meeting of the SOKA Group, National University, Seoul, Korea, June 23-29, 1999), mimeograph.

8. For the Latin American case, see Adriana Puiggrós, *Democracia autoritarismo en la pedagogía argentina y latinoamericana* (Buenos Aires: Galerna, 1986); Puiggrós, *Sujetos, disciplina y curriculum en los orígenes del sistema educativo argentino* (Buenos Aires: Galerna, 1990); Adriana Puiggrós et al., *Escuela, democracia y order (1916–1943)* (Buenos Aires: Galerna, 1992).

9. See Ari Antikainen, Jarmo Houtsonen, Juha Kauppila, Katja Komonen, Leena Koski, and Mari Käyhkö, "Construction of Identity and Culture through Education," *International Journal of Contemporary Sociology*, October 1999, 204–28.

10. David Held, ed., *Political Theory Today* (Stanford: Stanford University Press, 1991), 9. We draw in this section from Carlos Alberto Torres, *Education, Democracy, and Multiculturalism: Dilemmas of Citizenship in a Global World* (Lanhan, Md.: Rowman & Littlefield, 1998); and Nicholas Burbules and Carlos Alberto Torres, eds., *Education and Globalization: Critical Concepts* (New York: Routledge, 2000).

11. See C. A. Torres and R. Arnove, eds., *Comparative Education: The Dialectics of the Global and the Local* (Lanham, Md.: Rowman & Littlefield, 1999); Ari Antikainen, "Four Decades of Finnish Educational Sociology," *Scandinavian Journal of Educational Research* 14, no. 3–4 (1997): 397–411; Antikainen, "The Rise and Change of Comprehensive Planning: The Finnish Experience," *European Journal of Education* 25, no. 1 (1990): 75–82.

12. See Ari Antikainen, "Between Structure and Subjectivity: Life-Histories and Lifelong Learning," *International Review of Education* 44, no. 2–3 (1998): 215–34.

13. For instance, one of the editors of this handbook has conducted a systematic exploration of the beginnings of critical pedagogies and critical education in the United States, using biographical analysis. See C. A. Torres, *Education, Power, and Personal Biography: Dialogues with Critical Educators* (New York: Routledge, 1998).

REFERENCES

Antikainen, Ari. "Between Structure and Subjectivity: Life-Histories and Lifelong Learning." *International Review of Education* 44, no. 2–3 (1998); 215–34.

Antikainen, Ari. "Four Decades of Finnish Educational Sociology." *Scandinavian Journal of Educational Research* 14, no. 3–4 (1997): 397–411.

Antikainen, Ari. "The Rise and Change of Comprehensive Planning: The Finnish Experience." *European Journal of Education* 25, no. 1 (1990): 75–82.

Antikainen, Ari, Jarmo Houtsonen, Juha Kauppila, Katja Komonen, Leena Koski, and Mari Käyhkö. "Construction of Identity and Culture through Education." *International Journal of Contemporary Sociology*, October 1999, 204–28.

Boli, J., and F. Ramirez. "Compulsory Schooling in the Western Cultural Context." In *Emergent Issues in Education: Comparative Perspectives*, edited by G. P. Kelly, R. Arnove, and P. Altbach, 25–38. New York: State University of New York Press, 1992.

Burbules, Nicholas, and Carlos Alberto Torres, eds. *Education and Globalization: Critical Concepts*. New York: Routledge, 2000.

DiFazio, William. "Why There Is No Movement of the Poor." In *Post-Work: The Wages of Cybernation*, edited by S. Aronowitz and J. Cutler, 141–66. New York: Routledge, 1998.

Erikson, Robert, Erik J. Hansen, Stein Ringen, and Hannu Uusitalo, eds. *The Scandinavian Model: Welfare States and Welfare Research*. Armonk, N.Y.: Sharpe, 1987.

Freire, Paulo. *Pedagogy of the City*. New York: Continuum, 1993.

Giroux, Henry. *Schooling and the Struggle for Public Life: Critical Pedagogy in the Modern Age*. Minneapolis: University of Minnesota Press, 1988.

Gittlin, Todd. *The Twilight of Common Dreams: Why America Is Wracked by Culture Wars*. New York: Henry Holt, 1995.

Held, David, ed. *Political Theory Today*. Stanford: Stanford University Press.

Macpherson, C. B. *The Real World of Democracy*. Oxford: Clarendon, 1971.

Mayo, Peter. *Gramsci, Freire, and Adult Education*. London: Zed, 1999.

McCarthy, Thomas. *The Critical Theory of Jürgen Habermas*. Cambridge: MIT Press, 1979.

Meyer, John. "The Effects of Education as an Institution." *American Journal of Sociology* 83, no. 4 (1977): 55–57.

Morrow, Raymond Allen, and Carlos Alberto Torres. *Critical Theory and Education: Freire, Habermas, and the Pedagogical Subject*. New York: Teachers College, Columbia University, in press.

Morrow, Raymond Allen, and Carlos Alberto Torres. *Social Theory and Education: A Critique of Theories of Social and Economic Reproduction*. New York: SUNY Press, 1995.

Popkewitz, Thomas. *A Political Sociology of Educational Reform: Power/Knowledge in Teaching, Teachers' Education, and Research*. New York: Teachers' College, Columbia University, 1991.

Puiggrós, Adriana. *Democracia autoritarismo en la pedagogía argentina y latinoamericana*. Buenos Aires: Galerna, 1986.

Puiggrós, Adriana. *Sujetos, disciplina y curriculum en los orígenes del sistema educativo argentino*. Buenos Aires: Galerna, 1990.

Puiggrós, Adriana, et al. *Escuela, democracia y order (1916–1943)*. Buenos Aires: Galerna, 1992.

Smelser, Neil. "Contested Boundaries and Shifting Solidarities." *International Sociological Association (ISA) Bulletin*, Spring 1993, 5.

Thurow, Lester. *Building Wealth*. New York: HarperCollins, 1999.

Thurow, Lester. *Head to Head: The Coming Economic Battle among Japan, Europe, and America*. New York: William Morrow, 1992.

Torres, C. A. *Education, Power, and Personal Biography: Dialogues with Critical Educators.* New York: Routledge, 1998.

Torres, C. A., et al. "The State, Teachers Unions, and Educational Reforms in Six Pacific Rim Countries: Empirical Findings and Policy Recommendations." Presented at the international meeting of the SOKA Group, National University, Seoul, Korea, June 23–29, 1999. Mimeograph.

Torres, C. A., and R. Arnove, eds. *Comparative Education: The Dialectics of the Global and the Local.* Lanham, Md.: Rowman & Littlefield, 1999.

Torres, Carlos Alberto. *Education Democracy and Multiculturalism. Dilemmas of Citizenship in a Global World.* Lanham, Md.: Rowman & Littlefield, 1998.

Torres, Carlos Alberto. "La universidad latinoamericana: De la reforma de 1918 al ajuste estructural de los 1990." In *Curriculum universitario siglo XXI*, edited by C. Torres, R. Follari, M. Albornoz, S. Duluc, and L. Petrucci, 13–54. Paraná, Entre Rios: Facultad de Ciencias de la Educación, Universidad Nacional de Entre Rios, 1994.

Torres, Carlos Alberto. "Structural Adjustment, Teachers, and State Practices in Education: A Focus on Latin America." In *Educational Change and Educational Knowledge: Changing Relationships between the State, Civil Society, and the Educational Community.* Edited by T. J. Popkewitz and A. Kazamias. Albany: State University of New York Press, 1999.

Weiner, Lois. "Schooling to Work." In *Post-Work: The Wages of Cybernation*, edited by S. Aronowitz and J. Cutler, 185–201. New York: Routledge, 1998.

Wilensky, Harold L. *The New Corporatism: Centralization and the Welfare State.* Beverly Hills: Sage, 1976.

Wilensky, Harold L. *The Welfare State and Equality: Structural and Ideological Roots of Public Expenditures.* Berkeley: University of California Press, 1975.

I

SOCIAL THEORY AND METHODOLOGY

1

Sociological Theory of Education in the Dialectical Perspective

Honorio Martín Izquierdo and Almudena Moreno Mínguez

> The lesson for epistemology is this: Not to work with fixed concepts. Not to eliminate counterinduction. Not to be deceived into thinking that we have finally found the correct description of facts, when all that has happened is that some new categories have been adapted to old ways of thinking, which are so familiar that we interpret their frameworks as the frameworks of the world itself.
>
> The more solid, well-defined, and splendid is the building shaped by understanding, the greater is the need for life to flee from it towards freedom. We must endeavour to make sure that we do not lose our ability to make such a choice.
>
> —Feyerabend 1987, 40, 137

The aim of this work is to place the sociology of education within the general framework of sociology, bearing in mind that the main objective of this discipline is the study of the relationships between education and society. The contradictory character of these concepts leads us into a dialectic adventure analyzing the historical evolution of education and its intellection on the part of the sociology of education. The guideline behind this argument has been drawn up from the dialectic viewpoint, which attempts to encompass the social processes that have contributed to modeling the epistemological and methodological architecture on which the sociology of education is based and which responds to three key moments in the history of education:

1. Thesis: Education as a variable depending on the industrial society: meritocratic education in the functionalist sociology of education
2. Antithesis: Society as a variable depending on education: reproductive education in the critical sociology of education

3. Synthesis: The dual model of education: globalized education as opposed to multicultural education

The early thinkers responsible for the term "sociology" emerged from the maelstrom of nineteenth-century European society, where rapid social change, gradual differentiation, and complexity of society demanded the creation of institutions capable of structuring society, maintaining social order, and socializing individuals in values that made social integration possible. Therefore education became an essential tool in social articulation, socialization, and social control. The earliest references to the integrating function of education are in the work of Saint-Simon and Comte, later incorporated into the work of Durkheim. From this functionalist viewpoint, education is seen as a variable depending on social aspects, the immediate function of which is to maintain social order. In *Education and Sociology*, Durkheim carries out an exhaustive study of the historical relationship between education and society, setting out from the premise of the supremacy of social or collective aspects both over the individual as well as the phenomenon of education. Thus the institutionalization of schooling becomes the most suitable means of favoring the adaptation and integration of individuals to the social system, through the socialization of certain moral values.

Durkheim is the epistemological reference for functionalist sociology, as in his work he considers schooling as the principal means of integration, adaptation, and selection of the talents needed to manage industrial society. In this way and for the first time, the sociology of education distances itself from pedagogy and psychology, disciplines that stress the unidimensional aspect and individualization of the educational process, whereas the sociology of education stresses the relational and group character of the educational system.

Considering education as a balanced and functional social subsystem to meet the demands of the industrial society implies in itself a contradiction in the sense that research has shown that education does not always guarantee economic and social development or social equality. Within this context are many of the so-called critical interpretations, inspired by Marxist principles, which appear as the antithesis to the meritocratic conception of education. However, this critical sociology of education, in an attempt to demonstrate the negative effects caused by educational practice in society, is not able to objectivize the hidden mechanisms that reproduce and generate these differentiating effects in the process of education. Both the functionalist and the critical paradigms raise questions that are not resolved and have already been the subject of debate among the classics. In both perspectives, the link between education and society is seen from a single viewpoint, where the educational institution is considered as a kind of "black box," handing out qualifications and positions in society.

The complexity of social reality and the continuing emergence of new problems in the relation between education and society require a constant redefining of the aims of the study and methodologies used in research, in turn demanding the use of a plural approach to respond to the many challenges facing this discipline. In this tremendous effort on the part of the sociology of education to establish a rigorous theoretical framework that integrates the contradictory relationships between school and society, we have opted for the dialectic perspective of analysis in order to lay out the different objectives and methodologies of study that reflect current sociology of education. As a synthesis of this dialectic process we present the dual model of education[1] involving the so-called convergent sociology of education. Based on universal and globalizing concepts, it considers education a factor of progress, adaptation, integration, and selection of individuals in the information society. Its main objective is to study educational policy as well as the link between education and employment, and so on. Emphasis is also placed on the divergent sociology of education, the aim of which is the multicultural society and what is called education in diversity. The final goal of this perspective is to provide the basis for a kind of practical intervention in education that, in some way, allows individuals to display their uniqueness within the framework of a society of equals. From this dialectic viewpoint, we will carry out a brief overview of the different theoretical and methodological perspectives that have characterized research in the sociology of education to the present day, in order to define more accurately the aim of the discipline, since as Professor Lerena pointed out: "In order to define the goal of the sociology of education one must already have a sociological theory of education" (1985, 226).

The diagrams presented in figure 1.1 aim to synthesize the dual nature of the sociology of education, with regard to the paradigmatic development of the discipline and intellection of equal opportunities in the sociology of education. Our contribution to the diagram draws on what we have called the "dual model of education and equality of differences" as a binding element in the processes characterizing current education and therefore the sociological analysis of education.

INDUSTRIAL SOCIETY AND THE NEW FUNCTIONS OF EDUCATION

Although the origins of the social analysis of education date back to the eighteenth century when Rousseau published *Emile: or, On Education* (1762)—in which he expounds his model of negative education, revealing what was possible in human nature—it was not really until the publication of Durkheim's *Education and Sociology* (1956), when a primitive sociological analysis of education began. For him education is a function of society, moral education being the main structuring and binding factor in society. The final consolidation of the sociology of education came about with the publication of Parsons's 1959

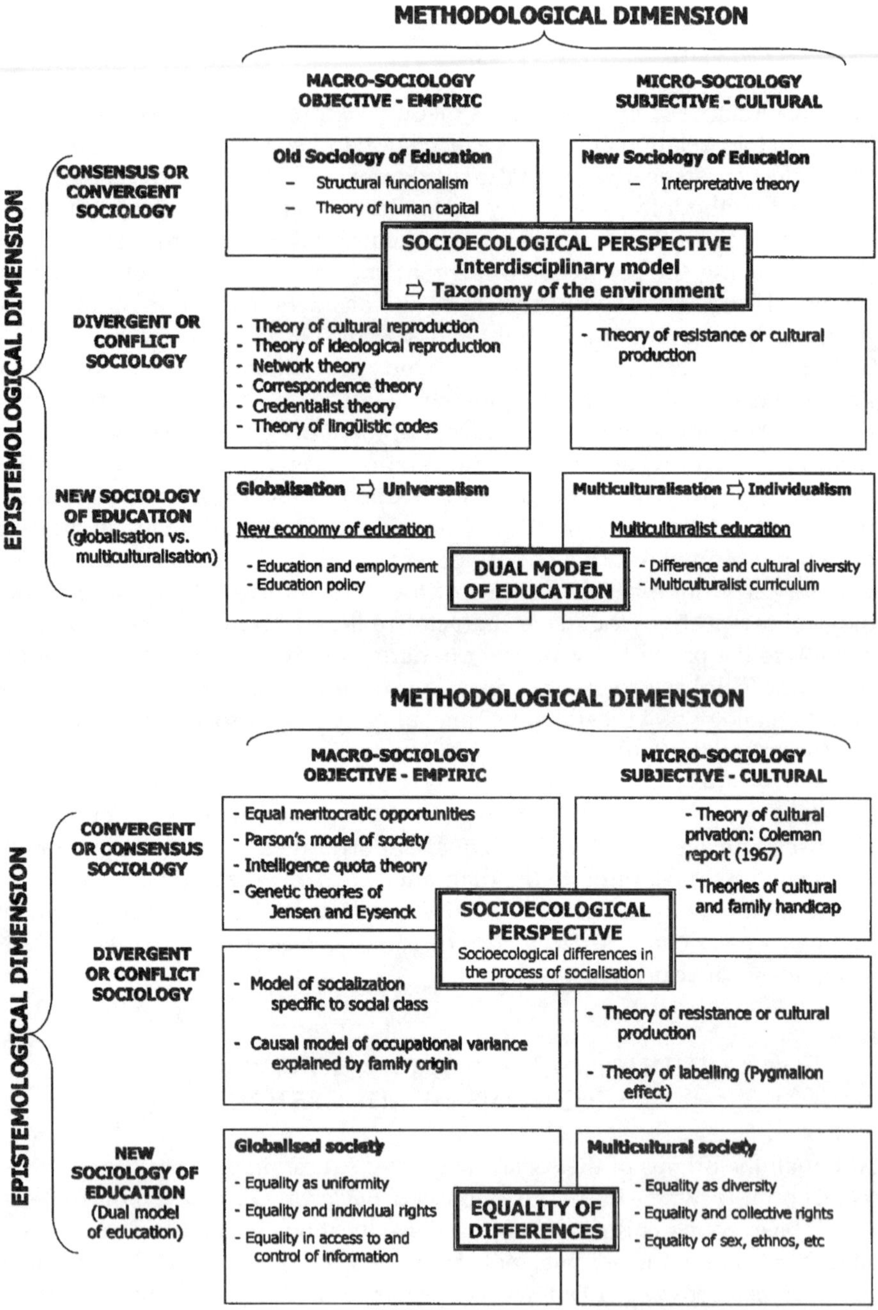

METHODOLOGICAL DIMENSION

	MACRO-SOCIOLOGY OBJECTIVE - EMPIRIC	MICRO-SOCIOLOGY SUBJECTIVE - CULTURAL
CONSENSUS OR CONVERGENT SOCIOLOGY	**Old Sociology of Education** - Structural funcionalism - Theory of human capital	**New Sociology of Education** - Interpretative theory

SOCIOECOLOGICAL PERSPECTIVE
Interdisciplinary model
⇨ **Taxonomy of the environment**

	MACRO-SOCIOLOGY	MICRO-SOCIOLOGY
DIVERGENT OR CONFLICT SOCIOLOGY	- Theory of cultural reproduction - Theory of ideological reproduction - Network theory - Correspondence theory - Credentialist theory - Theory of lingüistic codes	- Theory of resistance or cultural production
NEW SOCIOLOGY OF EDUCATION (globalisation vs. multiculturalisation)	**Globalisation** ⇨ **Universalism** <u>New economy of education</u> - Education and employment - Education policy	**Multiculturalisation** ⇨ **Individualism** <u>Multiculturalist education</u> - Difference and cultural diversity - Multiculturalist curriculum

DUAL MODEL OF EDUCATION

(left label: **EPISTEMOLOGICAL DIMENSION**)

METHODOLOGICAL DIMENSION

	MACRO-SOCIOLOGY OBJECTIVE - EMPIRIC	MICRO-SOCIOLOGY SUBJECTIVE - CULTURAL
CONVERGENT OR CONSENSUS SOCIOLOGY	- Equal meritocratic opportunities - Parson's model of society - Intelligence quota theory - Genetic theories of Jensen and Eysenck	- Theory of cultural privation: Coleman report (1967) - Theories of cultural and family handicap

SOCIOECOLOGICAL PERSPECTIVE
Socioecological differences in the process of socialisation

	MACRO-SOCIOLOGY	MICRO-SOCIOLOGY
DIVERGENT OR CONFLICT SOCIOLOGY	- Model of socialization specific to social class - Causal model of occupational variance explained by family origin	- Theory of resistance or cultural production - Theory of labelling (Pygmalion effect)
NEW SOCIOLOGY OF EDUCATION (Dual model of education)	**Globalised society** - Equality as uniformity - Equality and individual rights - Equality in access to and control of information	**Multicultural society** - Equality as diversity - Equality and collective rights - Equality of sex, ethnos, etc

EQUALITY OF DIFFERENCES

(left label: **EPISTEMOLOGICAL DIMENSION**)

Figure 1.1. Principal Paradigms in the Sociology of Education (top), Equal Educational Opportunities (bottom).

article "The School Class as a Social System," a point at which we can properly speak of the birth of the sociology of education. The meritocratic interpretation of education is developed within this framework.

Meritocratic Society

In the socioeconomic context of the mid-twentieth century, characterized by optimism and economic development, the meritocratic ideas of Parsons and Schelski emerged with intensity, and an attempt was made to provide the theoretical basis for the social functions fulfilled by education in mid-century American society. These functions ranged from the socialization of citizens in certain norms and values to the equal distribution of educational opportunities.

Parsons's outstanding contribution to the sociology of education is his analysis of school and society, in which he considers the classroom a subsystem of the social system, contributing to social order. These ideas are reflected in "The School Class as a Social System," published in 1959, taking up once again Durkheim's central idea (i.e., education as a process of acquiring social norms for social integration and moral balance of society), he suggests that the school and the family are the institutions charged with transmitting values and norms for forging the personality of the individual and favoring the development of certain roles imposed by industrial society. The school thus becomes the main legitimizing institution of meritocratic order. Very similar are the contributions of Dreeben (1990), who considers that learning the norms of independence, achievement, universality, and specificity in the classroom are fundamental for maintaining a consensus in terms of the functions to be fulfilled by schooling.

In this context of optimism in progress and technological development much work appeared from sociologists and economists insisting on the need to educate citizens in certain values to favor this economic and social development. Prominent in this line of thinking are techno-economic functionalism and the Theory of Human Capital, developed initially by T. W. Schultz in 1960. Most of the empirical work carried out in this context deals with the relations between the educational and productive system, laying special emphasis on social mobility. The idea that investment in education contributes to productivity and economic growth led to many studies aimed at linking economic growth with the spread of education. Becker's theory of human capital (1964) stressed the economic and social benefits provided by investment in education, as it has important redistributive effects.

In this model of meritocratic society, where the school becomes the main means of selecting the talents and elites who are to control and manage the process of economic development, unusual interest is aroused in equal educational opportunities and there is a gradual transformation of curricula, emphasizing an instrumentalist approach and fundamentally, the new function of education as a selector of talents and neutralizer of poverty and social inequality. From this viewpoint, equal opportunities are equated to equal access, which is a necessary condition for guaranteeing equality and social justice (Davies and Moore 1945).[2] Two other basic functions that education must perform in a meritocratic society are also derived from this premise: the selection of talents and equal opportunities.

EDUCATION IN THE FACE OF THE CONTRADICTIONS OF AN INDUSTRIAL SOCIETY

Education and Society from the Macrosociological Viewpoint: Critical Sociology

Criticism of the meritocratic model resulted from much of the work done on equal educational opportunities. Studies such as those of Blau and Duncan (1967), Coleman (1966), and Jencks (1972) reflect the sociopolitical concern of the time to achieve a more equal society.

Prior to the publication of these works, Dahrendorf (1957) aimed his criticism at the functionalist interpretation, according to which the educational system performed a neutral selective role in distributing educational opportunities: "Even today, certain criteria of adjudication, alien to the determination of the individual, play a vital role in the distribution of posts and positions" (Dahrendorf 1957, 95). In a later work, Dahrendorf (1968) emphasized how the bureaucratized meritocracy of Parsons and Schelsky's model of "equaled society" is a fallacy in the sense that it omits the introduction of factors such as the unequal educational offer between town and country, the lack of flexibility in the traditional educational system and the socializing role of the family, factors that have a decisive influence on educational selection and therefore on the attainment of equal educational opportunities.

The pioneering work of Dahrendorf (1957) paved the way for new empirical research on the relationship between family origin, social class, education, and academic and professional success that have come to be known as causal models of specific socialization and occupational mobility according to social classes. Prominent in this line of approach are the studies of Bourdieu and Passeron (1964), Blau and Duncan (1967), Dahrendorf (1957, 1968), Coleman (1966), Husen (1969), Müller (1975), Boudon (1973), Lerena (1976), and Carabaña (1983).

Special mention should be made of the work of Bourdieu and Passeron, since the introduction of the cultural dimension as a mechanism for the unequal reproduction of educational opportunities in terms of belonging to a certain social class meant a severe setback to meritocratic theories. However, the causal models used to verify empirically the relation between social origin and opportunities did not sufficiently explain this link. The application of Blau and Duncan's causal model for the United States demonstrated that the education and profession of the father only accounted for 18 percent of the variance, whereas the child's education, regardless of family origin, can only account for 24 percent of the variance, reflecting that 58 percent of the variance remains unexplained, which is in no way linked to the reproductive role of status (Blau and Duncan 1967, 202). Müller's research (1975) for the Federal German Republic confirmed these results.

In this regard, the Spanish case is worth mentioning, as considering only education and profession of the father, the variance explained is 44 percent (Carabaña 1983, 81), meaning that in Spain in the 1970s there was a certain link between family origin and opportunities.

The results of this research, together with the effects caused by the growth in unemployment in welfare states, the increase in public debt, and the appearance of overeducation, led to a questioning of, on the one hand, the premises of meritocratic functionalism and on the other, the theories of human capital by the critical paradigm, which considers school an area for reproducing inequalities and conflict. As a result of this, the supposed possibilities for social and occupational mobility in civil society depend on the arbitrariness of an unjust and unequal educational system. Criticism of functionalism is not uniform and is reflected in many different theories that analyze both Marxist and Weberian thinking.

Theories of Cultural Reproduction in Bourdieu and Passeron

Bourdieu and Passeron, from an analysis of the French educational system, attempted to show how cultural factors influence access to differential use of cultural and educational opportunities in terms of social class. The theories of Bourdieu and Passeron are based on the fact that the possession of a specific cultural capital is unequal and therefore leads to differential access to social and economic capital, thus contributing to cultural and social reproduction. In *Les Héritiers*, published in 1964, a picture is given of the unequal starting point of students in terms of social origin, explaining to a certain extent the different relation with academic culture. The aim of the work is thus to show how these cultural limits—attributed to family and social origin—are reflected in differential aptitudes which affect academic success or failure. This work still reflects some possibility of change with regard to this situation that ultimately disappears in *Reproduction* (1970), which shows how from the point of view of school everything is set out so that the "chosen few," who thanks to their cultural and social capital possess "the great culture," may succeed. To do this they introduce two basic concepts—cultural arbitrariness and symbolic violence—in order to defend the argument that all academic culture is arbitrary, since its validity comes solely from the fact that it is the culture of the ruling classes, imposed on the whole of society as if it were the only form of objective knowledge.

These two works stress the fact that academic culture is not neutral, since through the cultural arbitrariness and symbolic violence incorporated into teaching, the concept of domination linked to teaching is concealed, thus contributing to the reproduction of class inequalities. Thus the system of relations in educational domination guarantees the reproduction of a "habitus" as a cultural model enabling selection of individuals in terms of difference or similarity to the ruling cultural model (Bonald 1998, 77). Bourdieu and Passeron's analysis marked a significant advance with regard to merely materialistic analysis, as it introduced the cultural variable to identify the fact that the main obstacles encountered by students from the lower classes in their academic career are more cultural than economic. However their interpretations were not free from criticism since—as Willis says (1981, 442)—they conceive the educational system as a system of established and unalterable domination where "the agents, culture and diversity have been consigned to history." It is as if those who are dispossessed had no kind of culture, as "culture" is equated to "bourgeois culture," which ultimately makes any kind of countercultural or counterhegemonic action impossible (Willis 1981, 444). In short, what Willis is saying is that Bourdieu and Passeron's theory of cultural reproduction offers little hope of practical action and therefore of change.

Althusser's Theory of Ideological Reproduction

Althusser's (1972) idea of school as an ideological apparatus of the state heralded the starting point for the Marxist interpretation of education. Marxist thinking considers that the material conditions of existence determine culture, in this case education. According to Marx, the modern school contributes to the reproduction of social inequalities inserted into the model of capitalist production, as it accepts arbitrary legitimization of the inequality of knowledge imposed by credentials and selective qualifications and examinations (Lerena 1985; Jérez Mir 1990). Based on these principles, Althusser develops a theory of domination in which school and the educational system favor subordination to the dominant ideology so as to reproduce power and class relations: "In other words, school teaches certain skills, but also ways which ensure submission to the dominant ideology, or the domain of its application" (Althusser 1969). Along the same lines of interpretation, Gramsci (1971) affirms that the state is a system in which the hegemony of the bourgeoisie is mainly based on the intellectual and moral influence of this social group, as well as on the ideological impregnation of the whole of society. The interesting point about these contributions is that for the first time the consideration of school as an impenetrable "black box" is brought into question. In these Marxist perspectives, education forms part of the political and ideological superstructure, the function of which is to train consciences that fit the relations of the ruling production. Therefore, it is an institution depending on the state (Poulantzas 1975), which as an ideological apparatus has a twin role: on the one hand contributing to the reproduction of the productive forces through training in the skills and knowledge necessary for the smooth running of the productive process and on the other hand favoring the reproduction of ideologies through socialization and internalization of norms and values which sustain relations of production.

Economic Reproduction in the Baudelot and Establet Network Theory

Following along the lines of Althusser, Baudelot and Establet (1971) in their book *The Capitalist School in France* try to explain how school in its practice and teaching approach leads to a social differentiation that corresponds to social division at work. Through basic empirical work on dropping out of school in terms of age or level of education in the French educational system, Baudelot and Establet develop a theory on the reproductive and selective function of school. The bourgeois ideology of school is recreated by the teachers themselves, who from primary school favor the filtration of pupils into two different and closed school networks: the primary and professional network (PP) and the higher secondary network (SS). The former is shorter and allows access to the secondary occupational sector (low skilled and low paid) in the labor market. The second, on the other hand, provides access for prestigious professions to the cultural and economic elite. The main idea defended by these authors is that only certain social classes can access each "network," it being virtually impossible to pass from one network to another. Thus through teachers the internalization of the dominant ideology as an imposition of latent power is promoted. In this way, from the first days of school, interaction in the classroom has a very different effect on the children of the working classes than on the more well-to-do: "Vocabulary eliminates virtually all those terms which would allow working class children to understand and describe their family's living conditions. This being the case, we should not be surprised that a school environment which repeats, reinforces, prolongs and values the living conditions of the bourgeois family and that totally rejects the living conditions of the working class, might appear strange to working class children" (Baudelot and Establet 1971, 192). This initial differentiation in primary school is later reinforced and strengthened by the type of training in the primary and secondary professional network. Baudelot and Establet's goal is fundamentally to objectivize two kinds of culture that school offers to students in both networks through an analysis of what Althusser calls the "practices" and "rituals" of the school ideological apparatus. This analysis is completed in the work *Les étudiants, l'employé, la crise* (Baudelot et al., 1981), where there is criticism of the instrumental use made by the bourgeois of credentials, considering them as a kind of social circle that has been created to guarantee access by certain social groups to privileged positions and status. To a certain extent, it is a class strategy to legitimize and defend the privileges acquired through the educational system.

The Theories of Economic Correspondence

Bowles and Gintis (1976), with the publication of the book *Schooling in Capitalist America*, try to give greater theoretical consistency to the paradigm of the social networks, stressing the failure of reform in secondary education, since its application has continued to yield social relations equivalent to the social relations of production: "Social relations in education are a replica of the hierarchical division of work. Hierarchical relations are reflected in the vertical lines of authority which go from administrators to teachers and from teachers to students. . . . When we accustom the young to a series of social relations similar to those of the work place, school attempts to channel the development of personal needs towards these requirements" (Bowles and Gintis 1976, 175–76).

Bowles and Gintis take the theory of reproduction to an extreme, as in their opinion through ideological inculcation social relations are learned in school that correspond exactly to the social relations of production. In fact, the alienation experienced by students in school—in the sense that they do not control the content of their education—corresponds to the authoritarian practices of the productive system, it being the capitalist class that defines those educational models which best suit their own class interests.

Carnoy and Lewin (1985) widen the scope of this perspective and admit that school has a dual function: socializing in specific social codes that reproduce the relations of production and enable the internalization of values that maintain democratic and liberal culture, as a result of which they consider that education has a certain capacity for social transformation.

This vision allows us to explain some of the contradictions that can be seen between education and society which to date had remained hidden. Correspondence theories try to incorporate into the analysis of educational reality the contradiction that exists between the economic and political levels, a fact that transposed into the educational system yields the dual function that education must perform: to favor on the one hand the rights of the individual and on the other those of the capitalist system and property. However, these analyses lay the blame for the remote possibilities of change on structural factors, omitting the capacity for transformation which those in the classrooms have.

Collins's Credentialist Theory

From a neo-Weberian viewpoint, Collins bases his studies on the idea that educational expansion does not respond to changes in the productive framework nor to new occupational requirements. It should be remembered that Weberian sociology attempts to establish an equivalent theoretical relation between ideal types of domination and ideal educational types, from a historical analysis in which the symbolic domination exercised by the church has given way to the modern form of domination exercised by the bureaucratic state, characterized by the rationalization and bureaucratization of education in capitalist society. Ways of domination respond to specific forms of teaching and socialization of citizens. The characteristic feature of a bureaucratic society is that technical and economic rationalization require precision in the calculation of results, or, to put it another way, they impose the need for an objective expert to be selected through impartial tests called examinations of legitimization which certify these experts' access to positions of responsibility within the framework of a bureaucratized and technocratic culture.

Collins's findings—presented in *Credential Society* (1979)—confirm that the growth of bureaucracy fundamentally explains the demand for education and not the characteristics of the productive framework. In this way, Collins considers that education contributes to differentiation among groups, since through access to it credentials are awarded to access the best positions in the social structure. This leads some groups to press for a reevaluation of certain qualifications and a deevaluation of others, in such a way that school fulfills two functions that Weber identified at the time: preparation for the needs of bureaucracy and the creation of new ways of life and cultural styles (Hinojal 1991, 98). In this social context "what is learnt in schools has a much closer link to conventional norms on the concepts of sociability and the right to property than to instrumental and cognoscitive techniques" (Collins 1979, 26).

Symbolic Control and the Use of Linguistic Codes Depending on Social Class in Bernstein

Bernstein fits between the theories of reproduction and the new sociology of education. Bernstein's basic theory revolves around how class factors regulate the structure of linguistic communication in the family and therefore internalization in infancy of a specific sociolinguistic code, in such a way that class relations regulate what Bernstein calls the "limited and elaborate codes" in education that in turn determine success or failure at school. In this way, Bernstein is able to link the material and symbolic levels, or in other words, forms of power (domination) with forms of cultural transmission through school, since the latter tends to use a certain type of language and thus direct the development of roles, meaning that it is very likely that working-class children reproduce the linguistic code learned in the family of origin, which does not agree with the language used in school, possibly leading to academic failure (Bernstein 1975).

The educational code comprises "the underlying principles that make up the curriculum, pedagogy and evaluation" (Bernstein 1975, 46). This means that educational content and how it is transmitted and evaluated becomes the key to interpreting the mechanisms of cultural reproduction that are created in school: "How a society selects, classifies, distributes, transmits and evaluates the educational knowledge that it considers should be public, reflects both the distribution of power as well as the principles of social control. From this viewpoint, differences and change in the organisation, transmission and evaluation of educational knowledge should be an important area of sociological interest" (Bernstein 1975, 45).

Education and Society from the Microsociological Viewpoint: New Interpretative Sociology

The article published by Bowles and Gintis in 1981—where a review is made of the ideas put forward in *Schooling in Capitalist America*—is essential for a correct interpretation of how the new sociology of education has emerged. This work sets out from a critique of the dominant economic materialism in the first work. Although it may be true that there is a certain link between the social relations that exist in the capitalist system and relations in education, the latter is no longer considered merely as an epiphenomenon of the economic structure as had been put forward in capitalist teaching in America, since this principle of correspondence is explained in terms of the contradictions between democracy and capitalism. The contradictions that can be seen in the educational system are a projection of those seen in the state, where on the one hand the state is forced to promote the accumulation of capital (right of property) and on the other to legitimize democracy guaranteeing the rights of people, which in many cases are against the rights of property. Bowles and Gintis state that "this contradictory position of education explains the dual progressive/reproductive role (in which it promotes equality, democracy, tolerance, rationality, inalienable rights, on the one hand, while legitimizing inequality, authoritarianism, fragmentation, prejudice and submission on the other), and in part is the reflection of the tension existing in liberalism" (Bowles and Gintis 1981, 20–21).

From this review of the correspondence theory a consistent analytical framework may be derived for analyzing school as an area of structured social interaction. Thus, Bowles and Gintis manage to integrate the micro aspects—referring to social interaction—(skills, attitudes, etc.) with macro aspects (socioeconomic relations). The formula used for this is the objectivization of educational content, in other words, analysis of the curriculum: "Theses objectives may be divided into two complementary projects: democratization of the social relations of education and re–formulation of the question of democracy in the curriculum" (Bowles and Gintis 1981, 22). It is here where the important contribution of Bowles and Gintis to the new interpretative sociology of education is to be found, since they feel that educational reform requires a democratization of the curriculum, in such a way that students gradually come to control the spheres of education in order to neutralize the contradictions mentioned.

The publication of this article breaks with the pessimism and the logic that had characterized the theories of reproduction. Ten years earlier Young's book *Knowledge and Control* had been published, symbolizing the birth of the "interpretative paradigm," the aim of which was to reveal the underlying mechanisms of structuring involved in the social construction of educational knowledge, thus giving rise to the emergence of the new interpretative sociology of education (Young 1971, 3).

Conflict in the Theories of Resistance and Cultural Production

In this paradigmatic context resistance theories emerge that, contrary to what has been stated, start from a cultural analysis that has very little to do with the analyses of the theories of reproduction—as Willis pointed out: "Learning to Labor has been seen as an example of a neo-Marxist approach to education that explains the stability and spread of capitalist society, using a general notion of reproduction. With regard to certain important aspects, this vision is incorrect." In Willis's well-known study (1977) *Learning to Labor,* an attempt is made to respond to the question posed in the title: how do working-class children get working-class jobs? The difficulty answering this question is a result—as Willis says—of the fact that "they themselves consent to this" (Willis 1977, 11), fully aware of the low pay and sparse social recognition and consideration. This social fact is explained by Willis as the result of the social production in which the working class is located and culturally reproduces.

The aim of this work, therefore, is to show how a working-class identity is created that in some way contributes generation after generation to reproducing failure at school, accepted "voluntarily" as a means of identification and even as a means of resistance.

To a certain extent, the correspondence that exists between work, the family, and the organization of the school system itself makes it impossible for working-class children to obtain jobs other than working-class jobs.

In short, it may be said that through the use of qualitative techniques similar to those used in ethnography, Willis analyzes how working-class identity is created culturally in school by means of the resistance that pupils show toward intellectual work. In this sense, Willis's work provides a significant contribution to the sociological theory of education insofar as it "takes as a reference point what is missing or is only touched upon in previous theories: resistance" (Willis 1981, 447). Criticism of Willis's work is based on the fact that the resistance of working pupils is not reflected in any meaningful educational change, in other words, does not clarify what effects student resistance might have on the educational system.

Giroux has attempted to establish certain continuity with Willis's line of research by making a detailed analysis of the process of resistance and placing greater emphasis on the variables of "intention" and "effect" of resistance, in the sense that there may be the intention to resist without there being any counterhegemonic effects. On the other hand, counterhegemonic acts may be identified without there being any explicit intention (Bonald 1998, 148). Unlike Willis's analysis, his theory of resistance widens the possibilities of change beyond material determination of existence and stresses the role of teachers as transformative intellectuals: "Teachers need to develop a discourse and a set of hypotheses allowing them to act more specifically as transformative intellectuals" (Giroux 1990, 36).

The most notable thing about the resistance theories is that they incorporate the cultural variable as well as the action of the agents into the analysis of the processes of class reproduction, ethnos, and sex evident in school. However, numerous criticisms have been leveled at these theories, given their limitations in linking educational to social change, as well as the questionable empirical validity of the results obtained in the research.

Theorems of Symbolic Interactionism

The influences of the ethnomethodology of symbolic interactionism (referred to in the first part of this project) are seen in the sociology of education to a great extent. Interest in them is based mainly on the fact that they analyze dynamically the interactions occurring at a micro level, paying special attention to the symbolic significance of the interactions of the agents involved in the educational process (Woods 1983).

The study of the school as a relatively independent institution, of the interactions between pupil and teacher, and so on, have given rise to the generalization of concepts such as "survival strategy" (Woods 1977, 275), "labeling and negotiation processes" (Rist 1970; Riseborough 1988; Pollard 1984; Ball 1989), the so-called Pygmalion effect (Rosenthal and Jacobson 1968), or "adaptation strategies" (Hargreaves 1978) aimed at interpreting the symbolic relations maintained by teachers and pupils in the classroom. The strategy developed by the social actor himself is what gives sense to the actions and leads to specific practices.

In spite of efforts to draw up an interpretative model to allow a link to be established between structural factors (role of the state) and interaction in the classroom (attitudes of teaching staff and pupils), symbolic interactionism has not explicitly addressed the way in which agents incorporate social structures into their teaching practices. Therefore this perspective does not provide the suitable instruments to explain the origin and process of educational change (Halsey et al. 1980, 283).

One should not underestimate the theoretical contributions and methodologies that symbolic interactionism introduces into the analysis of the educational processes which take place in the classroom, since these are essential for analyzing the link between education and society, as well as between structure and action from a microsociological viewpoint.

Curriculum Theories

As a result of the publication of Young's book in 1971, a line of research was developed in the United States in the 1980s that centered on the analysis of the knowledge used and transmitted in the classroom. This has come to be known as sociology of curriculum, the aim of which is to critically analyze strategies for organization, production, and distribution of knowledge. The work of Anyon (1981), Popkewitz (1981), Taxel (1983), and Wexler (1982) reflects this. Along the same lines, using the Gramscian concept of hegemony, Apple (1979) undertook to study the role played by curriculum in creating and maintaining the ideological monopoly exercised by the ruling classes. To do this, he attempts to objectivize the social construction of the educational knowledge incorporated into hidden curricula, as well as the relations of power that have contributed to its development. With this, Apple is referring to the groups of interest who act as pressure groups in drawing up curricula and reports on the educational system, which are fundamental in educational reform.

Extending his analysis to the three levels of the curriculum (explicit, hidden, and in development) allows an examination of the influence of political economy on the production of the text, the practical application of the curriculum, and the tensions and contradictions characteristic of educational practice. On the other hand, social change and social demands require variables of sex, ethnos, and so on, to be integrated into curricula.

In spite of the progress made in epistemology and methodology, none of the theories mentioned here has been able to explain the processes which cause contradictions, nor has been able to develop a theory on the social consequences of the transformative action of those involved in the educational process.

The Sociology of Education as Opposed to the Dual Model of Education: Global versus Diversity

Epistemological and Methodological Challenges of Current Sociology of Education

The sociology of education faces important methodological and epistemological challenges that involve finding a consensus on the functions of education in postmodern society. Thus far we have seen how the discipline has been polarized around two major perspectives: the macro theory, which from different conceptualizations—functionalism and the theories of reproduction—has considered school as a "black box," and the micro perspective, which has dealt with the analysis of the actions of the agents involved in educational practice. None of these perspectives has been able to develop a theoretical framework to link what is transmitted and received by the recipients and transmitters in the educational system with a theory of social change.

Therefore, current sociology of education—sensitive to social change and contributions of sociologists such as Beck (1992), Habermas (1981, 1987), Giddens (1990), or Lash (1990)—is testing new theoretical and methodological perspectives that we have grouped together in what is called a dual model of education. Although these attempts have widened the field of analysis, they have not been able to neutralize the ambivalence that characterizes the sociology of education which, in essence, centers on the debate between considering the educational process as a form of social relation in which laws or general principles can be identified, and as an individualist, intuitive, and creative process in which different factors converge and the general results of which cannot be measured or predicted. If one is aware of this ambivalence and of the fact that education fulfills a dual role in current society (on the one hand guaranteeing social order—reproduction and accumulation—and, on the other, promoting democratization through the development of individual autonomy, active participation and respect for minorities and cultural diversity), we will then be in a position to draw up a sociological theory of education integrating both qualitative as well as quantitative approaches, together with the perspective of convergent education, characteristic of the globalized information society and of divergent education, reflecting a multicultural society. This latest version has led to a pedagogical debate that has supporters and opponents. Both perspectives are the obverse and reverse of democratic societies.

The paradoxes facing education in postindustrial democratic society are framed within the context of the social, economic and cultural change which is taking place in developed Western society. These contradictory processes occurring in the so-called society of knowledge are projected onto the theoretical and methodological body of the sociology of education, which is today more dualized than ever.

Therefore, from the dialectic synthesis we feel that the sociology of education faces a dual epistemological challenge since, on the one hand, it must respond to market globalization, which imposes a convergent education training individuals to occupy postmodern jobs, and on the other must integrate multicultural education as a model of divergent education, able to educate citizens in what has been called equality of differences, as a civic, tolerant, and nonexclusive form of culture. Whatever the case may be, educational sociologists seem to agree that this discipline must avoid any attempt at a holistic or relativist explanation of the link between education and society.

State education policy must therefore resolve the inherent contradictions of legitimization facing modern states as, on the one hand, governments fulfill the function of guaranteeing the process of accumulation and, on the other, of legitimizing the democratic process, favoring the integration and participation of all citizens from different social spheres without any kind of exclusion. Simplistic interpretations that oppose multiculturalism and globalization should be avoided as, although there is no global labor market, there is a global interdependence of work in the new economy, indicating that the multiculturalization of work in Western societies is yet another manifestation of globalization.

In the context of the logic of the globalization-multiculturalism dialectic, indicative of postmodern society, it is necessary to revise the traditional concepts of "social stratification," "segregation" or "equal opportunities" used in the work of Bowles and Gintis, Baudelot and Establet, or Bernstein, which basically deal with the differential access of individuals to different schools and levels of education depending on whether they belonged to a specific social class, ethnos, or sex. We must therefore start from the principle that it is impossible to draw up homogenous and universal curricula for all social groups, but rather that the different skills, motivations, cultural identities and interests of the pupils should be included. This involves rethinking the consideration of the classic equivalence between difference and inequality.

As a result, an approach has been developed concerning the adaptation and concept of multicultural education in postmodern society, whether dialogic or relativist, which has as many supporters as it does opponents. Some of the contributions labeled as feminist and postmodern stress the end of modernity and the importance of accepting difference as a requirement for ending practices of domination based on universal principles, leading to what Flecha (1999) calls the relativistic approach. These movements base their arguments on the absolute respect for difference that in many cases, more than putting an end to racism, creates another kind of so-called postmodern racism, totally opposed to the ethnocentrism of modern racism. On the other hand, the so-called dialogic approach based on the dialogic and communicative principles of the philosophy of Habermas and Freire would enable the integration of different cultural communities without the need to resort to vindication and conflict.

CONCLUSION

In this context new lines of thought and analysis are being developed relating to the functions that education must fulfill in postindustrial society. In a society that Beck defines as "risk," where education no longer guarantees social and occupational mobility as in industrial society, the latter must be able to redefine the objectives which it has historically been designated (normalization and socialization). Educational inequalities no longer refer exclusively to class and family origin, but to the skills individuals acquire for resolving problems deriving from sex (compatibility of family and professional work) or belonging to a specific culture. Individuals are today expected to be able to survive in the framework of a wide variety of global and personal risks, which are different and mutually contradictory (Beck et al. 1994, 21). Therefore, education must contribute to an individual's development so as to be able to dominate "risk opportunities." In a society of risk in which qualifications are devalued, educational inequality is more linked to what is taught than to the results obtained. An individual who is aware of the fragmentation of the universes that make up the "I" is in a better position to succeed in an ambivalent and contradictory society than one who is perfectly socialized and normalized in traditional values which, in general terms, are anachronistic in postindustrial society. This means that educational practice must embrace in its curricula the duality that is characteristic of this society (globalized-multiculturalized) to train individuals who are integrated and not segregated due to economic or cultural reasons in what Touraine (1992) has called the school of the subject.

In today's society, where individuals develop their personality from the internalization of antagonistic and contradictory ideas represented through virtual images, school and educators are faced with an important challenge that must lead them to a wider understanding of how knowledge is created, how identities are developed, and how values are expressed, values that uphold education and have been generated in many areas other than the traditional socializing institution, namely, the school. Therefore educators must be able to differentiate between both pedagogies and integrate into curricula basic aspects such as respect for human rights, principles of democratic integration, and respect for differences. As we advance in this educational field, it will be possible for "all" individuals to live together and learn in the same schools, showing their differences in equal conditions.

In many respects it is still an area of research unexplored by the sociology of education in which many questions are being raised, questions that have no easy answer, such as, What differences should be priorities for teachers and politicians? How can curricula be adapted to cultural diversity while avoiding stigmatizing educational practices? How can specific universal principles be maintained? What is understood by coeducation and intercultural education? These are just some of the questions that are giving rise to new research and promise an uncertain but intriguing future for the discipline. However, we must be alert to the undesirable consequences which the application in extremis of multiculturalism and its derivation in cultural relativism might have for science and the teaching practice.

These new perspectives for analysis emerging in current sociology of education, which we have presented as a synthesis in what we have called the dual model of education, more than being exclusive are in fact complementary, since they attempt to overcome the limitations and weaknesses of structuralist and functionalist interpretations of educational change. It is not a question, therefore, of opting for one perspective of analysis or another but of bearing in mind contributions and limitations for the analysis of the always contradictory relations between education and society.

As a postscript to these reflections, the following note by Touraine (1997, 230) might be worth bearing in mind. Offering a definition of multicultural education, it is close to the concept we have attempted to present in this work and guards us against the excesses of the relativist option in education:

> No multicultural society is possible without recourse to a universal principle which allows communication between culturally different individuals and groups. This universal principle might well be multicultural education as the most appropriate tool for combining equality and diversity. The main problem facing multiculturalism is radical cultural relativism in the name of the premise

"anything is valid" which might lead to many forms of control and domination. Therefore, multicultural education has a dual function: it must favor communication amongst groups and guarantee diversity within the limits morally and ethically recognized by democratic states, since multiculturalism must not be reduced to pluralism without limits.

NOTES

1. An approach is being developed in the sociology of education which, from the theoretical framework of sociology in Habermas, Giddens, Beck or Lash, among others, is attempting to provide the epistemological and methodological basis to what is called the dual model of society (Flecha 1997; Flecha 1999).
2. See reports by Clark (1962), Halsey et al. (1961), and Schultz (1983).

REFERENCES

Acker, S. 1994. *Gendered Education.* Buckingham, U.K.: Open University Press.
Alonso Hinojal, I. 1991. *Educación y sociedad: Las sociologías de la educación.* Madrid: Centro de Investigaciones Sociológicas.
Althusser, L. 1969. *For Marx.* New York: Vintage.
Althusser, L. "Ideology and Ideological State Apparatuses." In B. Cosin, ed., *Education, Structure and Society.* Harmondsworth: Penguin.
Anyon, J. 1981. "Social Class and School Knowledge." *Curriculum Inquiry* 11: 1–42.
Apple, M. W. 1979. *Ideology and Curriculum.* London: Routledge & Kegan Paul.
Apple, M. W. 1995. *Education and Power.* 2d ed. London: Routledge.
Ball, S. 1989. *Foucault and Education: Discipline and Knowledge.* London: Routledge.
Ball, S. 1999. *Politics and Policy Making in Education.* London: Macmillan.
Baudelot, C., and R. Establet. 1971. *L'école capitaliste en France.* Paris: Editions Maspero.
Baudelot, C., and R. Establet. 1989. *El nivel educativo sube.* Madrid: Morata.
Baudelot, C., et al. 1981. *Les étudiants, l'emploie, la crise.* Paris: Librairie François Maspero.
Beck, U. 1992. *Risk Society: Towards a New Modernity.* London: Sage.
Beck, U., A. Giddens, and S. Lash. 1994. *Reflexive Modernization, Politics, Tradition, and Aesthetics in the Modern Social Order.* Cambridge: Polity.
Becker, G. 1964. *Human Capital.* New York: National Bureau of Economic Research.
Bernstein, Basil. 1971. *Class, Codes, and Control.* Vol. 1. London: Routledge & Kegan Paul.
Bernstein, Basil. 1975. *Class, Codes, and Control.* Vol. 3. London: Routledge & Kegan Paul.
Blau, P. M., and O. D. Duncan. 1967. *The American Occupational Structure.* New York: Wiley.
Bonald, X. 1998. *Sociología de la educación: Una aproximación crítica a las corrientes contemporáneas.* Barcelona: Paidós.
Boudon, R. 1973. *L'Inégalité des chances.* Paris: Colin.
Bourdieu, P., and J. C. Passeron. 1964. *Les Héritiers.* Paris: Les Éditions de Minuit.
Bourdieu, P., and J. C. Passeron. 1970. *La Reproduction: Éléments pour une théorie du système d'enseignement.* Paris: Les Éditions de Minuit.
Bowles, S., and H. Gintis. 1976. *Schooling in Capitalist America.* New York: Basic.
Bowles, S., and H. Gintis. 1981. "Contradiction and Reproduction in Educational Theory." In R. Dale et al., eds., *Education and the State.* Vol. 1, *Schooling and the National Interest.* Lewes, U.K.: Falmer.

Carabaña, J. 1983. *Educación, ocupación e ingresos en la España del siglo XX.* Madrid: Ministerio de Educación y Ciencia.

Carnoy, M., and H. Lewin. 1985. *Schooling and Work in the Democratic State.* Stanford: Stanford University Press.

Clark, B. 1962. *Educating the Expert Society.* San Francisco: Chandler.

Coleman, J. S. 1966. *Equality of Educational Opportunity.* Washington, D.C.: U.S. Government Printing Office.

Collins, R. 1979. *The Credential Society.* New York: Academic Press.

Davies, K., and W. E. Moore. 1945. "Some Principles of Stratification." *American Sociological Review* 10, no. 2.

Dahrendorf, R. 1957. *Class and Class in Conflict in Industrial Society.* Stanford: Stanford University Press.

Dahrendorf, R. 1968. *Essays in the Theory of Society.* Stanford: Stanford University Press.

Dreeben, R. 1990. "La contribución de la enseñanza al aprendizaje de las normas: Independencia, logro, universalismo y especifidad." *Educación y Sociedad* 7.

Durkheim, E. 1933. *The Division of Labor in Society.* New York: Macmillan.

Durkheim, E. 1938. *L'évolution pedagogique en France.* Paris: Alcan.

Durkheim, E. 1956. *Education and Sociology.* New York: Free Press.

Feyerabend, P. 1987. *Contra el método.* Barcelona: Ariel.

Flecha, R. 1997. *Nuevas perspectivas críticas en educación.* Barcelona: Paidós.

Flecha, R. 1999. "Modern and Postmodern Racism in Europe: Dialogic Approach and Anti-Racist Pedagogies." *Harvard Educational Review* 69, no. 2: 150–71.

Giddens, A. 1990. *The Consequences of Modernity.* Stanford: Stanford University Press.

Giroux, H. A. 1983. *Theory and Resistance in Education.* South Hadley, Mass.: Bergin & Harvey.

Giroux, H. A. 1990. *Los profesores como intelectuales: Hacia una pedagogía crítica del aprendizaje.* Barcelona: Paidós.

Gramsci, A. 1971. *Selections from the Prison Notebooks.* (Q. Hoare and G. Nowell-Smith, eds.) New York: International Publishers.

Green, A. 1997. *Education, Globalisation, and the Nation State.* London: Macmillan.

Habermas, J. 1981. "Modernity versus Postmodernity." *New German Critique* 8, no. 1: 3–18.

Habermas, J. 1987. *The Philosophical Discourse of Modernity.* Cambridge: MIT Press.

Halsey, A., et al. 1980. *Origin and Destinations.* Oxford: Clarendon.

Hargreaves, D. H. 1978. "The Significance of Classroom Coping Strategies." In L. Barton and R. Meighan, eds., *Sociological Interpretations of Schooling and Classrooms.* London: Routledge & Kegan Paul.

Hargreaves, D. H. 1982. *The Challenge for the Comprehensive School.* London: Routledge & Kegan Paul.

Hinojal, A. 1991. *Educación y Sociedad: Las Sociologías de la Educación.* Madrid: CIS, Siglo XXI.

Husen, T. 1969. *Talent, Opportunity, and Career.* Stockholm: Almqvist and Wiksell.

Jencks, C. 1972. *Inequality.* New York: Basic.

Jérez Mir, R. 1990. *Sociología de la educación: Guía didáctica y textos fundamentals.* Madrid: Consejo de Universidades.

Lash, S. 1990. *Sociology of Postmodernism.* New York: Routledge.

Lerena, C. 1976. *Escuela ideología y clases sociales en España.* Barcelona: Paidós.

Lerena, C. 1985. *Materiales de sociología de la educación y de la Cultura.* Madrid: Grupo Cero.

Lerena, C. 1986. *Escuela, ideologia y clases sociales en España* 3rd ed. Barcelona: Ariel.

Martín Izquierdo, H. 1986. *Contexto socioecológico de la socialización infantil en los sociotopos urbanos de Valladolid.* Madrid: CIDE.

McCarthy, C., and W. Crichloe, eds. 1993. *Race, Identity, and Representation in Education.* New York: Routledge.

Müller, W. 1975. *Familie, Schule, Beruf.* Opladen: Westdeutscher Verlag.

Müller, W., et al. 1988. *Education and Class Mobility.* CASMIN Working Paper no. 14.

Page, R. 1987. "Teachers' Perception of Students: A Link between Classrooms, School Cultures, and the Social Order." *Anthropolgy and Education Quarterly* 18.

Parsons, T. 1959. "The School Class as a Social System: Some of Its Functions in American Society." *Harvard Educational Review* 29: 297–318.

Pollard, A. 1984. "Coping Strategies and the Multiplication of Differentiation in Infant Classroom." *British Educational Research Journal* 10, no. 1.

Popkewitz, T. S. 1981. "The Social Contexts of Schooling Change and Educational Research." *Journal of Curriculum Studies* 13, no. 3.

Poulantzas, N. 1975. *Classes in Contemporary Capitalism.* London: New Left Books.

Riseborough, G. F. 1988. "Pupils, Recipe Knowledge, Curriculum, and Cultural Production of Class, Ethnicity, and Patriarchy: A Critique of One Teacher's Practices." *British Journal of Sociology of Education* 9, no. 1.

Rist, R. 1970. "Student Social Class and Teacher Expectations: The Self-Fulfilling Prophecy in Ghetto Education." *Harvard Educational Review* 40: 411–51.

Rist, R. 1978. *The Invisible Children.* Cambridge: Harvard University Press.

Rosenthal, R., and L. F. Jacobson. 1968. *Pygmalion in the Classroom.* New York: Holt, Rinehart & Winston.

Rousseau, J. J. 1762. *Émile, ou De l'education.*

Schelsky, H. 1957. *Shule und Erziehung in der industrielle Gesellschaft.* Würzburg.

Schultz, T. W. 1960. "Capital Formation by Education." *Journal of Political Economy* 68: 571–83.

Schultz, T. W. 1961. "Investment in Human Capital." *American Economic Review* 51: 1–17.

Taxel, L. 1983. "The American Revolution: An Analysis of Literacy Content, Form, and Ideology." In M. Apple and L. Weis, eds., *Ideology and Practice in Schooling.* Philadelphia: Temple University Press.

Touraine, A. 1992. *Critique de la modernité.* Paris: Fayard.

Touraine, A. 1997. *Paurrons-nous vivre ensemble: Égaux et différents.* Paris: Fayard.

Wexler, P. 1982. "Structure, Text, and Subject: A Critical Sociology of School Knowledge." In M. Apple, ed., *Cultural and Economic Reproduction in Education: Essays on Class, Ideology, and the State.* Boston: Routledge & Kegan Paul.

Willis, P. 1977. *Learning to Labor: How Working-Class Kids Get Working-Class Jobs.* New York: Columbia University Press.

Willis, P. 1981. "Cultural Production Is Different from Cultural Reproduction Is Different from Social Reproduction Is Different from Reproduction." *Interchange on Educational Policy* 12, no. 2–3.

Woods, P. 1977. "Teaching for Survival." In P. Woods and P. Hammersley, eds., *School Experience: Explorations in the Sociology of Education.* New York: St. Martin's.

Woods P. 1983. *Sociology and the School: An Interactionist Viewpoint.* London: Routledge & Kegan Paul.

Young, M., ed. 1971. *Knowledge and Control: New Directions for the Sociology of Education.* London: Collier-Macmillan.

2

Explorations in the Systems-Theoretical Study of Education

Raf Vanderstraeten

This chapter attempts to highlight the relevance of systems theory, especially with regard to the sociological study of education. Attention will be paid to the analysis of face-to-face contacts in the interaction system of classrooms and to the macroanalysis of the educational system. The study of both micro- and macrolevel phenomena makes it possible to illustrate the wide-ranging potential of modern systems theory. Its basic idea is that social systems are autonomous systems, that is, systems that create and maintain their boundaries and establish realities sui generis. The basic characteristics of education are analyzed by focusing on the "nature" of these systems. As contemporary systems theory has not yet crystallized into a well-outlined theoretical and methodological approach, this study provides us with the challenges of a "work in progress."

THE INTERACTION SYSTEM OF EDUCATION

In this first part, I will indicate that social interaction creates a *new level on which reality is structured*. This interaction system is constituted by an intricate interplay of perceptual processes and communication among persons who are together. After the analysis of the systemic boundaries of face-to-face interaction, some of the restraints and possibilities of organizationally framed interaction in general and of classroom interaction in particular are discussed.

Perception/Communication

Following the German sociologist Niklas Luhmann, interaction systems "conceive of themselves as face-to-face interactions and use the presence of persons as a boundary-defining device. If new persons arrive, their communications have to be included into the system by some ceremonial recognition and introduction."[1] What is socially relevant is determined among those present. This means that interaction systems reserve for themselves the ability to decide who and what will *count as* being present. Interaction does not simply include everyone who is present and perceivable, and only these. Servants, for example, could be treated as absent, even when they were present in the same room. The waiter in a restaurant is sometimes present and sometimes absent—depending on whether he does or does not get included in the conversation among the dinner guests. The situation is similar for the individual who is momentarily left to her own resources, while a person to whom she has been talking answers a telephone call. Participation or inclusion in interaction does, in other words, not result from the mere presence of human bodies in a room. It is regulated by means of communication, and mostly by means of communication amongst those who are present. This system is an emergent reality that creates its own boundaries.

Through perception, interaction achieves the capacity for complementing explicit communication by (intended or unintended) indirect communication, where the risks of explicit action can be avoided. Indirect communication is, for example, important as a level for making sexual advances, but also for working out changes in theme, making an end to a contact, and so on. Equally important, reflective perceiving forces communication to go on. If you perceive that you are perceived and that this perception of being perceived is perceived, you have to assume that your behavior gains social relevance (whether this suits you or not). Reflective perception will force you to control your behavior as social behavior, that is, as communication. Even the communication of not wanting to communicate (e.g., looking out the window, hiding behind a newspaper) is communication. One *cannot not communicate* in an interaction situation. One must withdraw from the interaction if one wants to avoid communication.

Society has developed numerous patterns and social conventions that give form to interactions. This historical evolution seems to underpin the idea that interactions only specify societal norms and value orientations that provide for a normative consensus. Societal conventions often suffice to indicate and structure interaction systems. However, one can deviate from these conventions; rules can be broken, or the opportunities they create can be used selectively. For example, you meet someone you know and greet her—in order to get by her. Or you greet someone you know legitimately and are thus entitled to a greeting in return. But the greeting can be returned so as to display an unwillingness to engage in interaction. Some forms of interaction suggested by social conventions can be used to avoid interactions. The interaction system is autonomous with regard to the regulation of communication. There is a theoretical rationale for the separate treatment of interaction, for its treatment as a boundary-maintaining social system in modern times.

Organizationally Framed Interaction

One of the most dominant characteristics of modern society is the wide-spread proliferation of organizations. This historical development—often discussed in terms of rationalization and bureaucratization[2]—also touched on interaction. Interaction now predominantly takes place in organizational settings. For example, schoolteachers have replaced governors. But notwithstanding this organizational "framing,"[3] interaction cannot simply be "instrumentalized" for organizational purposes. It cannot simply be turned into a means that realizes particular organizational ends (as teachers know). On the other hand, organizations create a structure for the interaction, at the least because interaction now takes place *between the members of an organization*. To exemplify the impact of the organizational setting on interaction situations, and vice versa, some particular characteristics of organized interaction can be indicated.[4]

Interaction in organizations is often defined in terms of "work." One's presence at work is motivated by the benefits of organizational membership, not by the delights of the social interaction.[5] The possibility of social interaction depends in this account on the organization; interaction is regulated by the organization. However, organizational possibilities also depend on informal or deregulated interaction. The attitude toward tolerating professional mistakes, which Erving Goffman observed among many surgeons, for example, is from the perspective of the organization of the hospital itself a mistake.[6] In the interaction system of a surgical operation, however, this attitude fulfills important functions. Explicitly pointing to the mistake made by one of the surgeons would divert the attention of the participants. Moreover, it would impinge on the presentation of self of the addressee, and her reaction might really endanger the interaction. In particular cases, deregulated interactions can prove to be functional for the organization. More generally, it can be stated that the autonomy of the interaction system hinders its straightforward utilization in organizations. The organizational framing makes it possible to regulate interaction in terms of special conditions and special functions, but also allows for deregulated interaction. Regulation and informality come from the same root.

Within an organization, recurrent contacts between the members of the organization are evident. Joint membership guarantees the continuation of the interaction. It does not depend on the outcome of preceding interactions, or on individual willingness to participate. The relationship between the participants can be, and can remain, relatively neutral. Motives for being present exist independent of the interaction situation. A teacher does not return to a class because she likes to work with the class, but because the school organization makes arrangements for recurrent meetings. Presentations of self that nevertheless focus on previous interaction experiences almost inevitably ask for "critical" questions, for example, regarding someone's "real" motives. (Why does she praise us? What is she up to? What does she want of us?) Suspicion as to "real" motives develops almost automatically in these settings. The organization establishes premises that cannot—or only through paradoxical communication—be challenged in the interaction.[7] The improbability that a group of people (each of whom also fulfills other roles) recurrently meets seems to get normalized by organization, but in such a way that an explication in terms of "mutual sympathy" is excluded. In this sense, organization disrupts the connection between intensified social contacts and solidarity, which Emile Durkheim, and many social philosophers after him, presupposed.[8]

If one's presence in the interaction is guaranteed by the organization, a kind of motivational indifference gets normal. Particular commitment to organizational goals is not excluded, but it will become very visible. If mere presence is sufficient, the contrast of high commitment attracts all the more attention. In our postmodern society, this kind of situation is mostly observed by means of a scheme that distinguishes goals and motives. In organizations there are the goals for which one gives one's very best, and there are the motives behind one's behavior (e.g., careerist motives). Interestingly, the actor and the observer attribute the causes of behavior in different ways.[9] Actors typically indicate that they are interested in the work in itself. The organization normally also articulates targets whose realization is explicitly valued. But this does not preclude that observers discuss the actor's motives, and that eventually plans are made to thwart these presumed motives. Too diligent pupils often fall victim to the counterstrategies of their classmates. Apart from the problem of harassment, very little is known of the psychological impact of organizationally framed interaction.[10] It would, in my view, be worthwhile to study the impact of this goal/motive observational scheme on the way one indulges in one's work.

It would be wrong to infer from this brief characterization of organized interaction that "organization" has only led to the emergence of patterns of amoral behavior. It would also be wrong to infer that organizational structures only curtail interaction freedom. The relation between imposing restrictions on, and allowing the extension of, interaction freedom is more complicated. Organizational framing introduces restrictions that are able to provide for greater complexity. What is possible in normal societal interaction is not always possible in an organized setting. But particular organizational limitations sometimes enable the realization of a considerable surplus value in the interaction. The complexities of classroom education are a good example of this intricate interplay of interaction and organization systems.

Classroom Interaction

The "groundwork" for classroom interaction is laid outside the classroom, and outside the school. A large number of structural arrangements are beyond its control, such as the asymmetrical structure of the classroom (one teacher, a number of students of about the same age), the hierarchical relationship between teacher and pupils, the timetable, the subject matter that should be taught and learned. The customary spatial and architectural arrangements—rectangular rooms, aligned benches, pupils who face the teacher but not one another, and so on—complement this structural groundwork. Moreover, the value of schooling is widely promulgated and widely accepted as obvious in our Western society, though different groups may see its value differently. Because siblings and parents of children now at school have usually attended schools, schooling appears as a "natural" stage in growing up. The activities of the other teachers and the head in the classrooms, corridors, and hall also provide the foundation on which a teacher and her pupils build in the classroom.

However, this groundwork does not remove the necessity for the teacher to establish and defend her authority, and to create an environment that elicits learning experiences. In a older, but still noteworthy, article that focuses on strategies teachers adopt to establish their authority in the classroom, Martyn Hammersley wrote: "To the extent that the teacher successfully imposes an asymmetrical 'order' on classroom interaction, he turns his claimed authority into a fact to be reckoned with. By successfully demanding attention and disciplined participation, the teachers actually 'demonstrate' their competence as teachers, that they *are* teachers, and therefore their 'superiority' to pupils."[11] Most pupils know the "official" criteria and can judge their teacher's behavior accordingly. They are able to distinguish between good and bad, strong and weak, soft and strict teachers. "Any 'failure' to maintain 'discipline,' whatever the motive, is in danger of being seen as weakness, and thus lack of 'authority' and of being exploited by pupils."[12] These observations indicate that the system of classroom interaction *is constructed within the interaction* itself. It cannot be programmed, despite the structural and cultural "groundwork." However, *the interaction reflects these external conditions in itself.*

In comparison with other domains of social life, the educational system has hardly been able to establish and impose reliable forms of organizational control. Education is very "vulnerable." In classroom education, goals cannot be attained without the commitment of the pupils, while on the other hand this commitment *cannot be organizationally enforced.* The teacher is, as Dan Lortie noted, "expected to elicit work from students. Students in all subjects and activities must engage in directed activities which are believed to produce 'learning'. . . . The teacher therefore must 'motivate' students, within the constraints described, to work hard and, if possible, to enjoy their efforts. He cannot count on voluntary enthusiasm: the teacher must generate much of the positive feeling that animates purposeful effort. All this, moreover, must be accomplished within a group setting."[13] Educational organizations lack, as Lortie argued, an adequate and reliable technology. The results of particular interventions cannot be foreseen or planned in organizational headquarters. The sources of success or failure cannot be exactly identified. Education is highly dependent on the dynamics of the interaction system.

It is a general characteristic of the so-called people processing organizations (e.g., spiritual, medical, legal, or therapeutic systems of help) that organizational goals are difficult to achieve without the commitment of their clients. This characteristic might explain the high degree of professional autonomy and the importance of face-to-face interactions in the course of the "treatment."[14] There is, however, great variation within the professional organizations in this regard. Clients often enroll in "people processing" organizations because of biographical crises, and thus do not need to be urged on to collaborate. They long for this help and are willing to pay for it. Here, education finds itself in an exceptional position. Because children have to go to school (at least at the primary and secondary level), this source of voluntary enthusiasm or commitment mostly fails. Schools have to deal with a particularly critical audience. Accordingly, one finds numerous and often very inventive "opting-out" strategies in educational interactions, all of which make use of perception and the perception of perception. Pupils are continually engaged in reading the behavior of their teacher. Observing whether one is being observed or is temporarily out of the teacher's sight, hiding behind another one's back, pretending that one listens attentively, looking as if everything that is said is understood, and so on.

It is, in this context, interesting to point to some historical developments that have accompanied the generalization of classroom education. In the educational literature that appeared at the end of the eighteenth century, the very possibility of education in the classroom became an important topic. One doubted, for example, whether a teacher could exercise educational authority because there were no blood ties between the teacher and her pupils. Elsewhere, it has been argued that the generalization of classroom education depended on an organizational "deactivation" of the instability of educational relationships.[15] In this process of "restabilization," the curriculum fulfilled (and furthermore fulfills) an important role. The morphogenesis of the modern educational system encompassed a number of interrelated changes: the so-called discovery of the *child*, the professionalization of *teaching*, and the development of new curricular principles. It is no coincidence that these developments occurred in the same period and mutually reinforced each other. The triadic structure was indispensable for the morphogenesis of the modern system of education. Until today, the curriculum specifies what needs to be learned at school. This way, it unburdens the teacher; it reduces the tensions between teachers and pupils. In schools, one focuses on what needs to be learned. This organizational condition partly normalizes the improbability of educational interaction in the classroom.

In short, there develops an interaction system among those present in classrooms. Organizational arrangements have a bearing on this interaction. But they do not simply restrict degrees of freedom of the interaction. They

create opportunities that would not be available without the school organization. Restrictions on and extensions of these degrees of freedom go together and depend on each other.

THE FUNCTION SYSTEM OF EDUCATION

I now turn to the macrolevel of education. The following analysis deals with
what Talcott Parsons has called the "educational revolution," namely, the realization of mass higher education.[16] Demands for participation in higher
education have continued to increase during the twentieth century. Why
does this evolution occur within modern society?

From the outset, it is important to keep in mind that education is not the
only societal system to have expanded during the past decades. Similar evolutions are taking place elsewhere, for example, with regard to the demand
for health care, for legislation, or for political decision making. In fact, most
societal systems are confronted with expanding demands. This phenomenon
indicates that school expansion is less related to education and educational
policy as such, but the result of fundamental characteristics of modern society and thus open to general sociological analysis. On the basis of Luhmann's work, the following analysis focuses on two structural developments—functional differentiation and individualization—and indicates how
these developments contribute to the growth of the system of education.

Functional Differentiation

It is one of the general findings of classical sociology—which sought, at
the end of the nineteenth century, to grasp the nature of the "modern" in
contemporary societies—that social evolution coincides with greater social
complexity and increasing social differentiation.[17] Following Luhmann, this
statement is true but needs clarification.[18] Societies have first of all incorporated distinct *forms* of differentiation in the course of history. Degrees of differentiation and degrees of complexity are produced and mediated by these
forms of differentiation. Accordingly, it is the form (and not just the degree)
of differentiation that accounts for the continuous reproduction of the characteristics of modern society. Insight into these characteristics can be gained
by closely analyzing the modern form of societal differentiation.

Following Luhmann, modern society is not characterized by the forms of
segmentation or *stratification*, but by *functional differentiation*. Functional differentiation organizes communication processes around special functions to
be fulfilled at the level of society. One can think, in this regard, of the political function of producing collectively binding decisions, the economic function of securing the satisfaction of future wants, the religious function of interpreting the incomprehensible, the scientific function of acquiring

knowledge, or the function of educating human beings. "Since all necessary functions have to be fulfilled and are interdependent, society cannot concede absolute primacy to any one of them [as, e.g., to the upper ranks in stratified societies]. It has to use a second level of subsystem formation to institute the primacy of specific functions limited to a special set of system/environment relations."[19] In a functionally differentiated society, none of the primary subsystems can represent society in general. There is no point of view that would allow an overall perspective with universal validity. No function system can claim a position that transcends its particular function—not even the economy, the political system or religion. Instead, *function systems give primacy to their particular function.*

Each function system establishes a specific, highly selective set of system/environment relations. The specificity of its function is, however, combined with universalism.[20] The projection of universal relevance of its own function leads, as Luhmann indicates, to the *inclusion of the entire population.* In contrast with other forms of differentiation, the entire population now gains access to each of the social subsystems (e.g., through universal suffrage or compulsory education). Access to function systems becomes independent of any relation to other subsystems. Function systems have to treat their environments as environments of equals, while nothing but function can justify discrimination.[21] In other words, they can tolerate indifference toward almost everything, except very special features of their respective environments. The function systems do not depend on a complementary definition of their environment. Each subsystem can tolerate an open and fluctuating environment (so long as other subsystems fulfill their function). This has important advantages for the heightening of social complexity. In this sense, the form of differentiation mediates the degree of differentiation and of social complexity.

These evolutions have, as indicated, a wide-ranging scope. They do not only affect the educational system. A brief description of the medical system—which displays a particular resemblance with education (cf. infra)—may clarify this scope. At present, illness is no longer interpreted as an ill-fated relation to the world, or the consequence of disbelief or moral misbehavior. It is considered to be a specific defect in the normal physical or mental functioning of human beings, that can be identified with the help of the medical sciences, and that can be treated by specific techniques. Every individual is entitled to medical care—not just the upper classes of society. Moreover, the medical system not only strives for the healing of diseases but focuses on health. It follows a logic that holds out unlimited prospects of complete well-being *and* of medical interventions. According to the definition of the World Health Organization, "health is a state of complete physical, mental and social well-being and not merely the absence of disease or infirmity." As a consequence, the entire population is ill and needs to be treated. As with other subsystems, the medical system hypostatizes its own function. According to its proper perspective, neither politics nor religion, neither the economy nor education, but only the medical system itself is able to claim absolute primacy in society.

Developments within one subsystem may or may not jeopardize developments elsewhere in society. On the level of the function systems, there can be a simultaneous augmentation of autonomy and mutual dependence. There is no zero-sum principle; more freedom in one system does not need to imply less freedom in the others. Dependencies and independencies of function systems can expand together. Every subsystem is, in as far as it gains freedom for its *own* function, dependent upon the fulfillment of the *other* functions elsewhere within society. As Luhmann writes, "By specifying and institutionalizing functions, society *increases* its internal interdependencies. By loosening the structural complementarities of systems and environments and by providing for more and more indifference, society *decreases* internal interdependencies. It augments, in other words, internal dependencies and independencies at the same time."[22] For sure, modernization is not synonymous with progress.

Individualization

The preceding reflections focus on structural evolutions within modern society. They describe the development of a generalized "readiness" for expansion on the side of the function systems. But they do not yet explain the increasing demand on the side of the *individuals*. They do not explain why individuals raise their expectations (and raise their expectations about the fulfillment of their expectations). The hypothesis that underpins the following analysis is that contemporary processes of self-identification, and of the production of expectations and wishes, correlate with the social structure of modernity. According to well-known sociological analyses, modernity gives way to the increasing individualization of human beings.[23] This evolutionary process brings about, among other things, greater differences between the individual life worlds, increasing disparities between individual biographies and individual strategies for dealing with or avoiding role conflicts, and a more articulate awareness of personal uniqueness. Not the identity of, but the difference between individuals gets accentuated in complex and differentiated societies.

Since George H. Mead,[24] it has become clear that social structures mediate the constitution and actualization of the self. The way an individual experiences herself is dependent on the schemes that society makes available to present one's proper identity. In modern societies, schemes that allow us to think and talk about ourselves in terms of accumulated personal experiences have multiplied, and have become dominant. Important social institutions have developed that stimulate this kind of introspection, and that generate individual biographies—as, for example, diaries, psychoanalytic and therapeutic sessions, in-depth interviews in journals, in magazines, and on television. Individuals have to construct themselves within an authentic story of life. "Possessing a name and a place within the social framework in the form of general categories such as age, gender, social status and profession no longer suffices. . . . Rather, individual persons have to find affirmation at the level of their respective personality systems, i.e. in the difference between themselves and their environment and in the manner in which they deal with this difference—as opposed to the way others do."[25] The "burden of proof" rests in our contemporary society on individual shoulders.

Complementary to this description of the structural determinants of individualization in modern societies, additional questions need to be posed: How exactly do individuals constitute and preserve for themselves a particular identity? Which techniques do they use? In modern society, the self-identification of individualized individuals seems to take place (to a certain degree) by means of *expectations*, and the information or feedback these expectations provide—when they are fulfilled and when they are not fulfilled. An individual uses expectations as antennas for scanning the contingency of the environment in relation to herself. Her expectations produce the difference between success and disappointment, and this difference does not depend on these expectations alone. Expectations enable the gathering of information and the accumulation of experiences, and thus they contribute to the constitution and actualization of the self.[26]

Forming expectations is a simple technique. An expectation can be formulated without self-knowledge and without being familiar with the world—for example, by good luck. But "after a certain period of conscious life enriched by social experiences, completely random expectations cease to occur. . . . One is forced to orient oneself to one's own history of consciousness, however unique it may be."[27] In modern society, individuals are forced to adapt internally to the fulfillment or disappointment of their expectations. Each individual has to explain to herself the results; she needs to attribute success and disappointment to particular factors. The causes of fulfillment are, for example, attributed to oneself, and those of non-fulfillment to others.[28] One can, as a consequence, adapt one's level of expectations to one's experiences, or stick to one's original expectations and fall back into resentment or look for some kind of compensation.

This way of forming and dealing with expectations and the modern principle of functional differentiation clearly affect each other. Function systems seem to incite individuals to put forward their expectations and claims, insofar as these fall within their functional competence. For sure, they cannot legitimately reject these expectations. The fulfillment of their function is their raison d'être. And the entire population is actively or passively built into their operational perspective (inclusion). No school or university, for example, can reject the expectations of students to receive more and better education or training. On the other hand, no individual can gain an overall view of the overly complex operations of function systems. One can only follow the course of one's expectations and record whether what is expected really occurs. An individual's expectations enable a reduction in the "unmanageable complexity" of society, due to "the increasing diversification and particularization of familiarities and unfamiliarities."[29] They transform social complexity directly into individual fate. In this way, expectations and systems establish a kind of symbiosis. *They build a relationship that gives way to increasing growth.* Separated from each other, these elements would break down.

Educational Growth

The previous section sketches a fairly monochrome picture. It offers a general outline of the patterns of social differentiation and individual self-actualization in modern society. This outline can be, and needs to be, refined by focusing on the development of the *educational system* within modern society. In fact, the principle of functional differentiation itself indicates ways toward the respecification of our analysis. It points to the fact that the subsystems are directed toward different primary functions of the societal system, and that they thus display (to a certain degree) distinct characteristics. Function systems show both similarities and differences. Therefore, analyses are necessary to explain the particular characteristics of education vis-à-vis other function systems. Moreover, a similar sensitivity is needed for assessing the relevance of national data and national trends. Comparative perspectives allow us to color the picture of the evolution of educational participation in particular countries or regions.[30]

Starting point for this analysis is Luhmann's idea that society consists of communications, and *only* of communications. Individuals are no element or part of the societal system. The human body and the human psyche belong to the environment of society. Communication establishes a reality sui generis. This does not, of course, exclude the fact that social systems and individuals affect one another—as demonstrated in the previous sections. But organic, psychic and social systems consist of different networks of operations.

In the course of society's modernization, the systemic boundaries between human beings and the societal system have become outspoken. The human body and the human psyche have lost much of their immediate relevance for societal communication. The media of dissemination (writing, printing, and recently also electronic devices) enabled/enable an immense extension of the scope of the communicative process. And this process has clearly affected the form of social differentiation. "A societal system that is vertically differentiated according to the principle of stratification presupposes that societal differentiation is directed by kinds of persons, by their 'quality,' by their determination to live in specific castes or ranked groups. By contrast, with the transition to functional differentiation, the schematic of differentiation is chosen autonomously; it is directed only by the functional problems of the societal system itself."[31] Functional differentiation is a differentiation of communication systems.

Most function systems are, as a consequence, oriented toward problems within modern society itself (although they have, of course, an impact on society's environment). They organize networks of communication, and depend upon "symbolic media" (Luhmann) to fulfill their function—as, for example, politics on power, science on truth, the economy on property and money, or the family on love. The unique position of the educational system within society derives from the fact that education is *oriented toward society's environment*, that is, toward bringing about psychic and behavioral changes in human beings. It is only the medical system that occupies a similar boundary position. The medical and the educational systems are involved not only in the "socialization" of human beings as an adequate environment for social systems, but they also focus on human beings as such, namely, on the development of their capacities and on their health. They are (to a certain degree) concerned with the opportunities and problems proper to society's environment. Their ideals display a clear independence from societal concerns. In the educational system, the difficult relation (both in theory and in practice) between liberal education and vocational education provides a clear illustration of the conflict between the fulfillment of education's ideal of human development and the provision of qualifications which prepare for someone's professional life.[32]

An important consequence of this boundary position of the educational (and the medical) system might be, at first sight, a surprise. The boundary position explains why the values of human development (and health) are hardly contested within society. Human development is one of the few values that is looked upon as an ultimate value, and it has remained largely outside ideological controversies—in contrast with, for example, issues of (and governmental expenditures for) national defense, art collection, economic activities, religious services, or the organization of political life itself.[33] Because education does not merely involve communicative consequences, but is concerned with the *external conditions of the possibility of social systems*, there is little opposition to the ideals advocated. Accordingly, *there are only a few societal restraints on educational expansion*.[34] Of course, this does not mean that human development deserves preference in every kind of situation. This value expresses an abstract appreciation, and loses much of its relevance when it comes to the individual development of *other human beings*. Also, individuals do not always behave as if this value is an ultimate value (e.g., preferring a holiday over a conference). The rank order only applies to the communications with which the educational system asserts itself. But its application cannot easily be disputed by other function systems.

This situation has a correlate at the *individual level*. I have already indicated that society's "great transformation" (from stratification to functional differentiation) changed the conditions of inclusion within society. An individual's inclusion is no longer determined by her social origins or birth. Involvement in a function system is dependent on the circumstances—on the way inclusion is conditioned by the subsystems themselves. Each subsystem records, as a consequence, past accomplishments. For an individual, status and prospects for future involvement come to depend on previous events in the same system—as, for example, someone's economic position depends upon previous receipts and expenditure, or someone's scientific reputation on publications and citations. Inclusion takes, as Luhmann argued, the form of a career.[35] The concept of "career" should be understood in its broad sense, not just in terms of a succession of occupational positions within an organization. It includes stagnation or demotion. It might also refer to a career of diseases, or of crimes. A career is the temporal structure of the process of inclusion.

The career structure underlines the importance of decisions and outcomes in an individual's life. Henceforth, individuals feel triggered to put forward individual expectations and claims. This strategy enables them to distinguish themselves from what's common, or characterizes "the others."[36] The *accumulative structure* of a career provokes, at the same time, divergent evaluations of particular events and lifetime episodes. It enhances the relevance of the beginning of one's career, and leads to the dominance of the future over the present. Current choices and decisions get evaluated from the point of view of their future consequences, especially in one's earlier (school) years. This situation clearly stimulates individuals to invest in their education. Grades and certificates make a difference, although an educational career certainly does not neatly link up with, for example, an economic career. The hopes of manpower planning have not come true. In practice, diffuse relationships between training and selection for jobs tend to dominate.[37] Diploma inflation, underemployment, and overschooling have become widespread phenomena. Nevertheless, the social structure stimulates individuals to "go for it"—even when faced with counterfactual indications. The resultant process has been aptly described as "self-generating educational expansion."[38]

From the perspective of a theory of functional differentiation, the most obvious conclusion is that each function system creates the foundations for hypostasizing its *own* function, and that each function system stimulates individuals to put forward expectations and claims in its *own* functional domain. This point of view contradicts with approaches that discuss patterns of educational growth in the context of politics or of the economy.[39] The educational system is not a part of the economic system (such as the agricultural sector, or the computer industry); neither is it one of many subdomains of the political system. With this kind of sociological approach, important distinctions get blurred, while issues of streamlining educational growth are reduced to problems of policy planning and policy interventions.[40] The rationale of *political* decisions is always adjusted in the *educational* system. Political decisions produce effects in education, but they often do so in unexpected ways. Insisting on the autonomy of function systems and on the particular characteristics of the educational system makes it possible to avoid particular simplifications. However, the theory of functional differentiation should not lead to an underestimation of the interrelationships and interdependencies between the different function systems of society.

In sum, educational expansion is the result of an intricate interplay between individual expectations and characteristics of the educational subsystem. This interplay generates, in contemporary society, its own stimulation. The social order incites individuals to put forward their own individuality, and their individual career, as claims. The educational system does not and cannot limit itself to the expectations of individuals. According to its ideals (human development, *Bildung*, *perfectionnement*), ends can only be arbitrarily enforced. The particular patterns of educational expansion, of course, depend on particular conditions—such as the structure of the school system, legislation concerning compulsory school attendance, and so on. Political interventions make a difference. But these interventions will have unintended effects. The rationale of the political system is not the same as that of other societal subsystems. The educational system operates in its own way. It needs to translate external interventions into internal factual arrangements; it can only react autonomously.

CONCLUSION

In the first decades after World War II, systems-theoretical sociology was almost identifiable with Talcott Parsons's structural functionalism. Structural functionalism started from the assumption that social systems require a normative system that is internally coherent and broadly shared by its members. The stability of this normative system of order—which Parsons called a structural imperative—"explained" different social processes. From this perspective, the equilibrium of the system of society prescribed the function of education. Analyses of education focused on the fulfillment of its societal function. Researchers did not study the particular characteristics of an autonomous education system, but its instrumentality with regard to maintaining the equilibrium of society at large.

Nowadays, social systems theory has started to explore new directions. Systems theory is no longer concerned with stability, equilibrium or pattern maintenance. The preceding sections provide illustrations of this new approach with regard to educational phenomena. They illustrate the fruitfulness of social systems theory with regard to the level of educational interaction and the level of society and its subsystems. They use a highly complex theoretical framework, but also offer the corresponding analytical benefits.

NOTES

1. N. Luhmann, "The Evolutionary Differentiation between Society and Interaction," in *The Micro-Macro Link*, ed. J. F. Alexander et al. (Berkeley: University of California Press, 1987), 114; see also N. Luhmann, *Social Systems* (Stanford: Stanford University Press, 1995), 412–16; R. Vanderstraeten, "Observing Systems: A Cybernetic Perspective on System/Environment Relations," *Journal for the Theory of Social Behaviour* 31 (2001).

2. M. Weber, *Economy and Society* (Berkeley: University of California Press, 1978).

3. E. Goffman, *Frame Analysis* (Cambridge: Harvard University Press, 1975).

4. A. Kieserling, *Kommunikation unter Anwesenden* (Frankfurt a.M.: Suhrkamp, 1999), 335–87.

5. J. Habermas, *Technik und Wissenschaft als "Ideologie"* (Frankfurt a.M.: Suhrkamp, 1976).

6. E. Goffman, *Encounters: Two Studies in the Sociology of Interaction* (Harmondsworth, U.K.: Penguin University Books, 1961).

7. K. E. Weick, *Sensemaking in Organizations* (Thousand Oaks, Calif.: Sage, 1995).

8. See E. Durkheim, *De la division du travail social* (1893; Paris: PUF, 1930).

9. E. E. Jones and R. E. Nisbet, "The Actor and the Observer: Divergent Perceptions on the Causes of Behavior," in *Attribution: Perceiving the Causes of Behavior*, ed. E. E. Jones et al. (Morristown, N.J.: Central Learning Press, 1972).

10. See also R. Vanderstraeten, "Autopoiesis and Socialization: On Luhmann's Reconceptualization of Communication and Socialization," *British Journal of Sociology* 51 (2000): 581–98; R. Vanderstraeten, "The School Class as an Interaction Order," *British Journal of Sociology of Education* 22 (2001): 267–77.

11. M. Hammersley, "The Mobilisation of Pupil Attention," in *The Process of Schooling*, ed. M. Hammersley and P. Woods (London: Routledge & Kegan Paul, 1976), 111.

12. Hammersley, "Mobilisation of Pupil Attention," 112.

13. D. C. Lortie, *Schoolteacher: A Sociological Study* (Chicago: University of Chicago Press, 1975), 151–52. See also R. Dreeben, *On What Is Learned in School* (Reading, Mass.: Addison-Wesley, 1968).

14. A. Abbott, *The System of Professions* (Chicago: University of Chicago Press, 1988).

15. R. Vanderstraeten and G. J. J. Biesta, "How Is Education Possible? Preliminary Investigations for a Theory of Education," *Educational Philosophy and Theory* 32 (2001): 7–21.

16. See, for example, T. Parsons and G. M. Platt, *The American University* (Cambridge: Harvard University Press, 1974).

17. See, for example, G. Simmel, *Gesamtausgabe*, vol. 2, *Über soziale Differenzierung*, ed. O. Rammstedt (Frankfurt a.M.: Suhrkamp, 1989); Durkheim, *De la division du travail social*; T. Parsons, *The Social System* (Glencoe, Ill.: Free Press, 1951).

18. N. Luhmann, *The Differentiation of Society* (New York: Columbia University Press, 1982), 229–54; N. Luhmann, *Die Gesellschaft der Gesellschaft* (Frankfurt a.M.: Suhrkamp, 1997), 595–865.

19. Luhmann, *Differentiation of Society*, 236.

20. Luhmann, *Gesellschaft der Gesellschaft*, 375–76. See also T. Parsons, "Pattern Variables Revisited: A Response to Robert Dubin," *American Sociological Review* 25 (1960): 467–83.

21. See R. Stichweh, "Inklusion in Funktionssysteme der modernen Gesellschaft," in *Differenzierung und Verselbständigung: Zur Entwicklung gesellschaftlicher Teilsysteme*, ed. R. Mayntz, B. Rosewitz, U. Schimank, and R. Stichweh (Frankfurt a.M.: Campus, 1988),

261–93, R. Vanderstraeten, "Versäulung und funktionale Differenzierung: Zur Enttradi-tionalisierung der katholischen Lebensformen," *Soziale Welt* 50 (1999): 297–314.

22. Luhmann, *Differentiation of Society*, 237.

23. A. Giddens, *Modernity and Self-Identity* (Stanford: Stanford University Press, 1991), 70–108.

24. G. H. Mead, *Mind, Self, and Society*, ed. Charles W. Morris (Chicago: University of Chicago Press, 1934).

25. N. Luhmann, *Love as Passion* (Cambridge: Polity, 1986), 15–16.

26. N. Luhmann, *Essays on Self-Reference* (New York: Columbia University Press, 1990), 107–22; U. Beck, *Risikogesellschaft* (Frankfurt a.M.: Suhrkamp, 1986), 205–19. See also G. Bateson, *Steps to an Ecology of Mind* (New York: Ballantine, 1972).

27. Luhmann, *Social Systems*, 268–69.

28. See, for example, B. Weiner et al., "Perceiving the Causes of Success and Failure," in *Attribution: Perceiving the Causes of Behavior*, ed. E. E. Jones et al. (Morristown, N.J.: Central Learning Press, 1972), 95–120.

29. N. Luhmann, "Familiarity, Confidence, Trust: Problems and Alternatives," in *Trust: Making and Breaking Cooperative Relations*, ed. D. Gambetta (Oxford: Basil Blackwell, 1988), 105.

30. R. Vanderstraeten, "L'évolution de la scolarisation en Belgique: Vers une nouvelle perspective sur l'expansion du système éducatif," *Eduquer & Former* 2 (1996): 15–27; R. Vanderstraeten, "Educational Expansion in Belgium: A Sociological Analysis Using Systems Theory," *Journal of Education Policy* 14 (1999): 507–22.

31. Luhmann, *Social Systems*, 193. Another example might clarify this often disputed assumption. If, inside an organization, departments are set up around different external groups (e.g., customers or circles of persons to be cared for), this strengthens the influence of these groups on the organization; they find "their" representation in the organization. By contrast, if the structuring is chosen according to purely internal points of view, the autonomy of the organizational system increases.

32. See H. Silver, *Education, Change, and the Policy Process* (London: Falmer, 1990), 100–146; R. Vanderstraeten, *Leren voor het leven* (Leuven/Apeldoorn: Garant, 1995), 75–141.

33. One might consider, for example, the Universal Declaration of Human Rights, whose fiftieth anniversary has recently been celebrated. Most recent value surveys also underpin this outcome. With regard to assessments of the value of education, see D. Tyack and L. Cuban, *Tinkering toward Utopia: A Century of Public School Reform* (Cambridge: Harvard University Press, 1995).

34. R. Vanderstraeten, "Circularity, Complexity, and Educational Policy Planning: A Systems Approach to the Planning of School Provision," *Oxford Review of Education* 23 (1997): 321–32

35. N. Luhmann, *Soziologische Aufklärung 4: Beiträge zur funktionalen Differenzierung der Gesellschaft* (Opladen: Westdeutscher Verlag, 1987), 188–91; N. Luhmann and K. E. Schorr, *Reflexionsprobleme im Erziehungssystem* (Frankfurt a.M.: Suhrkamp, 1988), 277–82.

36. See P. Bourdieu, *La distinction: Critique sociale du jugement* (Paris: Les Éditions de Minuit, 1979).

37. H. Silver and J. Brennan, *A Liberal Vocationalism* (London: Methuen, 1987), 34–52.

38. J. W. Meyer, F. O. Ramirez, R. Rubinson, and J. Boli-Bennett, "The World Educational Revolution, 1950–1970," *Sociology of Education* 50 (1979): 245.

39. For example, M. S. Archer, *Social Origins of Educational Systems* (London: Sage, 1979).

40. Vanderstraeten, "Circularity, Complexity, and Educational Policy Planning."

3

Social Capital in Education:

Theoretical Issues and Empirical Knowledge in Attainment Research

AnneBert Dijkstra and Jules L. Peschar

In the past decades, much comparative research into educational attainment and stratification has been conducted. In these studies, a strong increase in average educational level in all countries has been observed (cf. Shavit and Blossfeld 1993). Still, the relatively strong effect of social background can be mentioned, although this effect seems to be decreasing in some countries if longer trends are taken into account. The relationship between level of education and job level has also become stronger in most industrialized countries, partly as a result of the increase in the level of education. Finally, diminishing returns of education have been observed.

On the basis of these findings, the argument is sometimes put forward that the impact of education as such is decreasing because of the steadily rising level of education. Since most people in modern Western industrialized countries have some certificate of secondary education, some authors believe that this criterion is slowly becoming irrelevant. However, this is a spurious argument. Education is at least as important—if not more—than before, because those who have not received an education are much worse off than those who have. And even people with a substantial amount of training cannot avoid being ranked by a future employer, as Thurow's (1975) labor queue theory suggests. From an individual perspective, therefore, it is quite rational to aim for the highest possible level of training in order to secure the best possible employment. From a societal point of view, however, the usefulness of this "rat race" may be questioned in situations where education is costly and jobs are scarce.

In the light of these observations, the debate about the distribution of educational opportunities is still highly relevant. In this chapter, we will discuss the developments around the concept of "social capital" in education. The concept of social resources or social capital—introduced in educational

58

attainment research around fifteen years ago—was quickly adopted in the sociology of education. Most authors regard it as a fruitful theory that may add new insights to our knowledge of processes involved in the distribution of educational opportunities and selection and allocation through education. In this chapter, we intend to make a contribution toward the evaluation of social capital theories and their empirical status in the light of our understanding of educational attainment and stratification processes. We will present an impression of the available empirical support for presumed effects of social capital on the distribution of educational attainment. We will also discuss the theoretical status of the concept of social capital as it is usually understood in studies of the distribution of educational opportunities.

SOCIAL CAPITAL IN EDUCATION

"Capital" for Education

One of the most researched issues in the sociology of education is the question to what extent social background influences educational achievement. There is widespread and frequently documented agreement that it does. But despite the intensive research effort, it is still largely unknown why this is so.

In the past decades, many studies have been devoted to the explanation of educational achievement, more specifically to its distribution among students from various social backgrounds. Research into determinants of educational attainment can be roughly divided into three categories. Studies conducted from a psychological point of view mainly focus on student competencies, for example, cognitive, motivational, or creative abilities. Ecological factors are also considered important. On the one hand, these are studied from an in-school perspective, for example, in school effectiveness research. On the other hand, ecological explanations have also been investigated from an out-of-school perspective, where (family) socialization research is the central paradigm for theoretical reflection and empirical research.

Concerning the distribution of educational opportunities, the main emphasis in the sociology of education during the past decades has been on the search for explanations based on the family background of students. The importance of the family for a successful educational career has been substantiated by a large volume of research. Classic examples are the studies by Coleman et al. (1966) and Jencks et al. (1972). Recent studies have shown that these insights have lost little relevance. Central to this line of research is the insight that the extent to which school careers are successful depends not only on the individual characteristics (e.g., their cognitive skills) of students, but is also connected with the position of their family within the social structure. The above summary of the basic educational opportunity model forms the basis of the socialization research tradition; it is represented in figure 3.1.

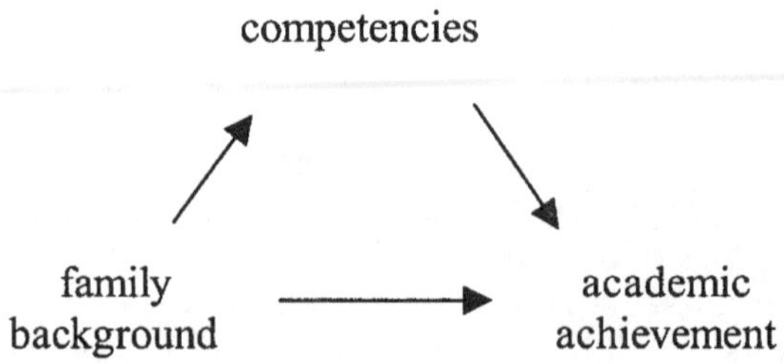

competencies

family   ⟶   academic
background   achievement

Figure 3.1.   Basic Model of Educational Opportunity

Although the family's social status appears to be a powerful indicator for
school success, it does not offer much insight into the factors that are responsible for the relationship between family background and educational
attainment. Socialization research focuses on revealing the mechanisms that
explain the distribution of educational achievement of students from different social backgrounds. What mechanisms are responsible for the relationship between background characteristics and school success? Which mediating variables explain the relationship between family environment and
educational attainment?

A substantial portion of socialization research concentrates on factors that
can be linked to the position of the family in the status hierarchy and that benefit a student's educational career. Families differ in the resources available to
them for supplying their children with qualifications that will enable them to
participate successfully in education. In this research approach, the means
available within the family are regarded as the intermediate factors between
family background and the student's educational career (see figure 3.2). These
mediating variables—the "resources" or "capital" available in the family—are
measures of various mechanisms that may influence academic achievement.

Financial, Human, and Cultural Capital

The first explanation put forward for socially different patterns of educational participation and achievement is financial resources—capital in the strict
sense of the word. Financial capital consists of the financial and other material
means available to a family that can be allocated to education. This can easily
be understood as a mediating variable. The higher the educational and occupational level of the family, the higher the budget for educational expenditure.

Human capital refers to the knowledge, skills, and capabilities that enable
an individual to act more effectively. Human capital is usually measured in
terms of the parents' education ("scholastic" capital). It can render a substantial contribution to a favorable starting position for children to participate successfully in education.

Other parental attributes that may benefit children have been called "cultural" capital. Although the concept of cultural capital was not widely ac-

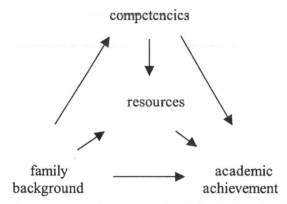

Figure 3.2. **Basic Resource Model of Educational Opportunity**

cepted until the 1970s (cf. Bourdieu and Passeron 1977), much of the extensive research into processes of socialization conducted in the past decades to explain the relationship between social background and educational opportunities may be regarded as research into the effects of cultural resources. The cultural capital approach attempts to explain the relationship between school success and family background by pointing to the cultural knowledge and attitudes of families that benefit a successful educational career. The motivational qualities of the parents, the linguistic characteristics of the family, and participation in cultural activities and reading behavior are examples of such cultural resources, and these differ according to social status (cf. Bernstein 1971; Kohn 1977; DiMaggio 1982). Research has shown that the link between the socio-economic background characteristics of students and their educational performance can be partially explained by the extent to which their families have cultural capital at their disposal (e.g., de Graaf 1989).

Despite the many studies based on this approach, our insight into the factors mediating the relationship between social background and educational career is by no means complete. This is illustrated by the—often disappointing—results of interventions aimed at the effects of family background to stimulate educational achievement. The unsatisfactory results have been explained by pointing to the inadequate theories and theoretically flawed empirical research on which these interventions were based (cf. Leseman 1989).

Social Capital

Although it is a more or less natural extension of human, financial, and cultural capital, a fourth type of resource has only recently received more attention. Known as "social capital," this kind of resource refers to means available to families that reside in human relationships. In particular the work done by James Coleman at the University of Chicago concerning the effects of social resources on the distribution of educational opportunities has received much attention. Coleman and his colleagues researched differences in educational achievement between public and private schools in the United States (Coleman, Hoffer, and Kilgore 1982). After having corrected for mediating variables, the differences they found continued to exist. In an interesting theory, Coleman and Hoffer (1987) suggest that the social capital available in the networks around Roman Catholic schools can explain the favorable performance of these schools.

In view of the influential role of the work of especially Coleman and Hoffer for the introduction of the concept of social capital in the sociology of education, we will begin our discussion of the usefulness of this concept for educational attainment research by presenting this theory at some length. In the rest of this section, we will describe the social capital concept suggested by Coleman to explain the inequality of educational opportunities and the context in which he presented this hypothesis. It soon turned out that these ideas were to inspire much of the research conducted into social resources in education. In the next section, we will continue our discussion by giving an impression of various empirical studies into the presumed effects of social capital; in the last section, we will discuss the theoretical status of the social capital concept as used in educational research.

Social Capital and Functional Communities

Refining earlier ideas about community impact on schools (Coleman 1961; cf. Lindenberg 2000), the explanation given by Coleman for the higher achievements of students of private schools centers on social resources supposedly available in the community around the school. To explain the favorable educational opportunities offered by Catholic schools in particular, Coleman and Hoffer (1987) point to the "functional communities" in which these schools are supposedly embedded. The social capital in such communities is regarded as an additional resource for children to achieve school success. Central to this approach is the notion that families differ not only in the extent to which they possess human and cultural capital, but also in their access to resources that reside in social relationships (Coleman 1988, 1990a). According to Coleman and Hoffer (1987), the social capital in the parental network of Catholic schools is related to the specific characteristics of the community around the school. Referring to classic studies such as *Middletown* (Lynd and Lynd 1929) and *Elmtown's Youth* (Hollingshead 1949), they point to the positive effects of closed networks that include several generations. Local communities such as Middletown and Elmtown, Coleman and Hoffer assert, are examples of functional communities. Characteristic features of such communities are relatively closed networks of mutual social relationships between generations and a dominant value system that is closely linked to the social structure. Such a closed network consists of relationships between parents who know one another and their children and other persons from the children's social environment. As far as the value system is concerned, it is not so much important that the community values are shared by everyone to the same extent, but that there exists a clear, dominant set of social values backed up by the community.

According to Coleman and Hoffer, such social capital available in the community provides parents with a grip on the social environment of their children, with respect to both their lives at school and their contacts with friends and other social activities. The homogeneous value system and the closed network create a uniform and effective pedagogical environment both through reinforcement beyond the direct control of parents (parents of friends and other adults known to the child) and through the school (a dominant set of values and the self-evident nature of roles). The social interaction within the parental community reinforces the parents' ability to monitor their children outside the family sphere and increases their opportunities for adequate supportive and corrective behavior. The social resources thus accrued in functional communities increase the chance of a successful school career. They compensate for the inadequate resources of students from deprived backgrounds and improve the educational opportunities of students from deprived social classes.

Coleman (1993) states that functional communities and the social capital inherent in them are increasingly under threat because of the influence of societal transformation processes. The greater separation of the workplace and the home, the fact that parents are no longer part of the same network throughout their lives, the increased number of working mothers, the decreased number of three-generation households, the increased number of single-parent families, and the strong influence of the mass media have all led to a decline of closed networks and dominant value systems (cf. Coleman 1987; Hoffer and Coleman 1990). As a result, it is assumed that functional communities nowadays exist only under specific conditions, such as those still existing in the more isolated, rural areas of the United States or schools that are part of specific social systems (Coleman 1985).

Contrary to the public schools, where, according to Coleman, the usually geographically determined functional communities have largely disappeared, most of the religious private schools in the United States—particularly, but not exclusively (cf. Berends and Dijkstra 1997), those of the Catholic denomination—retain the specific conditions for functional communities. Instead of geographically determined networks, it is the religious bond between parents that leads to more or less closed networks and "value communities." This is evident from the relatively strong ties parents have with Catholic schools, as illustrated by their involvement with the school life, volunteer work, and class visits (Coleman and Schiller 1992).

THE EMPIRICAL STATUS OF THE SOCIAL CAPITAL
CONCEPT IN EDUCATIONAL ATTAINMENT RESEARCH

Although their theory provides an appealing explanation, Coleman and Hoffer (1987) have not empirically tested the presumed effects of social capital. What is often overlooked in the reception of Coleman's social capital hypothesis is that the supposed relationship between educational opportunities and social capital is based on an ex post facto interpretation, while there has been no direct measurement of the assumed mechanism. Nevertheless, the theory has attracted much attention. The concept was rapidly adopted by many authors[1] and subsequently led to a large number of studies investigating the assumed relationship between the availability of social resources and educational achievement. In this section, we will discuss this research to give an impression of the great variety of the research conducted since the introduction of Coleman's social capital concept, with respect to both the highly diverse conceptualizations and operationalizations of this concept and the range of contexts studied. In the next section, which covers the theoretical basis of the concept of social capital, we will discuss to what extent the theory of social capital provides starting points for a categorization of this highly varied research effort.

Much of the educational research inspired by Coleman's social capital concept is strongly quantitative in nature. These studies often involve analyses of large datasets, as well as evaluation and case studies. Much of the research has concentrated on the American educational system, but the concept has also been applied to educational attainment and stratification research in other parts of the world. We will give an impression of studies based on American data and mention a few examples from other countries, with some emphasis on the Netherlands too.

Social Capital around American Schools

Much of the research conducted in the United States is based on large, nationally representative multipurpose datasets. It is not surprising that many of these studies used data from the National Education Longitudinal Study from 1988; the NELS cohort was offering the latest longitudinal student cohort data available after Coleman and Hoffer's theory was published, and contains several indicators of social resources. This cohort thus played an important role in the initial testing of the effect of social capital (e.g., Teachman, Paasch, and Carver 1997; Carbonaro 1998; McNeal 1999). The influence of social capital within specific migrants or minority groups has also been studied frequently with this dataset (e.g., Hao and Bonstead-Bruns 1998; Sun 1998; Portes and MacLeod 1999). Older datasets have also been analyzed with the social capital concept in mind. Without attempting to cover all the studies, we will give an impression of the results obtained from this American research.

Coleman's coauthor, Thomas Hoffer, used the Longitudinal Study of American Youth to analyze the role of social capital as an explanation for differences in school success. In a longitudinal study of the school careers of approximately six thousand students attending some fifty high schools in the late 1980s, Hoffer (1992) reported results that support the suggested effects of community characteristics on the availability of social resources. In terms of the social ties between parents and the amount of voluntary work done for the school, there appears to be less social capital available in urban than in suburban areas, although the support for a relationship with academic achievement is tenuous. A study based on the same dataset also reported that the strength of the relationships between parents is related to the academic performance of their children. These effects were particularly strong for smaller schools and schools in rural areas (Hoffer 1990).

Based on an analysis of the data of some eleven thousand students from the NELS datasets of the late eighties and early 1990s, Teachman, Paasch, and Carver (1997) also found positive effects. They reported relationships between high school dropouts in grades 10–12 and social capital. Social capital was measured with variables such as, for example, one- or two-parent family, the number of times the student changed schools, the degree to which his or her parents socialized with their friends' parents, and the interaction between parents and the school. Morgan and Sorensen (1999a) also used the NELS data, but they reported a negative effect of parental social capital. Their analysis concerned the relationship between math test scores and school-level measures of social capital, measured by variables like the involvement of parents with other parents, the number of close friends attending the same school, and the influence of parents on school policy. One of their conclusions was that the positive effect of Catholic schools on math achievement is hardly explained by parental involvement and social closure. They also found contrary effects of student friendship networks and schools where parents maintain close ties. Taken together, these effects canceled each other out. Carbonaro (1999), who used the same data but advocated the use of individual measures for social capital, also concluded that there is no support for a positive effect of intergenerational closure, but he did not find a significant negative effect either.[2]

Hofferth, Boisjoly, and Duncan (1998) based their study on data from the Panel Study of Income Dynamics and measured social capital in terms of the opportunities families have to obtain assistance (in the form of time or money) during "a serious emergency in your household" and the extent to which they offer such assistance to others. An analysis of data of some nine hundred adolescents collected at two points in time in the 1980s showed an effect of access to assistance provided by nonrelatives on the number of years of school attendance, although only within high-income groups. No effect was found for assistance offered by relatives. The effect of perceived access to assistance provided by friends was also found for college attendance, but not for high school graduation. Using the same data, Hofferth, Boisjoly, and Duncan (1999) concluded that—unlike the situation in family networks—providing assistance in friendship networks is related to access to assistance.

A longitudinal study conducted in the mid-1980s among some 250 adolescents born from teenage pregnancies investigated the effects of social capital in the form of educational support within the family, a network of friends, and help relationships (Furstenberg and Hughes 1995). The study shows positive effects on some—not all—indicators of educational and occupational success in early adulthood, but not for behavioral categories like delinquent behavior, early parenthood, and depression.

Smith, Beaulieu, and Seraphine (1995) used the High School and Beyond data collected in the 1980s—the same dataset used by Coleman and Hoffer (1987)—to investigate the contribution of social resources toward college attendance in rural communities and various types of urban communities. They operationalized social resources within the family by using variables such as working mothers, the number of parents in the family, and homework monitoring. The number of times the family changed residence and church attendance were used as measures of the social capital in the community. The authors reported hardly any effect for the first type of resources, although parental expectation of college attendance appeared to be a strong predictor. On the other hand, community social capital did have positive effects. The effects varied with the type of community.

Kahne and Bailey (1999) analyzed successful sponsor programs in which a tutor adopts a primary school class with pupils from deprived backgrounds and supports them by means of tutoring, monitoring, and the use of additional (also monetary) resources. According to these researchers, the success of such programs, as illustrated by a substantially increased chance of high school completion, may to a large extent be explained from the various forms of social capital available through the sponsor program: the building of relationships of trust, the creation of values conducive to education, and access to information.

Several authors consider the value of social capital, particularly for at-risk groups, as the primary perspective for an analysis of the relationship between social resources and school success. An example is a study by Portes and MacLeod (1999) of the achievements of second-generation immigrant students. The availability of social resources was measured with variables such as one- or two-parent family, involvement with the parents of friends, and a measure for parental involvement with the child's education. A comparison between the achievements of students who have at least one foreign-born parent and students from nonimmigrant families in the NELS cohort revealed some effects on achievement test scores and grade point average. However, these results did not contribute to the explanation of the achievements of immigrant versus nonimmigrant students. Data from the

NELS cohort was also used to analyze the educational opportunities of students with an East Asian background (Sun 1998). The variables representing within-family and outside-family social capital had varying effects on student test scores. Students from an Asian background mainly distinguished themselves by a strongly positive effect of the social capital available within the family. Stanton-Salazar and Dornbush (1995) studied the influence of social capital on the educational opportunities of Mexican high school students in the San Francisco–San Jose area. The availability of social resources was represented by several characteristics of the student network, like the social status of adults whom the students supposed would provide information-related support, the number of weak ties, and the proportion of non-Mexican friends. The researchers reported a positive relationship between various social-capital variables, grade level, and status expectations.

Social Capital around Other Societies' Schools

Outside the United States, too, research has been conducted into the influence of social capital on school success. We will give a brief impression of some of this research, carried out in a few countries. In this sketch, we will pay more detailed attention to a number of studies of the effects of social capital in the Dutch educational system. In the Netherlands, religion—which plays an important role in Coleman and Hoffer's (1987) argument and was used as an indicator for the availability of social resources—and religious segmentation have traditionally been important determinants of the organization of the educational system (cf. Dijkstra and Dronkers 2001). This religious segmentation resulted in a system in which the (dominant) private school sectors serve religiously segmented student bodies (Dijkstra, Driessen, and Veenstra 2001), offering a fruitful context for functional community effects.

Before describing various Dutch studies, we will first present the outcomes of some studies undertaken in other countries. An analysis of the data of approximately four hundred male graduates of elite universities in Seoul, South Korea, conducted in the early 1990s investigated the effect of the private social capital of the students—in the form of family and friends—and the institutional social capital on job success. The study concluded that it is not so much the private as the institutional social capital—the ties available through the university—that contributed to the level at which the graduate entered the labor market (Lee and Brinton 1996). In Canada, a study was conducted in 1976 among nearly five hundred students attending four schools in the Toronto metropolitan area. Thirteen years later, these students were interviewed again. The studies investigated the effect of social capital in the family and the community on the highest graduation level, the respondents' socioeconomic status, and other variables. The researchers used measurements such as parental support during

adolescence, the time the father spent with the family, maternal employment, and growing up in a two-parent family as indicators for the social resources available within the family. The (loss of) social capital available outside the family was represented by change of residence, where a distinction
was made between childhood and adolescence migration. The analyses
showed that migration had a negative effect on both educational performance and job level, with education mediating the effect on occupational status. It also appeared that the family's social capital, in the form of the
mother's support and the father's presence during adolescence, could mit-
igate the loss of social capital outside the family resulting from the family
moving to a different house. Conversely, the absence of social capital in the
family appeared to reinforce the negative effects of a change of residence
(Hagan, MacMillan, and Wheaton 1996).

To conclude this general discussion of the findings from empirical research into the influence of social capital on educational achievement, we
will give an impression of the results of analyses of data collected in the
Netherlands.

Van der Velden (1991) concentrated on secondary education and used the
mother's social participation and the social background of the grandfather
and family acquaintances as indicators for the availability of social capital.
Based on longitudinal data of more than five hundred students interviewed
twelve years after they had entered primary education, he investigated
whether there were indications for an effect of the social network on their
achievements in secondary education in the mid-1980s. No effects were
found for the mother's social participation or the occupational level of the
grandfather, but the extent of the social network and the social backgrounds
of the members of this network did have effects. Both factors appeared to
have a positive influence on achievement in secondary education. A study
conducted at orthodox Protestant schools in the second half of the 1980s
showed that these schools could be considered almost ideal examples of the
functional communities distinguished by Coleman. They were characterized
by strong ties between schools and semireligious institutions belonging to the
same denomination in which the church members participated actively and
frequently (Dijkstra 1992; Bosker, Dijkstra, and Peschar 1996). These analyses
concerned around five hundred students attending some twenty high
schools, whose school careers between the last year of primary education and
the second phase of secondary education was compared with the careers of
students from a national sample. The dependent variables were the achieved
educational level and the number of students who had to repeat a class or had
to be relegated to a lower school track. The study showed that the functional
community around the school had positive effects on school success, albeit
not across the board. The expectation that students would achieve better generally under the influence of the functional communities was not substantiated. The social resources in the functional community mainly appeared

to have an effect on the prevention of students repeating a class or being rel-egated to a lower school track. This effect was stronger for students from de-prived backgrounds. Dijkstra and Veenstra (2000) also investigated the role of social resources. They used the school career data of seventy-five hundred students in the first phase of secondary school, collected in the mid-1990s on 150 schools. In these analyses, social capital was measured by means of vari-ables representing the strength of the parental network around the school. Al-though these analyses again pointed to a relatively strong presence of social resources around orthodox religious schools, these resources did not appear to contribute to the explanation of differences in math scores.

The effects of social capital have also been investigated in primary educa-tion. In the mid-1980s, Van Liere and Maas (1994) analyzed the data of some six hundred pupils attending twenty primary schools to investigate the effect of the strength of the parental community on expected achievement in sec-ondary education. Their analysis showed that the relationship between parental community and the expected achievement level in high school mainly resided at the pupil level and could not be identified at the level of the school. Hofman, Hofman, Guldemond, and Dijkstra (1996) also studied the effect of social capital in primary education and tried to relate it to the re-lationships existing between the school, the school board, and the parental community. They concluded that the arithmetic scores of around seven hun-dred pupils attending ninety primary schools were related to the extent to which parents are connected to other parents and are actively involved in school affairs, and the influence of teachers, school managers, and parents on the decisions made by the school board. These variables appeared to explain a major portion of the (higher) performance of Catholic schools. Van Veen, Denessen, Van der Kley, and Gerris (1998) concentrated on the social capital within the family, which they operationalized as the nature and extent of the presence of the father and the mother in the child-rearing process. The analy-sis did not produce the expected effects on achievement in secondary educa-tion. On the contrary, slight parental presence appeared to have a positive in-fluence on the school career. However, an alternative interpretation of the same data focused on the positive effects found for the mother, which—as a representation of the social resources within the family—did point in the ex-pected direction (Glebbeek 1998).

THE THEORETICAL STATUS OF
THE SOCIAL CAPITAL CONCEPT

Although the concept of social capital was quickly adopted in educational stratification research, its value is still a matter of debate. Not only is the question sometimes raised whether the theory of social capital reflects mechanisms studied under different labels before, but it is particularly the theoretical basis underlying the concept that needs substantial elaboration. In particular, the question whether the concept of social capital is not too general to be productive as analytic tool and theoretical purposes, stands out.

Related Approaches

The insight that the social structure may be highly beneficial to individuals and groups is rooted in classic insights that may already be found in the works of, for example, Durkheim and Toennies. Around a century ago, Durkheim (1956) pointed to the close link between education and other social systems, for example morals, religion, and social stratification. Studies concentrating on the communities around, for example, Elmtown's schools in Morris (Illinois) or the schools near Crown Street in Liverpool are examples of the attention that has been paid to the social environment of schools ever since (Hollingshead 1949; Mays 1962). The ideas of Coleman, too, show interesting parallels with work done in connection with, for example, the ecology of human development model (Bronfenbrenner 1979; Cochran and Brassard 1979). A central element in this approach is the insight that child rearing is not separated from the wider environment, but is influenced directly and indirectly by relationships existing between the various spheres surrounding the child. The more relationships there are between these spheres and the greater the mutual trust between these spheres, the more effective the social context for child rearing and education will be. Aside from other differences with this model, the social capital hypothesis is mainly attractive for the opportunities it offers to refine a conceptual relationship between attributes of individual actors and the characteristics of the social structure in which actors operate (cf. Furstenberg and Hughes 1995; Greeley 1997).

At present, it is difficult to evaluate the criticism that the concept of social capital has hardly produced any new insights but is mainly an effective metaphor for (re)formulating current insights (cf. Portes 1998)—an example being the interpretation of research into the effects of one-parent families as social capital (e.g., McLanahan and Sandefur 1994). The social capital hypothesis would certainly be worthwhile if the concept should provide a theoretical perspective for generating new insights into the mechanisms underlying the distribution of educational opportunities, linking an integrative conceptualization of current knowledge to a fruitful analytic device for productive research. However, as the rest of this section will show, this promise is still to be fulfilled, despite the attractiveness of the concept.

Coleman's social capital is not "new" either, in the sense that other authors have also mentioned the role of social resources in the reproduction of social inequality.[3] Bourdieu in particular should be mentioned. He defined social capital as "the aggregate of the actual or potential resources which are linked to possession of a durable network of more or less institutionalized relationships of mutual acquaintance or recognition" (Bourdieu 1985, 248).[1] Coleman (1988) defines social capital in broader terms as "a variety of entities with two elements in common: they all consist of some aspect of social structures, and they facilitate certain actions of actors—whether persons or corporate actors—within the structure" (Coleman 1988, S98). Other influential conceptualizations of social capital—as expressed in the work of Putnam (1992), for example—have a different focus, but are less relevant in the context of educational stratification research (for a discussion of the various social capital theories, see, e.g., Portes [1998] and Morrow [1999]). A common feature of the various definitions of social capital is the notion that it "stands for the ability of actors to secure benefits by virtue of membership in social networks or other social structures," as Portes (1998, 6) formulates it. However, the way in which authors have developed these ideas, both theoretically and empirically, has been highly diverse.

Theoretical Problems

In the light of the above, it should not be surprising that the objection is frequently raised that social capital is a diffuse, "rather nebulous concept" (Morrow 1999) "used largely as a metaphor that encompasses existing sociological ideas" (Sandefur and Laumann 1998). This is not only due to the highly general and diverging definitions of the concept but also to its application to a wide range of areas and themes—family and youth, community life, work and organizations, and so on (for an overview, see Woolcock 1998). Various problems should be mentioned in this respect.

Diffuse Concept

To begin with, the influential, but relatively open definition provided by Coleman leaves room for a wide range of specifications. We have encountered some examples of this in the previous section. Coleman defined social capital in terms of its function ("a variety of entities [that] all consist of some aspect of social structures, and . . . facilitate certain actions of actors"), which also determines its value: "those aspects of social structure to actors, as resources that can be used by actors to realize their interests" (Coleman 1990a, 305). Coleman (1988) also distinguished various forms social capital may assume, such as obligations and expectations, the extent to which the social structure facilitates the flow of information and values upheld by means of sanctions. As factors that contribute to the creation—or destruction—of social capital, Coleman mentioned intergenerational closure, the stability of the social system, ideology, and depersonalized support systems (Coleman 1990a). Portes (1998) stated that this approach could easily lead to confusion and blurring of mechanisms, outcomes, and the social context in which social capital is created. He therefore warned against tautological statements in which what social capital is and what it does merge unnoticed (cf. Edwards and Foley 1997). Woolcock (1998) therefore advocated that the sources of social capital should primarily be taken as a starting point for the development of the concept. Conversely, Sandefur and Laumann (1998) linked up with Coleman's function-specific definition and focused on the benefits (rather than the forms) of social capital for obtaining a better insight into the relevant mechanisms. They mentioned the extent to which social capital facilitates the flow of information, the extent to which it strengthens personal autonomy, and its contribution to social solidarity as basic categories.

Another distinction in Coleman's theory of social capital (Coleman 1988) is the one between social capital within the family (also referred to as intrafamilial or family-based social capital) and social capital available outside the family (extrafamilial or community-based social capital). The social capital available within the family reflects the nature and intensity of the relationships between the family members. As we have seen in the previous section, many operationalizations of social capital concern this type of resource. In the context of the community, social capital resides in social networks that facilitate, for example, the exchange of information and the reinforcement of social values. At the conceptual level, Coleman (1990b) distinguished three social structural forms that generate social capital for child rearing: adult–child relationships, adult–adult–child relationships, and time-closure relationships. If there is social closure outside the family (e.g., relationships between a child and adults who in turn share relationships), this will lead to a consistent social setting for child rearing. Coleman (1990b) classified social structural closure in the form of continuity over time—which, implicitly, is a component of the other two forms too—as a separate category because of the importance of time-closure for the creation of investments and trust, as two important forms of social capital.

Collective and Second-Order Resources

The distinction between family-based and community-based social capital brings us to another reason for the possible emergence of a diffuse concept of social capital: the presence of various accesses to social capital. On the one hand, the concept of social capital in the literature refers to resources that become accessible through the relationships that individuals maintain with each other (e.g., Lin 1982). In many cases, social capital is understood as consisting of networks of social relations that may be effective for purposes of resource allocation. The effect of social class on educational outcomes can then be understood as the higher socio-economic classes having more opportunities to use their network to achieve better education for their children. On the other hand, social capital refers to collective resources available to anyone in the community (Coleman 1988). These two approaches seem to point to different mechanisms that create social capital. In the network approach, social capital is assumed to consist of second-order resources, re-sources of an individual with whom one enjoys a relationship and who makes these resources available. In that case, the production of social capital depends on three factors: the number of individuals in the network willing (or obliged) to help one, the strength of the relationships, and the nature of the resources these individuals may provide access to (cf. Flap 1995). This approach leads to definitions of the value of (an individual's) social capital as, for example, the one given by Snijders (1999): "the total expected value of the benefits that an individual can obtain from his ties with other individuals." Conversely, collective social capital is not based on individual "property rights" (e.g., the obligations of individual A to individual B). Instead, it resides in the community, for example the supervision of unattended children by other adults. In some social settings this is, and in other settings this is not, part of the community's normative structure (Coleman 1990a). Although sociology has a long tradition where the study of social networks is concerned (much less so, however, in the sociology of education), there is no common conceptual framework for relating social capital mechanisms operating in social networks or functional communities (Dijkstra and Peschar 1996).

Structural Holes and Structural Closure

The mechanisms underlying the social resources stored in social networks also require further reflection. The conceptual vagueness around the functioning of a central element in Coleman's social capital hypothesis—social closure—is a good case in point. Unlike Coleman and Hoffer (1987) who mention the positive effects of functional communities, Morgan and Sorensen (1999a) point to negative effects of closed communities through loss of autonomy and the exchange of redundant information. Besides "norm-enforcing schools" in which social closure supports child monitoring and the upholding of moral values, these authors distinguish "horizon-expanding schools" where most of the parents' ties lie outside the school community and provide access to resources in the wider community. The approach adopted by Burt (1999) reveals a similar tension. Unlike dense networks in companies that do not lead to positive effects, Burt showed that networks characterized by sparse ties and structural holes are effective. Burt related the apparent contradiction between these two approaches to the function that social capital should serve. Social closure facilitates communication and coordination, while networks characterized by structural holes give access to additional resources located outside the network. Social capital in the form of holes mainly facilitates connections between various resources, information, and so on, while social capital in the sense of closure may reinforce the internal functioning of the group. Podolny and Baron (1997) also stated that there is such a relationship between the characteristics of networks and the resources they generate.

Social Capital Is Neutral

The central role assigned to the function of social capital for a more detailed conceptualization of this concept is also illustrated by the work of Smith, Beaulieu, and Seraphine (1995). These authors make a distinction between structure and process as the formative elements of social capital. Structural factors (e.g., the presence of one or two parents in the family) influence the nature of the interaction that may or may not be beneficial to the goal pursued. Such a distinction between "channel" and "content" again illustrates that social capital is a "neutral" concept that does not determine the outcomes it facilitates. This also means that negative outcomes may occur. Besides the previously mentioned restrictive effects of closed communities,[5] other potentially negative effects can be distinguished, for example the restriction of freedom or opportunities, excessive claims by group members, or enforced conformity to group norms (Portes 1998).

Outcomes of Education

The last problem we will address here also involves the function-dependent specification of the concept of social capital. It concerns the identification of the domains that are relevant to the facilitative effect of social capital in educational settings.

There is another way in which the metaphor of capital has been applied to education. Particularly in economics but also in attainment and social stratification research, the education one has enjoyed is regarded as human capital. This investment made early in life may pay off later in life in terms of job or income. In the research practice, however, there are serious measurement problems when trying to quantify level of education as an indicator for human capital. This problem is most pressing in international comparative research, but it also exists in research that is restricted to one country.

Education is usually measured with a standardized scale. This is difficult because achievements in different educational systems or the certificates they confer cannot be compared directly. Researchers therefore assign a score to individuals that is related to their having a degree certificate, but it is well known that individuals with the same (type of) certificate may show a wide variation in performance. To avoid this problem, researchers usually adopt one of two solutions. Either the number of certificate categories is kept at a minimum, or education is coded as the number of years an individual has spent at a particular school or university. Both practices are less than perfect. Suppose, for example, that we should apply this approach to the domain of health. No doctor would be satisfied with the following indicator for health improvement: number of days spent in hospital or, even worse, the quality of the hospital. Anyone would agree that it would be better to rely on an individual indicator based on patient characteristics.

This analogy applies quite well to the domain of educational attainment. Within the framework of, for instance, the OECD a report on educational indicators is published every year. This report is based on educational levels and certificates awarded to graduates of schools and universities (OECD 2001). We have already noted how difficult such a comparison between national education systems is. Fortunately, information on individual achievement is also presented: for the most part achievements in mathematics, science, and/or native language skills. Nevertheless, these types of information only provide an incomplete picture, which means that little or nothing can be said about the effects of a particular type of education on individual achievement. Therefore, an alternative approach has been developed during the last few years. The most promising way out of this problem seems to be to avoid measuring achievement restricted to the subjects taught. Instead, competencies that transcend the school subjects—"cross-curricular competencies" (Peschar, in press)—are singled out. This type of competencies may be particularly essential for educational attainment and provides an important tool—in addition to conventional measures of educational achievement—for analyzing effects of the distribution of resources on the results of schooling. In fact, such information has been collected in the Programme for International Student Assessment (PISA) 2000 survey in some twenty-five countries already (OECD, in press).

Due to the function-specific definition of social capital, it is important to further specify the dependent variables used in educational attainment research. It is almost self-evident that achievements in the cognitive domain, in particular subjects that belong to the core curriculum, should be included. Depending on the level of education, the mathematical and linguistic domains thus play an important role. However, in the light of the remarks made above and given the socialization function of the school, it is also important to evaluate to what extent social capital may be a predictor of cross-curricular competencies and what role it may play in the socio-affective and normative-ethical domains. This means that a theory of social capital should address the question to what extent the social structure facilitates the attainment of the cognitive (core) curriculum—in terms of both core subject scores and cross-curricular competencies—and the socio-affective and normative-ethical domains of schooling.

At Halftime: Extra Playing Time?

Could the social capital hypothesis become the victim of its own success? Soon after its introduction in educational attainment research by Coleman fifteen years ago, researchers studying educational achievement and stratification began to regard it as an attractive, promising concept, and it was soon incorporated in research into the distribution of educational opportunities—and not only there. The social capital hypothesis was developed further to include all sorts of phenomena, domains, and levels, and was applied in highly diverse ways—in short, embraced as a regular cure-all. The question is whether the usefulness of the concept as a theoretical or analytical tool has been able to keep up with this reception.

When we look at the yields of the theoretical and empirical research so far, the conclusion seems inevitable that social capital is multidimensional in nature. We may even wonder if we can distinguish the contours of a common set of resources and mechanisms or if these only share the vehicle on which they rest—social relationships. Could this stretching of the theoretical framework become an obstacle to productive use? In other words, could the wide application of social capital that we are currently witnessing get in the way of productive, lucid, and unambiguous heuristic, conceptual, and operational applications? And will the ultimate conclusion be that the concept of social capital is not much more than an instructive metaphor?

Do not misread these remarks: our conclusion about the potential value of the concept of social capital is far from negative. The results of the empirical research briefly described in section 2 clearly illustrate that the concept, and particularly some of its aspects, can hold its own in the confrontation with empirical reality. The theoretical developments, too, give rise to the expectation that the concept may still provide productive leads for studies of educational attainment.

However, we have also observed that much of the empirical research is fragmentary and has resulted in shifting and hardly consistent pictures (cf. Peschar 1994; Dijkstra and Peschar 1996). Moreover, several of the studies produced what may be called contraindications. We have also seen that the fluid nature of the social capital concept still poses an obstacle to its theoretical development, and this impedes both the analysis of the mechanisms involved and rigorous empirical research. The concept has not been worked out in sufficient detail, is developing in divergent directions, and appears to become bloated. We therefore agree with the conclusion drawn by many authors that the concept requires further specification. As we have seen, various starting points have been proposed for further conceptualization. However, we have also noted that the currently available research outcomes make it unclear whether the development of taxonomies of effects and sources required for a more detailed specification of the mechanisms involved will not be so diverse as to prevent their incorporation in a concept that still has a distinct meaning.

We believe that a balanced judgment about the value of the concept of social capital will require yet more effort, both empirical and theoretical. There were good reasons for its positive reception, but there are also good reasons for the concerns expressed about its ambiguity, which makes it difficult to get a grip on the mechanisms that make social capital either a benefit or an obstacle. This means that our conclusion is necessarily rather pedestrian and that further conceptual development and empirical research will be required. Robert Nozick wrote, "There is room for words on subjects other than last words." That is a comforting note on which to conclude our discussion, because we think that the last word about this subject is still far ahead.

NOTES

This chapter was written as part of an exploratory study into effects of social resources in the Dutch educational system (SVO/NWO grants 93712 and SU/31489) and the research program Social Capital in Labor Markets and Education SCALE (NWO grant 510-05-0201). Reactions should be sent to A. B. Dijkstra, Department of Sociology, University of Groningen, Grote Rozenstraat 31, 9712 TG Groningen, the Netherlands. We would like to thank Matthijs de Vries, who provided valuable research assistance, and Sandra Dijkstra, who prepared the figures.

 1. Sandefur and Laumann (1998), for example, counted eighty-eight articles published between 1988 and 1998 that mention social capital in their titles.

 2. The conclusions drawn by Morgan and Sorensen (1999a) led to criticisms by Carbonaro (1999) and Hallinan and Kubitschek (1999). In response, Morgan and Sorensen (1999b) conclude that their primary conclusion, that the positive effect of Catholic schools cannot be explained in terms of social closure, has been refuted by their critics.

 3. Coleman (1990a) mentions Loury (1977), who introduced the concept of social capital as a measure for the resources that families or communities can call upon for the cognitive or social development of children. Woolcock (1998) refers to various older authors and mentions Hanifan's Community Center (Boston, 1920) as an early example of the use of the term "social capital" in the sense of resources accrued in social relationships.

 4. The contours of these ideas appeared earlier (Bourdieu 1980).

 5. Coleman, too, points to the potential costs of social closure in his work on social capital (e.g., Coleman 1987).

REFERENCES

Berends, M., and A. B. Dijkstra. 1997. "The Impact of Social Capital on Educational Opportunities in Cross-National Perspective." Paper presented to the annual meeting of the American Sociological Association, Toronto, August 9–13.

Bernstein, B. 1971. *Class, Codes, and Control.* London: Routledge.

Bosker, R. J., A. B. Dijkstra, and J. L. Peschar. 1996. "Social Capital and Educational Opportunities: Effects of Functional Communities in the Netherlands." Unpublished paper. Department of Sociology, University of Groningen.

Bourdieu, P. 1980. "Le capital social: Notes provisoires." *Actes de la recherche en science sociales* 3: 2–3.

Bourdieu, P. 1985. "The Forms of Capital." In *Handbook of Theory and Research for the Sociology of Education,* edited by J. Richardson, 241–58. New York: Greenwood.

Bourdieu, P., and J. C. Passeron. 1977. *Reproduction in Education, Society, and Culture.* London: Sage.

Bronfenbrenner, Urie. 1979. *The Ecology of Human Development: Experiments by Nature and Design.* Cambridge: Harvard University Press.

Burt, R. S. 1999. "The Network Structure of Social Capital." http://gsbwww. uchicago.edu/fac/ronald.burt/research.

Carbonaro, William J. 1998. "A Little Help from My Friend's Parents: Intergenerational Closure and Educational Outcomes." *Sociology of Education* 71: 295–313.

Carbonaro, W. J. 1999. "Opening the Debate on Closure and Schooling Outcomes: Comment on Morgan and Sorensen." *American Sociological Review* 64: 682–86.

Cochran, M. M., and J. A. Brassard. 1979. "Child Development and Personal Social Networks." *Child Development* 50: 601–16.

Coleman, J. S. 1961. *The Adolescent Society.* Glencoe, Ill.: Free Press.

Coleman, J. S. 1985. "Schools and the Communities They Serve." *Phi Delta Kappan* 66: 527–32.

Coleman, J. S. 1987. "Families and Schools." *Educational Researcher* 16: 32–38.

Coleman, J. S. 1988. "Social Capital in the Creation of Human Capital." *American Journal of Sociology* 94: S95–S120.

Coleman, J. S. 1990a. *Foundations of Social Theory.* Cambridge, Mass.: Belknap.

Coleman, J. S. 1990b. "Social Capital." In *The International Encyclopedia of Education Research and Studies,* edited by T. Husen and T. N. Postlethwaite. Oxford: Pergamon.

Coleman, J. S. 1993. "The Rational Reconstruction of Society." *American Sociological Review* 58: 1–15.

Coleman, J. S., et al. 1966. *Equality of Educational Opportunity.* Washington, D.C.: U.S. Government Printing Office.

Coleman, J. S., and T. Hoffer. 1987. *Public and Private High Schools: The Impact of Communities.* New York: Basic.

Coleman, J. S., T. Hoffer, and S. Kilgore. 1982. *High School Achievement: Public, Catholic, and Private Schools Compared.* New York: Basic.

Coleman, J. S., and K. S. Schiller. 1992. "A Comparison of Public and Private Schools: The Impact of Community Values." In *Independent Schools Independent Thinkers,* edited by P. R. Kane, 222–33. San Francisco: Jossey-Bass.

Dijkstra, A. B. 1992. *De religieuze factor, onderwijskansen en godsdienst* [The Religious Factor, Educational Opportunities, and Religion]. Nijmegen: ITS.

Dijkstra, A. B., G. Driessen, and R. Veenstra. 2001. "Academic Achievement in Public, Religious, and Private Schools: Sector and Outcomes Differences in Holland." Paper presented to the annual meeting of the American Educational Research Association, April 11, Seattle.

Dijkstra, A. B., and J. Dronkers. 2001. "State and Civil Society in Education: The Case of the Netherlands." In *Education between State, Markets, and Civil Society: Comparative Perspectives,* edited by H. D. Meyer and W. L. Boyd. Mahwah, N.J.: Lawrence Erlbaum, in press.

Dijkstra, A. B., and J. L. Peschar. 1996. *Sociaal kapitaal in het onderwijs: Een verkennende studie* [Social Capital in Education: An Exploratory Study]. Report to SVO. Groningen: Department of Sociology, University of Groningen.

Dijkstra, A. B., and R. Veenstra. 2000. "Functionele gemeenschappen, godsdienstigheid en prestaties in het voortgezet onderwijs" [Functional Communities, Religiosity, and Achievement in Secondary Education]. *Mens & Maatschappij* 75: 129–50.

DiMaggio, P. 1982. "Cultural Capital and School Success: The Impact of Status Culture Participation on the Grades of U.S. High School Students." *American Sociological Review* 47: 189–201.

Durkheim, E. 1956. *Education and Sociology.* New York: Free Press.

Edwards, B., and M. Foley. 1997. "Social Capital and the Political Economy of Our Discontent." *American Behavioral Scientist* 40.

Flap, H. 1995. "No Man Is an Island: The Research Program of a Social Capital Theory." Paper presented to the International Network Conference, London, July 6–10.

Furstenberg, F., and M. E. Hughes. 1995. "Social Capital and Successful Development among At-Risk Youth." *Journal of Marriage and the Family* 57: 580–92.

Glebbeek, A. C. 1998. "Commentaar bij artikel 'Gezin en schoolloopbaan'" [Comments on Article "Family and School Career"]. *Tijdschrift voor Onderwijsresearch* 23: 67–69.

Graaf, P. de 1989. "Cultural Reproduction and Educational Stratification." In *Educational Opportunities in the Welfare State: Longitudinal Studies in Educational and Occupational Attainment in the Netherlands*, edited by B. Bakker, J. Dronkers, and G. Meijnen, 39–57. Nijmegen: ITS.

Greeley, A. 1997. "Religious Structures as a Source of Social Capital." *American Behavioral Scientist* 40: 587–94.

Hagan, J., R. MacMillan, and B. Wheaton. 1996. "New Kid in Town: Social Capital and the Life Course Effects of Family Migration on Children." *American Sociological Review* 61: 368–85.

Hallinan, M. T., and W. N. Kubitschek. 1999. "Conceptualizing and Measuring School Social Networks: Comment on Morgan and Sorensen." *American Sociological Review* 64: 687–93.

Hao, L., and M. Bonstead-Bruns. 1998. "Parent-Child Differences in Educational Expectations and the Academic Achievement of Immigrant and Native Students." *Sociology of Education* 71: 175–98.

Hoffer, Th. B. 1990. "Parental Social Relations and Student Academic Outcomes." Paper presented at the annual meeting of the AERA, Boston.

Hoffer, Th. B. 1992. "Effects of Community Type on School Experiences and Student Learning." Paper presented at the annual meeting of the AERA, San Francisco.

Hoffer, Th. B., and J. S. Coleman. 1990. "Changing Families and Communities: Implications for Schools." In *Educational Leadership and Changing Contexts of Families, Communities, and Schools*, edited by B. Mitcell and L. L. Cunningham, 118–34. Chicago: University of Chicago Press.

Hofferth, S. L., J. Boisjoly, and G. J. Duncan. 1998. "Parents' Extrafamilial Resources and Children's School Attainment." *Sociology of Education* 71: 246–68.

Hofferth, S. L., J. Boisjoly, and G. J. Duncan. 1999. "The Development of Social Capital." *Rationality and Society* 11: 79–110.

Hofman, R. H., W. H. Hofman, H. Guldemond, and A. B. Dijkstra. 1996. "Variation in Effectiveness between Private and Public Schools: The Impact of School and Family Networks." *Educational Research and Evaluation* 2: 366–94.

Hollingshead, A. B. 1949. *Elmtown's Youth: The Impact of Social Classes on Adolescents.* New York: Wiley.

Jencks, C., et al. 1972. *Inequality: A Reassessment of the Effect of Family and Schooling in America.* New York: Basic.

Kahne, J., and K. Bailey. 1999. "The Role of Social Capital in Youth Development: The Case of 'I Have a Dream' Programs." *Educational Evaluation and Policy Analysis* 21: 321-43.

Kohn, M. L. 1977. *Class and Conformity: A Study in Values.* Chicago: University of Chicago Press.

Lee, S., and M. C. Brinton. 1996. "Elite Education and Social Capital: The Case of South Korea." *Sociology of Education* 69: 177–92.

Leseman, P. 1989. *Structurele en pedagogische determinanten van schoolloopbanen* [Structural and Pedagogical Determinants of School Careers]. Rotterdam: SAD.

Lin, N. 1982. "Social Resources and Instrumental Action." In *Social Structure and Network Analysis*, edited by P. Marsden and N. Lin, 131–46. Beverly Hills: Sage.

Lindenberg, S. 2000. "James Coleman." In *The Blackwell Companion to Major Social Theorists*, edited by G. Ritzer, 513–44. Oxford: Blackwell.

Loury, G. 1977. "A Dynamic Theory of Racial Income Differences." In *Woman, Minorities, and Employment Discrimination*, edited by P. A. Wallace and M. LaMond, 153–86. Lexington, Mass.: Lexington Books.

Lynd, R. S., and M. H. Lynd. 1929. *Middletown: A Study in American Culture.* New York: Harcourt.

Mays, J. B. 1962. *Education and the Urban Child.* Liverpool: University of Liverpool Press.

McLanahan, S., and G. Sandefur. 1994. *Growing Up with a Single Parent.* Cambridge: Harvard University Press.

McNeal, R. B. 1999. "Parental Involvement as Social Capital: Differential Effectiveness on Science Achievement, Truancy, and Dropping Out." *Social Forces* 78: 117–44.

Morgan, S. L., and A. B. Sorensen. 1999a. "Parental Networks, Social Closure, and Mathematics Learning: A Test of Coleman's Social Capital Explanation of School Effects." *American Sociological Review* 64: 661–81.

Morgan, S. L., and A. B. Sorensen. 1999b. "Theory, Measurement, and Specification Issues in Models of Network Effects on Learning: Reply to Carbonaro and to Hallinan and Kubitschek." *American Sociological Review* 64: 694–700.

Morrow, V. 1999. "Conceptualising Social Capital in Relation to the Well-being of Children and Young People: A Critical Review." *Sociological Review* 47: 744–65.

OECD. 2001. *Education at a Glance.* Paris: Organization for Economic Development and Cooperation.

OECD. In press. *Programme for International Student Assessment PISA: Initial Report.* Paris: Organization for Economic Development and Cooperation.

Peschar, J. L. 1994. "Capital in Education: Some Issues and Measurement Problems in Attainment and Comparative Research." Inaugural address on the occasion of the award of Doctor Honoris Causa in Economic Sciences, Budapest University of Economic Sciences, May 3.

Peschar, J. L. In press. "Cross-Curricular Competencies: Developments in a New Area of Educational Outcome Indicators." In *Comparing Student Achievement: The Role of International Assessment in Education Policy*, edited by J. Moskowitz and M. Stephens. Washington, D.C.: NCES.

Podolny, J. M., and J. N. Baron. 1997. "Resources and Relationships: Social Networks and Mobility in the Workplace." *American Sociological Review* 62: 673–93.

Portes, A. 1998. "Social Capital: Its Origins and Applications in Modern Sociology." *Annual Review of Sociology* 22: 1–24.

Portes, A., and D. MacLeod. 1999. "Educating the Second Generation: Determinants of Achievement among Children of Immigrants in the United States." *Journal of Ethnic and Migration Studies* 25: 373–96.

Putnam, R. D. 1992. *Making Democracy Work: Civic Traditions in Modern Italy.* Princeton: Princeton University Press.

Sandefur, R., and E. Laumann. 1998. "A Paradigm for Social Capital." *Rationality and Society* 10: 481–501.

Shavit, Y., and H.-P. Blossfeld, eds. 1993. *Persistent Inequality: Changing Educational Attainment in Thirteen Countries.* Boulder: Westview.

Smith, M. H., L. J. Beaulieu, and A. Seraphine. 1995. "Social Capital, Place of Residence, and College Attendance." *Rural Sociology* 60: 363–80.

Snijders, T. A. B. 1999. "Prologue to the Measurement of Social Capital." *La revue Tocqueville* 20.

Stanton-Salazar, R. D., and S. M. Dornbush. 1995. "Social Capital and the Reproduction of Inequality: Information Networks among Mexican-Origin High School Students." *Sociology of Education* 68: 116–35.

Sun, Y. 1998. "The Academic Success of East-Asian-American Students: An Investment Model." *Social Science Research* 27: 432–56.

Teachman, J., K. Paasch, and K. Carver. 1997. "Social Capital and the Generation of Human Capital." *Social Forces* 75: 1343–59.

Thurow, L. C. 1975. *Generating Inequality.* New York: Basic.

Van der Velden, R. K. W. 1991. *Sociale herkomst en schoolsucces: Het effect van culturele en sociale hulpbronnen op de schoolloopbaan* [Social Background and School Success: The Effect of Cultural and Social Resources on the School Career]. Groningen: RION.

Van Liere, C., and C. J. M. Maas. 1994. "Oudergemeenschappen en onderwijs" [Parental Communities and Education]. *Comenius* 14: 83–99.

Van Veen, K., E. Denessen, P. van der Kley, and J. Gerris. 1998. "Gezin en schoolloopbaan: Een onderzoek naar de invloed van cultureel en sociaal kapitaal in het gezin op de schoolloopbaan van kinderen" [Family and Educational Attainment: A Study on the Influence of Cultural and Social Capital in the Family on Educational Attainment of Children]. *Tijdschrift voor Onderwijsresearch* 23: 3–16.

Woolcock, M. 1998. "Social Capital and Economic Development: Toward a Theoretical Synthesis and Policy Framework." *Theory and Society* 27: 151–208.

4

Critical Ethnography and the Sociology of Education

Steve Jordan

For qualitative researchers in the sociology of education, and more broadly educational studies and the social sciences, the last quarter of the twentieth century represented a major turning point in the historical trajectory of their methodologies. Not only did this period witness an unparalleled interest and proliferation of these approaches to social inquiry, it also saw the emergence of vibrant theoretical debates over questions of methodology, method, and more generally, the ethics and politics of research. In education, the qualitative turn challenged the hegemony of "social arithmetic" (Nash 1997) and positivism, as well as giving powerful impetus to the generation of the new sociology of education (Young 1971). Looking back, the ascendancy of qualitative methodologies over this period created an alternative paradigm for social research, one that in many respects has been unparalleled in the recent history of either educational studies or the social sciences.

As we enter the new century, however, it appears that the excitement and possibilities for intellectual and social transformation signaled by the qualitative turn has slowed, if not entered a period of crisis. Thus, for the preeminent anthropologist George Marcus (1998), ethnography and other forms of qualitative research have simply become "stuck." From the perspective of educational ethnography, Norman Denzin (1997) has argued that contemporary ethnographic inquiry has entered its "sixth moment" characterized by a "triple crisis" of representation, legitimation, and praxis. This sense is shared by other authors (Delamont et al. 2000) who also surmise that qualitative research has reached something of a crossroads in its development. Significantly, while these authors are uncertain about the future trajectory of qualitative research, they nevertheless share the view that its methodological orientation will come from postmodernism. For Marcus and Denzin, for example, postmodernism will underpin the development of a critical ethnography for postmodernity.

The choice of the term "critical ethnography" to describe the postmodernist project is significant, as it has traditionally been used to denote forms of ethnographic and qualitative inquiry that represent a critique of conventional ethnography. In this respect, postmodernist ethnographies are critical, but in ways that are quite distinct from the theoretical approaches that originally gave critical ethnography its impetus almost three decades ago from within the sociology of education. My argument in what follows is that despite the ascendancy of postmodern approaches to qualitative research in the contemporary era, it is nevertheless necessary for sociologists of education to look beyond postmodernism in constructing forms of critical ethnographic inquiry. In doing this, they can not only reclaim certain aspects of the methodological traditions that originally inspired critical ethnography, but broaden debate and analysis of the contemporary processes that constitute globalization.

Consequently, in this chapter I have set myself three tasks. The first is to provide an overview of the origins of critical ethnography. While this shows how critical ethnography emerged out of the complex intersection of a number of intellectual and institutional arrangements, the overview focuses on the critique of positivism leveled against conventional ethnography. The second is to outline and critically evaluate the major theoretical traditions on which critical ethnography has drawn. As will become evident, I do this through an exploration of the politics of research that has defined modes of critical ethnographic inquiry. The last and most important section of the essay is concerned with how critical ethnography might contribute to the development of the sociology of education as we enter the new century. This argues for a more expansive and broader definition of the discipline to meet the challenges that global capitalism poses for both research and education in the contemporary world.

Before I proceed to my discussion of these themes, I should make clear that I have deliberately chosen not to draw a clear and unambiguous distinction between ethnography and qualitative research. While this distinction can be found in the literature, I believe it is not helpful and does not reflect the actualities of practice in the field. The point to grasp is that ethnography remains a contested and often loosely used concept within contemporary debate. Consequently, my approach is less concerned with defining terms than staking out an approach that is both critical and nonpositivist for the sociology of education.

THE CRITIQUE OF CONVENTIONAL ETHNOGRAPHY

From its inception critical ethnography was a peculiarly educational enterprise in that its origins and development arose mainly from the work of educational researchers and particularly sociologists of education (Carspecken

1996; Jordan and Yeomans 1995). Though it is difficult to be precise, its generation from within education occurred for four reasons. First, the rediscovery of Marxism in the 1960s and 1970s provided an alternative theoretical framework for analyzing and understanding the structure, organization and processes of schooling within capitalist society. Although this initially provided the impetus for a left functionalism epitomized by Bowles and Ginitis's (1976) concept of the "correspondence principle," other forms of Marxism began to gain ground. Most notable was the research conducted at the Centre for Contemporary Cultural Studies that used the political writings of the Italian Marxist Antonio Gramsci (1974) to generate the theoretical foundations for an interpretative Marxism that emphasized the study of the conditions of everyday life and culture through his concept of hegemony. The "culturalist Marxism" (Samuel 1981) that emerged from this work during the 1970s and 1980s, it should be noted, was itself inspired by developments in literary theory, historical, and feminist research (Rowbatham 1976; Scott 1987, 1988; Thompson 1968; Williams 1961).

Second, the social relations of educational research were—and continue to be—organized in different ways from those of mainstream disciplines such as sociology or anthropology that had claimed qualitative research as part of their tradition. That is, while educational research has shared much in common with mainstream social science and continues to borrow insights from its theoretical paradigms, its knowledge-producing practices have historically focused on the training and professional development of teachers and other educational practitioners. This has created an institutional matrix (in university schools and departments of education, and colleges of teacher training) that has valued theory as a means of informing educational practice, whether in teaching, management or policy development. In this way, forms of ethnographic research were particularly attractive to sociologists of education, not only as a means of prying open the "black box" of schooling (Woods 1988), but also as a way of conceptualizing how the complex practices of schooling and education might contribute to restructuring social theory.

Third, ethnography allowed researchers employing a Marxist or critical standpoint to get close up and observe in detail how particular sites, such as schools, classrooms, families, or youth subcultures, contributed to hegemony or its subversion. This would not only allow the generation of insiders' accounts of how educational inequalities were produced and legitimated, but would also point to contradictions and tensions that might constitute the basis for constructing emancipatory social practices. This also explains why ethnography has been embraced by feminist approaches to critical research (Ellsworth 1989; Lather 1991).

Last, education in both its institutional and discursive forms has, over the last quarter century, encouraged forms of critical research that not only are interdisciplinary but also eschew the insidious positivism characteristic of educational psychology. That is, its status as a field of inquiry and a form of professional practice, rather than a pure academic discipline, has meant that university schools and departments of education have traditionally focused on research that has explored the theory-practice nexus. This has allowed the emergence and exploration of a genre of research approaches organized around action and participatory research (Elliott 1998; Foley 1999; Kemmis 1993), and notions such as the reflective practitioner (Schon 1983) that are embedded in this nexus. Significantly these approaches have adopted a qualitative methodology, and they are invariably nonpositivist.

Positivism and Qualitative Research

The debate over positivism and its relationship to qualitative research in education has, over the last quarter century, been both complex and surprisingly enduring. As we enter the new century there is no indication that a "settlement" (Grace 1995) has been reached or that it has abated. While a detailed history of this debate is beyond the scope of this chapter, it is nevertheless important to understand how positivism has influenced the principles and practice of ethnography. In what follows I provide a brief overview of the contours and defining elements of the impact of positivism on both mainstream qualitative research and critical ethnography.

Williams (1983) has observed that it is "now virtually impossible to disentangle a popular sense of positivist from general arguments about empiricism and scientific method" (p. 238). Despite the grandstanding and hyperbole that surrounds the concept of positivism, the issue at stake is whether ethnography can be considered a scientific method and therefore legitimately assume its place among the social sciences. In this respect, the debate is essentially political, as it turns on what counts as acceptable knowledge, practice, and conduct by practitioners working within the field.

For these reasons we must be cautious about attempting to define positivism as if it were a tight and clearly demarcated epistemological approach. As Hammersley has emphasized, "The term 'positivism' refers to a wide range of theoretical and methodological ideas that overlap considerably with other positions" (Hammersley 1995, 245). Within mainstream qualitative research this "overlap" of ideas has been expressed through several key arguments. The first and one of the most enduring has been that the techniques of quantitative social science can be applied to qualitative research in its design, application, and procedures for data analysis. The effect of this can be seen in the organization and content of the many "handbooks" on qualitative methods (Miles and Huberman 1984; Yin 1989), but more particularly so in the growing number of software packages aimed at qualitative researchers (e.g., Scloari 1998).

A second argument that arises from the supposed isomorphism between qualitative and quantitative approaches is the idea that theory and method are quite separate and distinct aspects of social inquiry. Thus Burawoy has noted that in the "social sciences the lore of objectivity relies on the separation of the intellectual product from its process of production. . . . We are taught not to confound the process of discovery with the process of justification" (Burawoy et al. 1991, 8). That is, the procedures governing data collection and analysis are seen as a purely "technical" moment of the research process. Third, and related to the second, data collected is viewed as being devoid of any theoretical understanding that participants might bring to the study. The implication of this is that "Theory" can only be generated from inferences and causal relationships that the researcher brings to a study and the analysis of data. It is in this sense that qualitative researchers argue that theory is "grounded" in the data (Glaser 1968). For critical ethnographers, this bifurcation of theory and method has at least two negative implications. First, it legitimates and institutionalizes an asymmetrical relation of power by privileging the knowledge and expertise of the researcher over that of her subjects. Second, theory is reduced to and becomes an effect of method or technique. This not only impoverishes and limits possibilities for the generation of theoretical insight, it leads to a form of empiricism that questions the relevance of theory for educational research.

Third, the language and conceptual frameworks of mainstream qualitative research also reveal traces of positivism. This can be seen in the way in which many qualitative researchers have adopted and show an explicit concern with key conceptual terms of quantitative approaches, such as "measurement," "validity," "reliability," "generalizability," and so on. Even concepts that have more of an association with qualitative research, such as "triangulation," reveal a positivist methodology through their concern with ensuring multiple reference points for the validation of, significantly, "findings." This discourse continues to reproduce conceptual practices that are embedded within a positivist epistemology.

These effects—the emulation of quantitative methodology; the bifurcation of theory and method; its particular discourse—are by no means an exhaustive list of the impact of positivism on mainstream qualitative research. Forms of determinism that relegate human subjectivity to epiphenomena, whether functionalist or Marxist, can also emanate from a positivist perspective. In short, there should be no doubt that positivism remains a powerful ideology that continues to have a major impact on conventional qualitative research. Indeed, Tuhiwai Smith (1999) has argued from an indigenous people's perspective that it still defines the "Western" approach to research within the social sciences. As I suggested above, however, critical ethnographers have not been exempt from the effects of this ideology. This will become clear in what follows.

Critical Ethnography and Positivism

While critical ethnographers have broadly defined their position as post or nonpositivist, a strong positivist tendency is also evident. For example,

Thomas (1993) has argued that critical ethnography "is a style of analysis and discourse that is embedded within conventional ethnography. As a consequence, they share several fundamental characteristics." These are a "reliance on qualitative interpretation of data, core rules of ethnographic methods and analysis, adherence to a symbolic interactionist paradigm, and a preference for developing 'grounded theory'" (p. 3). This allows him to describe critical ethnography as "conventional ethnography with a political purpose" (p. 4). Significantly, he then goes on to assert that

> when done well, ethnography is as scientific and rigorous as quantitative social science or even the natural sciences. If a particular ethnographic study is not scientific, the problem lies with lapses of the researcher and not with the perspective. (p. 16)

In adopting this formula, Thomas reproduces an approach that understands critical ethnography as conventional ethnography plus critical theory. According to this, conventional ethnography's methods and procedures constitute the tools and techniques for producing empirical data which can then be interrogated using theoretical insights borrowed from critical theory. Superficially, this appears to be a logical and reasonable way of constructing a critical ethnography. However, I would argue that through its uncritical adoption of the "core rules of ethnographic methods and analysis," this approach actually reproduces several aspects of positivism that are characteristic of conventional ethnography.

The first is the assumption that conventional ethnography's methods and procedures are merely technical and free of theory. A second problem that arises concerns Thomas's assertion that critical ethnography will share a preference for the development of "grounded theory" (Glaser 1968). Yet, as Burawoy et al. (1991) point out, the adoption and acceptance of the research agenda associated with grounded theory implicates ethnographers in a conception of science modeled on the positivist principles of quantitative methodologies. Consequently, their argument is that grounded theory is heavily laden with positivist residues and this makes it a questionable addition to the methodological repertoire of a nonpositivist, critical ethnography.

Last, Thomas's (1993) desire for ethnography to be considered as "scientific and rigorous as quantitative social science or even the natural sciences" is a familiar juxtaposition that stems from a positivist outlook that many critical ethnographers would have difficulty subscribing to. It not only assumes that there is an isomorphic relationship between the theory and practice of ethnography and the quantitative/natural sciences, it also implicitly establishes a hierarchy of knowledge by making these exemplars for other forms of social inquiry. For Thomas, this view of ethnography as science also implies that bad or faulty ethnographies are the outcome of "lapses of the researcher and not with the perspective." Thus the perspective (or core rules) of ethnographic methodology are somehow considered to be independent, or at least autonomous, of the activities of the ethnographer. This separation attempts to establish an "ethic of objectivity" (Smith 1990a) that also negates the key concept of reflexivity that is common to nonpositivist versions of critical ethnography. I will return to the concept of reflexivity in the next section.

Thomas's approach to critical ethnography, therefore, is limited by an underlying commitment to a positivist methodology borrowed from what he understands to be the "core rules" of conventional ethnography. This turned on four issues: the separation of theory from method; the uncritical adoption of Glaser and Strauss's (1968) concept of grounded theory; an implicit acceptance of a hierarchy of scientific knowledge that gives undue primacy to the quantitative and the natural sciences; and (related to the third issue) the failure to recognize the complex reciprocal relationship between researcher and the research process expressed through the concept of reflexivity. Consequently, my argument is that Thomas's critical ethnography is severely compromised through its overt reliance on the methodology of conventional ethnography.

CRITICAL ETHNOGRAPHY AND THE POLITICS OF RESEARCH

As I indicated above, forms of critical ethnographic inquiry only began to emerge over the last quarter of the twentieth century. In his overview of its development, Quantz has convincingly argued that critical ethnography's initial impulse came from the unease that sociologists of education felt over their "accepted role of scholar as apologist for the status quo" during the late 1960s (Quantz 1992, 450). He then goes on to show how this sense of unease provoked a search for theoretical traditions and empirical research that challenged existing power relations and their associated social and political frameworks. While his account of the development of critical ethnography is meticulously researched, its scope is limited. Consequently, while this section of the chapter shares some ground with Quantz, it explores territory and themes that he does not explore or that emerged over the 1990s after his paper was published.

Over its short history critical ethnography has drawn on a wide array of theoretical traditions including phenomenology, symbolic interactionism, ethnomethodology, neo-Marxism, feminism, semiology, and cultural studies. In this respect, its development has not been unlike that of conventional ethnography whose methodologies have also been inspired by some of the same traditions. What has distinguished critical ethnography, however, is its explicit commitment to a politics of research that is antithetical to the core principles and practices of conventional approaches. This politics or critical orientation has several themes. First, in its early phase during the 1970s, critical ethnography focused on how ethnographic research could be connected with the wider political economy of capitalism. Studies such as Willis's *Learning to Labour* (1977) or Corrigan's *Schooling the Smash Street Kids* (1979), for example, were concerned with showing how local, context-specific studies of schooling revealed the contradictions, tensions, and struggles created by the State and capitalist social relations. Capitalism as context was, therefore, the starting point for critical ethnographies that drew primarily on Marxist social theory. Later studies, such as Foley's *Learning Capitalist Culture* (1990) have commenced from the same premise—albeit within a theoretical framework developed from the critical theory of Habermas (1987).

A second and connected theme is that of power and social inequality. Critical ethnography has consistently focused on revealing the sources and effects of power relations on the everyday world of people's lived experience. This stems from the recognition that the social is constituted by asymmetrical power relations in the workplace, the family, education, and, more broadly, within politics and civil society that systematically generate inequalities between individuals and groups. Whether these inequalities are seen as the effect of power/knowledge or capitalist relations of production, critical ethnography's method is to reveal how power infiltrates and organizes lived experience in ways that are congruent with the "relations of ruling" (Smith 1990b).

Third, the observation that the contemporary world is organized through often exploitative and oppressive social relations generates an ethical stance that marks a decisive break with conventional forms of ethnography. That is, where conventional ethnographers adopt a position of value neutrality (better known as the "prime directive" by fans of *Star Trek*), critical ethnographers believe that it is incumbent on them to engage those whom they study in a dialogue that consciously raises questions about the nature of their predicament and possibilities for emancipation. From this commitment emerges a politics of transformation that aims to enhance and empower subaltern groups through the research process itself; a heretical position that few conventional ethnographers are prepared to countenance.

A fourth key theme pursued by critical ethnography is the refinement, or restructuring, of social and political theory (Carspecken 1996). For critical ethnographers this concern arises from the observation that social and political theory is implicated in ruling Western capitalist societies. Consequently, they have turned to critiques of mainstream social science to inform their theory and practice. Most notable here is the work of anthropologists such as Asad (1986, 1994), Kabbani (1986), Said (1983, 1989, 1993), Tuhiwai Smith (1999) and that of the Canadian feminist and sociologist, Dorothy Smith (1987, 1990a, 1990b, 1994). Together, these critiques of anthropology and sociology have contributed to a reappraisal of the theoretical and methodological foundations on which these disciplines were founded. This is also a salient theme in the work of postmodernist ethnographers.

Postmodernism and Critical Ethnography

Within education one of the most receptive fields for postmodern ideas has been qualitative research (Delamont et al. 2000). Here, postmodern modes of analysis have not only introduced new concepts to critical inquiry (e.g., subjectivity, power/knowledge, normalization, simulacrum), they have also led to the creation of new journals, such as *Qualitative Studies in Education* devoted to the exploration of this genre of research. A key concept and theme that has defined this approach, and has been incorporated within both conventional and critical ethnography, is that of reflexivity.

Postmodernist concepts of reflexivity have increasingly influenced and shaped approaches to critical ethnography (Atkinson 1990; Delamont 1996; Denzin 1997; Marcus 1998; Packwood and Sikes 1996). The most significant impact of these concepts has been to promote a fundamental and pervasive skepticism toward forms of conventional ethnography that are either positivist in methodology, or still cling to realist notions of objectivity and truth. Postmodernist notions of reflexivity have also opened up possibilities for experimentation with new types of ethnographic practice such as auto/ethnography (Reed-Danahay 1997), the messy text (Denzin 1997) and different ways of representing and validating personal experience. Relatedly, it has driven standpoint epistemologies that have questioned the production of knowledge that claims to be foundationalist and, therefore, conventional notions of social theory (Lather 1991; Stanley 1990). In these ways postmodern constructs of reflexivity have increasingly displaced Marxism and critical theory as the dominant methodologies driving critical ethnography as we enter the twenty-first century.

While there can be no doubt that postmodernism has opened up new possibilities for the theory and practice of critical ethnography, it has also the potential to foreclose particular issues and questions for critical social research. First, there is the widespread and uncritical assertion that we now live under conditions imposed by postmodernity. Although this is often associated with the rise of post-Fordist regimes of accumulation, postmodernity remains a highly contested concept for describing the changes that have characterized the world economy over the last three decades. Indeed, there is a worrying tendency by some postmodernists to conflate the condition of postmodernity with the impact of neoliberalism (Hopenhayn 1995). Consequently, a number of critics have argued that it is ideological, as it deflects attention away from the fact that, despite contemporary transformations in economy and culture, it is still capitalism that prevails as the historically dominant social formation (Eagleton 1996; O'Neill 1995). Similarly, while the vocabulary or lexicon of postmodernism has been well adapted for use within cultural analysis and cultural studies, it is questionable whether it engages with "old" themes that were the hallmark of radical political economy, such as exploitation, class, capitalist accumulation, or even hegemony. Such concepts come out of a long historical tradition of collective and personal struggle that cannot simply be dismissed as passé. Indeed, one could argue that never have these analytical tools been more relevant than now under global capitalism.

Postmodern ethnographies are also particularly vague about history and historical process (e.g., Delamont et al. 2000; Denzin 1997; Marcus 1998). They appear to be so enmeshed within the simulacrum of postmodernity that their concepts of reflexivity become present-centric. Yet there exists an extensive and well-developed tradition of research that is suggestive of a "historical reflexivity" that would articulate well with the themes and methodology of critical ethnography (Thompson 1981, 1991). Finally, post-modernist ethnographies fail to engage with the concept of the State. This is a curious omission, as there now exists a substantial body of literature, in-formed by postmodernism, that is concerned with reconceptualizing the state as a form of political practice that inserts itself within everyday experi-ence and culture (Corrigan et al. 1987; Corrigan and Sayer 1985).

Despite these limitations, the impact of postmodernism on qualitative re-search from the 1990s appears to be not only reconfiguring the character, but displacing the traditional themes of critical ethnography. That is, where Marxism and critical theory once inspired it, now it appears to be defined by the "sign" of reflexivity. In the section that follows I will explore the impli-cations of my discussion of these issues in critical ethnography for the soci-ology of education.

CRITICAL ETHNOGRAPHY, GLOBALIZATION, AND THE SOCIOLOGY OF EDUCATION

A curious aspect of the development of critical ethnography is that its short history has coincided with the present crisis of capitalist accumulation. The nature of this crisis has had many dimensions and its effects have been far reaching, particularly for schools and educational systems across the globe (Robertson and Smaller 1996; Taylor et al. 1997). It has not only signaled the fin de siècle of social democracy, Keynesian economics, and the retreat of the (welfare) state, it has also generated revolutionary changes in government, politics, society, business, culture, and technology. One of the conceptual markers for this transformation of contemporary capitalism has been glob-alization, or more recently its cognate term, the "knowledge economy." As Castells (1999) has observed, the effects of globalization "are pervasive and cut across all spheres of human activity" (p. 45).

There can be no question that this historical process has challenged the con-ceptual and theoretical paradigms of the humanities and social sciences in fundamental ways over the last two decades. Further, as we enter the new century it is still the case that, "After twenty years of efforts to describe, analyse, and theorise the 'new society,' there is still a great deal of uncertainty about what this society is" (Castells 1999, 57). This "uncertainty" has not only subverted and questioned traditional modes of social inquiry that constituted the social sciences, it has also given impetus to new fields of study, such as those associated with cultural studies and postmodernism. The implications of what is called globalization for social research are, therefore, quite profound. In particular, it poses new challenges, themes and issues with which the sociology of education must engage. My argument is that critical ethnography can make a significant contribution to mapping out this project as we enter the new century. There are at least three ways that it can do this.

One of the most pressing issues that confronts sociologists of education, as Castells suggests, is quite simply what to make of the "new society" that appears to have emerged over the last quarter century. While there has been a great deal of work done that has attempted to theorize the character and dimensions of this society, there is still a noticeable absence of detailed, fine-grained ethnographies that show how it is being put together and works as a material and historical process. The absence of such ethnographies is attributable, I believe, to the postmodern turn in qualitative research I described above. Denzin's (1997) notion of the "postmodern cultural economy" exemplifies what I mean. He observes that

> humans live in a second-hand world of meanings. They have no direct access to reality. Reality as it is known is mediated by symbolic representation, by narrative texts, and by cinematic and televisual structures that stand between the person and the so-called real world. (p. xvi)

There can be no doubt that the contemporary world is saturated with synthetic images that have their origins in a cultural economy that affect and shape everyday experience. However, to argue (as Denzin does) that symbols, texts, and "televisual structures" should become the focus of ethnographic inquiry is to embrace a form of cultural reductionism that fails to understand how cultural processes are themselves embedded within, and an expression of, the contemporary accumulation process.

An alternative approach to this issue that evades a cultural reductionism is offered by Willis (1999; Willis et al. 1990) in his analysis of the "cultural commodity." Willis argues that the cultural economy of the late twentieth century is fundamentally capitalist and, therefore, still organized around the production of "mutifarious forms of new value" demonstrated by

> the way in which the capitalist cultural commodity circuit keeps dipping back into the streets and trawling the living culture for ideas for its next commodity, its next circuit. Capital's cultural producers remorselessly ransack the everyday in their never-ending search to find, embody, and maximise all possible use values in products. (1999, p. 158)

Thus where Denzin argues that critical ethnography should be aimed at the "world of televisual and cinematic narrativity and its place in the dreams, fantasies, and interactions of everyday people" (1997, xvi), Willis asserts that we need to "direct ethnographic attention to the practical moment of sensuous activity" (1999, 159) where value originates. Willis's analysis, therefore, takes us a step back by asserting the primacy of living labor power in the constitution of the new cultural economy. Aligned with this observation is his notion of how areas of common culture, that have not been commodified, can generate forms of informal cultural production that rely on "expressive labour power." For Willis, this realm represents a potential reservoir for the realization of practical activities and forms of consciousness that contradict and stand opposed to the instrumental and alienating character of work within the formal economy.

The value of Willis's analysis is that it eschews the tendency in postmodernist ethnography to view the cultural economy of global capitalism as a virtual reality; as a purely discursive world detached from the "grimy business of earning a living in the material labour process" (1999, 166). In this way it shifts critical ethnography away from the looking glass world of the postmodern simulacrum, urging us rather to think about and explore how that looking glass has been fabricated, for what purposes, and in whose interests. Such an approach wrenches critical ethnography away from its current trajectory under postmodernism in (re)asserting its connections with a historical materialism that gives primacy to political economy. The focus of inquiry then becomes how labor power, in its various forms, is being produced and shaped by the social relations of accumulation within an expanding globalized capitalism. However, while the responsibility for the preparation and reproduction of labor power has increasingly fallen on the education and training state over the last quarter century, Willis suggests that though "continuing as an important site for the playing out of crucial issues, schooling may be becoming increasingly marginal to the actual formation of subjectivity, identity, and culture" (1999, p. 140). Significantly, this theme has been echoed by other researchers working within the sociology of education (Delamont et al. 2000; McRobbie 1994). If this is so, then critical ethnography has a key role to play in mapping out new sites of study.

First, the increasing marginality of schooling to the formation of labor power/subjectivity suggests that the "new" sociology of education needs to reconsider the terrain that it has staked out as its own over the last three decades. While this has traversed a wide range of themes and issues including social stratification, gender, ethnicity, the family, youth culture, and so on, it has tended to pursue the study of these in relation to teachers, pupils, parents, and other groups commonly identified with the school or other formal institutions of education. What it has tended to neglect are both formal and informal sectors located outside of these institutions that appear to be increasingly important as sites for learning (Delamont et al. 2000; McRobbie 1994). I am thinking of current efforts to reenvision public and private enterprises as "learning organizations" (Argyris 1993; Senge 1990), the growth of work-based learning and training, and the proliferation of private providers for skills training in the formal economy (Jackson and Jordan 2000). Of equal importance are the community and voluntary sectors, NGOs, labor, environmental, and indigenous people's organizations that see education of their members and the wider population as a core function of their activities (Foley 1999; Swift 1999). These developments have not only created greenfield sites for critical ethnographic inquiry, they also reconfigure and expand the concept "education" in ways that are associated neither with schooling nor with the category of youth.

Exploring and mapping new educational sites that have emerged outside of formal schooling over the recent past also requires that sociologists of education critically reflect on their own conceptual practices, particularly in the boundary maintenance of their (sub)discipline. This would not only entail a careful and critical reappraisal of theoretical traditions and current research practice, but the adoption of a critical disposition toward the idea of a "sociology" of education as it has hitherto been constituted. McRobbie (1994), for example, has made a strong argument from a postmodern-feminist perspective that the sociology of education and cultural studies could be productively combined and rearticulated within critical educational studies. She asserts that while the sociology of education could offer this union its well developed and extensive array of methodological tools and empirical studies, it nevertheless lacks a vocabulary for describing, naming and analyzing the cultural economy of global capitalism. Thus sociology is unable to contend with concepts such as "fascination," "desire," and "subjectivity" because it is still fixed on the "material structuring of social processes" rather than with the "psychic processes which underlie social practice" (McRobbie 1994, 191). Cultural studies, on the other hand, has constructed a sophisticated lexicon for the interrogation of popular culture, but this lacks a consistent grounding in empirical studies that show how the relations of everyday life are connected with cultural forms. Further, it marginalizes concepts such as the state, social regulation, policy, and institutional practices that are central to an understanding of the social and political character of contemporary transformations. Nevertheless, these strengths and weaknesses, although in tension, can also be complementary and productive in the exploration of new fields of knowledge where "culture is a broad site of learning" (p. 66).

Although McRobbie's approach is suggestive of how sociologists of education might reconceptualize their problematic under the aura of a "resistance postmodernism" (McLaren et al. 1999) it does not indicate how this would be enacted through research. That is, while she argues that forms of critical ethnographic inquiry would be central to critical educational studies, she nevertheless does not tell us how this could be organized or implemented. Carspecken and Apple (1992) and Carspecken's (1996) work on this dimension of critical ethnography is particularly useful, as is that of a growing number of researchers who define themselves as "criticalists" (Fay Street

1992; McLaren and Farahmandpur 1999; Quantz 1992). However, while they elaborate methodological pathways for critical researchers to take, these nevertheless remain centered on schools and schooling. If we are to reconceptualize the category education, however, then sociologists of education need to look to research practices constructed for sites other than schools. One area of research that shares both methodological principles and a politics of research close to that of critical ethnography is participatory action research (PAR).

Primarily developed by community and adult educators, PAR has been used in a wide range of settings, including education, with different groups and communities (McTaggart 1991). The value of PAR lies not only in its well developed repertoire of methodological procedures and commitment to social justice, but in its capacity to generate critiques of contemporary capitalism from the standpoint of the groups and communities it involves in research (Hagey 1997). The democratic, participatory, and consensus-building research practices that PAR enacts effectively constitute a form of critical ethnography "from below." Thus PAR could act as a vital resource for sociologists of education in understanding how the political economy of global capitalism works through local cultures to construct new types of domination and hegemony. Of equal importance, PAR may also reveal how particular forms of informal learning might contribute to the generation of a counterhegemony through the struggles of green, neighborhood, women's groups, and indigenous people. (See Foley 1999; Swift 1999; Tuhiwai Smith 1999.)

Critical ethnography can, therefore, make at least three contributions to the sociology of education within the context of global capitalism. Following Willis's analysis of the cultural commodity, critical ethnography could be harnessed to exploring and mapping the contours of the new cultural economy that global capital has created. Second, this cultural map could contribute to reenvisioning the scope, central foci and themes of the sociology of education. Last, allied with PAR, critical ethnography could provide a powerful methodology from below for constructing research practices that would enable sociologists of education to analyze and detail new types of hegemony secreted by global capital across different sites within the new cultural economy.

CONCLUSION

This chapter has explored how critical ethnography has contributed to the knowledge producing practices of the sociology of education over the last twenty-five years. In tracing its development, I have noted how critical ethnography has been shaped by a complex amalgam of theoretical traditions, institutional arrangements and politics that together have provided the dynamic for its methodology and research foci. These have not so much produced a research tradition in the formal sense, rather, they contributed to a critical "discourse" (Quantz 1992) or "orientation" (Carspecken 1996) that has profoundly altered the discursive terrain of qualitative research and the sociology of education. Indeed, the advent of critical ethnography constituted one of the primary intellectual forces behind developments in the new sociology of education.

As I have shown, this "orientation" has undergone significant changes since its inception in the 1970s. Over the last decade in particular, it has increasingly been subject to the influence of postmodernism, as indeed has qualitative research and the sociology of education. While I am not prepared to dismiss the work of postmodern theorists as "junk theory" (Rikowski and McLaren 1999), I do nevertheless agree with Apple and Whitty (1997) that we have to be cautious, and therefore selective, over what can be usefully adapted from it for critical ethnographic research. As they point out, the current impact of neoliberal policies on education is rarely registered by postmodernists and poststructuralists, and where they are it is often to celebrate the choice, diversity, and difference that these policies supposedly create. My point is that while postmodernism may have some important contributions to make to critical ethnography through, for example, the concept and practice of reflexivity, it also may deflect attention away from historical and social processes that are currently driving global capitalism.

For this reason, I have argued that critical ethnographers need to reclaim some of the territory that they originally staked out within the new sociology of education. That is, rather than being transfixed by the images, texts and televisual structures of the postmodern simulacrum—which often renders a cultural reductionism—critical ethnographers need to revisit political economy. I am not thinking of the dismal structuralist notion of Bowles and Gintis's (1976) "correspondence principle," but Willis's (1999) concept of the "cultural commodity" that recenters living labor power as the source of value within the cultural economy of global capitalism. The implications for critical ethnography of Willis's analysis is that critical research should focus not on the virtual, looking glass world of postmodernity, but the social relations of contemporary accumulation that constitute the looking glass itself. Such an approach is suggestive of a complex integrative analysis that does not treat culture, ideology, "the text," images, or technology as separate categories, but rather understands them as part of the historical and material processes of capitalist accumulation that feeds off human labor power. Critical ethnography's strength, therefore, lies in its capacity to produce fine-grained ethnographies of how this process organizes and exploits human labor power in the production and consumption of cultural commodities under global capitalism (see McRobbie 1994; Willis 1999).

Finally, I have suggested that the transformations that global capital has brought require sociologists of education to review and reconsider their traditional themes, content and research foci. With Willis, I have suggested that this may entail looking to sites other than schools, thereby creating a more expansive concept of education for study and research. This will also necessitate sociologists of education to at least reconsider, if not reconceptualize, the content, aims, and themes of their discipline, as well as the theoretical and research traditions on which it has relied. In short, critical ethnography has a pivotal role to play in the formation of a new sociological imagination for the study of education in the new century.

NOTE

I would like to thank Elizabeth Wood for her helpful comments on this paper.

REFERENCES

Apple, M., and G. Whitty. 1997. "Structuring the Postmodern in Educational Theory." In *Postmodernism in Educational Theory: Education and the Politics of Human Resistance,* edited by D. Hill, P. McLaren, M. Cole, and G. Rikowski, 10–30. London: Tufnell.

Argyris, C. 1993. *On Organizational Learning.* Cambridge, Mass.: Blackwell.

Asad, T. 1986. "The Concept of Translation in British Social Anthropology." In *Writing culture: The Poetics and Politics of Ethnography,* edited by J. Clifford and G. E. Marcus, 141–64. Berkeley: University of California Press.

Asad, T. 1994. "Ethnographic Representation, Statistics and Modern Power." *Social Research* 61: 55–78.

Atkinson, P. 1990. *The Ethnographic Imagination.* London: Routledge.

Bowles, S., and H. Gintis. 1976. *Schooling in Capitalist America: Educational Reform and the Contradictions of Economic Life.* New York: Basic.

Burawoy, M., A. Burton, A. A. Ferguson, K. J. Fox, J. Gamson, N. Gartrell, L. Hurst, C. Kurzman, L. Salzinger, J. Schiffman, and S. Ui. 1991. *Ethnography Unbound: Power and Resistance in the Modern Metropolis.* Berkeley: University of California Press.

Carspecken, P. F. 1996. *Critical Ethnography in Educational Research.* New York: Routledge.

Carspecken, P. F., and M. Apple. 1992. "Critical Qualitative Research: Theory, Methodology, and Practice." In *The Handbook of Qualitative Research in Education,* edited by M. Le Compte, W. Millroy, and J. Preissle, 507–53. San Diego: Academic Press.

Castells, M. 1999. "Flows, Networks, and Identities: A Critical Theory of the Informational Society." In *Critical Education in the New Information Age,* edited by P. McLaren, 37–64. Lanham, Md.: Rowman & Littlefield.

Corrigan, P. 1979. *Schooling the Smash Street Kids.* London: Papermac.

Corrigan, P., B. Curtis, and R. Lanning. 1987. "The Political Space of Schooling." In *The Political Economy of Canadian Schooling,* edited by T. Wotherspoon, 21–43. Toronto: Methuen.

Corrigan, P., and D. Sayer. 1985. *The Great Arch*. London: Basil Blackwell.

Delamont, S. 1996. *A Woman's Place in Education: Historical and Sociological Perspective on Gender in Education*. Aldershot, U.K.: Avebury.

Delamont, S., A. Coffey, and P. Atkinson. 2000. "The Twilight Years? Educational Ethnography and the Five Moments Model." *International Journal of Qualitative Studies in Education* 13: 223–38.

Denzin, N. K. 1997. *Interpretive Ethnography: Ethnographic Practices for the 21st Century*. Thousand Oaks, Calif.: Sage.

Eagleton, T. 1996. *The Illusions of Postmodernism*. Oxford: Blackwell.

Elliott, J. 1998. *The Curriculum Experiment*. Buckingham: Open University Press.

Ellsworth, E. 1989. "Why Doesn't This Feel Empowering? Working through the Repressive Myths of Critical Pedagogy." *Harvard Educational Review* 59: 297–324.

Fay Street, A. 1992. *Inside Nursing: A Critical Ethnography of Clinical Nursing Practice*. New York: State University of New York Press.

Foley, D. 1990. *Learning Capitalist Culture*. Philadelphia: University of Pennsylvania Press.

Foley, G. 1999. *Learning in Social Action: A Contribution to Understanding Informal Education*. London: Zed.

Foster, P., R. Gomm, and M. Hammersly. 1996. *Constructing Educational Inequality*. London: Falmer.

Glaser, Barney G., and Anselm L. Strauss. 1968. *The Discovery of Grounded Theory: Strategies for Qualitative Research*. London: Weidenfeld & Nicholson.

Grace, G. 1995. *School Leadership: An Essay in Policy Scholarship*. London: Falmer.

Gramsci, A. 1974. *The Prison Notebooks*. London: Lawrence & Wishart.

Habermas, J. 1987. *The Theory of Communicative Action: A Critique of Functionalist Reason*. Cambridge: Polity.

Hagey, R. S. 1997. "The Use and Abuse of Participatory Action Research." *Chronic Diseases in Canada* 18: 1–4.

Hammersley, M. 1995. "Who's Afraid of Positivism? A Comment on Shilling and Abraham." *British Journal of Sociology of Education* 16: 243–46.

Hopenhayn, M. 1995. "Postmodernism and Neoliberalism in Latin America." In *The Postmodernism Debate in Latin America*, edited by J. Beverley, M. Aronna, and J. Oviedo, 93–109. Durham, N.C.: Duke University Press.

Jackson, N., and S. Jordan. 2000. "Learning for Work: Contested Terrain?" *Studies in the Education of Adults* 32: 195–211.

Jordan, S., and D. Yeomans. 1995. "Critical Ethnography: Problems in Contemporary Theory and Practice." *British Journal of Sociology of Education* 16: 389–408.

Kabbani, R. 1986. *Europe's Myths of Orient*. Bloomington: Indiana University Press.

Kemmis, S. 1993. "Action Research." In *Educational Research: Current Issues*, edited by M. Hammersley. London: Paul Chapman.

Lather, P. 1991. *Getting Smart: Feminist Research and Pedagogy with/in the Postmodern*. New York: Routledge.

Marcus, G. E. 1998. *Ethnography through Thick and Thin*. Princeton: Princeton University Press.

McLaren, P., and R. Farahmandpur. 1999. "Critical Pedagogy, Postmodernism, and the Retreat from Class: Toward a Contraband Pedagogy." In *Postmodernism in Educational Theory: Education and the Politics of Human Resistance*, edited by D. Hill, P. McLaren, M. Cole, and G. Rikowski, 167–202. London: Tufnell.

McLaren, P., D. Hill, and M. Cole. 1999. "Postmodernism Adieu: Toward a Politics of Human Resistance." In *Postmodernism in Educational Theory: Education and the Politics of Human Resistance,* edited by D. Hill, P. McLaren, M. Cole, and G. Rikowski, 203–13. London: Tufnell.

McRobbie, A. 1994. *Postmodernism and Popular Culture.* London: Routledge.

McTaggart, R. 1991. "Principles of Participatory Research." *Adult Education Quarterly* 41: 168–87.

Miles, M. B., and A. M. Huberman. 1984. *Qualitative Data Analysis: A Sourcebook of New Methods.* Beverly Hills: Sage.

Nash, R. 1997. *Inequality/Difference: A Sociology of Education.* Palmerston North: ERDC Press Massey University.

O'Neill, J. 1995. *The Poverty of Postmodernism.* London: Routledge.

Packwood, A., and P. Sikes. 1996. "Adopting a Postmodern Approach to Research." *International Journal of Qualitative Studies in Education* 9: 335–45.

Quantz, R. 1992. "On Critical Ethnography with Some Postmodern Considerations." In *The Handbook of Qualitative Research in Education,* edited by M. Le Compte, W. Millroy, and J. Preissle, 447–505. San Diego: Academic Press.

Reed-Danahay, D. 1997. Introduction to *Auto/Ethnography,* edited by D. Reed-Danahay, 1–9. Oxford: Berg.

Rikowski, G., and P. McLaren. 1999. "Postmodernism in Educational Theory." In *Postmodernism in Educational Theory: Education and the Politics of Human Resistance,* edited by D. Hill, P. McLaren, M. Cole, and G. Rikowski, 1–9. London: Tufness.

Robertson, S., and Smaller, H. 1996. *Teacher Activism in the 1990s.* Toronto: James Lorimer.

Rowbatham, S. 1976. *Hidden from History.* New York: Vintage.

Said, E. 1983. *The World, the Text, and the Critic.* Cambridge: Harvard University Press.

Said, E. 1989. "Representing the Colonised: Anthropology's Interlocutors." *Critical Inquiry* 15: 205–25.

Said, E. 1993. *Culture and Imperialism.* New York: Knopf.

Samuel, R. 1981. Afterword to *People's History and Socialist Theory,* edited by R. Samuel, 410–17. London: Routledge Kegan Paul.

Schon, D. 1983. *The Reflective Practitioner: How Professionals Think in Action.* New York: Basic.

Scloari 1998. *Nudist.* Thousand Oaks: Sage Publications Software.

Scott, J. W. 1987. "On Language, Gender, and Working-Class History." *International Labour and Working-Class History* 31, 1–13.

Scott, J. W. 1988. *Gender and the Politics of History.* New York: Columbia University Press.

Senge, P. 1990. *The Fifth Discipline: The Art and Practice of the Learning Organisation.* New York: Doubleday.

Smith, D. E. 1987. *The Everyday as Problematic: A Feminist Sociology.* Toronto: University of Toronto Press.

Smith, D. E. 1990a. *The Conceptual Practices of Power: A Feminist Sociology of Knowledge.* Toronto: University of Toronto Press.

Smith, D. E. 1990b. *Texts, Facts, and Femininity: Exploring the Relations of Ruling.* London: Routledge.

Smith, D. E. 1994. "The Relations of Ruling: A Feminist Inquiry." *Group for Research into Institutionalisation and Professionalisation of Knowlege-Production, GRIP.* University of Minnesota.

Stanley, L. 1990. *Feminist Praxis: Research Theory and Epistemology in Feminist Sociology.* New York: Routledge & Kegan Paul.

Swift, J. 1999. *Civil Society in Question.* Toronto: Between the Lines.

Taylor, S., F. Rizvi, and M. Henry. 1997. *Educational Policy and the Politics of Change.* London: Routledge.

Thomas, J. 1993. *Doing Critical Ethnography.* Newbury Park, Calif.: Sage.

Thompson, E. P. 1968. *The Making of the English Working Class.* Harmondsworth, U.K.: Pelican.

Thompson, E. P. 1981. "The Politics of Theory." In *People's History and Socialist Theory,* edited by R. Samuel, 396–408. London: Routledge & Kegan Paul.

Thompson, E. P. 1991. *Customs in Common.* London: Penguin.

Tuhiwai Smith, L. 1999. *Decolonizing Methodologies: Research and Indigenous Peoples.* New York: St Martin's.

Williams, R. 1961. *The Long Revolution.* London: Chatto & Windus.

Williams, R. 1983. *Key Words: A Vocabulary of Culture and Society.* Glasgow: Fontana.

Willis, P. 1977. *Learning to Labour: How Working-Class Kids Get Working-Class Jobs.* Aldershot: Gower.

Willis, P. 1999. "Labor, Power, Culture, and the Cultural Commodity." In *Critical Education in the New Information Age,* edited by P. McLaren, 139–69. Lanham, Md.: Rowman & Littlefield.

Willis, P., S. Jones, J. Canaan, and G. Hurd. 1990. *Common Culture: Symbolic Work at Play in the Everyday Cultures of the Young.* Buckingham, U.K.: Open University Press.

Woods, P. 1988. "Educational Ethnography in Britain." In *Qualitative Research in Education: Focus and Methods,* edited by R. Sherman and R. Webb. London: Falmer.

Yin, R. 1989. *Case Study Research: Design and Methods.* Newbury Park, Calif.: Sage.

Young, M. F. D. 1971. *Knowledge and Control.* London: Macmillan.

5

Sociocultural Approaches to Cognition:

Implications for the Sociology of Education

David MacLennan

.

Feminist philosophers have criticized mainstream philosophy for not acknowledging "the historical and cultural locatedness of the subject" (Fricker and Hornsby 2000, 8). One could imagine sociologists leveling the same charge against mainstream psychology—and until recently such a charge would have been valid. But over the last two decades, a concern with the locatedness of the subject—what the subject acquires from inhabiting a particular social setting—has become a central theme for some psychologists. These contextual psychologists reject the universal subject of mainstream psychology. Support for this approach has developed to a point where contextual psychologies have been accorded a status equal to that of earlier behaviorist and cognitive paradigms (Greeno at al. 1996; Greeno 1998).

The purpose of this chapter is to examine the treatment of the thinking/knowing subject—cognition, in short—by these contextual psychologies. Particular emphasis will be placed on what might be called a sociocultural approach to cognition and the contributions of a central figure: Russian Jewish psychologist Lev Vygotsky (1896–1934). Though the sociocultural approach to cognition has received surprisingly little attention in the sociology of education, it has a produced ideas and insights that are relevant to the discipline. My goal is to demonstrate that the activities of the thinking, knowing subject ought to be a central concern for the sociology of education and that in developing a research program in this area sociologists can benefit from the Vygotskian (or sociocultural) approach to cognition.

LOCATING THE THINKING/KNOWING SUBJECT
IN THE SOCIOLOGY OF EDUCATION

While the focus of this paper is the sociocultural approach to cognition, it is first necessary to locate cognition or the thinking/knowing subject in the sociology of education. There are a number of important reference points. The first is empirical research by sociologists investigating the relations between the social backgrounds of students—social class especially—and their educational attainment. Over the last thirty years, sociologists working in different national contexts have described a durable relation between class and educational attainment. But there is no consensus on why this relation persists. As Marshall and his colleagues put it: "Few would dispute that people's class of origin has a substantial influence on their educational achievements, but there is little agreement about the mechanisms by which this influence is effected" (1997, 144). A range of contributing factors have been proposed and these are summarized in Marshall et al. (pp. 137–44). They include the material circumstances of students' lives, bias among school personnel, issues of motivation and aspiration, rational assessment of the likelihood of success, inequalities in school resources, and differences in innate intelligence. It is worth noting that Marshall et al. do not refer to contextual psychologies or the sociocultural approach to cognition associated with Vygotsky.

Another reference point is the tradition of critical ethnography founded by Marxist ethnographer Paul Willis (1977). As against the determinism of reproduction theories, Willis introduced the idea of resistance. Both the cause and the vehicle of this resistance were at least partly cultural. On Willis's view, working-class males did not so much fail to be counted as knowers; they chose not to be counted, and in so doing celebrated an oppositional culture. However, research shows that difficulties in school begin very early, well before individuals could reasonably be said to *choose* to participate in an oppositional culture. This is not to exclude the possibility that an element of choice or agency is involved. But it is to insist that choices are constrained in relation to what individuals know or have learned, and hence on an educational career that has evolved over time and has a certain shape by the time learners *elect* to join particular subcultures. The importance of cognitive skills "formed at young ages" is stressed by sociologists like Farkas, who writes that "parental skills, habits and styles determine the very early cognitive skills of their children, and these influence the child's habits and styles via his/her estimation of the success they can expect from hard effort at tasks that both require and increase cognitive skill" (1996, 11). Farkas's argument is certainly compatible with a sociocultural view—and relevant to why some learners might elect to join school countercultures—but he makes no reference to Vygotsky in his bibliography.

A third reference point is the sociology of school knowledge (e.g., Young 1971). Early contributors to this research tradition showed how the curriculum was influenced by the biases, experiences, and standpoints of dominant social groups. A key research question was, What counts as knowledge? and abundant evidence was marshaled to illustrate a selective tradition, where the principles of selecting school knowledge were ethnocentric and tied in some way to dominant groups. It was possible to develop this argument focusing almost exclusively on texts (knowledge as a product) and devoting limited attention to the activities of knowing subjects (knowledge as a process). Yet even in the early days of this tradition it was clear to some of the contributors that the task of theorizing the knowing subject was relevant to their project. Nell Keddie, for example, believed that both knowledge and ability were socially constructed and hence that what counts as ability is partly a political question. But she also recognized that what differentiated some knowers from others is that they actually had different kinds of knowledge. As she puts it: "[students from cultural minorities fail] not only because of the meanings [standardized] tests have in the social context in which they are administered, but also because it seems patterns of thought, logic and perception have to be learnt rather than treated as the normal development of intelligence of any child" (1973, 12). Keddie's remark anticipates the sociocultural approach's emphasis on the relation between social settings and thinking.

A fourth reference point is the work of sociologists searching for a way to refute claims, like those advanced in *The Bell Curve* (1994), that differences in educational attainment reflect innate differences in intelligence. As against this view, Fischer et al. argue that educational inequalities are influenced by social inequalities and that what counts as intelligence can be learned—it is not simply a manifestation of a biological reality. To develop their argument, Fischer and his colleagues make use of what they call information processing models of intelligence. They suggest that these models can help us understand "what mental processes are involved when people solve problems" (Fischer et al. 1996, 47). However, they make no reference to contextual or sociocultural approaches to cognition, even though reference to the sociocultural approach would strengthen their argument significantly.

The works described above were published over the last three or four decades and raise a number of important questions. Some of the most important questions are: Why do certain categories of subjects fail to become knowers? Why do some subjects choose not to become knowers? Why are some subjects unlikely to be recognized as knowers? (I am indebted to Langton [2000] for this way of posing the questions.) These questions are not peripheral to the sociology of education. On the contrary: it would seem that they are, or ought to be, central to the discipline. But for whatever reason, sociologists have yet to take advantage of resources—particularly those of contextual psychologies—that would enable them to confront these questions in more productive ways.

This is not to say that sociologists have ignored the problem of the relation between social settings and the knowing subject. The problem has been addressed by figures like Bourdieu, whose importance to the discipline seems beyond dispute, and others, like Belenky et al., authors of *Women's Ways of Knowing* (1987; hereafter *WWK*), whose work has been very influential. Bourdieu's idea of the habitus, for example, highlights the role of early family experience—what might be called cultural socialization—in influencing an individual's way of knowing and expressing knowledge. Consider the following early statement of Bourdieu's position: "What the child received from an educated milieu is not only a *culture* . . . but also a certain *style* of relationship to that culture, which derives precisely from *the manner of acquiring it*. An individual's relationship to cultural works is [influenced by] the conditions in which he acquired his culture, the osmosis of childhood in a family providing good conditions for an experience of familiarity . . . which schooling can never completely provide"([1966] 1977a, 117).

At a general level, Bourdieu's position is quite compatible with the authors of *WWK*, who write: "The social forces that operate on a family during the daughter's formative years continue to shape her experience [or] The families . . . accurately reflect the environments that give rise to each of these ways of knowing. Individuals are typically supported by their families to develop only to a certain point, lingering on that level throughout much of their adult lives"(Belenky et al., 156). Compare the positions of Bourdieu and *WWK* with that of what is here called contextual psychology: "When individuals move from situation to situation, they carry histories of prior experience with them. These are histories of ways of behaving. They include the elaborated knowledge structures, along with affective and social propensities, developed in the course of tuning to prior situations. The way one enters a new situation is influenced by one's history of past situations"(Resnick 1994, 490).

What unites the work of Bourdieu, Resnick, and the authors of *WWK* are two basic assumptions. The first is an antiuniversalist assumption which asserts that the activities and experiences of knowing subjects in particular contexts influence both what and how they know. The second is a cultural assumption which asserts that, not discounting the possibility of some degree of singularity in the experiences of individuals, it is plausible to assert that individuals share activities and experiences as a result of their membership in social groups. It would be misleading to suggest that figures as diverse as Bourdieu and the authors of *Women's Ways of Knowing* agree on particular details or even on the methodological and political implications of these basic assumptions. Nor would it be accurate to suggest that the insights of contextual psychology can be simply imported into sociology. But contextual psychology has generated a wealth of useful resources, theoretical, methodological, and empirical. Many of these resources can be grouped under the heading "sociocultural approaches to cognition." I will describe these resources and indicate their relevance to sociologists wishing to explore the relation between social setting and the thinking/knowing subject.

KEY PROPOSITIONS

The following review of sociocultural approaches to cognition starts with a simple assertion: the human subject inhabits social settings and those social settings influence what kind of knower the subject becomes. Ideas related to this assertion may be developed with reference to three propositions.

1. Cognition is social: cognition and the acquisition of the ability to engage in cognition (learning) are social; one thinks and learns to think in relation to others; it follows that social relations, even those present early in the individual's lifespan, are important to learning and cognition.
2. Cognition is cultural: thinking depends on various cultural tools or artifacts; the most important tool is language, but other tools—maps, graphs, pictures, mathematical notation—are also important; it follows that different kinds of cognition might be associated with different cultures.
3. Cognition develops over time: as one acquires experience and knowledge in a particular domain, cognition changes; the thinking of experts is different from the thinking of novices.

Use of the terms "cognition" and "the knowing subject" may cause some confusion and no doubt it would be worthwhile to discuss the ways in which the terms are incommensurate. However, to simplify matters, phrases like "the knowing subject" and "the subject who engages in cognition" will be used interchangeably in this chapter. One further note of clarification is appropriate at this time. When discussing propositions special emphasis is placed on the work of Vygotsky. It is important to acknowledge that not all contextual psychologies derive exclusively from Vygotsky. Cultural psychology, for example, traces its origins to a number of sources of which Vygotsky is only one (Cole 1998; Shweder et al. 1998). Furthermore, research inspired by Vygotsky has evolved to a point where its relation to the founding figure is complex and problematic. Finally, as Bruner notes, the work of Vygotsky can be "aphoristic" or "sketchy" (1985, 23). As with any other rich body of research, there is plenty of room for interpretation and dispute. Still as a point of departure for a bridging of psychology and sociology, the work of Vygotsky stands as particularly valuable.

COGNITION IS SOCIAL: THE ACTIVITIES OF THE KNOWING SUBJECT ARE SOCIAL

Sociologists are aware of the difficulties associated with analytical distinctions between the social and cultural aspects of the social world. To be sure, many of the topics here discussed as social, topics like emotion and identity, could be discussed with reference to culture also. Nevertheless, I will adopt the position that while the social and cultural are integrally related, one can make analytical distinctions between them. The social refers to relations between subjects and the cultural refers to various products or artifacts, including language, used by subjects.

Having made this distinction it is necessary to acknowledge that Vygotsky's central insights into learning and cognition combine the social and cultural. This point is made by Kozulin in an effort to distinguish Piaget's cognitive individualism from Vygotsky's sociocultural approach. Kozulin describes how Piaget's perspective on cognitive ability highlights "the unassisted interaction between the child's mental schemas and the objects of the external world" (1998, 40). On Piaget's view, "The only requirement for the learning milieu is that it be sufficiently rich so that children have enough objects and processes to practice their schemas" (40). In contrast, Vygotsky stresses both the role of social relations in cognition and learning, and the role of cultural factors like symbolic representations. As Kozulin puts it:

> from Vygotsky's point of view, learning occurs in the collaboration between children and the adults who introduce symbolic tools-mediators to children and teach them how to organize and control their natural psychological functions through these cultural tools. In the process, the natural psychological functions of the child change, their nature becoming culturally and socially informed and organized. (1998, 40)

As this synopsis suggests, both the social and the cultural play an integral role in Vygotsky's conception of cognition and learning. In this section I devote particular attention to what Kozulin refers to as collaboration between adults and children. It will become clear however that this collaboration is not confined to adults and children. It encompasses a range of different collaborators with the common theme being some degree of asymmetry in the kinds of knowledge possessed by those involved. The point is that social relations between subjects influence how the less knowledgeable subjects, the novices to use a related terminology, think, learn, and demonstrate knowledge.

Vygotsky's most influential idea, the idea that best expresses his views on the social and cultural aspects of cognition, is the zone of proximal development (ZPD). Again the contrast between Vygotsky's views and those of Piaget is instructive. Kozulin maintains that for Piaget the key to understanding the cognitive ability is to set the child an "unfamiliar problem." Viewing the child in this context will enable the adult to "identify the *infantile* way of reasoning unaffected by the imitation of adult logic" (40). For Vygotsky, on the other hand, what is important is not the ability of the isolated child. It is rather what the child can do with the assistance of a more knowledgeable collaborator. In Vygotsky's words: "[ZPD is] the distance between the child's actual developmental level as determined by independent problem solving and the level of potential development as determined through problem solving under adult guidance or in collaboration with more capable peers" (cited in Duveen 1997, 79). With the right kind of assistance, or what came to be known as "scaffolding," some children are able to respond effectively to very complex cognitive challenges. On Vygotsky's view, this capacity for assisted performance should be the basis for understanding a child's ability and the likelihood a child will succeed in formal school settings.

Clearly the social aspects of cognition and learning are central to a Vygotskian perspective on the knowing subject. For many psychologists, Vygotsky offers "a perspective from which social relations and cognitive processes [can] be brought into a single productive framework" (Duveen, 78). I want to elaborate on this framework briefly before offering some more critical observations. Many researchers influenced by Vygotsky believe that change over time in a subject's thinking (ontogenesis) should be a central focus of inquiry. Tomasello's work—especially his discussions of the development of cognition in young children—is a particularly interesting application of Vygotsky. Tomasello demonstrates that even the cognition of very young children has an important social dimension. To clarify this social dimension, Tomasello introduces the idea of "social cognition," which he defines as "the ability of individual organisms to understand conspecifics as beings *like themselves* who have intentional and mental lives like their own" (1999, 5). He elaborates on the importance of social cognition to learning: "to socially learn the conventional use of a tool or symbol, children must come to understand why, toward what outside end, the other person is using the tool or symbol; that is to say, they must understand the intentional significance of the tool use or symbolic practice—what it is *for*, what *we*, the users of this tool or symbol, do with it" (6). In discussing the development of cognition over time, Tomasello offers a perspective that sociologists will recognize as distinctly Meadian. As children become more proficient symbol users, they learn to apply standards to themselves by viewing their own thinking from the standpoint of more accomplished collaborators. Thinking is thus social in the sense that children must learn to project themselves imaginatively into the minds of others. Or as Vygotsky understood it, they must internalize, make intrapsychological, a process that is originally interpsychological.

If social relations are so important to cognition in Vygotsky's view, how does he understand the distinctive features of these relations? Questions of this sort will be of interest to sociologists concerned with educational inequalities. A recent article makes some progress toward addressing these concerns by showing the emphasis Vygotsky placed on the affective or emotional aspects of cognition. Goldstein points out that in early compilations of Vygotskian texts discussions of the emotional aspects of cognition are not evident. More recent compilations show a different Vygotsky, one for whom emotion is crucial. Thus for Vygotsky it is not just social relations but the emotional tone of those relations that shapes the development of cognitive processes. As Goldstein puts it: "Vygotsky saw affect and intellect as interconnected and inseparable" (1999, 654). She maintains, further, that Vygotsky saw the tendency to view thinking out of context as a central flaw in psychology, and she cites Vygotsky on this point: "The separation of the intellectual side of our consciousness from its affective, volitional side is one of the fundamental flaws of all traditional psychology" (648). Goldstein concludes that while Vygotsky recognized the role of emotion and volition in cognition, he did not elaborate. It is therefore "up to us to do this work ourselves," and she identifies Nel Noddings's work on the role of caring in teaching and learning as a particularly useful resource.

Vygotsky's ideas about the role of social relationships in learning are supported by more quantitative traditions in psychology. In a review of recent research, Hartup and Laursen refer to findings that demonstrate links between the quality of early relationships and "competence in the social domain." One of the goals of this research is to explore the impact of early childhood experiences on subsequent experiences. They summarize this research in the following passage:

> Diverse assessments indicate that school engagement and grades are a function of relationship quality: Beginning in the nursery school and extending through secondary school, supportive relations with parents and friends predict higher levels of academic interest and abilities than conflict-ridden and contentious relationships do. (1999, 29)

Sociologists may be wary of potential cultural bias in the characterization of supportive relationships. They may also have concerns about research purporting to find links between past experiences and current actions, fearing that such arguments minimize the role of subjects as intentional agents. Nevertheless, even if these findings are treated with some skepticism, they do appear to build on Vygotsky and Noddings's emphasis on the emotional or affective dimensions of thinking and learning.

While studies of young children are clearly important, studies of adolescents may speak more directly to the interests of sociologists. In a critical review of some of Vygotsky's ideas, Duveen expresses concerns about possible limitations of Vygotsky's idea of the zone of proximal development. Duveen maintains that many of the criticisms of the ZPD converge on the idea of internalization. He cites Litowitz's characterization of this process: "cultural knowledge is transferred not from one person (adult) to another (child) but from two persons (the dyad) to one (the child) . . . the nonknower demonstrates equality in the dyad by becoming equally responsible for solving problems and accomplishing tasks" (cited in Duveen 1997, 80). In a criticism that anticipates a sociological response to such a scenario, Duveen draws attention to its basic assumptions: "The model emphasizes a sense of intersubjectivity based on mutual engagement in a joint activity which subordinates differences between the partners" (81). It seems that what is portrayed is something equivalent to a Habermasian ideal speech situation. In reality, such situations are rare. More often differences in power and culture work against intersubjectivity and mutual engagement. Thus according to Duveen the apprenticeship model, which has served as a concrete application of the idea of ZPD, has limited relevance to many school settings. It presupposes "well structured social processes," "a community of interest between novice and expert," and a "joint activity . . . which is meaningful to both parties." But as Duveen argues, "Some of the most persistent problems in secondary education . . . seem to arise precisely because the students do not recognize any community of interest with their teachers" (81).

While Goldstein's comments express a favorable assessment of Vygotsky's value to sociological research, Duveen sounds a more critical note. I tend to support a more favorable assessment, as will become clear in the next section. However, before discussing Vygotsky's views on the links between culture and cognition it is necessary to consider the problem of identity, a problem that clearly is both social and cultural. One of the most important insights into why some learners encounter difficulties at school or choose not to be counted as knowers focuses on the idea of identity. Some students do not engage in the practices of the school because those practices threaten their identities, their sense of who they are and what they stand for. Feminist psychologists, for example, describe a school system that fails to recognize a particular type of knower, a knower for whom the development of the self, construed holistically rather than atomistically, is particularly important. Sociologists have made similar arguments with respect to cultural minorities and working-class children.

One of the merits of the work of researchers whose work is influenced by Vygotsky is that it encourages us both to see the links between learning and identity, and to view the range of possible links on a continuum. At one end of the continuum are situations where identity is enhanced by sustained, effortful participation in practices recognized as worthwhile by the school. As Wenger puts it, "Learning—whatever form it takes—changes who we are by changing our ability to participate, to belong, to negotiate meaning. And this ability is configured socially with respect to practices, communities and economies of meaning where it shapes our identities" (1998, 226). Another possibility is where school participation threatens identity—the kind of situation described by Willis in his account of working-class males. A third possibility involves learners managing a double identity. The general point is expressed by Shweder and his colleagues: "A great deal of what happens in classrooms or testing situation has as much to do with maintaining or protecting one's identity as it has to do with the acquisition of academic skills" (1998, 917).

The relation between identity and learning will continue to be a central question in the sociology of education and researchers working in this area stand to benefit from developments in the Vygotskian tradition. It should be noted, however, that Vygotsky himself did not devote a great deal of attention to the problem of identity. According to Penuel and Wertsch, Vygotsky's sociocultural approach provides resources for thinking about identity but provides little guidance for understanding the specific problems of identity formation (1995, 84). Like Goldstein with her suggestions on caring and learning, Penuel and Wertsch point to more recent research—specifically that of Erikson—that they believe will help build on the Vygotskian approach. In a tentative synthesis which draws on both Vygotsky and Erikson, they "suggest that identity be conceived as a form of action that is first and foremost rhetorical, concerned with persuading others (and oneself) about who one is and what one values to meet different purposes. . . . It is always addressed to someone, who is situated culturally and historically and who has a particular meaning for individuals" (Penuel and Wertsch 1995, 91). With this formulation we arrive at a position that is relevant to sociologists studying school countercultures, though the sociocultural approach might insist that academic skills of students who join countercultures should not be ignored.

To conclude, in the Vygotskian tradition the activities of the thinking/knowing subject cannot be understood outside of the particular social context in which he or she is located. Social relations—relations between persons—are a crucial part of this context. Social relations are not something *added on* to a process of thinking and knowing that is solitary and internal. Even before the subject can speak, his or her relation to the world is influenced by his or her relations to adults in his or her immediate environment. The subject will carry memories of these early encounters into subsequent encounters and eventually into the encounters characteristic of school settings. Throughout the individual's lifespan, social relations influence the patterns of thinking and knowing a subject exhibits and what kind of thinker/knower the subject will become.

COGNITION IS CULTURAL

In the zone of proximal development, the child's relation to the objects of the world, and indeed to his or her own mental and emotional processes, is influenced by the activities and attitudes of copresent adults. But social relations are not the only aspect of the child's environment that influence his or her thinking and knowing. Just as important, as Kozulin notes, is the fact that adults introduce symbolic tools/mediators to children. With the help of adult instruction, these symbolic tools/mediators will change the child. The child's "nature," as Kozulin puts it, will become "culturally and socially organized" (1998, 40). The child will learn to use symbols (including language) in certain ways, to think in certain ways, and to become a certain kind of knowing subject.

In the same way that Vygotsky's views on the relation between knowing and social settings offer new ideas for sociologists, so too do his views on the relation between knowing and culture. At a general level Vygotsky's insights contribute to a fundamental rethinking of what sociologists mean when they use the term "culture." More specifically, they offer resources for exploring the proposition that there might be differences in cognition associated with cultural differences. This section focuses on the contributions of the sociocultural approach to the study of cultural differences in cognition.

To begin it is necessary to define what Vygotsky meant by symbolic tools/mediators—thinking tools. While language was the most important of the thinking tools, it was not the only symbol system Vygotsky associated with the idea of a thinking tool. Kozulin provides a useful summary of the Vygotskian view:

> According to Vygotsky and his followers, cognitive processes are formed in the course of sociocultural activities. As a result the individual comes into possession of a variety of cognitive processes engendered by different activities and requested by different types of activity. The radical change in cognition is associated in this model with the transition from one set of symbolic psychological tools to another. Psychological tools . . . include signs, symbolic and literacy systems, graphic symbolic devices, and formulae. Intercultural cognitive differences are attributed to the variance in the systems of psychological tools and in the methods of their acquisition practiced in other cultures. (1998, 102)

This perspective on intercultural cognitive differences offers a way to build on insights offered by authors like Keddie (1973) and others who thirty years ago argued against the idea of cultural deprivation. The term "cultural deprivation" was first used in the United States in the 1960s and was associated with a number of educational reforms (Head Start being the most important) intended to improve the educational performance of poor and minority children. Those using the term "cultural deprivation" were attempting to provide a cultural explanation for school failure, but their perspective involved assumptions about social and material deprivation as well. With respect to cultural factors, it was asserted that the family environments of some students lacked cultural artifacts associated with middle-class culture. With respect to social factors, it was asserted that the parents or caregivers of some students failed to engage in certain behaviors—reading to their children—that were common among middle-class parents. With respect to material factors, it was understood that some minority and poor children would be suffering the ill effects of malnutrition and other medical conditions associated with extreme poverty. The consequence of these various forms of deprivation was that such children did not develop socially and cognitively to the point where they were prepared to benefit from school activities. While the causes of their difficulties at school were seen to be complex, the term "cultural deprivation" was used to capture the central role of culture in causing these difficulties (Keddie 1973; Zigler and Meunchow 1992; Jenks 1993).

For the purposes of this discussion, a key assumption of the deprivation-ists should be highlighted: their concept of culture was ethnocentric and elit-ist. It was not the anthropological sense of culture—culture as a way of life—but culture defined with reference to the tastes and practices of educated elites. Put differently, one might say that the deprivationists worked with a universalist notion of Culture rather than a pluralist notion of cultures (to use Eagleton's distinction [2000, 37–38]). The deprivationists thus thought more in terms of culture superiority than cultural difference. This way of thinking carried over into their views on intercultural differences in cogni-tion. The thinking of minority students was inferior thinking: partly because of their cultural deprivation, such students had failed to develop cognitively, and this was the reason they encountered difficulties in school.

Controversies associated with the deprivationist thesis were many, and one of the most heated concerned the work of British sociolinguist Basil Bernstein (1971–1975). There was some disagreement about whether Bern-stein's research provided support for the deprivationist thesis. Bernstein had identified two different speech codes—a restricted code and an elaborated code—which he found more common among working-class and middle-class speech respectively. Bourdieu and Passeron found similar patterns in the speech of the working class, with its tendency to avoid abstraction and "move from particular case to particular case," in contrast to "bourgeois lan-guage" with its tendency "to abstraction, formalism, intellectualism and eu-phemistic moderation" (1977, 116). Under attack from the American linguist Labov (1973), who argued that the speech forms of black children exhibited a distinct logic (albeit a different logic than standard English), Bernstein seemed to equivocate on the question of the superiority of the elaborated code. But some commentators on Bernstein's work insist that the message is clear: "Unpalatable as it may be, the logic of Bernstein's sociolinguistic the-sis leads inexorably to the conclusion that those whose experience is regu-lated by a restricted code are, in terms of the demands necessarily placed on them by the school, linguistically deprived. . . . Within the framework of the existing class system, then, it would seem to follow that working class chil-dren lack something useful (an elaborated code made available to them 'as an *essential* part of their socialization within the family') that most middle class children possess" (Karabel and Halsey 1977, 65–66).

Whatever her views on Bernstein, sociologist Nell Keddie (1973) argued against the deprivationist thesis. Keddie's views, and the views of many of the contributors to her edited book, were based on a rejection of the distinc-tion between Culture (as in "high culture," for example) and cultures (as in the ways of life of different peoples). This rejection opens the door—at least on a theoretical level—to a new program of research. If one rejects assump-tions about the superiority of Culture over cultures, it follows that one would expect to find thinking, reasoning, and what might be called cognitive com-plexity in those other cultures. Over the last fifteen years, researchers exploring this proposition have produced a complex and diversified body of knowledge. Often taking their inspiration from Vygotsky, these researchers seek to understand how adults in non-Western cultures attempt to engender in their children the kinds of thinking and knowing valued in local settings. The research questions identified in a recent publication are typical: "(1) What are the activities that are available for children in their communities? (2) How do children engage in those activities? (3) What do children learn as a result of their engagement?" (Goncu 1999, 13; see also Moll 2000).

The value of this research is that it takes us beyond general claims about the equality of all cultures, as important politically as those claims may be. We are drawn into an inquiry that focuses more on the actual processes though which children and adolescents in diverse cultures are initiated into valued ways of thinking and learning. One of the most important findings of this research is that many forms of thinking are context bound (Garcia Coll and Magnuson 1999). Moreover, subjects who demonstrate cognitive complexity with respect to local topics may have difficulty coming to terms with the decontextualized forms of thinking valued by modern education systems. While their intellectual engagement with local environments is sophisticated, school personnel do not devote enough attention to building these forms of intellectual engagement into the school setting. The sociocultural approach to cognition provides new ways of appreciating innovative efforts to create bridges between different ways of communicating and different contexts of intellectual engagement.

To illustrate how such bridging might occur, it is useful to refer to Delpit's discussion of the classroom activities of "Martha Demientiff, a masterly Native Alaskan teacher of Athabaskan Indian students" (1997, 591). Demientiff's students "live in a small isolated rural village of less than two hundred people." They "are not aware that there are different codes of English." Introducing her students to "Formal English," Demientiff makes the following remarks:

> We have to feel a little sorry for [the speakers of "Formal English"] because they have only one way to talk. We are going to learn two ways to say things. Isn't that better? One way will be our Heritage way. The other will be Formal English. Then, when we go to get jobs, we'll be able to talk like those people who only know and can only really listen to one way. Maybe after we get the jobs we can help them learn how it feels to have another language, like ours, that feels so good. We'll talk like them when we have to, but we'll always know our way is best. (cited in Delpit 1997, 591)

For Vygotskians, language is the most important of the symbolic thinking tools. Hence the step from valuing different ways of communicating to valuing different ways of thinking and knowing is an obvious one.

There is one additional Vygotskian insight stemming from the idea of mediation that is relevant here. Mediation in the work of Vygotskians and authors like Feuerstein has both a cultural and a social dimension. Children move beyond their present understandings of the world with the help of symbol systems and with the help of the caring and knowledgeable adults in their environments. In encountering such mediated learning situations children learn to take advantage of the symbolic and interpersonal supports in their environment. Research has shown that even when there are differences between the culture of the school and that of children and their families, those children who have experienced socially and culturally mediated learning are better prepared to engage in school learning than children who have had not experienced supportive environments. This observation does not take us back to a naive deprivationist thesis. But it does alert us to issues, over and above cultural differences, that will influence how well children will do in school environments (Kozulin 1998, 67–68).

COGNITION DEVELOPS OVER TIME

Of the three propositions discussed in this chapter, the idea of cognitive development is perhaps the most difficult for sociologists to accept. The idea of cognitive development appears universalist at its very core and thus seems to work against efforts to understand the locatedness of the human subject, what the subject acquires by inhabiting a particular context. Yet while the idea of cognitive development does carry with it universalist assumptions, those assumptions may be challenged without losing an appreciation of how the thinking of individuals changes over time. The purpose of this section is to outline a sociocultural perspective on how thinking changes over time and to examine some recent research on the domain-specific nature of thinking.

Part of any developmentalist perspective on cognition is the notion of an ideal or endpoint toward which the development progresses. Often such ideals are expressed in an abstract and universalistic way. For example, Piaget refers to a capacity for abstraction or formal thought as the highest level of human cognition:

> in formal thought, there is a reversal of the direction of thinking between *reality* and *possibility* in the subjects' method of approach. *Possibility* no longer appears merely as an extension of an empirical situation or of actions actually performed. Instead it is *reality* that is now secondary to *possibility*. (Piaget, cited in Moshman 1998, 949)

Piaget's description of the ideal has much in common with what Bourdieu in a recent formulation (2000) calls the "scholastic disposition." In describing the "scholastic disposition," Bourdieu writes of the "*as if* posture," which he suggests "makes possible all intellectual speculations, scientific hypotheses, *thought experiments, possible worlds*, or *imaginary variations*" (12). Bourdieu maintains that the academic world thrives on and demands some version of this scholastic dispassion or habitus. He elaborates:

[The scholastic disposition] is what incites people to enter into the play-world of theoretical conjecture and mental experimentation, to raise problems for the pleasure of solving them, and not because they arise in the world, under the pressure of urgency, or to treat language not as an instrument but as an object of contemplation, formal invention or analysis. (2000, 13)

What differentiates Bourdieu's ideal from that of Piaget is that Bourdieu argues the scholastic disposition is not produced by some inner-directed process of development. It is the product, rather, of a process of socialization which takes place in particular cultural settings (settings which, among other things, are characterized by a "neutralization of practical urgencies and ends" [14]). Moreover, it is the interaction and congruence between experiences encountered in these settings and those encountered within the school that produce the ideal. It follows that the ideal, and hence the so-called cognitive development of the subject, cannot be understood outside the setting in which it occurs, and since the 1960s Bourdieu has written of the various "conditions of possibility," including early family socialization, which encourage the kinds of thinking, knowing, and communicating valued in academic contexts.

Vygotsky, like Bourdieu, rejects what he calls organismic views (which he attributes to Piaget). Such views portray cognitive development as shaped by inner mechanisms or forces. Vygotsky's central idea—the zone of proximal development—is an attempt to theorize the way in which the social and cultural factors of particular settings influence the ways of thinking exhibited by a particular child. In Vygotsky's view, instruction, both in and outside school environments, is of crucial importance to how children think. Having rejected organismic or inner-directed models of cognitive development, one might therefore question whether the term "development," as conventionally understood, actually applies to Vygotsky's work.

However, though Vygotsky rejects the developmentalist assumption of inner-directedness, he does endorse another developmentalist assumption: the notion of an ideal toward which development ought to progress. His views on this issue are expressed in his discussion of the child's acquisition of scientific concepts. On the one hand, Vygotsky expresses a favorable view of the "deferred imitation" (Van der Veer and Valsiner 1991, 345) characteristic of play. He writes: "Play is a source of development and creates the zone of proximal development" (cited in Van der Veer and Valsiner 1991, 345). On the other hand, Vygotsky does not hold a romantic view of learning which might assert that children left to their own devices would eventually discover the truths and insights conveyed more formally in school subjects and academic disciplines. For Vygotsky, the notion of progress in thinking and knowing is not in question. Thus he devotes particular attention to the relation between everyday concepts and scientific concepts in children's thinking. His central point is that the organization and use of scientific concepts differ from that of everyday concepts. Knowledgeable collaborators, in his view, ought to introduce to children scientific concepts. However, the important issue of the link between concepts and procedures was not examined by Vygotsky. This task was left to his Russian followers who insisted that children be "taught methods of scientific analysis . . . [which] become cognitive tools that mediate students' independent problem solving" (Karpov and Haywood 1998, 33).

To summarize, both Bourdieu and Vygotsky reject the notion of an inner-directedness, a universalist assumption associated with conventional accounts of development. While neither would dismiss biology as relevant to development, both stress the role of social and cultural factors in changes to thinking. Both would also recognize that cultural factors might influence which changes in thinking are valued in particular settings. However, both would endorse the views that progress in knowledge is possible—both, in other words, accept that there are ideals toward which learning ought to be directed. Such progress occurs both at the level of individuals and at the level of disciplines. Bourdieu's views on the latter kind of progress are summarized by Swartz: "[Bourdieu] embraces the Enlightenment tradition by contending that, even if reason is historical, it also has a capacity to produce forms of knowledge that transcend its own historical limitations" (1997, 252).

This point about the possibility of progress in knowledge is controversial and warrants further comment. To clarify the controversy, it may be instructive to make a distinction between realist views of knowledge—such as those of Bourdieu and Vygotsky—and constructivist views. With regard to constructivist views, feminists and others have stressed the role in the creation of knowledge of contextual factors such as gender and other social characteristics of knowers. Referring the role of such factors in science, constructivists hold that contextual factors "influence how scientists conceptualize their subject domain, what hypotheses they consider plausible, and what will count as evidence and *good reasons* in the evaluation of these hypotheses" (Wylie 2000, 167). In a constructivist view, contextual factors, more than *internal* disciplinary specific rules of evidence and logic, determine what counts as knowledge and what counts as progress in knowledge. A realist perspective, on the other hand, would accord noncontextual, disciplinary-specific factors greater weight, and would further insist that progress in knowledge occurs when that knowledge offers better explanations/deeper understandings of the world (or, to use analogy, when that knowledge more "successfully represents [or maps] the intended terrain" [Giere 1999, 215]).

It appears, then, that while constructivists might welcome the insights of Bourdieu and Vygotsky on the contextual character of thinking and learning—where contextual refers to the rejection of inner directedness—they would have serious concerns about the realist notion of progress in thinking, especially when the notion of progress is defined with reference to science. Constructivists might argue, for example, that the most important consideration in instruction is that children be engaged in practices of making meaning. Sharp distinctions between everyday concepts and scientific concepts cannot be justified on pedagogical or epistemological grounds. Furthermore, disciplinary specific rules of evidence and knowledge may have as much to do with contextual factors and social power as they do with *internal* disciplinary standards of validity.

These are important issues and they cannot be treated thoroughly within the constraints of this chapter. In a fuller account it would be necessary to demonstrate the complexity of Bourdieu's views on knowledge and the range of intermediate positions (between realism and constructivism) explored by feminist philosophers and others. However, rather than pursue these points here, I intend in the concluding paragraphs of this section to identify a program of research that has important implications for instruction. The key issue concerns the generic versus the domain-specific or disciplinary character of thinking. The ideal forms of thinking expressed by both Piaget and Bourdieu at the beginning of the section are very general in character. Over the last decade or so psychologists have begun to question this way of characterizing thinking. More specifically, they have tried to determine the extent to which thinking is best understood as a process involving certain very general features or a process that is more localized. They have, in other words, wondered whether there are domain-specific aspects of thinking (Hirschfeld and Gelman 1994). For example, the thinking of history, literature, and sociology may exhibit distinctive features and there may as well be both subdisciplinary as well as supradisciplinary (but not necessarily generic) ways of thinking. Moshman identifies three examples of supradisciplinary thinking: case-based reasoning (which would include analogical reasoning); law-based reasoning (which would include scientific reasoning); and dialectical reasoning, which he defines as "the deliberate coordination of inferences for the purpose of making cognitive progress" (1998, 961).

A recent overview by Shulman and Quinlan provides useful background information on the practical implications of this debate. They point to criticisms directed at generic "learning to think" programs. These criticisms were based on findings about the contextual character of thinking. Shulman and Quinlan quote Resnick, who argues as follows:

> The most successful programs are organized around particular bodies of knowledge and interpretation—subject matters, if you will—rather than general abilities. The treatment of the subject matter is tailored to engage students in processes of meaning construction and interpretation. . . . that can block the symbol detached from referent thinking that I have noted is a major problem in school. (cited in Shulman and Quinlan 1996, 417)

Pursuing the instructional implications of Resnick's remarks, Shulman and Quinlan suggest that researchers devote more attention to exploring the

kinds of thinking associated with particular school subjects or academic discipline. Recognizing that trends in this direction are already developing,
they write:

> In contrast to earlier forms of the psychology of school subjects, where either
> general or specific principles of learning or development were applied to sub-
> ject specific questions, we are witnessing the emergence of a new field where the
> analysis begins with an examination of the source discipline in its own terms—
> what is the thinking, wondering, feeling, reasoning, and collaborating which
> characterizes the work of history, mathematics or literature? (1996, 417)

The research program Shulman and Quinlan describe does not provide a
straightforward resolution to the broad range of issues—including emotion
and identity—discussed in this chapter. But it does allow us to move beyond
mainstream notions of cognitive development. In the same way a deeper
understanding of diverse cultures encouraged us to examine the unthought
assumptions associated with Culture, Shulman and Quinlan's emphasis on
the domain-specific character of thinking encourage us to examine the unthought assumptions associated with the idea of Development. Where the
questioning of Culture led to examination of how subjects become thinkers
and knowers in particular cultural settings, the questioning of Development
could lead to an examination of how subjects become thinkers and knowers
within particular school settings and more specifically, within the framework of norms and practices associated with particular academic disciplines
and subject matters. It may be that in addition to the scholastic dispositions
or habitus identified by Bourdieu there are dispositions or habitus associated
with particular bodies of knowledge and in a recent discussion Bourdieu
does refer to the specific habitus of particular fields (2000, 11). I should stress,
at this point, that one does not have to endorse a realist epistemology to be
interested in how subjects learn to think in the ways recognized by members
of academic disciplines. Put differently: research programs investigating the
social construction of knowledge can exist alongside research programs investigating why certain subjects reject, or learn to exhibit, distinctive ways of
knowing. Indeed, these two research themes intersect in the question of why
the knowledge produced by certain categories of knower, and certain ways
of knowing, is not considered legitimate or disciplinary knowledge.

Another issue pertaining to disciplinary thinking is the idea of expertise. Researchers have demonstrated that as individuals acquire expertise—increased
knowledge about the world—both their experience of the world and their
thinking change. As Sternberg et al. put it: "Experts and novices represent information differently, and experts engage in more sophisticated strategies and
performance monitoring than do novices" (2000, 4). In another context, Sternberg (1998) argues that a better appreciation of the nature of expertise will lead
us to rethink the notion of ability. Instead of viewing ability as some kind of
fixed capacity for thought, we should view ability as a kind of developing ex-

pertise. Clearly an understanding of the differences between the thinking of experts and the thinking of novices is crucial if we are interested in encouraging individuals to think in certain ways. Addressing the specific implications of these ideas for instruction, Resnick and Hal write, "although it is essential for children to have the experience of discovering and inventing, their experience must be one of disciplined invention—disciplined, that is, by knowledge and by established processes of reasoning and logic" (1998, 101). Many sociologists will insist that this "disciplined invention" be accompanied by an awareness of how social factors influence what counts as knowledge. The way forward, as suggested above, would seem to entail some combination of constructivist and realist accounts of knowledge.

To conclude, viewing thinking and changes in thinking in context enables us to break free of the notion of inner-directness associated with some forms of developmentalism. This is one of the main contributions of figures like Vygotsky and Bourdieu and it is a central insight of the sociocultural approach to cognition. However, both these figures have identified fairly abstract models of ideals toward which thinking is, or ought to be, directed (though it should be noted that Bourdieu does not endorse unequivocally the ideals associated with the scholastic disposition). Similar abstractions are found in many critiques of positivist thinking, where scientific reasoning becomes a target of criticism. Understanding the domain-specific features of thinking frees us from the overly abstract models which are either held out as ideals or rejected as ideological. But the emphasis on the domain-specific aspects of thinking need not commit us to extreme realist or constructivist accounts of knowledge. Finally, reestablishing the crucial link between knowledge (or expertise) and thinking provides us with new ways of exploring how the thinking of learners changes as they become more engaged in particular subject matters.

CONCLUSION

Just over a decade ago a review of the sociology of education identified the need for "a social theory of school learning" (Bidwell and Friedkin 1988, 467). In this paper I have identified several questions that remain central concerns for the discipline and that further highlight the need for a social theory of learning: Why do certain categories of subjects fail to become knowers? Why do some subjects choose not to become knowers? Why are some subjects unlikely to be recognized as knowers? The sociocultural approach to cognition discussed in this paper provides resources for sociologists seeking to answer these questions and to develop the social theory of learning called for by Bidwell and Freidkin.

The sociocultural approach starts with a basic assertion: the human subject inhabits social settings and those settings influence what kind of knower the subject becomes. This assertion can be elaborated with reference to three propositions: cognition is social; cognition is cultural; cognition develops over time. Research exploring these propositions was reviewed and implications for sociologists were highlighted. Particular emphasis was placed on the work of psychologist Lev Vygotsky. The work of Vygotsky and his followers serves as a crucial resource for anyone wishing to build bridges between sociology and psychology. Indeed, while Bourdieu does not cite Vygotsky, they have much in common. There are similarities as well between the work of the Vygotskians and work influenced by *Women's Ways of Knowing*.

The value of the sociocultural approach is not restricted to specific research traditions in the sociology of education. There is something for ethnographers wishing to understand how subjects become knowers. There is something for quantitative sociologists seeking more powerful explanations of class differences in educational attainment. There is something, finally, for theorists, for constructivists, realists, and those occupying the broad range of intermediate positions. The ability to participate in the knowledge-producing activities considered valuable in different social contexts impacts significantly on the life chances and social power of individuals and groups. A research program that contributes to our understanding of how that ability might be more widely distributed should appeal to sociologists and others pursuing broader goals of social justice.

REFERENCES

Belenky, M., B. Clinchy, N. Goldberger, and J. Tarulle. 1986. *Women's Ways of Knowing: The Development of Self, Voice, and Mind*. New York: Basic.

Bernstein, B. 1971–1975. *Class, Codes, and Control: Theoretical Studies toward a Sociology of Language*. 3 vols. London: Routledge & Kegan Paul.

Bidwell, C., and N. Friedkin. 1988. "The Sociology of Education." In *Handbook of Sociology*, edited by N. Smelser, 449–71. Newbury Park, Calif.: Sage.

Bourdieu, P. 1977a. "The School as a Conservative Force: Scholastic and Cultural Inequalities." In *Schooling and Capitalism*, edited by R. Dale, G. Esland, and M. MacDonald, 110–17. London: Open University Press.

Bourdieu, P. 1977b. *Outline of a Theory of Practice*. Cambridge: Cambridge University Press.

Bourdieu, P. 2000. *Pascalian Meditations*. Stanford: Stanford University Press.

Bourdieu, P., and J.-C. Passeron. 1977. *Reproduction in Education, Society, and Culture*. London: Sage.

Bourdieu, P., and L. Wacquant. 1992. *An Invitation to Reflexive Sociology*. Chicago: University of Chicago Press.

Bruner, J. 1985. "Vygotsky: A Historical and Conceptual Perspective." In *Culture, Communication, and Cognition*, edited by J. Wertsch, 21–34. Cambridge: Cambridge University Press.

Cole, R. 1998. *Cultural Psychology*. Cambridge: Harvard University Press.

Delpit, L. 1997. "The Silenced Dialogue: Power and Pedagogy in Educating Other People's Children." In *Education: Culture, Economy, and Society,* edited by A. Halsey, H. Lauder, P. Brown, and A. Wells, 582–94. Oxford: Oxford University Press.

Duveen, G. 1997. "Psychological Development as a Social Process." In *Piaget, Vygotsky, and Beyond,* edited by L. Smith, J. Dockerell, and P. Tomlinson, 67–90. London: Routledge.

Eagleton, T. 2000. *The Idea of Culture.* Oxford: Blackwell.

Farkas, G. 1996. *Human Capital or Cultural Capital?* Hawthorne, N.Y.: Aldine de Gruyter.

Fischer, C., M. Hout, M. Sanchez, M. Jankowski, S. Lucas, A. Swidler, and K. Voss. 1996. *Inequality by Design: Cracking the Bell Curve Myth.* Princeton: Princeton University Press.

Fricker, M., and J. Hornsby. 2000. Introduction to *The Cambridge Companion to Feminism in Philosophy,* edited by M. Fricker and J. Hornsby, 1–9. Cambridge: Cambridge University Press.

Garcia Coll, C., and K. Magnusen. 1999. "Cultural Influences on Child Development." In *Cultural Processes in Child Development,* edited by A. Masten, 1–24. Mahwah, N.J.: Lawrence Erlbaum.

Gardner, H. 1999. *The Disciplined Mind.* New York: Simon & Schuster.

Giere, R. 1999. *Science without Laws.* Chicago: University of Chicago Press.

Goldberger, N., et al. 1996. *Knowledge, Difference, and Power: Essays Inspired by Women's Ways of Knowing.* New York: Basic.

Goldstein, L. 1999. "The Relational Zone: The Role of Caring Relationships in the Co-Construction of Mind." *American Educational Research Journal,* Fall 1999, 647–73.

Goncu, A. 1999. "Children's and Researchers' Engagement with the World." In *Children's Engagement in the World: Sociocultural Perspectives,* edited by A. Goncu, 3–22. Cambridge: Cambridge University Press.

Greeno, J., A. Collins, and L. Resnick. 1996. "Cognition and Learning." In *Handbook of Educational Psychology,* edited by D. Berliner and R. Calfee, 15–46. New York: Macmillan.

Greeno, J., and the Middle School through Applications Project Group. 1998. "The Situativity of Knowing, Learning, and Research." *American Psychologist* 53: 5–26.

Hartup, W., and B. Laursen. 1999. "Relationships as Developmental Contexts: Retrospective Themes and Contemporary Issues." In *Relationships as Developmental Contexts,* edited by W. Collins and B. Laursen, 13–35. Mahwah, N.J.: Lawrence Erlbaum.

Herrnstein, R., and C. Murray. 1994. *The Bell Curve.* New York: Free Press.

Hirschfeld, L., and S. Gelman. 1994. *Mapping the Mind: Domain Specificity in Cognition and Culture.* Cambridge: Cambridge University Press.

Jenks, C. 1993. *Culture.* London: Routledge.

Karabel, J., and A. Halsey. 1977. Introduction to *Power and Ideology in Education,* edited by J. Karabel and A. Halsey, 1–85. Oxford: Oxford University Press.

Karpov, Y., and H. Haywood. 1998. "Two Ways to Elaborate Vygotsky's Concept of Mediation: Implications for Instruction." *American Psychologist,* January 1998, 27–35.

Keddie, N. 1973. Introduction to *The Myth of Cultural Deprivation,* edited by N. Keddie, 7–19. Harmondsworth, U.K.: Penguin.

Kozulin, A. 1990. *Vygotsky's Psychology: A Biography of Ideas.* Cambridge: Harvard University Press.

Kozulin, A. 1998. *Psychological Tools: A Sociocultural Approach to Education.* Cambridge: Harvard University Press.

Labov, W. 1973. "The Logic of Nonstandard English." In *The Myth of Cultural Deprivation,* edited by N. Keddie, 21–68. Harmondsworth, U.K.: Penguin.

Langton, R. 2000. "Feminism in Epistemology: Exclusion and Objectification." In *The Cambridge Companion to Feminism in Philosophy,* edited by M. Fricker and J. Hornsby, 127–45. Cambridge: Cambridge University Press.

Marshall, G., A. Swift, and S. Roberts. 1997. *Against the Odds? Social Justice in Modern Britain.* Oxford: Oxford University Press.

Moll, L. 2000. "Inspired by Vygotsky: Ethnographic Experiments in Education." In *Vygotskian Perspectives in Literacy Research: Constructing Meaning through Collaborative Inquiry,* edited by C. Lee and P. Smagorinsky, 256–68. Cambridge: Cambridge University Press.

Moshman, D. 1998. "Cognitive Development beyond Childhood." In *Handbook of Child Psychology,* edited by W. Damon and R. Lerner, 2:947–78. New York: Wiley.

Penuel, W., and J. Wertsch. 1995. "Vygotsky and Identity Formation: A Sociocultural Approach." *Educational Psychologist* 30: 83–92.

Resnick, L. 1994. "Biological and Social Preparation for Learning." In *Mapping the Mind: Domain Specificity in Cognition and Culture,* edited by L. Hirschfeld and S. Gelman, 474–93. Cambridge: Cambridge University Press.

Resnick, L., and M. Hal. 1998. "Learning Organizations for Sustainable Educational Reform." *Daedalus,* Fall, 89–118.

Shulman, L., and K. Quinlan. 1996. "The Comparative Psychology of School Subjects." In *Handbook of Educational Psychology,* edited by D. Berliner and R. Calfee, 399–422. New York: Macmillan.

Shweder, R., J. Goodnow, G. Hatano, R. Levine, H. Markus, and P. Miller. 1998. "The Cultural Psychology of Development: One Mind, Many Mentalities." In *Handbook of Child Psychology,* edited by W. Damon and R. Lerner, 1:865–938. New York: Wiley.

Sternberg, R. 1998. "Abilities Are Forms of Developing Expertise." *Educational Researcher* 27: 11–20.

Sternberg, R., G. Forsythe, J. Hedlund, J. Horvath, R. Wagner, W. Williams, S. Snook, E. Grigorenko. 2000. *Practical Intelliegence.* Cambridge: Cambridge University Press.

Swartz, D. 1997. *Culture and Power: The Sociology of Pierre Bourdieu.* Chicago: University of Chicago Press.

Tomasello, M. 1999. *The Cultural Origins of Human Cognition.* Cambridge: Harvard University Press.

Van der Veer, R., and J. Valsiner. 1991. *Understanding Vygotsky: A Quest for Synthesis.* Oxford: Blackwell.

Van der Veer, R., and J. Valsiner. 1994. *The Vygotsky Reader.* Cambridge, Mass.: Blackwell.

Vygotsky, L. 1962. *Thought and Language.* Cambridge: MIT Press.

Vygotsky, L. 1978. *Mind in Society.* Cambridge: Harvard University Press.

Vygotsky, L. [1934] 1994. "Academic Concepts in School-Aged Children." In *The Vygotsky Reader,* edited by R. Van der Veer and J. Valsiner, 355–70. Cambridge, Mass.: Blackwell.

Wenger, E. 1998. *Communities of Practice: Learning Meaning and Identity.* New York: Cambridge University Press.

Willis, P. 1977. *Learning to Labor: How Working-Class Kids Get Working-Class Jobs.* New York: Columbia University Press.

Wylie, A. 2000. "Feminism in Philosophy of Science: Making Sense of Contingency and Constraint." In *The Cambridge Companion to Feminism in Philosophy,* edited by M. Fricker and J. Hornsby, 166–84. Cambridge: Cambridge University Press.

Young, M., ed. 1971. *Knowledge and Control: New Directions in the Sociology of Education.* London: Collier-Macmillan.

Zigler, E., and S. Meunchow. 1992. *Head Start: The Inside Story of America's Most Successful Educational Experiment.* New York: Basic.

6

Decisive Moments and Key Experiences:

Expanding Paradigmatic Boundaries in the Study of School Effects

Gad Yair

> It is the *critical moment* when, breaking with the ordinary experience of time as simple re-enactment of a past or a future inscribed in the past, all things become possible (at least apparently), when future prospects appear really contingent, future events really indeterminate, the moment truly instantaneous, suspended, its consequences unpredicted and unpredictable.
>
> —Bourdieu 1988, 182

THE ORGANIZATION OF SCHOOLS AND THEIR EFFECTS

Schools exist to affect student outcomes. They are expected to teach, impart knowledge, and educate. They adopt diverse instructional and organizational means to affect individual students in cognitive and noncognitive domains. Yet schools are also expected to fulfill societal roles: to produce human capital; decrease social, ethnic, racial, and gender inequalities; socialize—for citizenship; and provide for myriad other goals. To achieve these goals, schools are rationally and bureaucratically organized, under the assumption that this is the best means to affect student and societal outcomes.

Despite vehement criticisms attacking rigidity in schools and repeated calls to humanize them, their organizational underpinnings are most likely to remain fastened to bureaucratic principles. Modern school systems have managed the immense variety in student populations—in age, ability, learning styles, and personal interests—by adopting rational universal means. The student body is divided by age (grade level), while students are socially promoted irrespective of their achievements. To further reduce variability, students are separated into ability groups, tracks, and school sectors. These arrangements attempt to match students' ability with appropriate educational opportunities while limiting undue social and racial biases in assignment. Furthermore, curricula in school are mostly hierarchically ordered, especially in mathematics, science, and foreign languages, with attempts at standardizing demands across schools, districts, states, and nations.

Reflecting the high expectations from schools, the study of school effects is one of the widest common denominators in the sociology of education. While the discipline covers diverse lines and methods of inquiry, it shares a common interest in the mechanisms that produce school effects. For example, studies of school effectiveness seek to uncover disciplinary climates and organizational factors that affect student achievement. Analyses of private–public differentials seek to investigate the long-term effects of sector differences in disciplinary climates and curricula on student achievements and expectations. Similarly, studies of gender, racial, and social inequalities seek to uncover organizational and curricular arrangements that intensify these inequalities. Studies on the effects of tracking, ability groups, selectivity, and streaming seek to disentangle the long-term effects of these arrangements on student learning outcomes.

PARADIGMATIC ASSUMPTIONS IN THE STUDY OF SCHOOL EFFECTS

While the literature on school effects is indeed immense in scope, few studies have focused directly on the underlying paradigmatic ideas of this corpus. Even the few conceptual studies of school effects have rarely explicated the causal mechanisms that produce the effects of schools on individual students. Superficially, most of this work is based on a trivial truism, namely, that when schools teach, students learn (at least a fraction of the time; see Yair 2000b). From this standpoint, differential school effects result from organizational variety in the provision of instruction, namely, in differential opportunities to learn.

Deeper scrutiny of the varied approaches in the sociology of education shows that they share a profound paradigm. This "cumulative" paradigm reflects the bureaucratic organization of schools and its corresponding assumptions concerning learning and school effects. These assumptions suggest that student learning is progressive, additive, cumulative, and predictable.

First, building on Carrol's model of school learning, it is assumed that exposure to learning opportunities determines student outcomes (i.e., the greater the exposure the higher the expected achievements; see also Dougherty 1996; Manlove and Baker 1995). Indeed, it is assumed that achievements are accumulated through longer exposure to educational stimuli and that inequalities mainly result from differential opportunities to learn. The practical corollary of this assumption is that when students fall behind their peers, they repeat the grade or are compensated by a longer school day.

Second, the cumulative paradigm assumes that learning is progressive or gradual, built step by step, mostly in a hierarchical order. Progress is not abrupt, and every lesson presupposes the previous one. Every step forward presupposes prior knowledge and student capacity. The bureaucratic organization of schools guarantees the progressive nature of learning by planning and coordinating curricula and standards.

Third, a cumulative paradigm assumes that instruction is a linear process, where units (i.e., hours, classes, and teachers) are equivalent and therefore exchangeable. Indeed, the study of school effects has a blind spot with regard to the literature on teacher effectiveness. It mostly ignores between-classroom variability, since teachers are viewed as exchangeable and replaceable. A corollary of this assumption is that learning outcomes can be planned and predicted—exactly because of the preemptive stance toward teacher effectiveness. It is assumed that teacher individuality and their unique relationships with students cannot be rationally organized, planned, and controlled.

Despite its pervasiveness, the cumulative paradigm has several limitations. First, it is difficult to reconcile its assumptions with the widespread belief that specific teachers do have profound influences on students' lives, with specific teachers making a difference in their students' lives. This motive is repeatedly shown in movies and is reflected in pervasive parental maneuvering of student assignments in schools.

Second, this paradigm cannot explain the efficacy of short-term intervention programs, extracurricular activities, and informal educational settings in affecting student outcomes, nor in nonlinear and rapid changes in their knowledge, values, and behavior. Actually, "cumulative studies" treat such rapid transformations and changes as "noise."

Third, the cumulative paradigm exhibits a simplistic and reductionist conception of learning. Essentially, most of the studies in the paradigm have a behaviorist overtone (instructional stimuli, student learning). They ignore complex psychological processes that underlie learning and are thus limited in its explanation. Fourth, the cumulative approach cannot fully explain "overachievement," namely, that some students know more than the opportunities they had in school. Finally, the cumulative approach is best suited for situations where instruction is bureaucratized, or as Perkins posits, when it is based on "a cold cognitive economy." In contrast, when instruction is based on "hot cognitive economies," a cumulative approach is severely limited in explaining its outcomes. Overall, these criticisms suggest that the ability of the cumulative paradigm to appreciate the varied underpinnings of school effects and their possible decisiveness in students' lives is clearly limited.

A BIG BANG APPROACH TO THE STUDY
OF SCHOOL EFFECTS

In an attempt to overcome the limitations of the cumulative paradigm, this chapter attempts to expand the study of school effects by borrowing from physics the metaphor of a "big bang." The astrophysical description of the universe as an outcome of a "big bang" has three interrelated ideas. First, the origin of all things (e.g., time and space) is traced to an unimaginable collision and explosion of a set of particles that caused the universe to expand ever since. Second, the types of forces that move the universe and the particles that constitute it were formed in an instant, at the same time with this formidable explosion. Finally, physicists argue that contemporary phenomena can be "reduced," traced back or explained by what happened in the very first seconds of the "big bang."

Using these ideas as a guiding metaphor, the "big bang" approach to educational effects suggests that some educational experiences enflame students' motivation and have strong, rapid, and decisive effects on their cognitive and noncognitive outcomes. These experiences may change predestined educational careers, empower students to break the habitus of their social class, and open otherwise hidden personal and social possibilities. Some of these activities are a jump station for social and occupational mobility. Others have lesser stratification effects yet practically determine specific educational majors and occupations.

Such "big bang" experiences achieve two tasks at the same time: They insulate students' attention from the encroachment of nonschool preoccupations—like peer pressure, home troubles, or work commitments. By buffering these "greedy" pressures, such instructional episodes equate opportunities to learn with their actual procurement. Second, and more importantly, these contexts produce extreme levels of motivation, encouraging participants to invest great effort in learning for its own sake.

These educational episodes can be likened to "positive traumas." Like other traumas, they mostly occur in short, intense, and decisive episodes. Yet, despite their focused happenstance, these episodes produce a variety of effects over the life course. Their effects cut across domains and time, recurring as persistent motivating predilections and interpretive cognitive schemata. Such decisive episodes explain the "surprise" that parents, teachers, and peers have when confronting individuals who have gone through such transformative contexts. They cause biographical discontinuities and breaks that make futile any previous efforts to mold and predetermine individuals' life course.

This perspective contrasts with the theoretical premises of the cumulative paradigm. First, this approach is sensitive to abrupt, strong, and transformative educational experiences and effects; it looks for abrupt insights, not slow growth. Instead of the slow but consistent model, this approach suggests that some contexts decisively affect participants and produce qualitative changes in a short time. Second, this approach looks for "nonlinear" effects, parallel-ing other studies of change that use "chaos" approaches. From this view-point, the prediction of specific school effects of such highly motivating con-texts might be extremely difficult. This approach is thus "open," in the sense that experiences cannot foreclose intended outcomes.

Third, this approach cannot assume that all students' experiences are equivalent and therefore exchangeable. On the contrary, it claims that some activities and teachers have unique effects on students, while others do not. Without extensive study of such settings, it may be extremely difficult to equate them even though they share underlying instructional properties that motivate students and produce their varied effects. Fourth, the "big bang" approach appreciates diverse developments in the study of motivation and learning, combining cognitive, affective, and conative factors in an inte-grated scheme. Finally, the present approach suggests that students' careers may reflect a small number of educationally decisive experiences that build on an infrastructure of rather slow, incremental, and linear processes. Con-sequently, in order to fully appreciate the capacity of schools to affect stu-dents, it is necessary to consider the interplay between additive, progressive, and cumulative factors and highly motivating teachers and activities that produce rapid yet decisive effects on student outcomes.

To compensate for the limitations of the cumulative paradigm, the remain-ing parts of this chapter develop the conceptual model presented in figure 6.1, proposed as a specific approach to the study of decisive educational episodes—one of possible others. It serves as an example for a "big bang" ap-proach to school effects. Since it is proposed as a supplement to the cumula-tive paradigm, future studies should ultimately combine the approaches to ex-plain more fully how schools, teachers and educational activities affect student outcomes. Furthermore, the analysis presented here acknowledges that expe-riences spread over a conceptual continuum—ranging from slow, tranquil, and additive experiences up to rapid, enflamed, and decisive ones.

The first part of the proposed model (causally the last) focuses on the wide spectrum of school effects, ranging from pragmatic decisions, personal changes, and moral choices, to behavioral changes. The second part analyzes three interrelated psychological mechanisms that imprint these episodes on students' memories. The third part focuses on instructional characteristics, seeking to show how they can intensify motivation. The fourth part of the model analyzes the social distribution of these effects, suggesting that while highly effective educational episodes are instructionally produced, they are also socially distributed. It suggests that middle-class and majority students enjoy greater access to highly effective educational settings, while lower-class and minority students have limited access to such settings and are thus more limited by their social position. The final section points out possible di-rections for future studies.

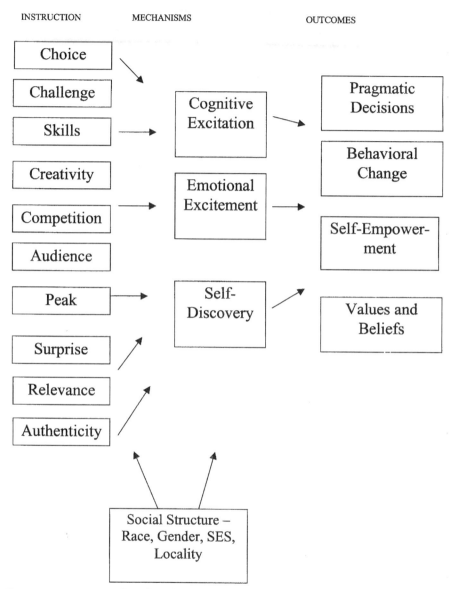

Figure 6.1.   Conceptual Model of Decisive School Effects

THE WIDE SPECTRUM OF DECISIVE SCHOOL EFFECTS

The study of educational effects has usually focused on achievements or attainments as a single criterion. While sociologists have suggested that schools affect more than one-dimensional achievement criteria, their call went mostly unheeded. There is reason to suspect that pragmatic and political interests and economically driven policy initiatives always boil down to a simple question: Are achievements rising or declining?

Although such interests are legitimate, narrowing the scientific study of school effects to achievements may have impeded possible developments in the understanding of how schools produce which kinds of effects, on what groups of students, and why. In contrast to the narrow cognitive focus of the cumulative paradigm, the data show that these highly motivating episodes affect a variety of cognitive and noncognitive educational outcomes. These outcomes range from pragmatic decisions about educational and occupational careers to self-empowerment and maturation, development of new moral values and beliefs, up to behavioral changes, which actually cut across all other outcomes.

Pragmatic Decisions

The rationale behind the use of achievements as the major criterion in the study of school effects is that they predict educational plans and ultimate attainments (Bidwell 1989, 479). In turn, educational attainments predict labor market outcomes, including earnings (hence it is important to study achievements). However, in some contexts and under specific conditions, schools can affect labor market outcomes while bypassing achievements or reversing the traditional causal process. In some highly motivating contexts, students may decidedly and quite early on choose a sphere of study or an occupation, and henceforth expend focused effort in school and plan their future educational trajectory to attain this highly valued choice. Under such conditions, educational and occupational aspirations drive achievements, not vice versa. Many adults indeed trace back their field of study, occupational choice, or decision to study in higher education institutes to a decisive educational episode. They remember a special activity, an outstanding teacher, or a series of educational activities that affected their future educational and occupational trajectories. Such episodes allowed them to set clear goals, clarify the necessary skills they needed to acquire, and motivated them to pursue hitherto blocked routes. Resulting from their heightened motivation, respondents described a series of actions they took to attain their valued goals.

Self-Empowerment

The "self" has an important position in the history of sociological thought. Psychologists have given this concept no lesser attention. The varied perspectives on the self suggest that it is a core concept in any attempt to describe and explain human behavior in social context. Furthermore, the emphasis on "self-as-outcome" (e.g., self-efficacy, self-concept, self-esteem) implies that people's sense of self decides their performance in specific or generalized domains. While there are empirical investigations of varied aspects of the self in educational settings, these studies mainly revolve around achievement self-concept.

The study of decisive educational episodes suggests that one of their major outcomes is self-empowerment, a broader concept than the popular idea of self-efficacy. The literature and preliminary results point to the operation of three facets of self-empowerment. First, highly effective educational settings allow participants to reevaluate themselves. With the backing of high expectations and trust, these settings unveil previously hidden capacities and vividly exemplify to participants their ability to overcome what were hitherto seen as unsurpassable limits. Second, these highly motivating contexts serve as a positive "reality check." Individuals learn to appreciate external demands and their ability to match them. They learn to appreciate the domains they excel in, and are thus encouraged to pursue new—sometimes unpredicted—trajectories and undertakings. In a way, participation in such episodes places a critical looking glass in front of people; they learn that they are different from what they had hitherto assumed. Finally, highly effective educational activities develop a belief in one's self, a growth in self-confidence and sense of efficacy. By empowering the self, these episodes encourage individuals to break away from predetermined life trajectories. In some cases, individuals learn to expose processes of social reproduction and envision alternative futures.

Values, Attitudes, and Beliefs

Schools and moral education are popularly seen as an oxymoron. While schools attempt to teach moral values through the teaching of civics, social studies, and history, there is a general suspicion that schools are actually amoral institutions. Even sociologists have rarely discussed the moral outcomes of schools, their analysis mostly drawing on hidden norms of life in classrooms and schools.

In contrast to the widespread ignorance of moral outcomes of schooling, the study of highly motivating experiences in school suggests that such activities do affect students' attitudes, beliefs, and moral values. Intense activities promote reflection and deliberation of previously held moral rules and religious beliefs. As a result, students are able to rationally choose among moral options and acquire new values and beliefs while relinquishing prior prejudices and values.

Behavioral Changes

Some school effect studies have looked at student behavior as an outcome (e.g., violence, sexual conduct) but rarely discussed causal mechanisms that explain specific behavioral outcomes. In contrast, the study of educationally decisive episodes suggests that they at times affect behavioral changes that constitute the basis on which people evaluate their sense of self and attitudes. Indeed, behavioral changes are inextricably related to the previously discussed outcomes. When individuals feel self-empowered, they extract information about their selves from newly adopted behaviors. Similarly, students experience moral changes when they see concrete changes in their behavior. In a way, then, behavioral changes are "correlated" with all other outcomes of intense educational episodes.

To conclude, this section has shown that in contrast to the narrow cognitive boundaries of traditional school effects studies, highly effective educational settings can indeed affect students' lives, leading to a wide variety of outcomes. It is now necessary to analyze how these varied effects come about.

MOTIVATIONAL MECHANISMS THAT AFFECT OUTCOMES

Based on prior approaches to the study of motivation, this section looks at three motivational mechanisms, each of which mediates the effects of instruction on student outcomes: (1) cognitive excitation, (2) emotional excitement, and (3) self-discovery.

Cognitive Excitation

Extreme motivating contexts enflame the "cold cognition" so characteristic of school learning circumstances. These contexts "defreeze" cognitive processes, reduce closure, and enable rapid acquisition of knowledge and insight. Motivating contexts animate intense curiosity and interest. They move individuals to pursue the unknown, producing a desire for learning and a craving for knowledge and understanding. Consequently, participants in these contexts are intrinsically engaged in learning. They invest huge efforts in their studies, investigate unknown domains and facts, and develop metacognitive structures ("learning on learning"). Finally, to the extent that curiosity and learning have materialized, insightful understanding can take place. People transform their understandings of physical and social phenomena, restructuring gestalts and old preconceptions.

Emotional Excitement

Successful instructional activities also trigger emotional experiences like happiness, enthusiasm, pleasure, excitement, love, and satisfaction. Participants find themselves emotionally moved by such activities, feeling emotional catharsis, excitement, and enthusiasm. Such experiences are apparent in an outburst of positive emotions that motivate individuals to invest great energy in learning activities. In different cases, love and identification with the activity can happen. In this rather calm and interior experience, people feel they love doing what they do and the people they do it with (e.g., a teacher, the subject matter, a partner). Such episodes can also be experienced as contentment, reflected in terms of happiness, satisfaction, and a sense of accomplishment.

Discovering One's Self

Due to social constraints, many individuals have difficulty in acquiring a realistic appraisal of their capacities and skills. Some are also influenced by environmental factors to acquire wrong evaluations of their abilities, character and moral worth. As a result, they fail to put their capabilities into action and to develop their skills to the utmost. In contrast, at the apex of highly challenging and motivating contexts, people find arenas for self-testing and the discovery of new abilities and interests. When evaluating their performance, feelings, and thoughts in these contexts, people may discover new information about their tastes, abilities, and inclinations. They discover new capacities and become more efficacious and self-assured.

As suggested earlier, highly motivating experiences are akin to "positive traumas." Their strong, varied, and long-lasting effects result from the ignition of cognitive excitation, emotional excitement, or self-discovery. When instructional settings succeed in exciting two or ultimately all three motivational mechanisms, they are more likely to affect such varied and long-term effects. It is now time to briefly discuss several instructional strategies that enflame the cold cognitions, flat emotions, and alienated selves so characteristic of ordinary school learning.

THE INSTRUCTIONAL PRODUCTION OF MOTIVATIONAL PEAKS

Preliminary investigations suggest that these motivational peaks have instructional preconditions. As figure 6.1 suggests, specific instructional strategies that teachers use incite different mechanisms of motivation and, as a result, help determine the outcomes of the setting or, more accurately, encourage students to decide on these effects. While the content (e.g., subject matter) and method of instruction (e.g., group work or whole class lecture) may have independent effects on motivation and learning, this section focuses on nine instructional strategies, each of which is hypothesized to affect a specific motivational mechanism. Theoretically, the combination of different strategies potentiates the instructional encounter by peaking all the motivational mechanisms.

Previous studies of situated motivation have shown that when students have a choice between tasks and are given autonomy in carrying out the activity, they are most likely to exhibit intrinsic motivation and interest in the activity. By freely choosing an activity, students become self-directed and involved in learning. Furthermore, the provision of challenging instructional tasks encourages students to invest great effort in learning. Students always aspire to rise to challenges—when faced with them. Otherwise, they are bored by dull activities or feel anxious from impending failure. By setting high yet attainable goals, teachers create conditions for optimal learning experiences.

Similarly, when teachers construct multiplex activities and where different students are able to use their skills, negative social comparisons are minimized while the motivation to prove one's self is increased. Similarly, when teachers require students to produce original creative work, the latter have to rely on their own strengths to prove that they can meet the challenge and succeed. Overall, challenging instructional settings that provide students with abundant choice, allow for use of multiple skills and evaluation criteria, and demand originality and creativity are highly likely to affect students' self-discovery and cognitive excitation.

In a different way, competitive arenas are likely to intensify emotional involvement. Competitions push students to excel as individuals and teams, and eliminate the dissociation of self and setting, thus producing "flow" and engagement. Furthermore, the presence of a significant audience also triggers student involvement. Such settings challenge students to put their best persona on stage, while at the same time supplying them with a sense of importance and agency.

Two other strategies evince similar effects. First, when instruction is based on a series of activities that progress toward a significant peak, students are likely to appreciate the worthiness of each part while showing continued interest in having a significant end-of-study peak. As in sports, long-awaited peaks structure persistence and motivation. Second, sudden surprises in the midst of learning can have decisive effects on students. Surprises invoke high emotionality yet also necessitate intense cognitive reappraisal of the self and one's past knowledge and values.

Finally, relevant and authentic instructional settings also kindle students' interest in learning. When students discern connections between school learning and their lives, they are likely to invest more effort and discover that they have interest in pursuing learning for its own sake. When activities resemble "real-life" tasks, they minimize students' mocking of learning and produce seriousness and thoughtfulness.

These analyses suggest that the organizational provision of instructional strategies affect the prevalence of motivational peaks in learning. It should be acknowledged, however, that students have different perceptions of instruction. Some may view an activity as challenging and allowing for creativity while others may perceive it as a boring, childish exercise. Student heterogeneity in social circumstances and interests challenges teachers and schools to find creative means to win their students' willful cooperation in learning. They have to tailor instruction to the concrete interests, capabilities, and social circumstances of their students. However, when schools make it difficult for teachers to use variety and creativity on a daily basis, they are likely to minimize motivation for most students and decrease the odds of decisive learning experiences. In contrast, when schools support teachers' autonomy, creativity, and professionalism to the fullest, they are most likely to push student motivation to the hilt. Under these conditions, the odds for the occurrence of decisive learning experiences go up.

THE SOCIAL DISTRIBUTION OF
INSTRUCTION AND ITS USAGE

Decades of sociological studies have shown that instruction is socially stratified and distributed. Relative to low socioeconomic status (SES) students, high SES students get to learn in better ability groups, higher school tracks, and more prestigious school sectors. These conclusions still hold, despite massive national efforts to decrease social inequalities in education.

There is room to believe that the provision of highly intense instruction is also socially distributed. Middle-class students seem to enjoy a greater number and more intense experiences relative to lower-class students. The former thus have many decisive opportunities for making pragmatic decisions, moral choices, and personal changes. They enjoy an educational trajectory that builds on their agency, allowing greater moratorium to find the most appropriate stations for their interests and capacities. In contrast, low SES students seem to experience few opportunities, and those that they do encounter are of lesser intensity than those of their peers. These students traverse a predetermined path, one in which their will and interests play a humble role at best. Consequently, they end up with a delimited sense of their capacities and interests, producing alienation from school and society.

Furthermore, these students are foreclosed by their position in the structure of society in a second, no less debilitating sense. The "big bang" model suggests that students' position in society also predisposes them to reap different benefits from highly effective educational episodes. This predisposition stems from at least three sources. First, social structures affect students' cultural capital, which is known to affect students' predisposition to engage with instruction and succeed in school. Second, new studies have shown that students' race and nonschool activities affect their engagement with instruction. Low SES and minority students have many external preoccupations when they sit in class. Their nonschool lifestyle determines their within-school experiences, suggesting that they reap fewer benefits from every opportunity. Finally, low SES students have fewer resources at home: less books, little space for learning, overcrowded houses, and in some cases even hunger and violence.

FUTURE RESEARCH AND
METHODOLOGICAL CONSIDERATIONS

The study of "big bang" educational episodes is in its infancy. At this time, the agenda for future work can only be sketched with four rough strokes.

First, empirical studies should determine how, where, and under what conditions decisive episodes occur. For example, do such episodes occur mostly in school, or are there other institutions where they take place? Can the factors that make school learning decisive be generalized to other institutions? Comparative studies can shed light on instructional strategies that incite these processes and determine the extent to which specific contexts specialize in producing specific effects.

A second task relates to the specification and description of the mechanisms that operate during these episodes. For example, are cognitive excitation, emotional excitement, and self-discovery the only mechanisms that mediate the effect of instruction on student outcomes? What are the direct and reciprocal effects of such mechanisms? Answers to such questions can produce a variety of theories and models that may describe different variants of "big bang" effects.

Third, a daunting challenge lies in deciphering the connection between past "positive traumas" and future outcomes. It is necessary to understand if and to what extent major decision stations in life (choosing type of track, major in college, occupation) can be accounted for by highly effective episodes, and to articulate exactly how.

Fourth, a macrosociological approach to the production and distribution of such school effects should be implemented. It is necessary to map the social and organizational production and distribution of highly effective instruction, and study the extent to which school and educational reforms change these distributions. Such studies can compare the extent to which public and private schools, religious sectors, educational streams and school tracks produce and socially distribute differential highly decisive opportunities.

REFERENCES

Abraham, John. 1995. *Divide and School: Gender and Class Dynamics in Comprehensive Education*. London: Falmer.
Adler, Chaim. 1996. *Report of the Public Committee on Extended School Day*. Jerusalem: Center for the Study of Public Policy in Israel.

Alexander, Karl L. 1997. "Public Schools and the Public Good." *Social Forces* 76: 1–30.

Baker, David P., and Deborah Perkins Jones. 1993. "Creating Gender Equality: Cross-national Gender Stratification and Mathematical Performance." *Sociology of Education* 66: 91–103.

Bandura, Albert. 1982. "Self-efficacy Mechanism in Human Agency." *American Psychologist* 37: 122–47.

Bandura, Albert. 1989. "Human Agency in Social Cognitive Theory." *American Psychologist* 44: 1175–84.

Bandura, Albert. 1997. *Self-Efficacy: The Exercise of Control.* New York: Freeman.

Barr, Rebecca, and Robert Dreeben. 1983. *How Schools Work.* Chicago: University of Chicago Press.

Bidwell, Charles E. 1965. "The School as a Formal Organization." In *Handbook of Organizations*, edited by James E. March, 972–1019. New York: Wiley.

Bidwell, Charles E. 1987. "Moral Education and School Social Organization." In *The Social Organization of Schools: New Conceptualizations of the Learning Process*, edited by Maureen T. Hallinan, 205–19. New York: Plenum.

Bidwell, Charles E. 1989. "The Meaning of Educational Attainment." *Research in the Sociology of Education and Socialization* 8: 117–38.

Bidwell, Charles E., and John D. Kasarda. 1980. "Conceptualizing and Measuring the Effects of School and Schooling." *American Journal of Education* 88: 401–30.

Bidwell, Charles E., and Jefferey Y. Yasumoto. 1999. "The Collegial Focus: Teaching Fields, Collegial Relationships, and Instructional Practice in American High Schools." *Sociology of Education* 72: 234–56.

Blossfeld, Hans Peter, and Yossi Shavit. 1993. *Persistent Inequality: Changing Educational Attainment in Thirteen Countries.* Boulder: Westview.

Borg, Walter R. 1980. "Time and School Learning." In *Time to Learn*, edited by Carolyn Denham and Ann Lieberman. Washington, D.C.: National Institute of Education.

Bourdieu, Pierre. 1986. "The Forms of Capital." In *Handbook of Theory of Research for the Sociology of Education*, edited by J. E. Richardson, 241–58. New York: Greenwood.

Bourdieu, Pierre. 1988. *Homo Academicus.* Stanford: Stanford University Press.

Brandsma, H. P., and J. W. M. Knuver. 1988. "Organizational Differences between Dutch Primary Schools and Their Effect on Pupil Achievement." In *School Effectiveness and Improvement*, edited by Bert Cremers, Tom Peters, and David Reynolds, 199–212. Cardiff: Rion.

Bryk, Anthony S., Valery E. Lee, and P. B. Holland. 1993. *Catholic Schools and the Common Good.* Cambridge: Harvard University Press.

Carrol, J. B. 1963. "A Model of School Learning." *Teachers College Record* 64: 723–33.

Casparis, Claudio. 1980. "A Theoretical Analysis of the 'Pygmalion Effect' and 'Self-Fulfilling Prophecies.'" *Zeitschrift-fuer-Sozialpsychologie* 11: 124–28.

Coleman, James S., Ernest Q. Campbell, Carol F. Hobson, James M. McPartland, Alexander M. Mood, Frederic D. Weinfeld, and Robert L. York. 1966. *Equality of Educational Opportunity.* Washington, D.C.: U.S. Government Printing Office.

Coleman, James S., and Thomas Hoffer. 1987. *Public and Private High Schools: The Impact of Communities.* New York: Basic.

Coleman, James S., Thomas Hoffer, and Sally Kilgore. 1982. *High School Achievement: Public, Catholic, and Private Schools Compared.* New York: Basic.

Csikszentmihalyi, Mihaly. 1975. *Beyond Boredom and Anxiety.* San Francisco: Jossey-Bass.

Csikszentmihalyi, Mihaly. 1990. *Flow: The Psychology of Optimal Experience*. New York: Harper & Row.

Csikszentmihalyi, Mihaly, Kevin Rathunde, and Samuel Whalen. 1993. *Talented Teenagers: The Roots of Success and Failure*. Cambridge: Cambridge University Press.

Cuttance, Peter. 1989. "The Effectiveness of Scottish Schooling." In *School Effectiveness and School Improvement*, edited by Bert Creemers, Tony Peters, and Dave Reynolds. Cardiff: Rion.

Daly, P. 1991. "How Large Are Secondary School Effects in Northern Ireland?" *School Effectiveness and School Improvement* 2: 305–23.

Darling-Hammond, Linda, and Jon Snyder. 1992. "Curriculum Studies and the Tradition of Inquiry: The Scientific Tradition." In *Handbook of Research on Curriculum*, edited by Philip W. Jackson, 41–78. New York: Macmillan.

Dauber, Susan L., Karl L. Alexander, and Doris R. Entwisle. 1996. "Tracking and Transitions through the Middle Grades: Channeling Educational Trajectories." *Sociology of Education* 69: 290–307.

De Graff, Nan Dirk, Paul M. De Graaf, and Gerbert Kraaykamp. 2000. "Parental Cultural Capital and Educational Attainment in the Netherlands: A Refinement of the Cultural Capital Perspective." *Sociology of Education* 73: 92–111.

Deci, Edward L. 1992. "The Relation of Interest to Motivation of Behavior: A Self-Determination Theory Perspective." In *The Role of Interest in Learning and Development*, edited by K. A. Renninger, S. Hidi, and A. Krapp, 43–70. Hillsdale, N.J.: Erlbaum.

Denham, Carolyn, and Ann Lieberman, eds. 1980. *Time to Learn*. Washington, D.C.: National Institute of Education.

Dougherty, Kevin J. 1996. "Opportunity-to-Learn Standards: A Sociological Critique." *Sociology of Education* 69: 40–65.

Dreeben, Robert. 1968. *On What Is Learned in School*. Reading, Mass.: Addison-Wesley.

Dreeben, Robert, and Rebecca Barr. 1987. "An Organizational Analysis of Curriculum and Instruction." In *The Social Organization of Schools*, edited by Maureen T. Hallinan. New York: Plenum.

Dweck, Carol S. 1999. *Self-Theories: Their Role in Motivation, Personality, and Development*. Philadelphia: Psychology Press/Taylor & Francis.

Eden, Dov. 1992. "Leadership and Expectations: Pygmalion Effects and Other Self-Fulfilling Prophecies in Organizations." *Leadership Quarterly* 3: 271–305.

Entwisle, Dorris R., Karl L. Alexander, and L. S. Olson. 1994. "The Gender Gap in Math: Its Possible Origins in Neighborhood Effects." *American Sociological Review* 59: 822–38.

Farkas, George, Robert P. Grobe, Daniel Sheehan, and Yuan Shuan. 1990. "Cultural Resources and School Success: Gender, Ethnicity, and Poverty Groups within an Urban School District." *American Sociological Review* 55: 127–42.

Gamoran, Adam. 1990. "Instructional Organizational Practices That Affect Equity." In *Leadership, Equity, and School Effectiveness*, edited by H. P. Baptiste, H. C. Waxman, J. W. Felix, and J. E. Anderson, 155–72, Newbury Park, Calif.: Sage.

———. 1992. "The Variable Effects of High School Tracking." *American Sociological Review* 57: 812–28.

Gamoran, Adam, and Robert D. Mare. 1989. "Secondary School Tracking and Educational Inequality: Compensation, Reinforcement, or Neutrality?" *American Journal of Sociology* 94: 1146–83.

Gamoran, Adam, and Matthew Weinstein. 1998. "Differentiation and Opportunity in Restructured Schools." *American Journal of Education* 106: 385–415.

Gardner, Howard. 1983. *Frames of Mind: The Theory of Multiple Intelligences.* New York: Basic.

Gardner, Howard. 1993. *Multiple Intelligences: The Theory in Practice.* New York: Basic.

Gaskins, Robert W. 1998. "The Missing Ingredients: Time on Task, Direct Instruction, and Writing." *Reading Teacher* 41: 750–55.

Goffman, Erving. 1956. *The Presentation of Self in Everyday Life.* Edinborough: University of Edinborough Social Science Research Center.

Goffman, Erving. 1962. *Asylums.* Chicago: Aldine.

Good, Thomas L., and Jere E. Brophy. 1986. "School Effects." In *Handbook of Research on Teaching,* edited by Merlin C. Wittrock, 570–602. New York: Macmillan.

Guiton, Gretchen, and Jeannie Oakes. 1995. "Opportunity to Learn and Conceptions of Educational Equality." *Educational Evaluation and Policy Analysis* 17: 323–36.

Hallinan, Maureen T. 1996. "Race Effects on Students' Track Mobility in High School." *Social Psychology of Education* 1: 1–24.

Hallinan, Maureen T. 1997. "The Sociological Study of Social Change." *American Sociological Review* 62: 1–11.

Kahane, Reuven. 1975. "Informal Youth Organizations: A General Model." *Sociological Inquiry* 45: 17–28.

Karweit, Nancy. 1988. "Time-on-Task: The Second Time Around." *NASSP Bulletin* 72: 31–39.

Kelly, Fernandez Patricia M. 1995. "Social and Cultural Capital in the Urban Ghetto: Implications for the Economic Sociology of Immigration." In *The Economic Sociology of Immigration,* edited by Alejandro Portes. New York: Russell Sage Foundation.

Kidder, Tracy. 1989. *Among Schoolchildren.* New York: Avon.

Kilgore, Sally. 1991. "The Organizational Context of Tracking in Schools." *American Sociological Review* 56: 189–203.

Kozol, Jonathan. 1991. *Savage Inequalities: Children in America's Schools.* New York: Crown.

Kruglanski, Arie W., and Donna M. Webster. 1996. "Motivated Closing of the Mind: 'Seizing' and 'Freezing.'" *Psychological Review* 103: 263–83.

Link, Charles R., and James G. Mulligan. 1986. "The Merits of a Longer School Day." *Economics of Education Review* 5: 373–81.

Mandeville, K. G. 1988. "School Effectiveness Indices Revisited: Cross-Year Stability." *Journal of Educational Measurement* 25:349–56.

Manlove, Jennifer S., and David P. Baker. 1995. "Local Constraints on Opportunity to Learn Mathematics in High School." In *Restructuring Schools: Promising Practices and Policies,* edited by Maureen T. Hallinan, 133–53. New York: Plenum.

Marcia, James E. 1993. "The Relational Roots of Identity." In *Discussions on Ego Identity,* edited by Jane Kroger, 101–20. Hillsdale, N.J.: Erlbaum.

Marcia, James E. 1994. "The Empirical Study of Ego Identity." In *Identity and Development: An Interdisciplinary Approach,* edited by Harke A. Bosma and Tobi L. G. Graafsma, 67–80. Thousand Oaks, Calif.: Sage.

Marsh, Herbert W., and Seeshing A. Yeung. 1996. "The Distinctiveness of Affects in Specific School Subjects: An Application of Confirmatory Factor Analysis with the National Educational Longitudinal Study of 1988." *American Educational Research Journal* 33: 665–89.

Mathews, Jay. 1999. "More Time at School Allotted to Schooling." *Washington Post,* March 29, B01.

McDonnel, Lorraine M. 1995. "Opportunity to Learn as a Research Concept and a Policy Instrument." *Educational Evaluation and Policy Analysis* 17: 305–22.

Mead, George Herbert. 1934. *Mind, Self, and Society.* Chicago: University of Chicago Press.

Mehan, Hugh. 1992. "Understanding Inequality in Schools: The Contribution of Interpretive Studies." *Sociology of Education* 65: 1–20.

Meyer, John W., and Brian Rowan. 1977. "Institutionalized Organizations: Formal Structure as Myth and Ceremony." *American Journal of Sociology* 83: 340–63.

Meyer, John W., and Brian Rowan. 1992. "The Structure of Educational Organizations." In *Organizational Environments: Ritual and Rationality,* edited by John W. Meyer and Richard W. Scott, 71–97. Newbury Park, Calif.: Sage.

Meyer, John W., Richard W. Scott, and Terrence Deal. 1992. "Institutional and Technical Sources of Organizational Structure: Explaining the Structure of Educational Organizations." In *Organizational Environments: Ritual and Rationality,* edited by John W. Meyer and Richard W. Scott, 45–67. Newbury Park, Calif.: Sage.

Mischel, Theodore. 1977. *The Self: Psychological and Philosophical Issues.* Oxford: Basil Blackwell.

Mohr, John, and Paul DiMaggio. 1995. "The Intergenerational Transmission of Cultural Capital." *Research in Social Stratification and Mobility* 14: 167–99.

Newmann, Fred, Helen M. Marks, and Adam Gamoran. 1996. "Authentic Pedagogy and Student Performance." *American Journal of Education* 104: 280–312.

Nuttal, D., Harvey Goldstein, R. Prosser, and Jon Rasbash. 1989. "Differential School Effectiveness." *International Journal of Educational Research* 13: 769–76.

Oakes, Jeannie. 1985. *Keeping Track: How Schools Structure Inequality.* New Haven: Yale University Press.

Oakes, Jeannie, and Gretchen Guiton. 1995. "Matchmaking: The Dynamics of High School Tracking Decisions." *American Educational Research Journal* 32: 3–33.

Page, Rebecca N. 1991. *Lower-Track Classrooms: A Curricular and Cultural Perspective.* New York: Teachers College Press.

Pajares, Frank. 1996. "Self-Efficacy Beliefs in Academic Settings." *Review of Educational Research* 66: 543–78.

Pajares, Frank. 1997. "Current Directions in Self-Efficacy Research." *Advances in Motivation and Achievement* 10: 1–49.

Pajares, Frank, and David Miller. 1994. "Role of Self-Efficacy and Self-Concept in Mathematical Problem Solving: A Path Analysis." *Journal of Educational Psychology* 86: 193–203.

Paris, Scott C., and Julianne C. Turner. 1994. "Situated Motivation." In *Student Motivation, Cognition, and Learning,* edited by Paul R. Pintrich, Donald R. Brown, and Claire Ellen Weinstein, 213–37. Hillsdale, N.J.: Erlbaum.

Perkins, David. 1992. *Smart Schools: Better Thinking and Learning for Every Child.* New York: Free Press.

Pintrich, Paul, R. W. Marx, and R. A. Boyle. 1993. "Beyond Cold Conceptual Change: The Role of Motivational Beliefs and Classroom Contextual Factors in the Process of Conceptual Change." *Review of Educational Research* 63: 167–99.

Portes, Alejandro. 2000. "The Hidden Abode: Sociology as Analysis of the Unexpected." *American Sociological Review* 65: 1–18.

Rejeski, Walter J., and William McCook. 1980. "Individual Differences in Professional Teachers' Attributions for Children's Performance Outcomes." 46: 1159–63.

Resh, Nura. 1998. "Track Placement: How the 'Sorting Machine' Works in Israel." *American Journal of Education* 106: 416–38.

Roscigno, Vincent J., and James W. Ainsworth-Darnell. 1999. "Race, Cultural Capital, and Educational Resources: Persistent Inequalities and Achievement Returns." *Sociology of Education* 72: 158–78.

Rosenbaum, James. 1980. "Track Misperception and Frustrated College Plans." *Sociology of Education* 53: 74–88.

Rosenshine, Barak. 1980. "How Time Is Spent in Elementary Classrooms." In *Time to Learn*, edited by Carolyn Denham and Ann Lieberman, 107–26. Washington, D.C.: National Institute of Education.

Rossmiller, Richard A. 1983. "Time-on-Task: A Look at What Erodes Time for Instruction." *NASSP Bulletin* 67: 45–49.

Sansone, Carol, and Carolyn Morgan. 1992. "Intrinsic Motivation and Education: Competence in Context." *Motivation and Emotion* 16: 249–70.

Schiefele, Ulrich, and Falko Reinberg. 1997. "Motivation and Knowledge Acquisition: Searching for Mediating Processes." In *Motivation and Achievement*, edited by Martin L. Maehr and Paul R. Pintrich. Greenwich, Conn.: JAI Press.

Schlechty, Phillip C. 1997. *Inventing Better Schools: An Action Plan for Educational Reform*. San Francisco: Jossey-Bass.

Schwartz, Norbert. 1998. "Warmer and More Social: Recent Developments in Cognitive Social Psychology." *Annual Review of Sociology* 24: 239–64.

Sizer, Theodor. 1984. *Horace's Compromise: The Dilemma of the American High School*. Boston: Houghton Mifflin.

Sizer, Theodor. 1992. *Horace's School*. Boston: Houghton Mifflin.

Smith, Frank. 1986. *Insult to Intelligence: The Bureaucratic Invasion of Our Classrooms*. Portsmouth: Heineman.

Sorenson, Aage B. 1989. "Schools and the Distribution of Educational Opportunities." *Research in the Sociology of Education and Socialization* 8: 3–26.

Sorenson, Aage B., and Maureen T. Hallinan. 1977. "A Reconceptualization of School Effects." *Sociology of Education* 50: 273–89.

Sternberg, Robert J., and Janet E. Davidson, eds. 1996. *The Nature of Insight*. Cambridge: MIT Press.

Stodolsky, Susan S. 1988. *The Subject Matters*. Chicago: University of Chicago Press.

Stodolsky, Susan S., and Pamela L. Grossman. 1995. "The Impact of Subject Matter on Curricular Activity: An Analysis of Five Academic Subjects." *American Educational Research Journal* 32: 227–50.

Swartz, David. 1977. "Pierre Bourdieu: The Cultural Transmission of Social Inequality." *Harvard Educational Review* 47: 545–55.

Teitler, Julien O., and Christopher C. Weiss. 2000. "Effects of Neighborhood and School Environments on Transitions to First Sexual Intercourse." *Sociology of Education* 73: 112–32.

Virginia State Department of Education. 1992. *Instructional Time and Student Learning: A Study of the School Calendar and Instructional Time*. Richmond.

Walberg, Herbert J. 1988. "Synthesis of Research on Time and Learning." *Educational Leadership* 45: 76–85.

Wayne, F. C., and Herbert J. Wallberg. 1980. "Learning as a Function of Time." *Journal of Educational Research* 20: 183–94.

Yair, Gad. 1995. "Equal Excellence: The Attainment of Excellence and Equality in Classrooms: A Multilevel Framework." In *Educational Advancement and Distributive Justice*, edited by Reuven Kahane. Jerusalem: Magnes.

Yair, Gad. 1997. "Implications of Within-School Variability: An Israeli Comparative Study." *Assessment in Education* 4: 225–48.

Yair, Gad. 2000a. "Educational Battlefields in America: The Tug-of-War over Students' Engagement with Instruction." *Sociology of Education* 73: 247–69.

Yair, Gad. 2000b. "Not Just about Time: Instructional Practices and Productive Time in School." *Educational Administration Quarterly* 36: 485–512.

Yair, Gad. 2000c. "Reforming Motivation: How the Structure of Instruction Affects Students' Learning Experiences." *British Educational Research Journal* 26: 191–210.

7

Biography, Life Course, and the Sociology of Education

Ari Antikainen and Katja Komonen

The mission of this chapter is almost impossible. We seek to examine, under the same title, two approaches usually understood to be distinct from each other. The biographical approach has been regarded as an *ideographical* and local method, while life course studies are considered *nomothetic* and based on a positivist position. In modern parlance, the former represents the emic and the latter the etic point of view. What legitimates our examination is the work of Habermas (1971, 1987). In his theory of knowledge and human interests, Habermas distinguishes between technical and hermeneutic interests, and in his communicative theory, a distinction is carried out between the "system" and the "life world." We argue that any analysis of social reality is insufficient unless both sides—the "outsider's" and the "insider's" point of view—are taken into account.

In the field of sociology, *The Polish Peasant in Europe and America*, by Thomas and Znaniecki (1918–1920), is the classic biographical study. Florian Znaniecki also published a two-volume textbook on the sociology of education. The first volume of his work deals with "educative society" and the second with "forming the educand" (Znaniecki 1928–1930; Wlodarek 1994). Unfortunately the text is available only in Polish. Znaniecki's work is located in an interesting way in the border area between G. H. Mead's symbolic interactionism and the Parsonsian sociology. His concept of the *humanistic coefficient* refers to what was later called the double hermeneutic nature of sociological phenomena: they are first interpreted by participants and then by researchers (Giddens 1976, 162). In educational research, the investigation of life experiences offers a way to study the very foundations of educative processes.

The work of the members of the Chicago School was influenced by the European humanistic tradition. Their case studies, theoretically grounded in G. H. Mead's social psychology and led by Robert E. Park, Ernest W. Burgess, and Everett C. Hughes, used personal documents in versatile ways. Howard Becker's study on teacher careers with its use of unstructured interviews represents the approach very well as late as the early 1950s (Becker 1970, 165–76). In his introduction to a new edition of Clifford Shaw's *The Jack Roller*, Becker (1970, 73) expresses a wish that was realized to some extent in the 1980s and later:

> We can perhaps hope that a fuller understanding of the complexity of the scientific enterprise will restore sociologists' sense of the versatility and worth of the life history. A new series of personal documents, like those produced by the Chicago School more than a generation ago, might help us in all the ways I have earlier suggested and in ways, too, that we do not now anticipate.

The concept and perspective of the life course was developed in an approach that Karabel and Halsey (1977) call "methodological empiricism" as recently as in the 1970s and 1980s. The aging population and the increasing demand for comparative studies in the globalizing world have accelerated the adoption of the interdisciplinary life course perspective.

How can we define the life course perspective and the biographical method? The subject of a life course study is an individual life or its trajectory. The intention is to describe and explain the social processes in which life courses are constructed, and also to link them to each other. On the macrolevel, the interplay between social changes and aging in successive cohorts is a central theme (Riley 1986, 154). In a biographical study, at least one of its data—known as *life documents*—is collected in the form of a story or narrative in order to understand the lives and actions of these people (Denzin 1989).

SOCIOLOGICAL STUDY OF THE LIFE COURSE

Instead of developmental tasks, the conceptual points of departure in sociological life course studies may include the stages or phases of the life course, transitions, life trajectories, sequences of social roles, and internal and external turning points generating change (Elder 1985, 17–18). However, the life course itself also resembles sequences of life following each other: different areas and spheres of life can indeed be analyzed as path-like trajectories where important life events function as turning points and often signify transition from one disposition or role to another (O'Rand and Krecker 1990, 241–44).

Transitions during the life course have been referred to as turning points or key experiences in life. They are parts of trajectories and provide them with meaning. A transition may happen either according to norms or in an unpredictable manner. In the former case, we are dealing with norm-related transition, that is, with transitions that can be expected to happen at a certain age. Such transitions include transition from primary to secondary education, from education to work life, marriage, and retirement. They are periods of change and growth when the person's conceptions of self and one's life change; some transitions become turning points in the individual's life and may redirect her life course and strengthen her identity. While transition into certain central roles can be compared to the fulfillment of developmental tasks, sociological life course theories do not expect that certain roles should follow each other in a fixed order (Clausen 1986; Elder 1985, 35; Hodkinson and Sparkes 1997, 39; Sikes, Measor, and Woods 1985, 57–58).

Life course studies examine life as the combined effects of a number of factors. The life course is not only about increasing chronological age. As a personal and social chain of events, it is a temporal and historical phenomenon that can be conceived of as a process in which the trends of an era, belonging to a particular generation, and the associated age-related differentiation are combined. In addition to the choices of the individual, her life course is governed by different social, and cultural, factors in particular by social institutions, economic structures, and the educational system (Clausen 1986, 8; Heinz 1992, 9; Giele and Elder 1998, 23).

Life course studies often use the concept of trajectory to refer to an individual's lifelong path in a certain sphere of life. The life course may then be divided into a work or a family trajectory. As well, the development of an individual's life course is conceptualized using the idea of career, which refers to one's progress in professional life or in a particular organizational hierarchy. From a sociological point of view, the notion of career may also refer to a lifelong sequence of tasks to be completed in work life, regardless of the level and type of the profession or the tasks. Although this concept usually concentrates on an individual's progress in one area of life, as an analytical tool it can be used in a much wider sense in referring to the different sequences of education and work, and transitions from one position to another in the different phases of an individual's life course (Elder 1985; Hodkinson and Sparkes 1997, 3; Kerckhoff 1993, 13).

Similarly, many career theories also understand the phases of career development as being normative and based on a human being's developmental stages. Seldom do they pay attention to social change or the whole life course of an individual. In the twenty-first century, we can question the applicability of the metaphors of trajectory and career, both of which were widely used in the 1980s to describe the transitions experienced by young people. More recently, researchers suggest that traditional careers are in the process of being replaced with different routes, paths, and bridges that are more individualized, more reflexive, more processual, and transformable by the individual. Also, the role of work, learning, and educational biographies has been emphasized. The metaphors of navigation and negotiation are used to emphasize both the individual's opportunities to choose from a wider variety of options and the risk of drifting through a period of transition (Watts and McNair 1995, 163).

The quantitative approach to life history has been developed as *event history analysis*. Mayer and Tuma (1990) describe this approach as a mode of research using statistical methods with the aim of clarifying the exact timing, duration, and location in the life course of events that have taken place within a certain period of time.

The life course perspective is, however, characterized by theoretical and methodological pluralism. A partial reason for theoretical pluralism is the interdisciplinary mode of research. Multilevel analyses, in which the action of the individual is examined in light of historical, social, and economic change, also contributes to theoretical pluralism. Methodological pluralism exists for similar reasons. Life course studies have used and benefited from, for instance, biographical approaches, follow-up studies, historical demography, prospective panel research, and event history analysis (O'Rand 1998, 66–67).

SCHOOLING AND THE CHANGE OF THE MODERN LIFE COURSE

Modernization has meant the institutionalization of the life course (Kohli 1985a; Meyer 1986). The self and the life course have become more individualized, while the definitions of transitions and age stages have become more unified. The whole life course is more homogenized and comprises four phases: childhood, education, work life, and retirement. As childhood and adulthood have been distanced from each other, the period of youth in between has expanded and changed together with changes in society and mass education.

The effects of expanded education can be seen in the life of an individual in a variety of ways. Although schooling locates the educated in the labor market, in different social strata, and influences social participation as well as the opportunity structure of welfare (Pallas 2000), it has not been able to transform the structural inequalities of race, class, and gender. European educational reforms have opened up social space and modernized social structures. Nonetheless, recent unemployment, today's labor markets, the inflation of educational credentials, and the fact that habitus distinctions have not disappeared have generated a kind of backlash (Alheit 1999). Thus, in addition to their economic resources, middle-class families' symbolic or cultural and social resources assist them in maintaining their privileged position (Bourdieu 1984; Power 1999). According to Chisholm and Hurrelmann (1995), the consequences of increased educational competition for the life situation of contemporary youth can be divided into three major groups. First, difficulty in coping with transitions successfully has led to the experience of personal inadequacy. Second, in hard competition practically all young persons face the risk of failure. Third, the sphere of activities and competence where one searches for "currency" to be used in the markets of the transition goes through expansion and inflation. Cote (1996) has pointed out that identity capital is about to surpass the role of human and cultural capital as the most central mobility resource.

Pluralization and postmodernization are the central contemporary social trends, not equalization. The same pluralization and fragmentation also concern youth's transition into adulthood and work life (Chisholm and Hurrelmann 1995).

THE UPS AND DOWNS OF BIOGRAPHICAL RESEARCH

The attraction and reward of biographical research lie in its ability to reach the life world of the subject who defines her own reality in her everyday life. Biographical research may open up new perspectives onto the making of meaning taking place at the level of symbolic processes and questions dealing with social action and cultural experiences. What is characteristic of biographical research is that it combines humanistic values with scientific aims. Also, it provides the silenced with a voice (Bertaux and Kohli 1984, 233; Denzin 1989, 82).

The Chicago School's studies used various combinations of different methods, including observation, personal documents, and informal interviews. *The Polish Peasant* by Thomas and Znaniecki (1918–1920) started this tradition. It draws on diaries, letters, and other personal documents. *The Polish Peasant* claims that in a process of change such as immigration, the individual, her family, and her community are all dependent on each other. This study was the first major sociological work to combine "the individual" with "the social." According to Thomas and Znaniecki, subjective life histories allow researchers to make generalizations concerning a particular social group. Their reflections on the relationship between the subjective and the objective led to the classic social psychological statement: "If men define situations as real, they are real in their consequences" (Thomas and Thomas 1938, 571).

Another early study analyzing the methodological foundations of the life history method is John Dollard's *Criteria for the Life History* (1949). For Dollard, life history offered a way to examine the relationship between the individual, culture, and social structures. In Dollard's view, the narrating subject must be seen as an exemplar of the more general cultural condition: "Detailed studies of the lives of individuals will reveal new perspectives on the culture as a whole which are not accessible when one remains on the formal cross sectional place of observation" (1949, 4).

From the end of World War II to the mid-1960s, interest in the use of the biographical method decreased, mainly because of the emergence and popularity of quantitative survey methods. In this period, theoretical models of the life course were developed, and a number of follow-up studies were conducted. The life course of an individual was understood to be connected with social change. It was thought that social development affects people of different ages in different ways, so the concepts of cohort, social age, and trajectory were introduced.

Since the 1970s, interest in the biographical method and its use has increased significantly. *Biography and Society*, based on the presentations by Bertaux's new ISA group Biography and Society, was published in 1981. Thompson's *The Voice of the Past: Oral History* saw the light of day in 1978. In general, the critique of positivism increased the popularity of qualitative research. The topics covered by biographical research have expanded, including such varying fields as elite groups, migration and class formation, intergroup relations, the poor and their living conditions, and cultural and social change.

Biographies are not just methodological tools and objects of study. Their role has been highlighted in studies based on theories of *reflexive modernization*, where questions of constructing and maintaining one's own life have become topical. Anthony Giddens (1991, 7–8) discusses the increase of self-reflexivity and the related increase in the autonomy of the biography, and Ulrich Beck (1992, 135) stresses the current transition from a standard to a *do-it-yourself* biography. They are not talking about the biographical method, however, but rather participating in a more metaphorical discussion concerning individualization and modernization. Indeed, Giddens (1991, 76) argued that a coherent self-identity requires a narrative, since the self is made visible in narrative.

Chamberlayne, Bornat, and Wengraf (2000) talk about the biographical turn, a term they employ to refer to the subjective or cultural turn in late modern society where the personal meanings the individual attributes to her action gain increasingly more weight. The attempt to give voice to marginalized groups, or those left outside dominant research paradigms in modern society, occupies a central place in today's biographical research.

The recent emphasis on the importance of biographies is part of a more general paradigmatic change. This change can be understood, in part, as an attempt to combine the analysis of the microlevel with that of the macrolevel, and in part as a sign that the issues of individualization, reflexivity, individuality, and identity have entered the center of research (Alheit 1999; Rustin 2000, 34–39). In an individualizing world, many social identities, including class, gender, generation, and race, appear to be less clear than before. Consequently, it has been argued that the production and reproduction of social identities takes place at the personal, subjective level, which forces the researchers to study society through the individual, her biography, and her world of experience. Thus biographies rooted in both social history and analysis of the individual personality, have offered a possibility to discuss experiences and processes amid social change. The biographical method is understood to be able to link the personal with the social. At the same time, as Erben (1998, 16) points out, researchers have discovered how difficult, and in the end impossible, it is to distinguish between the two in a straightforward manner.

DEFINING THE BIOGRAPHICAL APPROACH

The terms *life story* and *biographical narrative* usually refer to an individual's freely told, either written or spoken, story of her own life (Alheit 1994, 13; Denzin 1997). When the historical nature of the object under study is emphasized, researchers use the terms *oral history* (Thompson 1978), *life history* (Goodson 1981), or *personal history.* Although the terms *life story* and *life history* are often used as synonyms, there is a slight difference between them. While the former term refers to the individual's own subjective and often retrospective narrative of past events and their meaning, the latter is a more objective description of the individual's life course. In other words, life stories are connected to life history when the analysis locates them in their social, historical, economic, and situational context. Here the person's own story is often combined with other materials, including interviews with family members and official documents (Bogdan and Taylor 1975, 7; Goodson 1981, 67). As Titon (1980, 278) puts it, "A story is made, but history is found out."

The center of the biographical research interview is the individual. In discussing her life events, she is primarily expressing herself and her experiences, and secondarily is she commenting on society surrounding her. Thus the objective world gains its meaning in and through the individual's interpretation. The life story expresses those meaningful parts the narrator has selected as the content of her narrative, for instance, what she remembers, wants to tell, and finds important. The selection of the narrator is dependent on the hearer and the interview situation, too. Since, in this process, certain issues are chosen to be told and presented in a certain manner, it is not possible to tell a life story in exactly the same manner more than once, but there exists a possible narrative of past events for each occasion. The life story is varied in both content and narrative style: the individual has several stories to tell. Hence the narrator who describes what has happened has an authorizing role: what to tell and what to leave out (Connelly and Clandinin 1990, 5).

When a person tells her life story, she also explains her choices and expresses her subjectivity. Identity can be composed of the significant parts of the life story. When the individual narrates her life story, she provides an answer to the question, Who am I? (Gergen and Gergen 1983; Riessman 1993, 15). From a phenomenological perspective, the narratives of the individuals do not so much reflect reality as they create it by allowing individuals to give meanings to their past events and experiences, both collective and individual. Therefore, the meanings produced in life stories are not stable and universal but changing and contextual.

The central problematic of biographical research deals with the relationship between the individual and the collective. How can we discuss the unique and the individual, and the shared and the cultural at the same time? In what ways are individual experiences and sociohistorical contexts related to each other? Voices critical of biographical research have claimed that the emphasis on the individual and the specific means that too little attention is given to the social. However, Plummer (1996, 224) argues that in biographical research the polarization between the individual and the social is often artificial, since in life stories the two are always found intertwined. According to the view of interactionism, the individual and society are unified in collective behavior, and the self also expresses an idea of the other who is always present in all spheres of life.

Thus the social context is not something separate from the story, but it is realized in the individual's narrative. A story about the self is also a story about the world surrounding the self.

Events also need to be located in two frameworks: the original chronological one and the narrative one. Since narrativity is connected with language and its actual use, the student of biography has to reflect on the role and meaning of language as a medium of human understanding. Meanings are produced in cultural discourse, in fixed ways of speaking about particular issues. In this sense no meaning is private and subjective, but rather public and shared. According to this line of thinking, different cultural discourses "speak" in the life stories of individuals, and images produced in biographies are in many ways images of a particular society. That society and culture are always present in narratives can be seen in another way too. Life is always narrated in a particular way, guided by certain discourses, cultural and social rules, norms, and ideals. In addition, an individual tells about her life both in the framework of her own individual experiences and as a representative of a certain cohort, generation, class, and culture (Gergen and Gergen 1983; Randall 1996, 236–37).

If the narration of the life story is thought of as interaction between the interviewer and the interviewee, it can also be explored from this perspective. The interview setting always provides the teller with certain conditions that the researcher should seek to analyze.

In this sense, stories are delicate, and they are always told to someone with a certain purpose. Denzin (1989) argues on the basis of interpretive interactionism that the interviewer should try to identify in her own way with the world of the people she is studying, and to experience the problems of that world in the manner of those under study. She should seek elements that are renewable, structural, interactional, and meaningful in the social world of her subjects. The closer the contact between the researcher and the interviewer, the more difficult it is for her to hold on to theoretical premises that cannot be applied when studying the social reality of the individual or group being examined.

Traditionally, social scientific biographical research has defined autobiography as a sociohistorical document. Thus life has been examined with the help of a narrative considered as real history, as an *objective biography*. Today's researcher is not content to read biographies as mere life histories, as records of lived life, however, but seeks to pay increasingly more attention to the ways and conventions in which life is narrated, and the experienced and the lived described. The act of narrating one's biography can be considered a type of discourse: when an individual narrates her biography using language actively, she constructs her version of the events in her life and their meaning. From this perspective, a biography is a text and a cultural product, the same as a fictionalized biography. Life stories can be approached from a phenomenological point of view as subjective life stories. In this approach, the focus is on both *life as lived* and the experiential dimension of past events, *life as experienced*, or the subjective interpretation of objective experiences, and the way in which the individual understands and gives meanings to her own history (Bruner 1986, 6).

On the basis of these approaches, we can argue that there are two separate analytical ways to study life stories: *narrative analysis* and *the analysis of narratives* (Polkinghore 1995, 12). The former refers to the application of methods that examine language and its use in a detailed manner, such as discourse analysis, to the analysis of narratives as stories with meanings. The latter refers to approaches where narratives are gathered together and used as materials enabling one to explore the phenomenon under study.

BIOGRAPHIES RETURN TO THE SOCIOLOGY OF EDUCATION

Before the 1990s, the use of biographical methods in the sociology of education was surprisingly rare. Philip Jackson's "Life in Classroom" (1968) and Peter Woods's "Sociology and the School: Interactionist Viewpoint" (1983) were excellent ethnographies of school life, but they do not use biographical approaches at all. Becker's articles, based on his dissertation dealing with teacher careers in Chicago, and his coauthored ethnographical study of the culture of students of medicine are pioneering texts in the field (Becker 1970, 151–76). Becker studied topics considered important by the people he studied. He was informed by his subjects, yet not defined by them. In addition to observations, he used the open interview technique. In this approach, the informants define their situation and problems themselves, and the interviewer's questions shape the agenda of the interview. On the basis of Becker's writings, a number of concepts have entered the toolkit of sociologists: perspective, situational adjustment, and the ideal pupil, among others (Burgess 1995).

Goodson (1981) is one of the researchers who returned the biographical method to the sociology of education. Through his work, Goodson (1988, 1992) shows that commonly held views of the timelessness and interchangeability of teachers are not valid. Goodson's work links the teacher's personal biography with the history of society; for him, life history is a form of biography, but one located in its historical and social context. In his study, he talks about teachers, but he also talks to teachers as one speaks to active agents. The relationship between the researcher and those whom he researches is a mode of bargaining where both partners have something to give and take (Sikes and Measor 1992). The discussion between the researcher and those who provide her with biographies is particularly illuminating if the latter are also researchers. It can be even more so if they are critical researchers aiming at changing reality, whose biographies, if scratched, might also show a theory (Torres 1998).

In the study of adult education, the biography studies group of the European Society for Research on the Education of Adults (ESREA) has been particularly active (Alheit, Bron-Wojciechowska, Brugger, and Dominicé 1995). Its activities have demonstrated the national traditions of biographical research. Such traditions existed in Europe long before the return of the renewed sociological biographical methods. The question of the meaning of biography has become a challenge to adult education. Many recent developments have led to the recognition of the capacity for learning and education offered by biographicity, biographical knowledge, and qualifications. These include the aim of lifelong learning, recognition of the significance of informal educational processes, and the centrality of the questions of identity and otherness. While the social has become biographized in late modern society, environments of learning have changed in at least three ways: traditional life worlds have eroded, class-based milieus have broken down, and "normal" scripts for life have disappeared (Alheit 1999).

As far as we know, one of the few studies concerning the educational and learning biographies of people from different generations, with varying social and cultural backgrounds, was conducted in Finland, a society of particularly rapid change (Antikainen, Houtsonen, Huotelin, and Kauppila 1995; Antikainen, Houtsonen, Kauppila, Komonen, Koski, and Käyhkö 1999). While Finland's neighbor, Sweden, made the transition from an agricultural society to industrial capitalism in about one hundred years, Finland went through the same changes between 1960 and 1975. While the structures of the welfare state were shaken in the early 1990s, they did not entirely disappear, even though the economic depression was relatively deeper than that of the 1930s. In this sociohistorical context, the intergenerational differences are quite clear (Huotelin and Kauppila 1995) and education is a strong maker of identity. Learning biographies show significant learning experiences, even if they occur outside formal education and function as turning points, keeping lifelong learning going (Antikainen 1998). It has been pointed out, as well, that teacher support is particularly important for the construction of educational paths of working-class children, especially girls (Käyhkö and Tuupanen 1997). The research group claims that education has a plethora of meanings depending on the sociohistorical context and the life situation of the individual. These meanings are something that the technocratic evaluation of education characteristic of neoliberalist education policy is not able to achieve.

In addition to *class* and *race*, *gender* has become a central issue in both biographical studies and the study of the life course. Theories and models dealing with the life course and biographical knowledge have usually been based on data concerning men's lives. The concepts used and models presented cannot easily be applied to describe women's life courses since the central areas of adult life constitute different gender specific fields of action, commitment, and opportunity (Nilsen 1994). It has been pointed out that to study and interpret women's life courses requires an approach in which the life course is depicted as a whole and which includes the description and analysis of reproductive (family) factors in addition to the so-called productive factors (education and work) (Bjerén and Elgqvist-Saltzman 1994).

LIFE AS LIVED VERSUS LIFE AS TOLD

Recent debates in sociological biography studies consider the relationship between life as lived, and life as told. What is the relationship between one's life story and life course? Does such a thing as a *true* story really exist? These questions stem from the basic conflict involved in interview data: while it is the aim of the interview to detect the individual's own subjective world of experience, the researcher still hopes that the person's own voice is able to give a detailed description of what has really happened.

Usher (1998, 21) points out that the relationship between the lived and the told life is that of referentiality and constructivity. Attempts to deal with life stories as "real life" have been found to be problematic. A narrative explanation is always *retroactive*. Past events are explained retrospectively from the present, the end result of action. Since human memory is dynamic, the same person can interpret the same experience in different ways at different points in time. Neisser (1994, 1–2) states that while the *remembering self* is always an embodied social actor and thus, a part of real everyday life, the *remembered self* is always an interpretation and a construct.

Since biographies are deemed to be stories constructed from the present, Bourdieu (1987) criticizes their treatment as "life as lived". He talks about the "biographical illusion," referring to the idea that a coherent story does not correspond to a reality that is lacking in coherence and continuity. The narrator of a written biography, in particular, faces the problematic task of transforming the discontinuous into the continuous, and the fragmentary into the coherent, so that the text has a form. As a result, the point can be made that the more literary the story is, the less true it is likely to be.

In response to Bourdieu's critique, Denzin (1989, 62) argues:

> The point to make is not whether biographical coherence is an illusion or a reality. Rather, what must be established is how individuals give coherence to their lives when they write or talk self-autobiographies. The sources of this coherence, the narratives that lie behind them, and the larger ideologies that structure them must be uncovered.

Constructivists, for their part, emphasize the construction of life in language. They turn the focus onto the present, arguing that the past is always built and remembered in the terms of the present. From the perspective of the discursive character of life stories, narrativity, and the stories' relation to language, narration is seen primarily as a social and pragmatic act. After tellings and retellings, the story starts to live its own life, and the self becomes a changing audience, created in stories, to whom the story about the self is told (Bruner 1986, 11–12; Van Langenhove and Harré 1993, 96–97).

If an objective approach, embodied in the attempt to treat narrated life as real, and the related way of reading life stories as referential narratives of what has really happened, is not unproblematic, the same applies to the discussion life stories as texts that do not have any counterparts in real life. To break the bond between life and narrativity appears to lead to a problematic situation. It is as if the story told by an individual of her own life had no relationship to her own life; this would also abolish the relationship between the individual's identity and the life stories she has told.

How then to find a balance between the forms of life, lived and told? How to abandon the idea of life stories as facts without hitting the rocks of relativism? One can approach the truthfulness of life stories from an interpretative perspective, a perspective claiming that life stories are basically stories aiming at reality and truth. Here, truth is understood to stem from the unique perspective of the narrator. According to Roos (1994), the core of the life story cannot be found in the way in which it catalogues facts and events. What is more important is how these past events have been experienced, and how they have been constructed in consciousness. What matters is what is remembered, not what is forgotten. The truth is found in the experiences of the individual. Since people act according to what they believe to be true, their beliefs and experiences have a real meaning in their lives.

In the examination and assessment of life stories, one has to pay attention to their complexity as social and historical facts, as well as to their subjective representations and interpretations. When subjective experiences are chosen as the starting point of the analysis and the organization of materials, one has to realize the problem of the subjective document. A life story is not a direct reflection of what has happened, but a combination of what has been lived (the subjective) and what has happened (the objective). It has its conditions of production that limit and guide its genesis. Since a life story is some kind of a construction in the human mind, dependent on cultural rules and the use of language, it could be said to reflect theories of *potential lives*. Life stories are always constructions built in the interview setting, whose relationship with actual life events is mediated through the individual and the way in which she interprets and gives meanings to them. Thus it is not possible for anyone to recapture one's own life course as such, with all its phases, events, and experiences; all later interpretations of the meanings of events have shaped it into a different type of reality (Bruner 1986; McAdams 1996, 145).

Despite the fact that life as lived and life as told are not the same thing, the gap between them is not too wide. Yet, frequently, methodical debates concerning biographical research forget that life as action and life story as a narrative have their own rules and structures. They are not, and should not be, considered one and the same.

TOWARD A NEW SYNTHESIS?

The shared context of both life course and biography research traditions is contemporary social change. The traditional conception of the life course has been challenged in a variety of ways. Researchers, who rely on such terms as *individualization, choice*, and *risk*, or *biographization of social* have emphasized the diminishing linearity of the life course and its transformation into the more complex model prevalent in late modern societies. At the level of education, this can be seen in at least two ways: in the lengthening and expansion of education and in the shift from formerly stable careers into fragmentary, episodic, and experimenting educational paths, characterized by different transitions and ruptures related to educational and labor markets. The biography appears both as long-term plans and as a field of learning in which the life project and identity have to be reshaped flexibly on the basis of transitions in the life course.

Thus it can be concluded that social transformation is, once again, writing the history of the methods of the social sciences. Change in the life course and in everyday life, though slower than the change of social structure, cannot remain invisible regardless of the different approaches used to study it. This fact creates a possibility for dialogue, especially between those who conduct research into turning points and those who study transitions.

BIBLIOGRAPHY

Alheit, Peter. 1994. *Taking the Knocks: Youth Unemployment and Biography: A Qualitative Analysis*. London: Cassel.

Alheit, Peter. 1999. "On a Contradictory Way to the 'Learning Society': A Critical Approach." *Studies in the Education of Adults* 31: 66–82.

Alheit, Peter, Agnieszka Bron-Wojciechowska, Elisabeth Brugger, and Pierre Dominicé, eds. 1995. *The Biographical Approach in European Adult Education*. Vienna: Wiener Volksbildung.

Antikainen, Ari. 1998. "Between Structure and Subjectivity: Life-Histories and Lifelong Learning." *International Review of Education* 44: 215–34.

Antikainen, A., Jarmo Houtsonen, Hannu Huotelin, and Juha Kauppila. 1995. "In Search of the Meaning of Education: The Case of Finland." *Scandinavian Journal of Educational Research* 39: 295–309.

Antikainen, Ari, Jarmo Houtsonen, Juha Kauppila, Katja Komonen, Leena Koski, and Mari Käyhkö. 1999. "Construction of Identity and Culture through Education." *International Journal of Contemporary Sociology* 36: 204–28.

Beck, Ulrich. [1986] 1992. *Risk Society: Towards a New Modernity*. London: Sage.

Becker, Howard S. 1970. *Sociological Work: Method and Substance*. Chicago: Aldine.

Bertaux, Daniel, ed. 1981. *Biography and Society*. Beverly Hills: Sage.

Bertaux, Daniel, and Martin Kohli. 1984. "The Life Story Approach: A Continental View." *Annual Review of Sociology* 10: 215–37.

Bjerén, Gunilla, and Inga Elgqvist-Saltzman, eds. 1994. *Gender and Education in a Life Perspective: Lessons from Scandinavia*. Aldershot, U.K.: Avebury.

Bogdan, Robert, and Steven J. Taylor. 1975. *Introduction to Qualitative Research Methods: A Phenomenological Approach to the Social Sciences*. New York: Wiley.

Bourdieu, Pierre. 1984. *Distinction: A Social Critique of the Judgement of Taste*. Cambridge: Harvard University Press.

Bourdieu, Pierre. 1987. *The Biographical Illusion*. Working Papers and Proceedings of the Center for Psychosocial Studies, no. 14. Chicago.

Bruner, Edward M. 1986. "Experience and Its Expressions." In Victor W. Turner and Edward M. Bruner, eds., *The Anthropology of Experience*. Urbana: University of Illinois Press.

Burgess, Robert G., ed. 1995. *Howard Becker on Education*. Buckingham, U.K.: Open University Press.

Chamberlayne, Prue, Joanna Bornat, and Tom Wengraf. 2000. "Introduction: The Biographical Turn." In *The Turn to Biographical Methods in Social Science: Comparative Issues and Examples*. London: Routledge.

Chisholm, Lynne, and Klaus Hurrelmann. 1995. "Adolescence in Modern Europe: Pluralized Transition Patterns and Their Implications for Personal and Social Risks." *Journal of Adolescence* 18: 129–58.

Clausen, John A. 1986. *The Life Course: A Sociological Perspective*. Englewood Cliff, N.J.: Prentice-Hall.

Connelly, Michael F., and Jean D. Clandinin. 1990. "Stories of Experience and Narrative Inquiry." *Educational Researcher* 19: 2–14.

Cote, J. E. 1996. "Sociological Perspectives on Identity Formation: The Culture-Identity Link and Identity Capital." *Journal of Adolescence* 19: 417–28.

Denzin, Norman K. 1989. *Interpretive Biography*. Newbury Park, Calif.: Sage.

Denzin, Norman K. 1997. "Biographical Research Methods." In Lawrence J. Saha, ed., *International Encyclopedia of the Sociology of Education*. Oxford: Elsevier.

Dollard, John. 1949. *Criteria for the Life History*. New Haven: Yale University Press.

Elder, Glen H., Jr. 1985. "Perspectives on the Life Course." In *Life Course Dynamics: Trajectories and Transitions, 1968–1980*. Ithaca: Cornell University Press.

Elder, Glen H., Jr. 1998. "The Life Course as Developmental Theory." *Child Development* 69: 1–12.

Erben, Michael. 1998. "Biography and Research Method." In Michael Erben, ed., *Biography and Education: A Reader*. London: Falmer.

Gergen, Kenneth J., and Mary M. Gergen. 1983. "Narratives of the Self." In Theodore R. Sarbin and Karl E. Scheibe, eds., *Studies in Social Identity*. New York: Praeger.

Giddens, Anthony. 1976. *New Rules of Sociological Methods*. London: Hutchinson.

Giddens, Anthony. 1991. *Modernity and Self-Identity: Self and Society in the Late Modern Age*. Cambridge: Polity.

Giele, Janet Z., and Glenn H. Elder Jr. 1998. "Life Course Research: Development of a Field." In *Methods of Life Course Research: Qualitative and Quantitative Approaches*. Thousand Oaks, Calif.: Sage.

Goodson, Ivor. 1981. "Life Histories and the Study of Schooling." *Interchange* 11: 62–76.

Goodson, Ivor. 1988. *The Making of Curriculum*. London: Falmer.

Goodson, Ivor. 1992. *Studying Teachers' Lives*. London: Routledge.

Habermas, Jürgen. [1968] 1971. *Knowledge and Human Interests*. London: Heinemann.

Habermas, Jürgen. [1981] 1987. *Theory of Communicative Action*. Vol. 2, *Lifeworld and System: A Critique of Functionalist Reason*. Cambridge: Polity.

Heinz, Walter R. 1992. "Institutional Gatekeeping and Biographical Agency." In Walter R. Heinz, ed., *Institutions and Gatekeeping in the Life Course*. Weinheim: Deutscher Studien Verlag.

Hodkinson, P., and A. C. Sparkes. 1997. "Careership: A Sociological Theory of Career Decision Making. *British Journal of Sociology of Education* 18: 29–44.

Huotelin, Hannu, and Juha Kauppila. 1995. "Towards Generational Experiences of Education: Education in the Life Course of Finns." In Peter Alheit, Agnieszka Bron-Wojciechowska, Elisabeth Brugger, and Pierre Dominicé, eds., *The Biographical Approach in European Adult Education*. Wien: Wiener Volksbildung.

Hurrelmann, Klaus. 1989. "The Social World of Adolescents: A Sociological Perspective." In Klaus Hurrelmann and U. Engel, eds., *The Social World of Adolescents: International Perspectives*. Berlin: de Gruyter.

Jackson, Philip W. 1968. *Life in Classrooms*. New York: Holt, Rinehart and Winston.

Karabel, Jerome, and A. H. Halsey. 1977. "Educational Research: A Review and an Interpretation." In Jerome Karabel and A. H. Halsey, eds., *Power and Ideology in Education*. Oxford: Oxford University Press.

Kerckhoff, Alan C. 1993. *Diverging Pathways: Social Structure and Career Deflections*. Oxford: Cambridge University Press.

Kohli, Martin. 1985. "The World We Forgot: A Historical Review of the Life Course." In Victor W. Marshall, ed., *Later Life: The Social Psychology of Aging*. Beverly Hills: Sage.

Kohli, Martin. 1985a. "Die Institutionalizierung des Lebenslauf." *Kölner Zeitschrift für Soziologie und Sozialpsychologie* 37: 1–29.

Käyhkö, Mari, and Päivi Tuupanen. 1997. "A Life History Approach to Social Reproduction: Educational Choices among Young Working Class Finns." *Young: The Nordic Journal of Youth Research* 3: 39–54.

Mayer, Karl U., and Nancy Tuma. 1990. "Life Course Research and Event History Analysis: An Overview." In *Event History Analysis in Life Course Research*. Madison: University of Wisconsin Press.

McAdams, Dan P. 1996. "Narrating the Self in Adulthood." In James E. Birre, Gary M. Kenyon, Jan-Erik Ruth, Johannes J. F. Schroots, and Torbjorn Svensson, eds., *Aging and Biography: Explorations in Adult Development*. New York: Springer.

Meyer, John W. 1986. "The Self and Life Course: Institutionalization and Its Effects." In A. B. Sorensen, F. Weinert, and L. R. Sherrod, eds. *Human Development and the Life Course: Multidisciplinary Perspectives*. Mahwah, N.J.: Erlbaum.

Neisser, Ulrich 1994. "Self-Narratives: True and False." In Ulrich Neisser and Robyn Fivush, eds., *The Remembering Self: Construction and Accuracy in the Self-Narrative*. Emory Symposia in Cognition, no. 6. Cambridge: Cambridge University Press.

Nilsen, Ann. 1994. "Life-Lines: A Methodological Approach." In Gunilla Bjerén and Inga Elgqvist-Saltzman, eds., *Gender and Education in a Life Perspective: Lessons from Scandinavia*. Aldershot, U.K.: Avebury.

O'Rand, Angela M. 1998. "The Craft of Life Course Studies." In Janet Z. Giele and Glenn H. Elder Jr., eds., *Methods of Life Course Research: Qualitative and Quantitative Approaches*. Thousand Oaks, Calif.: Sage.

O'Rand, Angela M., and Margot L. Krecker. 1990. "Concepts of the Life Cycle. Their History, Meanings, and Uses in the Social Sciences." *Annual Review of Sociology* 16: 241–62.

Pallas, Aaron M. 2000. "The Effects of Schooling on Individual Lives." In Maureen T. Hallinan, ed., *Handbook of the Sociology of Education*. New York: Kluwer.

Plummer, Ken. 1996. "Symbolic Interactionism in the Twentieth Century: The Rise of Empirical Social Theory." In Bryan S. Turner, ed., *The Blackwell Companion to Social Theory*. Oxford: Blackwell.

Polkinghore, Donald E. 1995. "Narrative Configuration in Qualitative Analysis." In J. Amos Hatch and Richard Wisniewski, eds., *Life History and Narrative*. Qualitative Studies Series, no. 1. London: Farmer.

Power, Sally. 1999. "Educational Pathways into the Middle Class(es)." *British Journal of Sociology of Education* 25: 133–45.

Randall, William L. 1996. "Restorying a Life: Adult Education and Transformative Learning." In James E. Birren, Gary M. Kenyon, Jan-Erik Ruth, Johannes J. F. Schroots, and Torbjorn Svensson, eds., *Aging and Biography. Explorations in Adult Development*. New York: Springer.

Riessman, Catherine K. 1993. *Narrative Analysis*. Qualitative Research Methods Series, no. 30. Newbury Park, Calif.: Sage.

Riley, Mathilda W. 1986. "Sociological Perspective." In A. B. Sorensen, F. Weinert, and L. R. Sherrod, eds., *Human Development and the Life Course: Multidisciplinary Perspectives*. Mahwah, N.J.: Erlbaum.

Roos, Jeja-Pekka. 1994. "True Life Revisited. Autobiography and Referentiality after the 'Post.'" *Auto/Biography* 3: 1–16.

Rustin, Michael. 2000. "Reflections on the Biographical Turn in Social Science." In Prue Chamberlayne, Joanna Bornat, and Tom Wengraf, eds., *The Turn to Biographical Methods in Social Science: Comparative Issues and Examples*. London: Routledge.

Sikes, Patricia, and Lynda Measor. 1992. "Visiting Lives: Ethics and Methodology in Life History." In Ivor Goodson, ed., *Studying Teachers' Lives*. London: Routledge.

Sikes, Patricia J., Lynda Measor, and Peter Woods. 1985. *Teacher Careers: Crises and Continuities*. Issues in Education and Training Series, no. 5. London: Falmer.

Thomas, W. I., and D. S. Thomas. 1938. *The Child in America: Behaviour Problems and Programs*. New York: Knopf.

Thomas, W. I., and F. Znaniecki. 1918–1920. *The Polish Peasant in Europe and America*. Vols. 1–5. Boston: Gorham.

Thompson, Paul. 1978. *The Voice of the Past: Oral History*. Oxford: Oxford University Press.

Titon, Jeff T. 1980. "The Life Story." *Journal of American Folklore* 93: 276–92.

Torres, Carlos A. 1998. *Education, Power, and Personal Biography*. New York: Routledge.

Usher, Robin. 1998. "The Story of the Self: Education, Experience, and Autobiography." In Michael Erben, ed., *Biography and Education: A Reader*. London: Falmer.

Van Langenhove, Luk, and Ron Harré. 1993. "Positioning and Autobiography: Telling Your Life." In Nikolas Coupland and Jon F. Nussbaum, eds., *Discourse and Lifespan Identity*. Newbury Park, Calif.: Sage.

Watts, A. G., and S. McNair. 1995. "Towards a Strategy for Lifelong Guidance to Support Lifelong Learning and Work." In David C. A. Bradshaw, ed., *Bringing Learning to Life: The Learning Revolution, the Economy, and the Individual*. London: Falmer.

Woods, Peter. 1983. *Sociology and the School: Interactionist Viewpoint*. London: Routledge.

Wlodarek, J. 1994. "Florian Znaniecki's Sociology of Education." In Florian Znaniecki, ed., *What Are Sociological Problems?* Poznan: Wydawnictwo Nakom.

Znaniecki, Florian. 1928–1930. *Socjologia Wychowania I–II*. Warszawa: PWN.

8

Leading the Way:

The Development of Analytical Techniques in the Sociology of Education

Lawrence J. Saha and John P. Keeves

EDUCATIONAL RESEARCH AND THE SOCIOLOGY OF EDUCATION

Like other subfields in sociology, the sociology of education by and large reflects the theoretical and methodological fashions of the discipline as a whole. Thus the dominant theoretical paradigms in sociology have tended to guide the analysis of structural, institutional, and microlevel processes in the study of education. This has also been the case in research methods, as new analytical methods have been used to study educational problems.

An indication of the state of early research in the sociology of education is found in the historical development of the journal *Educational Sociology*, which underwent a name change in 1963 and came under the sponsorship of the American Sociological Association. The debates surrounding this transition reflect a concern that a takeover by sociologists might result in more theory than analysis of educational processes. Indeed at that time the outgoing editor confessed that the journal might hopefully draw sociologists out of their "cloistered environs" and get their hands dirty with the "raw meat" of education in a social context. (See Saha 1997 for a description of this event.)

From the very beginning of research into education, the conventional techniques of analysis began to point to the unique features in educational processes that required more sophisticated measurement instruments and statistical techniques to deal with them. Two methodological issues that received the notice of early educational researchers were the fallacy of imputing the correlations between groups to the correlations between the individuals that composed them (Robinson 1950), and the problem of measuring change in individuals (Burt 1937).[1]

In addition, since the 1960s there has been an increased awareness of the multivariate nature of educational processes. No longer is it sufficient to focus on one or two variables such as home background or peer group pressure in explaining educational outcomes, but clearly both have to be taken into account simultaneously to understand the dynamics of their interrelationships. The development of more complex analytical procedures has made this multivariate nature of educational processes, combined with the multilayered nature of educational structures within which these processes operate, a major focus of educational research.

A related but different development in educational research has been the increased interest in the measurement of variables. In 1938, a Committee of the British Association for the Advancement of Science examined the use of measurement procedures in psychology and the social sciences. They concluded that the techniques that had been developed could not satisfy completely the requirements of measurement. Even though the ordering operation and condition could be achieved by the methods employed, the additivity condition could not be checked (Ferguson et al. 1940). However, Ferguson (1942) and Lawley (1943) argued that by considering the performance of a person relative to the difficulty of the task, or the conjoint principle, this requirement could be satisfied.

With the development of computers and new statistical packages, greater attention has been directed to the development of more efficient, valid, and reliable measures of both educational outcome variables and those variables regarded as predictor variables. The increased use of multiple indicators rather than single indicators has required the increased use of scales, and the various techniques developed to constrict and evaluate these scales. The requirements for better levels of measurement in educational research have introduced to sociology a greater awareness and use of these procedures.

The developments that have occurred in educational research, particularly in the sociology of education, are having an impact on sociological research. These have come from the use of statistics, from advances in measurement, and from the analytical procedures employed to examine complex causal models that contain many variables involving data with a hierarchical structure.[2]

In this chapter we consider three major domains where the field of educational research has initiated and developed procedures that are changing not only the field of the sociology of education, but also that of sociology. These domains are (1) latent trait measurement, (2) causal modeling in a multivariate context, and (3) multilevel analysis. The latter is important because it examines (a) relationships at both the individual and the group levels, as well as interactions between the group and the individual, and (b) factors influencing both learning and development of the individual within the group. In the sections that follow, each of these domains is considered in turn and the contributions made by research workers in education and the sociology of education are examined.

Finally, this chapter discusses the regions and countries where these developments have largely taken place. Clearly there is now a relatively rapid transfer of new ideas and methodological advances from one region of the world to another. Scholars in particular regions of the world have been largely responsible for specific developments.

APPROACHES TO STATISTICAL ANALYSIS

During the twentieth century three distinctly different approaches to statistical analysis have gradually emerged (see Lindsey 1997). Statistical theory is not a unified field, and its different approaches are still highly controversial. This is in part a consequence of the different philosophical approaches to the nature of knowledge and to the epistemological foundations adhered to by different disciplines.

In the first half of the twentieth century the positivistic approach that general relationships could be directly induced from observation of the real world was widely accepted. In this context, Fisher (1954) advanced criteria for statistical significance based on testing the null hypothesis. However, this approach is now considered logically flawed because it is necessary to assume that the null hypothesis is true in order to apply a statistical test.

This approach was initially challenged by the Neyman-Pearson school of statistics, which argued that it was necessary for a choice to be made between the null hypothesis and an alternative hypothesis. Statistical inference was involved with the making of the choice. This approach strongly appealed to economists who had to make such choices, and to research workers in such fields as social medicine where practical decisions had to be made. However, this procedure does not generally apply to the social sciences and to educational research, which seek to explain the relationships between many variables, rather than make a clear decision that would have practical implications.

A third approach, followed by Bayesian statisticians, has argued that prior information is commonly available that should be taken into consideration in decision making. Most Bayesian statisticians have argued that classical significance testing has given misleading results; they would be prepared to follow new directions that have emerged, provided that prior knowledge was available for use in the analysis.

Fisher recognized two general approaches to the analysis of data. The first involved the systematic analysis of variance (Fisher 1935), best seen in both ANOVA and regression analysis procedures. However, he also recognized that if a model or hypothesis were formulated, and a generating distribution could be specified, then the model or hypothesis could be tested against data collected from the real world. Under these conditions maximum likelihood estimates of the parameters of the model could be calculated and compared with the observed data (Fisher and Yates 1938).

If there was little likelihood of agreement between the estimated parameters of the model and the observed data, the model should be rejected, and if there was a satisfactory level of agreement it should be accepted as adequate. Alternatively, two models could be readily compared under the maximum likelihood approach, and the model that best fitted the data could be accepted provisionally as the better model of the aspect of the real world under consideration. This approach would seem to avoid the logical problems involved in testing the null hypothesis.

This approach is increasingly being used in educational research and appears to have been developed by Lawley (1940) and Jöreskog (1967) within educational research for the testing of models that involved many variables. Subsequently, this approach was widely accepted by social science researchers involved in the examination of multivariate models. It should be noted, however, that the choices of a statistical approach, whether involving maximum likelihood methods, least squares procedures in the analysis of variance, the use of a hybrid strategy, or the general approach to statistical analysis and significance testing, are matters of personal preference (see Lindsey 1997).

Unfortunately these various approaches still give rise to widespread controversy. We see them in the criticism of thesis presentation and in comments by reviewers of articles submitted for publication in refereed journals. There is, however, a consistent way ahead that rejects positivism and adopts the epistemological approach of "coherentism," which has emerged from the use of multivariate modeling procedures.

Multivariate Relationships

Research in the social sciences faces the problem that in most situations there are many variables operating to influence several separate but related outcomes. The mathematical foundations of multivariate analysis were developed in the first half of the twentieth century by statisticians and mathematicians using matrix algebra. However, early psychological research, originally in the study of intellectual activity, examined the correlations between the performance of students on different tests of cognitive abilities. The developments that occurred in the use of factor analysis, both in Great Britain and the United States, attracted the attention of educational researchers. They applied these analytical techniques to a wide range of problems involving many variables, including the investigation of relationships between social background characteristics and school learning (Wiseman 1964).

However, an alternative approach to the investigation of social background factors and educational achievement developed around the use of regression analysis. Burks (1928) was the first to use a diagrammatic presentation of regression relationships to open up an area that slowly developed into the technique of path analysis by Wright (1934) in genetics and by Duncan (1966) in sociology. The complexity of the computations required in regression analysis led Fisher (see Tatsuoka 1997), who was an agricultural statistician, to develop simplified procedures involving the analysis of variance. This latter procedure found favor among psychologists, while regression analysis remained strongly favored by economists.

The widespread availability of electronic computers rapidly changed the field of data analysis in the 1960s. It also changed the financial support available for research in all branches of the social sciences, particularly education. The funding provided for educational research during the 1960s and 1970s led to the rapid advancement of many new statistical and analytic procedures in the field that pioneered the development of new techniques and approaches, which subsequently spread across the social sciences.

The field of educational research, in which it was relatively easy to collect large bodies of data from well-designed samples of students within schools on many predictor and outcome variables, made this field an excellent one for such developments to prosper. Three major studies facilitated these developments: (1) the Equality of Educational Opportunity Study (Coleman 1966) conducted in the United States, (2) the Plowden National Survey (Peaker 1967) undertaken in England, and (3) the First International Mathematics Study (Husen 1967) carried out by the International Association for the Evaluation of Educational Achievement (IEA) in twelve countries from the UNESCO Institute for Education in Hamburg, West Germany.

The first two of the above were one-off projects with clear completion dates. However, the IEA has continued to conduct cross-national studies of educational achievement from its headquarters in the Institute of International Education at the University of Stockholm, from 1970 to 1990, and from offices in the Netherlands in more recent years.

The innovative procedures employed in these three projects were the source of widespread debate and discussion. Moreover, these studies provided rich opportunities for secondary data analyses that permitted new analytical procedures to be developed and tested. It is, however, important to recognize that the many analytical procedures to emerge from these works have slowly spread to sociology, psychology, economics, and the other social sciences. The widespread impact of these developments clearly warrants a consideration, if brief, of each analytical technique.

Variance Components Analysis

One of the procedures that developed from the Equality of Educational Opportunity Study (Coleman et al. 1966), which was undertaken within the framework of least squares regression analysis, involved estimating the unique and joint components of variance. This work was reported by Mayeske et al. (1969) in *A Study of Our Nation's Schools* and by Mood (1971). However, Mood (1971) noted that under certain circumstances contributions to variance explained could be negative. This shortcoming led to the formation of blocks of variables of a similar kind, and the estimation of the unique and joint effects of the variable blocks. This use of block-wise regression analysis was employed by Peaker (1971) in the analysis of the Plowden follow-up data, and again by Peaker (1975) in reporting on the analysis of the IEA six-subject data in twenty-one countries.

Latent Variable Analysis

The idea of blocks of variables led to the advancement of procedures for combining observed variables to form latent variables, which in least squares regression analyses would reduce, if not eliminate, problems of multicollinearity, as well as form constructs that had greater validity and generality. In the first instance, a procedure known as canonical analysis, developed by statisticians in the 1930s but little used, was employed in educational research studies (Keeves 1972) to form either orthogonal or correlated latent variables from both predictor and criterion sets of observed variables.

This work was followed by Wold's (1976) and Noonan's (1976) use of partial least squares procedures to combine the observed variables in a block into a latent variable, using either a formative or a reflective mode, which corresponded to regression and factor analytic combinations respectively of the observed variables. About the same time, Jöreskog and Sörbom (1978) developed a maximum likelihood method to combine observed variables in a reflective or factor analytic mode to form latent variables in the analysis of multivariate models.

Path Analysis

Prior to Duncan's (1966) work in sociology on path analysis, Peaker had developed a rather crude approach to path analysis in terms of variance components that he used in the analysis of the Plowden National Survey data (Peaker 1967). In the report of the Plowden Follow-up Study, Peaker (1971) explained from first principles the basic ideas of path analysis as a pictorial representation of regression analysis. This approach was so controversial that his treatment had to be relegated to an appendix in the published report of the Plowden Follow-up Study.

However, Thomson (1949) had advanced this approach and taught the ideas of path analysis to educational students in Edinburgh in Scotland, some twenty years earlier. These ideas were quickly adopted in educational research (Keeves 1972; Comber and Keeves 1973) but were often challenged (Coleman 1975; Cooley and Lohnes 1976). Although generally accepted by sociologists, path analysis procedures are not widely acknowledged, even today, by psychologists who prefer to work with a decision-making statistical approach, rather than the modeling approach, to statistical analysis.

Both Wold (1976) and Jöreskog (1967), who were both at the University of Uppsala in Sweden, combined the techniques that they had developed for the formation of latent variables with a path analytic strategy. They used this approach to test and estimate the parameters of structural equation models using partial least squares and maximum likelihood procedures respectively. These strategies of analysis were initially tried out with data obtained from the IEA Headquarters at the University of Stockholm, Sweden. Jöreskog's (1967) maximum likelihood strategy, known as LISREL, has since been widely accepted as a strong approach to multivariate modeling in the social sciences.

Several similar programs have subsequently been developed, namely EQS (Bentler 1985), LISCOMP (Muthen 1987) and MPLUS (Muthen and Muthen 1998). The modeling approach to statistical analysis with its underlying co-herentist perspective is clearly employed in these analyses in which models are tested against data from the real world. Much of this developmental work has been undertaken by statisticians working within the context of ed-ucational research.

Confirmatory Factor Analysis

The initial approaches to factor analysis were exploratory in nature and were developed within the framework of ordinary least squares analysis. However, the introduction of the maximum likelihood strategy of data analysis, both by Thomson's students in Scotland (Lawley 1943) and by Jöreskog and Sörbom (1978) using the LISREL programs, which involve a modeling approach, have largely transformed the use of factor analysis as an analytical technique.

Instead of an exploratory approach, the use of LISREL demands a clearly specified model that is tested with a maximum likelihood procedure. The positivist perspective of exploratory analysis is rejected and the coherentist perspective of testing a well-specified model is rigorously pursued. It should be noted, however, that Carroll (1993), who developed the oblimin technique for least squares factor analysis, continues to use an exploratory approach with considerable success, rather than a confirmatory approach.

Modeling of Error

One of the major problems in social science research is the existence of er-ror in the measurement of the observed variables used in analysis. The for-mation of latent variables in data analysis serves to reduce the effects of er-ror in the analysis of data by optimizing the internal consistency or reliability of the latent variables that are formed. There is, however, another procedure that can be used in data analysis with structural equation modeling, namely, the modeling of error, either by correlating residual terms in a model, or by inserting an estimate of the error as a residual path for an observed variable. Most modeling programs permit the modeling of error and the estimation of parameters associated with error. This procedure was developed by Jöreskog and Sörbom (1978) in Sweden and used in the secondary analysis of IEA data by Munck (1979).

Procedures have also been developed, and are increasingly being used in computer programs for data analysis in educational research, that employ robust regression and empirical Bayes estimation procedures. These techniques serve to weight down those data that are found to have large components of error and to weight up those data that have small error components. Robust regression considers the outliers present in the data, and the empirical Bayes technique employs the reliability of the estimated relationship in the weighting of the data (Raudenbush and Bryk 1997).

Multilevel Analysis

As long ago as the late 1930s, E. L. Thorndike at Teachers College, Columbia University, warned of the problems encountered when correlations were estimated at the group level with data collected from individuals. Later, Robinson (1950), a sociologist, drew attention to ecological correlations obtained with aggregated data that might substantially inflate the estimates of relationships involving the behavior of individuals. In England, Peaker (1953) drew attention to the inappropriate standard errors obtained if schools were used as the primary sampling unit and students who were sampled from within schools were used as the secondary or micro unit of analysis. He devised procedures that made some allowance for the clustered nature of sample designs in educational research.

While sampling statisticians had devised procedures for correctly estimating errors in the calculation of mean values and proportions using complex formulas, little work was done on the estimation of errors for other statistics. Peaker (1967) developed procedures for the First IEA Mathematics Study conducted in 1964 that were used to estimate errors of mean values, as well as other statistics such as correlation and regression coefficients. Kish (1965) also examined the problem from the viewpoint of a sampling statistician in the United States.

Sampling Estimation Issues

Nevertheless, Coleman et al. (1966), in the Equality of Educational Opportunity study, aggregated data that had been collected at the student level and estimated the relationships at the school level. This led to widespread debate because major policies were advanced for educational practice on the basis of inflated estimates of the relationships. These in turn were a consequence of the sample design employed that was strongly nested in nature.

Peaker (1967), in his analysis of the Plowden National Survey data in England, recognized the problems associated with data aggregation and the use of a sample that involved a cluster sample design. He analyzed the data collected at the two complementary levels of the between student within school level, and the between school level. He purposefully avoided the between student across school level because of the errors involved in the disaggregation of school level data to the individual level. IEA research workers, led by Peaker, have been aware of the problems involved in the analysis of data that have been collected with a cluster sample design. These researchers have always sought to employ the best available procedures for the estimation of sampling errors, and for the estimation of parameters for relationships at both the individual and group levels.

Sociology is primarily concerned with relationships at a group level but commonly employs data collected at the individual level. However, these problems of analysis are generally not treated in sociological texts either as a substantive issue or as a concern with research methods. Moreover, until the late 1990s, a major package of computer programs, *Statistical Programs for the Social Sciences* (Norusis 1996), did not recognize the problems associated with a cluster or nested sample design.

A computer program, WesVar PC (Brick et al. 1996), was added to the SPSS computer programs but was not built into the main suite of programs. The analysis of relationships at the appropriate levels, when samples of a cluster or nested design are used, as is very common in sociological research, has not as yet been taken into consideration in most widely available computer packages that are employed in both social science and educational research studies.

Multilevel Relationships

The problems associated with the teasing out and estimation of relationships at different levels, and across two or more levels in data that involved a cluster or nested sample design, were largely ignored for a long period in educational and sociological research. Cronbach et al. (1976) drew attention to the problem, and many aspects of the problem were subsequently addressed by Burstein (1980). Earlier, Finn (1974) had developed procedures for the analysis of data, where an experimental or quasi-experimental design was involved, and where unequal numbers of students were clustered in treatment and control groups.

Although Finn's approach employs the use of the general linear regression model at two levels of analysis, it does not extend beyond a covariance adjustment. Thus it does not provide for the full regression analysis of the multilevel data that is generally collected, not only in large studies in the field of education but even in relatively small studies that do not employ a carefully balanced simple random sample.

These problems occur frequently in social and behavioral science research but are commonly overlooked. It is their obvious manifestation in schools, and classrooms within schools, and the sometimes very large design effects involved when student achievement is the criterion variable, that has led education researchers to become the major group involved in the development of statistical programs to analyze multilevel data in appropriate ways.

Three major programs have been constructed and are widely used to undertake the analysis of multilevel relationships. They were developed in an educational context but are now being used in other fields, including the social and behavioral sciences. The hierarchical linear modeling (HLM) program was developed in the United States. It analyzes data up to three levels, with cross-level interactions (Bryk, Raudenbush, Seltzer, and Congdon 1988). This approach to analysis involves maximum likelihood procedures, with the use of empirical Bayes estimation to provide for unreliability in the data. Data up to three levels are estimated separately but linked together in the iterative process. The program is extended to estimate criteria that are generated under normal, binomial, Poisson, and Bernoulli distributions.

A second program was developed in England that employs generalized least squares estimation (MLn) (Goldstein 1987). The analysis is undertaken using a single complex equation. In addition, Aitkin and Longford (1986) and Longford (1988) have developed an approach to multilevel analysis that uses the Fisher scoring algorithm. These programs employ a modeling approach to statistical analysis and provide for the comparison of models in terms of estimates of deviance. Several statistical packages have introduced programs that provide simplified approaches to multilevel estimation, generally based on least squares procedures.

Multilevel Path Analysis

The next major step forward in multilevel analysis involves linking together path analysis with multilevel analysis. Cheung, Keeves, Sellin, and Tsoi (1990) reported an initial attempt with educational data to construct and test a multilevel path model. Since that time Gustafsson and Stahl (1996) have developed the program STREAMS, which uses LISREL, EQS, or AMOS as the working program to examine path models, and factor analysis models at two distinct levels of analysis. However, this approach does not provide for cross level interactions which Cheung and his colleagues sought to provide. Likewise, Muthen and Muthen (1998) have developed a computer program M Plus that is similar in operation to STREAMS, but which makes provision for the analysis of categorical data under appropriate conditions within both path analytical and factor analytical approaches. These advancements had their origins in educational research in Sweden. With the rapid developments in the power of desktop computers, further advances in this area can be expected.

Longitudinal Data Analysis

Stability and change in both human and organizational characteristics provide important issues for research in education and the social and behavioral sciences. Here too, research in the sociology of education has contributed to general social science research.

Much has been written about the problems involved in the analysis of change, with procedures advanced to compensate for unreliability in the data. Willett (1988) drew attention to the shortcomings of the simple experimental design because of the unreliability of the data and the limited extent of change. He argued for the use of data from multiple occasions in the examination of change, so that the unreliability of the data could be accurately allowed for in analysis.

It is now clear that the multilevel programs referred to in the previous section can also be employed for the examination of change, with the measures of change analyzed at the lowest or micro level. While a linear relationship can be readily fitted to the change data, it is not necessary for the analyses to be restricted to a linear relationship, provided data are collected on a sufficient number, generally more than two, occasions. Moreover, the empirical Bayes procedure permits estimation where data are missing, which is a persistent problem in longitudinal studies where several occasions are involved in the recording of data.

The multilevel analysis procedures, now available, have the capacity to lead to marked advancement in general social science and behavioral research, where the systematic study of stability and change has in the past been limited by the lack of appropriate analytical procedures. Furthermore, the operation of some multilevel analysis programs, at three or more levels, allows for the introduction of the change data at the micro or intraindividual level, the examination of interindividual data at the meso level, and the consideration of organizational or group data at the macro level. Since the effects of groups are central to sociological enquiry, this development that allows for the investigation of group-level effects on individuals is of considerable importance. Moreover, the criterion variable need not be normally distributed but may be generated under a Bernioulli, Poisson, or binomial distribution.

ADVANCES IN MEASUREMENT

Reference has already been made to the fact that a committee of the British Association for the Advancement of Science (Ferguson et al. 1940) examined the use of objective tests, rating scales, and attitude scales in psychology and education. The committee queried whether the use of these procedures could satisfy the conditions of transitivity and additivity laid down by Campbell (1917) for measurement. One of the problems faced in measurement in the social sciences is the interaction between the person and the task in any attempt that might be made to measure. Lawley (1943), a Scottish educational psychologist, argued that if the unit of measurement allowed for this interaction or indeterminacy by using the performance of a person relative to the difficulty of a task, then this problem of interaction could be surmounted by what has become known as "conjoint measurement."

Lord (1952) extended the work of Lawley and formulated the ideas of latent trait theory for the purposes of educational testing in the United States. Subsequently, Rasch (1960) showed that the use of the logistic transformation, in its simplest form with a one-parameter model, could achieve measurement in the field of education that was independent of the particular set of items or tasks that were being used to obtain the measures. The measures would also be independent of the sample of persons who were being employed to calibrate the scale of measurement. The advantage of item response theory, or latent trait theory, with the one parameter model, namely, the difficulty levels of the items or the tasks that uses the logistic transformation, is that the scale scores obtained using this model are located on an interval scale with additive properties. Such a scale, now widely known as the Rasch scale, readily permits the equating of different sets of scores, and it provides for the measurement of change in human characteristics on an additive scale.

Since educational research is greatly concerned with factors that influence learning, the capability of measuring learning and development on an interval scale that has additive properties is extremely beneficial. Consequently, it is now possible to investigate systematically factors that influence learning and development which is the central problem of educational research, and that has widespread ramifications for the sociology of education and the field of sociology.

Both sociologists and psychologists are slowly accepting the advances that have been made in this domain, largely by education researchers. Moreover, the capacity for these ideas of measurement to be extended to the use of values, attitude, and rating scales, as well as for the measurement of performance, where several judges are involved, indicates that it will have widespread use in sociology during the coming decades.

CAUSAL MODELING IN A MULTIVARIATE CONTEXT

Research in education and the social sciences is primarily concerned with providing an explanation of events that occur in a regular way in the real world, without distorting the operation of the real world to collect the data as would be required if a tightly controlled experimental study were conducted. It is well recognized that causal inferences are difficult to determine from correlation data or from a quasi-experimental study or one carried out

in the natural environment. However, in the undertaking of a nonexperi-
mental study, a model that specifies causal relationships can be advanced
from theory and prior knowledge. The model then can be tested against empirical. If the model is found to be adequate and corresponds with empirical
observations, then it is appropriate to estimate the parameters of the model.

This strategy of investigation is employed within a coherentist theoretical
framework of the nature of knowledge, and it is facilitated by the use of
maximum likelihood procedures of statistical analysis. In addition, it is consistent with the modeling approach to statistics initially advanced by Fisher
(see Lindsey 1997). The approach to multivariate and multilevel modeling
has been developed in the main by education researchers. This approach is
finding increasingly wide use in the social sciences, in research studies
where the emphasis is not on making decisions in practical problem situations, or where conditional probabilities must be considered.

CATEGORICAL DATA ANALYSIS

While educational researchers have been active in the analysis of data that are
continuous or categorized in nature, educational research has not contributed
to the same extent to the analysis of data that are essentially categorical in nature. Developments in the analysis of categorical data have been largely undertaken in Europe and largely by sociologists. While educational researchers
often know something about log-linear models, and are gaining experience in
the use of logistic regression, there are procedures, about which they know
nothing, available for the analysis of categorical data. Examples of these procedures are configural frequency analysis, correspondence analysis, cohort
analysis, panel analysis, trend analysis, and the tobit model.

These techniques and procedures for data analysis have been developed
by sociologists and have not been taken up by educational researchers, particularly in the field of the sociology of education. Consequently, while this
chapter emphasizes the contributions of the sociology of education to the social sciences through the development of analytical procedures, there is still
much to be gained from the examination of the reciprocal process, by which
sociology has an impact on research into educational problems.

REGIONS OF THE WORLD IN WHICH MAJOR
DEVELOPMENTS OCCURRED

Let us now consider the regions of the world in which these developments
in education research and the sociology of education have occurred. Although the changes that have taken place have resulted from greatly increased computing power and electronic communication, it is the develop-

ment of new ideas that is of greatest significance. Consequently it is useful to consider the countries involved and, in doing so, to assess their contributions to change both in analytical procedures and theoretical perspectives.

Great Britain

In Scotland in the late 1930s and early 1940s there was a group of research workers in educational psychology led by Godfrey Thomson (1949), from the University of Edinburgh, who saw how to operationalize R. A. Fisher's ideas of maximum likelihood estimation. They related regression analysis to a path analytic approach and laid the foundations for many of the advances that have occurred since then.

Among this group Lawley contributed both to the problems of measurement and to the development of maximum likelihood estimation (Lawley 1949). Gilbert Peaker, a scholar at Cambridge University, not only recognized the nature of the multilevel problem but also developed the ideas of path analysis and the procedure of block wise regression analysis, which led to the formation of latent variable analysis. More recently, Harvey Goldstein, from London University, with a strong interest in longitudinal research studies, developed iterative generalized least squares procedures for the analysis of multilevel data (Goldstein 1987).

Scandinavia

The major European developments in quantitative data analysis in the study of education occurred primarily in Denmark and Sweden.

Denmark was the site of the development of item response measurement theory, through the education research work of Georg Rasch and his colleagues. The extent to which they were aware of the work of Lawley, on the other side of the North Sea in Edinburgh, is not clear. However, where Lawley tried to work with the normal function, Rasch saw the simplicity of working with the logistic function. He was able to make progress where Lawley had not been able to proceed in the absence of sufficiently powerful computers.

Much of the development in statistical analysis in Sweden took place at the Institute for International Education at the University of Stockholm where, under the leadership of Torsten Husen and T. Neville Postlethwaite, the International Association for the Evaluation of Educational Achievement (IEA) was based for twenty years. Already by the late 1960s and early 1970s a number of IEA studies used quantitative analysis for the comparison of mathematics learning across twelve countries (Husen 1967).

Educational research workers from many parts of the world were linked with these IEA activities, including David Walker from Edinburgh, Gilbert Peaker from England, J. B. Carroll from Harvard University and North Carolina in the United States, R. L. Thorndike from Teachers College, in New

York, and Benjamin Bloom, who with his many students from the Mesa Program at the University of Chicago, advanced the cause of the Rasch model in the United States. Many of Bloom's students were Australians who have made further advances in the field of Rasch measurement.

The impetus for the diffusion of the statistical developments of Wold and Jöreskog seems to have originated in relation to the IEA studies. Both Herman Wold and Karl Jöreskog, from Uppsala University, advanced the ideas of structural equation modeling with latent variables that transformed multivariate analysis and subsequently led to the developments in path modeling within multilevel analysis through the work of Bengt Muthen and Jan-Eric Gustafsson.

United States

The United States has the strongest coterie of educational research workers in the world, with key figures, such as James Coleman from the University of Chicago, having taken leading roles in education research and the sociology of education. However its contribution to the developments that have occurred during the past forty years has not been unique or commensurate with the size of the country or its strength in educational research.

The key work in the developments of multivariate analysis came from A. S. Brick at the University of Chicago and S. W. Raudenbush, initially from Harvard University and more recently from the University of Michigan. Ben Wright, also from the Mesa Program at the University of Chicago, has supported the developments in Rasch scaling in the United States, while educational research workers at the Educational Testing Service have developed more complex and less robust item response theory scaling procedures for use with achievement test data.

Australia

The Australian Council for Educational Research was founded in 1930 in order to promote research into education. While it is difficult to determine to what extent a link existed between the development of sociology and education research at that time, by 1962 the director did advocate incorporating a more sociological perspective into educational research (Saha 1990).

Although it is not clear to what extent one influenced the other, by the late 1960s considerable developments began to occur in the sociological study of education, which introduced new analytical techniques into sociological research generally. Two Australian educational research projects began in the late 1960s and early 1970s, which used newly developing techniques of block regression and path analysis. Both projects more or less introduced these techniques into general sociological use by the early 1970s.

The first of these was Australia's participation in the comparative study of science achievement by the International Association for the Evaluation of Educational Achievement (IEA) (Comber and Keeves 1973). In this project block regression, whereby clusters of variables were entered into the equation in a predetermined order, was used to identify the unique contributions of home background, school, and other influences on academic achievement.

The second was a Ph.D. project that studied gains in science and mathematics achievement (Keeves 1972). In both of these projects, the sociological study of education made valuable contributions to the use of quantitative techniques in Australian sociology generally so that by the mid-1970s these techniques began to appear routinely in the sociological literature. (See, for example, Broom, Jones, McDonnell, and Williams 1980.)

Since this early period, several Australians who have worked at the University of Chicago or had links with the Australian Council for Educational Research and IEA have developed and extended in a substantial way the use of Rasch measurement procedures. These educational research workers include David Andrich, Ray Adams, Geoff Masters, and Mark Wilson, all of whom have contributed in different and seminal ways to the use of Rasch measurement in practice.

The Netherlands

The Dutch, although not actively involved in the 1960–1980 period, have subsequently emerged as a group of research workers in education and the sociology of education who are innovative and supportive of the changes that have occurred and are occurring. Since 1990 the headquarters of IEA has been located in the Netherlands. This organization, with over fifty member countries scattered around the world, is not only continuing to contribute to analytical developments but is also disseminating ideas associated with the new techniques in the sociology of education.

CONCLUSION

The sociology of education, like its parent fields in education, is diffuse and at times controlled by ideology. Nevertheless, by drawing on developments in the area of educational research, the sociology of education has contributed extensively to advances in sociology and psychology during the past forty years. These developments have not occurred without sometimes fierce controversy in both the area of the sociology of education and the discipline of sociology.

A divide has been created in some regions between allegedly quantitative and qualitative perspectives, and between theoretical approaches and those focusing on social action and social change. However, the increased power of computers and the variety of ways in which they can be used with variables that involve both categorical and accurately measured data are giving rise to a reconciliation between opposing groups in some regions of the world. These developments have been accompanied by a rejection of positivism and a growing acceptance of a coherentist perspective, together with a clearer understanding of the nature of inquiry in the social and behavioral sciences.

NOTES

1. The first of these became known as the "ecological fallacy" in sociology (Robinson 1950). The second has generated increasing interest in longitudinal studies with multiple measurements over time where the measurement of change in educational performance has resulted in a better understanding of highly complex processes (Cronbach and Furby 1970; Goldstein 1979; Coleman 1981). We return to these issues later in the chapter.

2. The restriction of the consideration of these developments to what might be described as quantitative, as contrasted with qualitative analysis, is to seriously misunderstand the nature of the inquiry involved. As Kaplan has pointed out, "Quantities are of qualities, and a measured quantity has just the magnitude expressed in its measure" (1964, 20). However, the advances that are occurring are far deeper than the analytical techniques that are involved. They are concerned with the very nature of knowledge in the field of sociology and the rejection of positivism, as well as its replacement by coherentism with its implications for the analytical procedures employed in research.

REFERENCES

Aitkin, M., and N. Longford. 1986. "Statistical Modeling Issues in School Effectiveness Studies." *Journal of the Royal Statistical Society* A 149 (I).

Andrich, D. 1988. *Rasch Models for Measurement.* Newberry Park, Calif.: Sage.

Bentler, P. M. 1985. *Theory and Implementation of EQS: A Structural Equations Program.* Los Angeles: BMD Statistical Software.

Brick, J. M. P., P. James, and J. Severynse, 1996. *A User's Guide to Westar PC.* Rockville, Md.: Westat.

Broom, L., F. L. Jones, P. McDonnell, and T. H. Williams. 1980. *The Inheritance of Inequality.* London: Routledge & Kegan Paul.

Bryk, A. S., S. W. Raudenbush, M. Selzer, and R. T. Congdon. 1988. *An Introduction to HLM: Computer Program and User's Guide.* Mooresville, Ind.: Scientific Software.

Burks, B. S. 1928. *The Relative Influence of Nature upon Mental Development: A Comparative Study of Parent–Foster Child Resemblance and True Parent–Child Resemblance.* Chicago: National Society for the Study of Education.

Burstein, L. 1980. "Issues in the Aggregation of Data." *Review of Research in Education* 81: 258–63.

Burt, C. B. 1937. *The Backward Child*. London: University of London Press.

Campbell, N. R. 1917. *Foundation of Science: The Philosophy of Theory and Experiment*. New York: Dover.

Carroll, J. B. 1993. *Human Cognitive Abilities*. Cambridge: Cambridge University Press.

Cheung, K. C., J. P. Keeves, N. Sellin, and S. C. Tsoi. 1990. "The Analysis of Multilevel Data in Educational Research: Studies of Problems and Their Solutions." *International Journal of Educational Research* 14, no. 3: 217–19.

Coleman, J. S. 1975. "Methods and Results in the IEA Studies of Effects of School on Learning." *Review of Educational Research* 45, no. 3: 355–86.

Coleman, J. S. 1981. *Longitudinal Data Analysis*. New York: Basic.

Coleman, J. S., et al. 1966. *Equality of Educational Opportunity*. Salem, N.H.: Ayer.

Comber, L. C., and J. P. Keeves. 1973. *Science Education in Nineteen Countries: An Empirical Study*. Stockholm: Almqvist & Wiksell.

Cooley, W. W., and P. R. Lohnes. 1976. *Evaluation Research in Education*. New York: Irvington.

Cronbach, L. J., and L. Furby. 1970. "How Should We Measure 'Change' or Should We?" *Psychological Bulletin* 74: 68–80.

Cronbach, L. J., et al. 1976. *Research on Classrooms and Schools: Formulation of Questions, Design, and Analysis*. Stanford: Stanford Evaluation Consortium, Stanford University.

Duncan, O. D. 1966. "Path Analysis: Social Examples." *American Journal of Sociology* 72: 1–16.

Ferguson, A. G. 1942. "Item Selection by the Constant Process." *Psychometrika* 7: 19–29.

Ferguson, A. G., et al. 1940. "Quantitative Estimation of Sensory Events: Final Report." *Advancement of Science* 2: 331–49.

Finn, J. 1974. *A General Model for Multivariate Analysis*. New York: Holt, Rinehart & Winston.

Fisher, R. A. 1935.*The Design of Experiments*. Edinburgh: Oliver & Boyd.

Fisher, R. A. 1954. *Statistical Methods for Research Workers*. London: Oliver & Boyd.

Fisher, R. A., and Yates, F. 1938. *Statistical Tables*. Edinburgh: Oliver & Boyd.

Goldstein, H. 1979. *The Design and Analysis of Longitudinal Studies: Their Role in the Measurement of Change*. London: Academic.

Goldstein, H. 1987. *Multilevel Models in Educational and Social Research*. Oxford: Oxford University Press.

Gustafsson, J. E., and P. A. Stahl. 1996. *STREAMS User's Guide: Structural Equation Modelling Made Simple*. Goteberg: Goteberg University.

Husen, T. 1967. *International Study of Achievement in Mathematics: A Comparison of Twelve Countries*. 2 vols. Stockholm: Almqvist & Wiksell.

Huynh, Huynh. 1997. "Robust Statistical Procedures." In J. P. Keeves, ed., *Educational Research, Methodology, and Measurement: An International Handbook*, 657–62. Oxford: Pergamon.

Jöreskog, K. 1967. "Some Contributions to Maximum Likelihood Factor Analysis." *Psychmetrika* 32: 443–82.

Jöreskog, K. G., and D. Sörbom. 1978. *Lisrel IV: Analysis of Linear Structural Relationships by the Method of Maximum Likelihood*. Chicago: National Educational Resources.

Kaplan, A. 1964. *The Conduct of Inquiry: Methodology for Behavioral Science*. New York: Chandler.

Keeves, J. P. 1972. *Educational Environmental and Student Achievement.* Stockholm: Almqvist & Wiksell.

Kish, L. 1965. *Survey Sampling.* New York: Wiley.

Lawley, D. N. 1940. "The Estimation of Factor Loadings by the Method of Maximum Likelihood." *Proceedings of the Royal Society of Edinburgh* 60: 64–82.

Lawley, D. N. 1943. "On Problems Connected with Item Selection and Test Construction." *Proceedings of the Royal Society of Edinburgh* 61: 273–87.

Lawley, D. N. 1949. "The Maximum Likelihood Method of Estimating Factor Loadings." In G. H. Thomson, ed., *The Factorial Analysis of Human Ability,* 321–37 London: University of London Press.

Lindsey, J. 1997. "Significance Testing." In J. P. Keeves, ed., *Educational Research, Methodology, and Measurement: An International Handbook.* Oxford: Pergamon.

Longford, N. T. 1988. *VARCL: Software for Variance Components Analysis of Data with Hierarchically Tested Random Effects (Maximum Likelihood).* Princeton, N.J.: Educational Testing Service.

Lord, F. M. 1952. "A Theory of Test Scores." *Psychometric Monographs* 7.

Mayeske, G. W., et al. 1969. *A Study of Our Nation's Schools.* Washington, D.C.: U.S. Government Printing Office.

Mood, A. M. 1971. "Partitioning Variance in Multiple Regression Analyses as a Test for Developing Learning Models." *American Educational Research Journal* 8: 191.

Munck, I. 1979. *Model Building in Comparative Education.* Stockholm: Almqvist & Wiksell.

Muthen, B. O. 1987. *LISCOMP Analysis of Linear Structural Relations Using a Comprehensive Measurement Model.* Mooresville, Ind.: Scientific Software.

Muthen, B. O., and L. Muthen 1998. *M Plus: User's Guide.* Los Angeles: Muthen & Muthen.

Noonan, R. D. 1976. *School Resources, Social Class, and Student Achievement.* Stockholm: Almqvist & Wiksell.

Norusis, M. J. 1996. *SPSS User's Guides.* Chicago: SPSS.

Peaker, G. F. 1953. "A Sampling Design Used by the Ministry of Education." *Journal of the Royal Statistical Society* 116: 140–65.

Peaker, G. F. 1967. "The Regression Analysis of the National Survey." In Central Advisory Council for England, *Children and Their Primary Schools: A Report of the Central Advisory Council for Education.* Vol. 2, *Research and Theories.* London: HMSO.

Peaker, G. F. 1971. *The Plowden Children Four Years Later.* Slough: N.F.E.R.

Peaker, G. F. 1975. *An Empirical Study of Education in Twenty-One Countries: A Technical Report.* Stockholm: Almqvist & Wiksell.

Rasch, G. 1960. *Probabilistic Models for Some Intelligence and Attainment Tests.* Copenhagen: Danish Institute for Educational Research.

Raudenbush, S. W., and A. S. Brick 1997. "Hierarchical Linear Modelling." In J. P. Keeves, ed., *Educational Research, Methodology, and Measurement: An International Handbook,* 549–56. Oxford: Pergamon.

Robinson, W. S. 1950. "Ecological Correlations and the Behaviour of Individuals." *American Sociological Review* 15: 351–57.

Saha, L. J. 1990. "Towards an Australian Sociology of Education." In L. J. Saha and J. P. Keeves, eds., *Schooling and Society in Australia: Sociological Perspectives,* 3–13. Sydney: Australian National University Press.

Saha, L. J. 1997. "Sociology of Education: An Overview." In *International Encyclopedia of the Sociology of Education,* 106–17. Oxford: Pergamon.

Tatsuoka, M. M. 1997. "Regression Analysis of Quantified Data." In J. P. Keeves, ed., *Educational Research, Methodology, and Measurement: An International Handbook.* Oxford: Pergamon.

Thomson, G. H. 1949. *The Factorial Analysis of Human Ability.* London: University of London Press.

Willett, J. B. 1988. "Questions and Answers on the Measurement of Change." *Review of Research in Education* 15: 345–422.

Wiseman, S. 1964. *Education and Environment* Manchester. Manchester, U.K.: University Press.

Wold, H. 1976. "Soft Modelling by Latent Variables: The Nonlinear Iterative Partial Least Squares (NIPALS) Approach." In J. Gani, ed., *Perspectives in Probability and Statistics.* New York: Applied Probability Trust.

Wright, S. 1934. "The Method of Path Coefficients." *Annals of Mathematical Statistics* 5: 161–215.

II

SOCIOLOGY OF EDUCATION IN INTERNATIONAL CONTEXTS: REGIONAL FOCUS

9

Educational Policies and New Ways of Governance in a Transnationalization Period

António Teodoro

Schooling and literacy, even without trying to establish absolute implicating ties between them, constitute two human *inventions* derived from similar conditions.[1] By establishing the superiority of literacy over oral tradition, intellectual work over manual work, the spirit over the hand, the school system has achieved one of its greatest victories, thus becoming one of the key factors in the construction of modernity.

The relationship between schooling affirmation and literacy and the construction of modernity have been equated by several authors.[2] Related to the history of literacy, Justino Magalhães has questioned the connection between *literacy* and *historical development*, or, in other words, whether the transition from oral tradition to literacy meant a deep change in human thinking.[3] By way of response, Magalhães suggests that the hypothesis of literacy, although insufficient to trigger global change movements, nevertheless appears as a facilitating environment. If areas of dichotomy and rupture exist between oral tradition and literacy, there is above all an interaction and successive crossings, which have resulted in literacy reducing the power of representation of the word, replacing memory, and allowing a chasm between subject and object; that is, literacy appeals to intellectualization, oral tradition to sensory. Despite his critical reading of the *literacy myth*, Justino Magalhães supports the notion that the main contribution of literacy to *historical development* has been the creation of a disposition toward change and mobility in a broader sense.

> . . . literacy is a technology which allows for new ways of communication, administration and storage, as well as innovation regarding economic, political and cultural activities. The strengthening of writing against oral discourse relies on a number of tenets, some of them difficult to prove: (1) it is literacy rather than oral discourse that marks the rupture from archaism in the evolution of human societies; (2) it is along literacy that the distinction is made between

developed/learned peoples and primitive peoples; (3) literacy is synonymous with action, dynamics, change; (b) literacy and not oral tradition permits complex rational activities.[4]

The school system has been crucial in the expansion of literacy. Despite many practical difficulties and different rhythms of development, very early schooling became a global phenomenon that through *isomorphism* developed in the modern world.[5] Like all global phenomena, nowadays schooling has a local root, despite being a model constructed in a European context and only later became gradually widespread as the integration of different areas into the capitalist world economy occurred. The consolidation of the sixteenth- and seventeenth-century school model, rather than older learning ways, is the outcome of a long process developed within a complex network of social relationships and changes in representations and normative guidelines related to the world and humanity, as António Nóvoa points out, understandable in a framework where other aspects also emerge, namely, (1) the development of a new concept of childhood, (2) the appearance of a civilization of mores, (3) the establishment of a Protestant work ethic, and (4) the implementation of a disciplinary society, which resulted in locking children away in special spaces.[6]

It is in the tutelary shadow of the Church that the school model is shaped and improved over those three centuries deeply influenced by Reformation and Counterreformation. But the eighteen century, with its deep economic, social, and political changes, demands important cleavages in the educational area and society's organization.[7] In many countries, and through means not always peaceful, the state replaces the Church in education's control and will become the most important agent in the expansion of the school institution.

Throughout the nineteenth century school becomes a core element in linguistic and cultural homogenization, of invention of national citizenship, in short, the affirmation of the nation-state. As has been tirelessly stressed by the authors who support the perspective of the modern world system, school expansion is closely linked to that reality inevitable to the new stage of the economy in the capitalist world, the nation-state.

The ascendant nation-state form itself was fostered by a world political culture emerging from the conflicting dynamics of the world capitalist economy. The nation-state as a mode of political organization involves the formation of citizenship and the conferral of this status on individuals. Citizenship links individuals not merely to the state as a bureaucratic organization but, more importantly, to the "imagined community" that national states are expected to embody.[8] Mass schooling becomes the central set of activities through which the reciprocal links between individuals and nation-states are forged.[9]

The growing availability of school to all classes and social groups led to the consolidation of models of school organization and pedagogical organization able to accommodate an ever growing number of students. With this purpose a *grammar schooling*[10] has been developing since the nineteenth century capable of facing the challenge of *teaching many as if it were only one.*[11]

The school model first developed in Europe will become not just universal but almost the only one *possible* or *even conceivable.*[12] The analysis of how this school model was established and consolidated in the various world regions has become a privileged research field in comparative education. Being a subject of educational sciences, which may date back to early nineteenth century,[13] it was after World War II, however, that comparative education underwent a significant development and gained expression within educational sciences.

COMPARATIVE EDUCATION AND INTERNATIONAL ORGANIZATIONS: FROM MANDATE TO LEGITIMIZATION

The appearance of a vast system of international organizations of an intergovernmental nature, both within the United Nations—besides the United Nations itself other specialized organizations like UNESCO were created in the area of education, science, and culture or the IMF and the World Bank, in the finance and development support—and regarding economic cooperation within a specific geographic area—OECD is but an example—has given great encouragement to the internationalization of educational problems.[14] Devising educational policies, particularly in peripheral (or semiperipheral) countries within the world system, increasingly depends on legitimization and *technical support* of international organizations, which allowed, in the 1960s, for rapid spreading of the theories of human capital and educational planning, the hard core of modernization theories, so fashionable at that time of euphoria, where education became a compulsory instrument of *personal self-fulfillment*, *social progress* and *economic prosperity.*[15] The effort to establish a scientific rationality which permitted the formulation of *general laws* able to guide the reforming action in the education of each country was at the center of several initiatives—seminars, conferences, workshops, surveys, studies—conducted by all those international organizations, thus enabling the creation of several networks of contact, financing and exchange of information and knowledge among national political-administrative authorities, social actors, experts, and researchers.

The development of these networks relied on the concept of comparative education centered, according to António Nóvoa, around four essential issues: the ideology of progress, a concept of science, the concept of the nation-state and the definition of a comparative methodology. The first aspect, *ideology of progress*, is manifest in the equation *education = development*, that is, in the notion that the expansion and improvement of educational systems undoubtedly secures socioeconomic development. The second aspect, a *concept of science,* is based on the positivist paradigm of social sciences developed from the second half of the nineteenth century, which accords science—in this case comparative education—the role of establishing general laws on the working of educational systems, thus legitimizing the rhetoric of rationalization of schooling and efficiency of educational policies, considered the core of all reforming action. The third aspect, the *concept of the nation-state*, derives from the assumption of the *nation* as a privileged community of analysis, which in general leads to studies where attempts are made to underline, above all, the differences and similarities between two or more countries. The fourth and last, the *definition of a comparative methodology*, acquires its main dimension in the rhetoric of objectivity and quantification, which poses the problem of gathering and analyzing data and seldom (or never) that other question, namely, the construction itself of data and theoretical framework underlying them.[16]

Perhaps due to its origins, comparative education, in the paradigm that has been generalized by international organizations, has produced very limited knowledge, instead serving as a way for national authorities to legitimize their policies. An *instrumental positivism* prevails there, leading to what Thomas Popkewitz and Miguel A. Pereyra define as *epistemological fallacies* of comparative research.[17]

In this perspective the hypothesis defended here is that resorting to the *foreign* primarily works as an element of *legitimization* of options taken at a national level and very little as a serious effort toward the knowledge of the context of other experiences and realities.[18] Conversely, however, constant initiatives, surveys, and publications by international organizations can be considered to play a decisive role in *regulating* national educational policies, by establishing an *agenda* defining not only the priorities, but also the way problems should be equated and solved, which constitutes the establishment of a more or less explicit *mandate*,[19] depending on how central countries are.

LEGITIMIZATION AND MANDATE IN EDUCATIONAL POLICIES IN A SEMIPERIPHERAL EUROPEAN COUNTRY

That relationship between national educational policies and initiatives of *technical assistance* nature on the part of international organizations, which simultaneously assumes the character of legitimization and mandate, can well be illustrated through a situation like the one in Portugal, a semiperipheral country in the European context,[20] in the period from the end of the war to January 1, 1986, when it joined the European Economic Community/European Union (EEC/EU). Privileged relationships with various international organizations with intervention in the educational area can be located in that period, illustrating that dual relationship of legitimization and mandate: first, with the OECD until 1974; then with UNESCO, in the revolutionary crisis period of 1974–1975; after the *normalization* of the revolution, between 1976 and 1978, with the World Bank; and finally again with the OECD, in the period immediately before joining the EEC/EU. Table 9.1 presents an outline of the development of these privileged relationships.

Table 9.1 International Organizations and National Educational Policies: The Portuguese Case, 1955–1986

	1955–1974	*1974–1975*	*1976–1978*	*1979–1986*
Dominant international organization in technical assistance	OECD	UNESCO	The World Bank	OECD
Internal political support	*Estado Novo* industrial sectors, technocrats and liberals (as opposed to rural factions, regime's main stalwart in the left 1930s and 1940s)	Revolutionary political-military power + socialist, communist and revolutionary	Socialist Party	New right and *Bloco Central* Socialist Party + PSD [liberal party])
Dominant educational ideology	*Oecdism*	Education-democracy - citizenship, as synonym for *socialism*	*Normalisation* in the educational policy as the condition for a representative democracy	New emphasis on vocational courses and human resources education, as a result of European mandate
Main intentions / educational policy measures	Increased compulsory post-primary education, educational planning, administration modernisation, creation of new universities and reform of higher education	Democratic school management, democratisation of educational success, continuous education, end of social work division in access to and organisation of educational system	Shorter higher education courses access to universities limited (*numerus clausus*), power increase for central educational administration	(Re)creation of technical and professional education

OECD and the Mediterranean Regional Project: Economic Growth, Industrialization, and Educational Development

Portugal's participation in the European Recovery Program, the well-known American Marshall Plan of help to postwar Europe, reflects, in its hesitations and ambiguities, Salazar and his *Estado Novo* contradictions in regard to the new world order emerging from World War II.[21] Having early on shown their support to American Secretary of State George Marshall's initial statements leading to the plan named after him and having participated in the conferences that set it in motion, Salazar's government will, however, first refuse American financial support, arguing that it is not necessary to repair Portuguese economy.

Underlying this position, presented as a philanthropic attitude on the part of Portugal, as it allowed financial help to be preferably channeled to the countries devastated by the war, was strong opposition on Salazar's part to some of the economic and political tenets attached to the Marshall Plan: liberalization of world commerce, political union in Europe, and the U.S. attitude toward colonies belonging to impoverished European powers.[22] Salazar's policy involved pursuing the *nation* as a "primary nucleus, alive, which could not be reduced or assimilated, undoubtedly ready to co-operate, but equally ready to become autonomous should the need or a conflict arise"[23] and developing an economic policy benefiting not only the relationships with the African colonies, thus building the so-called *Portuguese economic area*, but also the relationships with Brazil and Spain and creating with these two countries, which one of Salazar's ministers of economy called Ibero-American block destined, together with the British Commonwealth, to become a new space preventing the advancement of North American dominance.

Despite its initial decision to refuse American financial aid, Portugal went on participating, although very modestly, in meetings and activities of the organizations created to put the Marshall Plan into practice, culminating in the creation of the Organization for European Economic Cooperation (OEEC), a resolution of the second Conference of Paris in 1948.[24] Due to diplomatic and financial and monetary reasons, however, the position of Salazar and the Portuguese government became untenable, giving rise to one of the most serious turnabouts in foreign affairs policies during the *Estado Novo*. Within a year, from September 1947 to September 1948, a change happened from a position of refusal to a *rush* for American financial aid, which came to be secured, first when a large-scale development program was presented requiring US$625 million and, later on, with an application regarding the specific program for 1949–1950, with an emphasis on acquisition abroad of equipment for five large areas, education being one of them.[25]

Accompanied, at home, by an increased influence on the part of *industrial entrepreneurs* in the control of key sectors of national politics, Portugal's participation in the Marshall Plan and the organizations derived from it, particularly OEEC/OECD, assumed a decisive importance regarding the transformation of the *Estado Novo*'s educational policies, by legitimizing the efforts and positions of those who were mainly concerned with labor's lack of qualifications and the ensuing need for a rapid expansion in educational offers. This participation put an end to the isolation to which the educational system had been subjected throughout most of the 1930s and 1940s, thus granting political and administrative authorities access to forums of debate and exchange of information and perspectives, which proved to be crucial in the evolution of concepts that have influenced educational policies since the 1950s.

The concerns evidenced by OEEC/OECD regarding education are closely linked with the economic sphere. The 1948 convention, which instituted OEEC, stated that the agreeing parties were to use in the most complete and rational way the workforce available. The need to give meaning to that item led to the creation of the European Agency of Productivity in 1953, still within OEEC and later, in 1958, to the establishment on a permanent basis of the Bureau of Scientific and Technical Personnel. In 1970, still under the impact of the launch by USSR of Sputnik, the first artificial satellite, the current Education Committee of OECD was created as a result of the fusion of several institutions devoted to science and training of scientific and technical staff. At the core of these decisions was the concept of science as the driving power of progress and that overcoming the shortage of qualified researchers and engineers would lead to long-term benefits in educational systems, bringing considerable changes not only in university studies but above all in the general education at the elementary and secondary levels.

The emergence within OEEC/OECD of the notion of education as a crucial issue for economic growth goes hand in hand with the birth and diffusion of the *theory of human capital* created by Theodore Schultz and clarified two years later in the supplement of the *Journal of Political Economy*, which already included other pioneering studies, including the one Gary Becker later published in *Human Capital* (1964), which has since then acted as *locus classicus* for the subject. The theory of human capital will become omnipresent in OECD works, assuming the statute of scientific (and economic) legitimization at a time of *euphoria* (according to Húsen) coincident with the spreading educational systems in the 1960s and 1970s.

Inspired by the long-standing habit common in economic policy, in 1958–1959 OEEC/OECD began to conduct yearly examinations aimed at evaluating the general situation of scientific and technical education, the dominant preoccupation at the time, as well as other problems specific to each member state. The procedure consisted of sending a small team of independent experts who would meet with the administration authorities and representatives of other concerned sectors. Based on these interviews the team of experts would write a report to be analyzed in a *confrontation meeting*, at the OECD headquarters, in which the top representatives of the country under scrutiny answered several questions posed by the *examiners* and by members of the OECD executive committee.

Following an examination of Portugal's educational policy conducted in 1959–1960, the OECD set into motion the most important—in financial and political terms and also due to the critical, conceptual, and methodological attention it received—operational program of its history, the Regional Mediterranean Project.[26] The initiative of this project belonged to the Portuguese minister of education, who, because he was concerned about devising a "cultural development plan, without which an economic development plan would be meaningless and useless,"[27] decided to ask OEEC for technical and financial support in order to establish the goals of the educational system in a way that would meet the needs for labor corresponding to the economic long-term aims of the country.[28] Because the initiative was considered one that might interest other southern European countries, themselves also OEEC/OECD members, the Regional Mediterranean Project came to include, besides Portugal, Spain, Greece, Italy, Turkey, and Yugoslavia.

Although it represented a mere academic exercise of planning, with little direct influence in the reforming political action, the Regional Mediterranean Project, however, decisively contributed to the consolidation of the *change* in the Portuguese educational policy of the 1960s and 1970s, by allowing the participation on a regular basis in the OECD activities of a vast number of technicians and political-administrative staff, and by receiving technical advice by international experts in most new projects launched,[29] precisely during that *golden period* of educational growth, inspired by an almost limitless belief in the economic value of education, first the vocational and scientific education, and later on also basic and general education as well. By ending Portugal's isolationism and creating the obligation to produce on a regular basis detailed reports about the situation of the economy and education, thus dramatically showing how distant the country was from others of its partners, that active participation in the OECD work made it possible for an educational ideology to develop, which Sacuntala de Miranda called *oecdism*,[30] which will represent the most important source of mandate and legitimization for the ideas and proposals of the sectors supporting the need for development, which had gradually become influential in the departments related to the economy, educational planning and workforce training.

UNESCO and Portugal, or the Search for International Legitimization at a Time of Revolutionary Crisis

From early on, the Portuguese Revolution of 1974, the Carnation Revolution that marked the end of dictatorships in Southern Europe,[31] assumed an anticapitalist or, at least an antimonopolist orientation. OECD, which had been playing a leading role in the technical assistance to the development of the Portuguese school system (and of political legitimization of its underlying political options), appeared, in the international context, as the organization of capitalist developed countries par excellence, with a clear option, in the area of its *recommendations* about educational policies, for linking educational systems to the needs of industrial growth and to the (capitalist) economic development in general.

After the initial period, during which some highest ranks of the military believed a certain continuity was still possible with the old regime, the revolution quickly took another course, in an attempt to respond to the pressure of grassroots social movements, who demanded a break with the past which, as far as education was concerned, meant a regime that had made educational development a secondary concern, for fear of its effects in the processes of social mobility.

As the *revolutionary process* coincided with the final phase of a period of *optimistic search for education*,[32] the educational policies of the provisional governments would focus on what Stephen Stoer and Helena Araújo call the axis *education-democracy-citizenship*.[33] In the case of the Portuguese revolution, democracy (and citizenship) would gradually become synonyms with *socialism*, as the "new name for peoples' freedom" and the "tool for the liberation of the exploited and oppressed."[34]

The international organization which, in the middle 1970s, as far as education and culture were concerned, was in better condition to respond to the hope for a new route (original or not) toward socialism, was undoubtedly UNESCO, at the time committed to fulfilling, in its intervention areas, to the deliberations toward the creation of a *new international economic order* (NIEO).[35]

> The political strategy behind the NIEO initiative was Third Worldist: it identified "underdevelopment" in the Third World as the result of historical conditions. Instead of blaming the victim, Third World spokespersons wanted the international community to acknowledge the inequality in the organization of the world economy. This strategy had its roots in the Third Worldism of the decolonization movement, where colonialism was blamed for global inequality.[36]

Portugal's relationships with UNESCO during *Estado Novo* had been flimsy at first and tempestuous later. Having ratified the UNESCO Founding Act only in March 1965, Portugal had announced its intention of abandoning that UN organization in June 1971, as a consequence of several decisions taken condemning Portugal and giving political and material support to the national liberation movements at war with Portuguese colonialism. After the revolution, Portugal resumed its membership of UNESCO in September 1974 in a context already marked by the recognition by the Portuguese government of the right to self-determination and independence of the peoples living in overseas territories under Portuguese administration.

Although Portugal had never stopped participating in regular activities of the OECD (and CERI) in the educational field, even pursuing some existing

projects under technical supervision of that organization, it would be UN-
ESCO that would produce the most significant work to legitimize the government's activity during the period of 1974–1975, by responding to Portuguese authorities' desire to redirect the educational system toward a "true
democratization and a real instrument for people's growth within a community that had chosen to reinforce its national independence and follow
the socialist road toward its development,"[37] and sending a mission, organized within its Division for Educational Policies and Planning, which visited
Portugal in May and June 1975.

The report made following that visit, *Éléments pour une politique de l'éducation au Portugal*, which came out very quickly, shows deep empathy with
what was happening in Portugal during that revolutionary period and a
significant agreement with the major guidelines of political action adopted
by the government toward the establishment of a *socialist society* and the reinforcement of *national independence*. Although it stressed the nonexistence
of a *global, integrated, and coherent* project in the educational area, evidently
when compared with other sectors of activity, it insisted on the need to define a strategy based, according to the UNESCO experts' proposal, on the
concept of continuous education, which would imply the following consequences:

1. suppressing the duality between formal education and nonformal education;
2. suppressing the separate educational areas, which produce social discrimination;
3. opening up the educational activities to the country's social, economic
   and political reality;
4. eliminating regional differences related to education;
5. engaging social movements in devising an educational policy and managing educational activities;
6. adapting curricula to the nation's social-economic goals: agrarian reform, workers' participation in companies' management, creation of
   cooperatives, etc.[38]

Like all reports by international organizations, *Éléments pour une politique
de l'éducation au Portugal* ended with a series of proposals covering not only
the various sectors and levels of formal education, but also professional
training, including sectors that at the time depended on the called Ministry
of Labor. Concerned about contributing toward a *global, coherent, and integrated* project, the UNESCO experts, following the 1960s and 1970s tradition
of education planning, wrote at length about the *planning work* for the reform. They therefore supported a definition of educational goals from *employment previsions*, insisted on a reorganization of the Ministry of Education's GEP (Studies and Planning Cabinet) in order to make it "the

instrument of the creation and co-ordination of planning activities" within the ministry,[39] and ended by minutely proposing the creation of an *institution* responsible for devising and implementing the reform.

The submission of the report in August 1975, at the peak of political-military confrontation related to definition of the future of the revolution, had little impact in the conduction of the Portuguese educational policy, except, perhaps, in the field of continuous education. But it undoubtedly represented, at the international level, an important factor in the legitimization of the most significant options taken in the area of Portuguese educational policy at that time of *revolutionary crisis*.[40]

The World Bank and Normalization of the Educational Policy

Once normalcy returned to the revolution—by transferring to the State the impasses in the creation of a social and political hegemony, until then present outside, in the grassroots movements and in the *Movimento das Forças Armadas* [Armed Forces Movement]—and joining the European Community was considered a national objective, an organization like UNESCO, at the time dominated by Third World and so-called socialist countries, certainly did not exhibit the credentials needed to act as an element that could legitimize the options of the winners of the revolutionary crisis. Due to circumstances outside the educational sphere, the World Bank was the first international organization to play the role of legitimizing the new orientations for the educational policy from the time when the organs of power born with the revolution became constitutional in 1976.

The temporary gap between social measures and wealth-generating policies that occurred in 1974–1975, together with the first oil crisis, led to a dramatic imbalance in national finances, which in turn created great difficulties in obtaining international investment vital for the balance of payments. The World Bank being one of the main institutions in the international financial system responsible for evaluating countries' financial health, with the obvious goal of assessing their capacity to honor their commitments, made visiting missions of that bank to various activity areas common, even during the period of *revolutionary crisis*.

The World Bank's presence in Portuguese educational policy after 1976 happened in a specific context: on the one hand, due to the need to find a *respectable* international source of legitimization for the option of replacing *politics with planning*, at a time when the topic of admission to the university was the key problem in the educational policy, both for public opinion and for government action; on the other hand, in a context of significant slowing down of public expenditure and cuts in social areas,[41] the possibility of securing external financing programs for reform projects deemed essential for the modernization of the educational system, which considered the training of human resources the key to successfully meet the European challenge.

The World Bank then represented the ideal solution for the Portuguese government's needs, as unlike the OECD, or any other international organization, it combined *consulting* with *assistance*, through money loans.

Although it had never before participated in projects in Portugal, the World Bank had been involved in education since 1962, its *Sector Policy Paper* considering it, in the functionalist tradition of the human capital theories, a *basic human need that sustains and accelerates global development*.[42]

After a quick evaluation of the Portuguese educational situation,[43] as the main educational reform, the World Bank advised the creation and launching of *short* higher education courses aimed at training qualified staff of an intermediate level. The proposal, vigorously defended by the World Bank experts, aimed at implementing an eminently technical education centered on a practical and specialized training, *narrow band* in the curricular jargon, where investigation activities as a heuristic process characteristic of higher education studies were explicitly absent. The Bank's proposals fully coincided with those of the Portuguese political-administrative authorities of that time, who strongly defended a policy centered on training human resources which would slow down the growing demand for university studies and lead toward technological, shorter and job-oriented courses.

The World Bank's participation in this project led to the approval of a US$47.9 million loan, aimed at building and equipping the colleges of the new polytechnic institutes, whose location had, in the meantime, been decided on, as well as postgraduation studies for their future professors, to take place in the United States. Later on, in the 1980s this special link with the World Bank would be kept in the field of university studies policies, especially in the *global reform program* for that educational area presented in 1989.[44]

Some years later, during an interesting debate on the World Bank's strategies and priorities, Joel Samoff pointed out the fact that there were no visible values or goals in the reports of that institution, but merely a standard diagnosis as starting point.[45] Stephen Stoer, who has dedicated some of his research work of the 1980s to this intervention of the World Bank in Portugal,[46] had previously argued, in a seemingly apparent contradiction, that the Bank's intervention in Portuguese education had been more *ideological* than *instrumental*.

This means that what counted most was the institution's support to the redefinition and re-establishment of the State (in other words, its contribution toward the process of normalization). In concrete terms this meant providing not only a model for educational development, based on the technical-functional theory, but also the external support to a country in dire need of rebuilding its image in order to rehabilitate itself vis-à-vis the international capitalist community. In the process of contributing to Portugal's "credibility," and as a result of the process of normalization, the World Bank also contributed to the rupture with the idea of "Portugal's transition to socialism."[47]

The OECD Again: A New Vocationalism Justified by the European Mandate

OECD's comeback to a dominant role in national education would take place at the beginning of the 1980s, as a result of Portugal's decision to apply for its integration in the group of OECD countries participating in the program *examination* of national educational policies. The express goal was to consider that exam, in the context of the preliminary studies for making its fundamental law, a kind of *external audit* to the educational situation, complementary of another *observation and reflection exercise* resulting from piecemeal contributions by a group of Portuguese experts, related to the situation and perspectives of the educational system.

The *exam* conducted by OECD experts at the beginning of the 1980s, in fact, would focus on a single point: criticism of the fact that national policies had neglected young people's vocational training. Defending technical and professional education as a *capital priority* of Portuguese educational policy, OECD advised the rapid creation of professional courses *from the age of fourteen*, adding, probably as a criticism of prior governmental options, proposed or supported by the World Bank, that "furthering access to polytechnic institutes is not a priority."[48]

The selection of priorities is particularly relevant when there are ambitious plans that may be frustrated by shortage of resources. Here lies the first dilemma in connection with the country's duality. A great emphasis is now laid on the development of the inner country rather than on the expansion of already established industry. Could that imply a similar priority in terms of professional training? Bearing in mind the fact that regional development demands modest qualifications on the part of individuals, requiring short training periods, possibly work-based, then perhaps priority should be given to the acquisition of specialized industrial qualifications.[49]

This position on the part of OECD entirely corresponded to what the political power at the beginning of the 1980s wanted to hear. In a context still deeply marked by the axis *education-democracy*, prevalent at the time of the revolutionary crisis (see table 9.1), the OECD report became the international document legitimizing that "top priority" which meant the (re)creation of the professional and technical-professional education, in an openly Fordist curricular framework. Despite having characteristics specific of each national reality, that priority corresponded to a tendency also observed in other European countries, characterized by several authors as a new *vocationalism*.[50] The notion underlying that orientation in the Portuguese case, as Stoer, Stoleroff, and Correia point out, was that "the offer of human resources with adequate qualifications is essential for the economy's modernization, and also that even in a situation of serious unemployment there are potential jobs vacant as a result of lack of specialized labor."[51] The state, according to these authors, assumes the role of *modernizing actor* by granting the educational system goals and functions related to the technological change and the economic modernization, that is, by legitimizing the economic role of the *democratic school*.

> The trend toward a professional/vocational education is present in educational policies of many European countries where mass schooling has developed. However, the emergence of a discourse legitimizing the changes inherent in this policy acquires a specificity which varies according to the characteristics of each one of them. Any analysis aiming at reconstructing the meaning of the debate produced in the 1980s around the restructure of the Portuguese educational system will face a diverse collection of texts appealing to the so called "modernization needs". This appeal to modernization is, in fact, the dominant element in the discourse on the educational system, and constitutes the slogan used to highlight the need to bridge the gap between school and active life, without needing to explain what is meant by active life or what is the nature of the relationships concerned.[52]

The formal adherence to EEC/EU, with the consequent participation in the common organizations in the technical and political areas, only served to reinforce the international legitimizing of that dislocation of priorities in the educational policy. European educational policies devised from Brussels were based on two *perversions*: the first one resulted from the overdetermination of education by the economic context and labor, as a consequence, to a large extent, of having arrived at the educational policies from broadening the concept of professional training; the second one resulted from the semi-clandestineness experienced by the Community concerning education, due to the fact that its founding treaties did not include any intervention in this area, thus preventing a true debate and democratic control, and originating an intervention deeply based on the experts' logic and on criteria of narrow economic rationality.[53] Assuming that the development of the educational system, as a determinant aspect of the construction of modernity, was based on a balance between *social regulation* and *social emancipation*, the European institutions' discourse concerning education at that time was predominantly based on a rationality concerned with social regulation.

The formal integration in the EEC/EU structures beginning in January 1986 enhanced the participation in projects, networks, and forms of transnational interaction favoring the affirmation of common languages and thought categories, which would constitute the core of the discourse on *educational reform*, the true alpha and omega of the whole national policy of the last third of the 1980s. As I have argued elsewhere,[54] the discourse on educational reform assumed the categories of ritual and rhetoric, aiming at legitimizing an image of school progress and modernization. The educational reform then acquired the status of *structural reform*, and it started being presented as the means par excellence that would enable the school system to face the challenges posed by European integration and the creation of the single market, by giving a decisive contribution to the economic sphere through the rapid increase in human resources' qualifications.

THE NEW FORMS OF TRANSNATIONAL REGULATION IN THE FIELD OF EDUCATIONAL POLICIES OR A LOW-INTENSITY GLOBALIZATION

As a persistent European idea, with its origin going back both to the Promethean concept of humans progressively taming nature and to the affirmation of an economy–capitalist world with Europe as its center, the *development* project rested on two main pillars: *technological transfer* and *education*.[55] If the recipients of development, that is, the peripheral and semiperipheral countries, may have had mixed feelings about central countries' promises of technological transfer, overall the pillar of education was unanimously considered the basis for social development and nation building, even when it led to the rejection and impoverishment of local cultures, looked upon as premodern and an obstacle to rationalization of economic development.

The development project started after World War II had the nation-state as its privileged ground. That project, where *modernization* was considered a universal ideal, offered an optimistic perspective for national economic development based on assistance programs of a bi- or multilateral kind, usually conducted by international organizations just established. In this perspective, development initiatives were the outcome of a process where, despite close links between national and international plans, it was the national space that constituted the fundamental political unit when it came to mobilizing populations and attaining the modernization ideal.

Strangely (or not), that *national* development project led to a global economic integration, which decisively from the *public debt crisis* of the 1980s, Philip McMichael's *lost decade*, moved the development terms from a predominantly national issue to a progressively global one. Development ceased to be a project capable of being conducted within the nation-state, based on the traditional stimuli to the national market, rather becoming more and more dependent on the world market, led by a *global managerialism* whose ten commandments are listed in the so-called *Washington Consensus* (1993): fiscal discipline, priorities in public expense, fiscal reform, financial liberalization, exchange rates, trade liberalization, direct foreign investment, privatization, deregulation, and property rights.

> Global managerialism refers to the relocation of the power of economic management from nation-states to global institutions. It may not be an absolute relocation, but neither is it a zero-sum game where "global" and "national" are mutually exclusive. Each folds into the other. Most important, national institutions embrace global goals. This is not clearly understood because nation-states still exist and their governments still make policy. It appears to the casual observer that because state exists, national projects must also. In this global context, that is not necessarily the case. Governments are quite often making policy on behalf of the global management officials of multilateral institutions as well as executives of transnational corporations and global bankers.[56]

That global development project—*globalization* is the generally accepted term—may be understood as something beyond the mere extension of the world system, according to Giddens,[57] or just the acceleration of the *transition age*, as Wallerstein[58] argues. Whatever the meaning, however, that new development project rests on two fundamental pillars, on the one hand a liberalization strategy and, on the other, the assertion of the competitive advantages axiom, based on a new concept of development, called *sustainable*, which eventually brings back to the front the neoclassic theory of human capital.

It is not surprising, thus, that Roger Dale argues that the most evident effects of globalization in educational policies result from the reorganization of states' priorities in becoming more competitive in order to attract investments of transnational corporations to their countries.[59] But, he adds, if globalization can change the parameters and direction of state policies in the educational field, that does not inevitably mean it has to overcome, or even remove, the political peculiarities of the nations (or any sectors). First, because globalization does not result from a country's imposition on another, possibly supported by the threat of a bilateral military action, but rather, and much more, the consequence of a supranational construction.[60] Second, because the consequences in educational policies are indirect, acting through national states, so that the new, distinct rules can be interpreted differently, which usually happens, according to the country's location within the world system. That does not mean, Dale adds, the weakening or dissipation of the power of states already powerful, but rather the strengthening of their capacity to collectively respond to the forces not one of them can, alone, individually control.

As a corollary of the argumentation presented, Dale advances two hypotheses: (1) it is possible to distinguish the effects of globalization in educational policies from those resulting from the traditional intervention forms by international organizations in the framework of the former developmental model; and (2) the effects of globalization on national policies are diverse and multifarious, rather than homogeneous and uniform.

In the developmental model, the organizations' technical assistance was (is) actively sought by the national authorities, especially as a way to legitimize internal options; on the other hand, the various differing reports presented by the international organizations constitute(d) a sort of more or less explicit mandate, depending on the countries' centrality. In the globalization project—and this is the hypothesis advanced in this chapter—the *globally structured agenda*[61] is defined above all having as nerve center the *great international statistic projects* and, in particular, the INES[62] project of the Center for Educational Research and Innovation (CERI) of the OECD.

Due to its impact on educational policies of the central countries (and on many countries located in the semiperiphery of the central areas), the project, developed around the construction and gathering of national educational indicators, assumes a particular relevance. Having as its most visible expression the annual publication of *Education at a Glance*, this OECD undertaking started as a consequence of a meeting held in Washington, in 1987, through the initiative and invitation of the American secretary of education and the OECD secretariat, attended by representatives of twenty-two countries as well as several experts and guest observers. The main point of the OECD agenda concerning education was, at the time, *quality in education,* which acted as a departing issue in the launch of INES project, possibly the most significant and important activity of that international organization in the whole of the 1990s.

Recognizing that the most complex problem was not so much the calculation of valid indicators but, rather, the classification of concepts, the representatives of the OECD member countries and the guest observers examined a series of over fifty possible national indicators, and ended by organizing them under four categories: (1) input indicators, (2) output indicators, (3) process indicators, and (4) human and financial resources indicators.[63]

Putting this project into practice allowed OECD to collect an important database about national educational indicators, which has made the publication of *Education at a Glance* possible since 1992. In that *glance,* besides traditional indicators, such as different schooling rates, the various levels of access to education, expenditure on education, teacher qualifications, a series of new indicators is presented with far-reaching consequences in the formulation of educational policies at a national level.[64] Those new indicators are presented by the OECD in a particularly significant way:

> In order to respond to the growing interest of public opinion and authorities, concerning schooling results, over a third of the indicators presented in this edition deal with these results both on a personal level and vis-à-vis the labor market, and with the evaluation of school efficiency. The indicators, based on the first international survey on adult literacy, give an idea of the level of adults' mastering of basic skills and the links between these skills and some characteristics of the educational systems. This issue also includes a complete series of indicators related to the results in Mathematics and Science, covering almost all OECD countries and are based on the Third International Study on Mathematics and Science. On the other hand, the indicators collected in the first survey of the INES project schools contribute to the expansion of the available database related to school efficiency.[65]

But even more significant are the future priorities presented for this project, which constitute a truly *global agenda* for future or ongoing reforms in several countries' educational systems at this point of century and millennium transition:

> First of all, figures about learning for life and its effects on society and economy are dramatically scarce. As countries can no longer count on the progressive expansion of initial education alone in order to meet the demand for new advanced qualifications, new indicators must help those in charge to improve the basis for learning for life. In order to do that databases must be created on job-based training, continuous and adult education, and on other kinds of learning outside the school. The factors influencing the types of knowledge acquisition along our life are difficult to grasp. Data on adult literacy . . . represent a first

step in that direction, as they provide information on the relationship between school curricula and the skills required by adults, and between learning and individual's jobs, whatever the age.

The evolution of information needs also demands an expansion of the database of results, namely those of students and schools. The sources of information should go beyond the mere analysis of results related to countries by trying to identify the variables influencing those results.[66]

The practical effects of this project are patent in several countries' educational policies at the end of the 1990s, where a similarity is evident regarding the options taken by national governments. But these effects, in the case of central countries, or countries belonging to central regions, are felt above all through the establishment of a global agenda rather than the affirmation of an explicit mandate,[67] as, for example, happens in sectors like financial activity, world trade, tourism, mass culture or the media.

We can, then, talk about degrees in the intensity of globalization. Defining globalization as "groups of social relationships which translate into the intensification of transnational interactions, be they interstate practices, global capitalist practices or transnational social and cultural practices." Boaventura de Sousa Santos proposes the distinction between *high-intensity globalization* for rapid, intense and relatively single-cause globalization processes, and *low-intensity globalization* for slower processes, more diffuse and more ambiguous in their causes, adding:

> The usefulness of this distinction lies in the fact that it makes it possible to clarify unequal power relationships underlying different ways to produce globalization, which are, therefore, crucial in the concept of globalization proposed here. Low-intensity globalization tends to prevail in situations where exchanges are less unequal, that is, where power differences are small (between countries, interests, actors or practices behind the alternative concepts of globalization). On the contrary, high-intensity globalization tends to prevail in situations where exchanges are very unequal and power differences are big.[68]

In education, the compulsory mediation by national governments in devising their respective policies, usually conditioned by strong internal social movements, makes it possible to argue that we are facing a possible paradigmatic example of *low-intensity globalization*.

HEGEMONIC AND COUNTERHEGEMONIC GLOBALIZATIONS: IN SUPPORT OF A PEDAGOGY OF POSSIBILITY IN THE IMPLEMENTATION OF EMANCIPATING POLICIES IN THE EDUCATIONAL FIELD

Stressing the fact that there is no genuine globalization, as what is generally designated as globalization is always a successful globalization of a certain localism, Boaventura de Sousa Santos mentions four ways of producing globalization, which originate the same number of forms, two of which are predominantly hegemonic, imposing themselves from top to bottom—as is the case with *global localism* and *local globalism*—and another two would be predominantly counterhegemonic, affirming themselves from the bottom up—as are what he calls *cosmopolitanism* and *common human heritage*.[69]

Globalization always presupposes localization. The main reason why a term is preferred to the other is that "hegemonic scientific discourse [tends to] prefer the history of the world from the winners' perspective."[70] In his attempt to seek alternatives to hegemonic answers to the crisis of the development theory, Philip McMichael proposes, based on a case study about the Chiapas rebels, the notion of *cosmopolitan localism* as a possible way to make a successful connection between the struggle for local rights and the world historic context.[71]

> To be sustainable, a global community must situate its constituent community needs within their world-historical context. That means understanding not only how the community has come to be within the context of global processes and relations (such as instituted markets), but also how its members can empower themselves through that context. And that includes ensuring that community empowerment means also empowering the individuals and minorities in those communities. It also means realizing that there are other communities with similar needs precisely because they are woven from similar world-historical threads.[72]

Contemporary societies are experiencing deep changes—of *bifurcation*, according to Prigogine—where *national space-time* has been quietly losing ground since the 1970s in relation to the growing importance of the *global and local spaces-times,* causing the national *social contract* crisis, which was the motive behind the development of modern central states as a paradigm of government legitimacy, social and economic welfare, security and collective identity. If globalization is understood as something beyond the mere continuation of the expansion of the economy-capitalist world, as Giddens insists, or just as the acceleration of the *age of transition*, as Wallerstein argues, it is important, anyway, to rethink the *development project* which was at the core of modernity building.

Boaventura de Sousa Santos argues for the need to formulate a *new social contract*, quite different from the modernity one, more comprehensive, covering "not only humanity and social groups, but also nature,"[73] which involves, in his opinion, a *democratic rediscovery of work*. In this latter direction goes Alain Touraine when he fights against the idea of the *end of work* and its replacement with a *leisure society* since, as he points out, what the last decades have shown is the growing withdrawal of the production society dominated by the market society. As a counterpoint to this opinion, Touraine argues that we are entering a *work civilization* where the boundaries between work, leisure and education may become increasingly thin.

> To conclude, we must admit that we have left a production society inspired by the great project of dominate nature, but that is no reason for us to abandon the idea that our society is anything other than a collection of markets and that the actors are anything but consumers, hence behavior is determined by the mass society. On the contrary, we are witnessing, following a period of really capitalist development, the rebirth of a production society, no longer industry-, but information-based, where technology plays a much more important role than in any past society and where, consequently, work problems, far from becoming secondary, will become more directly crucial than in the industrial society.[74]

A new social contract also implies the transformation of the national state in what Alain Touraine and Boaventura de Sousa Santos call the *newest social movement*. Such a proposal stems from the awareness that there exists an erosion of national state sovereignty and of its regulating capacities, since power is assumed to be exerted "within a network in a wider and more conflicting political field," through "a series of organizations and currents," where "the state co-ordination acts as the imagination of the center."[75] By considering that this new political organization *does not have a center*, Boaventura de Sousa Santos then argues that the *articulating state*—whose institutionalization still remains to be *invented*, he adds—should consider itself a newest social movement which stimulates the experimentation of alternative institutional designs which are not confined to representative democracy but rather illustrate what he calls *redistributive democracy*. The new *welfare state*, Boaventura de Sousa Santos concludes, is "an experimental state, and it the continuous experimentation with the active participation of citizens that guarantees the welfare sustainability."[76]

If that *new social contract* implies a redefinition of the role of the state (and the theories on it), it can also imply the replacement of the *contract* model itself. Habermas argues that the source of legitimization of modern juridical orders can only be found in the concept of *self-determination*: "it is necessary that citizens can at all times conceive of themselves as the actors of the laws they are subjected to as recipients."[77] This will lead, still according to Habermas to *the discussion or deliberation model* ending by replacing the contract's—the juridical community is not established by a contract, but rather due to an agreement reached through discussion.

Citizenship constructed on the basis of Habermas's concept of self-determination and without the exclusions of the postmodernity project may become the enzyme in the development of a democratic government concerned with social emancipation.[78] In such a context, the school system may become the core of the affirmation of citizenship in a communication society run in a dialogical way, always bearing in mind, however, that the school is an arena of struggle and compromise which cannot be changed by law or rhetoric, as Paulo Freire used to remind us.

The increased investment in education by national states, though necessary, is not enough for an emancipation policy which regards education as one of the most important empowerment factors, both individually and at the community level. In terms of current debate, marked, on the one hand, by the crumbling of the socialist thought and the conservative thought and, on the other, by the arrogant affirmation of neoliberalism as the indiscriminate expansion of the market economy, an emancipation policy for education will imply, in the opinion shared with R. Morrow and C. A. Torres, an attitude of resistance to rationalization of education as hegemonic goal under pretext of increased economic development or, in the Portuguese situation, of the need to overtake the *leading runners* in European integration.

In other words, resistance to equity and cultural education topics having been replaced by strategies geared toward the solution of economic demands, apparently more urgent. In this context, the critical education theories were forced to adopt an element of *conservation*, or even conservatism, in order to defend the most traditional educational functions and goals.[79]

In these days of paradigmatic transition, the state should become a field of *institutional experimentation*. Admitting that the school has some characteristics of *structural place*,[80] it may be argued that it constitutes a public space of institutional experimentation, where the future (and current) generations can be provided with new ways to plan the construction of a fairer world. A world, in Paulo Freire's symbolic words, "rounder, less angular, more humane and in which the great Utopia—*Unity in Diversity*—can materialise."[81]

Perhaps because of that, in the perspective of justice and social equity, it has become not just possible but necessary to adopt an educational agenda concerned with the construction of a democratic education and *educational cities* built on participation and democracy. Such an agenda, alternative to a so-called rationalization of educational structures and practices, imposed by the merchandising of the right to education and having in the international comparison of school results evaluation the legitimizing referent to its whole action, will certainly have as its core the transformation of the national state into a social movement, engaged in the strengthening of redistributive and participating democracy.

NOTES

1. The author thankfully acknowledges Stephen R. Stoer's and Luiza Cortesão's invaluable contribution and critical comments on an earlier version of this text, as well as the stimulating debate on this subject held not only with Steve and Luiza but also with José Alberto Correia, António Candeias, Manuel Matos, Ana Maria Seixas, Fátima Antunes, and Lucília Salgado, within the context of the investigation project,

204   *António Teodoro*

A Sociedade Portuguesa Perante os Desafios da Globalização: Modernização Económica, Social e Cultural [Portuguese Society vis-à-vis Globalization Challenges: Economic, Social, and Cultural Modernization], coordinated by Boaventura de Sousa Santos (Centro de Estudos Sociais, Coimbra, 1996–2000). The author also thanks Ana Maria Neto for his friendship and professional work in translating the Portuguese original.

2. See, e.g., André Petitat, *Production de l'école—Production de la société: Analyse socio-historique de quelques moments décisifs de l'évoultion scolaire en Occident* (Geneva: Droz, 1984).

3. Justino P. Magalhães, *Ler e escrever no mundo rural do Antigo Regime: Um contributo para a história da alfabetização e da escolarização em Portugal* (Braga: Universidade do Minho, 1994).

4. Justino P. Magalhães, *Ler e escrever no mundo rural do Antigo Regime*, 76.

5. See, e.g., Francisco O. Ramirez and Marc J. Ventresca, "Building the Institution of Mass Schooling: Isomorphism in the Modern World," in Bruce Fuller and Richard Rubinson, eds., *The Political Construction of Education: The State, School Expansion, and Economic Change*, (New York: Praeger, 1992), 47–59.

6. António Nóvoa, "História da Educação" (unpublished paper, Faculdade de Psicologia e Ciências da Educação da Universidade de Lisboa, Lisbon, 1994).

7. The greatest is, obviously, the one resulting from the French Revolution in 1789. On its consequences in the ideological plan, with the emergence of liberalism as ideological glue of economy in the capitalist world and, in the context of power, *the people taking their destiny into their hands*, see, e.g., Immanuel Wallerstein, *After Liberalism* (New York: New Press, 1995).

8. Benedict R. O'G. Anderson, *Imagined Communities: Reflections on the Origin and Spread of Nationalism* (London: Verso, 1983).

9. Ramirez and Ventresca, "Building the Institution of Mass Schooling," 49–50.

10. See, e.g., David Tyack and Larry Cuban, *Tinkering toward Utopia: A Century of Public School Reform* (Cambridge: Harvard University Press, 1995).

11. See, e.g., João Barroso, *Os liceus: Organização pedagógica e administração, 1836–1960* (Lisbon: Fundação Calouste Gulbenkian/JNICT, 1995).

12. António Nóvoa, *Histoire and comparaison (essais sur l'éducation)* (Lisbon: Educa, 1998), 52.

13. Comparative studies in various scientific areas, particularly in biology, but also in law, linguistics, or pedagogy, experienced a significant development at the beginning of the nineteenth century. In pedagogy, the breakthrough in what came to be the area of comparative education happened with Marc-Antoine Julien and his *Esquisse et vues préliminaires d'un ouvrage sur léducation comparée*, published in 1817 in Paris.

14. See Joel Samoff's seminal article "Institutionalizing International Influence," in Robert F. Arnove and Carlos Alberto Torres, eds., *Comparative Education: The Dialectic of the Global and the Local* (Lanham, Md.: Rowman & Littlefield, 1999), 51–89.

15. See Torsten Husén, *L'école en question* (Brussels: Pierre Mardaga, 1979).

16. António Nóvoa, "Modèles d'analyse en éducation comparée: Le cham et la carte," *Les sciences de l'éducation: Pour l'ère nouvelle*, no. 2–3 (1995): 9–61.

17. Thomas S. Popkewitz and Miguel A. Pereyra, "Estudio comparado de las prácticas contemporáneas de reforma de la formación del profesorado en ocho países: Configuración de la problemática y construcción de una metodología comparativa," in Thomas S. Popkewitz, ed., *Modelos de poder y regulación social en Pedagogia: Crítica*

comparada de las reformas contemporáneas de la formación del profesorado (Barcelona: Pomares-Corredor, 1994), 15–91.

18. One of the classical studies on comparative education, Bernd Zymek's *Das Ausland als Argument in der pädagogischen Reformdiskussion: Schulpolitische Selbstrechtfertigung, Auslandspropaganda, internationale Vertändigung und Ansätze zu einer vergleichenden Erziehungswissenschaft in der internationalen Berichterstattung deutscher pädagogischer Zeitschriften, 1871–1952* (Ratingen: Aloys Henn Verlag, 1975), quoted by Miguel A. Pereyra, "La comparación, una empresa razonada de análisis: Por otros usos de la comparación," *Revista de educación extraordinario: Los usos de la comparación en ciencias sociales y en educación* (1990), 23–76, already supported that hypothesis, based on an empirical work on the discussion concerning the educational reforms carried out in Germany between 1871 and 1952. Based on foreign references mentioned in German pedagogical journals, Zymek demonstrates that the attention given to foreign educational systems was not the result of a neutral scientific curiosity or a systematic investigation by pedagogues from those countries. Rather it was marked by a political-scholarly and scholarly-practical interest, seeking arguments to justify each moment's official political theses, presenting them as lacking party reproof, and, by showing their international character, responding to interests that were general and necessary.

19. Jurgen Schriewer classifies that kind of diffuse but present as *the semantic construction of world society*. Based on Niklas Luhmann's theory on self-reference social systems, Schriewer explains: "A reflective context, limited by political boundaries and/or by linguistic links externalises other reflective contexts which, in turn, refer yet to other contexts, with the result that they represent models and possible stimuli to one another. A network of reciprocal references then emerges from this accumulation of observations among nations. This network acquires its own autonomy, which transmits, confirms and accelerates the planetary universalising of reform representations, models, norms, criteria and options. Such a network becomes an element in the creation of a transnational semantics of pedagogical reform. From the point of view of knowledge sociology, this transnational semantics may be understood as the corelation of an evolutionary process caused by the dynamics of a functional differentiation in social systems, while it at the same time acts, as semantic construction of world society, on the social structures, transforming them, making them uniform and harmonising them" (Jürgen Schriewer, "L'éducation comparée: Mise en perspective historique d'un champ de recherché," *Révue française de pédagogie* 121 [1997]: 23–24).

20. On Portugal's position within the world system, see, among others, Boaventura de Sousa Santos, ed., *Portugal, um retrato singular* (Oporto: Afrontamento, 1993). On the consequences of that location, see António Teodoro, *A construção política da educação: Estado, mudança social e políticas educativas no portugal contemporâneo* (Oporto: Afrontamento, in press).

21. Salazar's misgivings and backwardness, never abandoned, are well illustrated in this ironic statement he made in November, 1947: "We are different from others due to the existing gap in our respective analysis of the current situation, but we do not pose any obstacles to any peacekeeping moves or international cooperation, and, modest as we are, we would like to constitute a constructive and useful element for everybody everywhere. We will not, therefore, refuse to rush around the world at top speed, taking part in meetings, conferences and conventions promoted by numerous, most active organizations" (Oliveira Salazar, "Miséria e medo, características do momento actual," in *Discursos e notas políticas*, vol. 4, 1943–1950 [Coimbra Editora, Coimbra, 1951], 302).

22. Franco Nogueira, one of Salazar's most influent foreign ministers and main biographer, correctly expresses the Portuguese dictator's fears: "The prime minister is suspicious of the Americans' goals: he fears the advances of the United States toward Europe constitutes imperial designs, rather than help; he fears that the American economic and financial supremacy in Western Europe may constitute an open door to European positions in Africa; and he is scared with the idea that the vulnerability of Portuguese structures may turn them into an easy prey to a powerful creditor, especially one who considers itself destined to world supremacy" (Franco Nogueira, *Salazar*, vol. 4, *O Ataque (1945–1958)* Livraria Civilização Editora Porto [1986], 89). To these determinant factors must be added his fears about making some statistical data available concerning Portugal's financial situation, namely, its gold reserves, as the problem of the gold received from Nazi Germany was still unsolved.

23. Oliveira Salazar, *Discursos e notas políticas*, vol. 4, *1943–1950*, 58.

24. Initially, the United States and Canada were observers at the OEEC, which theoretically only included European countries. In 1961, with the decision to change the OEEC into the Organization for Economic Cooperation and Development (OECD), did the United States and Canada formally become full-right members of the OECD.

25. Cf. Fernanda Rollo, *Portugal e o plano marshall* (Lisbon: Estampa, 1994).

26. Cf. George S. Papadopoulos, *L'OCDE face à l'éducation* (Paris: OECD, 1994).

27. Decree by the Portuguese minister of education on October 21, 1960. The capitalization exists in the original document.

28. The previously mentioned decree by the Portuguese minister of education of October 21, 1960, thus stated the goals of that analysis: "It has been considered not only fundamental but even indispensable to conduct a study on our needs in specialised labour, accompanying it with inquests on personnel needs, bearing in mind technical change and our adaptation to world economic growth."

29. Among others, the creation of the Ministry of Education's Educational Planning Bureau, the launch of television-based teaching (*Telescola*), the modernization of educational public administration, and the reform of higher education, with the creation of new universities, organized in departments, and the establishment of a new alternative, of a polytechnic nature.

30. Sacuntala de Miranda, "Portugal e o ocdeismo" (*Análise Psicológica*, 1, no. 2: 25–38).

31. Samuel Huntington goes even further: "The third wave of democratization in the modern world began, implausibly and unwittingly, at twenty-five minutes after midnight, Thursday, April 24, 1974, in Lisbon, Portugal, when a radio station played the song "Grândola Vila Morena." That broadcast was the go-ahead signal for the military units in and around Lisbon to carry out the plans for a coup d'état that had been carefully drawn up by the young officers leading the Movimento das Forças Armadas (MFA). The coup was carried out efficiently and successfully, with only minor resistance from the security police. Military units occupied key ministries, broadcasting stations, the post office, airports, and telephone exchanges. By late morning, crowds were flooding the streets, cheering the soldiers, and placing carnations in the barrels of their rifles. By late afternoon the deposed dictator, Marcello Caetano, had surrendered to the new military leaders of Portugal. The next day he flew into exile. So died the dictatorship that had been born in a similar military coup in 1926 and led over thirty-five years by an austere civilian, António Salazar, working in close collaboration with Portugal's soldiers" (S. Huntington, *The Third Wave: Democratization*

in the Late Twentieth Century [Norman: University of Oklahoma Press, 1991], 3). Still according to Huntington, *the first long wave of democratization occurred between 1828 and 1926, the second short wave of democratization between 1943 and 1962* (pp. 13–26).

32. Cf. Sérgio Grácio, *Política educativa como tecnologia social: As reformas do ensino técnico de 1948 e 1983* (Lisbon: Livros Horizonte, 1986).

33. Stephen R. Stoer and Helena Costa Araújo, "Educação e democracia num país semiperiférico (no contexto europeu)," in S. R. Stoer, ed., *Educação, ciências sociais e realidade portuguesa: Uma abordagem interdisciplinar* [Oporto: Afrontamento], 205–30).

34. The expression, which sums up a whole period of Portuguese history, was coined by Rui Grácio, *Educação e processo democrático em Portugal* (Lisbon: Livros Horizonte, 1981), 123.

35. On a closer plan, these deliberations resulted in the fourth Conference of Non-aligned Countries, held in Algiers in September 1973, where the decision was made to ask the Secretary-General of the United Nations to hold an extraordinary session of the General Assembly in order to analyse the "problems related to raw materials and development." This session, held from April 9 to May 2, 1974, by consensus approved the *Chart for the Creation of a New International Economic Order* and an action plan [resolutions 3201 (S-VI) and 3202 (S-VI), of May 1]. These two resolutions were completed, on 12 December 1974, with the acceptance, with six votes against and ten abstentions, of the *Chart of Economics Right and Duty of National States* [resolution 3281 (XXIX)].

36. Philip McMichael, *Development and Social Change: A Global Perspective* (Thousand Oaks, Calif.: Pine Forge, 1996).

37. UNESCO, *Éléments pour une politique de l'éducation au Portugal*, Consulting Services Provided to Member States Related to Educational Planning and Policies, no. ASMS/ED/EPP/002 (Paris: UNESCO, 1975), 1.

38. UNESCO, *Éléments pour une politique*, 41.

39. UNESCO, *Éléments pour une politique*, 66.

40. The expression was coined by Boaventura de Sousa Santos, *O estado e a sociedade em Portugal, 1974–1988* (Oporto: Afrontamento, 1990).

41. On this topic, see the seminal article by José Reis on the evolution of public expenditure, within political cycles and economic cycles, between 1958 and 1993 (José Reis, "Estado, instituições e economia: A despesa pública em Portugal," *Revista crítica de ciências sociais* 44 (1995): 47–59.

42. "Education plays several roles. First, it prepares and trains skilled workers at all levels to manage capital, technology, services, and administration in every sector of the economy. Experience has repeatedly shown that development projects are not well implemented unless investment of capital and transfer of technology are accompanied by adequate human knowledge and skills. Studies have also shown that economic returns on investment in education seem, in most instances, to exceed returns on alternative kinds of investment, and that developing countries obtain higher returns than the developed ones. Second, through trained personnel, developed methodologies, and institutional settings, education facilitates the advancement of knowledge in pure and applied fields. Third, as concern for the management of the environment, for conservation, for the use of energy, and for achieving a balance between human population and natural resources mounts, education will be expected to raise the consciousness of people and to provide knowledge, skills, and trained manpower to deal with environmental issues. Fourth, rapid economic growth, technological advancement, and social change transform the relationship between the individual and the society

and may tear down the traditional supports that have provided the social framework for the individual." (World Bank, *Education: Sector Policy Paper,* 2d ed. [Washington, D.C.: World Bank, 1985], 13–14)

43. World Bank, *Education Project: Republic of Portugal,* Staff Appraisal Report, no. 1807-PO, April 3, 1978.

44. World Bank, *Republic of Portugal. Higher Education. A Program of Reform.* Report no 7671-PO (draft confidential). April, 12, 1989. Washington, DC.

45. Joel Samoff, "Which Priorities and Strategies for Education?" *International Journal of Development* 16, no. 3 (1998): 249–71.

46. Stephen R. Stoer, *Educação, estado e desenvolvimento em Portugal* (Lisbon: Livros Horizonte, 1982); *Educação e mudança social em Portugal. 1970–1980, uma década de transição* (Oporto: Afrontamento, 1986).

47. Stoer, *Educação e Mudança Social,* 246–47.

48. OCDE, *Exames das políticas nacionais: Portugal* (Lisbon: Gabinete de Estudos e Planeamento/Ministério da Educação, 1984), 82.

49. OCDE, *Exames das políticas nacionais,* 183–84.

50. See, e.g., I. Bates, ed., *Schooling for the Dole? The New Vocationalism* (London: Macmillan, 1984); R. Dale, *The State and Education Police* (Milton Keynes, Philadelphia: Open University Press, 1989); R. Moore, "Education and the Ideology of Production," *British Journal of Sociology of Education* 2, no. 8 (1987): 227–42; G. Rees, H. Williamson, and V. Winckler, "The New Vocationalism: Further Education and Local Labour Markets," *Journal of Education Policy* 3, no. 4 (1989): 227–44. According to, for example, R. Moore, the characteristic that distinguishes and gives meaning to the *new vocationalism* is the way the content and curricular development, as well as its pedagogy, stem from a behavioral specialization of the *industry's needs,* in what is perceived to be the skills demanded by jobs. These skill are, still according to Moore, *mere rhetoric* aimed at working above all as a particular ideological representation. In the context of his country (United Kingdom), Moore argues that the *new vocationalism* consists, first of all, in a conservative alternative way of controlling the educational system, aimed at reducing its autonomy and becoming a production ideology regulating education, rather than an educational ideology supporting production.

51. Stephen R. Stoer, Alain D. Stoleroff, and José Alberto Correia, "O novo vocacionalismo na política educativa em portugal e a reconstrução da lógica da acumulação" *Revista crítica de ciências sociais* 29 (1990): 11.

52. Stoer, Stoleroff, and Correia, "O novo vocacionalismo," 46–47.

53. Cf. António Nóvoa, "L'europe et l'éducation: Éléments d'analyse sociohistoriques des politiques éducatives européennes," in T. Winther-Jensen, ed., *Challenges to European Education: Cultural Values, National Identities, and Global Responsibilities* (Sonderbruck: Peter Lang, 1996), 29–79.

54. See, e.g., António Teodoro, *Política educativa em Portugal: Educação, desenvolvimento e participação política dos professores* (Venda Nova: Bertrand, 1994); and "Reforma educativa ou a legitimação do discurso sobre a prioridade educative," *Educação, sociedade & culturas* 4 (1995): 49–70.

55. Cf. Philip McMichael, *Development and Social Change: A Global Perspective* (Thousand Oaks, Calif.: Pine Forge, 2000), 241–42.

56. McMichael, *Development and Social Change,* 132.

57. Anthony Giddens, *Beyond Left and Right: The Future of Radical Politics* (Cambridge: Polity, 1994).

58. Immanuel Wallerstein, "Globalization or the Age of Transition? A Long Term View of the Trajectory of the World-System," Fernand Braudel Center, 1999, http://fbc.binghamton.edu/iwtrajws.htm. In this text, Wallerstein assumes a violently critical position regarding the globalization rhetoric: "This discourse is in fact a gigantic misreading of current reality, a deception imposed upon us by powerful groups, and even worse one that we have imposed upon ourselves, often despairingly. It is a discourse that leads us to ignore the real issues before us, and to misunderstand the historical crisis within which we find ourselves. We do indeed stand at a moment of transformation. But this is not that of an already established newly globalized world with clear rules. Rather we are located in an age of transition, transition not merely of a few backward countries who need to catch up with the spirit of globalization, but a transition in which the entire capitalist world-system will be transformed into something else. The future, far from being inevitable and one to which there is no alternative, is being determinate in this transition that has an extremely uncertain outcome." Though I have taken into account Wallerstein's criticism, in this chapter I have used the concept of globalization, or, rather, globalizations in the sense proposed by Boaventura de Sousa Santos that we live in a *transitional time*, which he calls *late world system*: "The late world system is formed by three constellations of collective practices: the constellation of interstate practices, the constellation of global capitalist practices and the constellation of transnational social and cultural practices" (Boaventura de Sousa Santos, "Processos de Globalização," in *A sociedade portuguesa perante os desafios da globalização: Modernização económica, social e cultural* [Oporto: Afrontamento, 2000]).

59. Roger Dale, "Specifying Globalisation Effects on National Policy: A Focus on Mechanisms?" *Journal of Educational Policy* 14, no. 1 (1999): 1–17.

60. Very interesting is the distinction made by Roger Dale between globalization and *imperialism* or *colonialism*: "This may be an appropriate juncture at which to raise the issue of the difference between globalisation and 'imperialism' or 'colonialism', since it is quite plausible to suggest that the difference between globalisation and imperialism/colonialism is that what once happened only to third world or colonised countries is now happening to the most powerful states, previously the initiators rather than the recipients of external pressures on their national policies" (Dale, "Specifying Globalisation Effects," 8).

61. The concept is Roger Dale's ("Globalisation and Education: Demonstrating a 'Common World Educational Culture' or Locating a 'Globally Structured Educational Agenda'?" *Educational Theory*, in press).

62. Indicators of Educational Systems.

63. Cf. N. Bottani and H. J. Walberg, "À quoi servent les indicateurs internationaux de l'enseignement?" in CERI, *L'OCDE et les indicateurs internacionaux de l'enseignement: Un cadre d'analyse* (Paris: OECD/OCDE, 1992), 7–13.

64. See, e.g., the two areas privileged by the OECD at the end of the 1990s: assessment of school functioning and external evaluation of learning.

65. Center for Educational Research and Innovation (CERI), *Regards sur l'éducation: Les indicateurs de l'OCDE* (Paris: OCDE, 1996), 10.

66. CERI, *Regards sur l'éducation*, 11.

67. Let it be stressed that this statement only refers to central countries, or those located in central areas. In Third World countries, as Joel Samoff points out, there exists a true *institutionalization of international influence* in the most public of public policies, education: "Their mass is truly astounding: thousands of pages, many of them tables,

figures, and charts. These externally initiated studies of education in Africa undertaken during the early 1990s are most striking for their similarities, their diversity—of country, of commissioning agency, of specific subject—notwithstanding. With few exceptions, these studies have a common framework, a common approach, and a common methodology. Given their shared starting points, their common findings are not surprising. African education is in crisis. Governments cannot cope. Quality has deteriorated. Funds are misallocated. Management is poor and administration is inefficient. From predominantly Islamic Mauritania in the western Sahara to the mixed cultural, colonial, and political heritage of Mauritius in the Indian Ocean, the recommendations too are similar: Reduce the central government role in providing education. Decentralize. Increase school fees. Expand private schooling. Reduce direct support to students, especially at the tertiary level. Introduce double shifts and multigrade classrooms. Assign high priority to instructional materials. Favor in-service over pre-service teacher education. The shared approach of these studies reflects a medical metaphor. Expatriate-led study teams as visiting clinicians diagnose and then prescribe. The patient (i.e., the country) must be encouraged, perhaps pressured, to swallow the bitter medicine" ("Which Priorities and Strategies," 51).

68. Boaventura de Sousa Santos, "Processos da globalização."

69. See, e.g., Boaventura de Sousa Santos, *Toward a New Common Sense: Law, Science, and Politics in the Paradigmatic Transition* (London: Routledge, 1995); and "Por uma concepção multicultural dos direitos humanos," *Revista crítica de ciências sociais* 48 (1997): 11–32.

70. Boaventura de Sousa Santos, "Por uma concepção multicultural," 15.

71. Being a more recent event and constituting an important turning point in the understanding of the U.N. role in the new world order, it would be interesting to conduct a similar case study on the struggle of East Timorese people and the process leading to international recognition of their right to self-determination and independence.

72. McMichael, *Development and Social Change*, 256–57.

73. Boaventura de Sousa Santos, *Reinventar a democracia* (Lisbon: Gradiva/Fundação Mário Soares), 46.

74. Alain Touraine, "Nous entrons dans une civilisation du travail," Comunicação apresentada ao XIV Congresso Mundial de Sociologia, Montréal, 26 Julho–1 Agosto 1998. First version, not revised by the author.

75. Boaventura de Sousa Santos, *Reinventar a democracia*, 66.

76. Boaventura de Sousa Santos, *Reinventar a democracia*, 67.

77. Jürgen Habermas, *Droit et démocratie: Entre faits et normes* (Paris: Gallimard, 1997), 479.

78. This concept of enzyme is developed in Grupo de Lisboa, *Limites à competição* (Lisbon: Europa-América).

79. Raymond Allen Morrow and Carlos Alberto Torres, "Jürgen Habermas, Paulo Freire e a pedagogia crítica: Novas orientações para a educação comparada," *Educação, Sociedade & Culturas* 10 (1998): 129.

80. The concept of *structural place* was developed by Boaventura de Sousa Santos in *Toward a New Common Sense*: "At the most abstract level, a mode of production of social practice is a set of social relations whose internal contradictions endow it with a specific endogenous dynamic" (p. 420).

81. Paulo Freire, *Política e Educação* (Sao Paulo: Cortez), 36.

10

Constructing the Sociology of Education as a Unique Discipline:

The Cases of Mainland China and Taiwan

Jason C. Chang and Zhang Renjie

The sociology of education has gradually gained recognition as an academic discipline in both Mainland China and Taiwan over the past two or three decades. This is not to say that previously there was no interest in building a bridge between sociology and educational research in China. In fact, some Chinese academics had already brought about advances in so-called educational sociology during the first half of the twentieth century. Constrictions, however, created by the political split between Mainland China and Taiwan in 1949 caused these endeavors to stagnate. It was not until the 1970s that a field entitled "the sociology of education" emerged and took shape.[1] Since being reinstated a few decades ago, the field of sociology of education has been growing stronger and an increasing number of scholars have been entering it on both sides of the Straits. Not only have institutions of higher learning incorporated it as a unique discipline into their undergraduate and graduate programs, professional organizations have been set up to promote regular academic interchanges. Furthermore, it can be seen from time to time how the work of Cross-Straits (a general term describing both Mainland China and Taiwan) sociologists of education has impacted educational policies and practices.

While pleased with these accomplishments, sociologists of education from either side of the Straits are not complacent. Generally speaking, like sociologists of education in most developing countries, they want to go beyond a borrowed sociology of education, that is, merely copying and transplanting Western sociology of education. Most feel they should craft a distinctive sociology of education that suits their own social contexts. For example, Mainland scholars Ma and Gao (1998, 52–77) and Taiwan scholars Lee and Chang (1999) recently highlighted this issue, debating about how to best locate their respective sociology of education in the dialectics of internationalization and

211

indigenization (these terms are used by Mainland and Taiwan scholars in a way similar to globalization and localization, yet not totally the same). On November 19–23, 2000, Mainland China's National Council on Sociology of Education held its sixth Biennial Conference at Nanjing Normal University. As "internationalization and indigenization" and "methodology" were major themes, the Taiwan Association for Sociology of Education sent a delegation to take part in deliberations. Accordingly, it seems clear that both sides of the Straits face the common task of overhauling the sociology of education in accordance with their respective historical specificity, so as to create disciplines characterized by both worldwide standards and local effectivity.

This chapter aims at examining the overall development of the sociology of education in Mainland China and Taiwan. In order to provide a better understanding of the shifts in disciplinary framework, theoretical paradigms, methodology, and research topics, the authors selectively and critically reviewed pertinent reports and some major works, including books, journal articles, and research monographs, which were published or released by key sociologists of education from both sides of the Straits. Our analysis is organized into four parts and presented in the following sequence: (1) the emergence of sociological applications to education in Chinese society prior to 1949, (2) the construction of sociology of education as a unique discipline in Mainland China and Taiwan from 1949 to the present, (3) the relationship between sociology of education communities and the educational revamping praxes on both sides of the Straits, and (4) some controversial issues concerned with the future outlook for Cross-Straits studies in the sociology of education.

BRIEF HISTORY BEFORE 1949

Scholars on both sides of the Straits (Lee 1996; Wu 1998, 47; Gao 1993) agree that Tao Menghe (1888–1960), the late Beijing University professor and vice president of the Chinese Academy of Social Sciences, pioneered research in China on how society and education affect each other. His work *Society and Education* (Tao 1922) was the first book in Chinese to systematically discuss the relationship between education and society. Its publication marked the emergence of a new area of study and encouraged scholars to devote themselves to this field.

As of 1949, advancements were made on three major fronts (Gao 1993, 101–2; Ma and Gao 1998, 56–58), first, the translation of important works from the West. For instance, Tao's *Society and Education* was primarily based on F. R. Clow's *Principles of Sociology with Educational Applications* (1920) and the chapters on theoretical foundations of W. R. Smith's *An Introduction to Educational Sociology* (1917). The part concerned with practical applications in Smith's work was later translated and published in 1925 by Chen Qitian and entitled *Applied Educational Sociology*. Second, over twenty quality textbooks and academic works were compiled. In addition to that of Tao, other important works included Lei (1931), Shen and Wu (1931), Chen Qitian (1933), Lu (1934), and Chen Kemei (1947). Third, courses related to this new discipline were provided at some schools, including comprehensive universities and teacher education institutions.

An overview of the research conducted in this period reveals that, while some scholars tended to employ sociological knowledge to analyze the relationship between education and society as well as the process of education itself, there existed a disposition of integrating sociological and educational theories to extend new insights to cover what psychology (especially the so-called individualistic psychology) had fallen short in explaining educational practice (Gao 1993, 105–6; Ma and Gao 1998, 60). On the whole, the construction of the discipline by that time was basically normative in nature regardless of the route taken.

Regarding this point, we can get a general idea of what it meant from definitions applied to the discipline by some prominent scholars during this period. For example, Tao (1922) suggested that researchers apply materials, methods, and principles from sociology to inquire into the relationship between society and education and use the results to solve problems in education. Lu (1934) contended that this discipline should, through the lens of sociology, explore the relationships between education and other social institutions and look into ways to reform education. Chen Kemei (1947) believed that, as a science aimed at investigating the interaction between education and society, it has two main missions; first, to study the educational objectives of various social groups and, second, to probe the social objectives of education.

The reason that they proposed a new intellectual project in such a normative sense might have something to do with an ameliorative appeal to "save the nation through education." Chinese intelligentsia endeavored to realize this ideal during the first half of twentieth century to lift up their fellow countrymen who had been subjected to all types of chaos and devastation as the new nation struggled to build itself. It is not odd, therefore, to see scholars of that time urging the use of educational sociology "to dissect China's educational and social problems (such as crime, population quality, poverty, educational opportunity, and democracy), in hopes of finding ways to save the impoverished, the unenlightened, and the disadvantaged, and thereby save the nation via education" (Ma and Gao 1998, 61).

The normative shape can also be revealed from the methods these scholars used to accomplish their work. Despite the fact that they understood the necessity of applying surveys and statistics in carrying out research, they performed very little empirical study. Most continued to focus their analysis on historical records (Gao 1993, 106–7; Ma and Gao 1998, 60–61). In sum, although it is obvious that some progress in connecting educational research with sociology had certainly been made in pre-1949 China, we can hardly say that these pioneer scholars had already established a unique discipline in the modern scientific sense. Just as Wu (1998, 48) has argued, it resembled more a social philosophy of education and, moreover, its construct was simply a Chinese version of what existed in the West.

POST-1949 DEVELOPMENTS

China experienced civil war after World War II. The Chinese Socialists under Mao Ze Dong seized power in 1949, forcing Chiang Kai-shek's Nationalist government to relocate to Taiwan. This divided state of affairs has continued to the present and, with changes in government and an upsurge in indigenization in Taiwan, is growing in complexity.

As to sociology of education developments, while various schools of thought in Western societies were bustling with progress for the first twenty to thirty years after World War II, the situation in Mainland China and Taiwan was relatively stagnant. First of all, following in the steps of the Soviet Union, sociology in Mainland China fell into disgrace after 1949. In 1952, a nationwide teaching and research unit restructuring program removed sociology and related disciplines from institutions of higher learning. Government leaders with a biased understanding of sociology further made sociology off-limits during the Anti-Rightist Movement of the 1950s. Recommendations to reinstate sociology met with immediate criticism as they were seen as attempts to restore capitalism (Ma and Gao 1998, 62 and footnotes). It was not until 1979 that this situation saw improvement. In post-1949 Taiwan, some scholars who had worked in educational sociology in China, including Chen Qitian, Lu Shaoji, and Su Xiangyu, relocated to Taiwan with the Nationalist government. Since Taiwan schools did not offer classes in the subject at that time, they were unable to continue their research. Su Xiangyu, for example, later retired from teaching in the Taiwan University Psychology Department (Lee 1996, 99). Research in the target field got started in the early 1960s, when junior teachers colleges (or junior normal colleges as usually used by Taiwan educators, composed of three-year late secondary education and two-year tertiary education) began offering courses, though by and large course instructors still taught "educational sociology." A sociology of education with its modern connotations did not appear until after 1970. Developments in the discipline in both Mainland China and Taiwan are discussed in more detail below.

Mainland China

The sociology of education in Mainland China shared a fate similar to that of sociology. When sociology was reinstated in 1979, the sociology of education was also revived during this same year with the commencement of compilation of works to address developments, contents, and research orienta-tions of sociology of education in other countries.[2] In December 1981, the ed-itorial division of the periodical *Educational Research* of the Central Research Institute of Educational Science cohosted a symposium with the Research In-stitute of Sociology of the Chinese Academy of Social Sciences. Sociologists and educators were invited to share their views on the agenda regarding the reconstruction of the sociology of education[3]. As a result of this meeting, some scholars, especially those in education, began deliberating on the is-sues of recommencing teaching and research programs in sociology of edu-cation (Wu 1998, 48–49). With that, China launched the rebuilding of the dis-cipline.

First, in regard to the institutional aspect of the discipline construction, Nanjing Normal University led the way by offering classes in sociology of ed-ucation in February 1982. A number of normal universities (a traditional term used in Chinese societies to name the professional universities of education, which prepare secondary school teachers and related professionals) and some independent teachers colleges (four-year institutions of higher educa-tion that train preschool and primary teachers) followed suit. Shortly after-ward, Nanjing Normal University, Huadong (or East China) Normal Univer-sity, Beijing Normal University, and Hangzhou University began enrolling students into their sociology of education master's programs. Nanjing Nor-mal University and Huadong Normal University later received permission to offer doctoral programs in sociology of education.[4] In April 1989, Mainland China's first academic organization for this discipline, the National Council on Sociology of Education, was established in Hangzhou.[5] The first chairper-son elected was Professor Zhang Renjie and he continues to hold the position to the present. In November 1991, the council began to issue the *Sociology of Education Newsletter*, which was created to facilitate internal academic ex-change among its members, on a nonscheduled basis. If the offering of classes in colleges, the setting up of professional organizations, and the publishing of academic journals are seen as the criteria for the evaluation of a new disci-pline at the institutional level, then the process of rebuilding a sociology of education in Mainland China is now basically complete.

Concurrent with these institutional accomplishments were significant ad-vances in disciplinary foundations manifested for the most part in the fol-lowing three areas: First, the discussion of historical developments and the current status of the sociology of education in relevant developed countries. Examples of this include "Developments and Characteristics of Western So-ciology of Education" by Li (1983) and "Three Major Schools of Thought in Contemporary European and American Sociology of Education" by Wu (1986); second, the compilation of important works in the field of sociology of education, such as *Fundamental Readings in Foreign Sociology of Education* edited by Zhang (1989); third, the publication of sociology of education text-books and lexicographical works written by Mainland scholars themselves.[6]

Furthermore, many studies were carried out in the various subfields of sociology of education during the rebuilding period. According to *The Encyclopedia of Chinese Education: Collected Readings in Modern Educational Theories*, edited by Gu (1994), the studies in sociology of education selected from 1979 to 1991 by the collection can be divided into the following 14 categories: (1) subjects and methods of sociology of education, (2) technological revolution and education, (3) democracy and education, (4) culture and education, (5) population and education, (6) social stratification and education, (7) social change and education, (8) social problems and education, (9) the future and education, (10) socialization and education, (11) sociological analysis of school organization, (12) sociological analysis of classrooms, (13) sociological analysis of school successes and failures, and (14) reviews of sociology of education research in different countries. It is believed that these endeavors have laid a firm foundation for the steady progress of Mainland China's sociology of education, including its teaching and research.

As usually held, the most important measures of judging progress attained in a discipline like sociology of education are the breadth and depth of studies. These generally hinge, however, on the fundamental elements of the field itself, including disciplinary framework as well as built-in attributes and methodology. It is not surprising, then, that Mainland China's newly established sociology of education has placed a great deal of emphasis on these elements. Almost all of the National Council on Sociology of Education's biennial conferences, for instance, included these elements in their agendas.

As to disciplinary framework, most Mainland scholars have been engaged, to various degrees, with the modification of it in their writings. The majority of them did so on a minor or partial basis. Sometimes they added chapters to meet social changes, such as "New Telecommunications and Individual Socialization" and "Globalization and Education." Other times they reconsidered topics that seemed to stir no debate, such as "Sociology of Teachers" and "Family, School, and Students." Some scholars, nevertheless, sought to completely overhaul the field. To cite a recent, high-profile example, Wu (1998) wrote his book *The Sociology of Education* based on the concept that education is a subsystem of society. He attempted to delineate the overall structure of the discipline "sociology of education" in accordance with this perspective. His basic ideas are that, as a specific social subsystem, (1) the existence and operation of the education system must be interwoven with and circumscribed by the external social milieu at large; (2) the education system should have its own social structure and process internally; and (3) the education system is bound to impact outer society to a certain extent. He, therefore, advocates a sociology of education composed on four parts and organized in the following sequence: "The Theoretical Foundations of the Discipline," "Social Environment of Education," "Social Systems within Education," and "Social Functions of Education." Taiwan scholars Lee and Chang (1999, 293) critique this method of dealing with the discipline as similar to the "input-processing-output" model and, as such, it seems to have a logical framework. However, they continue, it obviously overlooks the "feedback" that is necessary for the inspection of the functioning of educational praxes and hence the transformation of it into new "input" resources.

As to built-in attributes, when sociology of education was first reinstated in Mainland China (before 1989), the focus was on whether or not it was a branch of education or of sociology, or a relatively independent, interdisciplinary field of study. The whole debate centered around not only the interrelationships of sociology of education, educational science, and sociology, but on whether or not the sociology of education is a "normative discipline," an "empirical discipline," or a "combination of the two." In other words, the entire controversy was concerned with the purpose and methodology of the sociology of education.

The debate lasted to the late 1990s and inspired the following view in 1999: "It behooves us to reflect upon many of the issues that emerged in the past 20 years during which the sociology of education was being restored. A mainstream view has never appeared in regards to the nature of sociology of education. In the sociology of education community, we find advocates of the 'normative' and the 'empirical' as well as those who support 'a combination of the two'" (Fang et al. 2000, 75). The authors believe that the holding of differing views is reasonable and healthy. Learning would suffocate otherwise (of course, the argumentation needs to be knowledge-based to be fruitful). We feel that the most important thing for Mainland China in this present stage is to endeavor to explore the possible directions of the sociology of education, instead of hoping one "mainstream" emerges to dominate. It is our profound hope that the key elements of the discipline, such as its framework, nature, and methodology, become clearer and sounder with advances in teaching and research.

Since 1979, the rank and file of sociologists of education in Mainland China has gradually increased in number. Furthermore, the scope of their research has expanded and the quality improved. Young scholars trained in the sociology of education are gradually becoming the backbone of the discipline. These trends became more marked after the publication (from October of 1999 on) of the Sociology of Education Series edited by Lu Jie and Wu Kangning of Nanjing Normal University. The first books in this series included *Sociology of the Curriculum, Sociology of the Classroom Teaching, Sociology of the Family Education,* and *Sociology of the Campus Life.* The following titles are scheduled for publication at later dates—*Theories and Methods of Sociology of Education, Sociology of Moral Education, Sociology of the Classroom, Sociology of Teachers, Sociology of School Organization, Sociology of Examination, Sociology of Regional Education,* and *Sociology of Information Network Education.* In sum, we feel that, in view of the above, the sociology of education in Mainland China has finally graduated from its initial stage during which the major emphasis was on the general introduction of the discipline as a whole, with minor emphasis on inquiries into the subfields, to a stage in which the emphasis has been completely turned around (Wu 1999, general preface, 2).

Taiwan

During the first five or six decades of the twentieth century, sociology of education research was almost nonexistent in Taiwan. It was not until 1960 that the president of Taichung Junior Teachers College and later Minister of Education Chu Hui-sen (1911) began promoting it by suggesting that it be made a required course for junior teachers colleges because of its value in teacher training. This marked the beginning of teaching and doing research in the sociology of education in Taiwan. Developments in Taiwan's sociology of education since then can be divided into three stages.[7] The first period or "initial stage" took place in the 1960s; the second "foundation-laying period" between 1970 and the mid-1980s; the current third or "expanding period" in the mid-1980s, specifically following the lifting of martial law in 1987.

In the 1960s, the initial stage of rebuilding the sociology of education, books related to this field were published for the first time ever in Taiwan (e.g., Chu 1963; Yin 1965; Tsao 1965) to meet local teacher training needs. By and large, research during this period consisted of organizing related literatures from the United States, Japan, and pre-1949 Mainland China for the purpose of writing introductory textbooks to satisfy the instructional needs of junior teachers colleges. Although scholars of the time recognized the importance of the scientific method, they seldom conducted empirical studies. This is due in part possibly to the fact that they were hampered by the lack of quantitative data in Taiwan during the initial stage and partly because of the relatively normative educational sociology tradition they inherited. Consequently, instead of a firm foundation built on empirical evidence that characterized their counterparts in the West, their contributions were limited to general "theoretical statements" (Lee and Chang 1999, 306). While these general theoretical statements might exist on paper only, research by Weng (1999, II-V-2~II-V-6) reveals that the sociology of education was not yet fully understood in Taiwan of the 1960s. Many works concerned with topics outside of this field, such as the welfare state, social education, school social work, divorce, and young romance, were listed under the title of this discipline in library's *Education Index*. Moreover, even papers dealing with psychology were included. The most probable reason for these misunderstandings is that the scope of the sociology of education was still ambiguous during the initial stage.

Entering the 1970s, the sociology of education in Taiwan was finally established on a scientific foundation. The leading figure of this period was the late professor Lin Ching-jiang (1940–1999), who held the office of minister of education during the last two years of his life. Other prominent figures include Taiwan Normal University Professor Chen Kuei-hsi and Kaohsiung Normal University Professor Lin Sheng-chuan. In 1970, Lin Ching-jiang wrote a paper pointing out five research areas in the sociology of education, including the social process and education, social structure and education, social changes and education, the social structure of schools and the relationship between school and community, and sociology of teaching. In 1972, when the discipline was made a required course in education departments in Taiwan universities, he published his influential book *Sociology of Education*. In addition to the above five areas, he added an introductory chapter in this book to delineate the meaning, development, and research methodology of sociology of education. Taiwan sociologists of education today recognize his as the first book defining disciplinary framework and initiating empirical research in the sociology of education in Taiwan.

Regarding disciplinary framework, we are not saying that everything was settled once Lin Ching-jiang defined the scope of sociology of education in Taiwan; rather that, at least in this second stage, most later research carried out in the sociology of education was carried out on the foundation he laid. As a matter of fact, the framework has gradually been enlarged and enriched by succeeding scholars in accordance with world trends and local advances in sociology of education studies. To cite an example, when Lin Ching-jiang (1972) first discussed "sociology of teaching," his arguments centered around the roles, groups, and status of teachers. Later, he (1979, 149–50) suggested that the theoretical framework of a sociology of teaching should encompass six categories: (1) analysis of the social functions of schools, (2) analysis of the relationship between teachers and students in schools, (3) analysis of the relationships among school organization, school culture, and teaching, (4) analysis of the community environment and the contexts of teaching in schools, (5) analysis of the roles of teachers and the characteristics of teachers' groups, and (6) research into the approaches for integrating sociology of teaching and instructional psychology. Discussions by Chen Kuei-hsi (1980) and Lin Sheng-chuan (1982), scholars representative of the foundation-laying period, almost never went beyond the scope marked out by these six categories. Chen, however, added another category: "patterns of classroom teaching." Later, when relevant research data was more readily available in Taiwan, they and their students supplemented various views to various degrees dealing with topics that they had neglected or had not yet fully discussed, such as sociology of educational knowledge and its implications for curriculum, teaching, and assessment (e.g., Lin Ching-jiang 1996; Chen Kuei-hsi et al. 1995; Chen Kuei-hsi 1998).

As to the empirical orientation of research, scholars of the foundation-laying stage, e.g., Lin Ching-jiang and Chen Kuei-hsi, did not exclusively reject the normative tradition, probably because they were education majors. Nonetheless, they all stressed that research in the sociology of education must adhere to scientific trends. Their works, therefore, usually contained official statistics, the quantitative analysis of others, as well as their own survey results. Lin Sheng-chuan, in particular, used a great deal of advanced inferential statistics in his research reports. With their positivist disposition, scholars of the foundation-laying period had another characteristic in common, that is, they unanimously believed in the structural functionalist consensus point of view. One possible reason for this is that they were passing on what they had learned, which in turn was from the same school of thought[8]; another is the staunch anticommunist political ideology of Taiwan at the time. During this time, it was forbidden to expound on theories related in any way to Marxism. Therefore, it is not surprising to see statements like "the consensus theory seems to suit the actual situation of Taiwanese society" (Chen Kuei-hsi 1990, 33) and "although the conflict model can augment our knowledge concerning the methodology of sociology of education, it is of no practical value in Taiwan" (Lin Sheng-chuan 1982, 24). Generally speaking, along the line of structural functionalism and positivist empiricism, the founding scholars of this stage strove to establish a disciplinary framework for the field, and the majority of their work as well as that of their followers focused on topics like educational opportunity equality, educational stratification, the status and roles of teachers, student (sub)culture, and student–teacher relationships (Lee and Chang 1999, 315).

Since the mid-1980s, especially since the lifting of martial law in 1987, Taiwan has experienced a surge in political-social movements and cultural flows. Sociology of education research entered its expanding period under such circumstances and has drawn an increasing number of talented scholars from younger generations during the past fifteen years or so. After searching the database of dissertation index at the Central Library in Taiwan, Tang (1999) discovered 209 doctorate and masters theses in sociology of education had been written between 1983, the year the library started keeping files of this sort, and 1999. The number of theses proliferated after 1987 and continued to grow steadily throughout the 1990s. With the rise in number of researchers, the topics under investigation have been expanded in both breadth and depth. For example, in addition to social class, some scholars began to discuss issues of educational stratification in terms of race and gender. While some others have approached curriculum issues from the perspective of sociology of knowledge, there are still some interested in examining policy issues on the base of a critical sociology of education. These new topics have been brought together in the book *Modern Sociology of Education* edited by Chen Kuei-hsi (1998).

There are two main differences in the construction of the discipline when compared with the previous stage. First, structural functionalism is no longer the sole agent. Chen Kuei-hsi's paper "Trends in the Sociology of Education" (1986), Chen Bo-chang's books on hidden curriculum (1987) and ideology (1988), and the translation work on sociological theories of education by Lee Jin-hsu (1987) triggered the discussion and argumentation of many "new" theories in Taiwan. Scholars have reviewed almost any theory that has ever existed, including Marxism, feminism, postmodernism, Weberian theory, reproduction theory, resistance theory, critical theory, dramaturgical theory, structuration theory, ethnomethodology, and so on. Second, quantitative empirical paradigm no longer acts alone. Simply put, if sociology can be categorized by its methodology into three distinctive traditions—empirical, interpretative, and critical (Huang Jui-chi 1996)—then we can find, in Taiwan's sociology of education circles during the expanding stage, some adherents who continued to support empiricism, while others espoused either interpretative or critical sociology. Many a scholar used more than one method to complete their research. It would sometimes seem arbitrary, therefore, to label the researchers as quantitative or qualitative in their orientations (Lee and Chang 1999).

Finally, it is worth mentioning that sociologists of education in Taiwan did not enjoy a professional association or journal of their own until the turn of the twenty-first century. With the growing number of researchers and the improving quality of their research since the 1980s, scholars dedicated to this field felt it increasingly difficult to form academic identity and make academic exchanges being as they were attached to other associations. For this reason, two unofficial gatherings were held in 1992 and 1993, but they were inconclusive as nobody was in charge. It was not until May 1999 under the impetus of the Graduate Institute of Education of Chung Cheng University that the first meeting of Taiwan Forum on Sociology of Education was convened. It was decided that this forum-style symposium would be held semiannually. Following suit, the Taiwan Association for Sociology of Education was finally established in Taipei in June 2000 with Professor Chen Kuei-hsi presiding. After its formation, the association both took over forum business and founded the semiannual *Taiwan Journal of Sociology of Education* issued for the first time in June 2001. With this, all the basic work necessary to establishing the sociology of education as a discipline was finally completed and, accordingly, the sociology of education in Taiwan entered a new era.

CONNECTING RESEARCH AND POLICY

After World War II, Western sociologists of education, concerned with maintaining the academic purity of their field, seldom focused research on the improvement of educational practices. Even with the gradual increase in the prevalence of sociology of educational policies since 1980, some were still worried that the field might become practically oriented (e.g., Shilling 1993). In comparison, despite the fact that they, too, had been debating the elimination of a normative educational sociology, Mainland China and Taiwan sociologists of education have never been able to entirely purge its influence. Lin Ching-jiang (1981, 9), for example, feels that "without research into 'what should be', the analysis of 'what it is' is of no use; without finding out 'what it is', the principles and rules of 'what should be' are simply empty talk. These two ways of thinking can complement each other." For many scholars on both sides of the Straits, it is not incompatible to consider practical applications when carrying out basic research in sociology of education.

Three major models have evolved in Mainland China and Taiwan for connecting research and policy: First, sociologists of education, hoping to exert a positive influence, are becoming increasingly concerned with educational policies. As Zhang (1996) once contended, part of the authentic value of educational research, which includes the sociology of education, is embedded in "providing educational policy-making with a scientific basis and forward-looking insights," instead of "simply expounding on what some 'government official' has said." In other words, while paying attention to educational policies, sociologists of education must firmly maintain their professional standing. Furthermore, the objective of their research, or more specifically, the sociological analysis of educational policy, is to constructively criticize and challenge policies rather than blindly glorify them or rubber-stamp them. Since research of this kind demands clear and concrete evidence, it usually examines ongoing policies or those already done. Weng's review (1996) of Taiwan's teacher education reforms and Chang's critique (2000a) of the indigenization-based policy of local studies programs in Taiwan are typical examples.

Second, sociologists of education are being consulted more and more by policy makers to provide professional viewpoints to help form better policies. This is because in today's society, all things related to the public good as well as personal rights ultimately need to be made transparent. Policy making behind closed doors will no longer stand up against challenges. An increasing number of policy makers on both sides of the Straits, therefore, are coming to realize that policies must have a foundation supported by deliberate research and more and more sociologists of education are being consulted or are commissioned to carry out policy research related to their specialty. Consultation and research of this type are generally carried out in advance of or during the formulation of education bills or development plans. For example, it was under the recommendation of scholars that "Modernizing Educational Research" was incorporated into the original draft of the Guangdong Provincial Education Modernization Index System. To site another example, work in educational reform for Taiwan's indigenous peoples over the past few years has benefited a great deal from the expertise offered by sociologists of education like Tan (1998) and Chang (2000b).

Third, education policy makers and sociologists of education are carrying out joint research to realize educational programs. This connection is usually initiated when the government plans to promote relatively large-scale education or curriculum experiments. For example, Mainland sociologist of education Zhang headed a special project by Mainland China's Ministry of Education entitled "An Experimental Research on the Integrated Liberal Arts

Curriculum of General Senior High Schools in Guangdong Province." The research team consisted of education policy makers, curriculum-theory specialists, instructional-theory specialists, and schoolteachers. With almost no "reference framework," this group established a teaching material system of integrated liberal arts in terms of major subsystems of society following recommendation and discussion from team members. Completed over a period of over four years, the research results, scheduled for publication in 2001, are divided into four parts: theories, teaching materials, experiments, and related data. The research findings show that 24.3 percent of students surveyed were "very interested," while 74.3 percent, for a total of 98.6 percent in positive answers, were "interested" in teaching materials in "contemporary Chinese society" (Zhang and Feng 1999).

In addition to the three models described above, Taiwan does something that is indeed rare in the world, that is, sociologists of education are directly responsible for formulating and implementing education policies. As mentioned above, Chu Hui-sen in the initial period and Lin Ching-jiang in the foundation-laying period held the office of minister of education in charge of the highest-ranking educational policy-making organ. Lin Ching-jiang, in particular, took full advantage of the opportunity to put into practice his sociology of education viewpoints. According to his student and a leading figure during the expanding period Chen Bo-chang (2000), the education reform measures based on Lin Ching-jiang's sociology of education viewpoints and implemented during his term in office (1998–1999) can be divided into five main categories: First, establishing recurrent education and community college systems to promote lifelong education; second, creating more channels for entering late and postsecondary schools to reform the distorted college entrance examination system; third, realizing concrete plans to equalize educational opportunities by improving education for indigenous peoples as well as those with special needs; fourth, setting up a multichannel lifelong in-service education system for teachers to reinforce their professional knowledge; fifth, reforming curriculum and instruction by drawing up a nine-year primary and early secondary school curriculum, carrying out comprehensive high school curriculum experiments, and reducing class sizes. Despite his passing away, the policies formulated during his term are still being implemented. For instance, with the concerted efforts of education policy makers and a research group led by Chen Bo-chang, the nine-year primary and early secondary school curriculum is scheduled to be enacted in the fall of 2001.

CONCLUSION

A comprehensive observation of the evolution of Cross-Straits' sociology of education since the 1970s shows that, although it has indeed made headway and things are starting to take shape, it is undeniable that we have a great deal of work before us, especially when compared to the West. While the West has been able to compile large volumes of work beginning in 1971 (Ball 2000), we are still awaiting the advent of more quality research (Ma and Gao 1998; Lee and Chang 1999; Tang 1999). While some say that Western sociology of education has left the fringes to join mainstream sociology or social sciences (Saha 1997), we are concerned that its counterpart here might still be marginalized (Tang 1999). While the West has shown solid work in exploring new theoretical perspectives (Torres and Mitchell 1998), we are still unduly emphasizing quoting and transplanting (Weng 1999; Tang 1999), structural functionalism (Lee and Chang 1999), and social philosophical statements (Wu 1998, 50). While sociology of education in the West has incorporated various research approaches (Noblit and Pink 1995), we are still promoting empirical studies (as in Mainland China) (Ma and Gao 1998) or encouraging researchers to engage in exploring methodological issues (as in Taiwan) (Lee and Chang 1999). As Western sociology of education has experienced a number of paradigm wars and the interdisciplinary trend has blurred its boundaries (Ball 2000, xxxi), we are searching for disciplinary borders and identities (Fang 2000; Lee and Chang 1999).

In view of the above comparisons, Cross-Straits' sociology of education appears relatively immature and seems to be bogged down at the "primary level." But when we look at how it is thriving, we believe it to be a very promising field. To further complete its disciplinary construction, four areas of work deserve our attention.

Dialogue between Sociologists and Educators

Most Cross-Straits' sociology of education research has been done by educators working at teacher education institutions (Ma and Gao 1998; Tang 1999; Luo 1987). Sociologists involved in this field, as increasing in number, are employed for the most part in comprehensive or research-type universities.[9] The difference between the unique tasks of institutions to which sociologists and educators each belong, plus the less than satisfactory amount of interaction between them, contributes to the impression that sociology of education headed by sociologists is theory minded, and that headed by educators is more practical. Some scholars have attempted to clarify and reconcile this dualism (Lee 2000). In fact, when we view sociology of education developments over the past few decades, sociologists have not necessarily concerned themselves with basic or empirical studies; nor have educators only dealt with applied or normative studies. This is especially true following the emergence and prevalence of interpretative theory, critical theory, poststructuralism, postmodernism, and postcolonialism. The line between research paradigms adopted by sociologists and educators is no longer obvious. Moreover, the rise of policy sociology makes it increasingly possible that the theoretical and practical purposes of sociology of education will eventually be reconciled (Whitty 1997). Consequently, Mainland China and Taiwan should begin emphasizing dialogue between sociologists and educators in sociology of education research. It should not, however, become an excuse for debating how many types of sociology of education there are or which is more "correct"; rather, it should facilitate the sharing of viewpoints and specialties. They should build on this knowledge to avoid misunderstandings and boost cooperation, while finding new topics and adding vitality to sociology of education research on both sides of the Straits.

Dialogue between Macro-orientation and Micro-orientation

Influenced by American sociology, research in the sociology of education on both sides of the Straits has been conventionally categorized as either macro- or micro-oriented. The macro-oriented approach discussed the operation of social structure and its relation to education while making references to either the consensus or the conflict theories. The micro-oriented approach, on the other hand, makes use of branches of interpretative theory and symbolic interactionism to analyze social interaction within schools and its relation to teaching and learning. This division of labor started out well enough but grew to impress some scholars as partial and biased. The reason, they maintain, is that the macrosocial structure and the microinteraction process correspond to each other; when cut abruptly in half, each succeeds in partially facilitating research work but fails to reveal the whole picture. In fact, the consensus and conflict theories can also serve the purpose of explaining social interactions, such as that between teachers and students at the microlevel, while interpretative theory falls nothing short of reflecting social structure, such as social class at the macrolevel. The problem at hand, therefore, is to reinforce dialogue between the macro- and microorientations to strike a balance between the two. In this respect, Collins's (1981) efforts on locating the microfoundations for macro sociology, Ritzer's (1996, 487–561) ponderings on the integration of macro and micro orientations, and Lee and Chang's (1999) attempt to link up macro and micro perspectives with the social functions of education as the meso-dimension are all worth further consideration. Also, the way European sociology deals with the issues of opposition and integration between structure and agency, as shown in the structuration theory or in the dialectics between reproduction theory and resistance theory, might point to another direction in which we can manage to cross the border between macro- and microorientations.

Dialogue between Quantitative Research and Qualitative Research

The debate as to whether quantitative or qualitative research is "better" has been a point of contention across the Straits for the past decade or so. As we see it, this debate is pointless since different methods have different origins, functions, and limitations. Attacks on other research methods brought about by a lack of understanding of their epistemological foundations are detrimental to academic research. Generally speaking, quantitative research echoes an etic viewpoint that owes its origins to positivist empiricism and focuses on inferring abstract generalizations by directly quoting or modifying present theories. Qualitative research, on the other hand, implies an emic point of view which is derived from interpretative paradigms and stresses the understanding of specific contexts through directly stepping into or participating in the living world to grasp meanings. Imagine, if you will, two types of researchers—outsiders and insiders. The former might consist of university professors while the latter of schoolteachers. They share an interest in exploring gender interaction of students in the schoolteacher's school. These two type of researchers, however, may choose to apply either an etic or emic perspective in their research. When combined, as shown in Lee and Chang (1999), we could come up with an ideal type consisting of four research approach categories: outsider-etic, insider-etic, outsider-emic, and insider-emic. Although no single method adequate for dealing with all topics exists, we can employ each of these approaches to bring forth a critical dialogue on the target scenario, say, the gender interaction of students. These, then, might act as different windows or paths enabling us to attain a multifaceted and closer look at the phenomenon. We sincerely hope the encounters of the positivist or quantitative research and the interpretative or qualitative research in Cross-Straits' sociology of education proceed in this manner so as to complement each other and converge existing theories and changing practices. This is obviously a long-term goal.

Dialogue between Internationalization and Indigenization

Research in sociology of education across the Straits has followed for the most part in the wake of Western trends since the 1970s (or possibly even from as early as the pre-1949 period). It has only been in recent years that scholars on both sides of the Straits have started indigenizing the sociology of education. Take the ever-mounting credentialism for example. We can explain this peculiar kind of populism in Chinese societies, which overemphasizes getting into the best schools and climbing to the highest rung possible on the ladder of education, with the Western ideas such as meritocracy and human capital theory. Yet we cannot overlook the importance of the roles played by traditional Chinese respect for "intelligentsia gentry" and traditional Chinese culture of "family face" (Tang 1999). Therefore, more and more scholars believe that sociology of education research has to be conducted within the specific historical-cultural contexts of societies to keep it from losing its identity and subjectivity to its Western counterparts. In so doing, however, we do not mean to reject or exclude Western-based theories. Indigenization is not equivalent to seclusion, nor is localization synonymous with self-satisfied ultraconservatism. We are simply trying to improve our understanding of our own educational praxes by taking into account our unique histories and social realities. Living in an age of globalization, it is especially difficult to steer clear of outside influences, let alone our own interest in transferring our influence to other parts of the world by winning international recognition for our accomplishments. Therefore, we need to keep abreast of global trends, even as indigenization continues to take root. This does not mean blindly following the lead or hanging on to the coattails of the West; rather, it is to widen our horizons to facilitate communication and to keep pace with this ever evolving world. That is why in almost all of meetings of the Taiwan Forum on Sociology of Education over the past two years, a point has been made to invite globally renowned sociologists of education, such as Michael Apple, Peter McLaren, Carlos Torres, Geoff Whitty, and Michael Young. Their participation ensures a dialogue between internationalization and indigenization.

One last thing, we believe that dialogue between sociologists of education on either side of the Straits should be increased. Over the past ten years or so, we have opened up contact, visited each other, and co-compiled a *Reading* (Li, Bai, and Lee 1992). In November 2000, the mainland's National Council on Sociology of Education asked the Taiwan Association for Sociology of Education to send a delegation to participate in its biennial conference in Nanking. The two sides reached agreements on the exchange of information, cooperation in research, and regular visits. This coauthored article, among the first of its kind, was made possible by the work mentioned above and is consequently a result of constructive and substantial dialogue across the Straits. We appreciate the experience brought about by this cooperation and wish to contribute more to its success. In a word, we hope that by engaging more scholars from both sides of the Straits in broader and more profound dialogues and interchanges, the sociology of education in Mainland China and Taiwan will continue to improve.

NOTES

1. Although some scholars in Taiwan of the 1960s pointed out that we should not neglect the "social" nature of education (e.g., Chu 1963; Yin 1965), their research centered on the normative tradition of educational sociology. Significant works in step with global trends did not begin appearing until the early 1970s (e.g., Lin 1972).

2. Including Zhang Renjie, "New Areas in Educational Sciences," *Educational Research* 3 (1979); Zhang Renjie, "Four Research Trends in Sociology of Education," *Foreign Education Information* 3 (1979); Zhong Qiquan, "Developments in the Sociology of Education," *Foreign Education Information* 3 (1979); and Ma Jixiong, "An Introduction to Educational Stratification Theory," *Foreign Education Information* 4 (1979).

3. See "Education and Society Symposium Minutes," *Educational Research* 3 (1982).

4. In Mainland China, not every university teacher can become an adviser for master's or doctorate students. To become one, university teachers who are sufficiently

accomplished in their field of study must be reviewed and approved by the government. There are currently only three advisers for doctorate students in the field of sociology of education in Mainland China. They are Professors Lu Jie and Wu Kang-ning at Nanjing Normal University (Wu is dean of the University's College of Educational Science) and Professor Zhang Renjie (also director) of Guangzhou University Research Institute of Educational Science (he, together with his Ph.D. program, moved to this Institute from Huadong Normal University).

5. In 1991, Mainland China's Sociological Association also established a Research Consortium on Sociology of Education, headed by Professor Li Yixian of Beijing University. It began publishing its *Newsletter* in 1992. Relatively speaking, this organization does not seem to be as active as the National Council on Sociology of Education and has not held any academic activities for years.

6. The main textbooks included *The Sociology of Education*, co-edited by Lu Jie and Wu Kangning, (Beijing: People's Education Press, 1990), and *The Sociology of Education*, written and edited by Dong Zefang, (Wuchang: Huazhong Normal University Press, 1990). Zhang Renjie edited the *Dictionary of Education: The Sociology of Education Volume* (Shanghai: Shanghai Education Press, 1992).

7. Taiwan scholars, including Tang (1999), Weng (1999), Lee and Chang (1999), recently reviewed the development of this field. Tang did not divide it into clear stages nor did she give the stages names, but the divisions she employed were very similar to those of Weng. Weng felt that the period from 1945 to 1970 was marked by inheritance and misunderstandings; the transplanting and importing of foreign theories defined the years 1971 to 1986; and from 1987 to 1998 was the plural development period. Lee and Chang divided the stages as follows: 1960 to 1972 was the "initial period"; 1972 to the early 1980s the "foundation-laying period"; and the "transition period" spanned from then to the late 1990s. These classifications were integrated and used for this paper.

8. Lin Ching-jiang, during his studies in Taiwan, was one of the students of Professor Hsieh Cheng-fu. Professor Hsieh received his doctorate in sociology in France and was a follower of Emile Durkheim's functionalism. After receiving his doctorate in the United Kingdom in 1968, Lin Ching-jiang began teaching sociology of education at Taiwan Normal University Graduate Institute of Education. Chen Kuei-hsi was one of his first students. Lin Sheng-chuan also graduated from this institute.

9. It is worth noting that, as most Cross-Straits' teacher education institutions and comprehensive universities merely offer courses or programs related to sociology of education, the Nan-hua University in Taiwan set up a Graduate Institute of Sociology of Education in 1997. It was the first teaching-and-research unit of this field and is still the only one in Mainland China and Taiwan. Most of its faculty members are sociologists, and they are also members of the Taiwan Association for Sociology of Education.

CHINESE REFERENCES

Chang, Jason C. 2000a. The local studies programs in Taiwan. In *Multicultural education: Issues of ours and experiences of others*, 63–102. Taipei: Shi-ta Books.

Chang, Jason C. 2000b. *The cultivation and promotion of aboriginal professionals: Towards a long-term planning and programming.* A research project sponsored by The Executive Yuan Council of Aboriginal Affairs, Taiwan.

Chen, Bo-chang. 1987. *Curriculum research and educational reform.* Taipei: Shi-ta Books.

Chen, Bo-chang. 1988. *Ideology and education.* Taipei: Shi-ta Books.

Chen, Bo-chang. 2000. The praxes of sociology of education and educational reform. In Lee, Chian-hsing, ed., *Lin Ching-jiang's educational thought and its praxes*, 73–91. Kaohsiung: Lee-wen Culture Co.

Chen, Kemei. 1945. *Educational sociology.* Shanghai: World Publishing.

Chen, Kuei-hsi. 1980. *Sociology of education.* Taipei: San-min Publishing.

Chen, Kuei-hsi. 1986. Trends in the sociology of education. In Taichung Junior Teachers College Alumni Editing Team, ed., *Academia and thought: Interdisciplinary research in education*, 301–41. Taipei: Wu-nan Books.

Chen, Kuei-hsi. 1990. *The study of sociology of education.* Taipei: Shi-ta Books.

Chen, Kuei-hsi, ed. 1998. *Modern sociology of education.* Taipei: Shi-ta Books.

Chen, Kuei-hsi, Kao, Chiang-hua, and Chang, Ttze-yan. 1995. *The sociology of education.* Taipei: Open University.

Chen, Qitian, trans. 1925. *Applied educational sociology.* Shanghai: Zhonghua Publishing.

Chen, Qitian, trans. 1933. *An introduction to educational sociology.* Shanghai: Zhonghua Publishing.

Chu, Hui-sen. 1963. *Educational sociology: Research of the perspective of educational sociology and its implementation.* Taipei: Fu-hsing Books.

Fang, Jianfeng, et al. 2000. A review of educational theories in this century: Minutes from the seventh Annual Conference of the National Council on Educational Foundations. *Educational Research*, no. 3. This conference was held on November 22–24, 1999, Shanghai.

Gao, Xuping. 1993. The sociology of education in Mainland China. *Modern Education* 83: 101–16.

Gu, Mingyuan, ed. 1994. *The encyclopedia of Chinese education: Collected readings in modern educational theories.* Vol. 1. Wuhan: Hubei Education Press. The part on sociology of education was edited by Lu Youquan.

Huang, Jui-chi. 1996. *Critiquing sociology: Critical theory and modern sociology.* Taipei: San-min Publishing.

Lee, Jin-hsu, trans. 1987. *Sociological interpretations of education.* Taipei: Kuei-kuan Publishing. Written by David Blackledge and Barry Hunt, 1985.

Lee, Jin-hsu, trans. 1996. A review of the sociology of education written in "Chinese." *Fokuang Journal*, opening issue, 97–116.

Lee, Jin-hsu, trans. 2000. "Two" sociologies of education? Paper presented at the sixth biennial conference of Mainland China's National Council on Sociology of Education, November 19–23, 2000, Nanjing Normal University.

Lee, Jin-hsu and Chang, Jason C. 1999. The studies of sociology of education in Taiwan: Retrospect and prospect. In Taiwan Normal University Department of Education's National Chair Professor of Education, ed., *Educational sciences: Internationalization and indigenization*, 283–345. Taipei: Yang-chih Culture Co.

Lei, Tongqun. 1931. *Educational sociology.* Shanghai: Commercial Press.

Li, Yixian. 1983. Developments and characteristics of western sociology of education. *Developments in Foreign Education* 6 (1983).

Li, Yixian, Bai, Jierui, and Lee, Jin-hsu, eds. 1992. *Selected readings of western sociology of education*. Taipei: Wu-nan Books.

Lin, Ching-jiang. 1970. The sociology of education. In *Yun Wu Dictionary of Social Sciences*, vol. 8, *Education*, 23–46. Taipei: Commercial Press.

Lin, Ching-jiang. 1972. *Sociology of education*. Taipei: Taiwan Books.

Lin, Ching-jiang. 1979. On improving teaching efficiency: A sociological perspective. In Taiwan Normal University Graduate Institute of Education, ed., *Sociology of education*, 127–53. Taipei: Wei-wen Publishing.

Lin, Ching-jiang. 1981. *A new look at the sociology of education: Research in the interrelationship of society and education in Taiwan*. Taipei: Wu-nan Books.

Lin, Ching-jiang. 1996. Sociological analysis of the knowledge of teaching. In *Educational ideas and educational development*, 363–70. Taipei: Wu-nan Books.

Lin, Sheng-chuan. 1982. *Sociology of education*. Kaohsiung: Fu-wen Publishing Co.

Lu, Shaoji. 1934. *Educational sociology*. Shanghai: Commercial Press.

Luo, Da-han. 1987. A historical analysis of the studies in sociology of education. *Research of Education and Psychology* 10: 125–47.

Ma, Hemin and Gao, Xuping. 1998. *Research of sociology of education*. Shanghai: Shanghai Education Press.

Shen, Guanqun, and Wu, Tongfu. 1931. *A General introduction to educational sociology*. Shanghai: Nanjing Books.

Tan, Guang-ding. 1998. Formulating educational and cultural policies for aboriginal people. A research project sponsored by the Executive Yuan Council of Aboriginal Affairs, Taiwan.

Tang, Mei-ying. 1999. A review of the development of sociology of education in Taiwan. Paper presented at the first meeting of the Taiwan Forum on Sociology of Education, held by Chung Cheng University Graduate Institute of Education, on May 15–16, 1999, Chiayi, Taiwan. In *Conference Handbook*, pp. II-VII-1~II-VII-16.

Tao, Menghe. 1922. *Society and education*. Shanghai: Commercial Press.

Tsao, Hsian-kun. 1965. *Principles of educational sociology*. Taipei: Taiwan Provincial Taipei Junior Teachers College.

Weng, Fu-yuan. 1996. A review of Taiwan's teacher education reforms in the early 1990s: Dialogue between structure and policy. In Teacher Education Society and Comparative Education Society, eds., *New issues of teacher education*, pp. 1–24. Taipei: Shi-ta Books.

Weng, Fu-yuan. 1999. A preliminary analysis of the developments of the sociology of education over the past sixty years in Taiwan. Paper presented at the first meeting of the Taiwan Forum on Sociology of Education, held by Chung Cheng University Graduate Institute of Education on May 15–16, 1999, Chiayi, Taiwan. Printed in *Conference Handbook*, pp. II-V-1~II-V-12.

Wu, Kangning. 1986. Three major schools of thought in contemporary European and American sociology of education. *Educational Research* 9.

Wu, Kangning. 1998. *The sociology of education*. Beijing: People's Education Press.

Wu, Kangning. 1999. *Sociology of the classroom teaching*. Nanjing: Nanjing Normal University Press.

Yin, Yun-hua. 1965. *Educational sociology*. Taichung: Taiwan Provincial Taichung Junior Teachers College.

Zhang, Renjie. 1989. *Fundamental readings in foreign sociology of education*. Shanghai: Huadong Normal University Press.

Zhang, Renjie. 1996. The authentic value of educational research. *Educational Research* 3.

Zhang, Renjie, and Feng, Dongwen. 1999. On the compilation and experiment of teaching materials of an integrated liberal arts curriculum for general high schools. *Educational Research and Experiment* 1.

ENGLISH REFERENCES

Ball, S., ed. 2000. *Sociology of education: Major themes.* 4 vols. London: Routledge.

Collins, R. 1981. On the microfoundations of macrosociology. *American Journal of Sociology* 86: 984–1014.

Noblit, G. W., and W. T. Pink 1995. Mapping the alternative paths of the sociology of education. In W. T. Pink and G. W. Noblit, eds., *Continuity and contradiction: The futures of the sociology of education,* 1–29. Cresskill, N.J.: Hampton.

Ritzer, G. 1996. *Sociological theory.* 4th ed. New York: McGraw-Hill.

Saha, L. J., ed. 1997. *International encyclopedia of the sociology of education.* Oxford: Elsevier Science.

Shilling, C. 1993. The demise of sociology of education in Britain? *British Journal of Sociology of Education* 14, no. 1: 105–12.

Torres, C. A., and T. R. Mitchell, eds. 1998. *Sociology of education: Emerging perspectives.* Albany, N.Y.: State University of New York Press.

Whitty, G. 1997. Educational policy and the sociology of education. *International Studies in Sociology of Education* 7, no. 2: 121–35.

11

Education in a Transition Society:

Growing Inequality

David Konstantinovski

Many realms of Russian society life have changed significantly in the last decade. It was hoped that the 1990s would be the period of democratization in Russia. However, now that the consequences of the changes have become more or less clear, the society has realized that these consequences are not quite what was expected.

It became clear that in the years supposedly leading to democratization of society, the opposite effect occurred—social inequality did not decrease and even grew. The official statistics show impressive figures of differentiation in terms of property possession, growth of unemployment, and poverty (RF 1999, 107, 114, 120–25, 132, 155–56).

In this connection, new conditions must inevitably intensify social differentiation of young people, particularly in the education field. The influence comes from both the global factors of contemporary Russian reality and from the pressure on the education system from interested groups having the necessary potential (Konstantinovski and Khokhlushkina 2000). Voluntarily or not, the education system gets involved in the processes of social selection. Logically, the selection effects in education are supposed to become more apparent and more severe. Since the significance of the educational system is increasing and the prognosis is that it will keep increasing, the social processes within this system attract more attention, first, the problem of orientation and social behavior of young people, especially—orientation toward receiving some or other levels of education and actual opportunities for that. The contradiction between declared equal rights for education and the real social differentiation in educational field is rightfully considered a global, societal problem.

This problem could be of significance for any society. It turns out to be especially urgent in contemporary Russia. Questions of democracy, equal opportunity, and social mobility are extremely keen in a transitional society when social instability is high. Following the example of liberal societies, the country invariably gets both positive and negative consequences. We have to study and evaluate (from scratch, based on our own materials) the new social mechanisms, the conflicts, and the ways to settle them. This chapter studies the main social problem that Russian youth meets in secondary education and in moving from secondary school graduation to higher education in Russia—the problem of social differentiation. This problem is evidenced in the results of studies conducted from the 1960s to the present.

It is necessary to analyze the dynamics over a long period, since the problems facing post-Soviet youth today have roots in the Soviet past and are a modification of what we had in the Soviet period. The current situation can be interpreted and understood correctly and clearly only if its genesis is analyzed.

BASIC APPROACHES TO THE RESEARCH

Opportunities that society opens up to citizens at some period of its development are a resource that is used in different ways and needs to be considered both as the reflection of opportunities in orientations and the way the opportunities are mastered (or appropriated) by individuals in the life course. Opportunities in the educational field constitute a highly important resource, especially for youth. We can study the orientation toward certain kinds of opportunities in the educational field by strata and actual distribution of realization of certain variants in probability among various social strata.

The myth of equal opportunity is highly attractive. Equality has been humankind's ideal for centuries. Every epoch in history witnessed different people of different social status concerning themselves with this ideal. Every philosopher devoted his works to this question or at least expressed his views on it. Social associations, politicians, and political parties keep manipulating this ideal. We can criticize utopias and neglect speculations, but we can't give up the ideal.

The equality problem is invariably related to the educational system because of its functions. The first point is the importance of fair distribution of potential opportunities in the educational field: opportunities to learn, to study, to get knowledge and qualifications. The second point is that education, profession, and qualifications are not just terminal values (i.e., values in themselves); they are instrumental values as well—the way to achieve goals, investment capital for a life career. The one who gets opportunities in the educational field secures to a certain extent his or her social mobility, and access to other social values and prosperity.

To get social status, you have to master a social role. Shakespeare said "all the world's a stage," so the higher, more complicated (and usually more attractive) the status, the more difficult the roles we have to master ("all the men and women merely players"). The mastering of a social role and social status in a developed society is actually determined by study in educational institutions, by passing through the formal educational system. Education was not and is not a warranty of life success (in Russia or in other countries), though education can significantly influence the possibility of success. Education has both symbolic and practical significance and determines the life career of a person to a great extent.

The way the humankind has gone so far shows that the problem of equality is still important. E. Durkheim wrote in 1897 about the "naive authors" who believed that this problem would vanish itself after "the economic property inheritance disappears" (Durkheim 1897). It seems that today, more than one hundred years later, this opinion is still correct concerning the promises made by some people and expectations of other (more numerous) people.

The problem of differentiation in the educational field is central to education researches. It is present in general works focused on social situation in educational field (Archer 1978; Collins 1978; Popkewitz 1991). It was elaborated in works concerning this critical issue (Bidwell 1995; Coleman 1968, 1995; Whitti and Edwards 1995). The problem of complexity, dependence of social processes in educational field on many factors, ambiguity, and the dynamics prediction difficulties of the processes are generally mentioned. Cross-impacts of social structure, economic, demographic, political, and cultural factors and the educational field cause situations important in the development of society that require continuing research efforts. The creation of the next generation's human capital by investments of social and financial capitals, problems of social justice in the new social reality, perspectives of schooling, education as a value in different strata, and so on, are studied; the distinctive features of social processes in educational systems of many countries are analyzed. Comparisons of data from East European countries (Gospodinov, Shubkin, and Andics 1986), as well as between the Soviet Union and the United States (Dobson 1988; Trow 1988) are of interest. Showing up the national specific, its determination by complex characteristics of different countries allows us to study various aspects of social conditionality of youth opportunities in the educational field.

This problem developed in French sociology,[1] where basically two kinds of interpretation were considered. One kind of interpretation assumed that legitimation of social status transmission, necessary for inequality reproduction, takes place in education; in this connection declaring equal opportunities is not the true object of the education system, but just a mystification (Bourdieu and Passeron 1964, 1970). Another kind of interpretation supposed that educational policy is really trying to promote scholarship but meets with failure, as the family does not show proper interest: the family has no guarantees of the teenager obtaining the required degrees and corresponding social goods (Boudon 1973, 1974; Baudelot and Establet 1989).

The myth of equal opportunity along with other myths was an important part of the ideology in Soviet Russia. It was supported by official propaganda not only through slogans but also through statistics data, which must look convincing. In particular, data on representation of industrial and farm workers, women, and national minorities in the educational system were published as a proof of equal opportunity.

Soviet society wasn't free from unequal opportunities in its educational system, in status transmission, and in other phenomena common in other societies. It was earnestly shown by V. Shubkin (1968). Later these problems were developed in a research project (Konstantinovski and Shubkin 1977) continuing into the present (Konstantinovski 1997, 1999).

Two groups of questions are important for Russian educational field analysis. The first one is related to differentiation level. Has the social differentiation in the Russian educational system remained constant? Has it decreased or increased in terms of general changes in the country? What about the situation in school and higher education fields in this respect? Another group of questions is on interpreting differentiation. Does it affect the absence of real education accessibility for everyone, with people of humble birth not able to overcome social filters, who must make way for children of elite and close to elite groups to the educational institutions giving high qualification and prestige professions? Or is the reason the lack of striving for education, due to a lack of faith in achieving future success? Or maybe teenagers from lower classes don't aspire to higher positions in society; perhaps young people and their parents do not want their children to receive high level of education?

We require certain empirical data in order to estimate this. The surveys' results can provide material for an approach to resolving these questions applying to Russian specifics.

The study of education accessibility for all strata is important to both scholarly and practical approaches. It is considerable even in itself, within the confines of sociology of education, and for social mobility, social structure, and social changes researches. Furthermore, information from a society changing quickly gives peculiar possibilities for researchers. Besides that, this problem is an important indicator of the state of society on the whole. In particular, it is essential for social tension level evaluation. Therefore such surveys have considerable significance for practice.

The Situation in the Educational Field: Post-Soviet Period

For the last ten to fifteen years the whole complex of factors has influenced orientations and social behavior of youth in the educational sector. It was determined by various political, economic, and other changes in the country.

On the one hand the situation turned out to be more favorable to training. It happened for certain reasons. The demographic processes nature affected: the number of school-age youth has been changing very gradually without any sudden shifts, as it had before. The fact that higher educational institutions and colleges met the wishes of youths interested in qualifying for prospective professions was also affected; as a result of education decentralization, educational institutions were able to raise enrollments and start providing education being demanded by the labor market professions.

But a series of facts made the situation more severe than before. One of the most important reasons is worsening living conditions. Poverty is an everyday reality for a large part of the population (RF 1999, 141, 166, 586–87). From this derives the intensification of survival issues: it is not possible to seek an education when you have to earn to help your family.

As a result of economic recession the demand for labor decreased: the demand for general labor, particularly youth labor, and for young specialists in many professions (RF 1999, 107, 114, 120–25, 132). Youth experience problems in finding jobs in a changing and competitive labor market, especially in the current Russian economy. Youth is in a difficult situation because it must compete with groups having more qualifications and experience. Those groups have more chances in the labor market. Youth receives only the worst positions, possibly moving into deviant and criminal pursuits. This also has to affect orientations and social behavior of youth in the educational field.

Besides that, the role of education in social mobility processes has changed. In addition, the transformation of value orientations of the society related to general changes in the country took place. Due to the causes mentioned above, the prestige of education and of many highly qualified occupations shifted differently in different strata (Konstantinovski 1999, 53–54).

Pluralization of education has been in progress. Pluralism is necessary for the educational system, but it must have social character. Consequently, differentiation of educational institutions into privileged and mass became more profound (Cherednichenko 1999, 18–19). We have various kinds of schools and higher educational institutions now, and their hierarchy reflects social differentiation. Numerous children, especially from lower strata, are not winners in this situation.

The level of state guarantees in the educational field has become lower; the former state line for introduction of universal secondary education (eleven years of learning) has changed to the line for basic (incomplete secondary) education (nine years of learning) (RF Law 1966);[2] federal and local financing has diminished. Paid education was introduced, and as living standard fell, it decreased the chances of sizable part of youth for receiving quality education. The hierarchy of "elite" and "cheap" educational institutions took shape as a result. The "golden sieve" appeared in education, and only children of well-to-do families have any chance to surmount it.

Information Basis of the Research

The research includes a study of both orientations of upper-grade students in a daytime secondary school and real opportunities of school graduates in a thirty-five year period from the 1960s to present. This is a study of cohorts following one another. The research program provides for a study of different young people groups—urban and countryside, boys and girls, children of families belonging to different social-professional groups.[3] The method creates an information basis for comparison of young people's intentions and their actual lives.

A distinctive feature of the research is that we study both static "snapshots" of orientations and actual lives of young people in certain periods, certain social conditions; and the dynamics of orientations and social behavior in relation to changes in Russia. The database created is a result of recording of some parameters (attitude to occupations, future plans of young people, actual distribution of young people in the educational system, and so on) in the changing environment: different demographic situations, labor market situation, and so on (the conditions of a "natural experiment"). Such an approach brings sociological researches together with those that are usually conducted in science, for example, in physics. The observations began long before the recent transformations in the life of the country, and they continue at the present moment. This makes it possible to observe the effects of those transformations: to reconstruct the phases that preceded the current situation and to trace the correlation between the changes in the parameters we are interested in, and global changes in Russian reality.

The information basis of the research is a composition of data. It includes the results of surveys and data from official state, corporate, and local statistics. The statistical materials we use came not from published information but from initial data, and our analysis is based on those data.

The data from surveys combine materials from questionnaire and objective information. At the first stage we gave the questionnaire survey to daytime secondary (complete) schools. We asked upper-grade students in their last months of schooling about their opinion on occupations, about their wishes and expectations for future profession and education, and so on. We recorded detailed personal social-demographic information on each upper-grade student. At the second stage we recorded information on the actual life way of every interviewee after the person graduated and made his first life steps outside school (about six months later).[4]

The research based on this method was been carried out in Novosibirsk Oblast since the 1960s. The research was also carried out in other Siberian regions, in Leningrad Oblast, several regions in Central Russia, and some republics of the former USSR. Here we use the materials from research in the Novosibirsk Oblast in 1963, 1983, 1994, and 1998. This region is a developed industrial and agricultural area, and its capital is one of the largest cities in Russia. These data were compared to data of studies in several other regions.

The samplings were made in such a way that different young people groups—upper-grade students in daytime secondary schools of regional centers, cities, and towns, settlements and countryside villages—were represented proportionally to a share of each group in the total number of students in the schools of the region in a certain year. Every information array is actually a model of the overall aggregate. The database for every year includes information on one thousand or more respondents. The samplings were made as combined, multistage.

Social Selection at School

The children of Soviet elite families traditionally received the most effective level of education and the most effective professions (concerning the life success, which was conceived as official recognition in the course of an official career). Proximity to official power, privileged social status, culture capital, financial advantages, declared and latent benefits—quite a number of factors worked for social groups at the top levels of the social hierarchy. This created conditions for reproduction of the parents' high social status and growing social mobility.

Let's analyze the social selection process in secondary school formerly and now. The results at that stage of selection can be traced by analysis of structure of young people becoming upper-grade students in a secondary school. Those teenagers have already managed to reach this crucial border of Russian educational system and have gained the access to finishing secondary (complete) school and then to going up to the higher levels of education in order to get the desired social status.

Social structure of upper-grade students (and later school graduates) was analyzed by aggregated groups, the status was determined by their parents' positions in respect to authority, financial standing, occupational and employment characteristics, and education level. These groups were studied: children of administrators of high, middle, and minor ranks (regional, party, industrial, and other administrators); children of specialists (highly qualified employees, excluding administrators)—university degree people who do intellectual work; children of white-collar workers—intellectual work employees with general or specialized secondary education; children of industrial and agricultural blue-collar workers—people who do physical labor that doesn't require a high level of education.[5] This type of aggregating has had a long tradition both in Russian society and Russian sociology.

As figure 11.1 shows, the share of administrators' children in Novosibirsk Oblast in the early 1960s made up less than one-tenth of the total number of the upper-grade students in the daytime secondary schools. Specialists' children, about one-fourth; in sum, approximately one-third of the total number. Blue-collar workers' children—over one-third of the total number and white-collar children, just below one-fourth.

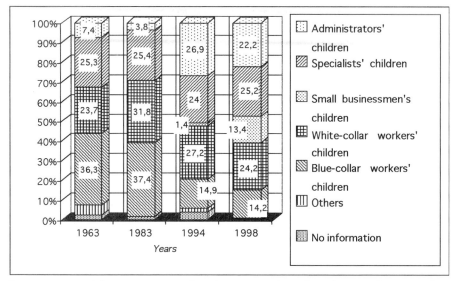

Figure 11.1   Social Structure Dynamics of Upper-Grade Students in a Daytime Secondary (Complete) School (%), Novosibirsk Oblast.
Note: The "small businessmen" category was absent during the Soviet period.

At the beginning of the 1980s the social structure of upper-grade students in a daytime school changed slightly. There were official actions aimed at social engineering in the country: the authorities tried to make secondary education universal (general). Every teenager was supposed to receive an equivalent of secondary education. Table 11.1 displays relative shifts in the upper-grade students' structure. The share of administrator's children reduced twice. The share of white-collar children increased by one-third. The replenishing source of students for the realization of universal education actions is obvious.

The changes, which have taken place for the past years, are very significant both in quantitative indices and social meaning. In 1994 the share of

Table 11.1.   The Quote Change of Various Groups among Upper-Grade Students in a Daytime Secondary (Complete) School (%), Novosibirsk Oblast

Groups	1963–1983	1983–1994	1994–1998
Administrators' children	-48.6	+- 607.9	-17.5
Specialists' children	+- 0.4	-5.5	+5.0
Small businessmen's children	0.0	0.0	+857.1
White-collar workers' children	+34.2	-14.5	-11.0
Blue-collar workers' children	+3.0	-60.2	-4.7

Notes:
1. The calculations were done the following way: difference between figures of the last year and the initial year was compared with figures of the initial year (percentage).
2. The "small businessmen" category was absent during the Soviet period.

administrators' children exceeded one-fourth of the total upper-grade students in the Oblast (figure 11.1). The relative increase of the administrators' children's share was 600 percent (table 11.1). It has increased 7 times against the early 1980s and 3.5 times against the early 1960s. The administrators' children took the share of other groups, at the same time the share of blue-collar workers' children fell 2.5 times. Comparisons between the Novosibirsk survey and other studies show that such processes are observed in other regions too (Konstantinovski 1999, 91–92).

The year 1998 witnessed a rapidly growing share of small businessmen's children. In 1994 their share was 1.4 percent, in 1998, 13.4 percent. Who are their parents? They are former engineers and technicians who used to work at military-industrial facilities (as result of the Novosibirsk Oblast industry specifics). Now those people have become small traders, store and workshop owners, and so on. The share of small businessmen's children in the structure of upper-grade students is nearly equal to that of blue-collar workers' children. As for the rest, the structure remains the same as it was in 1994.

The results were verified by local research—repeated research (replications of our research) at the same schools. It was possible due to the database that had records on schools where a single survey at some period of time was made and records on schools where replications in different years took place. The calculations made for some schools (which admit children of some local city district) confirmed the general sampling results. In order to verify the results, calculations for settlements with different urban saturation were additionally made. The results were the same: the social structure of upper-grade students has slightly changed, the administrators' children took the share of other groups, at the same time the share of blue-collar workers' children fell (Konstantinovski 1999, 81–82).

But perhaps changes in social structure were the sole source of this leap? In other words, the increasing share of administrators' children and the decreasing share of blue-collar workers' children were caused by the fact that many former industrial and agricultural blue-collar workers have set up their own businesses and have transferred into administrators' group.

This hypothesis was verified in different ways and was rejected. Let's check, for example, the education level of parents who were recorded in 1994 as administrators. Seventy-six percent of that group had a university degree. Therefore if they hadn't been administrators they would have been recorded as specialists, not blue-collar workers, and more than 8 percent of administrators who had secondary professional education would have been recorded as white collar. The supposition that three-fourths of the present administrators used to be university degree experts who worked as blue-collar workers doesn't seem credible.

The detected changes reflect, to some extent, changes in the social structure of society, but the analysis shows that they are related mostly to growing social differentiation in the educational field.

Census data, which include information about the population's level of education, can help us verify the results and continue our analysis. Let's compare parents' structure with the educational structure of population (i.e., structure of population by education level). Compare the share of teenagers with either highly educated parent in the number of secondary school upper-grade students in the region with the share of highly educated population in the total population of the region. Here we can assume that we make a comparison similar to that based on social-professional family status—to compare indirectly the share of highly educated administrators' and specialists' children in the number of upper-grade school students with the share of higher educated administrators and specialists in population. Since highly educated specialists can be referred to this category, what about the administrators? Our study demonstrated that most parents who are administrators have completed higher education; on the whole 90 percent of the parents who are administrators and specialists have graduated from a higher educational institution.

According to the microcensus of 1994, the share of people with higher education in the Novosibirsk Oblast population over fifteen years of age made up 13.5 percent (RF Education 1995, 216); in Russia it was 13.3 percent (RF 1995, 119).[6] For the people who are most likely to have children as upper-grade students in a secondary (complete) school, the university degree share varied very greatly. The only group that exceeded the level of one-fifth (21.9 percent) was a group forty-five to forty-nine years of age; this group includes just 5 percent of the total Russian population (RF 1995, 119). Of course, here, as in analogous comparisons, the calculations are based on some assumptions. Our assumption is that every person in those groups has at least one child who could be an upper-grade student in a secondary school in the current year. In Novosibirsk Oblast that group (45–49 years of age) also had the maximum figures: 21.6 percent of population (RF Education 1995, 216). The research of upper-grade students in Novosibirsk Oblast showed that over 40 percent of administrators' and specialists' children had both or at least one parent with higher education.

In addition, we can compare the dynamics of the population's educational structure and the dynamics of the students' structure. The question is, Can the census data on educational level of the population prove the conclusion about the growing social differentiation in school?

We should select the age-groups that are most likely to have children who are upper-grade students in a secondary school: potential, or hypothetical, parents of upper-grade students. The age of that group is thirty to fifty-nine years, according to Russian census data structure.

Our estimation is based on the microcensus of 1994 (RF Education 1995, 216). Since we are to compare 1994 and 1983 but there was no census in 1983, we have to resort to interpolation based on 1979 and 1989 censuses. The figure for 1983 is calculated by primary data of the Russian State Statistics

Committee (Goskomstat). The interval is ten years. The assumption was that in that period of time the share of university degree people increased linearly.

The share calculated by the census data includes the population of all social strata. That's why in order to make the correct comparison with upper-grade students, we have figured out the share of upper-grade students whose parents with university degrees belong not only to administrator and specialist groups, but to other groups as well (including small businessmen, pensioners, unemployed, and others).

The compared shares of population with higher education in the Oblast (potential, hypothetical university degree parents) and upper-grade students with university degree parents (i.e., real university degree parents whose children are upper-grade students in a secondary school) are given in table 11.2.

As you can see, the ratio of the share of upper-grade students with university degree parents to the share of potential parents with university degrees increased 1.5 times for the period from 1983 to 1994. Of course, the calculations were based on some assumptions. Nevertheless, the results of the calculations show that census data prove the conclusion of growing social differentiation in the field of secondary school education.

Official actions aimed at universal secondary education[7] resulted in a growing number of students in upper grades of secondary school. The larger part of every age cohort had been graduating from secondary school. At the beginning of the 1960s, an average of less than 30 percent of people who had completed a daytime basic (former incomplete secondary) school graduated from a daytime complete secondary school every year; twenty years later, the figure practically doubled (based on primary data of the Russian State Statistics Committee).

The last decade witnessed significant changes in schooling. Pupils left school more often at all grades, the so-called dropouts (or so-called sifting in Russian). Figure 11.2 displays typical examples. The dropout rate was quite low and stable in the early 1980s. It began growing in 1986–1987, when the first economic and social changes came to the country. The dropout rate

Table 11.2. Educational Structure of the Population and of Parents Whose Children Are Upper-Grade Students in Secondary (Complete) Schools, Novosibirsk Oblast

Indices	1983	1994
The share of higher-educated population in Novosibirsk Oblast (30–59 years of age), %	12.8	18.9
The share of upper-grade students in secondary (complete) schools with at least one higher-educated parent, %	26.3	54.9
The ratio of the share of upper-grade students with at least one higher-educated parent to the share of higher-educated population	2.0	2.9

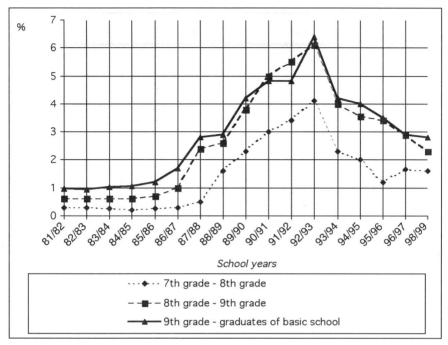

Figure 11.2.   Falling Dropout Rate (%), Russia
Source: Primary data of Russian State Statistics Committee (Goskomat).
Note: Figure shows the difference in the number of students as of the beginning of the school year, and in the case of last curve students at the beginning of ninth grade and those graduating from a basic school at the end of this school year due to the nine-year study length at basic (former incomplete secondary) postgraduate student schools of Russia.

peaked in the early 1990s. In the past years it has declined, though it is still several times higher than the 1980s level.

Statistical data can help us analyze the movement of an age cohort in school from the first grade to the upper grades. Let's follow the cohort that graduated from eleventh grade (secondary complete daytime school) in 1994. Of the total number of pupils who began studying in the first grade, 85.5 percent completed the basic school; 45.6 percent entered the senior grades of secondary (complete) school. Some students then quit studying and just 41 percent of that cohort passed all the stages and earned the certificate of secondary (complete) education.

Let's compare the information on the cohort that graduated from secondary (complete) school in 1994 and the cohort that graduated from secondary (complete) school in 1983 (table 11.3). We compare the paths and, to a certain extent, the fates of the two cohorts (because their choices influence their further life ways). One of them achieved the age of presumptively graduating from any kind of secondary school in the early 1990s, and the other, eleven

Table 11.3. The Number of Students at the Beginning of the School Year and Graduates from Schools (%), Russia

Year-Length of Secondary (Complete) Education	Entered First Grade	Graduated from Basic School	Entered the Senior Grades of Secondary (Complete) School	Graduated from Secondary (Complete) School
1973/74–1982/83	100.0	102.9*	59.7	57.2
1984/85–1993/94	100.0	85.5	45.6	41.0

Source: Primary data of Russian State Statistics Committee (Goscomstat).
*The number of students includes pupils remaining in the same form for second year and migrants; so total percentage may be more than 100.

years earlier. We compare to what extent they used the general education (received the opportunities from society and realized them) in proper time and proper form (the most common in the contemporary world form—daytime school).

No doubt, the second cohort made less intensive use of general education in the mid-1990s (and maybe later) than the cohort of the early 1980s. Even the number of students graduating from basic school was higher in the early 1980s than in the 1990s. The dropout rate from different school grades results in a sad figure—2 million kids and teenagers neither study nor work (RF Youth 1996, 37).

The dynamic of the dropout rate has a social character. Back in early 1980s, secondary (complete) school graduations increased by an unequal number of youth from various social strata (demonstrated by the 1963 and 1983 surveys). In 1990s dropout process, undoubtedly, some groups are presented as small streamlets, and others as big rivers. Trend of changes of secondary (complete) upper-grade students' social structure was demonstrated (as it was stated above) in our research.

Here we witness a kind of inequality that has the same peculiarity as disposition (inborn features) inequality. We can't choose what we are born. We can't choose the epoch to be born. Some cohorts enter life when they are welcome in educational institutions and can get jobs, when the state is interested in them and can take good care of them, when they are desired children in the family of society. Other cohorts are born in time of limited vacancies, poor resources, unstable values, and vague prospects.

From the Preferences to Intentions: Inequality Perception

Gathering of information on professions' appeal for upper-grade students was held according to method of survey (Shubkin 1970, 268–70; Konstantinovski 1999, 338–39). They were asked to measure appeal of professions of different scopes of activity and of different educational requirements from the list of tens (of fifty in 1990s). Findings allow us to form a picture of how the world of professions is reflected in the consciousness of young people (and hence the world of corresponding social statuses). The questionnaire also contained questions on what respondents are going to do after finishing school: to study, work, or combine study and work; if to study then where and so on.

Thus we received an opportunity to consider aspirations of upper-grade students by two indices. One of them (attitudes to professions expressed in appeal points) emphasizes variants of life career being the most desirable or preferable.[8] On this data basis we can study youth *preferences*, taken as some imaginary choice; high appeal points were conceivably given to professions, which young people would prefer if there were no limitations, on the one hand, such as material living conditions and competition from contemporaries, and on the other hand, such as personal abilities, scholarly achievements; and other elements of reality, acting as regulators. Another index *(intentions)* gives us information on personal plans of upper-grade students that they are going to realize.[9]

Survey results already in 1960s showed that the professions appealed differently to upper-grade students of different social groups. The higher the parents' social status and education level, the more appealing are occupations of qualified mental work requiring a high level of education. At the same time striving toward education continuation is apparent in all groups of upper-grade students. The school, adjusting students' orientations, may have its effect here.

The pursuit of education as a main feature of upper-grade orientations developed most dramatically in 1990s and is distinctly demonstrated by data from recent surveys. In the 1990s the upper-grade students became a very homogeneously orientated cohort. This is clear: in fact, they are teenagers who have already passed intensive selection, and their rather exact and mostly similar strivings have been already set. They arrived in the final school phase in order to move further. In each considered group the most appealing professions are the same. Upper stages of the occupational hierarchy are represented by occupations that require a high level of education: lawyer, physician, economist, foreign language translator, programmer, and others. There are of course some differences between group orientations. For example, workers' and peasants' children, as distinct from others, included shop assistant among the most appealing professions. But on the whole, unanimity of upper-grade students is present from whatever families they come. For example, the most appealing occupation—lawyer—was identified by all groups together from 6.9 to 7.5 scores at the beginning of the 1980s (Konstantinovski 1999, 269–76), and from 8.4 to 8.9 scores at the end of the 1990s. Thus we have every reason to justify the conclusion that orientations for occupations that presuppose higher education are observed in each group. These orientations are the most preferable, that is, they predominate over orientations toward lower levels of education, and these orientations are distributed in each group of youth almost equally.

The personal plans of upper-grade students' distribution, unlike professions appeal data, shows much greater differentiation and, moreover, of a certain kind.

Institutes of higher education are always the main objective of people who graduate from secondary (complete) school, and other educational institutes are chosen by those who are not among the leaders of the cohort. Differentiation of personal plans in relation to social-professional status was stated in all surveys. The higher the parents' status, the stronger the orientation to a high level of education among other future plans of upper-grade students.

In 1990s—through equalized preferences—differentiation of intentions turned out to be pronounced. Figure 11.3 dramatically demonstrates: the share of people, planning to enter higher educational institutions from any group is higher, the higher parents' social status is. Workers' and peasants' children are oriented primarily to secondary special (colleges) and primary professional education (vocational-technical schools). This correlation is found in each surveyed region.

On the given data we can see how young people, while setting (molding) their personal plans according to an appraisal of substantial reality elements, adjust their aspirations in relation to set occupational prestige structure. Obtained survey data allow us to assume that the differences between preferences and intentions of teenagers are due not just to the fact that they have different inclinations, take a sober view of their abilities, and so on. Finishing school and clarifying their future plans, teenagers examine their true opportunities in the social relations system, within which they enter independent life, and so some part of young people restrain their strivings.

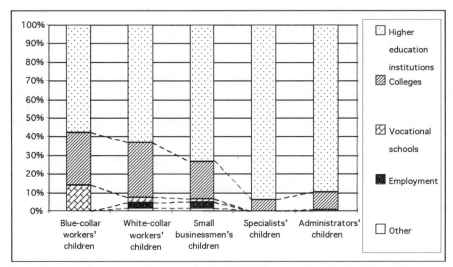

Figure 11.3.   Structure of Upper-Grade Students' Personal Plans (Those Who Plan as % of Group): Distribution by Parents' Social-Professional Status, Novosibirsk Oblast, 1998

From Intentions to Life Steps: Facing the Reality

Now we use the third index—*actual life steps* of youth. Life steps distribution by social-professional status of secondary (complete) school upper-grade students is also differentiated. In addition, differentiation again becomes more profound on the transition from personal plans to life steps. For example, 77.8 percent of administrators' children became higher school students, from 89.9 percent of those who planned (86.5 percent realized plans), and just 39.1 percent of workers' and peasants' children from 57.8 percent who had such plans (67.6 percent of teenagers managed to realize their aspirations) in 1998.

The findings presented in figures 11.4 and 11.5 show the disparities on entering higher education. Secondary (complete) school graduation is required to apply to higher educational institutions. Figure 11.4 contains the information about administrators' and specialists' children. The percentage of administrators' and specialists' children among the upper-grade students who plan to enter higher education is higher than the percentage of these groups among all the upper-grade students. And the percentage of administrators' and specialists' children among the graduates who entered higher education is more than the percentage of these groups among the upper-grade students who plan to enter higher education. This correlation is revealed in each of our surveys. Figure 11.5 demonstrates the quotas of white-collar and blue-collar children. Comparing figure 11.4 and figure 11.5 exposes that the correlation types are inverse: children from upper groups strive more intensively and have more possibilities for entering higher education than

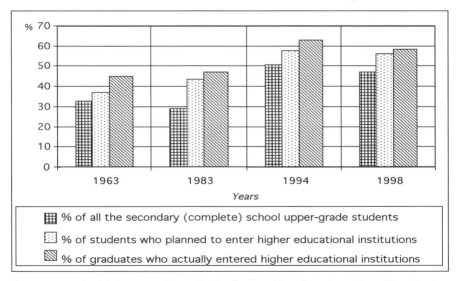

Figure 11.4. **Social Structure Dynamics in the Transition from Secondary (Complete) to Higher Education: Administrators' and Specialists' Children, Novosibirsk Oblast**

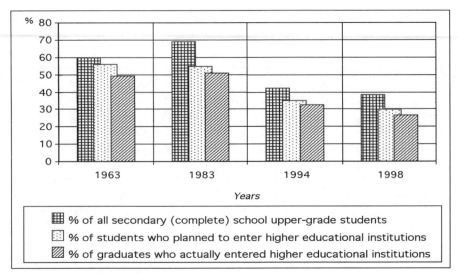

Figure 11.5 Social Structure Dynamics in the Transition from Secondary (Complete) to Higher Education: White-Collar and Blue-Collar Workers' Children, Novosibirsk Oblast

children of families low on the social scale, and the disparities in attending higher education are obvious. The findings of surveys carried out in several regions are similar (Konstantinovski 1999, 187). This data clearly reveals the overall pattern of relative advantage.

Table 11.4 demonstrates the first life steps of youth after they graduated from secondary (complete) school in Novosibirsk Oblast in 1998. Previous years witnessed a similar situation (Konstantinovski 1999, 191–94). The table demonstrates the correlation between parents' social and professional status and the chances for their children to enter various educational institutions. We can see who gets into higher education institutions, and who enters institutions giving lower qualification. It's clear that higher education institutions are filled more with youth from higher society strata, it is an "econiche" for this part of youth.

A comparison of the structure of freshmen with the population structure was carried out. The study was the same as the one conducted among secondary (complete) school graduates (see above).

Table 11.5 shows figures of 1983 and 1994: the share of people aged thirty to fifty-nine with university degrees in the population of Novosibirsk Oblast (based on materials of population censuses); the share of secondary (complete) school graduates, who have at least one parent with higher education, in the total number of secondary (complete) school graduates, who entered a higher education institution at the year of school graduation (the figures are taken from surveys, the shares are calculated as of the mass of graduates in the whole, including all presented groups); the correlation between these two indices in the last row.

Table 11.4. The First Life Steps of Youth after They Graduated from Secondary (Complete) School, Distribution by Parents' Social Status (%), Novosibirsk Oblast, 1998

Group	Higher Education Institution	College	Vocational School	Employ-ment	Other	No Informa-tion	Total
Administrators' children	77.8	15.2	4.0	1.0	1.0	1.0	100
Specialists' children	83.2	11.5	0.9	0.9	0.9	2.6	100
Small business-men's children	66.7	25.0	3.3	1.7	3.3	0.0	100
White-collar workers' children	50.0	26.9	10.2	3.7	3.7	5.5	100
Blue-collar workers' children	39.1	28.1	23.4	3.2	3.1	3.1	100

The results of calculations (of course with unavoidable assumptions) allow us to make the following conclusions. The fact that the share of freshmen with higher-educated parents is greater than the share of potential higher-educated parents (by almost three and half times) proves the existence of differentiation mentioned in the above listed survey materials. But the fact that in transmission from secondary (complete) school graduation to the higher education field the degree of differentiation is changeless, means that the structure of school pupils changes earlier and the structure of secondary (complete) school graduation has already formed by the moment of graduation. In the analyzed decade, due to transformations in the society, the intensification of social selection (the essence of this intensification is to increase differentiation) occurred at early stages of learning, at a school stage. As a reminder, the analyzed increase (in secondary school) grew almost 1.5 times between 1983 and 1994 (table 11.2).

Table 11.5. Educational Structure of the Population and of Parents Whose Children Graduated from Secondary (Complete) School and Entered Higher Education the Same Year, Novosibirsk Oblast

Indices	1983	1994
The share of higher-educated population in Novosibirsk Oblast (30–59 years of age), %	12.8	18.9
The share of children graduated from secondary (complete) school and entered higher education the same year, who have at least one high-educated parent, %	43.5	63.8
The ratio of the share of children graduated from secondary (complete) school and entered higher education the same year, who have at least one higher-educated parent, to the share of higher education population	3.4	3.4

Discussion

It is obvious that resources provided by Russian society today as opportunities in the domestic educational system are used to different extents by different social groups.

During the process of orientation and social behavior setting, young people are making next sequential steps from abstraction to reality, from preferences prevalence—to the synthesis of both "internal" and "external" factors, applied to individual specifics.[10] At that, mainly deliberately or mainly intuitively (without complete information) individuals make some summation and come to the result that defines content at the transition from each previous step of orientation and social behavior setting to each next one. And step by step, as we have seen on empirical data, the differentiation becomes more profound in the upshot.

When young people make their first attempts to realize their personal plans, the moment of facing reality (and sometimes colliding with it) occurs. In actuality, it has not been reflected in the consciousness of a young man nor has he considered it in his personal plans. But here he must face the proper actuality, the way it is and in its full measure. As presented by survey data, the interaction with educational field reality happens differently for people from different social groups and has different consequences. Here the inequality approves itself visibly, and just as it has been formed by social conditions to a certain moment.

Formation of intentions about life course choice after finishing school occurs on the basis of the image of the world of professions, indirectly representing social statuses; here the young man must soberly consider reality, his opportunities in particular, his chances of getting some level of education or acquiring some profession. The process of intention formation can be rightfully regarded as a part of the socialization process (however we think of this term today), and furthermore as an important one. In considering research results, we must find that teenagers from groups occupying not the higher stages of social hierarchy, on the phase of socialization, substantially have to become aware of existing inequality that particularly shows itself in the educational field, and to fit their life strategy to reality, in the light of inequality. Conceivably, consideration of reality factors, including consideration of social inequality, definitely shows itself at the transition phase from preferences to intentions.

We must keep in mind that even at the stage of preference formation young people might consider the limiting reality factors. If it is so, we can propose that some part of young people, especially from strata far from the social top, takes into account its chances of reaching some positions in the society and therefore lowers orientations as early as on the stage of preferences formation.

Subject to considerations mentioned above, it is rightful to assume that not only at the phase of finishing secondary (complete) school, but at the previous steps of school education something similar occurs. In deciding on the practicability of staying in school or leaving it, teenagers and their parents decide at different phases of school education, subject to several actual factors, including the chances of receiving a certain educational level and corresponding statuses in future. This feature develops brightly in dropout dynamics.

On the whole, there is evidently a basis on which the following interpretation of existing educational differentiation in Russia is possible. (In our interpretation we consider that the differentiation is remaining and becoming more profound under the influence of falling living conditions, unemployment, education, and highly qualified jobs' prestige changes, introduction of paid education, and other factors, mentioned above.)

Differences in orientations and social behavior of youth in the educational field are a corollary and a reflection of differentiation in society. Partly, teenagers and their parents don't show interest or the necessary energy for realizing the series of opportunities provided by the educational system (*do not want*). They either do not have the motivation to reach for higher positions in the society or do not obtain the means of reaching these positions through education. Attitude to education, as evidenced by the whole series of researches (including ours), is related with the value system prevailing in the social group.

Partly, inequality of opportunity in getting an education shows itself more brightly in the higher educational field. As a result, the equalizing of chances and providing of a "social elevator" by means of education do not happen in most of cases, but the legitimation of social status transmission and inequality reproduction happens predominantly. The system fails those who *are not able* to overcome barriers in order to use the opportunities theoretically or potentially provided for all members of society. Here we see motivation toward achieving higher positions in the society by the means of education but socially imposed barriers inhibit its realization.

Those who lower their aspirations are adjoined to these categories of educational actors because they don't hope to overcome barriers; these are people who *do not want because are not able* (or think so, i.e., predict they will not be able). This is a result of their perception of reality—of recognizing and accepting it. There is a certain motivation to achieve higher positions in society by the means of education, but intentions are adjusted by awareness of social barriers.

Of course, obtained results have limitations, as every sociological research has. At the same time we should keep in mind that results have been derived from considering strong relationships, revealed in surveys, being repeated for thirty-five years and in several regions; and by the means of quantitative measurement of three indexes: preferences, intentions, and actual life steps.

CONCLUSION

Contemporary Russian youth understands well what transformations take place in society. Youth from upper groups have the potential necessary to realize this understanding. For decades Soviet youth wanted to become scientists, engineers, physicians (Shubkin 1970, 190–92). Now lawyers, economic and financial specialists, and programmers have the highest level of attractiveness (Konstantinovski 2000, 124–31). Youth of elite families move others aside and get the best positions in entering higher educational fields. Children of administrators outstrip others in entering professions of economy and finance; children from other groups receive professions with low perspectives for life career more often (Konstantinovski 2000, 189–90).

The differences in secondary school graduation rates among various groups plus strata inequality in access to higher education give us a picture of the current problems facing Russian youth and education. A stratification of chances in higher education in its basic configuration is similar to that of the Soviet period and to that found in other industrialized countries. But in Russian schools we notice a rapid growth in social disparity lately.

When looking into the future and considering the state of the economy, the transformation of the educational system, and the general situation in the country, the conclusion comes that in the immediate future the identified trends will continue. Today it is mostly children of yesterday's and the new elites, children of other social groups with a relatively high status who enter higher education and acquire high qualification professions, preferably in economics, finances, and law; it is they who will become the leaders of tomorrow's Russia.

Young Russians today are unlikely to get high positions in society through the meritocratic model, including education. "Hereditary princes and hereditary beggars" can become the rule of Russian society. A totalitarian or authoritarian regime, ingratiating itself with the people, would certainly adopt a populist attitude in this respect too; but as the experience of the Soviet period proves, the higher stratum privileges will continue, but in a more covert form.

Democratization was declared as one of the most important goals of Russian educational reformation. However, these aspirations have met some difficulties having complex social sources in a transition society. This is related to the contemporary general transformation of Russia, particularly the modification of the Russian educational system.

NOTES

The surveys were made in a research project under the direction of Professor Vladimir Shubkin in the Center for Sociology of Education and Youth (the chief scientist at present is the author of this paper), Institute of Sociology, Russian Academy of Sciences.

1. The works of French sociologists are popular in Russia. Diversified analysis of educational sociology development in France, summating and predicting, is made by Derouet (1999).

2. Recently the transition from eleven-year to twelve-year secondary (complete) education has been discussed. It concerns prolonging apprenticeship for one year for those who receive secondary (complete) education, but it does not touch mass education.

3. Due to volume limits, this article doesn't contain materials on particularities of urban and rural youth problems or gender particularities.

4. We do not consider here those who leave the upper grade without graduating.

5. Here are examples to show the way we processed the information received during the survey. The total personnel of an industrial enterprise was divided into the following groups: director, chief engineer, and machine-shop manager are referred to the administrator group; machine-shop and construction department engineers are the specialist group; accountants, clerks, stockmen are the white-collar group; turner and stamp operator are the blue-collar worker group. The personnel of a hospital: administrators—director, head physician, heads of departments; specialists—physicians; white-collar workers—nurses, hospital attendants; blue-collar workers—ambulance driver, cleaning people.

If a schoolchild is referred to some group, that means both (or at least one of) his or her parents are of that group. The higher parental status was considered determining. For example, if the father is a university teacher and the mother is a laboratory assistant with specialized secondary education, the child is referred to the specialist group. We based this on the results of our research: orientations and social behavior in the educational sphere correlates with data (attributes) of the parent with higher status. Such an approach has certain limitations, though the necessary analysis could be done.

6. It was the last Russian census to the present time.

7. The program that the Communist Party adopted at the twentieth party congress in 1956 provided for measures aimed at universal secondary education. The decision was confirmed by the following resolutions and the 1972 resolution of the Central Committee of the Communist Party and USSR Ministry Council, "On Completing the Transition to the Universal Secondary Education," was adopted.

8. Such interpretation of occupational prestige and preferences is in the article (Hyman 1966, 497).

9. Both indices can be understood as orientations. Additionally, first one indeed represents information on occupational prestige, and another can be taken as expectations.

10. Such an interpretation as applied to occupational choice is in Ginzberg 1951.

REFERENCES

Archer, M. 1978. *Social Origins of Educational Systems.* London: Sage.

Baudelot, C., and R. Establet. 1989. *Le niveau monte: Réfutation d'une vieille idée concernant la prétendue décadence de nos écoles.* Paris: Seuil.

Bidwell, C. E. 1995. "Schools, Faculties, and Equality of Educational Opportunity." In *Educational Advancement and Distributive Justice: Between Equality and Equity*, edited by R. Kahane, 99–116. Jerusalem: Magnes Press/Hebrew University.

Boudon, R. 1973. *L'inégalité des chances: La mobilité sociale dans les sociétés industrielles.* Paris: Armand Colin.

Boudon, R. 1974. *Education, Opportunity, and Social Inequality: Changing Prospects in Western Society.* New York: Wiley.

Bourdieu, P., and J.-C. Passeron. 1964. *Les héritiers: Les étudiants et la culture.* Paris: Les Éditions de Minuit.

Bourdieu, P., and J.-C. Passeron. 1970. *La reproduction: Eléments pour une théorie du systéme d'enseignement.* Paris: de Minuit.

Cherednichenko, G. A. 1999. "The Reform of Secondary School" [Reforma srednei shkoli]. *Sociological Journal* [Sociologicheskii Zsurnal] 1–2: 5–21. In Russian.

Coleman, J. S. 1968. "The Concept of Educational Equality." *Harvard Educational Review* 38: 7–23.

Coleman, J. S. 1995. "Social Change and the Loss of Social Capital: Implications for Children." In *Educational Advancement and Distributive Justice: Between Equality and Equity*, edited by R. Kahane, 17–31. Jerusalem: Magnes Press/Hebrew University.

Collins, R. 1978. *The Credential Society: An Historical Sociology of Education and Stratification.* New York: Academic.

Derouet, J.-L. 1999. "Sociology of Education: In Search of Society" [Sociologija obrasovanija: v poiskah obshestva]. *Journal of Sociology and Social Anthropology* [Zhurnal sociologii i social'noi antropologii], Sankt-Peterburg, special ed., 179–90. In Russian.

Dobson, R. B. 1988. "Higher Education in the Soviet Union: Problems of Access, Equity, and Public Policy." In *State and Welfare, USA/USSR: Contemporary Policy and Practice*, edited by G. W. Lapidus and G. E. Swanson, 17–60. Berkeley: Institute of International Studies, University of California.

Durkheim, E. 1897. *Suicide.* Chapter 5. [Russian edition: Diurkgeim E. Samoubiistvo M: Mysl', 1994, p. 235.]

Ginzberg, Eli, et al. 1951. *Occupational Choice: An Approach to a General Theory.* New York: Columbia University Press.

Gospodinov, K., V. Shubkin, and J. Andics, eds. 1986. *Social Problems of the Young Generation Today: International Comparative Study.* Sofia: Institute of Youth Studies.

Hyman, H. H. 1966. "The Value Systems of Different Classes." In *Class, Status, and Power*, edited by R. Bendix and S. M. Lipset, 488–99. New York: Free Press.

Konstantinovski, D. 1997. La transmission des statuts et le systeme de l'enseignement en Russie. In *Formation des élites et culture transnationale*, edited by D. Broady, N. Chmatko, and M. de Saint Martin, 47–62. Stockholm: FUKS, Lrarhgskolan.

Konstantinovski, D. 1999. *Inequality Dynamics: Russian Youth in Changing Society: Orientations and Paths in Educational Field (from 1960s to 2000)* [Dinamika neravenstva: Rossiiskaja molodezh' v meniajush'emsja obsh'estve: orientatsii i puti v sfere obrasovanija (ot 1960-h godov k 2000-mu)]. Moscow: Editorial URSS. In Russian.

Konstantinovski, D. 2000. *Youth of 90s: Self-determination in New Reality* [Molodezh' 90-h: samoopredelenie v novoi real'nosti]. Moscow: CSE RAE. In Russian.

Konstantinovski, D., and F. Khokhlushkina. 2000. "The Formation of the Social Behaviour of Young People in the Sphere of Education." *Russian Education and Society* 42, no. 2: 26–58.

Konstantinovski, D., and V. Shubkin. 1977. *Youth and Education* [Molodezh' i obrazo vanie]. Moscow: Nauka. In Russian.

Popkewitz, T .S. 1991. *A Political Sociology of Educational Reform: Power/Knowledge in Teaching, Teacher Education, and Research.* New York: Teachers College, Columbia University.

RF [Russian Federation]. 1995. *Russian Statistical Yearbook. Statistical Collection* [Rossiiskii statisticheskii ezhegodnik. Statisticheskii sbornik]. Moscow: Goskomstat Rossii. In Russian.

RF. 1999. *Russian Statistical Yearbook. Statistical Collection* [Rossiiskii statisticheskii ezhegodnik. Statisticheskii sbornik]. Moscow: Goskomstat Rossii. In Russian.

RF Education. 1995. *Education of Russia Population (by Data of Microcensus 1994). Statistical Collection* [Obrasovanie naselenija Rossii (po dannim mikroperepisi naselenija 1994 g.). Statisticheskii sbornik]. Moscow: Goskomstat Rossii. In Russian.

RF Law. 1966. Federal Law "On Inclusion of Alterations and Additions into the RF Law 'About Education'" [O vnesenii izmenenii i dopolnenii v zakon RF "Ob obrazovanii"]. In *Collection of RF Legislation* [Sobranie Zakonodatel'stva RF] 3: 150. Moscow: Juridicheskaja literatura. In Russian.

RF Youth. 1996. *Youth Situation in Russian Federation* [Polozhenie molodezhi v Rossiiskoi Federatsii]. Moscow: Gos. Komitet RF po delam molodezhi. In Russian.

Shakespeare, W. *As You Like It* 2.7 [Russian edition: Kak vam eto ponravitsja, in *Polnoe sobranie sochinenii*, 5:47.] Moscow: Iskusstvo, 1959.

Shubkin, V. N. 1970. *Sociological Experiments* [Sotsiologicheskie opiti]. Moscow: Mysl'. In Russian.

Shubkin, V. N., et al. 1968. "Quantitative Methods in Sociological Studies of Problems of Job Placement and Choice of Occupation." *Soviet Sociology* 7, no. 1: 3–24.

Trow, M. 1988. "American Higher Education: Past, Present, and Future." In *State and Welfare, USA/USSR: Contemporary Policy and Practice*, edited by G. W. Lapidus and G. E. Swanson, 61–92. Berkeley: Institute of International Studies, University of California.

Whitty, G., and T. Edwards. 1995. "Social Justice and Education in a New Era: Rhetoric and Reality." In *Educational Advancement and Distributive Justice: Between Equality and Equity*, edited by R. Kahane, 32–46. Jerusalem: Magnes Press/Hebrew University.

12

Education, Power, and the State:

Successes and Failures of Latin American Education in the Twentieth Century

Carlos Alberto Torres

THE CENTURY OF EDUCATION: PRELIMINARY CONSIDERATIONS

Eu sustento que a unica finalidade da ciencia esta em aliviar a miseria da existencia humana.

—Bertolt Brecht[1]

The twentieth century is marked by the extension of educational opportunities to children as well as to youth and adults in all social sectors in Latin America. The twentieth century has been the century of education, and the role of the state in the promotion of public education has been decisive in reaching this objective. In this century, particularly in the last five decades, limited public resources have been spent in the provision of basic education for children, youth, and adults; the years of obligatory schooling have been extended significantly; initial and preschool education was provided to an increasingly broad gamut of families, especially families possessing few resources; access for children with learning deficiencies or disabilities was facilitated in Latin American classrooms; and equal opportunity for the poor, immigrants, and indigenous peoples, as well as for girls and women, were substantially improved. Without doubt, the twentieth century is marked also by the femininization of the educational enrollment.

Along with the expansion of educational opportunities, improvement in efficiency took place, exemplified in the increased capacity to retain students in the initial and middle levels of the system, and in the capacity to promote them so that they continue advancing in the school system, arriving eventually in postsecondary school and completing postsecondary studies in ever increasing numbers. At the same time, the themes of quality and relevance of education have been a secular preoccupation of thinkers, public intellectuals, teachers, leaders of teachers' unions, and members of the governmental bureaucracies. These concerns echo the demands expressed daily in schoolyards and classrooms as well as in public forums by parents of different social sectors deeply interested in the education of their children.

The Latin American population, like most of the world population, accepted the Enlightenment argument, amply disseminated by the liberal states, that education constitutes a building block for progress and a good in and of itself. This modern premise reinforces itself with theoretical developments of the discipline of economics of education, whose repercussions in Latin America will be reviewed later in this chapter. The central aspect is that people believe there are not great possibilities of social advance without better educational standards. That is, education appears not only as consumption but as an investment with individual and social high rates of return that vary according to the educational levels. One can conclude from this viewpoint that a more educated population will be a population with greater levels of social tolerance and conviviality, more productive and competitive in the national and international markets. In the end, to say it in the sociological jargon, the Enlightenment will argue that higher levels of education will produce a better society composed of more satisfied, responsible, and productive individuals.

This expansion, diversification, and amplification of educational opportunities has been seen as a condition sine qua non for the expansion of the imperative Kantian categories of social justice and individual responsibility in the society in its entirety, especially in the different versions of the welfare state. The expansion and universalization of education appears not only as a sign of modernity or a sign of greater rationality of social action but, paradoxically, also as a precondition of the two.

However, equity, quality (including effectiveness, equality, and efficiency), and relevance of education continue to be critical questions of educational systems. Toward the end of the century, Latin American states were prisoners of the contradictions of Latin American development and of their own logic of bureaucratic action, and still healing the wounds of the double crisis of external debt and fiscal crisis of the state that have lasted since the 1980s,[2] like a burden impossible to overcome. They found it even more difficult to attack the existing problems in the educational world, especially given the difficulties in educational financing and, as we will see further on, in the function of political philosophies and educational agendas that seek the privatization of education through user fees, vouchers, or charter schools, a movement that may signal the abandonment of state's responsibilities in financing public education.

Consequently, the expansion, diversification, and improvement of educational systems, which we would like to denominate, rhetorically, the triumphs of education, are obscured by the miseries of Latin American education. The elementary and secondary educational systems of the region continue to be segregated by social class, where the poor study in public schools and the middle and upper classes flourish educationally in private institutions. With few exceptions in the countries of the region, initial education and preschooling, decisive in the cognitive constitution of boys and girls, although it has been expanded notably compared with the beginning of the twentieth century, when this education was a privilege of very wealthy families, it is not within the reach of the majority of the poor populations of the continent. Illiteracy continues to be an enormous problem, like a medusa of multiple heads, where the disadvantage of women and the indigenous sectors with respect to the literacy of the rest of the society grows. Bilingual education, though expanded consistently in the last three decades, still doesn't reach the level necessary to serve the large majority of indigenous populations to be fully bilingual. Regrettably adult education, which used to be a central preoccupation, at least in the rhetorics of certain government alliances and social movements in the 1960s and 1970s, has been relegated into a marginal area in policy terms in the 1980s, in spite of the growing demand and significance of the problem, practically languishing as a public political issue toward the end of the century. In a certain sense, the situation of illiteracy, with dimensions much more complex given the demands of cybernetic literacy and the advances in communication, locates the problem of functional, cybernetic, and computational literacy, practically at the same problematic level as functional literacy was an educational problem to be dealt with around the turn of the nineteenth century and the beginning of the twentieth (Torres 1990). Like a Greek tragedy of eternal return, and in spite of the advances in scholarship, we observe a new crisis of the demand for adult education when we enter in the new century. Teacher training, and especially teacher pay, continue to be the Gordian knots of educational policies, much more hastened facing the transformations of the neoliberal state policies. The politics of curriculum aiming at promoting scientific and humanistic education of the population confront unusual challenges with the technological advances and the knowledge explosion in a world growing more globalized and segmented by class. This curriculum crisis is compounded by the strong discrimination of race, class, and gender in Latin American educational systems. Furthermore, this crisis is aggravated by the fact that some regional markets remain outside the dynamics of globalization, removed from the circuits of production, accumulation, circulation and consumption of the world system, with the educational, social, political and economic repercussions that this implies. The links within education and work, with the shortcomings in the work markets and employment, reaching in Argentina (as confirmed by official statistics) 16 percent of the economic active population, as well as growing levels of poverty, especially among the less educated inhabitants of the region, is another theme hastened by current public policies. We saw the end of the century with innumerable conflicts in higher education in Latin America; with Chilean university students taking to the streets to demand more funds; with public Brazilian universities recuperating after several months of strike without obtaining the majority of their objectives; with the University of Buenos Aires, threatened by financial austerity policies by a government trying to meet the demands of the International Monetary Fund to the point of risking closing their doors by the first of October 1999, two months before the normal end of the academic year if the economic adjustment was to be carried out; and with the National Autonomous University of Mexico (UNAM) in a strike that lasted several months, with a student social movement that summoned in its massive mobilization more than a quarter million people in the streets, and the resolution of the conflict was as expected, the police entering the UNAM campus, detaining students, the resignation of the University President, and the appointment of another university president. These and many other similar situations reflect what has happened in the region's universities in the last years. These stories tell us that the Latin American public university continues fighting for its identity in confronting the new century, debating within its honorable reformist tradition, and the complexities of negotiating with political regimes each time less interested in supporting their public universities. Moreover, the public universities find themselves struggling to understand and manage the new pressures of globalization and their repercussions in local politics.

The greatness of public education in this century ran the risk of being blinded by the miseries of public politics that renounce their liberal democratic tradition, with potential damage in the education of citizens, one of the central responsibilities of the state in education. This chapter offers empirical evidence and normative and analytical arguments, showing the progress, but also the backward steps, the triumphs and the miseries of Latin American education. In doing so, it also highlights ideas that have yielded significant fruit and contributed to create educational traditions of distinction, and signaling, in their final section, some of the principal challenges for education in the new century. The risk that we confront, ostensibly, is that the breakdown of the agreement for public education may signify and, worse indeed, perhaps anticipate the breakdown of the democratic pact in Latin American societies.

STATE AND EDUCATION: UNITY IN DIVERSITY

> All systems are false, Marx as much as Aristotle—even when both can have seen the truth.
>
> —Max Horkheimer[3]

The civil wars ended in the last of the nineteenth century, culminating in the process of national reorganization that the Latin American countries concluded around 1880. The Latin American educational systems were created a little after the newly independent nations established their borders, created unified armed forces, promulgated national constitutions based in liberal principles coming from the English Magna Charta, the American Revolution, and the French Revolution. Additionally, language policies in defense of Spanish or Portuguese as national languages were linked to the sovereignty of the country. The final step in the constitution of the new nations was, of course, the establishment of a gradual and progressive extension of the obligatory and free primary education to all the social sectors.

Education, in the invention of the liberal illustration, was a responsibility of the state, acting *in loco parentis*. In the twentieth century, three great political regimes have predominated, with the exceptions obviously, of the abundant revolutionary experiences in the region. The twentieth century has been also the century of social revolutions in Latin America. These state models represent different styles of state authoritarianism (i.e., authoritarian populism, corporatism, or military dictatorships). Although these situations, very common in Latin American politics, have altered whatever image of a pure form of liberal democratic government may exist, the main administration of state has been marked by these three state movements with important educational implications. Let me, theoretically, suggest few insights into the state–education relationship in the region.

We find first the oligarchic liberal state, a conservative state that emerged in the region between 1880 and 1920 and, depending on national histories, lasted until the end of World War II and underwent the important crisis of 1929 that reoriented the geopolitical axis of Latin America, displacing Great Britain from power and signaling the growing presence of the United States in the region. It was this liberal (though deeply conservative) state controlled by landowner oligarchies and based on electoral fraud that gave the original impulse to public systems of education. Next, dressed in distinct robes, the developmentalist state emerges from the middle of the 1940s until approximately the crisis of the 1970 and 1980s—newly with the huge historical variabilities and national conditions—reflecting consistent patterns of forced modernization of national societies with the ruling axis of the state; the notion of education as human capital was decisive for the expansion of schooling systems. Even when the developmentalist state was replaced by military dictatorships like Argentina, Brazil, Chile, Uruguay, these technocratic models based on human capital theory were not replaced and coexisted side by side with spiritualist models inspired by conservative Catholic humanism in education. Finally came the great rupture of the 1980s, with the fiscal and debt crisis, giving way to models of structural adjustment and economic stabilization, and to the neoliberal state in the region with open markets, deregulation, decentralization, and privatization of education.

If one tried to find parallel models of public Latin American education with educational transformations of the world systems, one would be able to say that the liberal model of public education prevails since the middle to end of the nineteenth century until the crisis of 1929, giving way to models of compensatory education where public education plays a decisive role in developing state models that, with the historical, economic, and atavistic peculiarities of the region, resembles forms of the welfare state, with the landmark of Roosevelt's New Deal. Finally we find the neoliberal state of the 1980s in Latin America that corresponds, pari passu, to the neoconservative experiences in the developed world (Thatcher, Reagan, Mulrony governments), with their enormous international impacts on the educational agendas advanced particularly by international organizations. The end of the century in Latin America is marked by the globalization of education and the presence of the hegemonic agenda of neoliberalism in education.

Certainly, this highly aggregated historiographic periodization presents very complex difficulties for the analysis of the links between state and education, not only because of the national peculiarities but also because of the dynamics of structural transformation in the region, although similar, this agenda doesn't necessarily impact in identical terms all the countries, the educational models, the financing of education, or the main guidelines of educational policies. Certainly there is a parallel between state models and educational models, but to remember one of the teachings of Marx, the social formations, as well as the modes of production, never die before the new social form is born. On the contrary, social formations superimpose each other, they juxtapose one another, they survive over time and cohabitate, in an amalgam very rebellious for the understanding of the historic imagination that invites caution in the historic analysis.

Clearly the beginnings of Latin American public education have sufficient elements in common to justify a generic analysis like the one proposed here. Yet in the realm of sociology of education there is enough evidence to argue that educational transformations in the world system toward the end of the twentieth century both homogenize and fragment drastically all the systems of schooling, including the modus operandi, models of public education, patterns of educational transformation in general (including private education), the strategies of educational transformation and educational reform, school administration, and the broad principles of teaching and learning. Unity in diversity of educational experiences in the region can be the motto of this conversation about greatnesses and miseries in Latin American education in the twentieth century.

EXPANSION AND CRISIS OF LATIN AMERICAN EDUCATION: THE END OF THE CENTURY

In a sense, this is a game of never-ending mirrors.

—Immanuel Wallerstein[4]

I have argued elsewhere (Torres and Puiggrós 1997, 6–8) that the expansion of education in Latin America was linked to the early stage of industrialization in the 1950s and 1960s and that represents one of the highest rates of educational growth in the world. Between 1960 and 1970, the rate of growth of higher education and of middle education was 247.9 percent and 258.3 percent, respectively, amply documented by UNESCO (1974, 167, 227). However, the growth of primary education, which crowned the force of expansion of the system during the century, although significant, was much more modest than the other levels, reaching 167.6 percent. The literacy rates remained relatively consistent in the majority of the countries of the Latin American area (UNESCO 1971). One study ended about the end of the 1970s shows a significant continuity in this pattern of educational development (UNESCO/CEPAL/PNUD 1981).[5] In this spirit, the Chilean investigator Ernesto Schiefelbein, analyzing the financing of education, argues that the four decades preceding the 1990s represents a significant progress for the Latin American democracies throughout: "(i) expansion of access to education for the majority of children that reach school age, (ii) extension of the years of schooling; (iii) betterment in the quick access to school; (iv) nutritional provision and care to a very large number of poor children; (v) increase in the provision of minimum input for the schooling and elimination of the differential channels for social levels" (Schiefelbein 1997, 32). This optimistic diagnosis, clear as it is, doesn't reflect any overconfidence if one might consider the high rates of repetition of the region and the drop out rates.[6]

In spite of secular growth of the educational system in terms of rates of enrollment especially in primary education, the rate of growth of educational spending, adjusted for inflation, diminished in the 1980s. The Venezuelan educator Fernando Reimers shows that between 1975 and 1980 total spending on education increased in all the countries of the region. However, between 1980 and 1985, total spending in real terms decreased in twelve of the eighteen countries studied (Reimers 1990, 16).[7] Reimers argues that in contrast with the previous successes in expansion of public education, the last two decades signify a fall in the school quantity and quality in the region. According to Reimers's research, the Ministry of Education in the region saw itself forced to sacrifice equity and efficiency in order to reduce educational spending under political pressures of structural adjustment. Those budget cuts affected in a disproportionate manner primary education and reflect on limited resources in terms of teaching materials, school buildings, and falling rates of enrollment (Reimer 1991, 325–38).[8] A natural consequence of those adjustments is that the decrease in educational spending alienated the organizations of the teaching profession, especially to the unions of schoolteachers and university professors, creating new areas of conflict in school–state relations in terms of the formation, operationalization, and evaluation of the public politics in education (Carnoy and Torres 1994; Torres 1998).

As Reimers and Tiburcio signal,

> An analysis of the changes in public financing of education in Latin America between 1970 and 1985 concludes that the adjustment took a disproportionate cut

in the educational spending as a percentage of governmental spending in education or as a percentage of the Gross National Product. Within the education, the spending in capital or infrastructure suffered in a disproportionate manner as well as made it all the items that were not linked to salary, while many countries reduced even more disproportionately the spending on primary education. A study of the financial crisis in Central America between 1979–89 concludes that the majority of the countries (with the exception of Honduras) showed a tendency to spend a smaller percentage of the GNP in education, then the salaries of the teaching profession has depreciated in real terms with a loss of around two-thirds of its worth, and that the end of the decade the majority of the educational budget goes to pay salaries. (Reimers and Tiburcio 1993, 22)

A similar analysis for Brazil and Mexico shows that the fall in the educational budget took place "in a scenario of growth of the governmental sector in relative terms of the PBI" (Reimers and Tiburcio 1993, 37). For reasons much more clear in terms of teacher salaries subsidizing the educational expansion, and not as much in terms of reduction of the educational expenditure per se, a similar phenomenon has been detected in Mexico through a historic and longitudinal analysis of teacher salaries in the decades 1940 to 1980 (Morales-Gómez and Torres 1990).

The next section is an attempt to synthetize and analyze some of the key educational theories that have prevailed in Latin American environments during the twentieth century, which to some extent explain key developments in educational reforms in the region.

EDUCATIONAL THEORIES IN LATIN AMERICA: A CRITICAL OVERVIEW

I give for a metaphor all of the syllogisms, with their ergo correspondents that allow them to freeze in the scholastic decanter; the metaphor teaches me more, illuminates me more and, above all, I find heat under it, as the imagination only at fire works.

—Miguel de Unamuno[9]

It's convenient, at the end of the century, to take stock of the ideas that animated the educational debates in the region during the last century. Yet, given the limitations of space in this chapter, this analysis cannot be exhaustive. Running the risk of making an economy of analysis that violates reality, I have preferred to synthesize, without doing justice to these ideas and traditions, the pedagogical debate in terms of great lines of thought, which on occasion intersect, on occasions oppose one another, on occasions merge in an eclectic array of politics and thought of individuals and institutions. This eclecticism allows paradigms to borrow pedagogical concepts from one another in a very libertarian manner. But this is justly the nature of reality, or at least how we can perceive it on the surface. The chaotic, the confusing, the intense, the impassioned, and the normative coexist intimately with the systematic and methodical, the ordered, the synthetic, and the analytical. That which follows is an intent to briefly formalize the distinctive lines of these traditions, without any pretension of exhaustiveness.

A DIFFICULT TRANSITION? FROM PEDAGOGICAL POSITIVISM, SPIRITUALISM, HUMANISM, AND NORMALISM TO THE ECONOMY OF EDUCATION AND HUMAN CAPITAL THEORIES

The school systems of Latin America reflect an extraordinarily eclectic mixture of philosophical and pedagogical thoughts that, in a complex amalgam, oriented the discussions on education, especially between the transition of the end of the past century, or we say, at least, since the generation of the 1880s, until the appearance of the model of the "New School" in Latin America. An incredibly interesting mix is the pedagogical spiritualism, on occasions linked to Catholic education, including a conservative tone, and the logic of pedagogical positivism. As Moacir Gadotti (1998) points out, these orientations find their origins in liberal pedagogical principles from Rousseau to Pestalozzi, Herbart, and the education premises that came from the French Revolution.

It is impossible to realize, in few pages, the history of the pedagogical ideas in Latin America; perhaps it will be an impossible chore in spite of interesting intents to synthesize those processes from a historical perspective (Puiggros 1996; 1997; Cucuzza 1996). In large part, this tradition is mixed with the practice of normalism, the Sarmintinean image of the teachers or, better said, the female teacher, as constructor from the classrooms of the nation, forger of minds and souls, true missionary of the Enlightenment. Curiously enough, drawing from the positivistic foundations of the logic of normalism, and later from the transition to a scientificist model in education with the insertion at the end of the 1970s of the political economics of education, the new versions of educational planning supported in positivist epistemological principles that had lengthy history in the region, and adapting them, curiously, in a paradoxical turn of history, so to speak, to the theories of human capital.

The pedagogical and philosophical model of normalism looked to sustain a homogeneous system and a homogeneous pedagogical subject, ignoring in great measure the differences in pedagogical subjects, a difference that was not only segmented by class, gender, religion, or ethnicity, but was ever mounting with the growing international migration of the turn of the twentieth century from Europe that modified, quite dramatically, the demographics of the populations, particularly in the Southern Cone of Latin

America. Normalism was conceived of as a system where there would have been a great level of control in a highly centralized system. With a great sense of optimism in the civilizing task of school, fundamentally, and without questioning the oligarchic foundations of conservative regimes that brought to life the foundations of the modern Latin American schools, normalism adopted, with the differences and the specific readings of liberalism adapted to the conservative necessities of oligarchic politics, a model of positivist orientation to combat the tendencies of the traditional humanist or spiritualist curriculum that had a historic force in education much further from its heuristic possibilities (Puiggros 1990).

Positivism reflects a collection of propositions of how to carry out scientific work. Knowledge, for positivism, exists in three distinct levels of abstraction and therefore generalization: to the level of particular observation, to the level of the laws and empirical generalizations, and to the level of theoretical definitions. In general terms, the explanations are based on the possibility of establishing regularities, or a pattern of uniformities that can be differentiated from the accidental generalizations or the laws. Insofar as the positivistic explanations come from the natural sciences and not from the social sciences, the epistemology of positivism is confronted with the principle of ambiguity from the social sciences. In the natural sciences, an event that does not conform to a rule of universality invalidates the rule; in the social sciences, this is virtually the case of practically every event, insofar as the social reality is open, and every event is, potentially, of an idiosyncratic nature—phenomenology will take this to an extreme. The epistemological problem of avoiding discrete events invites positivism to consider notions or models of statistical probability more than generalizations starting from the laws. These, at their time, should be different from generalization of empirical observations, which places under discussion the most dense theme of how to move from the level of empirical observations to the definitions of causality, without having to base itself in interpretations, that for the positivists would be to accept a metaphysical model, something unacceptable for this paradigm. From this standpoint arise the hypothetical deductive models, where reality is converted in a collection of logical constructions (or mathematics, using a different language) more than a set of real entities. The problem, unsolvable at times for positivism, is how to differentiate an observation from a theory, in equal manner, how one can distinguish itself, and this a central epistemological premise, a value judgment from an empirical judgment. Finally, to end this brief epistemological rendezvous, positivism has serious difficulties in understanding the transformation of nonlineal events, or the profound discontinuity from the phenomena of real life. In the same manner, the singularity and subjectivity of the investigator is ignored in function of a omnicomprehensive notion of social objectivity. Positivistic pedagogical thinkers argue that there is a fundamental social order motivating a dynamic of transformation from social reality. This order is discernible

with the rigorous and objective application of the specific method of the social sciences. This method, obviously, reflects the premises of all the scientific
methods linked to the model of the natural sciences; this is a method based
in foundationalism, objectivity, the search for control and the manipulation
of variables, experimentalism (or, better said, given the historicity of the social processes and the ethical difficulties of working with human subjects,
quasi-experimentalism), universality, and rationality.

In a curious twist of fate, the culmination of this process of relying on a
method and a logic that would eliminate the spiritualist biases of Latin
American pedagogical thought and that radically affected the experience of
normalism, was the theory of human capital. This model is based on the neoclassic economic theories that postulate the benevolence of self-interest. This
is to say that individuals are rational, that they make their decisions, always
in function of a deliberate economic calculation (even when the decisions
they may make are mistakes), and that the pursuit of totally self-centered interests will result, in final instance, in a benefit for society on the whole.
("Benevolence" 1998, 80; Pescador 1994, 167). This theory was not originally
a theory about the investment and return of education, but was born as a
theory trying to explain that the rates of growth of education in world development have been the result of satisfying the growing demand for workers with greater and better capabilities and skills in an employment market
expansion and increasingly differentiated by specializations. (Torres, Pannu,
and Bacchus 1993, 3–32). As Pescador points out, "The traditional definition
of human capital comprehends the abilities, the talent and the understandings of an individual, and since times past the economists have identified
human capital analyzing only its origins of investment and particularly education. In great measure, the bibliography identifies education more as human capital than important in its own sense" (1994, 163).

The theory of human capital considers that the expense of education of the
individual consists of two components, one of consumption and another of
investment (Pescador 1994, 163). In the latter case everything is based on a
theory of choice (rational choice) and the maximization of profits under certain restrictions. From here arises the powerful concept of the rates of return
on an investment in education which, since disseminated in the bureaucratic-
educational environment of Latin America, have constituted an unavoidable
reference in the educational decision-making process. The rates of return, or
rates of profitability, permit the calculation of economic results starting from
the costs that we incur in education, as much from individuals (rates of private return) as from society (rate of social return). Among the most interesting results of this model are the following:

1. Not all educational levels have the same type of profitability in the investment (under the premise that the marginal profit in the possible result of investing in a unit more than a specific product; in this case, one

measures approximately the marginal profit of an individual to decide to have an additional year of education).

2. "The cost of opportunity tends to diminish as it extends to each level of education" (Pescador 1994, 165).
3. There is a strong bias in the models of investment where one considers that virtually all earnings "constitute exclusively yields from the investment in some form of human capital" (Pescador 1994, 166).

In the models of distribution of the income, the theory of human capital argues that "the income of the people constitutes in this way the yield of their investments in human capital, for which its distribution depends on the distribution of the investment of human capital and its corresponding rate of yield" (Pescador 1994, 166).

It cannot be doubted that these neoclassic premises in education, joined to the structural-functionalist models regarding the functionality of education (Morrow and Torres 1995, Torres 1989; 1990), provided many of the keys of intellectual rationality for the allocation of resources and the formulation of educational politics in the world. However, in spite of the restriction of space, it is advisable to point to the consideration that this theory is subject to question, both in terms of its political orientation and theoretical and methodological grounding. This theory had enormous force in the 1950s and 1960s, extending into the present times, in constant reincarnations, in many of the economic formulations of neoliberalism in education.

First, in the measure that the educational opportunities have increased more rapidly than the labor opportunities, this has resulted in a true inflation of credentials in terms of classification of manual labor; the educational threshold of the professions has risen systematically in the last four decades to a global level. From this situation one may question the link between education and productivity; already many more individuals look for more education in order to augment their chances of employability, that is to say, to better their position in the employment line of those looking for better jobs. This theory of the line in education, and the notion divulged in the 1970s of the "diploma disease," poses difficult questions to answer from the statistical models of human capital. For instance, does education increase the product (individual and social) or simply assign individuals to jobs of higher and more complex technological requirements, that in turn are those of greater productivity and potential income? Is public education simply a subsidy for employers, that is to say, to socialize the costs of producing people trained to satisfy the necessities of companies? Does the educational credential legitimize an unequal social structure, and in as much contribute to the reproduction of unequal labor roles? These themes invite an analysis that goes beyond the analytical possibilities of the theories of human capital and of the economics of education in itself. These questions, and many more that remain in the inkwell (or should we say in the keyboard) due to lack of space invite us to develop a political economy of education.

THE "NEW SCHOOL"

As Moacir Gadotti correctly pointed out, the movement of the "New School," which has in the North American philosophy and pedagogy of John Dewey as one of its most remarkable thinkers, comes from a distinguished tradition including such intellectuals as Adolphe Ferriere, Edouard Claparede, Jean Piaget, and William Heard Kilpatrick. The New School represents the most vigorous movement of renovation of education in the twentieth century since the creation of the public bourgeois school (Gadotti 1998, 147). Developing a directivist pedagogy sui generis centered in the child and not in the directivist and instructional work of the teacher, the philosophy of the new school proposed that education was the propeller of social change valuing self-transformation and the spontaneous activity of children. This model makes two pedagogical pillars of the notions of experience and activity. One learns by doing, would be the Deweyian maxim, and based in a pragmatic posture, looked to augment the educational outcome from the child starting from his experience rather than from a teachers-centered motivation. The principles of initiative, originality, and cooperation were advanced as key to liberate the potential of the individual and changing the social order, seeking an education that will reformulate democracy (Dewey 1981). Obviously, the impact of this thought in the Latin American pedagogical environments still resounds with enormous force. It is little known that Dewey was consulted immediately after the Mexican Revolution on how to adapt the principles of the New School to the educational principles of the revolution. Much more widely known is the impact that the New School had in Brazil with the administration of Anixio Texeira, associated with the modernization of Brazilian education, reaching even to reverberate in the some of the positions that Paulo Freire later took.[10]

Dussell and Caruso point out that in spite of the impact that in the last instance the notion of the New School had, in the first decades of this century it was a marginal thought.

> It's not a surprise that during the first decades of this century the diffusion of ideas of Dewey were led by liberal and radical pedagogues who, in a distinct manner, confronted the status quo. Many of them considered the North American educational system and the pedagogies coming from the United States a model example for reforming a country where the oligarchy owner of the land governed a fraudulent democracy. Industrialism and popular participation were the lights of the city for them. However, its global administration led them to not consider the differences and the fights that had given form to the North American curriculum. (Dussell and Caruso 1997, 108)

After World War II, a renewed incorporation of Dewey in the Latin American pedagogical panorama, as pragmatic philosopher, took place but without displacing definitively the positions of spiritualism and humanism, still hidden in the different education layers of teacher training institutions and Ministries of Education, especially in the Southern Cone.

The appearance of the models of popular education and the experiences and theories of Paulo Freire in the cold decades of the 1960s and 1970s altered radically the educational proposals. However it is clear that both the spiritualist authoritarian approach and the humanist perspective continue reappearing in the Latin American pedagogical environment time and time again, especially the first model associated with dictatorial experiences.

PAULO FREIRE AND POPULAR EDUCATION

The paradigm of popular education has been born from the radical models of education, many of which are linked to the experiences of Paulo Freire in Brazil in the 1960s. The common characteristics of popular education have been discussed by distinct analysts and synthesized in other places (Gadotti and Torres 1993; Torres 1995a, 1995b). This pedagogy, personalized in the figure of philosopher of education and pedagogue Paulo Reglus Neves Freire, was initially developed in Brazil and Chile, spreading itself with vigor in the Southern Cone and reaching Mexico, the United States, and Canada, but influencing innumerable education programs around the world; it may suffice to cite only some, like the literacy campaigns in Guinea-Bissau, Cabo Verde, São Tome e Principe, Nicaragua and Mexico, or adult education programs in Tanzania and South Africa.

Popular education comes from a political and social analysis of the life conditions of the poor and of their most visible problems (like malnutrition, unemployment, health problems), and intends to arrive at an understanding, both at the level of individual and collective consciousness, of these conditions. It bases educational practices in collective and individual experiences, taking very seriously the previous knowledge acquired by the populations, and works in groups more than on an individual basis. The concept of education that those programs offer is intimately related with capabilities or concrete classifications that intend to teach to the poor, for example, reading, writing, and arithmetic, and seek to inspire in the participants a sense of pride, dignity, and confidence in themselves in order to reach a political and social level of autonomy. Finally, those plans can be originated by governments with relation to rural integrated development plans as in Colombia and the Dominican Republic (Torres 1995a), or as the same experience of Paulo Freire in front of the Municipal Secretary of Education of São Paulo 1989–1991 during the administration of the Workers Party (PT) demonstrates it (O'Cadiz, Wong, and Torres 1998), or as in Nicaragua with the popular education collectives (Arnove 1986) and can direct themselves as much to adults as to children.

A pedagogical emblem for the focus of Paulo Freire and the pedagogy of the oppressed (Torres 1995b; Gadotti 1989; Rodrigues Brandao 1981) is that the key problems of education are not methodological or pedagogical but political. The educational programs that are designed through the inspiration of this model, with strong historical presence in the field of adult education and literacy, try to be established in instruments or mechanisms of politico-pedagogical collaborations with the socially subordinated sectors. It is a pedagogy for social transition and, therefore, defines its educational activity as a "cultural action" whose central objective can be summarized with the term "conscientization." In its most radical version, the specificity of the conscientization resides in the development of critical consciousness and class practice, that is to say, appears as part of the "subjective conditions" of the process of social transformation or, in traditional terminology, social revolution.

In strictly educational terms, its intention is a nonauthoritarian pedagogy. Teachers and students are at the same time students and teachers linked by a pedagogical dialogue characterized by a horizontal relationship. The educational program can be carried out as much in the classroom as in a "cultural circle" in informal or nonformal settings, and the transmission of ideas and understandings takes place starting from the previous knowledge of the educated. Among the fundamental characteristics of this focus one finds its historical resistance to work within the educational systems, given their suspicion on the role of the apparatus of the capitalistic state and the bureaucratic organization of educational practice. To the degree that the state and school represent places where relations of domination are hidden, with a strong presence of hidden curriculum, this pedagogy advocates, in many of its versions, by the creation of de-schooling alternatives à la Illich, including fairly anti-intellectual positions—making possible, on occasions, as Freire lamented in a conversation with me, the presence of a movement that he characterized as "basism," which implies the rejection of formal knowledge and authority, and the acritical celebration of popular knowledge as the only origin of pedagogical work (Torres 1994). It's interesting to remark that this paradigm seeks to establish nonstate alternatives inserted in the heart of civil society. In consequence, many of its representatives work politically and professionally close to political parties, or in universities and centers of research, as well as in organizations that are Church-related.

Clearly this pedagogical invention, linked to the notion of cultural revolution in the 1960s, is a model diametrically opposed to the predominantly neoliberal model in Latin American education, which constitutes, paradoxically, the culmination of the most conservative and capitalist positions in Latin American education, and a flagrant contradiction with the liberal tradition and the spirit of public education, obligatory and free, that predominated the continent since the last century.[11]

It is worth pointing out, in turn, as a precaution, that although the neoliberal agenda is intimately linked to the neoclassic economic principles that prevail in diverse regulatory institutions of capitalism like the World Bank, the International Monetary Fund, and diverse foundations of the advanced industrial capitalist world and organizations of bilateral help, there is an "elective affinity" to use a Weberian language, with the postures of the neoliberal governments of the region, the majority of which adopted the guidelines of this agenda. In the case of a distinguished liberal tradition like the postrevolutionary Mexican state, although the typically neoliberal economic politics did not have the same level of interference and control in the economy, especially during the government of Carlos Salinas de Gortari, the limits and possibilities of educational transformation in the country are clearly influenced by key principles of the neoliberal tradition. The recent triumph of a conservative populist candidate, overthrowing the Revolutionary Institutional Party that ruled the country for more than seventy-six years, makes it very difficult to estimate the next direction of education in Mexico. However, the new president has already indicated his interest in "total quality models," managerial solutions, and open market philosophies guiding his future government.

THE NEOLIBERAL AGENDA:
THE AGENDA OF PRIVATIZATION

The analytic premises of the hegemonic neoliberal agenda, well represented in diverse international organisms like the World Bank, can be categorized under the etiquette of supply-side economics. Two political premises guide this agenda: the notion of privatization of public education and the reduction of public expenditure. Obviously these political orientations are not incompatible, and privatization can be considered an important strategy for the reduction of public sector expenditure. The notion of privatization requires an additional explanation. These politics are crucial elements in the reforms that promote the liberalization of the market. On one side, they reduce the pressure of public expenditure through the privatization of the enterprises of the public sector. On the other side, privatization is a powerful tool to depoliticize the regulatory practices of the state. Privatization plays a central role in the political arsenal of neoliberalism because: "purchase of service contracting is both an administrative mechanism for addressing the particular issues of the social legitimacy of the state involved in direct social services and an attempt to borrow from the managerial ethos of private enterprise (and entrepreneurial development) systems of cost benefit analysis and management by objectives" (Culpitt 1992, 94).

Neoliberals and neoconservatives argue that the state and the market are two diametrically opposed social systems, and that both are real options for providing specific services (Moran and Wright 1991). Why is there a preference for the market over the state? The neoliberals consider the markets more versatile and efficient than the bureaucratic structures of the state for countless reasons (Torres 1996, 1998; Torres et al 1999). Neoliberals argue that the markets respond more rapidly to technological changes and the social demand than the state. The markets are seen as more efficient and cost-effective than the public sector in the provision of services. Finally, market competition will produce greater "accountability" for the social investment than bureaucratic politics. Together with these political preferences the neoliberals link privatization of public enterprises with the solution of the problem of external debt. After all, in a certain version of the neoliberal ideology, the state enterprises "were responsible for creating the Latin American debt problem and, more importantly . . . their privatization may help resolve that problem" (Ramamurti 1991, 153). However, it's worth remarking that the process of privatization is not free from contradictions. For example, Ramamurti (1991, 168) suggested that "it is by no means certain that substantial efficiency gains will be realized in the long run by privatizing large [enterprises of the state] with high market power." A second source of conflict has to do with the regulatory mechanisms:

> given Latin America's poor record of government regulation and the lack of established procedures for resolving regulatory disputes (other than by informal pressures and behind-the-scenes negotiations), it is difficult to be optimistic about the quality of regulation after privatization. Governments may renationalize some of these industries in the future, by choice or by necessity. Were that to happen, foreigners might have to be compensated for their investments at rates much higher than those received at the time of privatization, thus creating a potentially large outflow in the future. Such conflicts could also damage relations with private investors, causing a recurrence of outward capital flight, at worst. (Ramamurti 1991, 169)

A final commentary concerning this generic philosophy of privatization: Many of its proponents seek an antistatistical perspective more than a true perspective of privatization with enhancement of market competition. In other words, the question is, Do these policies generate true competition in diverse markets or constitute a strategy to replace the monopoly that the state enterprises has, in specific areas of the economy, with a similar monopoly but this time in charge of select private enterprises?

In terms of specific education policies, the neoliberal agenda seeks an amalgam of positions, all of which are represented in the policies of the World Bank. For example, it seeks the democratization of schooling, increased participation of women and children in education, a very laudable objective located at the heart of liberal politics for equality. But there is sufficient information to show that what is given with one hand may be taken back with the other: the rhetoric of equality via the educational policies of the World Bank support the education of women but, on the other hand, women are exactly those who have paid the highest price due to the policies of structural adjustment all over the world, and Latin America is no exception (Cavanagh, Wysham, and Arruda 1994; Emeagwali 1995; Caufield 1996).

Two specific policies, prioritization of basic education and an emphasis on the question of educational quality characterize also the educational agenda of the World Bank. However, as José Luis Coraggio points out, given the fact that the World Bank is composed primarily by economists and not by educators, the final objective of education policies is economic efficiency, liberalization of the markets, and globalization of capital, all of which harbor an overemphasis on quantitative methods to measure the success of educational policy. Using strict economic criteria (e.g., the rates of return based on personal income), it is suggested that one additional year of private education in the lowest levels of the system (e.g., primary schools) produces a greater increase in future earnings than at the higher levels of the educational system. Therefore one may conclude very quickly that the investment in basic or primary education will result in greater increases in the gross national product than investment in any of the other levels without counting, of course, on the obsession that World Bank specialists have with viewing the investment in higher education in Latin America, in particular, as a subsidy to the elites. For Coraggio, however, the problem is that a net increase in the national product assumes that the principle of the country is a "reservoir" of qualified, cheap, and flexible workers who can produce goods and services for export. The real increase in the investment, however, will not take place in the pockets of those productive workers, but in the pockets of the consumers of those goods and services who are localized in the industrialized world (Coraggio 1994, 168). A similar problem has been expressed in other analyses; considering the premises of the preparatory documents for the Jomtien Conference, it has been almost a decade, and while no measurable change in basic education has been observed in the region, some of the Jomtien recommendations have had important implications for higher education in the region, subject to new policies of performance-based evaluations (Torres 1991, 1–20; Morales-Gomez and Torres 1994; Reimers 1990).

Neoliberalism has been associated with the notion of globalization, and this in turn may impact the overall operation and performance of the educational systems in the region (Burbules and Torres 2000). It is therefore appropriate to ask how has globalization impacted the formulation of educational politics in Latin America? Clearly, there are three aspects where globalization, especially based on a neoliberal model may have impacted Latin American education: at the level of the political economy of educational financing, in terms of the linkages between education and work, and through the creation of a movement for standards of international academic excellence, with its implications at the level of evaluation, curriculum, higher education, or teacher training.

In terms of the political economy of education, as I pointed out earlier, the neoliberal model reflects an international agenda of educational research and investment that preaches privatization as an educational solution, as much for the correction of deficiencies of the state investment in education as for confronting the fiscal crisis of the state. This has driven different instruments of educational financing, like vouchers, to favor certain technocratic instruments of analysis and educational planning like the rates of return in education, and certain experiences of educational decentralization, like the charter schools. Many of these political instruments, with their distinct variants, have assumed the position of models and hegemonic premises—and therefore nonnegotiables—in the formulation of educational politics. It is interesting to observe how the Chilean experience in education constitutes an early and archetypical model of this neoliberal orientation.

In terms of the links between work and education, it is clear that the old mechanisms of educational planning have been buried with a properly expedited death certificate. But also it is clear that there are not precise answers in regard to educational planning. Given the technological change of the last decades, the changes in the politics of investment of governments, especially the reduction of the public sector, and especially the constant transformations in the dynamics of the job markets, how to make education respond clearly to the dynamics of the job market continues to be a true enigma. Even more, it is not clear if these dynamics can be anticipated with sufficient time to adjust the educational products to the satisfaction of the necessities of the market—an old utopia of the educational planners—even though it is clear that there is a relative autonomy of education that we should respect, independent to the demand of the market, so that education may be an instrument of enlightenment (cognitive and moral, clearly) and not merely a public policy whose virtue is exclusively based in its ability to enhance the employability and productivity of the workforce. The theme of technological policies to enhance in Latin American countries the linkages between universities and the business world continue to result in apparently unsolvable dilemmas. Finally, it is clear that in the job markets, the workers who receive the highest compensation in terms of income are the symbolic analysts, very well defined in the book by Robert Reich (1992). Without the increasing production of symbolic analysts, in which higher education has a grand task, it is impossible to capture a greater share of the economic resources of the international system, and therefore it is almost equally impossible to expand the ability to redistribute resources via social policies.

In the end, the hegemonic neoliberal model has driven within the educational environment a movement for the creation of educational standards via international standards of educational performance that have impacted practically all of educational levels, from preschool to the university. Regrettably, this movement for standards has been used more as an instrument of control than as tool for educational benefits. Putting forth a specific definition of educational quality, this movement has produced substantive modifications in educational settings, contributing each time more tests and exams for the evaluation of learning, and in the same mechanisms for the evaluation of systems. A clear example of this movement is the evaluation models of higher education implemented in Argentina by the Ministry of Education in clear programmatic communication with the World Bank educational designers during the administration of Carlos Menem, a situation that has not really changed during the government of de LaRua.

As I have pointed out elsewhere,

> There are new forces oriented to the transfer of the cost of services to the users; to reorient the educational investments toward the areas that the World Bank has considered to offer the greatest rates of return, that is primary and basic education; to reduce the cost of education, affecting salary levels and, in as much, the training of teachers (considering overeducated as a university training that would generate salary expectations higher than the countries can finance); and promoting the decentralization of educational services as a method of redefining the relationship between education and power between the national (federal), provincial, and municipal governments. (Torres 1994c, 14)

Although those three grand effects in Latin American educational politics are discernible, their goodness is disputable. The impact of the neoliberal globalization on the upper class, on the specific activities that the teachers carry out with the children inside classrooms—what do we know of what happens in the classroom once the door is shut closed? And of course in the localities at the margins of the international system there is still heated material for academic and political discussion. The situation could not be more paradoxical. For example, in whichever school hall, whether it be in the most remote and isolated rural area of the province of Jujuy, in Argentina or the state of Chiappas, in Mexico, or in the heart of the federal capital in Argentina, or the federal district of Mexico City, we may find a teacher, who if he or she is competent and committed, is naturally a producer and diffuser of universal knowledge, and therefore a transmitter of the globalization of knowledge. However, this same teacher, upon questioning the premises of the neoliberal globalization model, as much in its politico-pedagogical message as in terms of the relation of the pedagogical and dialogical link that he establishes with his students, could confront globalization daily in her classroom practices. One has to admit that we know very little of what happens in classrooms everyday, and for that it is necessary to implement more educational research into this level of the system, both in curricular and pedagogical terms; however, it would not be very risky to imagine that if the majority of the teachers are represented by the teacher unions of the region, they are decidedly opposed to neoliberal globalization, as empirical comparative research in the Pacific Rim seems to indicate (Torres et al. 1999).

One cannot doubt that the neoliberal mechanisms of globalization can be systematically critiqued, that their benefits as public policy can be disconfirmed by empirical investigation, and that some of their negative effects on education can be reversed with a different political philosophy and an alternative educational policy. The dispute for the nation, which is also a dispute for education and the citizenry, is a task that corresponds to the civic movements, the social movements, to political parties that oppose the neoliberal model, and to the teacher unions that have carried, in many parts of the world, the weight of the confrontation against neoliberalism. As it is obvious, the results of the social conflict of this importance cannot be appraised in the short term, even though some of the negative consequences for education begin to be clearly seen.

TOWARD A NEW EDUCATIONAL UTOPIA?

> The impossibility of an uncontested canon results from the impossibility of defining a single, integrated, nonproblematic and descriptive social and pedagogical identity in the culture of the West.
>
> —Morrow and Torres[12]

> We had the experience but missed the meaning / And approach to the meaning restores the experience.
>
> —T. S. Eliot[13]

These quantitative changes, together with profound qualitative changes, affect Latin American education at practically all levels, in such a manner that the traditional models cannot realize the complexity of the changes and explain them thoroughly. Without attempting to give a complete account of these new challenges, which have been formulated elsewhere (Torres and Puiggrós 1997, 12–22), it would be appropriate to at least mention in their most elemental form the most salient aspects of the Latin American educational crisis.

There is a profound crisis in the understanding of which is the pedagogical subject to be educated. That which could be dominated by an endemic crisis of the systems is reflected in a real and symbolic dislocation between the discourses of the teachers and the students, that is reflected also in a dislocation, also of magnitude, between the discourses of new generations (which in the developed world has been dominated by the Nintendo generation) and adult generations. This cultural dislocation in school settings adds to the proverbial issues of equality and relevance of education, equity, equality, and social mobility as well as discrimination. It does not treat only the secular problems, even not resolved of the educational system, that were accustomed to heated discussion on the betterment of schooling, how to be the repetition, the dissertation the quality of education, the relevance of education. That which now confronts us is a strong crisis of legitimacy in the educational systems in terms of their effectiveness, that is to say, the effectiveness of the educational agents per se, including the teachers, parents, and private and public educational institutions.

There is a rupture in the symbolic public link between generations; this perhaps may give rise to crisis that supersedes the secular deficiencies of the system, in spite of the achievement of education, and that goes further than the same miseries that we have observed here. What appears before our eyes, as educators preoccupied as much with the dailyness and practice of education in the classroom as by the general directions, orientations, nature, financing of educational politics, is how education becomes inserted in the organic crisis of Latin American societies, even more so when the process of globalization[14] enlarges the processes, universalizes the symbols, exacerbates the emotions, complicates the options, and shows new dynamics that are increasingly more difficult to extend to the common population. Of course, this is not to say that intellectuals and technicians, as well politicians, those who, with honorable exceptions, do not qualify in any of the previous categories. The presence of the means of communication, in particular, creates new combinations between popular traditional cultures, a popular transnationalized culture, and the political cultures developed by the state institutions of the region, on occasions drastically confronted by the institutions of civil society and social movements as well as the unions. This is to say, simply, while there is an enormous dispute over identity, and a totally agonizing process in the context of the dispute for ego recognition between individuals (which creates all types of tensions as well as contradictions, some unresolvable), there is also a rupture in the school walls, which already cannot protect the children from pedagogically inappropriate influences. There is also a strong crisis in the logic of modernity, prevalent in the schools, that creates other types of conflicts, including at the symbolic analytic level, in the treatment of educational themes in the classroom. There are countless indicators that point to the complexity of this crisis, including growing difficulties in the teaching of a read-writing of a youth culture created around the manipulation of cybernetic and mediating visual symbols, the growing obstacles for learning the scientific and technical disciplines (the crisis in teaching mathematics in Latin America reaching unimaginable dimensions years back), there is, simply, a profound breach in the transmission of culture and "official" knowledge (Apple 1993). Obsolete school rituals, opposing discourses, problems in the definition of the cultural capital of the school, disappearance of fictitious borders, crisis in the concepts of citizenship and democracy, growing disparity between the educational models and the job market, and finally, a most complex gamut of factors have brought Latin American education, at the beginning of the twenty-first century, to the edge of the abyss. Clearly neoliberal politics, to say it in a tragicomic manner, offers educational systems a step forward in their own demise.

In another work (Torres and Puiggrós 1997, 19–23) we made an assessment of education, considering various facts to which I would now like to refer. It is necessary to tackle distinct themes for this process of educational review, incorporating the notions of unequal and combined development in

Latin America, with clear expressions in art and the humanities, with some of the most advanced studies in the production of scientific thought, coexisting with premodern, peripheral, marginal, and pre-Columbian cultures. These cultures are marked by profound linguistic and cultural discontinuities, within which, with respect to the more sophisticated segments of the culture of modernity and postmodernity, and of course with respect to the cultural capital that dominates schools; that is to say that cultural melange of mestizos, indigenous peoples, and European cultures, largely Spanish and Portuguese, that created the hybridized cultures analyzed by Argentine researcher Nestor Garcia Canclini in several works (García Canclini 1982, 1990). In education, this is complicated in confronting what one Argentine historian of education, Gregorio Weinberg (1984), called the asyncronicity of the Latin American educational models. The notion of difference à la Derrida (1989) and about the notion of *otredad* that now, still in private backrooms, I am afraid, brings us to rescue the existentialist thought, combined with the powerful postmodernist direction about the political culture as a culture of difference, offers perspectives, theoretical and political, increasingly more necessary, far ahead of what political positivism can offer.

The notion of hegemonic crisis in Latin American democracies continues to stimulate thought on the crisis of school systems in Latin America. We should have to unthink the notion of pedagogical subjects (as much teachers as students) in the new social, cultural, and political formations emerging in Latin America in this century that, according to some intellectuals of the New Left, end with a clear indication of the end of utopia (Jacoby 1999). This crisis invites, clearly, a reconsideration of the role the state plays in public education and how the new politics of privatization can produce obscene results, far from any image of public decorum. The "new problems" of the "new times" that the school systems are living with in the region, differ, greatly, from the expectations and solutions of the 1950s, to refer us simply to the middle of the century. How can we educate street children, a group increasing in numbers in the metropolises and peripheral urban areas of Latin America? How does the drug trafficking culture affect the scholastic task? How are the private communication and information networks affecting the status, the confidence, and the accessibility of the scholastic knowledge in the region?

The notion of the pedagogical subject, and his links with the social and pedagogical structures of Latin America, although one could conceive in terms of the sociological and political models studying the links between social agency and structure, require an increasingly refined thought to understand the subtleties (as much in the conceptual construction as in the social construction of the historical experience) of the fight for identity, including preoccupations, every day more charged, in the pedagogy considering the multiple and asyncratic parallel determinations of class, race, ethnicity, sexual preference, religion, gender, and regionalism.

The role of the conditioned states in Latin America (Torres 1996) continues to be problematic as much for democracy as for education. The old Sarmiento adage of "educating the sovereign" preceded educational thought in Latin America and converted into the heraldry of normalism that conditions, even more so, the rhetorics and the practices of the regional states. The notion of oppression (of that "sovereign") that Paulo Freire installed, for a time and for always, into the Latin American pedagogical discourse. With great pride we should note the contribution of Paulo Freire's Latin American thought in the insertion of the pedagogy of the oppressed into the politico-pedagogical worldwide debate, which should guide the political reflection that is the role of the state in education in the next century. It is a relevant theme, especially now that poverty and educational inequality has been more crucial, as has already been pointed out by Argentinean sociologist Daniel Filmus (1999). To rethink pedagogy of the oppressed and the conditioning of the Latin American states, it is necessary to rethink the centrality of education in the cultural project of a society and state in Latin America, especially in light of cultural fractures, the borders of identities, and the front lines of cultural battles.

This rethinking of the notion of knowledge implies the renewal of the notion of power, and therefore the notion of citizenship and democracy (Torres 1998). It remains to be said that the fight for education is not simply a technocratic activity calmly implemented on the bureaucratic desks, or agitatedly negotiated in the school classrooms, ministerial cloisters, and union backrooms. Neither is it simply a fight for better educational opportunities for individuals. The fight for education is a question of state; it is a fight for the defense of democratic pact.

NOTES

1. Cited in Carlos Rodriques Brandao, comp., *Pesquisa participante* (São Paulo: Editora Brasilense, 1981), 1.

2. The diagnosis of the World Bank for the period 1970–1987 shows that of the seventeen most indebted countries in the world, twelve are in Latin America (Argentina, Bolivia, Brazil, Chile, Colombia, Costa Rica, Ecuador, Jamaica, Mexico, Peru, Uruguay, and Venezuela; World Bank, 1989). The importance of the external debt for the region cannot be underestimated. The Economic Commission for Latin America (ECLA, CEPAL in the Spanish acronym) estimated that in the year 1987, for example, the countries of the region altogether transferred toward the exterior to pay services for the debt, a total amount equivalent to 2 percent of the gross regional product (CEPAL 1987).

3. Latin America continues to have high rates of functional illiteracy. Official data, not always reliable, allow us to divide the countries into four large groups: those with less than 10 percent illiteracy in their population, between 10 percent and 20 percent, between 20 percent and 30 percent, and more than 30 percent. In the first group we

find (data for 1995), Argentina (3.8 percent), Chile (4.8 percent), Colombia (8.7 percent), Costa Rica (5.2 percent), Cuba (4.3 percent), Ecuador (9.9 percent), Panama (9.2 percent), Paraguay (7.9 percent), Uruguay (2.7 percent), and Venezuela (8.9 percent). In the second group we find Bolivia (16.9 percent), Brazil (17.6 percent), the Dominican Republic (17.9 percent), Mexico (10.4 percent), and Peru (11.3 percent). In the third group, El Salvador (21.5 percent) and Honduras (27.3 percent). Finally, in the fourth group we find Guatemala (44.4 percent), Haiti (55 percent), and Nicaragua (34.3 percent). It can be said that the illiteracy of women and indigenous groups is larger than the distribution in the population, and that the imbalance between urban and rural illiteracy is often, in the rural areas, three times that in the urban areas (Wilkie, Aleman and Ortega 1998, 185–87).

4. Max Horkheimer, *Eclipse of Reason* (New York: Oxford University Press, 1947), 198.

5. Immanuel Wallerstein, "Social Science and the Quest for a Just Society," *Américan Journal of Sociology* 102, no. 5 (1997): 1241–57, cited on page 1254.

6. For the beginning of the 1990s, the rates of repetition are the following: Brazil 45 percent, other countries of South America 36.3 percent; Central America and Panama, 39.5 percent; the Gulf of Mexico (Dominican Republic, Cuba, and Mexico), 38.6 percent; countries of the Anglo Caribbean, 18.7 percent. The rate of repetition for the entire region is 41.2 percent (UNESCO-OREALC 1991). A report by the Center for Educational Studies in Mexico argues that between 1980 and 1986, only 52 percent of the children in primary school completed their grade level, and that the dropout rate rose from 10.3 percent in 1986 (Morales-Gómez 1989). The highest rates of repetition in the first three years of primary school (for 1994–1995), one finds in the following countries: Brazil (18 percent), the Dominican Republic (17 percent), Guatemala (16 percent), Peru (15 percent), Haiti (13 percent), Honduras (12 percent), Uruguay (10 percent), and Venezuela (11 percent). (Wilkie, Aleman and Ortega 2000, 190–91).

7. The total spending on education measured as a percentage of the government spending is the following (1993–1995): Argentina 4.5 percent, Bolivia 6.6 percent, Brazil 1.6 percent, Chile 2.0 percent, Colombia 3.7 percent, Costa Rica 4.5 percent, the Dominican Republic 1.9 percent, Ecuador 3.4 percent, El Salvador, 2.2 percent, Guatemala 1.7 percent, Haiti 1.8 percent, Uruguay 2.8 percent, Venezuela 5.1 percent. In contrast the United States spends 5.3 percent (Wilkie, Aleman and Ortega 2000, 225–27).

8. It should not surprise anyone that in spite of the enormous advances in mandatory education in Latin America, the differences between the developing world and the developed world are abysmal. For example, in 1966, an enormously symbolic year for distinct reasons on the world level, the developed countries, with about one-third of the planet's inhabitants and one-fourth of the world's children, spent $120,000 million on social programs, while the developing countries as a whole, with an infinitely larger population, spent only 10 percent of that amount: $12,000 million. This difference in social service spending increases on education, even more when we consider the decrease in investment in education in recent years, may have reached greater proportions. For example, in 1980, total public spending on education in some Latin American countries in relation to the gross national product was 3.6 percent in Argentina, 4.4 percent in Bolivia, 4.4 percent in Mexico, and 7.8 percent in Costa Rica. In 1985 Argentina had fallen to 2.2 percent, Bolivia to 0.5 percent, Mexico to 2.6 percent, and Costa Rica to 4.7 percent (Torres and Puiggrós 1997, 13). Nei-

ther is this decline strange when the average annual growth of the gross domestic product per capita in the region from 1961 to 1970 was 2.6 percent, surpassing in many societies of the region the rate of growth of the population. In 1971–1980, this growth rate rose to 3.3 percent to decrease (-1.1 percent) from 1981 to 1989, a period that economists perhaps too lightly refer to as the lost decade of development (Morales-Gómez and Torres 1990, 19).

9. Cited in Ramón Gómez de la Serna, *Don Miguel de Unamuno: Retratos completos* (Madrid: Aguilar, 1961).

10. In a conversation with Paulo Freire in his house in São Paulo, two years before his death, he confided in me that one of his aspirations was to write a history of the New School in Brazil, an educational movement that he appreciated enormously and considered in some sense a precursor to his own work and orientation.

11. Due to the importance today in Latin America of the neoliberal research, evaluation, and policy formulation agenda, I will dedicate a larger segment of this chapter than I have dedicated to the previous theories and agendas.

12. Raymond Allen Morrow and Carlos Alberto Torres, *Social Theory and Education: A Critique of Theories of Social and Cultural Reproduction* (New York: State University of New York Press, 1995), 428.

13. T. S. Elliot, "The Dry Salvages," in *The Four Quartets* (1943; reprint, New York: Harcourt, Brace, 1971), 24.

14. Globalization has been defined by David Held as the intensification of global relations that bind distant localities such that what happens at the local levels is affected by phenomena originating many miles away and vice versa (Held 1991). Held suggests that globalization is the product of the emergence of a global economy, the expansion of the transnational ties among economic units creating new forms of collective decision-making, the development of quasi-supranatural intergovernmental institutions, the strengthening of communications transnationalization, and the creation of new military and regional orders.

REFERENCES

Apple, Michael. 1993. *Official Knowledge: Democratic Education in a Conservative Age.* New York: Routledge.

Arnove, Robert. 1986. *Education and Revolution in Nicaragua.* New York: Praeger.

"The Benevolence of Self-Interest." 1998. *Economist,* December 12, 80.

Burbules, Nicholas, and Carlos A. Torres, eds. 2000. *Education and Globalization: Critical Analysis.* New York: Routledge.

Carnoy, M., and C. A. Torres. 1994. "Educational Change and Structural Adjustment: A Case Study of Costa Rica," in Joel Samoff, ed., *Coping with Crisis: Austerity, Adjustment, and Human Resources,* 64–99. London: UNESCO-CASSELL.

Caufield, Catherine. 1996. *Masters of Illusion: The World Bank and the Poverty of Nations.* New York: Henry Holt.

Cavanagh, John, Daphne Wysham, and Marcos Arruda. 1994. *Beyond Bretton Woods: Alternatives to the Global Economic Order.* London: Pluto/Institute for Policy Studies/Transnational Institute.

CEPAL. 1987. *Panorama económico de América Latina.* Santiago: LC/C 1481.

Coraggio, José Luis. 1994. "Human Capital: The World Bank's Approach to Education in Latin America." In J. Cavanagh et al., *Beyond Bretton Woods: Alternatives to the Global Economic Order*. London: Institute for Policy Studies/Transnational Institute/Pluto Press.

Cucuzza, Héctor Ruben, ed. 1996. *Historia de la educación en debate*. Buenos Aires: Miño y Davila.

Culpitt, Ian. 1992. *Welfare and Citizenship: Beyond the Crisis of the Welfare State?* London: Sage.

Derrida, Jacques. 1989. Cómo no Hablar? Y Otros Textos [How not to Talk? and other Texts]. Barcelona: Anthropos.

Dewey, John. 1981. *The Philosophy of John Dewey*. Edited by John J. McDermott. Chicago: University of Chicago Press.

Dussell, Inés, and Marcelo Caruso. 1997. "Dewey under South American Skies: Some Readings from Argentina." In Carlos Alberto Torres and Adriana Puiggrós, eds., *Latin American Education: Comparative Perspectives*, 103–23. Boulder: Westview.

Filmus, Daniel. 1999. *Educación y desigualdad en América latina de los 90s. ¿Una nueva década perdida?* Buenos Aires: Flacso. Mimeograph.

Elliot, T. S. 1971. "The Dry Savages." In *The Four Quartets*. 1943; reprint, New York: Harcourt, Brace.

Emeagwali, Gloria T., ed. 1995. *Women Pay the Price: Structural Adjustment in Africa and the Caribbean*. Trenton, N.J.: Africa World Press.

Gadotti, Moacir. 1989. *Convite à leitura de Paulo Freire*. São Paulo: Editora Scipione.

Gadotti, Moacir. 1998. *Historia de las ideas pedagógicas*. Mexico: Siglo XXI, 1998.

Gadotti, Moacir, and Carlos Alberto Torres, ed. 1993. *Educación popular: Crisis y perspectivas*. Buenos Aires: Miño y Davila.

García Canclini, Néstor. 1982. *Culturas populares en el capitalismo*. Mexico: Nueva Imágen.

García Canclini, Néstor. 1990. *Culturas híbridas*. Mexico: Grijalbo.

Gómez de la Serna, Ramón. 1961. *Don Miguel de Unamuno: Retratos completes*. Madrid: Aguilar.

Held, David. 1991. *Political Theory Today*. Stanford: Stanford University Press.

Horkheimer, Max. 1947. *Eclipse of Reason*. New York: Oxford University Press.

Jacoby, Russell. 1999 *The End of Utopia*. New York: Basic Books.

Morales-Gómez, Daniel. 1989. "Seeking New Paradigms to Plan Education for Development: The Role of Educational Research." *Prospects* 19, no. 2: 192–204.

Morales-Gómez, Daniel, and Carlos Alberto Torres. 1994. "Education for All: Prospects and Implications for Latin America in the 1990s." In Carlos Alberto Torres, ed., *Education and Social Change in Latin America*. Melbourne: James Nicholas.

Moran, Michael, and Maurice Wright. 1991. *The Market and the State: Studies in Interdependence*. New York: St. Martin's.

Morrow, Raymond Allen, and Carlos Alberto Torres. 1995. *Social Theory and Education: A Critique of Theories of Social and Cultural Reproduction*. New York: State University of New York Press.

O'Cadiz, Pilar, Pia Linquist Wong, and Carlos Alberto Torres. 1998. *Democracy and Education: Paulo Freire, Social Movements, and Education Reform in São Paulo*. Boulder: Westview.

Pescador, José Angel. 1994. *Teoría del Capital Humano: Exposición y Crítica*. In Carlos A. Torres and Guillermo González Rivera, eds., *Sociología de la educación: Corrientes contemporáneas*, 161–72. Buenos Aires: Miño y Davila.

Puiggrós, Adriana. 1990. *Sujetos, disciplina y curriculum en los orígenes del sistema educativo argentino, 1885–1916.* Buenos Aires: Galerna.

Puiggrós, Adriana. 1996. *¿Qué pasó con la educación argentina? Desde la conquista hasta el menemismo.* Buenos Aires: Kapeluz.

Puiggrós, Adriana. 1997. *Imperialismo, neoliberalismo y educación en América Latina.* Buenos Aires: Paidos, 1997.

Puiggrós, Adriana. 1998. *La educación popular en América Latina: Orígenes, polémics y perspectivas.* Buenos Aires, Miño y Davila.

Ramamurti, Ravi. 1991. "Privatization and the Latin American Debt Problem." In Robert Grosse, ed., *Private Sector Solutions to the Latin American Debt Problem.* New Brunswick, N.J.: Transaction/North-South Center/University of Miami.

Reich, Robert. 1992. *The Work of the Nations: Preparing Ourselves for Twenty-First Century Capitalism.* New York: Vintage.

Reimers, Fernando. 1990. *Educación para todos en América Latina en el Siglo XXI. Los desafíos de la estabilización, el ajuste y los mandatos de Jomtien* [Education for All in Latin America on the Twenty-first Century. The challenges of stabilization, adjustment and the Jomtien mandates]. Paper presented in the workshop on "pobreza, ajuse y supervivencia infantil" organized by UNESCO in Peru, December 3–6, 1990.

Reimers, Fernando. 1991. "The Impact of Economic Stabilization and Adjustment in Latin America." *Comparative Education Review,* no. 35, May 1991, 325–328.

Reimers, Fernando. 1994. "Education for All in Latin America in the Twenty-First Century and the Challenges of External Indebtedness." In Carlos Alberto Torres, ed., *Education and Social Change in Latin America.* Melbourne: James Nicholas.

Reimers, Fernando and Luis Tiburcio. 1993. Education, adjustment and reconstruction: options for change: a UNESCO policy discussion paper. Paris: UNESCO.

Rodrigues Brandão, Carlos, ed. 1981. *Pesquisa participante.* São Paulo: Editora Brasiliense.

Schiefelbein, Ernesto. 1997. "Financing Education for Democracy in Latin America." In Torres, C.A. and Puiggros, a., eds., *Latin American Education: Comparative Perspectives.* Boulder, Colo.: Westview Press.

Torres, Carlos Alberto. 1989. "El mundo de Talcott Parsons y la educación (I): El pensamiento sociológico funcionalista y la educación primaria." *Revista brasileira de estudos pedagógicos,* January–April, 55–64.

Torres, Carlos Alberto. 1990. "El mundo de Talcott Parsons y la educación (II): El pensamiento sociológico funcionalista y la educación superior." *Revista brasileira de estudos pedagógicos* 70: 428–34.

Torres, Carlos Alberto. 1991. "A Critical Review of Education for All (EFA) Background Documents." *Perspectives on Education for All,* Ottawa, IDRC-MR295e, April, 1–20.

Torres, Carlos Alberto. 1994. *Estudios Freireanos.* Buenos Aires: Libros del Quirquincho.

Torres, C. A. 1994. "La universidad latino Américana: De la reforma de 1918 al ajuste estructural de los 90s." [Latin American University: From the Reform of 1918 to Structural Adjustment in the 1990s] In C. Torres, R. Follari, M. Albornoz, S. Duluc, and L. Petrucci, eds., *Curriculum Universitario Siglo XXI,* 13–54. Argentina: Facultad de Ciencias de la Educación, Universidad Nacional de Entre Rios, Argentina.

Torres, C. A. 1995a "Estado, políticas públicas e educação de adultos." [The State, Public Policy and Adult Education]. In Moacir Gadotti and José E. Romão, *Educação de*

Jovens e Adultos. Teoria, prática e proposta, 16–24, São Paulo, Cortez Editora and Instituto Paulo Freire.

Torres, C.A. 1995b. "Estado, Privatização e Política Educacional. Elementos para uma crítica do neoliberalismo." [The State, Privatization and Educational Policy. Elements for a critique of neoliberalism]. In Pablo Gentili, ed., *Pedagogia da exclusão. Crítica ao neoliberalismo em educação*, 109–136, Petrópolis, RJ, Editora Vozes.

Torres, C. A. 1996. *Las secretas aventuras del orden: Estado y educación*. Buenos Aires: Miño y Dávila Editores.

Torres, C. A. 1998. *Education, Democracy, and Multiculturalism: Dilemmas of Citizenship in a Global World*. Lanham, Md.: Rowman & Littlefield.

Torres, Carlos Alberto, Seewha Cho, Jerry Kachur, Aurora Loyo, Marcdela Mollis, Akio Nagao, and Julie Thompson. 1999. "Political Capital, Teachers' Unions, and the State: Value Conflicts and Collaborate Strategies in Educational Reform in the United States, Canada, Japan, Korea, Mexico and Argentina." Manuscript, UCLA.

Torres, Carlos Alberto, Rajinder S. Pannu, and M. Kazim Bacchus. 1993. "Capital Accumulation, Political Legitimation, and Educational Expansion." In A. Yogev and J. Dronkers, *International Perspectives on Education and Society*, 3–32. Greenwich, Conn.: Jai Press.

Torres, Carlos Alberto, and Adriana Puiggrós. 1997. "The State and Public Education in Latin America." In C. A. Torres and Adriana Puiggrós, eds., *Latin American Education: Comparative Perspectives*. Boulder: Westview.

UNESCO. 1971. Conferencia de ministros de educación y ministros encargados de ciencia y tecnología en relación con el desarrollo de América Latina y el Caribe. Venezuela, December 6–15, Caracas, Venezuela. [Conference of ministers of education and acting ministers for science and technology in relation to the development of Latin America and the Caribbean.] Caracas: UNESCO.

UNESCO. 1974. *Evolución Reciente de la Educación en América Latina*. [Recent Evolution of Education in Latin America]. Santiago de Chile: UNESCO.

UNESCO-OREALC. 1991. *Situación educativa en América latina*. Santiago: UNESCO-OREALC.

Wallerstein, Immanuel. 1997. "Social Science and the Quest for a Just Society." *American Journal of Sociology*, March, 1241–57.

Weinberg, Gregorio. 1984. *Modelos educativos en la historia de America latina*. Buenos Aires: Kapeluz.

Wilkie, James Wallace, Eduardo Aleman, and Jose Guadlupe Ortega. 2000. Statistical abstract of Latin America, Volume 36. Los Angeles: UCLA Latin American Center Publications, University of California.

World Bank. *World Development Report 1990*. 1989. Oxford: Oxford University Press/World Bank.

13

Institutionalized Legitimate Informational Capital in the Welfare State:

Has Policy Failed?

Martin D. Munk

Have the opportunities enjoyed by different birth cohorts changed over the years? Why has the trend of durable educational and social reproduction continued over the years? These questions are answered not merely in relation to the level and composition of informational capital, but particularly in relation to social position. This is measured in the years between 1980 and 1995, a period characterized by unemployment and political alterations. To what degree does inequality exist over time *between* members of different birth cohorts in relation to key issues such as general education and adult education and work experience and unemployment? It is important to explain variations of inequality over time, as measured by life chances and odds ratios for entering different educational and social positions. I use cohort studies of inequality based on large registers (Denmark as a case). The purpose is to illustrate variations and invariations. The sociocultural analysis has been the primary focus in many studies over the last ten to twenty years. Some of those studies have contributed to a greater understanding of contextual variations. However, another type of analysis has been overlooked to some degree: the cohort-historical approach (Dex 1991; Elder 1985). The cohort perspective demonstrates that social structure is not unchangeable. It seems in a way that the methodology of cohort studies supports the idea of a changing society, not merely in terms of broad concepts such as globalisation and individualisation, but also in terms of concrete empirical results.

One of the political goals that is inherent to the welfare state is to promote equality and equal opportunities for all citizens. In a recent paper one goes so far as to speak about equal outcomes (Roemer et al. 2000). One major aim has been to create possibilities for people to enter and complete different kinds of education, to strengthen the link between education and work, to formalize the process of qualification, to reduce poverty and inequality as well as to promote educational and social mobility. However, several new investigations in Europe show that inequality increases, or at least remains stable (Fritzell 1999; Gustafsson/Johansson 1999; Halleröd 1999). This trend is typically measured in terms of economic inequality, either as disposable income or market income, as the dependent variable, as well as the opportunity to gain access to education and chances of attaining different levels of employment. All in all, inequality is increasing. Inequality, especially social reproduction, considering the relationship between education and social position, seems to be persistent. The analysis is based upon a theoretical framework in which the concept of social space is central (Bourdieu [1979] 1986). A social space corresponds to the space of lifestyles, the space of social positions, the space of the social trajectory, but also by forms of welfare capital. Welfare capital refers to forms of social benefit opportunities. This means that social positions are simultaneously structured by symbolic, materialised and social benefit relationships (Munk 2000).

EDUCATIONAL AND LABOR MARKET POLICIES

The transformation of the welfare state has been a major issue, as related to the topics of unemployment and marginalisation, opportunities and education. Besides focusing on general welfare programs and policies, increasing attention has been given to general education and adult education. This has often been related to the activation of those outside the labour market as a means to deal with unemployment. However, this may be a contradiction to some degree, since a greater supply of education can correspondingly create greater inequality regarding opportunities in the labour market (Morris and Western 1999, 632ff.). In recent years, there has been a progressively stronger focus upon the future role of education as a key factor in coping with changing labour markets in which competitiveness is—and becomes increasingly—more crucial. Governments have conducted a more regulated policy concerning education that is in line with the slogan of "education, education and education," formulated by British Prime Minister Tony Blair, as a means to solve problems of exclusion and unemployment. The trend of the re-institutionalisation (more students and changed systems) of the Educational System is notable. The policy change may be characterised as a shift from "culture" to market efficiency, a new rationality. Furthermore, the development of education is illustrated by reappearing junctures of system reforms over the last 200 years. Different levels of education can be perceived as social historical constructions, articulated as interests of certain social classes, as a reaction or an answer to changes in living conditions. More fields of education have been constituted as public/mass education subsidised by the state and they were institutionally and economically legitimised (Boli and Ramirez 1986; Wallerstein 1999).

This new institutionalisation, considered as a constraint, is probably important for the strategies by which every individual agent endeavours to maintain, or even change, its position in society. I am particularly thinking of two remarkable quasi-political constructions in the field of education (related to the new labour market policy of activation): On the one hand, an increasing use of adult educational systems, mostly by the skilled and semi-skilled. On the other hand, a homologizing of higher education (towards an Anglo-Saxon system with bachelors, master's and Ph.D. degrees). The first trend seems to be a way of relegating agents with less convertible capital to positions, or at least occupations, where they can be "kept busy." The second trend seems to act as a tool for more privileged groups to maintain or expand acquired capital. Previously it was possible to obtain many academic positions, also within the university system itself, merely with a master's degree (formally six years of study, but usually accomplished after eight years of study). Now younger people are expected to get a Ph.D. degree just as in America, England, France and other countries. This implies that academics without a Ph.D. are less attractive in the academic institutions, not only in universities but also in ministries and other bodies of public administration. The second trend is partly due to an increasing number of students attending higher education, and subsequently more and more young people have obtained a master's degree at the university.

SOCIAL REPRODUCTION: DENMARK AS A CASE

A point of departure for the present analysis is a study by Erik Jørgen Hansen (1995). Comparing several Danish studies of social recruitment and opportunities, one finds a better chance for working-class people to obtain further university education. However, it is still much lower than in privileged social groups (Hansen 1997, 12–13). Internationally there is a strong tradition for the study of the relationships between social origin, educational level and social position (Shavit and Müller 1998; Breen and Goldthorpe 1999; Shavit and Blossfeld 1993; Kerckhoff 1993; Prandy 1998). In some of those studies it has been shown that not only educational level, social origin and gender influence specific employment chances but also educational track and specific cohorts (Buchmann and Sacchi 1998, 419–421; Blossfeld 1986; Krahn and Lowe 1999). The present cohort study of social reproduction is based upon registers from Statistics Denmark, especially the years of 1980, 1985, 1990 and 1995 regarding covariates and outcome variables. Particularly, birth cohorts born in 1954, 1959 and 1964 are analyzed at the age of thirty-one years. Categorical dummy variables were social origin, gender, education, employment status, applying tabulations and logistic regression analysis.

Does the importance of higher education increase or decrease for certain social groups? Can adult education compensate for a low level of general education or act as a kind of extra capital? How does adult education act as a vehicle of qualification for different social groups? In the following, social reproduction is primarily measured by life-chances in trajectories of different social origin change over time will be illustrated, especially for different birth cohorts (see table 13.1). A social trajectory is defined as the series of positions successively occupied by the same agent or group of agents in successive spaces (Bourdieu [1992] 1996, 258). All trajectories could be understood as travels through society, and the many individual histories are equivalent with families of intragenerational trajectories.

SOCIAL ORIGIN, EDUCATION AND JOB POSITIONS

Cross-tabulations (not shown) show that younger generations, in a sense, are in a more competitive situation than was the case in the years after 1945. There are more competitors on the labour market with an academic degree or other kinds of education. At the same time, analyses show that the association between certain origins and education is decreasing. Individuals from privileged classes seem to avoid a demanding trajectory in academic fields (descending social mobility), or they have other converting strategies that allow them to enter new sectors compared to the culture of their social origin, including groups without further description. Strategies of reconversions[1] are defined as practices by which every agent endeavours to maintain or even change its position in society, a means of keeping up with societal changes. Perhaps some upper class children find manual positions (Ishida et al. 1995, 148) as well as positions as consultants. All in all, there seems to be a new trend of divisions within social classes and cohorts.[2] Young people have increasingly obtained further education, possibly indicating a delayed *social selection process* regarding the transition from education to social position. Higher and longer education does not necessarily lead to academic or executive positions. This is also the case for women. This could in fact indicate that the new educational policies, legitimised by the state, are coherent with this process. But women in younger cohorts (1964 compared to 1954) have higher probabilities for success in academic institutions, which corresponds to a similar pattern in Norway, at least concerning colleges (Nordli Hansen 1999).

I made an analysis of outcomes using a socio-economic nominal scale going from the position out of labour market to academics and managers, but focusing on academics and skilled workers. In table 13.1, where the outcome is social position, especially regarding the chance of becoming an academic or executive manager, shows that individuals born in 1959 are 31 percent more likely to succeed than those born in 1964. The birth cohort of 1954 also

Table 13.1. Logistic Regression of Social Origin, Highest Education, Sex, Unemployment, Adult Education, Cohort, and Work Experience on Social Position at Age 31

	Academics/Director		Skilled Worker	
	Parameter Estimates	Odds Ratios	Parameter Estimates	Odds Ratios
Intercept	-4.44 (0.06)	0.01 (0.01,0.01)	-1.38 (0.07)	0.25 (0.22, 0.29)
Basic education/Gymnasium	-0.09 (0.03)	0.92 (0.86,0.98)	-2.10 (0.02)	0.12 (0.12,0.13)
Vocational education	0.00 (0.00)	1	0.00 (0.00)	1
Long/academic education	3.07 (0.03)	21.45(20.40,22.54)	-3.71 (0.08)	0.02 (0.02, 0.12)
Men	0.00 (0.00)	1	0.00 (0.00)	1
Women	-1.12 (0.02)	0.33 (0.31,0.34)	-2.44 (0.02)	0.09 (0.08, 0.09)
Cohort = 1954	0.06 (0.03)	1.06 (1.00,1.11)	0.84 (0.03)	2.31 (2.19, 2.43)
Cohort = 1959	0.27 (0.02)	1.31 (1.25,1.37)	0.35 (0.02)	1.42 (1.37, 1.48)
Cohort = 1964	0.00 (0.00)	1	0.00 (0.00)	1
Father academic	0.87 (0.04)	2.38 (2.22,2.56)	-0.51 (0.03)	0.60 (0.56, 0.64)
Father employed	0.60 (0.04)	1.83 (1.70,1.97)	-0.30 (0.03)	0.74 (0.70, 0.78)
Father artisan	0.40 (0.04)	1.49 (1.39,1.61)	-0.17 (0.02)	0.84 (0.80, 0.88)
Father skilled	0.32 (0.04)	1.38 (1.26,1.50)	0.13 (0.03)	1.14 (1.09, 1.20)
Father unskilled	0.00 (0.00)	1	0.00 (0.00)	1
Father out of LF	0.25 (0.04)	1.28 (1.18, 1.38)	-0.15 (0.03)	0.86 (0.82,0.90)
Work exp. 0 years	-1.74 (0.15)	0.18 (0.13, 0.23)	-2.20 (0.21)	0.11 (0.07, 0.17)
Work exp. <1 years	0.00 (0.00)	1	0.00 (0.00)	1

Table 13.1. Logistic Regression of Social Origin, Highest Education, Sex, Unemployment, Adult Education, Cohort, and Work Experience on Social Position at Age 31 (continued)

	Academics/Director		Skilled Worker	
	Parameter Estimates	Odds Ratios	Parameter Estimates	Odds Ratios
InteWork exp. 1 years	0.68 (0.18)	1.98 (1.39, 2.81)	-0.77 (0.33)	0.46 (0.24, 0.89)
Work exp. 1-5 years	0.20 (0.05)	1.23 (1.11,1.35)	0.76 (0.07)	2.15 (1.87, 2.46)
Work exp. 5-10 years	0.11 (0.05)	1.11 (1.01,1.22)	1.27 (0.07)	3.55 (3.09, 4.07)
Work exp. +10 years	0.10 (0.05)	1.11 (0.99,1.23)	1.63 (0.07)	5.12 (4.45, 5.90)
Unemployed yes	0.00 (0.00)	1	0.00 (0.00)	1
Unemployed no	0.42 (0.03)	1.52 (1.43,1.61)	-0.59 (0.02)	0.55 (0.53, 0.58)
Adult education yes	0.00(0.00)	1	0.00 (0.00)	1
Adult education no	0.38(0.02)	1.47 (1.41,1.53)	-0.47 (0.02)	0.63 (0.61,0.65)
	Deviance (value/DF): 2.5/ Pearson Chi-square: 5828.3		Deviance (value/DF): 2.0/Pearson Chi-square: 8991.4	

Note: "Best model." I checked for interaction between covariates. Logit is the link function. The distribution is binominal. N (1954) = 69,514, N (1959) = 67,706, N (1964) = 76,490. 1124 are totally missing. Standard error, confidence interval (95 percent), in parentheses. N (AC/D) = 16590, N(SKW) = 23841.

had a better chance of entering academic and executive positions. However, university education still has a great impact upon one's chance of becoming an academic or executive manager. The success of this type of trajectory increases with at least one year of work experience. The odds ratio is nearly doubled compared to the odds ratio of the reference group with less than one year in the labour force. In this trajectory, it is obviously not an advantage to complete different kinds of adult education.

Social origin continues to play a major role in the process of obtaining a social position as an academic or executive manager. The odds ratio for social origin is 2.38 in the instance that one's father is an academic or executive manager, which in fact is higher without controlling for the highest educational level as a variable. In other words, the effect of origin declines when the parameter of highest/longest education is active in the model. This is comparable with the situation in other countries (Erikson and Jonsson 1998a, 25; 1998b). But there are differences between elite and normal university education (Nordli Hansen 1999). Thus the children of executive managers and academics have better opportunities to gain access to higher education than do the children of skilled or unskilled parents (even though the opportunities enjoyed by the latter have apparently increased between 1947 and 1976; Hansen 1997). After this period the trend has increased to some extent; not in the sense that fewer and fewer obtain a university degree—to the contrary. But seen in relation to social origin there is still an unequal distribution of both access to, and completion of, higher education. Meaning that the children of managers and academics are "closer" to the university system. In addition, younger generations still have a *smaller chance* of entering the social position of academics. I also controlled for the experience of unemployment between the age of twenty-six and thirty-one, which in fact further indicates a difference in the odds ratio, implying that persons with less than one year of unemployment have a much higher chance of entering the position of academic.

SOCIAL GROUPS WITH LITTLE CAPITAL

When considering the position of the skilled worker, another picture emerges (see table 13.1). Work experience in particular seems to have an impact on whether or not a person enters the position of skilled worker. Not surprisingly, the older generations have a greater chance of entering this position, the reason being that in the past it was more common to follow a traditional vocational trajectory. The logistic regression analysis points out that both vocational and adult education have importance for entering the position of skilled worker. However, at the same time there also seems to be an association between skilled worker and unemployment between the ages of twenty-six and thirty-one (more than a year).

Logistic regression analysis shows that a combination of formal vocational training (four years) and adult education can be of help in some
cases. But in the last five to ten years the vocational educational system
has been changed towards a more academic curricula, partly as promoted
by Danish Unions, with the aim of "keeping up" with new demands in the
labour market (new technology, flexibility and adaptation). However, if
the vocational system is merely redefined towards a more "academic"
mixture, there is a risk of creating greater social selection in the educational system.

Ahead, a crucial problem is that adult education does not cancel out the
risk of unemployment (see Jensen and Jensen 1996), despite some positive
results for younger individuals during the recent years (Statistiske Efterretninger 1999), also found in the present study of cohorts. If one divides the
groups to be analysed into more homogeneous segments (e.g., skilled and
unskilled together as one group), rather than heterogeneous segments, one
finds some support for using adult education. But often unskilled and those
outside the labour force with little or no formal education seem to be somewhat hindered from opportunities to make progress in their working life.
This is true unless the employment conjunctures are very good, but the relative distance between non-educated and educated remains concerning the
risk of becoming unemployed.

To conclude, obtaining different levels of education and employment
still depend on social origin and gender, as well as cohorts. Apparently,
there is also an effect of cohorts regarding the chances for achieving specific educational and social positions (see also Elstad 2000). While the Danish educational system has expanded during the last twenty to thirty years,
more and more people from different social classes attend and accomplish
progressively higher and further education. Even if a greater number of
students whose parents do not have an academic education have been ad-
mitted into the university system, education continues to play a major
function in the process of the social reproduction. At the same time, a number of children, especially from the working class, still enter groups of
unskilled workers and groups outside the work force. In fact, a growing
number of children, especially those from working class conditions, enter
groups of unskilled workers or groups outside the labour force. Young
people with less legitimate capital are facing a "vulnerable" life, indicating
that it is difficult to change the direction of one's life trajectory (Blossfeld
and Stockmann 1999, 13).

Measured in terms of the opportunity to get different jobs, including people with educational degrees, there still seems to be a tendency to social inequality. Several logistic regression analyses were modelled to elucidate
these claims (Marshall, Swift, and Roberts 1997; tables can be obtained by the
author).

IS INFORMATIONAL CAPITAL BECOMING CRUCIAL?

Cultural (educational = informational) capital is only reproduced in a relative manner. It fact, it is correct, in terms of absolute figures, that there are many more students in the (higher) educational system (Goldthorpe 1996a, 487). This paradox is also notable in a European perspective. I would explain this paradox by referring to the logic of legitimised policymaking, to the logic of social differentiation, and what is termed conditionality, referring to policies forcing nearly everyone into the educational system. Thus, in the social process of differentiation, education contributes by producing new social trajectories, but not necessarily new durable social positions. Societal processes have led to a greater struggle in the field of education, as educational capital becomes more crucial for all. Many agents have changed their strategies towards the system of education to be consecrated. Take, for example, the children of firm owners who inherited economic capital and firms, who have typically changed their strategies towards the system of education. The MBA phenomenon also exemplifies this trend. Another feature is the internationalisation of university studies, where an increasing number of students go abroad in the course of their studies, a trend which has rapidly developed over the last fifteen years (Broady, Börjesson, and Palme 1998; Broady and de Saint Martin 1997).

In other words, a change of the "reproduction of social structures," the point being that the upper class develops alternative strategies according to the "diploma-devaluation," which accentuates the problem of education and labour market. It is relevant to stress what the *dynamics of supply/demand* is really about. The traditional formulation of this relationship is not adequate in the attempt to explain processes of mobility, as many researches of labour market have stated (Boje 1986). What essentially is more important, is the question about scarcity:

> It is the symbolic scarcity of the title in the space of the names of professions that tends to govern the rewards of the occupation (and not the relationship between the supply of and demand for a particular form of labour). . . . it is not the relative value of the work that determines the value of the name, but the institutionalized value of the title that can be used as a means of defending or maintaining the value of the work. (Bourdieu 1985, 733)

Speaking in general terms, investments in educational capital and other forms of capital can shape the conditions for converting social positions in order to make up new pathways (Buchmann/Sacchi 1998). Not in a straightforward way, however. The social selection trend comprises the effects of *class habitus* and of *inflation of titles*. Exams and titles become more and more conclusive, crucial in the process of social differentiation (Young 1958; Collins 1979).[3]

THE REPRODUCTION OF FAMILIES

Lately the position of families has been addressed as an important part of the welfare state (Goldthorpe 1996a), the social reproduction of families. The social space is a place for the struggles of families, that is, maintaining and improving their social positions. The space consists of three dimensions: "the volume of capital, composition of capital, and change in these two properties over time, manifested by past and potential trajectory in the social space"[4] (Bourdieu [1979] 1986, 114). Strategies of reproduction depend on the composition and volume of capital and different means such as inheritance, customs, labour market, systems of education and so on, which are mediated in relation to agents' expectations for the future. Agents are positioned according to a state of distribution of the specific capital, which has been accumulated in the consequence of previous struggles. Several social scientists are aware of this problem. They point out that a population with a generally higher education will, under pressure, effect strong families to invest more in their children's education, as to defend their position (a "defensive expenditure"), investments which are necessary merely to maintain advantages (Goldthorpe 1996a, 494).

If the conditions of capital relations are changed it is necessary to adapt the strategies of reproduction through the reconversions of capital to other forms of capital, for example by converting economic to informational capital (Bourdieu [1979] 1986, 136–37; Hansen 1995, 240–41). It is possible in certain circumstances to reconvert inherited cultural capital to educational capital (Bourdieu [1979] 1986, 80–81, 125ff.):

> reconversions correspond to movements in a social space which has nothing in common with the unreal and yet naively realistic space of so-called "social mobility" studies. The same positivistic naivety which sees "upward mobility" in the morphological transformations of different classes or fractions is also unaware that the reproduction of the social structure may, in certain conditions, demand very little "occupational heredity." This is true whenever agents can only maintain their position in the social structure by means of a shift into a new condition (e.g., the shift from small landowner to junior civil servant, or from craftsman to office worker or commercial employee). (Bourdieu [1979] 1986, 131)

Sociologists and scholars have seen the study of mobility as the principal part of the efforts to show how social structures function and how one should explain individual movements in society (Featherman and Hauser 1978). However, principal problems in those studies are lacking recognition concerning that mobility is a process going on within the social space with distances, and that social mobility is identified as upward mobility even if we are talking about a shift from small landowner to administrator in the civil service. There are concrete problems in this context in terms of structural mobility, as empirical investigations of social structures indicate and support the argument that social mobility is essentially an expression of changing structures and not a picture of dynamic individuals who can possibly break with social boundaries. The problem with structural mobility could be solved by focusing upon "career trajectory" (Blackburn and Prandy 1997, 500; Bourdieu 1974; Erikson and Goldthorpe 1992; Strauss 1971; Sørensen 1986). Since the 1980s, researchers have emphasized a work-life-perspective when studying mobility (Sørensen 1986; Erikson and Goldthorpe 1992, chap. 8; Rosenfeld 1992). The last type is to some degree parallel to the way Bourdieu formulates an alternative theory. However, Sørensen is building upon a rational choice theory (Coleman 1988) and Bourdieu is relying on a theory of habitus (Bourdieu 1977, 72).

The studies of social mobility have not recognised that the social space provides at least two or three different movements (Bourdieu [1989] 1996, [1992] 1996). Firstly there are vertical movements, proceeding within the *same* field, for example, from a teacher to a professor in the educational field; secondly there are horizontal movements between *different* fields, for example, from a teacher to a shopkeeper. Thirdly there are crossing movements, for example from artisanal petite bourgeoisie to a writer. It means that vertical movements only require an increase in capital that is already valid and dominates within the structure of profit in a specific field. Processes of mobility are not just movements between fathers and sons; they exist in different fields and these fields will be historically transformed, thereby contributing to the reproduction of the social space (Bourdieu [1989] 1996, 136–39). It is not enough to study the shift of jobs. One must also investigate the shifts of fields and conversions of different kinds of capital. A shift from one trajectory to another depends on different collective events, such as wars or major crises, or by individual events such as "random" meetings and business, neglecting different kinds of contacts and connections. There are *specific effects of social trajectories.*

The convertibility of different forms of capital is the basis for the strategies aimed at ensuring the reproduction of capital and the position in the social space through the smallest number of conversions. The decisive moment is the ease with which the different forms of capital are converted and transmitted, and the incommensurability between different forms of capital causes great uncertainty for all holders of capital, as everyone wants to lose as little as possible.

SOCIAL STRUCTURES AND WELFARE REGIMES

The driving explanatory model is the model of social space. The structure in the space is defined by the distribution of capital, of properties and characteristics. This implies that class is not only defined by its position, but defined through criteria as profession, income, educational level and by secondary properties such as religion, race, a certain gender distribution, geographical distribution, ethnic belonging and so on. Eventually class is defined by the structure of relations between all relevant properties:

> The model of social space . . . is not only limited by the nature of data used (and usable), particularly by the practical impossibility of including in the analysis structural features such as the power which certain individuals or groups have over the economy, or even the innumerable associated hidden profits. If most of those who carry out empirical research are often led to accept, implicitly or explicitly, a theory which reduces the classes to simple ranked but non-antagonistic strata, this is above all because the very logic of their practice leads them to ignore what is objectively inscribed in every distribution. A distribution, in the statistical but also the political-economy sense, is the balance-sheet, at a given moment, of what has been won in previous battles and can be invested in subsequent battles; it expresses a state of the power relation between the classes or, more precisely, of the struggle for possession of rare goods and for the specifically political power over the distribution or redistribution of profit. (Bourdieu [1979] 1986, 245)

But the principle of welfare regimes (Esping-Andersen 1999) probably also affect the general picture of social reproduction. For example, Denmark has its own model with a high rate of women in the labour market and children in day-care institutions as a regulator in relation to the market of commodities, civil society and decommodification (Esping-Andersen 1990). Perhaps more adequately described by the concept of recommodification (Bonoli, George, and Taylor-Gooby 2000, 48–49), seen in light of changed welfare and labour market policies.

THE DISTRIBUTION OF (INFORMATIONAL) CAPITAL

The distribution of capital is not just given: there is a more or less democratically regulated (Weber [1922] 1978) struggle for capital in the power field (a mixture of the cultural, political, economic and bureaucratic field).

According to Hedström/Swedberg (1998), it is also necessary to analyse the *social mechanisms* of the structural tendencies, as for example the distribution of capital. In all societies there are struggles for scarce and attractive resources; people reconvert different kinds of capital into social positions in order to construct new pathways. This mechanism can be termed as a *structural homology*, which is a very particular relation of causal interdependence between specific areas in society, such as education and the labour market (Bourdieu [1989] 1996, 263). This will imply a rather closed structure with an opposition between the "old" and the "new" individuals who enter and act in the labour market. It is thus difficult to enter a field and obtain a permanent position, not only because of personal and organisational structures (e.g., embeddedness) (Granovetter 1985; Tilly 1998), but because of symbolic barriers which correspond with a multitude of settings. So when, for example, a firm or an institution demands groups or a single individual, the social mechanism operates (the foundation of inequality), in spite of state policies. The point being that state policies, old as well as new, are in fact a part of the structural homology. This contributes to unequal distributions of legitimate capital, even if the disadvantaged classes and generations in the Danish welfare state, compared to other kinds of welfare states, have better living conditions and rights to social benefits from public institutions and possibilities for adult education (especially the skilled workers). "Since inequality in general, is strongly connected to class inequality, a successful social policy can be expected to decrease the inequality between classes" (Erikson 1990, 258). But eventually the interdependence between the labour market and the educational field, mediated by the power field, is strongly connected to the establishment and reproduction of the welfare state. In sum, it seems that structural "effects" are still operating, also within the welfare state with its very large and expanded social programs, even if those programs have been reformed. This means that the creation and construction of a particular welfare state has led to the support of groups with less capital, thereby modifying the distance and transforming the relations between social classes. However, there is still a relative gap between social classes, in spite of political, social and organisational structures of redistribution (see Taylor-Gooby 1999). As a matter of fact, the basic structure in society operates according to its own rules and laws; it reinforces hierarchies in places and fields, and it contributes to unequal distributions of legitimate capital. This is especially the case within the power field, where two dominating groups continue to dominate the others, outside the power field (Bourdieu [1989] 1996). This is particularly the case in France, where institutions such as Grandes Ecoles are very significant, contributing to the reproduction of the corps, through the unequal distribution of titles in accordance with social origin. In other words, there is a strong relationship between the reproduction of the field of power and the field of universities.

CONCLUSION

One can conclude that social inequality, as related to education, still exists. Obtaining different levels of education and jobs still depends on social origin, gender, work experience and to some degree adult education. Generations born in the mid 1960s are less advantaged than generations born in the mid- and late 1950s, as measured by the time when the birth cohorts were thirty-one years old. This invariance and variation combined with changed policies connected to institutions of education and labour markets probably explain much of the variation in the linkage between social origin, education and occupation.

The social mechanism of structural homology seems to be a means of providing a general answer regarding the persisting reproduction of social inequality, which can be interpreted as a reproduction of the relative distance between groups. But the situation might also be influenced by new ways of organising social life. In fact, new cleavages correspond to new forms of inequality (lack of effects), which means that levels of social mobility and educational inequality basically remain as earlier. New forms of capital, resources and admissions are now at stake. In this sense, social inequality can increase over time, though further studies of younger cohorts might reveal other patterns. Competition in the labour market could well decline as a result of demographic changes and fewer young individuals. "Globalisation" may nevertheless abolish this trend, which is likely to take different directions, depending on areas and sectors. Further studies will have to concentrate upon more detailed life trajectories, especially regarding younger cohorts. The point being that both the supply and demand sides should be taken into consideration.

To conclude, it is difficult to trace the effects of new "policy regimes," that is, concepts with some resemblance to the "welfare regime" concept. Many countries have experienced various substantial changes in welfare policies relating to education. I do not find clear evidence that policy changes have reduced the problems of educational and social inequality. But good economic and employment conjunctures can be linked to less unemployment in several countries. This has partly, probably, to do with the trade-off between equality and employment (Esping-Andersen 1999, 180–84), the policy of equality and unemployment.

NOTES

This project was supported by a grant from the Danish Research Council (no. 9700145).

1. Converting is sometimes used in connection with religious conversions, as from Protestant to Catholic. However, here I use the concept directly coupled to strategies related to reproduction and survival. The concept of reconversion was developed as a reaction towards theories of social stratification and mobility. Firstly, by introducing the scheme of social and cultural reproduction (Bourdieu and Passeron [1970] 1977), which is not a mechanical theory, especially not after having supplemented the theory with the concept of *strategies of reconversions* (Bourdieu et al. 1973, 1978). Finally, by concluding with the concept of social space (Bourdieu [1979] 1986).

2. Furthermore a fairly good log-linear model shows that it was reasonable to analyze social origin, education, position and cohort at the same time (see also Jonsson 1993; Marshall et al. 1997).

3. Goldthorpe 1996b points out Young's satiric book about meritocracy as the one which started the basic study of how education functions in the social structure as credentials.

4. The theoretical space of habitus.

REFERENCES

Blackburn, R. M., and K. Prandy. 1997. The reproduction of social inequality. *Sociology* 31, no. 3: 491–509.

Blossfeld, Hans-Peter. 1986. Career opportunities in the Federal Republic of Germany: A dynamic approach to the study of life course, cohort and period effects. *European Sociological Review* 2: 208–25.

Blossfeld, Hans-Peter, and Reinhard Stockmann. 1999. The German dual system in comparative perspective. *International Journal of Sociology* 28: 3–28.

Boje, Tomas. 1986. Segmentation and mobility: An analysis of labour market flows on the Danish labour market. *Acta Sociologica* 29, no. 2: 171–78.

Boli, J., and F. O. Ramirez. 1986. World culture and the institutional development of mass education. In *Handbook of Theory and Research for the Sociology of Education*, edited by J. G. Richardson, 65–90. London: Greenwood.

Bonoli, Giuliano, Vic George, and Peter Taylor-Gooby. 2000. *European Welfare Futures: Towards a Theory of Retrenchment*. Cambridge: Polity.

Bourdieu, P. 1974. Avenir de classe et causalité du probable. *Revue française de sociologie* 15, no. 1: 3–42.

Bourdieu, P. 1977. *Outline of a Theory of Practice*. Cambridge Studies in Social Anthropology, no. 16. Cambridge: Cambridge University Press.

Bourdieu, P. [1979] 1986. *Distinction: A Social Critique of the Judgement of Taste*. London: Routledge & Kegan Paul.

Bourdieu, P. 1985. The social space and the genesis of groups. *Theory and Society* 14, no. 6: 723–44.

Bourdieu, P. [1992] 1996. *The Rules of Art*. Cambridge: Polity.

Bourdieu, P. [1989] 1996. *The State Nobility*. Cambridge: Polity.

Bourdieu, P., and L. Boltanski. 1978. Changes in social structure and changes in the demand for education. In *Contemporary Europe: Social Structures and Cultural Patterns*, edited by S. Giner and M. S. Archer, 197–227. London: Routledge & Kegan Paul.

Bourdieu, P., L. Boltanski, and M. de Saint Martin. 1973. Les stratégies de reconversion: Les classes sociales et le système d'enseignement. *Information sur les sciences sociales* 12, no. 5: 61–113.

Bourdieu, P., and J.-C. Passeron. [1970] 1977. *Reproduction in Education, Society, and Culture*. London: Sage, 1990.

Breen, Richard, and John H. Goldthorpe. 1999. Class inequality and meritocracy: A critique of Saunders and an alternative analysis. *British Journal of Sociology* 50: 1–27.

Broady, D. M., Mikael Börjesson, and M. Palme. 1998. Go west! Swedish higher education and transnational markets. Paper presented at Empirical Investigations of Social Space conference, Cologne, 7–9 October.

Broady, D., and M. de Saint Martin, eds. 1997. *Formation des élites et culture transna-tionalisation* (Colloque de Moscou, 27–29 April 1996), Centre de sociologie de l'éd-ucation et de la culture, École des Hautes Études en Sciences Sociales, Paris/Forskningsgruppen för utbildnings-och kultursociologi, ILU, Uppsala Uni-versitet.

Buchmann, Marlis, and Stefan Sacchi. 1998. The transition from school to work in Switzerland. In *From School to Work: A Comparative Study of Educational Qualifica-tions and Occupational Destinations,* edited by Y. Shavit and W. Müller, 407–42. Ox-ford: Clarendon.

Coleman, J. 1988. Social capital in the creation of human capital. *American Journal of Sociology* 94 (supplement): S95–S120.

Collins, R. 1979: *The Credential Society.* New York: Academic.

Dex, S., ed. 1991. *Life and Work History Analyses: Qualitative and Quantitative Devel-opments.* Sociological Review Monograph, no. 37. London: Routledge & Kegan Paul.

Elder, G. H., ed. 1985. *Life Course Dynamics, Trajectories, and Transitions, 1968–1980.* Cornell: Cornell University Press.

Elstad, J. I. 2000. Social background and life chances in Norway: Persisting inequali-ties throughout the twentieth century. *Yearbook of Sociology* 5, no. 1: 93–119.

Erikson, R. 1990. Politics and class mobility: Does politics influence rates of social mobility? In *Generating Equality in the Welfare State: The Swedish Experience,* edited by Inga Persson, 247–65. Oslo: Norwegian University Press.

Erikson, R., and J. Goldthorpe. 1992. *The Constant Flux.* Oxford: Clarendon.

Erikson, R., and J. O. Jonsson. 1998a. Social origin as an interest-bearing asset: Fam-ily background and labour-market rewards among employees in Sweden. *Acta So-ciologica* 41: 19–36.

Erikson, R., and J. O. Jonsson. 1998b. Qualifications and the allocation process of young men and women in the Swedish labour market. In *From School to work, A Comparative Study of Educational Qualifications and Occupational Destinations,* edited by Y. Shavi and W. Müller, 369–406. Oxford: Clarendon.

Esping-Andersen, G. 1990. *The Three Worlds of Welfare Capitalism.* Cambridge: Polity.

Esping-Andersen, G. 1999. *Social Foundations of Postindustrial Economics.* Oxford: Ox-ford University Press.

Featherman, D. L., and R. M. Hauser. 1978. *Opportunity and Change.* New York: Aca-demic.

Fritzell, J. 1999. Changes in social patterning of living conditions. In *Nordic Social Pol-icy,* edited by Mikko Kautto, 159–84. London: Routledge & Kegan Paul.

Goldthorpe, J. H. 1996a. Class analysis and reorientation of class theory: The case of persisting differentials in education. *British Journal of Sociology* 47, no. 3: 481–505.

Goldthorpe, J. H. 1996b. Problems of "Meritocracy." In *Can Education Be Equalised? The Swedish Case in Comparative Perspective,* edited by R. Erikson and J. O. Jonsson, 255–87. Boulder: Westview.

Granovetter, M. 1985. Economic action and social structure: The problem of embed-dedness. *American Journal of Sociology* 91: 481–510.

Gustafsson, B., and M. Johansson 1999. In search of smoking guns: What makes in-come inequality over time in different countries? *American Sociological Review* 64: 585–605.

Halleröd, B. 1999. Economic standard of living: A longitudinal analysis of the economic standard among Swedes, 1979 to 1995. *European Societies* 1: 391–418.

Hansen, E. J. 1995. *En generation blev voksen.* Report 95:8. Copenhagen: Socialforskningsinstituttet.

Hansen, E. J. 1997. *Perspektiver og begrænsninger i studiet af den social rekruttering til uddannelserne.* Report 97:17. Copenhagen: Socialforskningsinstituttet.

Hedström, P., and R. Swedberg, eds. 1998. *Social Mechanisms: An Analytical Approach to Social Theory.* Cambridge: Polity.

Ishida, H., W. Müller, and J. M. Ridge. 1995. Class origin, class destination, and education: A cross-national study of ten industrial nations. *American Journal of Sociology* 101, no. 1: 145–93.

Jensen, Anne M., and P. Jensen, 1996. *The Impact of Labour Market Training on the Duration of Unemployment.* Aarhus: Centre for Labour Market and Social Research.

Jonsson, J. O. 1993. Education, social mobility, and social reproduction in Sweden: Patterns and change. In *Welfare Trends in the Scandinavian Countries,* edited by E. J. Hansen, S. Ringen, H. Uusitalo, and R. Erikson, 91–118. New York: M. E. Sharpe.

Kerckhoff, Alan C. 1993. *Diverging Pathways, Social Structure, and Career Reflections.* New York: Cambridge University Press.

Krahn, H., and G. S. Lowe. 1999. School-to-work transitions and postmodern values: What's changing Canada? In *From Education to Work: Cross-National Perspectives,* edited by W. R. Heinz, 260–83. Cambridge: Polity.

Marshall, G., A. Swift, and S. Roberts, 1997 *Against the Odds?* Oxford: Clarendon.

Morris, M., and B. Western, 1999. Inequality in earnings at the close of the twentieth century. *Annual Review of Sociology* 25: 623–57.

Munk, M. D. 2000. The same old story? Reconversions of educational capital in the welfare state. In *Jahrbuch für Arbeit und Bildung* (Education and Work) 1999–2000, *Deregulierung der Arbeit: Pluralisierung der Bildung?* edited by Axel Bolder, Walter R. Heinz, Günther Kutscha, 87–98. Opladen: Leske & Budrich Verlag.

Nordli Hansen, M. 1999. Utdanningspolitikk og ulikhet. In *Tidsskrift for samfunnsforskning* 2: 172–203.

Prandy, K. 1998. Class and continuity in social reproduction: An empirical investigation. *Sociological Review* 46, no. 2: 340–64.

Roemer, J. E. 2000. To what extent do fiscal regimes equalize opportunities for income acquisition among citizens? Available at http://pantheon.yale.edu/~jer39.

Rosenfeld, R. 1992. Job mobility and career processes. *Annual Review of Sociology* 18: 39–61.

Shavit, Y., and H.-P. Blossfeld, eds. 1993. *Persistent Inequality: Changing Educational Attainment in Thirteen Countries.* Boulder: Westview.

Shavit, Y., and W. Müller. 1998. *From School to Work: A Comparative Study of Educational Qualifications and Occupational Destinations.* Oxford: Clarendon.

Statistiske Efterretninger. 1999. SE 5 (U & K). Copenhagen: Statistics Denmark.

Strauss, A. L. 1971. *The Contexts of Social Mobility.* Chicago: Aldine.

Sørensen, A. B. 1986. Theory and methodology in social stratification. In *Sociology: From Crisis to Science? The Sociology of Action,* edited by U. Himmelstrand, 69–95. London: Sage.

Taylor-Gooby, P. 1999. Bipolar bugbears. *Journal of Social Policy* 28: 299–303.

Tilly, Charles. 1998. *Durable Inequality*. Berkeley: University of California Press.
Wallerstein, Immanuel. 1999. The Heritage of Sociology: The Promise of Social Science. *Current Sociology* 47: 1–41.
Weber, M. [1922] 1978. *Economy and Society*. Berkeley: University of California Press.
Young, M. 1958. *The Rise of the Meritocracy, 1870–1933*. London: Thames & Hudson.

III

CRITICAL ISSUES IN SOCIOLOGY OF EDUCATION

14

Making Sense of Education Reform:

Global and National Influences

Geoff Whitty and Sally Power

In recent years, many nations have sought to reformulate the relationship between government, schools and parents. Our own research has looked at the growing emphasis on parental choice and school autonomy in England, Sweden, Australia, New Zealand and the United States (Whitty et al. 1998), but similar policies are being pursued or advocated elsewhere. To what extent are these policies comparable? Can they be said to constitute a coherent trend? And, if so, what does it signify? Is the widespread emergence of devolutionary policies nothing more than a series of local responses to local crises, or does it indicate a more profound restructuring of relations between state and civil society on an international scale?

The almost simultaneous emergence of similar reforms across continents has led some to suggest that the current restructuring of education needs to be understood as a global phenomenon. Indeed, it has been argued that this trend is part of a broader economic, political and cultural process of globalisation in which national differences are eroded, state bureaucracies fragment and the notion of mass systems of public welfare, including education, disappears. But, rather than embrace such grand theories wholeheartedly, we need to consider whether contextual specificities are at least as significant as any broader cross-national developments. In other words, we need to explore the degree of commonality and coherence within the education reforms of different countries before going on to consider the extent to which we are witnessing a fundamental change in the governance of national systems of education.

Policy-makers are often criticised for looking overseas for solutions to domestic problems in the naive belief that policies designed in one context can be unproblematically transported elsewhere. Those involved with analysing these policies also need to be wary of decontextualising reforms. To compare across countries without recognising the distinctive historical and cultural dimensions of policies is to risk "false universalism" (Rose 1991) whereby similarities are spotted without reference to the context in which they were developed.

Certainly, any cross-national comparison needs to acknowledge the differences in the degree and manner in which education is being restructured. The extent to which responsibility has been devolved downwards differs greatly both between and within countries. The reforms in New Zealand have eliminated all intermediate levels of decision-making between central government and schools. This has resulted in a situation where extensive powers have been delegated to schools, but many have also been retained by, even consolidated within, central government. Recent reforms in England have been less dramatic, but are probably closest to this mode of devolution in so far as grant-maintained schools in particular bypass the intermediate level influence of local education authorities (LEAs) and stand in an unmediated relationship with central government. While schools in New Zealand have more powers than any of the other fourteen countries in an OECD (1995) study, mainstream public schools in the United States have the second fewest. Federal government there is deemed to have no decision-making powers, while even state governments have relatively few. Decision-making is concentrated at local levels, but principally within the district rather than the school. Within the Swedish public education system, decision-making is now concentrated at the local levels, but, unlike in the United States, it is divided evenly between the school and the district. Sweden is, of course, of particular interest in this respect, having traditionally been a rather centralised, regulated and relatively successful educational system, which nevertheless has reduced the degree of prescription in its national curriculum and embarked on a process of restructuring through devolution and choice. The first stage of devolution was down to local government level, but there has subsequently been experimentation with competition and choice between individual schools, including state funding of private schools. This was taken furthest under a center/right government in the early 1990s, and more recent social democratic government has retained the main elements of the reform but tried to find a better balance between collective and individual interests (Miron 1993).

We clearly need to acknowledge differences in the political complexion of reforms that may look similar. In England, New Zealand, Sweden, Australia and the United States, or at least in individual states within these last two countries, devolution, institutional autonomy and school choice have often become associated with a conservative agenda for education. Yet, support for at least some aspects of these policies is by no means limited to New Right politicians who argue that social affairs are best organised according to the general principle of consumer sovereignty. Indeed, some of the early moves to devolution in Victoria, Australia, in the 1980s were talked of in terms of professional and community empowerment, even though more recent policies there have been associated with a New Right marketising agenda (Angus 1995). This was also the case with some of the devolution initiatives in New Zealand in the 1980s, despite the fact that subsequent reforms there too have been more concerned with fostering market freedom than with equity (Grace 1991; Gordon 1992). In both countries, governments of different political complexions have supported reform, albeit with somewhat different emphases. In the United States, the Chicago reforms were originally supported by a curious alliance of black groups seeking to establish community control of their local schools, white old-style liberals who had become disillusioned with the performance of the School Board, New Right advocates of school choice and some former student radicals of the 1960s. Similarly, radical reformers of many shades of opinion are currently looking to the U.S. charter school movement as the way to create their own "educational spaces" (Wells et al. 1996). In Sweden, while the balance has shifted back to a concern with equity issues with the return of a Social Democratic government, there has been cross-party support for the general direction of the reforms. And, even in England and Wales, where the reforms were most closely and consistently associated with the New Right Thatcher and Major governments, some of the key elements are being kept in place by the New Labour administration under Tony Blair.

Much of this confusing complexity derives from the many shades of meaning behind apparently similar policies. Not only do concepts like devolution and choice enter into different relationships with each other, they are "multi-accented" concepts or "sliding signifiers" in their own right. As Lauglo (1996) points out, in discussing "decentralisation," it should not be thought of as a unitary concept. Indeed, he identifies eight alternatives to the conventional bureaucratic centralism of mass education systems, four of which reflect different political legitimations for redistributing authority and four which reflect different arguments concerning the quality of education provision and the efficient use of resources. These alternatives are variously, and often simultaneously, emphasised within each of our countries. Liberalism, or more accurately neo-liberalism, is evident within all of them, but perhaps most particularly in England and Wales where it has become closely articulated with the so-called new public management combining what Lauglo terms "market mechanisms" and "management by objectives." Such developments are also strongly in evidence in New Zealand and in some states in the United States and Australia. However, justifications for decentralisation within some American districts, such as Dade County, Florida, can be seen as being related to pedagogic professionalism—at least within the reforms of the 1980s—while professional control was also an aspect of Swedish reforms at that time. A further feature of some justifications surrounding restructuring has been references to the democracy of local participation. This often takes the form of local populism, however, rather than participatory democracy. Any cross-national discussion of educational restructuring needs therefore to bear in mind a wide range of variance. Educational reform is being conducted within contexts with different histories, different constitutional and administrative arrangements and different political complexions. Moreover, the nature and extent of decentralization, and the ways in which policies are interconnected, vary both within and between countries.

However, while such variance needs to be acknowledged, it should not obscure the common factors. It is clear from the above discussion that there are common trends across countries. As Fowler (1994) comments, despite the large body of "exceptionality literature," "important variations among institutions and cultures do not erase deeper similarities"—particularly between advanced industrial democracies. Despite the differences, there does appear to be considerable congruence in the policies in many different countries. Within the range of political rationales, it is the neo-liberal alternative which dominates, as does a particular emphasis on market type mechanisms. This decentralisation via the market is also articulated with justifications of quality and efficiency, drawing on the discourse of the new public management with its emphasis on strong school management and external scrutiny—made possible by the development of performance indicators and competency-based assessment procedures reinforced in many cases by external inspection. These developments in education policy reflect a broader tendency for liberal democracies to develop along the lines of what Gamble (1988) has called the "strong state" and the "free economy." This strong state increasingly "steers at a distance" and the notion of the free economy is extended to a marketised "civil society" in which education and welfare services are offered to individual consumers by competing providers rather than provided collectively by the state for all citizens. In other words, bureaucratically provided welfare is increasingly being replaced by welfare distributed through "quasi-markets" (Levacic 1995).

ACCOUNTING FOR POLICY CONVERGENCE

Even though these directions in education policy have not penetrated all countries (Green 1994), and have so far had only limited influence in countries like Japan, the similarity between the broad trends in many parts of the world suggests that education policy may well be witnessing something more significant than passing political fashion. In seeking to understand the similarities between policies, a range of explanations can be invoked. At one end of the continuum are those that highlight the role of individual policy-carriers, and at the other end are theories of globalisation and post-modernism where the traditional role of the nation state is overridden by multi-faceted international restructuring. Of course, these various explanations may not be mutually exclusive, but each emphasises a different locus of change which may have important implications for the possibility of generating potential alternatives to current policies.

One form of explanation is that ideas developed in one context have been copied in another. To some extent, neo-liberal policies have been actively fostered by international organisations, for example by the IMF and the World Bank in Latin America and Eastern Europe (Arnove 1996). But informal modes of transmission are probably more common (Whitty and Edwards 1998). There is certainly evidence to suggest that when education policy-makers formulate proposed reforms they look to other countries for inspiration and justification. Kenneth Baker, English secretary of state for education under Margaret Thatcher, drew inspiration for the City Technology College experiment from reports about and personal visits to specialist schools in New York City and elsewhere in the United States. Conversely, Britain's grant-maintained schools policy apparently inspired some charter school legislation in the United States, notably in California, where the state superintendent is said to have been impressed by the policy following a brief visit to the United Kingdom. With reference to Australia and New Zealand, Smyth (1993) claims that Victoria's *Schools for the Future* framework bears an "even plagiaristic" resemblance to New Zealand's policy blueprint *Tomorrow's Schools*, which, he claims, was itself "hijacked directly from Thatcher's England." Seddon (1994) argues that Australia in general has displayed "a dependent and subservient preoccupation with developments in the UK and USA" (p. 4). Finally, Miron (1993) suggests that the centre-right coalition in Sweden looked to Thatcherite England for its inspiration, but then itself sought to become a "world leader" in fostering choice policies in education.

Although policy borrowing has clearly been a factor in the move toward choice within devolved systems of schooling, it only begs more questions. What gives these particular policies such widespread appeal across different countries and different political parties? To what extent does their appeal stem from a disillusionment with existing modes of education provision, or does it rather reflect a more general crisis within the state or even a shift of global proportions?

Some observers suggest that the reforms can be understood in terms of the transportation of changing modes of regulation from the sphere of production into other arenas, such as schooling and welfare services. They point to a correspondence between the establishment of differentiated markets in welfare and a shift in the economy away from Fordism toward a post-Fordist mode of accumulation which "places a lower value on mass individual and collective consumption and creates pressures for a more differentiated production and distribution of health, education, transport and housing" (Jessop et al. 1987, 109). Ball (1990), for example, has claimed to see in new forms of schooling a move away from the "Fordist" school toward a "post-Fordist" one—the educational equivalent of flexible specialisation driven by the imperatives of differentiated consumption replacing the old assembly-line world of mass production. These "post-Fordist schools" are designed "not only to produce the post-Fordist, multi-skilled, innovative worker but to behave in post-Fordist ways themselves; moving away from mass production and mass markets to niche markets and 'flexible specialisation' . . . a post-Fordist mind-set is thus having implications in schools for management styles, curriculum, pedagogy and assessment" (Kenway 1993, 115).

Kenway (1993) herself actually goes further and regards the rapid rise of the market form in education as something much more significant than post-Fordism; she therefore terms it a "postmodern" phenomenon, accentuating the nexus between the "global" and the "local." Although notoriously difficult to define, within the realm of social relations, post-modernity is usually associated with processes of globalisation, the rise of new technologies, the breakdown of old collectivities and hierarchies and sometimes an increase in social reflexivity. Part of the appeal of the recent education reforms may thus lie in their declared intention to encourage the growth of different types of school, responsive to needs of particular communities and interest groups. They may seem to connect to the aspirations of groups who found little to identify with in the "grand narratives" associated with modernist class-based politics. In this sense, the reforms might be viewed as a rejection of all totalising narratives and their replacement by "a set of cultural projects united [only] by a self-proclaimed commitment to heterogeneity, fragmentation and difference" (Boyne and Rattansi 1990, 9). In other words, support for schools run on a variety of principles could reflect a broader shift from the assumptions of modernity to those of postmodernity.

However, there are various problems with these "new times" theses. They are not only "notoriously vague" (Hickox 1995) but also tend to exaggerate the extent to which we have moved to a new regime of accumulation. The more optimistic versions also exaggerate the benefits of the changes. Neo-Fordism may therefore be a more appropriate term than post-Fordism (Allen 1992), while Giddens's concept of "high modernity" probably captures the combination of change and continuity rather better than that of "post-modernity" (Giddens 1991). Indeed, new cultural forms and more flexible modes of capital accumulation may be shifts in surface appearance, rather than signs of the emergence of some entirely new post-capitalist or even post-industrial society (Harvey 1989).

EXPORTING THE "CRISIS"

To that extent, the reforms may be better seen as new ways of dealing with the vagaries of capitalism. In this situation, the state's dominant mode of regulation is changing to one of "steering at a distance." To various degrees, the reforms have been prefaced with allegations that bureaucratically controlled education is both inefficient and unproductive. Systems of "mass" schooling were seen to have "failed" on a number of counts. They have disappointed those who see education as a route to a more equitable society as differences in educational outcomes continue to reflect differences in socio-economic status. Mass systems of public education are also deemed to have been unproductive in terms of economic returns, as is evident in frequently aired concerns about educational standards and international competitiveness. The new arrangements for managing education and other public services can be seen as new ways of tackling the problems of accumulation and legitimation facing the state in a situation where the traditional Keynesian "welfare state" is no longer deemed viable (Dale 1989).

In particular, there are two directions along which the state needs to secure legitimacy. One relates to the need to conceal, or at least displace responsibility for, the shortcomings and inherent inequities of capitalism itself. The second relates to the requirement that it legitimates its own activities—for instance, disguising its relationship with capital through a position of benign neutrality. As capitalism fails to bring prosperity and opportunity, there is a danger that people will "see through" not just the structural problems of education systems, but the basis of the mode of production. In many Western countries, the 1980s saw rising unemployment rates and, while some groups prospered throughout the decade, the gap between rich and poor grew wider.

Through explaining economic decline and enduring poverty in terms of failures within the state infrastructure, attention is deflected away from the essential injustices and contradictions of capitalism. The management of the public sector is called into question and the demands for reform prevail. The generation of policy alone becomes part of the solution. As Apple (1996) argues, governments "must *be seen* to be doing something . . . [r]eforming education is not only widely acceptable and relatively unthreatening, but just as crucially, 'its success or failure will not be obvious in the short-term'" (Apple 1996, 88; his emphasis). But, whereas in the past, the attempts to restore legitimacy may have involved increasing bureaucratisation and greater "expert" intervention, these processes are now seen as the problem rather than the solution. Bureaucratic control of education, it is suggested, stifles responsivity to the needs of business and industry.

It is also possible to argue that the current move toward school decentralisation arises from the state's inability convincingly to present public education as a means of promoting a more equitable society and redistributing real opportunities. Such a position is taken by Weiss (1993) who draws on the work of Weiler (1983) to suggest that, in Germany, devolution is the latest in a series of strategies used by the state to legitimate its policies and practices. He suggests that policies of school autonomy and parent empowerment leave conflict to be dealt with at lower levels of the system, with the higher administrative structures appearing uninvolved, and therefore, above reproach. Malen (1994) too uses concepts drawn from Weiler's (1989) work on decentralisation to suggest that site-based management in the United States may have considerable political utility for managing conflict and maintaining legitimacy.

Whether decentralisation is seen as a complete abdication of responsibility by the state, "a deliberate process of subterfuge, distortion, concealment and wilful neglect as the state seeks to retreat in a rather undignified fashion from its historical responsibility for providing quality public education" (Smyth 1993, 3), or a selective withdrawal from areas in which it has difficulty succeeding, such as equality of opportunity (Nash 1989), making educational decision-making the responsibility of individual institutions and families is an effective strategy for "shifting the blame." The failure of individual schools to flourish as "stand alone" institutions can be attributed to poor leadership or teaching quality. Similarly, unequal educational achievement among students can be explained through poor parenting—either through failing to exercise the new entitlement to choose effectively, or failing to engage with schools as active partners and participants. The burden of sustaining meritocratic ideology is shifted from the shoulders of government.

Fragmenting public systems of education may not only legitimize the political authority of the state and the credibility of capitalism as the most feasible mode of production, it may also be an example of the way in which the state, during periods of gross economic pressure, seeks ways to cut back on public expenditure generally in order to privilege the needs of capital (e.g., through tax cuts) and thus provide the best possible conditions for sustaining productivity and maximising profit. Certainly, the reforms have not been followed by increased investment into education beyond initial "pump-priming" money or cash incentives for favoured schemes. The trend toward self-management of schools often brings little more than "the capacity to 'manage' specific resources and centrally determined policy at the school site within the context of increasingly contracting state revenues" (Robertson 1993). Some observers claim that devolution is "not what it purports to be— it is a budget cutting exercise masquerading under the banner of schools getting more control of their own affairs" (Smyth 1993).

THE CHANGING ROLE OF THE STATE

However, it seems clear that, although the extent of any underlying social changes can easily be exaggerated by various "post-ist" forms of analysis, both the discourse and the contexts of political struggles in and around education *have* been significantly altered by recent reforms. Not only have changes in the nature of the state influenced the reforms in education, the reforms in education are themselves beginning to change the way we think about the role of the state and what we expect of it. Green (1990) has pointed to the way in which education has not only been an important part of state activity in modern societies, but also played a significant role in the process of state formation itself in the eighteenth and nineteenth centuries. The current changes in education policy may similarly be linked to a redefinition of the nature of the state and a reworking of the relations between state and civil society.

At one level, the new policies foster the idea that responsibility for education and welfare, beyond the minimum required for public safety, is to be defined largely as a matter for individuals and families. Not only is the scope of the state narrowed, but civil society becomes increasingly defined in market terms. As many of the responsibilities adopted by the state during the post–World War period begin to be devolved to a marketized version of civil society, consumer rights increasingly come to prevail over citizen rights.

Although some aspects of education have been "privatized" not so much in the strictly economic sense as in the sense of transferring them to the private decision-making sphere, others have become a matter of state mandate rather than local democratic debate. Despite the rhetoric about "rolling back" or "hollowing out" the state, certain aspects of state intervention have been maintained, indeed strengthened. The strong state is a minimalist one in many respects but a more powerful and even authoritarian one in others.

New modes of regulation reflect a shift from conventional techniques of coordination and control on the part of large-scale bureaucratic state forms and their replacement by a set of "discursive, legislative, fiscal, organizational and other resources" (Rose and Miller 1992, 189), what Foucault might have termed moral or disciplinary technologies. But, although these devices may appear to some people to offer considerable scope for local discretion compared to the "dead hand" of centralised bureaucracies, they also entail some fairly direct modes of control, albeit in a different modality. For example, the devolution of funding to schools on a per capita basis requires schools to attempt to maximise their rolls. Schools which do not attract students are penalised in a direct fashion by the withdrawal of funding and staffing resources. And the publication of test results and school inspection reports potentially provides a powerful link between the requirements of the "strong state" and the actions of individual schools and parents in the marketplace.

Particularly helpful in understanding how the state remains strong while appearing to devolve power to individuals and autonomous institutions competing in the market is Neave's (1988) account of the shift from the "bureaucratic state" to the "evaluative state." This entails "a rationalization and wholesale redistribution of functions between center and periphery such that the center maintains overall strategic control through fewer, but more precise, policy levers, contained in overall "mission statements," the setting of system goals and the operationalisation of criteria relating to "output quality" (p. 11). Rather than lead to a withering away of the state, the state withdraws "from the murky plain of overwhelming detail, the better to take refuge in the clear and commanding heights of strategic "profiling" (p. 12). In some cases, this brings about the emergence of new intermediary bodies—trusts, agencies and quangos [quasi-autonomous non-governmental organizations]—which are directly appointed by and responsible to government ministers rather than under local democratic control. Such agencies are often headed by a new breed of government-appointees who tend to have a higher public profile than conventional state bureaucrats and have had a significant role in setting new political agendas through close contacts with the media. The evaluative state also requires significant changes to be made at the institutional level. Schools and colleges have to develop new modes of response which require new structures and patterns of authority. In particular, it seems to encourage strong goal-oriented leadership at the institutional level, involving a shift from the traditional collegial model to that of the "chief executive" and "senior management team."

Neave (1988) suggests that the evaluative state does not represent any one ideological viewpoint. Its key characteristic is a move away from government by "bureaucratic fiat." Yet there are close links between what he describes and Pusey's (1991) concept of economic rationalism in which education is framed as a commodity and education policy becomes the means by which it can be more efficiently and effectively regulated and distributed in relation to an overriding concern with economic objectives, so that the market becomes the ascendant metaphor and there is a clear permeation of business values and vocabulary into educational discourse (Marginson 1993). At the same time education is, in some respects, brought more directly and effectively under the control of central government agencies. Sweden, UK and New Zealand, and many states in America and Australia, have introduced competency-based performance indicators as a means of measuring educational output. Although justified in terms of consumer information and public accountability, these programs enable government to scrutinize more effectively educational expenditure and productivity while at the same time blocking alternative definitions of what counts as appropriate learning.

In Australia, Marginson (1993) claims that the emphasis on economic objectives entails a distancing of education from social and cultural domains. In practice, though, there is often another component to current policies that needs to be taken into consideration. The New Right in many countries is a coalition of neo-liberal advocates of market forces and neo-conservative proponents of a return to "traditional" values (Gamble 1983). The balance between the neo-liberal and neo-conservative aspects of contemporary conservatism varies between and within countries. However, where neo-conservatives are strong, they expect the education system to foster particular values, especially among those whose adherence to them is considered suspect. The criteria of evaluation employed are thus not only those of economic rationalism, but also those of cultural preferences. This is particularly the case where there is perceived to be a threat to national identity and hegemonic values either from globalisation or from supposed "enemies within," who are sometimes seen to include "bureau-professionals" and members of the "liberal educational establishment."

McKenzie (1993) argues that British governments have "actually increased their claims to knowledge and authority over the education system whilst promoting a theoretical and superficial movement toward consumer sovereignty" (p. 17). Although other countries have not been as prescriptive as Britain, many governments at state or national level have tightened their control over the curriculum in terms of what is taught and/or how this is to be assessed and inspected. This central regulation of the curriculum is not only geared toward standardizing performance criteria in order to facilitate professional accountability and consumer choice within the education market-place, it is also about trying to maintain or create national identities. In England and Wales, the formulation of the National Curriculum has been underlain by a consistent requirement that schools concentrate on British history, British geography and "classic" English literature. During its development, the influential Hillgate Group (1987) expressed concern about pressure for a multicultural curriculum and argued for "the traditional values of western societies" underlying British culture which "must not be sacrificed for the sake of a misguided relativism, or out of a misplaced concern for those who might not yet be aware of its strengths and weaknesses" (p. 4).

Thus, although some theories of globalization hold that the state is becoming less important on economic (Reich 1991), political (Held 1989) and cultural (Robertson 1991) grounds, at the present time there is little to support the postmodernist predictions of Usher and Edwards (1994) of the decline of the role of the state in education, at least in relation to the compulsory phase of provision. While this phenomenon of a strengthened state alongside policies of devolution and choice is particularly evident in Britain, similar trends can be identified in many countries (Gordon 1995; Apple 1996; Arnove 1996). Even if we concede that there has been a reduction in the profile of the nation state as an international entity and a convergence of policy approaches, there is nothing to suggest that it has yet conceded its grip on areas of internal regulation.

Yet these particular political responses to globalization and the situation confronting modern nation states are not inevitable. The specific policies are not simply explicable as irresistible outcomes of macro-social change. As indicated earlier, the particular combination of policies discussed here has been heavily influenced by the interpretations of such changes offered by various pressure groups from the New Right. We should remember that neither enhanced choice nor school autonomy is necessarily linked to a conservative agenda and that such measures have, in other circumstances, sometimes been part of a more progressive package of policies. Indeed, as noted earlier, some of the reforms actually originated in a different tradition, but have subsequently been incorporated and transformed by a rightist agenda. And while we should not underestimate the significance of those changes which are evoked—but inadequately characterized—by terms such as post-Fordism and post-modernity, we should not assume that the policy responses that are currently fashionable are the most appropriate ones. In many countries, the political left was rather slow in recognizing the significance of the changes and thus allowed the right to take the initiative. This, in turn, has had serious consequences for the direction in which reform has gone and for the particular forms of subjectivity which they encourage. But it has also generated some potential contradictions that may be exploited by those seeking an alternative agenda.

THE HIDDEN CURRICULUM OF REFORM

For example, the emphasis on competition and choice that the New Right has brought to the reforms has an associated "hidden curriculum" of marketization. Ball (1994) claims that "insofar as students are influenced and affected by their institutional environment, then the system of morality 'taught' by schools is increasingly well accommodated to the values complex of the enterprise culture" (p. 146). Old values of community, co-operation, individual need and equal worth, which Ball claims underlay public systems of comprehensive education, are being replaced by values that celebrate individualism, competition, performativity and differentiation. These values and dispositions are not made visible and explicit, but emanate from the changing social context and permeate the education system in myriad ways.

In some cases, the messages of the market and the preferences of governments complement each other. In other instances, however, market forces may contradict, even undermine, the "old-fashioned" values and sense of nationhood that governments ostensibly seek to foster. This contradiction may reflect more than the ideological distance between neo-conservatism and neo-liberalism. It could represent the tension between attempting to maintain a stable and strategic center in an increasingly fragmented and atomized context. The market, as Marquand (1995) reminds us, is subversive—it "uproots communities, disrupts families, mocks faiths and erodes the ties of place and history."

To some extent the potential subversion of the market is contained through strong regulatory measures. But neo-conservative agendas may be increasingly compromised by the growing presence of corporate interests in the classroom. Whereas the school curriculum has traditionally transcended—indeed actively distanced itself from—the world of commerce (see Wiener 1981), the growth of self-managing schools and the promotion of market forces within education is forging a new intimacy between these two domains. In the United States, for instance, the commercial satellite network Channel One offers schools free monitors on condition that 90 percent of students watch its news and adverts almost every day. Molnar (1996) cites a wide range of examples where corporate business entices schools to promote its products. In many countries, there are schemes whereby equipment can be purchased with vouchers from supermarket chains, the take-up of which is enhanced as a result of budget constraints and the removal of public control (Roberts 1994). Harris's (1996) report on the Australian Coles program reveals not only the vast amount of time teachers can spend counting dockets, but also the promotional space occupied by visible tallies and scoreboards as well as the advertising on the computer equipment eventually acquired. Such promotions are particularly attractive to schools in need of extra resources. In England, schools have been given clearance to sell space for advertising, and the proliferation of commercially sponsored curriculum materials and promotions has been such that an independent organisation designed to protect consumer interests has published a good practice guide for teachers, governors, school boards and parents (National Consumer Council 1996).

Advertising in schools is likely to provoke a number of anxieties. Those on the left will be concerned that curriculum materials portray a partial, and inaccurate, account of business interests. In this connection, Molnar (1996) quotes a study guide on banking which defines "free enterprise" as the symbol of "a nation which is healthy and treats its citizens fairly." One international survey of corporate products in the classroom found that "the biggest polluters of the environment—the chemical, steel, and paper industries—were the biggest producers of environmental education material" (Harty 1994, 97). Neo-conservatives, on the other hand, may be critical of the cultural threat of what is sometimes called "McDonaldization." There are fears that schools will develop "an anti-intellectual emphasis" and "a consumptionist drive to purchase status goods." Indeed, Harty alleges that the permeation of multinationals "contributes to a standardised global culture of material gratification . . . [which will] impinge on the cultural integrity of whole nations" (Harty 1994, 98–99). In this scenario, far from encouraging students to appreciate the particularities of their regional or national inheritance, schooling becomes implicated in the training of desires, rendering subjects open to the seduction of ever changing consumption patterns and the politics of lifestyling.

Thus, there are often contrasting messages coming from the overt and the hidden curricula. While at the level of direct transmissions, students are meant to be taught the neo-conservative values of the cultural restorationists (Ball 1990), the context in which they are taught may undermine these canons. The content of the lessons emphasizes heritage and tradition, but the form of their transmission is becoming increasingly commodified within the new education market place.

This tension is discussed in a paper by Bernstein (1997). He argues that the increasing deregulation of the economic field and the increasing regulation of what he terms the symbolic field are generating new forms of pedagogic identity, in contrast to both the "retrospective" identity of old conservatism and the "therapeutic" identity associated with the child-centered progressivism that was evident in England and the United States in the 1960s and 1970s. An emergent "decentered market" identity embodies the principles of neo-liberalism. It has no intrinsic properties, and its form is dependent only upon the exchange value determined by the market and is therefore infinitely variable and unstable. A "prospective" pedagogic identity, on the other hand, attempts to "recenter" through selectively incorporating elements of old conservatism. It engages with contemporary change, but draws upon the stabilizing traditions of the past as a counterbalance to the instability of the market. While a decentered market pedagogy might be seen to foster "new" global subjects, a prospective pedagogy seeks to reconstruct "old" national subjects, albeit selectively in response to the pressures of the new economic and social climate. Thus, there may be an emphasis in the overt curriculum on "imagined communities" of the past at the same time as real collectivities are being atomized in a culture of individual and institutional competition.

Green (1996), who believes we are seeing "partial internationalisation" rather than rampant globalisation, claims:

> It is undoubtedly true that many of the advanced western states find it increasingly difficult to maintain social cohesion and solidarity. Growing individualism and life-style diversity, secularisation, social mobility and the decline of stable communities have all played a part in this. . . . In some countries, where markets and individualism have gone furthest in dissolving social ties, there is reason to wonder whether national solidarism has not vanished beyond recovery. (p. 41)

Although Green himself acknowledges that states still retain strong control over the regulation of education systems through strategic performance-based funding, he argues that there has been a narrowing in the scope of educational ends where "broader national educational objectives in terms of social cohesion and citizenship formation have become increasingly confused and neglected, in part because few western governments have a clear notion of what nationhood and citizenship mean in complex and pluralistic modern democracies" (Green 1996, 58).

Inasmuch as the current wave of reforms mark a response by nation states to deal with the fundamental, and increasingly apparent, social and economic crises by which they are beleaguered—both from within and without—devolution can provide only a temporary solution. As Weiss (1993) argues, the conflicts and disparities within the education system are too deep-seated to be resolved by simply shifting the blame down the line. As the processes of polarization become sharper and the failure of local initiatives more transparent, the structural limitations of the new educational policies will be reexposed. In this context, Green (1996) argues that even the current degree of responsibility taken by governments for public education may not be enough "as the social atomization induced by global market penetration becomes increasingly dysfunctional. With the decline of socially integrating institutions and the consequent atrophy of collective social ties, education may soon again be called upon to stitch together the fraying social fabric" (p. 59). While the demise of some forms of national solidarity may be long overdue, the general atrophy of collective ties and consequent loss of notions of citizenship which Green predicts must surely be cause for concern. The issue then becomes one of establishing how education might best help reconstruct the social fabric and who shall influence its design.

SEEKING ALTERNATIVE FUTURES

The impact of these developments on coming generations may only be a matter of conjecture at this stage, but it does seem clear that the very structures of education systems and their associated styles of educational decision making impinge upon modes of social solidarity and forms of political consciousness and representation. However, rather than seeing the future in terms of resurrecting elements of old conservatism in the face of rampant marketisation, we should surely take the opportunity to consider how we might develop new and more genuinely inclusive collectivities for the future and put equity back on the agenda. In other words, we need to consider whether there are alternative prospective identities that we might wish to foster.

David Hargreaves (1994) argues that, while we should be happy to encourage a system of independent, differentiated and specialized schools to reflect the increasingly heterogeneous nature of modern societies, we should also reassert a sense of common citizenship by insisting on core programmes of civic education in all schools. This idea is now being actively pursued by the New Labour government in Britain, as one of the ways in which it wishes to revise the Conservative government's National Curriculum. Our own view is that such proposals pay insufficient attention not only to the effects of quasi-markets in exacerbating existing inequalities between schools and in society at large but also underestimate the power of the hidden curriculum of the market to undermine any real sense of commonality. The very exercise of individual choice and school self-management can so easily become self-legitimating for those with the resources to benefit from it and the mere teaching of civic responsibility is unlikely to provide an effective counterbalance. Attention therefore also needs to be given to the development of an alternative "hidden curriculum," through the development of new sets of relations within schools and beyond them.

More specifically, if we want students to learn democratic citizenship we need to put in place structures of learning which embody those principles. In other words, as Apple and Beane (1999) put it, we need to develop more genuinely democratic schools. However, changes *within* schools are unlikely to be able to counter the hidden curriculum of marketization coming from competition *between* schools and within civil society. We therefore need to think of alternative ways of organising political and economic life in the face of the macro-sociological changes that are occurring. Foucault points out that what he called new forms of association, such as trade unions and political parties emerged in the nineteenth century as a counter-balance to the prerogative of the state, and that they formed a seedbed for the development of new ideas on governance (Kritzman 1988). We need to consider what modern versions of these collectivist forms of association might now be developed as a counter-balance not only to the prerogative of the state, but also to the pre-rogative of the market.

Too little serious thinking of this type has yet been done, notwithstanding Giddens's espousal of a "third way" that supersedes both social democracy and neo-liberalism (Giddens 1998). In Britain, despite claims that its policies embody that Third Way, the New Labour government has adopted largely rightist policies in its approach to education. Meanwhile, those still on the Left have done little yet to develop a concept of public education which looks significantly different from the state education that some of us spent our ear-lier political and academic careers critiquing for its role in reproducing and legitimating social inequalities (Young and Whitty 1977). Even if the social democratic era looks better in retrospect, and in comparison with current policies, than it did at the time, that does not remove the need to rethink what might be progressive policies for the next century. As Hatcher (1996) argues, "It would be profoundly mistaken to respond to the Right's agenda, based on differentiation through the market to widen social inequalities, by clinging to a social-democratic statist model which serves fatally to depoliticise and de-mobilise those popular energies which alone are capable of effectively chal-lenging the reproduction of social class inequality in education" (p. 55).

If new approaches are to be granted more legitimacy than previous ones, we need to consider what new institutions might help to foster them—initially within a new public sphere in which ideas can be debated, but potentially as new forms of democratic governance themselves. Clearly, such institutions could take various forms and they will certainly need to take different forms in different societies. They will no doubt be struggled over and some will be more open to hegemonic incorporation than others. Some may actually be cre-ated by the state, as the realization dawns that a marketized civil society itself creates contradictions that need to be managed. Thus, there is likely to be both a bottom-up and a top-down to create new institutions within which struggles over the content and control of education will take place.

In England, there has been some discussion about ways of democratizing the state and civil society. Geddes (1996), following Held (1989), contrasts le-gal democracy (modern neo-liberal democracy in a free market system), competitive elitist democracy (the conventional representational party sys-tem), pluralism, neo-pluralism (quasi-corporatism), and participatory de-mocracy. Like many people working in this field, he sees the future in terms of attempts to combine the virtues of different approaches. In particular, he seems to favour combining representative and participatory democracy, by such devices as decentralizing the policy process and establishing commu-nity councils, citizens' juries, and opinion panels.

Similarly, in the United States, there are moves to encourage new "forms of group representation that stand less sharply in tension with the norms of democratic governance" (Cohen and Rogers 1995, 9) than the sorts of unaccountable "factions" that are currently able to take advantage of both the market and existing state forms. Cohen and Rogers take the view that it is possible to improve the practical approximation of even market societies to egalitarian democratic norms. They argue that, by altering the status of "secondary associations" within civil society, associative democracy can "improve economic performance and government efficiency and advance egalitarian-democratic norms of popular sovereignty, political equality, distributive equity and civic consciousness" (p. 9).

In every society, we shall now have to ask what are the appropriate constituencies through which to express community interests in the twenty-first century, and thus provide the conditions for what Mouffe (1989) argues strong democracy needs—an articulation between the particular and the universal in a forum for "creating unity without denying specificity." In the specific field of education, there is a similar need to develop new contexts of democratic decision-making in civil society, which are more genuinely responsive and inclusive than either the state or market forces. Community education forums have been suggested in both England and New Zealand, but we need to give careful consideration to the composition, nature and powers of such bodies if they are to prove an appropriate way of reasserting democratic citizenship rights in education in the late twentieth century. They will certainly need to respond to critiques of the class, gender and racial bias of conventional forms of political association in most modern societies.

We have to confront these issues as a matter of urgency since, at the level of rhetoric (though not reality), the reforms of the New Right *have* probably been more responsive than their critics usually concede to those limited, but nonetheless tangible, social and cultural shifts that have been taking place in modern societies. A straightforward return to the old order of things would be neither feasible nor sensible. Thus, if we are to avoid the atomization of educational decision-making, and associated tendencies toward fragmentation and polarization, we need to create new collective and experimental contexts within civil society for determining institutional arrangements that are genuinely inclusive.

Of course, this cannot be seen as an issue for schools alone. As Gerald Grace has argued, too many education reformers have been guilty of "producing naive school-centered solutions with no sense of the structural, the political and the historical as constraints" (Grace 1984, xii). Unfortunately, this is true of some contemporary approaches to school improvement (Mortimore and Whitty 1997). We need to recognize that struggles over the form and content of education cannot be divorced from broader struggles over the nature of the sort of society that we want all our children to grow up in. But to say that is not to say that human agency is unimportant in determining the nature and direction of change. As we have seen, members of New Right networks helped to spread neo-liberal policies around the globe during the 1980s and 1990s (Whitty and Edwards 1998). It is equally important that those who contemplate alternative responses to global developments share and develop their ideas and experiences with like-minded people throughout the world, while recognising that specific policies must be grounded in the history and culture of particular national and local contexts.

NOTE

This chapter was delivered at a meeting of the Westermarck Society, University of Joensuu, Finland, March 1999. Parts of the chapter were based on work carried out with Professor David Halpin of Goldsmiths College, University of London. See Whitty et al. 1998. An earlier version of this chapter was published in *International Journal of Contemporary Sociology* 36 (1999), no. 2: 144–62, and is reprinted by permission.

REFERENCES

Allen, J. 1992. "Post-Industrialism and Post-Fordism." In S. Hall, D. Held, and T. Mc-Grew, eds., *Modernity and Its Futures*, 169–220. Cambridge: Polity.

Angus, M. 1995. "Devolution of School Governance in an Australian State School System: Third Time Lucky?" In D. S. G. Carter and M. H. O'Neill, eds., *Case Studies in Educational Change: An International Perspective*. London: Falmer.

Apple, M. W. 1996. *Cultural Politics and Education*. Buckingham, U.K.: Open University Press.

Apple, M. W., and J. Beane, eds. 1999. *Democratic Schools*. Buckingham, U.K.: Open University Press.

Arnove, R. 1996. "Neo-Liberal Education Policies in Latin America: Arguments in Favor and Against." Paper delivered to the Comparative and International Education Society, Williamsburg, March 6–10.

Ball, S. J. 1990. *Politics and Policy-Making in Education: Explorations in Policy Sociology*. London: Routledge.

Ball, S. J. 1994. *Education Reform: A Critical and Post-Structural Approach*. Buckingham, U.K.: Open University Press.

Bernstein, B. 1997. "Official Knowledge and Pedagogic Identities: The Politics of Recontextualising." In I. Nilsson and L. Lundahl, eds., *Teachers, Curriculum, and Policy: Critical Perspectives in Educational Research*, 165–80. Umea, Sweden: Department of Education, Umea University.

Boyne, R., and A. Rattansi, eds. 1990. *Postmodernism and Society*. London: Macmillan.

Cohen, J., and J. Rogers, eds. 1995. *Associations and Democracy*. London: Verso.

Dale, R. 1989. *The State and Education Policy*. Buckingham, U.K.: Open University Press.

Fowler, F. C. 1994. "The International Arena: The Global Village." *Journal of Education Policy* 9, no. 5–6: 89–102.

Gamble, A. 1983. "Thatcherism and Conservative Politics." In S. Hall and M. Jacques, eds., *The Politics of Thatcherism*. London: Lawrence & Wishart.

Gamble, A. 1988. *The Free Economy and the Strong State*. London: Macmillan.

Geddes, M. 1996. *Extending Democratic Practice in Local Government*. Greenwich: Campaign for Local Democracy.

Giddens, A. 1991. *Modernity and Self-Identity*. Cambridge: Polity.

Giddens, A. 1998. *The Third Way: The Renewal of Social Democracy*. Cambridge: Polity.

Gordon, L. 1992. "The New Zealand State and Education Reforms: 'Competing' Interests." Paper presented to the American Educational Research Association, San Francisco, 20–24 April.

Gordon, L. 1995. "Controlling Education: Agency Theory and the Reformation of New Zealand Schools." *Education Policy* 9, no. 1: 55–74.

Grace, G., ed. 1984. *Education in the City*. London: Routledge & Kegan Paul.

Grace, G. 1991. "Welfare Labourism versus the New Right." *International Studies in Sociology of Education* 1, no. 1: 37–48.

Green, A. 1990. *Education and State Formation*. London: Macmillan.

Green, A. 1994. "Postmodernism and State Education." *Journal of Education Policy* 9, no. 1: 67–83.

Green, A. 1996. "Education, Globalization, and the Nation State." Paper presented at Education, Globalization, and the Nation-State: Comparative Perspectives symposium at the World Congress of Comparative Education Societies, University of Sydney, July 1–6, 1996.

Hargreaves, D. H. 1994. *The Mosaic of Learning: Schools and Teachers for the Next Century*. London: Demos.

Harris, K. 1996. "The Corporate Invasion of Schooling: Some Implications for Pupils, Teachers, and Education." *AARE SET: Research Information for Teachers*, 2.

Harty, S. 1994. "Pied Piper Revisited." In D. Bridges and T. McLaughlin, eds., *Education and the Market Place*. London: Falmer.

Harvey, D. 1989. *The Condition of Postmodernity*. Oxford: Basil Blackwell.

Hatcher, R. 1996. "The Limitations of the New Social Democratic Agendas." In R. Hatcher and K. Jones, eds., *Education after the Conservatives*. Stoke-on-Trent, U.K.: Trentham.

Held, D. 1989. "The Decline of the Nation State." In S. Hall and M. Jacques, eds., *New Times: The Changing Face of Politics in the 1990s*, 191–204. London: Lawrence & Wishart.

Hickox, M. 1995. "Situating Vocationalism." *British Journal of Sociology of Education* 16: 153–63.

Hillgate Group. 1987. *The Reform of British Education*. London: Claridge.

Jessop, B., et al. 1987. "Popular Capitalism, Flexible Accumulation, and Left Strategy." *New Left Review* 165: 104–23.

Kenway, J. 1993. "Marketing Education in the Postmodern Age." *Journal of Education Policy* 8, no. 1: 105–22.

Kritzman, L. D., ed. 1988. *Foucault: Politics/Philosophy/Culture*. New York: Routledge.

Lauglo, J. 1996. "Forms of Decentralization and Implications for Education." In J. Chapman et al., eds., *The Reconstruction of Education*. London: Cassell.

Levacic, R. 1995. *Local Management of Schools: Analysis and Practice*. Buckingham, U.K.: Open University Press.

Malen, B. 1994. "Enacting Site-Based Management: A Political Utilities Analysis." *Educational Evaluation and Policy Analysis* 16: 249–67.

Marginson, S. 1993. *Education and Public Policy in Australia*. Cambridge: Cambridge University Press.

Marquand, D. 1995. "Flagging Fortunes." *Guardian*, July 3.

McKenzie, J. 1993. "Education as a Private Problem or a Public Issue? The Process of Excluding 'Education' from the 'Public Sphere.'" Paper presented to the International Conference on the Public Sphere, Manchester, 8–10 January

Miron, G. 1993. *Choice and the Use of Market Forces in Schooling: Swedish Education Reforms for the 1990s*. Stockholm: Institute of International Education.

Molnar, A. 1996. *Giving Kids the Business: The Commercialization of America's Schools*. Boulder: Westview.

Mortimore, P., and G. Whitty. 1997. *Can School Improvement Overcome the Effects of Disadvantage?* London: Institute of Education.

Mouffe, C. 1989. "Towards a Radical Democratic Citizenship." *Democratic Left* 17: 6–7.

Nash, R. 1989. "Tomorrow's Schools: State Power and Parent Participation." *New Zealand Journal of Educational Studies* 24, no. 2: 113–28

National Consumer Council. 1996. *Sponsorship in Schools*. London: National Consumer Council.

Neave, G. 1988. "On the Cultivation of Quality, Efficiency, and Enterprise: An Overview of Recent Trends in Higher Education in Western Europe, 1968–1988." *European Journal of Education* 23: 7–23.

OECD. 1995. *Decision Making in 14 OECD Education Systems*. Paris: OECD.

Pusey, M. 1991. *Economic Rationalism in Canberra*. Cambridge: Cambridge University Press.

Reich, R. 1991. *The Work of Nations: Preparing Ourselves for 21st Century Capitalism*. London: Simon & Schuster.

Roberts, P. 1994. "Business Sponsorship in Schools: A Changing Climate." In D. Bridges and T. McLaughlin, eds., *Education and the Market Place*. London: Falmer.

Robertson, R. 1991. "Social Theory, Cultural Relativity, and the Problem of Globality." In A. D. King, ed., *Culture, Globalization, and the World-System*. London: Macmillan.

Robertson, S. L. 1993. "The Politics of Devolution, Self-Management, and Post-Fordism in Schools." In J. Smyth, ed., *A Socially Critical View of the Self-Managing School*. London: Falmer.

Rose, N., and P. Miller. 1992. "Political Power beyond the State: Problematics of Government." *British Journal of Sociology* 43, no. 2: 173–205.

Rose, R. 1991. "Comparing Forms of Comparative Analysis." *Political Studies* 39: 446–62.

Seddon, T. 1994. "Decentralisation and Democracy." Paper presented to the National Industry Education Forum seminar, Melbourne, 26 August.

Smyth, J, ed. 1993. *A Socially Critical View of the Self-Managing School*. London: Falmer.

Usher, R., and R. Edwards. 1994. *Postmodernism and Education*. London: Routledge.

Weiler, H. 1983. "Legalization, Expertise, and Participation." *Comparative Education Review* 27: 259–77.

Weiler, H. 1989. "Education and Power." *Educational Policy* 3: 31–43.

Weiss, M. 1993. "New Guiding Principles in Educational Policy: The Case of Germany." *Journal of Education Policy* 8, no. 4: 307–20.

Wells, A. S., C. Grutzik, S. Carnochan, J. Slayton and A. Vasudeva. 1999. "Underlying Policy Assumptions of Charter School Reform: The Multiple Meanings of a Movement." *Teachers College Record* 100, no. 3: 513–35.

Whitty, G., S. Power, and D. Halpin. 1998. *Devolution and Choice in Education: The School, the State, and the Market*. Buckingham, U.K.: Open University Press.

Whitty, G., and T. Edwards. 1998. "School Choice Policies in England and the United States: An Exploration of Their Origins and Significance." *Comparative Education* 34, no. 2: 211–27.

Wiener, M. J. 1981. *English Culture and the Decline of the Industrial Spirit, 1850–1980*. Cambridge: Cambridge University Press.

Young, M., and G. Whitty, eds. 1977. *Society, State, and Schooling*. Lewes, U.K.: Falmer.

15

Civil Society as Equilibrium:

Governance and Choice in Education between Private Delivery and Central Regulation

AnneBert Dijkstra and Jaap Dronkers

In the international discussion about enlargement of parental choice and private deliverance of education, the Dutch arrangement is often regarded as a unique system. Central to this arrangement is the constitutionalised principle of "freedom of education." This principle has resulted in approximately 70 percent of parents sending their children to schools established by private associations and managed by private school boards, yet fully funded by the central government. In the opinion of national interest groups as well as experts (e.g., van Kemenade et al. 1981; Hermans 1993) this freedom of education and equal financing of public and private education from public funds makes the Dutch system exceptional. Foreign observers are also of this opinion, as illustrated by the last OECD review of Dutch education, in which the arrangement of freedom of education and the underlying compartmentalised organisation of society has been designated as unique (Organisation for Economic Cooperation and Development [OECD] 1991). The Dutch system developed in a century from a relatively secular school system, dominated by the national government at the beginning of the last century, to a plural system, with private school sectors dominated by religious groups. According to international observers, "the evolution of the Dutch system of education is unique in the Western World" (James 1989, 179)—this history is also regarded as remarkable.

This international interest in the Dutch arrangement (and a few others, e.g., the Danish system) often has the debate about parental choice and public financing of private education for a background. For several societies, the analysis of the effects that are to be expected of enlargement of parental choice and privatisation in education is often based on analytical evaluations or small-scale experiments (e.g., the Milwaukee Parental Choice Program in the United States; cf. Witte 1993). Yet the Netherlands offers an "experiment" in private production of education on a national scale that includes the entire education system and is a century old. As Brown (1992, 177) so concisely puts it: "The Netherlands is the only country with a nation-wide school choice program." In the choice debate, the Dutch experiment is advanced as an argument in pleas to come to more private deliverance of education in other countries (e.g., Dennison 1984) or as a warning to not go down that road (e.g., Walford 1995). The apparently unique features of the Dutch system evidently offer points of departure to arguments for as well as against enlargement of freedom of education and private production of education. A number of years ago, Glenn (1989) warned that references to the Dutch situation are "often with little factual basis," underlining that a proper insight in the Dutch system is necessary, before more general "lessons" can be learned. In this chapter, we will discuss some characteristics of the system of schooling in the Netherlands, as well as recent developments in this long-standing nationwide experiment of private deliverance of education.

SYSTEMS OF CHOICE AND CENTRAL REGULATION

Parental choice of a school for their children was one of the most important topics in nineteenth-century Netherlands. The political struggle between the liberal, dominant class and the Catholic and orthodox Protestant lower classes gave rise to Christian-democratic parties that have held central political power since the start of the twentieth century until the mid-1990s.

This political struggle was not unique to the Netherlands but the unintended result of three interacting processes: the struggle between the state and the established churches in Continental Europe; the fight between the eighteenth-century ancien regime (mostly with one state church and suppressed religious minorities) and the nineteenth-century liberal state (which claimed to be neutral to all churches); and the emergence of new social classes in the nineteenth century (skilled workers, craftsmen, labourers) that rejected the dominant classes, either liberal or conservative. Nor was the outcome of these three interacting processes unique to the Netherlands. In several Continental European societies (Austria, Belgium, France, some German *Länder*) these processes had more or less comparable results, with public and religiously subsidised school sectors offering parents a choice between schools of the same curriculum and usually under comparable financial costs for the parents. For good reasons, these processes had a quite different effect in the United Kingdom (Archer 1984) while other societies, like the United States, have never experienced these long conflicts over school between the state and the church, or the ancien regime and the liberal state.

In the Netherlands, choice between religious and public schools was not only an educational choice; it was closely connected to other choices in life—voting, church activities, membership in clubs, unions, newspapers, etc. The choice between public and religious schools was linked to the choice between the Catholic, orthodox Protestant and public subcultures, or "pillars," as they were called in the Netherlands (for a description of this "pillarisation" in Dutch society, see Post 1989). A consequence of these religious grounds for the rise of subsidised schools was that parental choice on educational grounds (quality of schooling in public and religious schools) did not exist during the first half of the twentieth century. Religious considerations and the belonging to a specific sub-culture were dominant, with perhaps only some elite groups the exception to this rule. Free parental choice of school was a religious choice. Since religious socialisation was seen as closely connected to education, this freedom of parents to choose a public or religious school under equal financial conditions was known as "freedom of education," a concept which originally referred to one of the basic human rights formulated during the French Revolution. Initially, this concept of "freedom of education" referred to the freedom to teach without church approval, contrary to the situation of the ancien regiem. Later, it came to mean freedom of persons and juridical bodies to establish and maintain schools of different denominations under equal conditions to public schools maintained by the state (cf. Box, Dronkers, Molenaar and de Mulder 1977).

The religious, political and social contrasts at the time of the so-called School Conflict that reached its peak around the turn of the century, have greatly affected the structure of the pillarised education system. Convinced of the dilution, as they saw it, of the Christian character of the public school, nineteenth-century supporters of Christian education strove for their own schools. After the attainment of this freedom of education in the 1848 constitutional amendment, the conflict then moved to government financing of private schools. The School Conflict was finally ended with the "Pacification" of 1917, which provided the financing of private schools from general funds, laid down in the constitution. The freedom of education amendment and the provision of public funding represent the basic historical background of the contemporary framework within which private-religious schools in the Netherlands operate and continues to be a delicate political issue until today. As a result, the constitutional sections on education has not been undergoing any change, despite its old-fashioned wording and inapplicability to current issues (e.g., recent tendencies towards ethnic segregation since the arrival of new minority groups in Dutch society, cf. Karsten 1994) and despite later revisions of the Dutch constitution, its old-fashioned wording being too sensitive to change without reviving the school conflict of the nineteenth century.

The constitutional education article states that "education shall be an object of constant solicitude on the part of the government." In this, the constitution prescribes the equal subsidizing by the state of all school sectors; they are subjected to strong control of equal examinations, salary, capital investment, etc. by the national state (see also James 1989). Although the constitution only sets out the funding of primary education, later legislation expands this public funding to all types of education, including schools for higher vocational training, until the Protestant and Catholic universities were also subsidised by the state on the same footing as public universities in 1972, all without any change to the constitution.

The Dutch educational system is considered unique in several other aspects when compared to other European countries with similar state-subsidised religious and public school sectors. First, in most such countries the religious schools are of one denomination, mostly Catholic or the former Protestant state church. This is not the case in the Netherlands, whose creation in the sixteenth-century religious wars resulted in a large Catholic minority within a moderate Protestant state. As the outcome of the nineteenth-century political struggle, there have existed since the 1920s three main private sectors, a Catholic, a Protestant and a non-religious private school sector, all with independent private school boards, besides some small private religious sectors and the public sector, the latter governed by local municipalities. Within the Catholic and Protestant school sectors, there are national umbrella organisations which also function as lobbies, but they do not replace the autonomous boards, nor do they co-ordinate all Protestant or Catholic schools. These boards generally have the juridical form of a foundation, with a high degree of self-selection of new board members.

Second, the principle of freedom of education or parental choice under conditions of equal funding was enshrined in the constitution of 1917. The interesting point to note is that the Netherlands has almost the only educational system with equal subsidies and treatment for religious and public schools. From the Dutch point of view, certain debates in other societies on parental choice or vouchers closely resemble debates on this topic in the Netherlands in the second half of the nineteenth century. Those debates focused among others on the lower quality of religious schools or the alleged elite characteristics of such schools and the unfairness of paying taxes for public schools and extra money for the preferred religious school or the appropriatness of public funding of religious schools.

Third, the equal subsidizing of all religious and public schools has promoted a diminution of prestigious elite schools outside the state-subsidised sector. As a consequence of equal subsidizing and prohibited use of extra funds for teacher grants, smaller classes, etc., there does not exist an institutionalised hierarchy of schools within each school type, such as in most Anglo-Saxon societies (the English public schools or independent grammar schools; the Ivy League, or the difference in the quality between schools in the poor inner cities and those in the wealthy suburbs in the United States).

RELIGIOUS SCHOOLS IN SECULAR SOCIETIES

From the middle of the twentieth century onwards, the religious substructures or pillars in Dutch society broke down rapidly. In 1947 only 17 percent of the population did not officially belong to any church; by 1995 the proportion had increased to 40 percent. The same trend can be seen in the votes in favor of Christian-democratic parties in national elections: in 1948, 55 percent; in 1994, less then 30 percent of the vote. The extent of secularisation in the Netherlands is considered being one of the highest in western societies (Greeley 1993). The first thing one might expect to have resulted is a decline in institutions such as religious schools that depend on religious affiliation for their recruitment. Although such a decline occurred in a number of organisations and institutions (unions, journals, clubs, hospitals), it did not affect the educational system. In 1950, 73 percent of all pupils in primary education were attending a non-public school; in 2000, 68 percent.

How then can one explain the non-disappearance of religious education or the failure of public schools to attract the growing number of children of non-religious parents (cf. Dronkers 1992)? This issue of legitimacy is also of interest to modern societies characterised by an increasing number of religious schools and increasing pressure for public funding and perhaps even more so in societies with a not very active religious population. The Dutch case might offer some insights into the mechanisms of stability or increase in religious schooling in not particularly religious societies. Out of several explanations and theories explaining this paradox suggested in the literature (cf. Dronkers 1995) we will shortly address some mechanisms that might add to the explanation of the continuing existence of religious schools in Dutch society (for a detailed account, see Dijkstra, Dronkers and Hofman 1997).

Segregation

Differences in student intake explain, on average, only one-third of the outcome differences between schools. After controlling for the differences in student intake, the differences in effectiveness between public and religious schools are roughly the same as before controlling. Religious schools do not on average have a better qualified student intake, so this second explanation is not a good one for the attractiveness of religious schools.

Central Regulation

A second suggested explanation is the strong position of religious schools through political protection by the Christian-democratic party, by laws protecting freedom of education and by the dense (administrative) network of the organisations of religious schools. This hypothesis has some validity. The central position of the Christian-democratic party on the Dutch political map till halfway the 1990s made it possible to maintain the pillarised school system and the religious schools within that system, despite the society's decreasing secularisation and even to establish new religious schools in areas with low number of active church members. Nevertheless, this mechanism can't fully explain the flourishing private religious school sectors because the Dutch system enables parents to "vote with their feet." Despite all regulations and the strong formal position of religious schools, parents can favour other school sectors without facing serious spatial or financial barriers because of the free choice of schools (the Dutch system, among other things, does not contain catchment areas) and the equal governmental funding of public and private schools.

Schools are financed according to the number of pupils enrolled and the way to establish a new school is to find enough parents who will send their children to that school of a given denomination. Several groups of parents (orthodox Protestant, evangelical, Islamic, Hindu) have recently used this mechanism of "voting with their feet" with success against the powerful, already established organisations of private religious schools to found schools of their own religious preference. The essential question here is therefore why non-religious parents did not use the same mechanism to increase the number of non-religious schools or the number of pupils attending them. It is hard to argue that these parents are less powerful or less numerous than the orthodox Protestant, evangelical, Islamic, or Hindu parents and their organisations—actually, the opposite might be true. Non-religious parents are on average better educated and have more links with the established political parties than the groups mentioned before. What we conclude from this is that non-religious parents no longer feel deterred by the religious socialisation of religious schools—that is, to the extent religious schools still offer such socialisation (cf. Vreeburg 1993)—and thus do not see the need to change to non-religious schools. If this is true, the mechanism of protection is not sufficient to account for the continuing existence of religious schools.

Administration

There are slight differences in educational administration between public and religious schools (Hofman 1993) and they can explain some of the outcome differences, despite the enforced financial equality and strong control by the state. It is not the formal differences in educational administration, but on the average the stronger informal relations between board and teachers in the religious schools which explains partly the better performance of their pupils and thus the attractiveness of religious schools for non-religious students and parents (Hofman et al. 1996).

Values

A fourth explanation is that irreligious parents prefer religious socialisation because they still appreciate the religious values to which they no longer adhere. However, it is clear from longitudinal research that the number of adherents to religious values among Dutch adults is decreasing, which is in contrast to the stability of recruitment of religious schools. Only a minority of parents (about 30 percent, depending on the local situation) give religious reasons for choosing a religious school for their children. If the appreciation of religious values by irreligious parents were an effective explanation of their choice of a religious school, the percentage of religious reasons should be higher. However, the values-oriented character of religious schools leads them to stress secular, non-religious values as an important aspect of schooling in the broader sense (Germans would call this *Bildung* and the French *éducation*). Public schools with their neutral status tend to avoid discussion on value-oriented topics and stress instruction instead. Irreligious parents who prefer schooling to have a broad scope rather than a more narrow instructional purpose thus choose the modern religious school for its breadth, which they consider an aspect of educational quality, rather than for religious values.

Neither Protestant nor Catholic churches have a major influence any longer on the curriculum of most religious schools and religious education has declined to the point where it simply gives factual information on various world views. One good reason for this breakdown of religious socialisation is the scarcity of teachers who are religious and willing to undertake that religious socialisation. The lack of religious teachers in the Netherlands can be explained by the positive relationship between level of education and degree of traditional religiousness. A majority of pupils in religious schools have not an active religious background and their parents do not want them be socialised into a religion they do not belong to. But they do not object to cognitive information on various world views. There is a happy conjuncture between the impossibility of religious schools to provide religious socialisation and the small number of parents still wanting it. Thus, these schools offer as next best cognitive information on world views (which a teacher who is not religious can give as part of cultural socialisation, although it is often still known under the old curriculum title of religious education) and non-religious parents can accept information on world views as part of cultural socialisation (despite its old-fashioned title). The forced neutrality of public schools and the secular values-oriented character of religious schools explains partly the attractiveness of the latter schools.

Another explanation offered for the attractiveness of religious schools is their (on average) mild educational conservatism, compared to the (on average) more progressive tendency of public schools. Among the reasons for this mild educational conservatism is the different exposure of public and private schools to social policy initiatives around the school. The board of public schools is the council of the municipality. These councils might favour educational experiments in order to accomplish political goals because education is one of the major instruments of policy makers to promote desirable developments. Although boards of private religious schools are often in indirect ways connected with the more moderate political parties, boards of private schools have less direct connections with policy makers and represent—mostly indirectly—more parents. Therefore they will feel less need for educational experiments for political reasons. Another difference between public and private schools is that the first have less opportunity to avoid pressure from the national government because they cannot use the principle of freedom of education as a shield to protect themselves. Religious schools can only be obliged to conform to educational experiments if they are forced to by national law which declares the educational experiment a quality condition necessary to qualify for public funding. In all other cases, religious schools can only participate in educational experiments on a voluntary basis.

Effectiveness

Dutch research contains evidence of positive effects of Catholic and Protestant schooling on academic achievement (for a review, see Dijkstra 1992). These differences, all adjusted for differences in the student intake of public and private schools, are reported in terms of educational outcomes measured as dropout, test scores, degrees, attainment, etc. Although, as in other societies, the debate to what extent these differences are of any substance remains unsettled, private religious schools do distinct themselves by a reputation for offering educational quality, which, as research shows, is an important motive in the process of parental choice favouring religious schools in The Netherlands.

Closely related to the reputation of academic quality of religious schools is the argument of a deliberate educational choice. A deliberate choice for an "unconventional" school (as compared to a "traditional" choice for a common school) will increase the possibility of this "unconventional" school becoming a community in which students perform better. Depending on a deliberate educational choice and the self-selection following from such a choice, both religious and public school can become a community with shared values and dense social ties affecting student achievement, as suggested by Coleman and Hoffer (1987). Roeleveld and Dronkers (1994) found evidence that schools in districts in which neither public, Protestant nor Catholic schools attracted a majority of the students, the effectiveness of schools was the highest, after taking student composition into account. In districts without schools having a dominant position on the educational market, there is no such thing as a "conventional" school choice and thus the parental choice is more deliberate. In districts in which public, Protestant or Catholic schools had either a very small share of the market (<20 percent) or a very large one (>60 percent of all students), the effectiveness of these schools was lower. In these district the "conventional" school choice is most common and the parental choice more traditional.

Especially after the secularisation of Dutch society peaked from the 1960s onwards, religious schools were forced to compete for students for other than religious motives and they could no longer rely on their recruitment along the religious, pillarised lines in society. For religious schools, a deliberate educational choice became important. Religious schools were on average better equipped for this competition because of their history (during the nineteenth century, Dutch religious schools won the struggle partly on the pupil market) because of their private governance and administration (more flexibility compared to public schools under authority of the local government, cf. Hofman 1993) and because of their reputation of educational quality (Dijkstra, Dronkers and Hofman 1997). Perhaps public schools also lost this battle because their leading advocates expected the religious school sector to break down automatically, as a consequence of the growing secularisation and irreligiousness of Dutch society.

EDUCATIONAL INEQUALITY, REGULATION AND COSTS

Inequality

As already mentioned, the equal funding of private and public schools has promoted the diminution of prestigious elite schools outside the state-subsidised sector. The equal financial resources of religious and public schools has prevented a creaming-off of the most able students by either the public or the religious schools. Before the 1970s, the choice of a religious or public school was not made on educational, but on religious, grounds. As a consequence, the longtime existence of parental choice didn't increase educational inequality in Dutch society.

The educational differences between religious and public schools are recent and could be the start of a new form of inequality, despite efforts of the Dutch administration to diminish unequal educational opportunities. Differences between parents in their knowledge of school effectiveness, which correlates with their own educational level, can perhaps be seen as the basis of this new form of inequality (Dijkstra and Jungbluth 1997). In the Netherlands, as well in other European societies, the importance of deliberate choice of parents to promote the educational opportunities of their children seems to be an important element in understanding the persistence of educational systems with religious school sectors as substantial components, despite secularisation. But also in a school system without private religious sectors of some size, knowledge of school effectiveness by parents can be an important factor.

Regulation

The system of equal funding has led to a high degree of central regulation and a relatively uniform curriculum and structure. While the private sector is considered responsible to determine the philosophical or religious direction of their education, the government is given responsibility to oversee and guarantee the general quality of schooling. Although the central government is not allowed to determine the exact content of the curriculum, nor the specific texts and pedagogy, the government does have significant control regarding standards of quality, such as teacher qualifications, working conditions and salaries, curriculum subjects and the time allotted for each, the use of finances and the examinations given to all students at key transition points (cf. OECD 1991, 16). Because of these centralised standards and the equalisation of resources available to both private and public schools, there is a relatively high degree of uniformity as well as equality between private and public school sectors. The standardised exams given at key transition points and the diplomas granted by schools (which indicate a similar level of achievement) mean that students are able to move in and out of different sectors with relative ease. Thus, while the Dutch system is designed to give parents significant choice regarding the philosophical or religious orientation of schools, there is considerably less choice as to the level of resources a school has and the academic quality that is often associated with such funding (cf. Naylor and Dijkstra 1997).

Costs and Economies of Scale

Another explanation for the demand for private schooling may be the financial differences between school sectors. Dutch schools do not differ greatly in their fees. Religious schools charge certain extra fees, which are mostly used for extra-curricular activities. The choice of parents here can hardly be influenced by financial considerations. The irrelevance of financial criteria for choice during a school career is shown in various educational attainment studies (de Graaf 1987). Financial differences do not adequately explain the existence of religious schools.

A dual educational system, however, is not less expensive. Koelman (1987) estimated the extra costs of the Dutch system of both public and religious schools at about Gld.631 million per year for primary education only. The extra costs come from the many small schools of different sectors existing in one community, given the small minimum number of pupils necessary to maintain a school. Efforts by the government to reduce these costs are promoting larger schools by increasing the minimum number of pupils in a school. In secondary education this has led to a fusion of schools in larger units, but the mergers have been mostly within the given boundaries of the public and religious sectors (with some tendencies to merge Protestant and Catholic schools into one Christian school). However, in primary education this fusion movement partly collapsed because the government could not raise the minimum number of pupils to a sufficient level. The main cause of the failure has been pressure from smaller communities, who have feared losing their only school. In contrast to the higher cost of maintaining small schools (public or religious) are the lower overhead costs of most religious schools, which are not obliged to use the more expensive services of their municipalities but can shop around to obtain the cheapest and most effective assistance for administration, repairs, building, cleaning, etc. Religious schools also use more voluntary help (owing to their more direct link with parents), which also lowers overhead costs. A total balance sheet of the lower overheads costs of religious schools and the higher costs of maintaining a multisector school system has never been agreed, as the figures are disputed by all sides.

Toward a New Equilibrium?

In the Netherlands, a new form of religious schooling was introduced by the establishment of Islamic schools operating in the Dutch context, although their number is not yet very large. The motives for establishing Islamic school are comparable to those given by Protestant and Catholic parents during the School Conflict in the nineteenth century. Since the constitution and educational laws were developed to accommodate these religious based educational preferences, the Dutch system essentially allows for the establishment of schools organised around new denominations, despite objections raised in the current political debate. Besides problems regarding the actual establishment of Islamic schools (the mobilisation of parents, religious and cultural differences among the communities the schools want to serve and the lack of qualified Islamic teachers), especially the consideration that segregation will hamper the integration of Islamic children into Dutch society is raised as an argument against an Islamic school sector. The strongest opposition on this basis comes from advocates of public rather than Catholic and Protestant schools, since the integration of all religious groups into one school has always been the ideal of public schools.

On the whole, the Dutch case doesn't indicate that private religious schools do produce more educational inequality then public schools, as long as these religious schools are treated in the same way by the state as the public schools and as long as the religious schools are not allowed to collect extra resources for their schools.

Recent developments suggest that the disparity between the supply of schooling (organised around religious diversity) and demand of schooling in a predominantly secular society (see section III) might lead to some adjustments in the regulations regarding the establishment of private religious schools in the near future. Especially noticeable was a report published by the Dutch Educational Council (the so-called Onderwijsraad, an influential advisory council to the national government) which might become the marker of an important change in the current system of choice. The Educational Council, commonly seen as powerful "watchdog" regarding the arrangement of freedom of schooling, is proposing the adjustment of the educational system to the new social realities of Dutch society. In effect, the report radically re-interprets the design of the system of choice in education (Leune 1996; Onderwijsraad 1996). The Council argues no longer taking the religious charter of the school into account in the planning of the educational establishment, but to base this solely on a quantitative criterion, thus removing all criteria regarding the need for a religious or philosophical foundation for schools from legislation.

Although the Educational Council (Onderwijsraad 1996, 95) puts the existence of discrepancies between the supply of schools and educational preferences of parents into perspective and is of the opinion that the current situation offers a sufficient balance between supply and actual demand, the Council recognises a cause for drastic adaptation of the school planning and suggests founding and maintaining schools only on the basis of a numerical criterion. The main reason for the proposed adaptation is to tune the teaching activities more to the parental wishes, although arguments in the field of retrenchment should not be left out, be it, that they are seldom mentioned.

In practice, this will not so much mean the foundation of new schools. In the current system, the denomination of the school also plays a part in the funding of a school that wishes to change (or merge) its religious direction, when, for example, the student population has changed its identity. In a system in which a religious or philosophical charter is no longer a criterion for state funding, it is becoming easier to realise parental preferences through adaptation of the school's religious charter (Netelenbos 1997, 11–14). So, by providing for diversity along other dimensions than the religious or philosophical lines, according to parental demands, it is hoped that the system would allow for more of a linkage between changing parental preferences and the teaching activities. Furthermore, the system would be more consistent, no longer having as its rationale the religious diversity which Dutch society no longer exhibits.

With the adaptation of the educational infrastructure based on religion to a demand-driven system, the evolution of the current religiously based system to an otherwise structured system, based on other than religious preferences, be they ideological, pedagogical, educational or based on any other diversity, could lie ahead. By basing the founding and closing down of schools on a quantitative criterion, the balance between educational consumers and suppliers is thought to tip in favour of the first.

Regarded in the field of education and world view this would mean, that the educational supply is no longer sorted on the basis of denomination and the ideological diversity behind it, but that, now more than ever, the actual need defines the composition of the supply of schools. Different to a division of the stream of pupils based on religious diversity and a preprogrammed system of schools for the religious mainstreams, the decreased importance of religion and the enlargement of cultural diversity is reason to rid the organisation of the supply of as many impediments as possible, in order to create maximal freedom to whom ever manages to mobilise sufficient support for a school of the proposed identity, as is the idea behind this development towards adjustment of some religious parts in the current arrangement of choice.

The school, however, is not only responsible for the passing on of culture, but is also a selective and reproductive instrument. Prestige, power and possessions have been unequally distributed in society and educational achievements play an important part in the acquisition of these. Getting ahead in the labour market and the division of chances in life are highly influenced by scholastic achievements, which closely corresponds to socio-economic background. Education, therefore, is an important instrument for the justification and reproduction of the inequality of power, social status and income. The school, through this, becomes a scene of battle of social groups centered on securing their position within the hierarchy of status of enlarging their part in the division of scarce means (see, for example, Bowles and Gintis 1976). This means that not only is education a market where buyers and suppliers together decide on the setting of the transferral of standards and values, but also an arena, in which social groups meet to battle for the scarce social means.

This gives rise to the question what implications the intended enlargement of the freedom of educational consumers in the Netherlands will have for the arena in which social groups meet face to face in the competition for scarce means. What does enlargement of educational freedom mean for the reproduction of social inequality? (For more information, see also Dijkstra and Jungbluth 1997.)

DISCUSSION

The Dutch case shows that promoting more parental choice in education and more competition between schools can be a good way to improve the quality of teaching, to decrease the level of bureaucracy in and around schools and to reduce the costs within schools. The Dutch case also shows that it is possible to strike a fair balance between the parental freedom of school choice and the aims of a national educational policy. It assumes, however, the equal funding and treatment of public and private religious schools by the state. Advocates of a strong market orientation and the absence of the state in education tend to forget these important conditions of equal treatment and subsidizing. Without these conditions, the introduction of religious schools will produce less quality of teaching for the average student, more educational inequality and a less balanced provision of societal relevant education. A balanced combination of the forces of the market and the state produces a better education for a larger part of the population than a reliance on either the state or the market. In the latter case the missing counter-balances against the inevitable negative aspects of either a powerful state or an almighty market will produce a suboptimal result.

The developments outlined earlier make the Dutch experiment interesting because of, among other things, the question why parents in a secularised society do not favour education that is managed by the government on behalf of that society, but favour education managed by private organisations. This preference seems also to be demonstrable in other modern societies and it is growing. There seem to be complementary explanations available, as discussed above. Schools run by private non-profit organisations will eventually, in equal circumstances, have more chances to have a more effective management and a social network around those schools, than schools that are run by local or national governments. These explanations cannot be seen as separate from the problems governments have to effectively produce and allocate in the long term quasi-collective goods in the areas of education, the arts and social services. Particularly the two-sided character of these quasi-collective goods is important in this. These are goods that neither the market nor the state is able to produce and allocate both efficiently and effectively. Private non-profit organisations seem to be able to deal better with the two-sided character of these quasi-collective goods than private, profit-seeking organisations or public organisations, so that the former can produce quasi-collective goods, under equal circumstances, more effectively and efficiently than the state or profit organisations.

What does this mean for the future of systems of choice? The most likely development seems to be that it continues to exist, but in a transformed shape. The ideological and religious legitimisation of private non-profit organisations will move more and more to the background. This will happen, however, without the legitimisation being publicly renounced by all because religion and ideology still form the building blocks of society. In those cases where that religious legitimisation will be abandoned, it will be traded in for one that will refer to the efficiency of the education offered. This efficiency does not need to relate only to school results, but also to the measure in which the school offers protection against the dangers of modern society. The legitimisation of this efficiency will probably be rather multiform: ranging from ideological attention to a certain didactics and from a religious identity to a certain social-cultural composition of the student population. Because private non-profit organisations may offer this efficiency in providing adequate surroundings more easily, there will not be a movement in the direction of an increase in education managed by local or national government. On the contrary, schools that are at the moment being managed by a local or national government, might increasingly try to transform into schools managed by private non-profit organisations, or something resembling this. In short, the most likely development of public and denominational education might be a transformation to a type of non-religious or non-denominational education.

The role of the national and local government has become rather important in all of this. Regarding the optimal production and allocation of the quasi-collective good, which because of its nature cannot be left fully to the free market, the government is given the role of allocator of the collectively financed costs of the initial education, of guard of the quality of the initial education and of determiner of the scale and the duration of the initial education. These roles are not new to the Dutch government: it has fulfilled these roles since the education legislation of the Batavian Republic. But the role of administrator of education is because of the anticipated transformation, transferred to private nonprofit organisations.

This transformation of private production of education based on religious and ideological organisations to a system based on private non-profit organisations might also create new problems. Private delivery of education by nonprofit organisations does not automatically lead to an economically efficient organisation of education. A situation with too many small schools under the responsibility of too many private non-profit organisations leads via one with a large number of small schools to scale inefficiencies and therefore to an expensive educational system and economic inefficiency. On the other hand, large non-profit organisations, which each manage many large schools, will no longer be very efficient because frequent and intensive contacts with the internal sections in the school and with external authorities, will diminish (cf. Hofman, Hofman, Guldemond and Dijkstra 1996). The cause of this is the necessary increase of bureaucracy and legal rigmarole. The chances to form a functional community in and around the school will also diminish. Therefore, it will remain the task of the government, as provider of the collective means for education, to continually find the balance between efficiency and effectiveness.

Private nonprofit organisations have another classical drawback: they may fall into the hands of a certain elite in society. The managerial control of education may, in such a situation, become an uncontrollable instrument of power. The current denominalisation of education is a good illustration of just such a situation: there is a close bond between administrators of denominational education and the (Christian-democratic) political party that took up a central position in the Dutch political landscape for a long time. This classical drawback of private non-profit organisations makes permanent action of the national government necessary, to prevent unproductive power

340 *AnneBert Dijkstra and Jaap Dronkers*

concentrations in education. If the transformations of education systems toward a more private production of education takes place too quietly, or is dominated by rhetoric and symbolism, this disadvantage might work out even more seriously. Solutions, like handing power of administration over to parents or schools, will also have to indicate which groups will have to receive this power, in situations where parents or schools do not have adequate administrative or marketisation resources at their disposal. Given the inequality between schools and parents, it is unlikely that all schools and groups in society will be able to summon the force to administrate effectively.

REFERENCES

Archer, M. S. 1984. *Social Origins of Educational Systems*. London: Sage.
Bowles, S. and H. Gintis. 1976. *Schooling in Capitalist America: Educational Reform and the Contradictions of Economic Life*. London: Routledge.
Box, L., J. Dronkers, M. Molenaar, and J. de Mulder. 1977. *Vrijheid van onderwijs* [Freedom of education]. Nijmegen: Link.
Brown, F. 1992. "The Dutch Experience with School Choice: Implications for American Education." In P. W. Cookson Jr., ed., *The Choice Controversy*, 171–89. Newbury Park, Calif.: Corwin.
Coleman, J. S., and T. Hoffer. 1987. *Public and Religious High Schools: The Impact of Communities*. New York: Basic.
de Graaf, P. 1987. *De invloed van financiele en culturele hulpbronnen in onderwijsloopbanen* [The influence of financial and cultural resources in education careers]. Nijmegen: ITS.
Dennison, S. R. 1984. *Choice in Education*. London: Institute of Economic Affairs.
Dijkstra, A. B. 1992. *De religieuze factor: Onderwijskansen en godsdienst* [The religious factor: Educational opportunities and religion]. Nijmegen: ITS.
Dijkstra, A. B., and P. Jungbluth. 1997. "The Institutionalization of Social Segmentation? Segregation of Schooling in the Netherlands." Paper presented to the Thirty-third World Congress of the International Institute of Sociology, Cologne, July.
Dijkstra, A. B., J. Dronkers, and R. H. Hofman, eds. 1997. *Verzuiling in het onderwijs: Actuele verklaringen en analyse* [Pillarisation in education: Current explanations and analysis]. Groningen: Wolters-Noordhoff.
Dronkers, J. 1992. "Blijvende organisatorische onderwijsverzuiling ondanks secularisering" [Persistent organisational pillarisation in education]. *Beleid en Maatschappij* 19: 227–37.
Dronkers, J. 1995. "The Existence of Parental Choice in the Netherlands." *Educational Policy* 9: 227–43.
Glenn, C. L. 1989. *Choice of Schools in Six Nations*. Washington, D.C.: U.S. Government Printing Office.
Greeley, A. M. 1993. "Religion around the World Is Not Dying Out." *Origins* 23: 49–58.
Hermans, C. 1993. *Vorming in perspectief: Grondslagenstudie over identiteit van katholiek onderwijs* [Education in perspective: Study of the foundation of the identity of Catholic schooling]. Den Haag: ABKO.

Hofman, R. H. 1993. *Effectief schoolbestuur: Een studie naar de bijdrage van schoolbesturen aan de effectiviteit van basisscholen* [Effective school administration: A study on the impact of school boards on the effectiveness of primary schools]. Groningen: RION.

Hofman, R. H., W. H. A. Hofman, H. Guldemond, and A. B. Dijkstra. 1996. "Variation in Effectiveness between Private and Public Schools: The Impact of School and Family Networks." *Educational Research and Evaluation* 2: 366–94.

James, E. 1989. "The Netherlands: Benefits and Costs of Privatized Public Services." In G. Walford, ed., *Private Schools in Ten Countries: Policy and Practice*, 179–99. London: Routledge.

Karsten, S. 1994. "Policy on Ethnic Segregation in a System of Choice: The Case of the Netherlands." *Educational Policy* 9: 211–25.

Koelman, J. B. J. 1987. *Kosten van verzuiling: Een studie over het lager onderwijs* [The costs of pillarisation: A study for primary education]. Den Haag: VUGA.

Leune, J. M. G. 1996. "The Meaning of Government Legislation and Funding for Primary and Secondary Schools with a Religious Character in the Netherlands." Paper for a colloquium on the Ambiguous Embrace of Government, Erasmus University, Rotterdam, November.

Naylor, W., and A. B. Dijkstra. 1997. "Private Schooling in the Netherlands: The Institutionalization of Directional Diversity." Paper prepared for the annual meeting of AERA, Chicago, March.

Netelenbos, T. 1997. *De identiteit van de school in een pluriforme samenleving* [The identity of the school in a plural society]. Den Haag: OCW.

Onderwijsraad. 1996. *Advies richtingvrij en richtingbepalend* [Direction-free and determination of direction]. The Hague: Onderwijsraad.

Organization for Economic Cooperation and Development (OECD). 1991. *Reviews of National Policies for Education*. Paris: OECD.

Post, H. 1989. *Pillarization: An Analysis of Dutch and Belgian Society*. Avebury, U.K.: Aldershot.

Roeleveld, J., and J. Dronkers. 1994. "Bijzondere of buitengewone scholen?" [Special or typical schools?]. *Mens en Maatschappij* 69: 85–108.

Van Kemenade, J. A., P. L. M. Jungbluth, and J. M. M. Ritzen. 1981. "Onderwijs en samenleving" [Education and society]. In J. A. van Kemenade et al., eds., *Onderwijs: Bestel en beleid* [Education: system and policy], 95–242. Groningen: Wolters-Noordhoff.

Vreeburg, B. A. N. M. 1993. *Identiteit en het verschil: Levensbeschouwelijke vorming en het Nederlands voortgezet onderwijs* [Identity and the difference: Religious education in Dutch secondary schools]. Zoetermeer: De Horstink.

Walford, G. 1995. "Faith-Based Grant-Maintained Schools: Selective International Policy Borrowing from the Netherlands." *Educational Policy* 10: 245–57.

Witte, J. F. 1993. "The Milwaukee Parental Choice Program." In E. Rasell and R. Rothstein, eds., *School Choice: Examining the Evidence*, 69–109. Washington, D.C.: Economic Policy Institute.

16

Women and Education in Europe

Ingrid Jönsson

"Women Are Catching Up with Men" ran the headline of a recent press release from Eurostat. The headline refers to present trends in educational attainment in the EU member states (Eurostat 1997b). Women have to a larger extent than men used the expansion of the educational systems taking place during recent decades. The gender gap is closing but large differences still remain among generations and social classes (Shavit and Blossfeld 1993).

The overall level of education is increasing and upper secondary education is now becoming the norm and the attainment gap between countries is closing (OECD 1998). In this chapter, I will only refer to statistics on the national level and will not go deeper into differences between regions. Regional differences are still significant due to different levels of economic development as well as varying social and cultural traditions (Duncan 1996). I will focus on increased educational attainment among women and point to some interesting variations among European countries. My main concern is to broaden the understanding of women's increased educational attainment by relating it to recent economic, demographic, social and cultural changes. A presentation of general contemporary trends in educational participation will be followed by a discussion focusing especially on Germany, Portugal and Sweden and on women's changing position as citizens.

EDUCATION AS A PART OF THE WELFARE STATE

According to T. H. Marshall, social citizenship is the last stage of full citizenship and includes the rights to economic security and welfare (Marshall 1950). Marshall argued that civil, political and social rights developed steadily from the eighteenth century. Marshall's primary concern was the development of citizens' rights in relation to class, and the analysis falls into disarray when gender is included. Women did not get access to any of the three kinds of rights at the same time as men. Nor did women reach them in the same order as men did (Lister 1990, 1997; Walby 1990, 1997).

Paid employment has replaced the right to carry arms as the basis for access to social rights. Both forms have exclusionary effects on women, but the growth of the welfare states entails an emancipating potential for women (Sainsbury 1996). The construction of the welfare states is therefore of special significance to women, the possibility of living independently of husband and marriage and participating in public life. In this process, education plays an important role.

The eligibility for social benefits and the existence of public services differ across welfare regimes (Esping-Andersen 1990). Social benefits can be obtained on the basis of one's own eligibility or on the eligibility of a family member's labour market participation, citizenship, residence or needs. Even though European welfare systems include elements from all kinds of entitlement systems, there are national characteristics due to historical, cultural, economic, political and social circumstances. Feminist researchers claim that women's care and household work is neglected in all three kinds of welfare regimes constructed by Esping-Andersen. In all welfare regimes, such work is done by women—to varying degrees as unpaid work in the family or as paid work on the market or within the public sector (e.g. Siim 1988; O'Conner 1993; Orloff 1993; Borchost 1994; Daly 1994; Sainsbury 1996). When discussing women's citizenship rights, account should be taken of the fact that women's structural positions and experiences differ from those of men. Full citizenship rights are primarily based on participation in the labour market and in the public sphere (Lister 1990, 1997; O'Conner 1993, 1996; Walby 1990, 1997). Sainsbury (1996) claims that universal social benefits are most favorable to women's independence.

Historically, lower social classes and women had limited access to education due to economic conditions, cultural norms and formal laws. Nowadays, such obstacles have been abolished, but having formal and legal rights does not mean that all citizens participate on equal terms. In practice, class, gender and race are still of crucial importance. In this chapter, I will mainly focus on gender but when data allow, I will refer to the interaction of class and gender. In many countries, equalizing educational opportunities has been on the political agenda during the post-war period. In Sweden, such ideas go as far back as the nineteenth century but were not formally implemented until the introduction of comprehensive schooling in the 1960s. The post-war reform strategy was to create equal opportunities for all children irrespective of sex, social background and geographical residence (Jönsson and Arnman 1989). Also in the other Nordic countries, Portugal, parts of Germany and the UK, comprehensive education was introduced during compulsory school years and in some countries at post-compulsory level as well. In Sweden, the most recent reform strategy to narrow the social gap between those who take general and vocational programs was to introduce a basic amount of general subjects as well as some orientation towards working life on both types of programs. Both types of programs qualify a person for higher education. In other countries, the school systems are still selective and dual (Littlewood and Jönsson 1996). In the middle of the 1990s, large variations in organization and number of school years still exist at both compulsory and upper secondary level. Compulsory education lasts for eight years in some of the south European countries compared to eleven years in the UK and Luxembourg. In Belgium, Germany, the Netherlands and Austria, compulsory schooling lasts for at least nine years of full-time studies followed by another two to three years of part-time duration. In the Nordic countries, the formal length of compulsory schooling is nine years but in practice, upper secondary education is more or less compulsory due to a high rate of youth unemployment. In 1997, 95 percent of all seventeen-year-olds attended upper secondary education in Sweden. In spite of school reforms, class inequalities are found to be persistent and equalization occurring during limited periods of time (as, e.g., in Sweden and the Netherlands during the 1970s) is to a larger extent attributed to improved living conditions rather than to educational reforms (Shavit and Blossfeld 1993).

Large differences in educational attainment are still found among European countries. In 1996, compulsory education is still the most frequent level of education in Portugal (80 percent), Luxembourg (71 percent), Spain (70 percent), Italy (62 percent) and Greece (56 percent), while upper secondary education is becoming the most frequent attainment level in Austria (63 percent) Germany (60 percent), the UK (55 percent) and the Scandinavian countries (55–44 percent). The lowest rate of tertiary education is found in Austria (8 percent), Italy (8 percent), Portugal (10 percent), Luxembourg (11 percent) and Spain (18 percent), while the highest rates are found in Sweden and Norway (27 percent), followed by the Netherlands (23 percent), Denmark (22 percent), the UK (22 percent) and Finland (21 percent). The level of education of the workforce is higher than among the population as a whole (OECD 1998). There are comparatively more women in less educated categories with the exception of Portugal, Sweden and Finland. Only modest equalization has taken place between social classes while a general trend of convergence is found between men and women.

In spite of a convergence in the level of education between men and women there are still marked differences in employment rates between women according to educational attainment levels. For men, such differences are smaller. Employed women aged 25–39 had better educational qualifications than men, 26 percent having university degrees compared to 22.5 percent of men, while the proportion of upper secondary education was the same (47 percent). For men, the average educational level does not differ for men in work or outside the labour force, while the level of education for employed women is higher than for non-working women with the exception of Germany and Luxembourg. The difference is especially marked in the southern European countries, Ireland and France. The educational level among unemployed women is lower than that of unemployed men. Many women with low level of education do not enter the labour market (Eurostat 1995). The educational gender difference is most clearly seen in female-dominated occupations (office, sales and service activities), where 74 percent of women in 1995 had at least upper secondary education compared to 70 percent of men. Among higher skilled occupations (managerial, professional and technical jobs), the differences are less pronounced. However, in all EU member states with the exception of Germany, Luxembourg, the Netherlands and the UK, the relative number of women with at least upper secondary education in these jobs was higher than for men. In male-dominated jobs the attainment level of men exceeded that of women in most European countries (Eurostat 1995).

INCREASE OF EDUCATIONAL PARTICIPATION AMONG WOMEN

Historically, women gained access to education later than men and were in many countries—even well into the twentieth century—excluded from public upper secondary and higher education. Feminist researchers claim that less effort has been put into the quality of female education than into that for males (Kyle 1979; Lundahl 1986; Fürst 1990). Although formal obstacles to women's participation have now been abolished, the organization of the educational systems affects levels of women's educational attainment and choice of programs. Different female and male preferences in education persist alongside a rise in the number of female students. Measures taken to change traditional education patterns are mostly directed towards women. Women are also more inclined to make non-traditional choices, such as to study technology, while men very seldom choose programs leading to traditional female jobs such as caring.

Women in Upper Secondary Education

The level of qualification beyond basic schooling has risen over the last twenty-five to thirty years. Women have especially gained from this improvement. In 1975–1976, there were 81 females to 100 males in upper secondary education. In 1981–1982, the number of females had risen to 93 per 100 males and in 1993–1994 the number of females exceeded that of males (101/100) (table 16.1).

When upper secondary education is broken down into general and vocational programs, interesting gender differences appear. In all countries with

Table 16.1.   Trends in Female Participation: Upper Secondary Education Females per
100 Males

Country	1975–1976	1981–1982	1993–1994
EU 15	81	93	101
B	97	102	97
DK	95	91	101
D	78	81	85
GR	77	85	93
E	96	02	96
IRL	102	100	103
I	80	96	99
L	n.a.	n.a.	n.a.
NL	65	85	84
A	72	80	84
P	89	114	111
FIN	115	119	125
S	99	109	114
UK	77	99	115

Source: Eurostat 1997a.

the exception of the UK, Finland, Spain and Sweden, male students outnumber female students enrolled in vocational programs. Vocational training has also remained sex-segregated to a larger extent than general education. In countries like Austria, Germany and the Netherlands, where 70–78
percent of upper secondary education is organized as vocational training,
the rate of males is particularly high (table 16.2).

Vocational education is mostly school-based, but work-placed vocational
training in combination with time spent in education/training institutions
exists in Denmark, Germany, the Netherlands and Austria. In Denmark and
Germany time is shared between the two locations. In the Netherlands and
Austria pupils spend most of their time at the workplace with some time
spent in an education/training situation (Eurostat 1997c). The work-based
programs are located in private industry as well as in the public sector. As
compared with men, German women attend shorter training courses, which
are concentrated in a relatively small number of occupations (Blossfeld
1987). The types of programs chosen by males and females are very traditional; males mainly opt for industry and trade while females prefer programs within the service sector (SAF 1996). In Germany, the number of available trainee places for women is smaller than the number of applicants.
Women more often than men are trained in full-time vocational schools. In
Finland, Sweden, Greece, Spain and Portugal, the vast majority of initial vocational training takes place in education/training institutions.[1]

In all European countries, females predominate in general education. The
predominance is especially pronounced in Denmark, France, Greece, France,
Italy, Portugal, Finland and Sweden. The expansion in the number of fe-

Table 16.2. Proportion of Students In General and Vocational Upper Secondary Education and Rate of Females, 1993–1994

	General Programs	% Females	Vocational Programs	% Females
EU 15	41	53	59	48
B	32	45	68	47
DK	46	57	54	44
D	22	53	78	44
GR	67	55	33	34
E	59	53	41	52
F	58	55	42	44
IRL	77	51	23	49
I	27	56	73	47
L	n.a.	n.a.	n.a.	n.a.
A	22	55	78	45
P	77	58	23	45
FIN	46	54	54	53
S	46	54	54	53
UK	42	58	58	50

Source: Eurostat 1997a.

males at the upper secondary level and their choice of academic tracks facilitate their transition to higher education, while male upper secondary students to a larger extent choose a vocational education preparing them for a specific occupation (Shavit and Blossfeld 1996). Female students leave upper secondary school with higher average marks than male students do, which increases their chances in the selection process for higher education.

Women in Higher Education

In the 1970s, women were in the minority in higher education in all member states and have remained so in Germany, the Netherlands, Austria and Greece. In Belgium, Ireland and the UK there are now almost as many women in higher education as men, while women outnumber men in Denmark, Spain, France, Italy, Portugal, Finland and Sweden. In all fifteen member states, the number of students attending higher education has increased from about 8 million in 1984–1985 to about 12 million in 1994–1995 (table 16.3).

It should, however, be pointed out that the statistics from Eurostat cited above include all kinds of higher education, which means they cannot be split up into non-university, shorter and longer higher education.[2] In all member states, gender differences are found in enrollment in different kinds of tertiary education. Women are, with few exceptions, over-represented in non-university tertiary education. Such programs are often shorter in duration and focus on specific areas of the labour market with a traditionally strong female presence. In shorter university programs, females are also

Table 16.3.　Trends in Female Participation: Higher Education Females per 100 Males

	1975–1976	*1981–1982*	*1993–1994*
EU 15	..	80	90
B	64	76	97
DK	88	98	105
D	62	72	73
GR	58	74	88
E	57	83	104
F	90	105	120
IRL	53	67	93
I	64	77	106
L	n.a.	n.a.	n.a.
NL	48	70	86
A	63	76	89
P	89	147	132
FIN	82	89	113
S	..	108	120
UK	65	59	100

Source: Eurostat 1997a.

over-represented (with the exception of Finland). The reverse gender relation is found in longer university education in Austria, Belgium, Denmark,
Germany, the Netherlands and Sweden. The most pronounced difference is
found in Germany and the smallest in Denmark and Sweden. In Portugal,
more females than males study at this level. In all European countries, men
outnumber women at the Ph.D. level (OECD 1996).

The length of university education varies from three years in the UK (the
English and Welsh B.A.) to five years in Germany (Diplom) and the Netherlands (Doctorandus). As a consequence the "normal" graduation age varies
from twenty-one years in Spain, Portugal and the UK, twenty-four years and
older in Finland and Sweden to the age of twenty-six in, for example, Germany. The transition age is often higher in countries which do not offer
shorter university courses.

In all European countries, women and men choose different fields of study
leading to different sectors of the labour market. At the tertiary level, social
sciences are the most popular field of study among both sexes (26 percent females and 28 percent males) while the second largest field, engineering and
architecture, is male-dominated (chosen by 28 percent of the male and 7 percent of the female students). The reverse is found for humanities, applied
arts and religion (chosen by 17 percent of the female and 9 percent of the
male students) and for medical science (chosen by 14 and 7 percent respectively) (Eurostat 1997d).

University students come to a very large extent from families with direct
experience of academic education. The same trend is found in all EU member states but is more pronounced in Portugal (73 percent), France (68 per-

cent), Spain (63 percent) and Italy (61 percent) than in Denmark (30 percent), Finland (37 percent) and the Netherlands (43 percent). In Sweden, as many as 55 percent of the parents of students in higher education had a university education themselves (Eurostat 1997d).

LABOUR MARKET PARTICIPATION IN RELATION TO EDUCATIONAL ATTAINMENT

Labour market participation is higher among men, as compared to women, and increases with higher education for both men and women. Highly qualified women work outside the home to about the same extent as men with the same educational background. In all countries, women with higher education have a paid job. With the exception of the Nordic countries, France and Portugal, there are substantial gender differences in economic activity among men and women with only compulsory educa- tion. A recent trend in Sweden as well as Germany points to a decline in labour market participation among women with low education (Klammer and Ochs 1998; Stark 1996). The crisis of the labour market in Germany in the 1990s also had the result that highly trained women were insuffi- ciently absorbed in the labour market (Klammer and Ochs 1998). Female unemployment is with few exceptions higher than that of men in most Eu- ropean countries.

A differentiation into younger and older women points to a considerably higher labour market participation rate among younger women. Economic activity among women and men aged twenty-five to thirty-nine—the age when most families have their children—points to differences in labour mar- ket participation related to gender as well as educational level.

Behind the figures in table 16.4, one can perceive variations in the con- struction of the welfare systems and cultural traditions with implications for women. In countries with low female economic activity, especially among women with at most compulsory schooling, few public measures are taken to facilitate women working outside the home. In countries with high rates of female economic activity irrespective of educational level, some kind of tax-subsidized childcare provision often exists. This social service facilitates women's going to work and makes it economically worthwhile to have a paid job as compared to when the care for children is privately paid for. In poorer countries (e.g., Portugal), women with a low level of education are forced to work outside the home out of economic necessity (Ruivo et al. 1998). Care for children is not publicly organized but provided by the fam- ily or informally organized. In countries like Germany and the UK, where women often take breaks from the labour market when having children, they often experience downward mobility after returning to work (Rubery, Smith and Fagan 1999).

Table 16.4.   Economic Activity Rate for Men and Women, Aged 25–39 by Highest Level of Education, in the EU Member States, 1995

	Compulsory Education		Upper Secondary Education		Higher Education	
	M	W	M	W	M	W
B	91	62	96	82	96	90
DK	87	65	94	82	96	90
D	91	56	91	75	87	84
GR	96	49	96	63	96	86
E	93	54	93	70	93	84
F	94	67	97	83	95	87
IRL	90	45	96	69	96	85
I	91	47	88	70	92	84
NL	83	52	96	71	95	87
A	92	70	94	79	95	93
P	95	76	90	79	98	96
FIN	87	68	90	79	95	85
S	95	76	93	87	94	90
UK	91	63	95	76	97	87

Source: Eurostat 1997e.

The rise of women's labour market participation in recent decades is attributed to married women's entrance into the labour market. Labour market participation among single women is, however, still higher than that of married women. Single as well as married women in the lower age groups have a paid job more often than women of older generations. The relatively low rate of labour market participation among the youngest women is related to their higher participation in education and training. The larger variations in labour market participation among older women mirror variations in the time when married women in larger numbers entered the labour market in different countries (table 16.5).

EXPLANATIONS OF DIFFERENCES IN FEMALE PARTICIPATION IN EDUCATION

Expansion of the Educational Systems

There are several factors contributing to variations in women's educational and labour market participation presented in the previous text and tables. The level of education among men as well as women is affected by the economic development in a country and the level of resources allocated to education. In southern Europe, basic education is still the most frequent level of education while upper secondary education is the most common level in the northwestern part of Europe. Such variations might be explained

Table 16.5. Economic Activity Rates for Women in Some Selected Age Groups in EU Member States, 1995

	20–29	25–29	30–34	35–39	40–44	45–49	50–54	55–60
B	55	82	77	74	67	57	42	22
DK	75	77	82	85	90	86	72	58
D	70	74	72	74	77	74	68	47
GR	52	63	62	60	56	46	39	29
E	58	71	64	59	54	44	34	25
F	57	80	79	78	80	76	68	45
IRL	69	75	64	55	48	43	35	26
I	49	60	60	60	55	48	36	20
NL	77	77	69	67	66	61	48	29
A	74	79	77	77	75	69	60	28
P	56	78	80	80	76	69	60	42
FIN	63	73	80	83	88	88	81	56
S	67	81	86	89	91	93	91	79
UK	70	73	70	74	78	78	71	56

Source: Eurostat 1997f.

by differences in economic development, while social and gender differences have to be explained differently.

Social inequalities are due to differences in cultural capital and economic constraints. The equalization occurring in Sweden and the Netherlands is explained by equalization of material living conditions and cultural lifestyles rather than by school reforms (Shavit and Blossfeld 1996). Equality of opportunity in education irrespective of sex and socio-economic background has been on the political agenda in many European countries during the post-war period. One conclusion to be drawn from the figures presented in this chapter and from the results presented by Shavit and Blossfeld (1993) is that social selection to higher education is persistent. Based on the results of a Swedish case study, Shavit and Blossfeld (1996) claim that "the increases in women's rates of educational participation have set a limit on the extent to which educational institutions could reduce selectivity. This, in turn, has limited the increase in attendance rates of lower class men and women" (p. 250). The attainment rate among middle class men is not commented on.

In older generations, men are on average better educated than women are. Among younger generations, a reverse gender gap is developing at secondary and tertiary levels. When tertiary education is broken down into non-university, university programs of varying duration and into subjects chosen by men and women, traditional gender patterns persist. The expansion of jobs within the service sector and semi-professional occupations plays an important role for the increase of women in education above compulsory level (Blossfeld 1987).

Germany and Portugal are two countries deviating in a conspicuous way from the average general trend in female participation. In Germany, there are only 85 and 73 females per 100 males in upper secondary and higher education, compared to 111 and 132 respectively in Portugal. In Sweden, the attendance rate amounts to 144 females per 100 males in upper secondary education. In higher education there are 120 females per 100 males. It should however be kept in mind that the proportion of the population with tertiary education is more than twice as high in Germany and Sweden as in Portugal (Eurostat 1997a). The expansion of education at these two levels has been used to a larger extent by females than males in Sweden and Portugal. In Sweden, women have predominated among university students since the beginning of the 1980s. In Portugal, women outnumbered men at about the same time while the male dominance still exists in Germany. Portuguese education was reformed and expanded after the fall of the dictatorship. Also in the German educational system, women are increasing in numbers but men still outnumber women (Klammer and Ochs 1998).

The Structure of the Educational System

The structure of the educational system has an impact on the participation of men and women at different levels and on different programs. In Germany, Austria, the Netherlands and Italy, between 70 and 78 percent of upper secondary education is organized as vocational training. A large part of the vocational training is work-based in these countries. The rate of female students in vocational training is also lower in some of these countries (42–45 percent) than in Sweden, Finland and the UK (50–54 percent), where vocational training is primarily school-based. Females and males have different preferences of educational and labour market sectors. In all European countries females are in the majority in general upper secondary education. This educational choice often leaves them in a less favorable situation in relation to the labour market but in a more favorable position in relation to higher education. To be able to get a job women have to be more qualified than men. As has previously been pointed out, women are often better qualified than men in the same kind of jobs.

In the EU countries, the rate of female unemployment is higher than that of males. There is a correlation between unemployment and educational level. The unemployment rate is higher among lower than higher educational groups but on every level females are in the majority. The same situation is found in all the member states. The risk of becoming long-term unemployed increases with low education and with age. The risk is higher for women than for men.

The length of university education is another possible factor of relevance. A five-year education might be less attractive for women than the choice of a shorter university education as women and men anticipate their future in different ways (Malmgren [1982] 1985; Esseveld and Goodman 1984). Although women in most European countries see themselves as working

Table 16.6.   Unemployment Rate by Educational Level and Gender in EU Countries, 1995 (%)

	Compulsory Education	Upper Sec Education	Higher Education
Men	12	6.5	5
Women	15.5	10	7.5

Source: Eurostat 1995.

women, most of them also perceive themselves as future mothers carrying the main responsibility for the care of children (Cwejman and Fürst 1988; Oechsle and Zoll 1992; Tobio 1997).

Public Social Services

Depending on their position in the labour market, and their educational and social background, women adopt different strategies to reconcile family and work. Cultural traditions and the nature of the welfare system as well as the structure of the labour market are important factors influencing their actions. Slow progress in providing outside services to meet domestic responsibilities (mainly child care and care for the sick and elderly) acts as a brake on women's professional ambitions and limits their mobility (André 1996). Depending on the nature of the welfare system, women might hesitate to choose a long university education. In practice, this might be a choice between family and work or at least a postponement of having children. It is obvious, however, that educational level plays an important role for the rate of labour market participation among women.

In a recent study carried out by the German Minister of Equal Opportunities, it is claimed that 25 percent of women's investments in education are wasted as women are discriminated against in the labour market. Young women are not being employed as they are expected to leave the jobs when having children (quoted in Fölster 1996). Women in West Germany seem to be confronted with a choice between family and career, as 25 percent of them remain childless (Maier 1993, quoted in Einhorn 1997). The labour market participation rate of women aged twenty-five to thirty-nine with different educational background varies in an interesting way between Germany, Portugal and Sweden. Most of the highly educated women in Sweden and Portugal (90 and 96 percent respectively) work outside the home compared to 84 percent in Germany. The labour market participation rate declines at lower educational levels but the difference between low and highly educated Swedish and Portuguese women is smaller than in many other European countries. Some 76 percent of low-educated women in Sweden and Portugal have a paid job compared to 56 percent in Germany, 54 percent in Spain and 52 percent in the Netherlands. Even lower rates are found in Ireland (45 percent), Italy (47 percent) and Greece (49 percent) (Table 16.4). The table points to the fact that Portuguese and Swedish women in age groups with small children more often work outside the home than, for example, German women. Statistics also show that only 11.6 percent of Portuguese women work part-time as compared to 39.8 percent of Swedish women and 33.8 percent of German women. In Germany, there are also women working short part-time (less than nineteen hours or paid less than DM600 per week), which is not included in labour market statistics. Nor do they qualify for social benefits. Women probably hold most of these approximately 7 million jobs. Such jobs enable them to adapt to child care and household responsibilities (Fölster 1996). In Portugal as well, there are many women not included in the official labour market statistics as they work in the informal labour market (Stratigaki and Vaiou 1994). In Sweden, most women work long part-time hours, which qualifies them for full social benefits. The number of females in part-time jobs increased in the EU member states with the exception of the Scandinavian countries and Portugal during 1983–1995 (EC 1998).

Ideologies of Motherhood

Ideologies of motherhood and families are rooted in a historical, cultural and political context (Leira 1992). Since the late 1960s, Swedish women have been regarded and treated as individuals in the welfare system and seen as working mothers. Each individual is supposed to support herself or himself and social rights are individualized. Public support is organized to make it easier for women to work outside the home. The provision of tax-paid child-care facilities for small children and young schoolchildren was expanded to meet the needs of working mothers. A generous parental leave scheme and labour regulations which give working mothers the right to part-time work while the children are small serve to explain the high rate of labour market participation among Swedish women. Working part-time is one way of managing both work and family without leaving the labour market.

In Germany, taking care of children is seen as a task for the family performed by women. Women's waged work plays a secondary role to that of men. The breadwinner family model frees the man from care and household work. Women's social security and social status are based on the husband's (Pfau-Effinger 1994). German women are not treated separately in the social security or tax system. The German feminist movement has paid less attention to paid labour than to policies which concern unpaid and invisible domestic activities (Ostner 1993). However, the situation is changing as women increasingly are participating in training and paid employment, which challenges the "housewife marriage" (Pfau-Effinger 1994). The increasing number of women working outside the home has to solve the situation according to their own means. Middle- and upper-class women use other women (immigrants, low-educated women, au-pair girls etc.) to help with household and care work while working class women have to rely on unpaid support from women in their family network. The patriarchal structure is left untouched (Rerrich 1996). The influence of different ideas of motherhood is still noticeable in former East and West Germany (Ostner 1994; Gerhard 1999).

In Portugal, the situation of women started to change in the 1960s and 1970s as a consequence of industrialization, internal and external labour market migration, men's participation in the Colonial War and the end of Salazar's dictatorship. An official agreement from the 1940s between the state and the church formed the background to a very traditional and conservative ideology of women's roles in society. The fall of Salazar in 1974 decreased this overwhelming influence of the Catholic Church and caused a break with traditions (André 1996). The Portuguese tax system is similar to that in Germany and access to social benefits are unevenly spread as they are connected to different employment conditions. Public provision of childcare facilities is scarce and women have to rely on relatives and private provisions.

Full Citizenship for Women

The critique of the way Marshall defined full citizenship points to the fact that women's situation in the public sphere cannot be understood without reference to household and care work. In practice, women's labour market participation is affected by the construction of the welfare systems. This also affects women's possibility to live an autonomous life. Feminist researchers have brought up women's situation in relation to private and public dependency and also pointed out that men's dependence on female care and household work is neglected in the discussion (Sainsbury 1996). In, for example, Germany, the welfare system makes women dependent on their husbands. In Scandinavia, women are dependent on the state, not as clients as in liberal welfare regimes, but as consumers and employees (Hernes 1984).[3]

Education can be seen as a means to reach more autonomous living conditions for women. A strong correlation exists between education and labour market participation. Social benefits connected to labour market participation are normally larger and easier to negotiate than social benefits traditionally allocated to women on the basis of motherhood (Orloff 1993). Portugal and Germany belong to a similar tradition. Access to social benefits is reached on the basis of labour market participation. In Portugal, the system is characterized by relatively generous benefits for those belonging to the labour force and by lacking social protection for those remaining outside (Ferrera 1996). The expansion of jobs within the public sector in Portugal opened a labour market for educated women. The economic and political changes starting in the 1970s have contributed to a changed attitude to education among females.

CONCLUSION

To conclude, variations in educational participation among women must be understood in a wider perspective. Reforms of the educational system influence female participation but changes in political, social and cultural traditions as well as changes in the labour market are of greater importance. Demographic changes consisting of an increasing number of elderly people, a decrease in birth rates and in the number of large families and a higher rate of divorce, in addition to increasing demands for qualifications, are of special importance to women. A fairly large number of women already participate in paid labour and the participation rate is expected to rise as a consequence of low birth rates leading to future shortage of labour. Women with higher educational qualifications more often work outside the home than women do with lower qualifications. Unemployment hits the latter group harder. In relation to such recent trends in demographic and labour market development, education is of special importance to women. Higher educational qualifications facilitate more rewarding positions in the labour market, increased access to public life and a larger degree of independence.

NOTES

An earlier version of this chapter was published in *International Journal of Contemporary Sociology* 36 (1999), no. 2: 144–62, and is reprinted by permission.

1. Vocational training in Sweden is school-based and the time spent at the work place is included in the curriculum.

2. ISCED is an international standard classification of education. The following levels are used:

    ISCED 0: pre-primary education
    ISCED 1: primary education
    ISCED 2: lower secondary education
    ISCED 3: upper secondary education
    ISCED 5, 6, 7: higher education

ISCED 5 requires the completion of upper secondary education but does not generally lead to a university degree. ISCED 6 covers programmes leading to a first university degree or equivalent. ISCED 7 covers programmes to a second, postgraduate university degree. In Eurostat (1996), the presentation of higher education is not divided into ISCED 5, 6 and 7.

3. Esping-Andersen (1990) classifies different welfare systems into three different kinds of welfare regimes. The notion of regime refers to the qualitatively different arrangements between the state, the market and the family. He makes clusters of Western welfare states into liberal, conservative and social-democratic welfare systems. The liberal welfare regime is found in the US and in the UK since the 1970s. The conservative welfare regime is found in, for example, Germany and finally, the social-democratic welfare regime is found in the Scandinavian countries.

REFERENCES

André, I. M. 1996. "At the Centre of the Periphery? Women in the Portuguese Labour Market." In *Women of the European Union: The Politics of Work and Daily Life*. Edited by M. D. García-Ramon and J. Monk. London: Routledge.

Ball, J. S., and S. Larsson. 1989. *The Struggle for Democratic Education: Equality and Participation in Sweden*. New York: Falmer.

Berggren, A.-M. 1996. *Kvinnorna och välfärden*. A-M. Stockholm: Forskningsrådsnämnden.

Björnberg, U. 1992. *European Parents in the 1990s: Contradictions and Comparisons*. New Brunswick, N.J.: Transaction.

Blossfeld, H.-P. 1987. "Labour Market Entry and the Sexual Segregation of Careers in the Federal Republic of Germany." *American Journal of Sociology* 93, no. 1: 89–118.

Borchorst, A. 1994. "Welfare State Regimes, Women's Interest, and the E." In *Gendering Welfare States*. Edited by D. Sainsbury. Thousand Oaks, Calif.: Sage.

Cwejman, S., and G. Fürst. 1988. *Tonårsflickors väg: Strategier i klyftan mellan ideologisk könsneutralitet och könssegregerande politik*. Göteborgs Universitet: Sociologiska Institutionen.

Daly, M. 1994. "Comparing Welfare States: Towards a Gender Friendly Approach." In *Gendering Welfare State*. Edited by D. Sainsbury. London: Sage.

Duncan, S. 1996. "The Diverse Worlds of European Patriarchy." In *Women of the European Union: The Politics of Work and Daily Life*. Edited by M. D. García-Ramon and J. Monk. London: Routledge.

Einhorn, B. 1997. "The Impact of the Transition from Centrally Planned to Market-Based Economies on Women's Employment in East Central Europe." In *Promoting Gender Equality at Work: Turning Vision into Reality for the Twenty-First Century*. Edited by E. Date-Bah. London: Zed.

Erikson, R., and J. O. Jonsson. 1996. *Can Education Be Equalized? The Swedish Case in Comparative Perspective*. Boulder: Westview.

Erskine, A., with M. Elchardus, S. Herkommer, and J. Ryan. 1996. *Changing Europe: Some Aspects of Identity, Conflict, and Social Justice*. Aldershot, U.K.: Avebury.

Esping-Andersen, G. 1990. *The Three Worlds of Welfare Capitalism*. Cambridge: Polity.

Esseveld, J., and S. Goodman. 1984. *Students' Vision of Their Future: How a Hierarchical Society Becomes Reproduced*. Lund: Lund University.

European Commission. 1998. *The Future of Work in Europe*. Brussels: Employment and Social Affairs, DGV.

Eurostat. 1992. *Labour Force Survey 1990*. Luxembourg.

Eurostat. 1995. *Employment in Europe*. Luxembourg.

Eurostat. 1997a. *Education across the European Union: Statistics and Indicators*. Luxembourg.

Eurostat. 1997b. *Report on Education: Women Are Catching Up with Men, but Traditional Differences Remain*. Press release no. 27/97. Luxembourg.

Eurostat. 1997c. *Key Data on Vocational Training in the European Union*. Luxembourg.

Eurostat. 1997d. *Key Data on Education in the European Union*. Luxembourg.

Eurostat. 1997e. *Statistics in Focus, 1997/1*. Luxembourg.

Eurostat. 1997f. *Labour Force Survey 1995*. Luxembourg.

Ferrera, M. 1996. "The 'Southern Model' of Welfare in Social Europe." *Journal of European Social Policy* 6: 17–37.

Fölster, S. 1996. *Barn och äldreomsorg i Tyskland och Sverige: Tysklandsdelen: Välfärdsprojektet.* Stockholm: Socialdepartmentet.

Fürst, G. 1990. *En ny gymnasieskola för flickor och pojkar: Jämställdhetsperspektiv på den nya gymnasieskolans linjestruktur.* Göteborgs Universitet: Sociologiska Institutionen.

García-Ramon, M. D., and J. Monk. 1996. *Women of the European Union: The Politics of Work and Daily Life.* London: Routledge.

Gerhard, U. 1999. "Social Policy and Motherhood: The East-West-German Case." Paper presented at meeting of the Thematic Network on Working and Mothering Social Policies and Social Practices, Frankfurt, 22–26 April 1999.

Hernes, H. 1984. "Women and the Welfare State: The Transition from Public to Private Dependency." In *Patriarchy in Welfare Society.* Edited by H. Hernes. Oslo: Universitetsförlaget.

Hernes, H. 1984. *Patriarchy in Welfare Society.* Oslo: Universitetsforlaget.

Jones, K. G., and A. G. Jónasdottír. 1988. *The Political Interest of Gender.* London: Sage.

Jönsson, I., and G. Arnman. 1989. "Social Segregation in Swedish Comprehensive Schools." In *The Struggle for Democratic Education: Equality and Participation in Sweden.* Edited by J. S. Ball and S. Larsson. New York: Falmer.

Klammer, U., and C. Ochs. 1998. *The Development of Gainful Employment of Women in Germany.* Düsseldorf: WSI.

Kyle, G. 1979. *Gästarbetarska i manssamhälle: Studier om industriarbetande kvinnors villkor i Sverige.* Stockholm: Publica.

Leira, A. 1992. *Welfare States and Working Mothers: The Scandinavian Experience.* Cambridge: Cambridge University Press.

Lewis, J. 1993. *Women and Social Policies in Europe: Work, Family, and the State.* Aldershot, U.K.: Edward Elgar.

Lister, R. 1990. "Women, Economic Dependency, and Citizenship." *Journal of Social Policy* 19, no. 4: 445–67.

Lister, R. 1997. *Citizenship: Feminist Perspectives.* London: Macmillan.

Littlewood, P., and I. Jönsson. 1996. "Schooling and Social Justice: Some Current Trends." In *Changing Europe: Some Aspects of Identity, Conflict, and Social Justice.* Edited by A. Erskine, with M. Elchardus, S. Herkommer, and J. Ryan. Aldershot, U.K.: Avebury.

Lundahl, L. 1986. *Flickors utbildning för hem och yrke: Några skolpolitiska skiljelinjer.* Lund: Lunds Universitet.

Maier, F. 1993. "Frauenwerbstätigkeit in der DDR und der BRD—Gemeinsamkeiten und Underschiede." In *Politische Ökonomie des Teilens,* 22. Berlin: Fachhochschule für Wirtschaft—Forschung.

Malmgren, G. [1982] 1985. *Min framtid: Om högstadieelevers syn på framtiden.* Lund: Symposion.

Marshall, T. H. 1950. *Citizenship and Social Class and Other Essays.* Cambridge: Cambridge University Press.

OECD. 1996. *Education at a Glance.* Paris: OECD.

OECD. 1998. *Education at a Glance.* Paris: OECD.

Oechsle, M., and R. Zoll. 1992. "Young People and Their Ideas of Parenthood." In *European Parents in the 1990s: Contradictions and Comparisons.* Edited by U. Björnberg. New Brunswick: Transaction.

O'Conner, J. 1993. "Welfare State Regimes: Theoretical and Methological Issues." *British Journal of Sociology* 44, no. 3: 501–18.

O'Conner, J. 1996. "From Women in the Welfare State to Gendering Welfare State Regimes." *Current Sociology* 44, no. 2 (Summer).

O'Reilly, J., and C. Fagan, eds. 1998. *Part-Time Prospects: An International Comparison of Part-Time Work in Europe, North America, and the Pacific Rim*. London: Routledge.

Orloff, A. A. 1993. "Gender and the Social Rights of Citizenship." *American Sociological Review* 58, no. 3: 303–28.

Ostner, I. 1993. "Slow Motion: Women, Work, and the Family in Germany." In *Women and Social Policies in Europe: Work, Family, and the State*. Edited by J. Lewis. Aldershot, U.K.: Edward Elgar.

Ostner, I. 1994. "Back to the Fifties: Gender and Welfare in Unified Germany." *Social Politics*, Spring.

Pfau-Effinger, B. 1994. "The Gender Contract and Part-Time Work by Women: Finland and Germany Compared." *Environment and Planning* 26: 1355–76.

Rerrich, M. S. 1996. "Modernizing the Patriarchal Family in West Germany: Some Findings on the Redistribution of Family Work between Women." *European Journal of Women's Studies* 3: 27–37.

Rubery, J., M. Smith, and C. Fagan. 1999. *Women's Employment in Europe: Trends and Prospects*. London: Routledge.

Ruivo, M., et al. 1998. "Why Is Part-Time Work So Low in Portugal and Spain?" In *Part-Time Prospects: An International Comparison of Part-Time Work in Europe, North America, and the Pacific Rim*. Edited by J. O'Reilly and C. Fagan. London: Routledge.

SAF. 1996. *Tysk yrkesutbildning i förändring: Det duala utbildningssystemet*. Stockholm: Sveriges Tekniska Attachéer & Rådet för Arbetslivsforskning.

Sainsbury, D. 1994. *Gendering Welfare States*. London: Sage.

Sainsbury, D. 1996. *Gender Equality and Welfare States*. Cambridge: Cambridge University Press.

Shavit, Y., and H.-P. Blossfeld. 1993. *Persistent Inequality: Changing Educational Attainment in Thirteen Countries*. Boulder: Westview.

Shavit, Y., and H.-P. Blossfeld. 1996. "Equalizing Educational Opportunity: Do Gender and Class Compete?" In *Can Education Be Equalized? The Swedish Case in Comparative Perspective*. Edited by R. Erikson and J. O. Jonsson. Boulder: Westview.

Siim, B. 1988. "Towards a Feminist Rethinking of the Welfare State." In *The Political Interest of Gender*. Edited by K. G. Jones and A. G. Jónasdottír. London: Sage.

Stark. A. 1996. "Arbete och arbetsmarknad i ett könsperspektiv på Sverige." In *Kvinnorna och välfärden*. Edited by A.-M. Berggren. Stockholm: Forskningsrådsnämnden.

Stratigaki, M., and D. Vaiou. 1994. "Women's Work and Informal Activities in Southern Europe." *Environment and Planning* 26: 1221–34.

Tobío, C. 1997. "Women's Strategies and the Family-Employment Relationship in Spain." Paper presented at the ESCR seminar on Women's Search for Identity in Contemporary Europe, University of Bath, November 1997.

Walby, S. 1990. "Is Citizenship Gendered?" *Sociology* 28, no. 2: 379–95.

Walby, S. 1997. *Gender Transformations*. London: Routledge.

17

North and South Contrasted:

Cultural Similarities and Differences in Affective Education

Yaacov J. Katz, Alkistis Kontoyianni, Peter Lang, Isabel Menezes, Sean R. St. J. Neill, Arja Puurula, Shlomo Romi, Claudia Saccone, Lisa Vasileiou, and Lennart Vriens

In previous reports of our affective education study from twelve European and Mediterranean countries we discussed transnational communalities and revealed similar constructs in attitudes toward teaching responsibilities and values (Neill 2000; Puurula et al. 2001; Puurula 2000). The aim of this chapter is to extend the analysis of the previous chapters and describe the differences in attitudes between teachers and students of northern and southern European countries toward teaching responsibilities and the values that the school is supposed to promote. Are there educationally relevant differences or similarities of teaching practices between north and south? While discussing the rationale of the concept of Mediterranean Rim for comparative educational analysis Cowen (1998, 69) presents strong arguments:

> The educational "genealogies" of many of the countries in the Mediterranean Rim are out of time. That is less metaphorically, the educational codings of many of the countries of the Mediterranean Rim are in a sociological time which is not that of the late twentieth century.

Despite increasing global similarities in teaching traditions and curricular structure, marked regional differences due to distinctive historical trajectories and socio-economic circumstances are evident (Meyer et al. 1992; Ossenbach-Sauter 1996; Esteve 1999; Brock and Tulasiewicz 2000; Le Métais 1999).

Sultana (1998) mentions examples of the similarities in compulsory educational systems in the Mediterranean countries: educational centralisation, the importance of religion, the parallel systems of denominational schools, the issue of women's education, and finally economic underdevelopment. The long histories of colonialism and dictatorships around the Mediterranean Rim have created concerns about the nature of contemporary cultural identity, and in many countries education has a dual task to promote national identity and economic well-being of the same standard as the other European countries (Cowen 1998; Persianis 1998).

Since the Industrial Revolution the idea of economic progress, social order and modernity were the incentives for compulsory schooling for all (Green 1990; Pollard et al. 1994; Hendrick 1997). In the nineteenth century this led in almost every modern country to a knowledge-based and verbalistic curriculum that left little room for the youngsters' own individual development. The basic purpose of modern curricula of the nineteenth century was to form citizens through "the moral curriculum code" according to the frame factor theory of Lundgren (1972, 1991).

At the turn of the nineteenth and twentieth century the Reformpedagogik, the New Education Movement and the Progressive Education Movement put this idea of a school for a mainly academic curriculum into question and stressed that the school should be a place for the individual development of children (Selleck 1972; Cha 1992; Benavot et al. 1992). The moral code was replaced by the "the rational curriculum code," and later by "the civic code" after World War II. Only since the late 1960s has the "modern unique individual" in some countries surpassed society as the fundamental source of legitimisation for schooling (Simola 1998). An important question can be raised: are southern and northern countries of Europe at different stages in their curriculum code development?

The century that started with scholarly writings about "the century of the child" has thus changed from "pedagogical individualism" (child-centered education directed to the needs of a student group) towards "administrative individualism" (Sultana 1992; Popkewitz 2000). Hargreaves (1990) discusses the culture of individualism in the English secondary school; by the 1980s team or house spirit were much less popular, as compared to the post-war period. Other indices of the growth of administrative individualism are the development of pastoral care, personal and social education and tutor groups which actually promote the welfare of the individual rather than that of the collective and a child as a member of a group. The dominant market ideology produced slogans such as "back to basics," "effective education," and "standards for quality" and denounced child centeredness as ineffective and lacking quality (Donmore 1979; Thornell 1979; Galton et al. 1999).

Paradoxically, during the same period, when constructivist theories of learning prevail, the actual limitation of neoliberal thought at policy level has caused evident changes in the role and tasks of a teacher. In many European countries—both north and south—the trend of the 1990s was towards managerialism. Teachers were not seen as pedagogues but as "designers of the learning environments of the individual learners," persons in charge of "individual study plans," "mere obedient and loyal civil servants," "compliant technicians" (Simola 1998; Klette 2000; Helsby 2000; McCulloch 2000; Esteve 1999).

AFFECTIVE EDUCATION DEFINED

The debate between child- and curriculum-oriented educators has shaped the conceptual development of education during the twentieth century. In the 1960s and the early 1970s the child-centered movement had a high level of influence with the rise of critical pedagogy (Cunningham 1988). The other, curriculum-oriented trend concentrated on the specification of curricular targets. The idea of the affective as an important domain of education originated in the humanistic-oriented psychology and psychotherapy of the 1950s. Bloom's (1956) and Krathwohl's (1964) taxonomies distinguished three domains of educational objectives: the cognitive, the affective and the psycho-motor.

Teachers are continually challenged by other aspects of teaching and learning than purely cognitive: motivation and emotion, values and norms, physical and social. Besides this, social and societal problems like bullying, dropout youngsters, racism and prejudices require a more elaborated concept of education, to give a real democratic introduction for the new generation into the adult world. Affective education is an increasingly important aspect of European school practice (Marland 1980; Pring 1984; Power 1996). Lang et al. (1998) propose the following working definition:

> By "affective education" is meant that part of the educational process that concerns itself with attitudes, feelings, beliefs and emotions of students. A further important dimension goes beyond the individual students and concerns the effectiveness of their relationships with others, thus interpersonal relationships and social skills are recognised as central to affective education.

Affective education research has covered mainly four topics: self-concept, interpersonal perspective taking, moral development and sense of community (Nucci and Lee 1992). Hoz and Kainan (1999) describe affective education as a means of developing students' abilities to cope with emotional aspects of their lives. This may be a too narrow definition. "Affective education" has in recent years also become popular as a term for more limited conceptions—equivalent to "values education" or "education for emotional intelligence." Narrower conceptions can lead to neglect in practice of important areas which are included in the wider definitions of affective education; for example, Steinberg (1976) defined affective education as a means for the development of society.

Affective education has been realised in contrasting practices (Lang et al. 1998). Beane (1993) points to the importance of integrating the dimension of the affect in the total educational program. It is necessary for the development of the "whole" student; it is integrated with almost every other aspect of learning and schooling. In this sense, a theory of learning or schooling that ignores affect is incomplete and inhuman.

THE MODEL OF CULTURAL VARIATIONS OF VALUES

Educational activity is an expression of national life and character, and pedagogy is a window on national culture of which it is a part (Alexander 1999). Prosser (1999) distinguishes four broad categories of school culture, and his definition of "wider culture" as contrasted to "generic culture," "unique culture," and "perceived culture" comes nearest to our understanding. "Wider culture" emphasises the relationship between a nation's culture and the culture of its schools. In this chapter, we will elaborate the influence of "culture" on the response of people socialised in the educational systems of nine countries, approaching "culture" as a system of shared beliefs and values. We will not consider, for example, organisational aspects of culture.

Among other writers in the long tradition starting from the anthropological definition of Tylor in 1871, Aloni (1997) presents a sociological definition of the term: Culture represents a system of values, objectives, knowledge, skills and feelings constituting societal norms in different fields of interaction specific to an individual society. Also, culture is to be understood within a specific historical frame of reference, unique to a particular society (Nicholas 1991; Mosa 1999; Benham and Heck 1993; Broadfoot et al. 1993).

Hanna et al. (1999) consider that because every culture exists within a context (basing themselves here on the ideas of Scharfstein [1989]) the ability to traverse and move fluidly among contexts is a function of "wisdom." Each culture is in itself a context and contains an entire set of internally consistent symbols and meanings. For both the individual and members of the society as a whole, the way of experiencing the world incorporates values, attitudes, opinions and concepts which derive from these symbols and meanings.

Figure 17.1 displays our preliminary model for the study. The decision-making process starts from the values participants hold—we considered these would vary between south and north, reflecting national and regional cultures. These values pass through a filter of social background, related to age, experience including training experience, status, gender etc.—so that a young female primary teacher will have rather different views to an experienced male secondary science teacher, despite their shared cultural traditions. The decisions they make about their own responsibilities, and the responsibilities they feel others should take will therefore differ—but will also differ from those which their counterparts in other countries would make.

According to Inglehart's survey of "world values" (1990), the northern countries value "post-modern," individualistic values like balance, independence, tolerance, imagination, change, responsibility, trust for people and value of the environment, while southern countries place higher value on "modern" values like religion, obedience, family values, respect for parents and national pride. The second European value study (1990–1991) states that economic development leads to a shift in the direction of individualism (Ester et al. 1993). Thus modern society will gradually converge in the direction

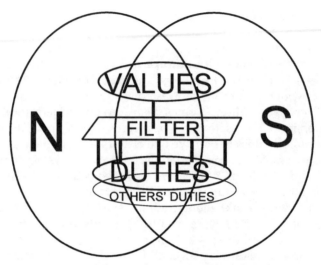

Figure 17.1.   Preliminary Theoretical Model for the Study

of an individualized value system regarding basic values such as religion, morality, politics and work ethics. The value system of modern society tends to be fragmented rather than cohesive and collectivist, and in the long run will exhibit a coherent pattern of individualized value systems in all domains of behavior, including education and teaching. However, this hypothesis of value fragmentation did not get support from the empirical findings of the study.

Individualism/collectivism have long been considered one of the major themes of cross-cultural studies. Triandis and Chen (1998) point out that there existed an implicit suggestion that some other theme might emerge in the 1990s within social psychology, but the 1990s proved to be even more fertile ground for the development of theory around these constructs.

Following the theory of Hofstede (1980) nations are distinguished by four dimensions: power/distance, masculinity/femininity, individualism/collectivism, and uncertainty/avoidance. Here individualism implies a loose social framework in which people take care of themselves, as opposed to collectivism, which stresses the importance of social groups. In individualistic cultures identity and emotional independence from the group organisation are maintained, and it is strongly believed that individual decisions have primacy. In collectivist cultures identity resides in the social system or subsystem. In individualistic cultures school education aims at giving students the means for continuing, lifelong learning while in collectivist societies emphasis is on how to do (Hofstede 1986).

According to his empirical findings, northern cultures are more individualistic and feminine/nurturant; geographical latitude and individuality-collectivism correlates .75*** and masculinity-femininity -.31* (Hofstede 1998). The countries of our study are listed in table 17.1 according to these two dimensions. There is a more accurate match between the south-north perspective studied in our report and the individualism-collectivism dimension than the masculinity-femininity dimension.

Criticism of Hofstede has focused on the vague definition of the four dimensions and on the restricted samples from IBM employees. In the Chinese culture Hofstede's individualism-collectivism scale appeared as the dimension of integration (Merkens 1996). Sagy et al. (1999), commenting on Triandis's theoretical framework, found that in Israeli society, different ethnic and religious groups were significantly differentiated on the individualism-collectivism dimension.

Schools influence their students in relation to democratic values, the rights and freedoms of individuals (John and Osborn 1992). Collaboration between teachers promotes the adoption of progressive values and increased understanding of their students, thereby setting the stage for the development of better relationships with students (Bruner 1996; Gitlin 1999). The traditions of teacher training differ between countries; primary level teachers being mainly trained in humanistic pedagogical traditions, whereas secondary level teachers are trained mainly with a subject-oriented, academic ethos. In some countries primary-level teachers work mainly in pairs or teams, while secondary teachers usually work as individuals. Secondary teachers, therefore, usually lack a culture of sharing teaching responsibilities for the needs of individual children or groups, which is normal at the primary level (Nias 1989; Hargreaves 1994; Niemi and Kohonen 1995; Esteve 1999). These "universals" related to educational phase show considerable variation between countries, however.

Table 17.1. Countries Discussed in This Chapter Listed in Order of Two of Hofstede's Dimensions

Individualism	Masculinity
Great Britain (3)[1]	Italy (2)
Netherlands (4)	Greece (6)
Finland (9)	Great Britain (8)
Ireland (11)	Ireland (9)
Israel[2]	Israel[2]
Italy (12)	Finland (12)
Spain (14)	Spain (14)
Greece (16)	Portugal (15)
Portugal (17)	Netherlands (16)
Collectivism	Feminist (nurturant) societies

Notes
1. Numbers in parenthesis are ranked among all countries in Hoppe's report (1998, 33).
2. Not included in the reference source.

RATIONALE OF THE STUDY

The research tasks of the study are, having reflected on the concepts of school culture as related to the culture of the society, to study the differences and similarities between north and south European teachers' and students' thoughts on education, especially views on values, responsibilities and teachers' professional satisfaction. In this study we compare northern countries (England, Finland, Ireland, Netherlands and Northern Ireland) and southern (Greece, Israel, Italy Portugal and Spain) of the main questionnaire data gathered in 1998.

METHODOLOGY

Instrument

Two questionnaires were devised, one for teachers, and the second, matching it as far as possible, for students, to allow direct comparison between the views of teachers and students. Except in the first, social background section, all attitudes were assessed by five-point Likert scales. The first section in both questionnaires asked for the social background information, and the second section asked about a wide range of affective education responsibilities. Teachers were asked both how important it was that they themselves should carry out these responsibilities, and how important that others in the school should carry them out. Students were asked only how important it was that the teacher should carry the responsibility out. Two further sections covered professional satisfaction and dissatisfaction (teachers only), and educational values, and their importance in education.

Procedure

Colleagues in each country were asked to administer the questionnaire to 200 students of top primary and lower secondary age in their classes, and 100–150 teachers of these age-groups, for completion individually (opportunity samples). The age-range of students was limited to 11–12 years (elementary/primary schools) and 15–16 years. As far as feasible, male and female numbers were to be equal. Teachers were selected from among those teaching the two age-groups of students selected. The samples were drawn from urban schools. Two more criteria were applied: first, that all participant schools would represent the main type/types of school found in a particular country, and second, that neither school should be exceptional in terms of socio-economic intake, examination results, or other key variables.

In practice samples that are used in this sub-analysis of the preliminary data are 1818 students and 1100 teachers (the numbers of students and teachers for each country being as follows: England 154/69, Finland 231/153, Greece 228/153, Ireland 119/83, Israel 349/126, Italy 200/200, the Netherlands 189/144, Northern Ireland 202/90, Portugal 146/82). Certain threats of validity should be mentioned: it was more difficult to get co-operation from schools in England, as they were under heavy pressure from educational reforms. Also, responses could have been affected by particular events at the time of data collection. In the Netherlands data was collected between two important structural developments in educational policy which provoked considerable debate and concern among teachers. In Greece the questionnaires were administered soon after a substantial raise in teacher salary. In Israel the research was carried out in a situation of sharp public debate concerning controversial issues of peace, while in Ireland and Northern Ireland the research was conducted against the background of the developing peace process.

The analysis of the results (SPSS) was carried out in the University of Warwick Institute of Education by the Warwick team with support from and consultation with the other members of the research group. The analyses reported here are made with ANOVA and discriminant analyses. In discriminant analysis groups (in this case north and south) are identified *a priori*. Discriminant analysis considers all the variables together and identifies the variables which most clearly discriminate the two groups.

The main dimensions of the study are:

Educational values
  A. two individual factors
    1. personal values (e.g., "motivation for life," "openness," "flexibility" and "creativity")
    2. autonomy and tolerance (e.g., "critical thinking," "personal autonomy," and "democratic citizenship")
  B. one collective factor
    1. social values (e.g., "honesty," "fairness," "moral values," and "respect for others")
Teaching responsibilities
  A. one individual factor
    1. prevention and support (e.g., "supporting students with family problems," "supporting students with personal problems," "teaching protection from abuse," and "helping abused children")
  B. two collective factors:
    1. positive classroom climate (e.g., "all should experience success," "academic feedback," "promote positive classroom behavior," and "help students who are not working well"

2. parental involvement (e.g., "involve parents in social activities," "involve parents in academic activities," "good teacher–parent contacts," and "discuss progress with parents")

Professional satisfaction

1. professional satisfaction (positive ratings, both extrinsic and intrinsic)
2. intrinsic dissatisfaction (negative ratings of within-school aspects such as relationships with students and colleagues, lesson success etc.)
3. extrinsic dissatisfaction (negative ratings of aspects external to the school such as pay, public esteem, educational policy changes, and relations with parents)

Univariate Comparisons of North and South

Teachers

Teachers in the north were slightly more likely to be teaching in secondary schools (p <.05), but there were no significant differences in the subjects taught and whether they were class teachers or not. Southern teachers were significantly more likely to be female (p <.00) and were more experienced (p <.00); the latter especially reflected the large number of very experienced teachers in the Italian sample. There were also fewer part-time teachers in the south (p <.00).

Students

There was no significant difference for sex, but students in the south were older (p <.00).

Univariate Analyses of Factors

Teachers

Scores were significantly higher for south for personal values (p <.00), social values (p <.00) and especially for autonomous citizenship (p <.00). They were also higher for the responsibilities of positive classroom practice (p <.00), prevention and support (p < .00) and, especially, parental involvement (p <.00). Southern teachers also rated the responsibility of others in the school for positive classroom values higher (p <.01); this difference was even more marked for the responsibilities of others for prevention and support (p <.00) and for those of others for promoting respect and parental involvement (p <.00). This implies that northern teachers were more prone to take personal responsibility, rather than see these responsibilities as collective ones for all in the school; in this sense they were more autonomous. The differences were more marked for the lower-priority factors (parental involvement, especially, and prevention and support).

However, the results for the teachers' job satisfaction section suggest that there is a tendency for more exaggerated responses in the south: southern teachers scored higher on professional satisfaction (p <.00) but also on extrinsic (p <.05) and, especially, intrinsic dissatisfactions (p <.00).

Students

Unlike teachers, students showed no regional difference in their rating of personal values or social values. There were no significant regional differences for positive classroom practice, or prevention and support, but southern students rated parental involvement and related responsibilities slightly higher than did their northern counterparts (p <.05). This indicates a slight tendency to modern, rather than post-modern, thinking among southern students. However the overall conclusion has to be that, in contrast to teachers, students replies indicated less regional differences.

Discriminant Analysis

Teachers

The histograms show an overall higher scoring for south; the distributions for both regions are fairly close to normal, with some irregularities in the distribution. Overall, 68.2 percent of "grouped" cases were correctly classified, with south being more accurately classified than north (74.9 percent as opposed to 61.2 percent). This is a recurring pattern, and may relate to the differentiation between the "Anglo-Saxon" countries (England and the two sections of Ireland) and the other northern countries (Finland and the Netherlands) shown on the Hofstede scales above, suggesting this group is less unitary in its approach than south. The discriminating variables can be listed in order of their pooled within-groups correlations with the canonical discriminant function—this shows how much each contributed to the discrimination:

1. the responsibilities of others for involvement with parents (r = .54)
2. the value of autonomous citizenship (r = .49)
3. teachers' own responsibility for dealing with parents (r = .46)
4. intrinsic dissatisfactions (r = -.42)
5. the responsibility of others in the school for prevention and support (r = .38)

These differences can be seen as representing a collectivist or modern perspective in the south, with greater emphasis on involving parents, as representatives of the community, both as the teacher's individual responsibility and as an overall responsibility of others in the school.

Southern respondents also scored higher for the importance of social values for students and professional satisfaction with conditions of service, and personal values for students, while north scored higher for extrinsic professional dissatisfactions (pay, public esteem etc.). However there is also a marked difference in scores for the core responsibilities which teachers rate as their own highest priorities: for positive classroom practice and prevention and support; the responsibilities of others for positive classroom practice show a less marked difference. Both the emphasis on social values and positive classroom practice can be seen as modernist responses in the south. The greater satisfaction with professional conditions in the south can also be seen as a conformist modernist viewpoint, in contrast to the more disaffected individualistic northern teachers.

If we consider possible social background explanations for these differences, we find there are significant differences between regions related to teacher sex (with more female teachers in the south; south also has full-time, as opposed to part-time posts and more experienced teachers. Here again, the contribution of the Italian teachers, who are experienced women, is apparent. Given that women rate values and responsibilities higher across the sample as a whole, this raises the possibility that apparent regional differences in fact relate to differences in the proportion of women in the two regions. Differences related to sector and subject specialisation are much less marked; the southern sample contains fewer secondary teachers and correspondingly more class teachers; the various subject specialisms are correspondingly less represented in the south. There is however considerable overlap between north and south in the histogram of distributions, and the patterns of distribution are extremely irregular for both groups, with south having the wider range. Again south was more accurately predicted than north, with 68.4 percent correctly classified as against 57.9 percent, the overall classification for the two groups being 63.3 percent correct.

Students

The histograms show distributions approaching normality for the overall sample and both sub-samples; south has a higher mean but greater deviation. It is therefore not surprising that overall discrimination is poorer than for the teachers, with 61.0 percent of cases being assigned to the correct groups overall; once more south (65.0 percent) is more accurately assigned than north (56.9 percent). Discriminating variables can be listed in order of their pooled within-groups correlations with the canonical discriminant function:

1. parental involvement responsibilities ($r = .66$)
2. positive classroom ($r = .21$)
3. prevention and support responsibilities ($r = -.14$),
4. personal values ($r = -.16$)

This pattern suggests a differentiation between an emphasis on affective and personal aspects, both for values and teachers' responsibilities, in the north, and academic responsibilities (both positive classroom practice and links with parents could be interpreted in this way) in the south. In other words southern students appear to have a somewhat narrower, more academically focused version of education, as opposed to a more inclusive, whole-child version in the north. This is consistent with the view of northern students as post-modernist, while their southern contemporaries remain modernist, but with a much less marked difference than their teachers.

A comparison of social background effects showed that students in the south were older than those in the north but sex differences were negligible. Differences were relatively slight, with 57.0 percent of southern cases correctly classified, as opposed to 55.4 percent of northern cases. We may therefore conclude that social background effects were of limited importance in the case of students. However there remains a possibility that the effects mentioned above related to the age-differences between the samples, with south having a rather lower proportion of primary-age students (this group being more concerned with the affective aspects of education) whereas secondary students, who make up a slightly higher proportion of the southern sample, are more career and therefore academically oriented.

DISCUSSION

We may summarize the main results as follows. Teachers' attitudes differ markedly between the regions; 68.2 percent of "grouped" cases were correctly classified, with south being more accurately classified than north (74.9 percent as opposed to 61.2 percent). These differences can be seen as representing a collectivist, southern perspective, with greater emphasis on involving parents, as representatives of the community, both as the teacher's individual responsibility and as an overall responsibility of others in the school, greater emphasis on positive classroom practice, social values and professional satisfaction. Or to use the curriculum code theory of Lundgren (1991), the southern respondents prefer rational curriculum code while the northern respondents see "civic code" or even "an individualistic code" as an ideal.

Southern students are more varied in their attitudes than those in the north; south has a higher mean but greater deviation so that the lowest, as well as the highest, values relate to south. As a result, overall discrimination is poorer than for the teachers, with 61.0 percent of cases being assigned to the correct groups overall; once more south (65.0 percent) is more accurately assigned than north (56.9 percent). In other words the southern students appear to have a somewhat narrower, more academically focused version of education, as opposed to a more inclusive, whole-child version in the north. This is consistent with the view of northern students as more post-modernist, while their southern contemporaries remain modernist.

We may summarize and elaborate these ideas by the model in figure 17.2. As can be seen, modernist ideas are primarily collectivist, in contrast to the individualistic ideas of post-modernism. However, we have used separate terms to describe the intermediate position. In the south, the intermediate position represents a transitional stage between modernism and the post-modernism towards which south appears to be moving; as can be seen, southern students are further along this transition than their teachers, though they remain predominantly in the intermediate, "semi-post-modern" position. In the north, however, teachers are fully post-modern, but their students are less post-modern; however their position is different from that of south. Whereas the southern semi-post-modern position is one in which individualism is increasing, responsibility for hard work by students continues to have a collectivist element, represented by the importance of parental involvement. In the north, we consider hard work by students to be related primarily to the need for individual, especially economic, success; so similar behaviour proceeds from different, more individualistic motives—the need for a good career. Different educational "generations" place different values on education, related to economic and cultural pressures at the time they are educated (Antikainen et al. 1996). We have therefore termed this category "prequel-modernism"— though it reverts to an apparently traditional pattern of behaviour, it is informed, like the prequel to a film, by earlier experience of "later" developments in the historical sequence.

The results of this study require some care in interpretation. There is, firstly, the problem that, for teachers, the scores for south tend to be higher overall, and this may be due to unavoidable differences in the profiles of the samples from the two regions. This may account for the difference between the regions in key teaching responsibilities. However there do appear to be real differences between the regions, when these imbalances in the samples, and the inadequacies of questionnaire methodology, have been taken into account. These questions will be explored more in further analyses of the data using more sophisticated statistical analyses methods (Neill forthcoming. a,b).

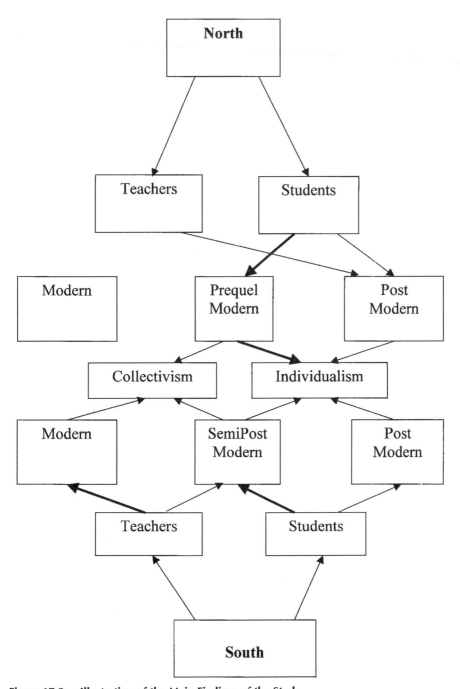

Figure 17.2.   Illustration of the Main Findings of the Study

CONCLUSION

We need to look, first, at the difference between teachers and students, and how these may reflect differences between both the generations and north and south. These differences can be interpreted by the contrast between the concepts of modernity and post-modernity, concepts which have created considerable philosophical debate in recent years. As Hargreaves (1994, 38) points out in his book about teachers' changing work and culture in the post-modern age, it is possible to concentrate on post-modernity as a social condition, not post-modernism as an aesthetic, cultural and intellectual phenomenon.

We may conclude, first, that there is a difference between the attitudes of southern and northern teachers towards the values schools should promote, and to their own teaching responsibilities and those of others in their schools. On the other hand, students show much less marked regional differences. The first finding is in line with the theories of Hofstede (1998), Triandis (1995) and Trompenaars (1994), and the immanent socio-cultural difference of collectivistic and individualistic orientation is the key to the finding. Out of this comes the greater reported importance of the community, as represented by parents and the other staff of the school ("the responsibilities of others"), to teachers in the south. This is backed up by other evidence that in collectivist cultures teachers pay greater attention to groups (Hamilton et al. 1991).

The views of teachers seem to have a limited effect on students who emerge from education as European citizens, confirming the results of Inglehart (2000). Inglehart's explanation is that youngsters tend to be more globalised whereas their elders have "nationalised" tendencies, due to the adoption of nationally specific materialistic values, related to the particular aspects of materialism which confer status in a specific society. Similarly, Osborn (1999) showed that while there was continuing evidence of the influence of national context on student perceptions of schooling, there was a clear suggestion of increasing globalisation of many concerns. This is reflected in the strong national differences between teachers in different countries, compared to the lack of differences between their students. Inglehart also considers that younger age-groups in America and other post-modern societies currently remain less materialistic than their parents' generation. The shift from materialist to post-materialist values is only one aspect of a shift from modern to post-modern values, as a shift which has occurred in the countries of north. Post-modern values are uncommon in most Mediterranean countries, which are still moving from traditional to modern values. This appears to be a secular change; as the students grow older and enter adult life, they would be expected to become less materialistic and culturally influenced than previous generations. The limited coherence, in our results, of the values which teachers promulgate, and the values adopted by students, stems from a mechanism by which children develop more globalised views, in resistance to socializing influences pushing them towards a more regionalized adult culture. The more skeptical attitudes of students, compared to their teachers, in our results confirms findings in other studies (Kulik 1997; Martello 1998; Bergin and Walworth 1999; Aksoy 1998).

We now need to consider these ideas which have swept up teachers, but have left their students largely unaffected. Philosophy has become caught up in a web of polemic between modernism and post-modernism, individualism and collectivism, self and society; education is centrally involved in such issues. Individualism is formulated in terms of post-modernist arguments and it may be explained as the liberal construction of the individual through education and the politics of difference (Habermas 1987; Peters and Marshall 1996; Foucault 1986). The individualism-collectivism (community) dichotomy is reflected in a series of binary oppositions which have been crucial in setting the terms of debate for recent reforms: private-public; separated self–shared self; male-female; self-other; market-state. Yet, according to Young (1990), the terms individualism-collectivism are major constructs which share a common logic which permits them to define each other negatively.

Individualism can be contrasted with individuality; in Hargreaves's (1994) view individuality (implying personal independence and self-realisation) is educationally desirable, as individualism (implying anarchy and social atomisation) is clearly not. Individualism takes the form of autonomy, where isolated teachers work in their own classrooms without immediate support from colleagues, insulated from outside pressures; as Stoll (1999) suggests this pattern is increasingly difficult to maintain under current conditions, where there is greater outside control and accountability, and pressure for social control and collegial responsibility.

Thus the individualism-collectivism continuum is that which distinguishes between teachers in north and south, but also between teachers and their students. Students are globalised in contrast to their teachers, but this globalisation takes the form of a continuing attachment to modern, rather than post-modern values. School students may increasingly be adopting "prequel-modern" educational values and views on the teacher and student role, while happy to adopt post-modern technology, such as mobile telephones, and post-modern values in other spheres.

The explanations used to describe differences between teachers and students in north and south should be seen in a "conservative" perspective, especially in light of the way Soeters (1994) deals with the issues of culture in European society. He discussed the results of Hofstede's original study and compared them to the findings of a replication study conducted by Hoppe about twenty years later. On the basis of the findings of both studies, Soeters suggested that there appears to be a considerable heterogeneity of culture in different European countries and that there is a strong measure of recalcitrance regarding cultural changes. Thus culture evolves, develops and changes only very slowly, indicating that the existing differences in culture among European countries are not easily changed or modified, nor are culture gaps easily bridged.

NOTE

Core funding for initial research was secured from the UK Economic and Social Research Council, sufficient to support a series of research meetings and analysis of the questionnaire; the University of Warwick supported a research meeting, via funds provided by the National Union of Teachers. The University of Helsinki also supported a research meeting for the group. The following institutions also contributed to the participation of national members: Department of Teacher Education, University of Helsinki; Foundation for Science and Technology, Portugal; Institute for Community Education and Research, Bar-Ilan University, Israel.

REFERENCES

Aksoy, N. 1998. Opinions of upper elementary school students about "good teachers." Paper presented at the twenty-ninth annual meeting of the Northeastern Educational Research Association, Ellenville, N.Y.

Alexander, R. 1999. Culture in pedagogy, pedagogy across cultures. In R. Alexander, P. Broadfoot, and D. Phillips, eds., *Learning from Comparing: New Directions in Comparative Research.* Wallingford: Symposium.

Aloni, N. 1997. Cultural education in a multi-cultural society. *Matzav Ha'Inyanim Beth Berl Academic Journal* 7: 3–6. In Hebrew.

Antikainen, A. Houtsonen, J. Kauppila, and H. Huotelin. 1996. *Living in a Learning Society.* London: Falmer.

Beane, J. 1993. *A Middle School Curriculum: From Rhetoric to Reality.* Columbus, Ohio: National Middle Schools Association.

Benavot, A., Y.-K. Cha, D. Kamens, J. Meyer, and S.-Y. Wong. 1992. Knowledge for the masses: World models and national curricula, 1920–1986. In J. W. Meyer, D. H. Kamens, and A. Benavot, eds., *School Knowledge for the Masses.* London: Falmer.

Benham, M. K. P., and R. H. Heck. 1993. Political and cultural determinants of educational policy making: The case of native Hawaiians. Paper presented at the annual meeting of AERA, Atlanta, April 1993.

Bergin, J. W., and M. Walworth. 1999. Developing a course in secondary level classroom behavior management: A study. Paper presented at the seventy-ninth annual meeting of the Association of Teacher Educators, Chicago.

Bloom, B. S. 1956. *Taxonomy of Educational Objectives: The Classification of Educational Goals—Handbook 1: Cognitive Domain.* London: Longman.

Broadfoot, P., M. Osborn, M. Gilly, and A. Bûcher. 1993. *Perceptions of Teaching: Primary School Teachers in England and France.* London: Cassell.

Brock, C., and W. Tulasiewicz, eds. 2000. *Education in a Single Europe.* London: Routledge.

Bruner, J. S. 1996. *The Culture of Education.* Cambridge: Harvard University Press.

Cha, Y.-K. 1992. The origins and expansion of primary school curricula: 1800–1920. In J. W. Meyer, D. H. Kamens, and A. Benavot, eds., *School Knowledge for the Masses.* London: Falmer.

Cowen, R. 1998. Thinking comparatively about space, education, and time: An approach to the Mediterranean rim. In A. K. Kazamias and M. G. Spillane, eds., *Education and the Structuring of the European Space.* Athens: Seirious Editions.

Cunningham, P. 1988. *Curriculum Change in the Primary Schools since 1945.* London: Falmer.

Donmore, R. 1979. Back to Basics now and 20 years ago: A comparison of two movements. *Educational Leadership* 36, no. 8: 555–58.

Ester, P., L. Halman, and R. de Moor. 1993. *The Individualizing Society: Value Change in Europe and North America.* Tilburg: Tilburg University Press.

Esteve, J. M. 1999. Teachers confronted with social and educational change. In H. Niemi, ed., *Moving Horizons in Education: International Transformations and Challenges of Democracy.* Helsinki: Helsinki University Press.

Fischer, A. H., A. S. R. Manstead, and P. M. Rodriguez Mosquera. 1999. The role of honour-related versus individualistic values in conceptualising pride, shame, and anger: Spanish and Dutch cultural prototypes. *Cognition and Emotion* 13, no. 2: 149–79.

Foucault, M. 1986. *The Care of the Self.* Harmondsworth, U.K.: Penguin.

Galton, M., L. Hargreaves, C. Comber, D. Wall, and A. Pell. 1999. *Inside the Primary Classroom: 20 Years On.* London: Routledge.

Gitlin, A. 1999. Collaboration and progressive school reform. *Educational Policy* 13, no. 5: 630–58.

Green, A. 1990. *Education and State Formation: The Rise of Educational Systems of England, France, and the USA.* London: Macmillan.

Habermas, J. 1987. *The Philosophical Discourse of Modernity.* Cambridge: MIT Press.

Hamilton, V.L., P. C. Blumenfeld, H. Akoh, and K. Miura. 1991. Group and gender in Japanese and American elementary classrooms. *Journal of Cross-Cultural Psychology* 22, no. 3: 317–46.

Hanna, F .J., F. Bernak, and R. Chi-Ying Chung. 1999. Towards a new paradigm for multi-cultural counselling. *Journal of Counselling and Development* 77 (Spring): 125–34.

Hargreaves, A. 1994. *Changing Teachers, Changing Times: Teachers' Work and Culture in the Post-modern Age.* London: Cassell.

Hargreaves, D. H. 1990 *The Challenge for the Comprehensive School.* London: Routledge.

Helsby, G. 2000. Multiple truths and contested realities: The changing faces of teacher professionalism in England. In C. Day, A. Fernandez, T. E. Hauge and J. Möller, eds., *The Life and Work of Teachers: International Perspective in Changing Times.* London: Falmer.

Hendrick, H. 1997. Construction and reconstructions of British childhood: An interpretative survey, 1800 to the present. In A. James and A. Prout, eds., *Constructing and Reconstructing Childhood.* London: Falmer.

Hofstede, G. 1980. *Culture's Consequences: International Differences in Work-Related Values.* Beverly Hills, Calif.: Sage.

Hofstede, G. 1986. Cultural differences in teaching and learning. *International Journal of Intercultural Relations* 10: 312–20.

Hofstede, G., ed. 1998. *Masculinity and Femininity: The Taboo Dimensions of National Cultures.* London: Sage.

Hoppe, M. H. 1998. Validating the masculinity/femininity dimension on elites from 19 countries. In G. Hofstede, ed., *Masculinity and Femininity: The Taboo Dimensions of National Cultures.* London: Sage.

Hoz, R., and A. Kainan. 1999. Caring in educational systems: A response to husbands and Lang. *European Educational Researcher* 5, no. 1: 36–38.

Inglehart, R. 1990. *Culture Shift in Advanced Industrial Society.* Princeton: Princeton University Press.

Inglehart, R. 2000. Globalization and post-modern values. *Washington Quarterly* 23, no. 1: 215–29.

John, P. D., and A. Osborn. 1992. The influence of school ethos on pupils' citizenship attitudes. *Educational Review* 44, no. 2: 153–65.

Klette, K. 2000. Working-time blues: How Norwegian teachers experience restructuring in education. In C. Day, A. Fernandez, T. E. Hauge, and J. Möller, eds., *The Life and Work of Teachers: International Perspective in Changing Times.* London: Falmer.

Krathwohl, D. R. 1964. *Taxonomy of Educational Objectives: The Classification of Educational Goals. Handbook 2: Affective Domain.* London: Longman.

Kulik, L. 1997. Sex-typing of occupations in the Israeli educational system: Students versus teachers. *Journal of Career Development* 24, no. 2: 103–14.

Lang, P. 1998. Towards an understanding of affective education in a European context. In P. Lang, Y. Katz, and I. Menezes, eds., *Affective Education: A Comparative View.* London: Cassell.

Lang, P., Y. Katz, and I. Menezes, eds. 1998. *Affective Education: A Comparative View.* London: Cassell.

Le Métais, J. 1999. Values and aims in curriculum and assessment frameworks: A sixteen-nation review. In R. Moon and P. Murphy, eds., *Curriculum in Context.* London: Sage.

Lundgren, U. P. 1972. *Frame Factors and the Teaching Process: A Contribution to Curriculum Theory and Theory on Teaching.* Stockholm: Almqvist & Wiksell.

Lundgren, U. P. 1991. *Between Education and Schooling: Outlines of a Diachronic Curriculum Theory.* Victoria: Deakin University.

Marland, M. 1980. *Pastoral Care: Organising the Care and Guidance of the Individual Student in a Comprehensive School.* London: Heinemann.

Martello, C. 1998. *Self-Perceived Levels of Responsibility in Seventh-Grade Students.* Research Report no. 143. University of Michigan.

McCulloch, G. 2000. The politics of the secret garden: Teachers and the school curriculum in England and Wales. In C. Day, A. Fernandez, T. E. Hauge, and J. Möller, eds., *The Life and Work of Teachers: International Perspective in Changing Times.* London: Falmer.

Merkens, H. 1996. Youth at risk: Attitudes and value concepts among young people in Europe at a time of social change. In D. Brenner and D. Lentzen, eds., *Education for the New Europe.* Providence: Berghahn.

Meyer, J. W., D. H. Kamens, and A. Benavot. 1992. *School Knowledge for the Masses.* London: Falmer.

Mosa, A. A. 1999. Culture in education and mass media: Conformation or confrontation. *Educational Media International* 36, no. 1: 37–40.

Neill, S. 2000. Teachers' and students' views on affective responsibilities: International similarities and national differences. *Curriculum and Teaching* 15, no. 2: 5–28.

Neill, S. A. Forthcoming. Cultural patterns and differences in teachers' views on affective education between north and south: A structural model.

Nias, J. 1989. *Staff Relationships in the Primary School: A Study of Organizational Culture.* London: Cassell.

Nicholas, R. W. 1991. Cultures in the curriculum. *Liberal Education* 77, no. 3: 16–22.

Niemi, H., and V. Kohonen. 1995. *Towards New Professionalism and Active Learning in Teacher Development: Empirical Findings on Teacher Education and Induction.* Research Series A 2. University of Tampere, Department of Teacher Education.

Nucci, L., and J. Lee. 1992. Affective education. *Encyclopedia of Educational Research,* 1:42–43. New York: Macmillan.

Osborn, M. 1999. National context, educational goals, and pupil experience of schooling and learning in three European countries. *Compare* 29, no. 3: 287–301.

Ossenbach-Sauter, G. 1996. Democratisation and Europeanisation. In D. Brenner and D. Lentzen, eds., *Education for the New Europe.* Providence: Berghahn.

Persianis, P. 1998. Cultural resistance to the structure of the European space in Greece and Cyprus. In A. M. Kazamias and M. G. Spillane, eds., *Education and the Structuring of European Space.* Athens: Serios Editions.

Peters, M., and J. Marshall. 1996. *Individualism and Community: Education and Social Policy in the Post-modern Condition.* London: Falmer.

Pollard, A., P. Broadfoot, P. Croll, M. Osborn, and D. Abbott. 1994. *Changing English Primary Schools? The Impact of the Educational Reform Act at Key Stage One.* London: Cassell.

Power, S. 1996. *The Pastoral and the Academic: Conflict and Contradiction in the Curriculum.* London: Cassell.

Popkewitz, T. P. 2000. Reform as the social administration of the child: Globalization of knowledge and power. In N. C. Burbules and C. A. Torres, eds., *Globalization and Education: Critical Perspectives.* New York: Routledge.

Pring, R. A. 1984. *Personal and Social Education in the Curriculum.* London: Hodder & Stoughton.

Prosser, J. 1999. The evolution of school culture research. In J. Prosser, ed., *School Culture.* London: Paul Chapman.

Puurula, A. 2000. Teachers' job satisfaction and affective education in twelve countries. *Curriculum and Teaching* 15, no. 2: 29–48.

Puurula, A., S. Neill, Y. J. Katz, S. Romi, I. Menezes, L. Vriens, and P. Lang. 2001. Teacher and student attitudes to affective education: A European collaborative research project. *Compare* 31, no. 2: 165–86.

Sagy, S., E. Orr, and D. Bar-On. 1999. Individualism and collectivism in Israeli society: Comparing religious and secular high school students. *Human Relations* 52, no. 3: 327–48.

Scharfstein, B. 1989. *The Dilemma of Context.* New York: New York University Press.

Selleck, R. J. W. 1972. *English Primary Education and the Progressives, 1914–1939.* London: Routledge & Kegan Paul.

Shamai, S., and Z. Ilatov. 1998. Attitudes of Israeli and Canadian students towards new immigrants. *Education and Society* 16, no. 1: 27–36.

Simola, R. 1998. Rationalism of hopes: A discursive basis for a world culture of educational reforms? In A. M. Kazamias and M. G. Spillane, eds., *Education and the Structuring of European Space*. Athens: Serios Editions.

Soeters, J. 1994. Management and cultural diversity in Europe. In L. Bekemans, ed., *Culture: Building Stone for Europe 2002*, 169–88. Brussels: European University Press.

Souza, P. R. 2000. Values education and cultural diversity. In M. Leicester, C. Modgil, and S. Modgil, eds., *Systems of Education: Theories, Policies and Implicit Values*. London: Falmer.

Steinberg, J. M. 1976. *Educational Growth in the Classroom: Implementing Affective Education through the Process of Confluency*. Stockholm: Almqvist & Wiksell International.

Stoll, L. 1999. School culture: Black hole or fertile garden for school improvement? In J. Prosser, ed., *School Culture*. London: Paul Chapman.

Sultana, R. G. 1992. Personal and social education: Curriculum innovation and school bureaucracies in Malta. *British Journal of Guidance and Counseling* 20, no. 2: 164–86.

Sultana, R. G. 1998. The Mediterranean: A New Focus for Comparative Studies? In A. M. Kazamias and M. G. Spillane, eds., *Education and the Structuring of European Space*, 73–94. Athens: Serios Editions.

Thornell, J. G. 1979. Reconciling humanistic and basic education. *Clearing House* 53: 23–24.

Triandis, H. C. 1983. Dimensions of cultural variations as parameters of organizational theories. *International Studies of Management and Organization* 12: 139–69.

Triandis, H. C. 1995. *Individualism and collectivism*. Boulder: Westview.

Triandis, H. C., and X. P. Chen. 1998. Scenarios for the measurement of collectivism and individualism. *Journal of Cross-Cultural Psychology* 29, no. 2: 275–90.

Trompenaars, F. 1994 *Riding the Waves of Culture*. New York: Irwin.

Tylor, B. E. 1871. Primitive Culture. www.britannica.com/bcom/eb/article

Young, I. M. 1990. *Justice and the Politics of Difference*. Princeton: Princeton University Press.

18

Citizens in the Text?

International Presentations of Citizenship in Textbooks

Sinikka Aapola, Tuula Gordon, and Elina Lahelma

Education is a strongly national project, informed by an ideology of raising "good citizens" and preparing young people for adulthood. In Western democracies ideas of adulthood and citizenship are characterised by tensions between egalitarianism and inequality. Despite the official statements toward promoting equality, formal equality is diffused by relations of power and axes of inequalities based on gender, social class, ethnicity, disability and sexual orientation. These inequalities are structurally, spatially and culturally constructed as well as embodied and they have various consequences. Unless inequalities are actively challenged, school practices may actually result in reinforcing them (e.g., Skeggs 1997).

Textbooks offer an interesting view on the notion of citizenship in education. They are an institutionalised form of authoritative texts, although their position in teaching varies. Textbooks formulate perceptions of the world by offering categorizations for the readers. They construct citizenship in two main ways: explicitly, in presenting certain views of people—representations of citizenship—and implicitly, in the way the texts are constructed. We shall look at both these aspects.

Our main emphasis is to explore the discursive representations of citizenship and embodiment in school textbooks, and their intertwined associations with a hierarchical social organisation of (presentations of) age and gender. Our chapter is based on a comparative reading of a sample of biology textbooks published in the 1990s from four countries: Finland, Great Britain, Sweden and the United States.

CONCEPTUALIZING CITIZENSHIP
AND EMBODIMENT IN EDUCATION

Schools are expected to educate future citizens who are capable of associated rights and responsibilities. Citizenship in education, however, is often an abstraction that does not incorporate social and cultural differences (cf. Jones 1990; Pateman 1988). Several studies suggest that citizenship education tends to focus rather narrowly on the realm of the political at the expense of family and embodiment (Stone 2000). Broadening the abstract conceptions of citizenship, we consider students as knowing, cultural, gendered, embodied and sexual citizens as well as political, legal and social citizens (Gordon et al. 2000). These citizens are constructed in everyday practices in schools.

In political theory citizenship is analysed through the concept of the social contract, which has been used to explain the formation of nation states. It refers to collective co-operation among men in the cultural sphere, which was distinguished from the natural sphere, where everyday wants and needs were located. In the natural sphere competition, self-interests and self-sufficiency are seen to rule. Men stepped beyond the natural sphere of bodies and emotions to promote joint interests in the collective sphere (Pateman 1988). Initially women, children, the disabled and working-class men and men of colour remained in the natural sphere, while white, upper- and middle-class able-bodied men rose to the cultural sphere. The cultural sphere was seen as a place where minds were capable of submerging bodies, the abstract was able to negate the concrete.

T. H. Marshall (1963) divided citizenship into political, legal and social. Formal citizenship rights have now been extended to include all adults, including women and other minority groups, but their relationship to social, cultural and embodied citizenship remains uncertain. Children and young people are usually not included in it either. The welfare states have nurtured social citizenship, the aim of which is to bridge the gap between the cultural and the natural sphere and to redress inequalities. Equality in the political sphere is not sufficient if people are not equal in the market. These inequalities are addressed through social citizenship, whereby unequal economic distribution is compensated for through welfare policies.

It has been suggested that social citizenship needs to be extended (c.f. Jones 1990; Gordon et al. 2000a) and the hierarchical nature of embodied relationships needs to be re-addressed. Social rights submerge the materiality of bodies and the insubstantiality of emotions; therefore, the concept of citizenship needs to be extended to include embodiment.

Bodies reproduce, although the reproduction is mainly located in the female body. The route to reproduction is accomplished by representing developing bodies as biological. This is intertwined with a hierarchical social organisation of age and gender. When the material bodies become citizen's bodies, they undergo a process of sanitisation and elimination of difference and become self-evident naturalised bodies. School students confront the representations of citizenship in classrooms, where a range of embodied practices take place (Gordon et al. 2000).

In schools, students are usually positioned as citizens-to-be, and while they learn to exercise their future rights, the emphasis is often more on duties and responsibilities. According to the Finnish curriculum document the school is "to develop attitudes and capabilities in students which will make it possible for them to function as active, critical and responsible citizens" (NBE 1994, 17). The current British curriculum documents suggest more active citizenship for youth: "Citizenship encourages pupils to become helpfully involved in the life of their schools, neighbourhoods, communities and the wider world" (QCA 1999, 28; in Callender and Wright 2000, 216). Callender and Wright (2000) note, however, that recommendations and most of the recent literature on citizenship education are silent on the educational contexts in which learning about citizenship is to take place. Discussion about citizenship education is highly prioritized in many countries (Torney-Purta et al. forthcoming). Education for citizenship requires contributing to students' competence to act as conscious agents in society. In the curricula it often is a cross-curricular theme, included in the teaching of various subjects, for example, history, religion and geography.

In the curricula of Finnish comprehensive school (NBE 1994), cross-curricular themes include aspects of citizenship education (for example, international education, consumer, family and health education). The important core is, however, included in the year-nine subject "knowledge about society," which has specific textbooks. The practice in Sweden is rather similar. In Britain citizenship can be taught in the core subjects of the National Curriculum, through personal and social education, and through "immersion in the corporate life of the school" (NCC 1990, 5). Specific textbooks are not regularly used. In the United States, the practice varies, but, for example, in California the History-Social Science Framework (1987) includes elements of good citizenship.

RESEARCH ON TEXTBOOKS

School texts are based on particular ideas of learning and teaching, of school student and reader. Textbooks are produced specifically for school use, distributed through commercial channels, and routinely used in classrooms. The importance of textbooks in teaching and learning varies in different countries, depending on the prevailing pedagogical ideologies and between school subjects, but they are often in the centre of teaching activity (Apple and Christian-Smith 1991).

In Finland, there is a strong tradition of centralised school organisation. Textbooks have followed the suggestions made in the curriculum documents, and they were controlled by the National Board of Education until the early 1990s. Despite the change towards decentralization, which brought more autonomy to schools on the contents of curriculum (Antikainen 1990; Lahelma 1993), the practices do not change rapidly. In 1996 external evaluators of the Finnish comprehensive school (Norris et al. 1996) noted that authority and expertise were still located in teachers and textbooks, teachers did not extensively produce materials, and resources of school libraries were scarce. Ethnographic research in Finnish secondary schools suggests that the contents of textbooks often structure the syllabus (Gordon et al. 1999). However, Finland's case should not be over-emphasised as an extreme example on reliance on textbooks; similar observations have been made in other countries too (e.g., Foley 1990).

Despite the often central position of textbooks in teaching, there are relatively few studies on the worldview they mediate, especially from a critical point of view (see Apple and Christian-Smith 1991). As Pöggeler suggests, political influence is present in all textbooks, not just in particular subjects (Pöggler 1985; cited in Johnsen 1993, 69–70).

In our analysis we draw on feminist educational theory and critical discourse analysis. We see textbooks as active in constructing the social reality by offering value-laden definitions and categorizations, linked to wider social and cultural structures, relations and processes (e.g., Fairclough 1993). Certain versions of the world are presented as legitimate in hegemonic discourses, while others may be silenced or challenged (e.g., Weedon 1997). Discourses can be used to subjugate (groups of) people in the society, as, for example, sexist and racist discourses make obvious. Discourses create various subject positions—locations organized around systematic conceptual repertoires. (Davies and Harrè 1990, 46–59.) Some subject positions open more possibilities for agency and negotiation, while others are more restricted.

LOOKING FOR CITIZENSHIP IN TEXTBOOKS

Our main focus is on biology textbooks, but first we discuss a sample of Finnish and Swedish textbooks of citizenship education. Thus we illustrate different ways to include adolescence, gender, and embodiment in education.

There were two Finnish textbooks of citizenship education in our sample. In both of them youth is discussed in specific sections, while the rest of the chapters deal with institutions wielding power in society. This structure positions youth outside other institutions, which is openly pointed out in a subtitle in one of the books: "A young person lacks power." Students learn, for example, that young people "are ready to bear responsibility, but mainly for themselves" (Lehtonen et al. 1999, 11).

These examples illustrate two more general tendencies in the books: the readers are not granted a competent position in relation to knowledge about youth, and youth are not granted a position of responsible citizens. Sections on youth also include information about important age limits, which demonstrate youth as a period of legal steps towards adult citizenship, giving them more rights and duties each year. Embodied changes, such as the legal age limits for the right to have sex, are not included. The section "Individual, Family and Society" in one of the sample books includes a story of the trajectories of a girl and a boy from their childhood families to their joint new home, employment and parenthood. Sexual citizenship (Gordon et al. 2000a) is not addressed explicitly, but a self-evident heteronormative story is presented (see Lehtonen 1997).

Both of the Finnish textbooks discuss gender explicitly in a few paragraphs, and their focus is especially on gender equality. The general message seems to be a celebration of the situation of Finnish women who "received the right to vote—first in Europe" (Metsäkallas et al. 1999, 198). It is claimed that equality reigns because "the law of equal opportunities decrees that men and women have to be treated equally in the labor market," while there still may be problems in sharing domestic duties (Lehtonen et al. 1999, 58). Nordic gender equality is demonstrated with statistics suggesting women's active participation in the labor market and politics.

Elsewhere in the text gender is not addressed. Drawings and their subtexts suggest, however, that entrepreneurs and police officers are men, as well as labor union activists and criminals. A tragicomic—but telling—example is a subtitle: "President: The Father of the Country" (Metsäkallas et al. 1999, 219). Only a year after the publication of this book the first female president stepped into power in Finland.

We found the Finnish textbooks rather inadequate in their analysis of society and in their distribution of knowledge. The Swedish book in our sample was rather different, offering more active subject positions to the young readers. Two goals are stated: first, to provide knowledge to advance understanding about the society: including relations of power, finance and democracy. The second goal is to help students search for knowledge themselves (Hedengren 1997, 7).

Difference to the Finnish books is evident: this book poses more questions than closed answers, and students are urged to "think more" and "search further by themselves." For example, they are asked to look at representations of women and men in the media, and to reflect on their relation to body images (Hedengren 1997, 44–45). Students are also asked to consider the double standards for girls' and boys' sexual behavior (Hedengren 1997, 43). Unlike those in the Finnish book, the questions posed provide the young readers opportunities to reflect on their citizenship as gendered and embodied.

In his study on references to "democracy" in Swedish social science textbooks, Anderberg (1981; cited in Johnsen 1993) argues that textbooks have three inherently contradictory requirements: the school democracy requirement, the report requirement and the education requirement. This means that the textbooks should be written so that they become part of the school's democratic system, as well as objectively present the topic in question, and encourage students to practice democracy. As a result, the books have to avoid so many factors that they lack their own subjective, explicitly explanatory portrayals of democracy as a phenomenon (Anderberg 1981; cited in Johnsen 1993, 117). It seems that the new Swedish textbook has succeeded in this task better than the Finnish ones.

We have several reasons to look for representations of citizenship in biology textbooks. First, we aim to extend the concept of citizenship to embodiment, and biology deals most concretely with issues such as the physical body, and even the social context of that body. Biology/natural science is also a compulsory subject in middle school in all the countries in our study, whereas almost all other subjects may be voluntary. It is also a subject where textbooks are used as a rule.

Sections on puberty and adolescence, reproduction and sexuality are of major interest to the young readers, as they are just facing physical and social changes. Young people are looking for their position in the society, and in defining adolescence, biology textbooks are in fact defining it for them.

We have analyzed how citizenship is constructed, and how citizens' bodies are represented in the textbooks. We have paid attention to the concepts used, as well as to textual styles and visualizations. Among the questions we have presented to the texts were: how do textbooks define adolescence? How do they construct gender differences? What kind of subject positions are constructed for young people?

We have looked particularly at representations of adolescence and sexuality, as these are closely connected with representations of citizenship and embodiment. Bodily development and (hetero)sexuality are among the most important dimensions defining young people and their social position. On the other hand, bodily maturity has no importance in the official definitions of young people's citizenship.

Our emphasis is on Finland, but we have included books from Sweden, another Nordic country with a comprehensive school system. Moreover, we have examples of textbooks from the United States and Britain, as their organization and contents of schooling are well known and influential all over.

Comparisons between textbooks from different countries are difficult due to the varying pedagogical traditions and differences in curriculum, as well as to the historical and social contexts and economic processes that affect the production and use of textbooks in a particular country. The target groups of the textbooks in our sample also vary slightly in age, although all are used in the middle school level. The presentation styles in the books also vary enormously.

FINNISH TEXTBOOKS

In Finnish comprehensive school the biology curriculum is to include human organisms, vital functions and their changes, the human life cycle, sexuality, and social relationships (NBE 1994). Thus not only the physical functions of the body, but even wider dimensions of human sexuality and the life cycle are deemed relevant. The objectives of biology teaching include students learning to accept their development, coming to know themselves and understanding differences between people (NBE 1994). It seems, however, that all these themes have not been mediated to the textbooks as equally important. For this article we have analyzed all biology textbooks that were generally used in Finnish secondary schools (for 13–16-year-old students) in the late 1990s (see the appendix).

Puberty/adolescence is described first and foremost as a physical, bodily event, linked to hormonal changes and maturation of sex organs. However, there is usually also some discussion about the mental changes connected to adolescence. One of the books locates adolescence in the life course, discussing its psychological, physical and social aspects:

> The psychological and physical changes are strong particularly in adolescence. The young person disengages her/himself from the parents and childhood playmates, gains independence. This may cause disputes between the young person and his/her parents. That can cause feelings of guilt, depression. Towards the end of adolescence, the young person gets more interested about other people and the environment. At the same time s/he is looking for his/her place in the society and as a sexual being. (Rönkä et al. 1994, 257)

Adolescence is depicted as a time of big changes that may have negative emotional and social consequences for the young person. It is associated with emotional turmoil, but here it is not reduced to purely biological processes such as hormone production; it is suggested that social reasons may also affect the way an adolescent feels or acts. In most of the descriptions, however, physical development (i.e., hormonal imbalance) is named as the only cause of the turbulence. The link from the body to the young person's mind/psyche is presented as direct: changes in the teenager's body supposedly cause embarrassment and confusion, and social problems may follow (see Aapola 1997). This is a problematic view, as it does not take into account the manifold social circumstances of young people's lives (see Hill and Fortenberry 1992).

Puberty is defined as the development of "sex features" and reproductive capacities. Gender differences are located in the physical sex characteristics, unproblematized. According to the biology textbooks, physical maturation accentuates gender differences. Girls are said to reach puberty earlier. Signs of masculinity are emphasised in relation to boys' development: deepened voices, growing facial hair, increase in height and muscular strength. Girls' appearance is said to become more feminine: their hips widen and breasts grow. Menarche is mentioned and, often, discomfort and pain that supposedly follow it.

Gender differences are presented as absolute, not average and relative: "boys grow taller than girls and their muscles are stronger," it is announced. Social gender differences are either not mentioned, or they are stereotypical and un-problematized: "boys are interested in girls and sex and girls are interested in clothes and want to impress boys" (Koski and Koski 1994). Similarities in girls' and boys' development are not discussed as often as the differences.

Transition from childhood to adulthood in Finnish textbooks is defined within the spheres of physical and mental development and sexuality. Other social spheres besides family and friends are not taken up. As a rule, puberty/adolescence is linked with the "growing interest towards the opposite sex," which is supposed to "awaken" as the hormones start to spread in the body.

> Descriptions of human sexuality in the textbooks are dominated by references to physiological functions and sex organs. Feelings, desires and fears are not elaborated on. The cultural and psychological dimensions of sexuality are thus not discussed, such as values and norms linked with sexuality, or the commercialization of sex and double morality. Everyday sexuality, and problems young people frequently face in starting their sex-lives are not addressed. Contraception methods are usually introduced, as well as sexually transmitted diseases. Heterosexuality is clearly the norm, but usually textbooks also briefly discuss homosexuality (see Lehtonen 1997). Only one of the books refers to social aspects of sexuality: The society regulates people's sexual behavior with the help of various habits, rules and prohibitions. In different cultures these maybe very different. There may also be very different individual perceptions and opinions regarding sexual behavior. (Rönkä et al. 1994, 142)

Even within the same text, different, sometimes contradictory discourses are evoked. In the Finnish biology textbooks, womanhood and manhood are defined by physical development, especially by reproductive capacity. Linking adolescence with reproductive maturation implies the possibility of sexual activity, but this issue is rarely addressed directly. Usually it is hinted that sex is not meant for young people, although their bodies are now becoming mature enough for reproduction.

It is implied that "adulthood" is linked with social processes, not biological ones: one has to "become an independent adult before one can form a family." Girls in particular are warned to control their desires. Adulthood is also connected to psychological processes, with becoming "mature" and "independent." Adulthood is usually depicted as positive and is linked with autonomy, freedoms and citizenship rights which have been a male privilege until this century (see Gordon 1994).

SWEDISH TEXTBOOKS

There are two Swedish biology textbooks in the sample. They differ from other books in their take on human development and sexuality, if not in their approach to other subjects. Their discussions on adolescence, human sexuality and romantic relationships are the most extensive. Puberty/adolescence is defined as a period in a young person's life, marked by rapid physical changes, but even more importantly, by social changes, especially the onset of romantic and sexual relationships.

In *Biologi/Spektrum* (Fabricius et al. 2000) Sweden is described as a model country of open sex education. However, readers are reminded that this openness has not always been there. There is an interesting referral to historical changes in the attitudes towards masturbation. Sex organs are described (with detailed pictures), and physical development and menstruation are discussed. The formation of romantic and sexual relationships is covered at length. Social and legal aspects of sexuality, even controversial issues such as abortion, violence and prostitution, are mentioned, which is a rare exception.

The Swedish textbooks define sexuality in a remarkably similar way, although one of the books is more comprehensive in its discussion of the life course and sexual relationships. However, they approach adolescence, as well as young people's sexuality, differently. The older book uses mainly biological discourse and defines puberty as the maturation of sex organs and "the awakening of the sexual drive" (Linnman et al. 1993, 244). Psychological changes are also mentioned. Adolescence is defined an "in-between" time, when the young person is still a child in need of help from the parents, but developing into an adult, and wanting their rights. It is depicted as a time of many changes and growing independence, but mainly in negative terms, bringing conflicts with parents and difficulties in understanding oneself:

(The adolescent) has one foot in childhood and the other one in the adult's world. One does often not feel at home anywhere, which makes one feel abandoned and misunderstood. (Linnman et al. 1993, 245)

The more recent textbook *(Biologi/Spektrum)* offers a more positive view to youth. Although adolescents are said to go through feelings of uncertainty, it is suggested that they can trust their own experiences and get help from their friends, parents and teachers (Fabricius et al. 2000, 117).

Youth is depicted as first and foremost a crucial time in forming romantic relationships. A normative developmental lineage is constructed: young people are said to first love from a distance, and "really" fall in love only later, wanting to have his/her feelings met. Issues related to taking contact, breaking up and jealousy are discussed at length, resorting to psychological and romantic discourses. Young people's relationships are described as valuable and important, although sometimes difficult (Fabricius et al. 2000, 120–25).

In both Swedish textbooks sexual relationships are described as a potential source of joy and fulfillment, but the older textbook presents young people's relationships more negatively, as "superficial," formed only to satisfy a "strong sexual drive" (Linnman 1993, 248). In both books a successful adulthood means becoming more responsible in one's relationships and in the end with having a child and forming a family. There are normative timetables; the teenager should not have a child while still at school:

> For a teenager going to school (the pregnancy) can feel like a big catastrophe. Many make difficult decisions about abortion or their parents take care of the child.—All children should have the right to be born welcome!" (Fabricius et al. 2000, 343)

The "teenager's" situation is described gender-neutrally, without investing the whole responsibility of preventing pregnancy to the girl (see Aapola 1999).

Sexuality is discussed in terms of "sexual drive," suggesting its biological nature. Within this discourse, the normative form of sexuality is heterosexuality. The stable heterosexual couple is presented as the ultimate level of relationships, the result of a long maturation process. In the older textbook homosexuality is discussed mainly in negative, even homophobic terms, as "caused by a failure in childhood sexual development" (Linnman et al. 1993, 251–52). In the more recent textbook (*Biologi/Spektrum*), both hetero- and homosexual relationships are discussed as romantic—not just sexual—relationships, and homosexuality is defined an equally normal sexual orientation: "Most fall in love with someone of the opposite sex, but about one in ten with someone of the same sex. In each case, the feelings are the same. To be homosexual is as natural as to be heterosexual" (Fabricius et al. 2000, 126).

It is acknowledged that homosexuals have not always been treated well in the society. The name of the local organization promoting sexual equality is given, and readers are encouraged to call if they have questions (Fabricius 2000, 126–27).

The Swedish textbooks use in their discussions of adolescent embodiment not only biological discourse, but psychological, social and legal discourses and even romantic discourse, which is unusual. They contain references to historical changes in the attitudes surrounding sexual behavior, showing that even "scientific facts" and legal issues are open for debate. Controversial topics are brought up, although rather neutrally.

There is a strong emphasis on the evolving romantic and sexual relationships of young people, and less on other social aspects of growing up. Adulthood is equated with the formation of a stable (heterosexual) couple and having a child. Gender differences beyond physical characteristics are not addressed: teenagers are constructed as a group going through the same kind of uncertainties, regardless of gender. The only social gender differences that are brought up concern prostitution and rape.

Representations of embodiment in the Swedish textbooks vary widely, from images of sex organs to photographs showing young people in social situations, and on to descriptions of deep and satisfying emotions associated with a loving sexual act. Even disabled bodies are mentioned as equally deserving of a "rich love life." The citizen's body in these books is not gender-specific, except in relation to reproduction.

Not many agentic positions are opened up for the readers, other than that of an uncertain teenager looking for love. The most important responsibilities one has concern protecting oneself and one's sex partner against unwanted sex acts, premature pregnancies and diseases by carefully planning the sex act and acquiring the necessary preventive devices, and "listening to" one's partner. Sometimes the reader is urged to get more information regarding issues of interest. The reader is directly reminded of particular social citizenship rights within the Swedish law, especially in relation to homosexual rights and rape.

TEXTBOOKS FROM THE UNITED STATES

The two U.S. textbooks in our study share many similarities but differ markedly from the European ones. The U.S. books are massive, covering six hundred to eight hundred pages each, with an abundance of topics. They are clearly meant to be studied during several years. Their textual style is very scientific, and they are full of microscope photographs, drawings of cells, tables and figures, while there are few images of people and the human environment.

The U.S. books consist of several different parts: first, core texts, divided in dozens of chapters. Second, there are suggestions for various experiments the students can conduct. Both books include sections where the scientific process is brought into light. *Modern Biology* (1998) includes sections introducing scientists and sections consisting of magazine articles discussing issues that touch on biology. *Life Science* (1991) includes a section in which various issues concerning biological research such as animal testing are discussed, and another on careers and hobbies based on natural science. The students are presented with various possibilities to learn more about biology. Also, the uses of scientific knowledge in the society are discussed, contrary to other biology textbooks we analyzed.

The core texts in the U.S. books are far removed from everyday life. They are strictly natural scientific texts, limiting themselves into discussing the minutiae of physical phenomena, such as the endocrine system, and omitting all references to the experiential level, actions of human individuals not to mention human communities, the societal and cultural level.

There is very little in these otherwise very detailed texts about gender differences, human life course, sexuality and puberty/adolescence, although they can hardly be considered irrelevant topics within biology. In the United States, there have been constant debates around classroom censorship, and sex education is a controversial issue. The biology textbooks thus limit their discussion of sexuality to describing the reproductive system, without any reference to sexual orientation and the like. As a result, the reader is left with a very simplified picture of human sexuality. As the textual style is very scientific, the reader is offered no positions from which to act, other than to conduct experiments on the phenomena described. The relation of these phenomena to everyday life is left out. The text is authoritative, constructing a top-down relationship, where the expert teaches a non-expert, who is to learn the text.

TEXTBOOKS FROM GREAT BRITAIN

In our sample, there are three biology textbooks from Great Britain (see appendix to this chapter). One of the most interesting biology textbooks in the sample is *GSCE Double Award Biology* (Gater and Wood-Robinson 1997). In the introduction, the authors talk directly to readers, encouraging them to seek out further information and use their imagination: "Any book can give only a certain amount of information, so you should try to develop confidence in searching for information from a variety of sources both in and out of school" (Gater and Wood-Robinson 1997, v).

The book makes extensive use of illustrations, ranging from cartoons to photographs of athletes in action and anatomical drawings of the human body. Contrary to the other textbooks in our sample, several illustrations show colored people of all ages, and both male and female characters appear.

The layout of the book is reminiscent of a youth magazine: the text is frequently interrupted with pictures, separate boxes, "newspaper clippings" and questions. Each subchapter ends with suggestions for exercises applying biological principles to everyday phenomena. The textual style in general uses lots of everyday expressions, metaphors and terminology. The starting point is nearly always in a phenomenon linked to the reader's everyday life (Gater and Wood-Robinson 1997).

Puberty/adolescence and sexual relationships are discussed briefly in a subchapter about human reproduction. Puberty is equated with reproductive maturity. Menstrual cycle is explained, with a warning to be "careful." Heterosexual intercourse is depicted as "making love," as a shared physical and emotional experience, with responsibilities for both partners. Pregnancy is described as a potentially "wonderful condition, for both mother and father," and the whole section actually opens with a woman describing her birthing experience. This is one of few occasions that a biology textbook uses experiential discourse (Gater and Wood-Robinson 1997, 176).

Biology (Jones and Jones 1997) is quite different from its counterpart. It uses scientific discourse, and its illustrations are mainly anatomical drawings and microscopic photographs. It also has pictures of men and women of various ages, and to some extent from different cultures, in various social situations. In relation to human reproduction, a range of issues are included: fertilisation, pregnancy and birth, growth and development and birth control. Sexual relationships are not separated from reproduction and pregnancy, except for the mention of birth-control methods.

Puberty and adolescence are discussed in the subchapter on "growth and development." Adolescence is defined as a time of many physical changes controlled by hormones. Changes are listed gender-specifically: "In girls, the breasts begin to develop and menstruation begins. In boys, the testes and penis grow larger, and the voice breaks" (Jones and Jones 1997, 97). It also said that adolescence tends to start earlier for girls. Even shared changes are mentioned: growth of bodily hair, increased action of sweat glands and acne.

Adolescence is also linked with changes in the young person's thinking: on the positive side, intellectual development and a great capacity for learning, but also feelings of insecurity. The end of adolescence is marked by thinking, not physical development: "It is not possible to say how long it (adolescence) lasts, but probably most people feel they are fully adult by the age of eighteen" (Jones and Jones 1997, 97). Adolescence is thus linked with both physical and psychological changes.

There is a passing reference to young women in the chapter on birth control; they are told to avoid intercourse:

> When a girl reaches adolescence, she begins to release an egg from her ovaries once a month. If a single sperm reaches an egg in the oviduct, then pregnancy may result. The safest way to make sure that this does not happen is to avoid sexual intercourse. (Jones and Jones 1997)

However, a whole variety of contraceptive devices is introduced, which makes this caution seem odd, as the explicit reasons why a young woman should avoid sexual relations are not discussed. The social discourse of youth is lacking, and so are many other issues concerning the social, cultural and moral aspects of sexuality as well.

CITIZENS IN THE TEXT

In our analysis of the biology textbooks, we have studied the discourses, concepts and categories that have been used particularly in the context of human reproduction, sexuality and adolescence. We have been especially interested in the representations of adolescence and gendered embodiment, as well as subject positions that are made available for young people, and their implications in terms of agency (see Davies and Harrè 1990) and social citizenship.

Human reproduction is considered a key part of the high school biology curriculum in all the countries in the study. However, sexuality, puberty and adolescence do not seem to have an equal importance: many books refer to them in passing. Biology textbooks usually do not separate sexuality from reproduction: sexual intercourse is often discussed only in the immediate context of pregnancy. As a result, almost all the social, cultural and moral issues surrounding sexual relationships are left out, with some exceptions. Sexuality is reduced to heterosexual intercourse, and even that is often presented as merely involving the male and female sexual organs, not as a meeting between people.

Gender differences are reduced to "sex characteristics," and they are essentialised: it is implied that they can be derived purely from biology (Aapola 1997), and the social, cultural and historical aspects of the gender system are not discussed. In most of the biology textbooks, men and women are presented as potential fathers and mothers in the reproduction process only. The biology textbooks construct an ideal embodiment of masculinity, marked by big size and muscular strength, and of femininity, marked by curves. Only Scandinavian textbooks discussed social and cultural issues related to gender and sexuality. The Swedish textbooks even discuss homosexuality at length, whereas most other biology books make next to no reference to sexual orientation.

Puberty and adolescence are presented briefly, as the onset of sex hormone production and reproductive maturity. If youth is approached more widely, it is defined as a time period marked by drastic physical changes and emotional imbalance, based on hormones. Some books offer tables depicting normative timetables of physical development. The Scandinavian textbooks again differ from others by discussing youth more extensively, as a life phase involving major social and psychological changes.

There is very little in the biology textbooks regarding agency of human individuals or communities. That is illustrated well by the visual images dominating the textbooks: anatomical drawings of sex organs and illustrations of naked, anonymous female and male bodies abound. The dominant discourses are biological and scientific; experientiality is left out. This accentuates the functions of cells, organs and the like at the expense of human activity.

There is a lack of discussion regarding the relationship between biology and social issues in biology textbooks, although they touch on many controversial issues such as sex education, the environment and genetics. If citizenship education is to be immersed in all school subjects, the biology curriculum does offer several possibilities to discuss issues concerning citizenship and agency, as well as the social and cultural aspects of biological phenomena, but they are not taken up.

The adult–child relationship and its power implications are clearly visible in school textbooks. Their textual style is authoritative. The statements are represented as the only truth; the conditions and background of knowledge constructions are left out. Usually young readers are positioned as passive; their views are not deemed worth discussing, and typically they are not encouraged to exercise agency as citizens.

There is variation among books in the same country, and generalizations have to be cautious. However, on the basis of this study it seems that the Scandinavian books, as well as the British textbooks, offer more agentic positions to the reader/student than the U.S. textbooks, and their representations of embodiment are also more varied.

Representations of citizenship are connected to constructions of embodiment and to discourses of puberty, adolescence and gender. The focus in biology textbooks is on physical development, linking growing up with the maturation of sexual organs. However, young people's sexuality is usually not discussed directly. This implies that having a grown-up body does not bring the social rights of an adult citizen; they are linked with heterosexual relationships, family and economic independence, having a job and becoming a parent. Alternatives routes to adulthood and citizenship are either not discussed at length, or are presented as problematic, as in the case of homosexuality.

Citizenship is defined somewhat differently for girls and boys, although on the level of school curricula texts equality is promoted. On a closer look, the traditional gender system remains unchallenged in the textbooks (cf. Lahelma 1993). Gender differences are constructed as natural, biological, and the social, multifaceted dimensions of masculinity and femininity are not discussed. This is analogous to the way that adolescence is constructed as a natural, biological process, without acknowledging the social dimensions of age (see Aapola 1999).

The discourse of social citizenship submerges the materiality of bodies. The body of a citizen is constructed as a specific body. Implicit is an unexamined assumption about able-bodied, gendered, white, heterosexual bodies. That people are different and bodies are socially and culturally constructed, should not be ignored in educational practices, textbooks included.

APPENDIX: TEXTBOOKS ANALYZED

Finland

Koski, Erkki, and Anna-Liisa Koski. 1994. *Koululaisen perustieto: Oppilaan tietosanakirja.* Helsinki: Painatuskeskus.

Lehtonen, Olli, Harri Rinta-aho, Sakari Tiainen, and Eero Waronen. 1999. *Horisontti: Yhteiskuntaoppi.* Keuruu: Otava.

Leinonen, Matti Teuvo Nyberg, and Olavi Vestelin. 1997. *Koulun biologia* 9.New edition, 1–7. Keuruu: Otava.

Metsäkallas, Pirkko Titta Putus-Hilasvuori, Jari Ukkonen, and Jukka-Pekka Tanska. 1999. *Nykyaika: Yhteiskuntatieto.* Porvoo: WSOY.

Rikkinen, Jouko Pekka Hannula, Helena Samuli, and Juha Venäläinen. 1996. *Värikäs luonto* 9. Porvoo: WSOY. 1–2 painos.

Rönkä, Antti, Eila Jeronen, Kirsi Arino, Annikki Lappalainen, and Antero Tenhunen. 1994. *Eliöt ja elämä: Biologian käsikirja.* Porvoo: Weilin+Göös.

396   *Sinikka Aapola, Tuula Gordon, and Elina Lahelma*

Great Britain

Gater, S., and V. Wood-Robinson. 1997. *GSCE Double Award Biology*. London: John Murray.
Jones, Mary, and Geoff Jones. 1997. *Biology*. Cambridge: Cambridge University Press.
Sears, J., and S. Taylor. 1994. *Life and Living: Key Stage 4*. N.C.: Hodder & Stoughton.

Sweden

Fabricius, Susanne, Fredrik Holm, Ralph Mårtensson, Annika Nilsson, and Anders Nystrand. 2000. *Biologi/Spektrum: För grundskolans senare årskurser*. Stockholm: Liber.
Hedengren, Uriel. 1999. *I händelsernas centrum: Samhällskunskap förgrundskolans senare år*. Falköping: Almqvist & Wiksell.
Linnman, Gunnel, Nils Wennerberg, and Gösta Birger Rodhe, 1993. *NO-Biologiboken: Faktabok för högstadiet*. Uppsala: Almqvist & Wiksell.

United States

Atkin, Beth M., et al. 1993. *Modern Biology*. Orlando: Holt, Rinehart, and Winston.
Warner, Linda A., Sherry A. Lawson, Loretta Kett Bierer, and Tracey L. Cohen. 1991. *Life Science: The Challenge of Discovery*. Toronto: C. Heath.

REFERENCES

Aapola, Sinikka. 1997. "Mature Girls and Adolescent Boys? Deconstructing Discourses of Adolescence and Gender." *Young* 5, no. 4: 50–68.
Aapola, Sinikka. 1999. *Murrosikä ja sukupuoli: Julkiset ja yksityiset ikämäärittelyt*. [Puberty/Adolescence and Gender: Public and Private Formulations of Age.] Suomalaisen Kirjallisuuden Seuran Toimituksia 763. Helsinki: SKS.
Antikainen, Ari. 1990. "The Rise and Change of Comprehensive Planning: The Finnish Experience." *European Journal Education* 25, no. 1: 75–82.
Apple, Michael, and Linda Christian-Smith. 1991. "The Politics of the Textbook." In M. W. Apple and L. K. Christian-Smith, eds., *The Politics of the Textbook*. New York: Routledge.
Callender, Christine, and Cecile Wright. 2000. "Discipline and Democracy. Race, Gender, School Sanctions, and Control." In Madeleine Arnot and Jo-Anne Dillabough, eds., *Challenging Democracy. International Perspectives on Gender, Education, and Citizenship*. London: Routledge.
Davies, Bronwyn, and Rom Harré. 1990. "Positioning: The Discursive Production of Selves." *Journal for the Theory of Social Behavior* 20, no. 1: 43–63.
Fairclough, Norman. 1993. "Critical Discourse Analysis and the Marketization of Public Discourse: The Universities." *Discourse and Society* 4, no. 2: 133–68.
Foley, Douglas. 1990. *Learning Capitalist Culture*. Philadelphia: University of Pennsylvania Press.
Gordon, Tuula. 1994. *Single Women: In the Margins?* London: Macmillan.

Gordon, Tuula, Janet Holland, and Elina Lahelma. 2000. *Making Spaces: Citizenship and Difference in Schools*. London: Macmillan.

Gordon, Tuula, Elina Lahelma, Pirkko Hynninen, Tuija Metso, Tarja Palmu, and Tarja Tolonen. 1999. "Learning the Routines: Professionalization of Newcomers in Secondary School." *International Journal of Qualitative Studies of Education* 12, no. 6: 689–706.

Hill, Robert F., and Dennis J. Fortenberry. 1992. "Adolescence as a Culture-Bound Syndrome." *Social Science and Medicine* 35, no. 1: 73–80.

Johnsen, Egil Borre. 1993. *Textbooks in the Kaleidoscope: A Critical Survey of Literature and Research on Educational Texts*. Oslo: Scandinavian University Press.

Jones, Kathleen. 1990. "Citizenship in Woman-Friendly Polity." *Signs* 41: 781–812.

Lahelma, Elina. 1993. *Policies of Gender and Equal Opportunities in Curriculum Development: Discussing the Situation in Finland and Britain*. Research Bulletin 85, Department of Education, University of Helsinki. Helsinki: Yliopistopaino.

Lees, Sue. 2000. "Sexuality and Citizenship Education." In Madeleine Arnot and Jo-Anne Dillabough, eds., *Challenging Democracy: International Perspectives on Gender, Education, and Citizenship*, 259–77. London: Routledge.

Lehtonen, Jukka. 1997. "Heterosexuality in the School: Curricula and Student Resistance." Presentation at the Sociology of Education Workshop, European Sociological Association Conference, University of Essex, August 1997.

Marshall, T. H. 1963. *Sociology at Crossroads*. London: Heinemann.

NBE. 1994. *Framework Curriculum for the Comprehensive School 1994*. National Board of Education, Painatuskeskus, Helsinki.

NCC. 1990. *Curriculum Guidance 8: Education for Citizenship*. London: HMSO.

Norris, Nigel, Roger Aspland, Barry MacDonald, John Shostak, and Barbara Zamorski. 1996. *An Independent Evaluation of Comprehensive Curriculum Reform in Finland*. Yliopistopaino, Helsinki: National Board of Education.

Osler, Audrey, H.-F. Rathenow, and H. Strakey, eds. 1995. *Teaching for Citizenship in Europe*. Straffordshire, U.K.: Trenthan.

Pateman, Carole. 1988. *The Sexual Contract*. Cambridge: Polity.

Skeggs, Beverley. 1997. *Formations of Class and Gender*. London: Sage.

Stone, Lynda. 2000. "Embodied Identity: Citizenship Education for American Girls." In Madeleine Arnot and Jo-Anne Dillabough, eds., *Challenging Democracy: International Perspectives on Gender, Education, and Citizenship*. London: Routledge.

Torney-Purta, Judith, R. Lehman, H. Oswald, and W. Schulz. Forthcoming. *Citizenship and Education in Twenty-Eight Countries: The Civic Knowledge and Engagement of Adolescents*.

Weedon, Chris. 1997. *Feminist Practice and Poststructuralist Theory*. 2d rev. ed. Oxford: Basil Blackwell.

Index

Note: Page references to tables and figures are indicated by "t" and "f," respectively.

Index

National Council on Sociology of Education (Mainland China), 212, 215, 216, 227
National Curriculum (England and Wales), 315, 319, 383
National Education Longitudinal Study (NELS), 64, 65, 66, 67
nation state. *See* state
Neave, G., 313, 314
Neisser, Ulrich, 153
NELS. *See* National Education Longitudinal Study
neoconservatism: market values and, 316, 317; and values, 314
neoliberalism, 270–76; and educational devolution, 307–8; educational policies of, 272–73; globalization and, 273–76; market versus state in, 271–72; and pedagogic identity, 317–18
the Netherlands, 325–40
New Deal, 3, 261
New Education Movement, 361
new international economic order (NIEO), 191
New Labour, 307, 319, 320
New Right, 306, 307, 314, 315, 316, 321
New School movement, 268–69
Neyman-Pearson school of statistics, 162
NIEO. *See* new international economic order
Nintendo, 276
Nodding, Nel, 108
Noonan, R. D., 165
normalism, 264–65
Nóvoa, António, 184, 185
Nozick, Robert, 76
null hypothesis, 162

occupational mobility, 26, 27
OECD. *See* Organization for Economic Cooperation and Development (OECD)
oecdism, 190
OEEC. *See* Organization for European Economic Cooperation

Onderwijsraad. *See* Dutch Educational Council
oral history, 149
oral tradition, versus literacy, 183
Organization for Economic Cooperation and Development (OECD), 10, 11, 75, 185, 186, 189–90, 191, 194, 195–96, 198–99, 325
Organization for European Economic Cooperation (OEEC), 188–89, 190
organizations, interaction in, 44–45
Osborn, M., 374

Paasch, K., 65
Panel Study of Income Dynamics, 65
PAR. *See* participatory action research
parental choice. *See* school choice
Park, Robert E., 144
Parsons, Talcott, 7, 23, 25, 26, 48, 55, 143
participatory action research (PAR), 95
Passeron, Jean-Claude, 1, 7, 26, 27–28, 112
path analysis, 165–66, 169
Peaker, Gilbert, 165, 167, 168, 173
pedagogic identity, 317–18
pedagogy of the oppressed, 269–70, 279
Peneul, W., 109–10
People's Republic of China. *See* Mainland China
Pereyra, Miguel A., 186
personal history, 149
Pescador, José Angel, 266
Peschar, J. L., 68
Pestalozzi, Johann Heinrich, 264
Piaget, Jean, 106, 114, 115, 268
PISA. *See* Programme for International Student Assessment
Plowden Follow-up Study, 165
Plowden National Survey, 164, 165, 168
Plummer, Ken, 150
pluralism, and culture, 112–13
Podolny, J. M., 73
policy-making, 222; educational responsibility and, 312–13; national comparisons of, 308–10
Polish Peasant in Europe and America, The, 9, 143, 147

About the Contributors

Sinikka Aapola. Researcher, Department of Sociology, University of Helsinki, Finland, and postdoctoral research fellow, Academy of Finland.

Ari Antikainen. Professor of sociology of education, Department of Sociology, University of Joensuu, Finland.

Jason C. Chang. Associate professor of sociology of education, Department of Education, Taiwan Normal University.

AnneBert Dijkstra. Senior researcher at the Department of Sociology and the Interuniversity Center for Social Science Theory and Methodology, University of Groningen, the Netherlands.

Jaap Dronkers. Professor of social stratification and inequality, European University Institute, San Domenico di Fiesole (FI), Italy.

Tuula Gordon. Researcher, Helsinki Collegium for Advanced Studies, University of Helsinki, Finland.

Honorio Martín Izquierdo. Professor of sociology of education at the Universidad de Valladolid (Spain), Ph.D. in philosophy, University of Bonn, and Ph.D. in philosophy, Universidad de Valencia.

Steve Jordan. Assistant professor and codirector of graduate programs (Culture and Values/Educational Leadership), Department of Integrated Studies in Education, Faculty of Education, McGill University.

Ingrid Jönsson. Associate professor, Department of Sociology, Lund University, Sweden.

John P. Keeves. Professorial fellow, Institute of International Education, Flinders University, Adelaide, South Australia.

Katja Komonen. Researcher, Department of Sociology, University of Joensuu, Finland.

David Konstantinovski. Professor of sociology, State University of Humanistic Sciences, and head of the Sociology of Education and Youth Department, deputy director, Institute of Sociology, Russian Academy of Sciences.

Elina Lahelma. University lecturer, Department of Education, University of Helsinki, Finland, and academy fellow, Academy of Finland.

David MacLennan. Department of Social and Environmental Studies, University College of the Cariboo, Kamloops, British Columbia, Canada.

Almudena Moreno Mínguez. Professor of sociology of education in the Universidad de Valladolid (Spain). Graduate in sociology, Universidad Complutense de Madrid.

Martin D. Munk. Associate professor of sociology; researcher of welfare distribution at the Danish National Institute of Social Research, Copenhagen.

Jules L. Peschar. Professor of sociology of education at the University of Groningen, the Netherlands.

Sally Power. Professor of education and head of the School of Educational Foundations and Policy Studies, Institute of Education, University of London.

Lawrence J. Saha. Reader in sociology, School of Social Sciences, the Australian National University; editor of *Social Psychology of Education: An International Journal.*

António Teodoro. Professor of sociology of education, director of Educational Department, Lusophone University, Lisbon.

Carlos Alberto Torres. Professor of social sciences and comparative education, UCLA, Graduate School of Education and Information Studies, and director, Latin American Center.

Raf Vanderstraeten. Senior researcher, Faculty of Sociology, University of Bielefeld, Germany.

Geoff Whitty. Professor of education and director of the Institute of Education, University of London.

Zhang Renjie. Professor and director, Research Institute of Educational Science, Guangzhou University.

Gad Yair. Lecturer, Department of Sociology and Anthropology and School of Education, Hebrew University of Jerusalem, Israel.

The Affective Education Research Group consists of European researchers who have worked together since 1996. The following writers contributed to chapter 17:

Yaacov J. Katz, professor, and **Shlomo Romi,** Ph.D., Bar-Ilan University, School of Education, Israel.

Alkistis Kontoyianni, professor of drama in education, University of Thessaly, Faculty of Human Sciences, Department of Early Childhood Education, Volos, Greece.

Isabel Menezes, professor, University of Porto, Faculty of Psychology and Education, Portugal.

Arja Puurula, professor, University of Helsinki, Faculty of Education, Department of Teacher Education, Finland.

Claudia Saccone, professor, Universita'degli studi del Molise, Language Department and European projects, Italy.

Peter Lang, senior lecturer, **Sean R. St. J. Neill,** Senior Lecturer, and **Lisa Vasileiou,** doctoral researcher, University of Warwick, Institute of Education, United Kingdom.

Lennart Vriens, professor, Faculty of Social Sciences, Utrecht University, the Netherlands.